Abortion Bibliography

for 1978

Abortion Bibliography

for 1978

The Whitston Publishing Company
Troy, New York
1980

PREFACE

Abortion Bibliography for 1978 is the eighth annual list of books and articles surrounding the subject of abortion in the preceeding year. It appears serially each fall as a contribution toward documenting in one place as comprehensively as possible the literature of one of our central social issues. It is an attempt at a comprehensive world bibliography.

Searches in compiling this material have covered the following sources: *Abstracts on Criminology & Penology; Abstracts on Police Science; Access; Air University Library Index to Military Periodicals; Alternative Index; American Humanities Index; American Reference Books Annual; Applied Science & Technology Index; Art Index; Bibliographic Index; Biological Abstracts; Biological & Agricultural Index; British Humanities Index; Business Periodicals Index; Canadian Education Index; Canadian Periodicals Index; Catholic Periodical & Literature Index; Communication Abstracts; College Student Personnel Abstracts; Completed Research in Health, Physical Education, & Recreation; Criminal Justice Abstracts (form: Crime & Delinquency Literature); Criminal Justice Periodical Index; Cumulative Book Index; Cumulated Index to Nursing Literature; Current Index to Journals in Education; Dissertation Abstracts International: A. Social Sciences & Humanities; Dissertaion Abstracts International: B. The Sciences & Engineering; Education Index; Environment Abstracts; Environment Index; Essay & General Literature Index; Government Reports Announcements and Index; Hospital Literature Index; Human Resources Abstracts; Humanities Index; Index Medicus; Index to Legal Periodicals; Index to Jewish Periodicals; International Bibliography of the Social Sciences; International Nursing Index; Journal of Human Services Abstracts; Library of Congress Catalog: Subject Catalog;*

Library of Congress Catalogs: Films & Other Materials for Projection; Media Review Digest; Monthly Periodical Index; PAIS; Philosophers Index; Popular Periodical Index; New Periodicals Index 1978; Nursing Literature (now—Nursing and Allied Health Literature); Masters Abstracts; Index to Periodical Articles Related to Law; Population Sciences: Index of Biomedical Research; Psychological Abstracts; Readers Guide to Periodical Literature; Religion Index One: Periodicals (form: Index to Religious Periodical Literature); Sage Urban Studies Abstracts; Social Sciences Index; Social Work Research & Abstracts (form: Abstracts for Social Workers); Sociological Abstracts; The Wall Street Journal Index; and Women's Studies Abstracts.

The bibliography is divided into two sections: a title section in alphabetical order; and a subject section. Thus, if the researcher does not wish to observe the subject heads of the compiler, he can use the title section exclusively. The subject heads have been allowed to issue from the nature of the material indexed rather than being imposed from Library of Congress subject heads or other standard lists.

Countries are listed alphabetically under subjects: "Abortion: Africa," etc.; with states listed alphabetically under "Abortion: United States: Arkansas," "California,"etc.;drugs are listed under the specific drug involved; entries evolving from *Biological, Psychological* or *Sociological Abstracts* are so indicated with abstract number cited; and all abstracts of news stories appearing in The New York *Times Index* include story length indicators: (L) long, (M) medium and (S) short. Editorials, editorial page columns and reviews will not include this indicator. In addition, each *Times* entry concludes with date, page, column, (e.g., May 1, 1:8 means the article was published on May 1, page 1, column 8). Sunday sections, other than the main news section, are identified by Roman numerals following the date (e.g., May 6, IV, 3:4 means the numeral IV indicates the "News of the Week in Review" section).

The Book section includes Government Publications and Monographs.

The Subject Heading Index includes page numbers.

Since Whitston's *Population Bibliography* series has ceased with the publication of the 1976 [1979] supplement, the *Abortion Bibliography* series, with this eighth annual listing, has begun to include subjects peripheral to but closely allied with the subject of abortion which traditionally had been covered in that earlier series: Birth Control, Contraceptives and Contraception, Sterilization, and the like. We hope that this added inclusion will enhance and prove useful to the coverage of the subject of Abortion.

TABLE OF CONTENTS

LIST OF PERIODICALS CITED

AORN Journal. Association of Operating Room Nurses, Inc.
Acquisitions Medicales Recentes
Across the Board
Acta Anotomica
Acta Biologica et Medica Germanica
Acta Chirurgica Belgica
Acta Cytologica
Acta Dermato-Venereologica
Acta Endocrinologica
Acta Europaea Fertilitatis
Acta Hepato-Gastroenterologica
Acta Morphologica Neerlando-Scandinavica
Acta Obstetrica y Ginecologica Hispana-Lusitana
Acta Obstetricia et Gynecologica Scandinavica
Acta Physiologica Polonica
Acta Physiologica Scandinavica
Acta Vitaminologica et Enzymologica
Actas Luso-Espanolas de Neurologia y Psiquiatria
Adolescence
Advances in Chromatography
Advances in Experimental Medicine and Biology
Advances in Lipid Research
Advances in Planned Parenthood
Advertising Age
African Journal of Medical Sciences
African Studies Review
Air Force Times
Akron Law Review
Akusherstvo i Ginekologiia
America
American Academy of Political and Social Science

American Baby
American Bar Association Journal
American Biology Teacher
American Druggist
American Economic Review
American Economist
American Family Physician
American Heritage
American Industrial Hygiene Association Journal
American Journal of Clinical Nutrition
American Journal of Clinical Pathology
American Journal of Community Psychology
American Journal of Comparative Law
American Journal of Diseases of Children
American Journal of Economics and Sociology
American Journal of Epidemiology
American Journal of Jurisprudence
American Journal of Law and Medicine
American Journal of Nursing
American Journal of Obstetrics and Gynecology
American Journal of Orthopsychiatry
American Journal of Physical Anthropology
American Journal of Psychiatry
American Journal of Psychology
American Journal of Public Health
American Journal of Surgery
American Journal of Surgical Pathology
American Medical News
American Pharmacy
American Sociological Review
Anaesthesist
Anatomical Record
Andrologia
Anesthesia and Analgesia
Angewandte Chemie
Angiology
Angle Orthodontist
Annales Chirurgiae et Gynaecologiae Fenniae
Annales de Medecine Interne
Annales d'Endocrinologie
Annales d'Oto-Laryngologie et de Chirurgie Cervico Faciale
Annali dell' Ospedale Maria Vittoria di Torino

Annals of Allergy
Annals of Human Genetics
Annals of Internal Medicine
Annals of Ophthalmology
Annual Review of Medicine
Annual Survey of American Law
Antimicrobial Agents and Chemotherapy
Archiv fuer Geschwulstforschung
Archiv fuer Toxikologie
Archiv fur Gynaekologie
Archives de Maladies du Coeur et des Vaisseaux
Archives of Environmental Health
Archives of Sexual Behavior
Archives of Surgery
Archivio di Ostetricia e Ginecologia
Archivio Italiano di Anatomia e di Embriologia
Arizona Law Review
Arkhiv Anatomii, Gistologii i Embriologii
Arthritis and Rheumatism
Arzneimittel-Forschung
Ateneo Parmense [Acta Biomedica]
Atlas
Australasian Nurses Journal
Australian and New Zealand Journal of Surgery
Australian Family Physician
Australian Journal of Biological Sciences

Bangkok Bank Monthly Review
Bangladesh Medical Research Council Bulletin
Biochemical and Biophysical Research Communications
Biochemical Journal
Biochemical Pharmacology
Biochemical Society Transactions
Biological Psychiatry
Biology of the Neonate
Biology of Reproduction
Biomedical Mass Spectrometry
Black Enterprise
Boletin Medico del Hospital Infantile de Mexico
Bollettino Chimico Farmaceutico
Boston University Law Review

Brain Research
Bratislavske Lekarske Listy
British Journal of Anaesthesiology
British Journal of Cancer
British Journal of Clinical Pharmacology
British Journal of Criminology
British Journal of Dermatology
British Journal of Obstetrics and Gynaecology
British Journal of Pharmacology
British Journal of Preventive and Social Medicine
British Journal of Psychiatry
British Journal of Social Work
British Journal of Surgery
British Medical Bulletin
British Medical Journal
British Poultry Science
Brooklyn Law Review
Bruxelles-Medicale
Bulletin de Medicine Legale et de Toxicologie Medicale
Bulletin des Societes d'Ophthalmologie de France
Bulletin of The American Protestant Hospital Association
Bulletin of The Pan-American Health Organization
Business Insurance

California Nurse
California Western International Law Journal
Canadian Journal of Hospital Pharmacy
Canadian Journal of Physiology and Pharmacology
Canadian Journal of Public Health
Canadian Medical Association Journal
Cancer
Cancer Research
Cancer Treatment Reports
Capital University Law Review
Casopis Lekaru Ceskych
Catholic Digest
Catholic Lawyer
Catholic Mind
Cell and Tissue Research
Central African Journal of Medicine
Centro Latinoamericano de Demografía. Boletín Demográfico

Ceskoslovenska Gynekologie
Ceskoslovenska Otolaryngologie
Ceylon Medical Journal
Chemical and Engineering News
Chemical Week
Chicago Studies
China Quarterly
Chirurg
Christ to the World
Christian Century
Christianity and Crisis
Christianity Today
Ciba Foundation Symposia
Circulation
The Civil Liberties Review
Clergy Review
Clinica Chimica Acta
Clinical and Experimental Immunology
Clinical and Experimental Pharmacy & Physiology
Clinical Endocrinology
Clinical Genetics
Clinical Nephrology
Clinical Obstetrics and Gynecology
Clinical Oncology
Clinical Pharmacokinetics
Clinical Pharmacology and Therapeutics
Clinical Science and Molecular Medicine
Colorado Nurse
Columbia Journal of World Business
Columbia Law Review
Commentary
Commonweal
Community Mental Health Journal
Comptes Rendus des Seances de la Societe de Biologie et de Ses
    Filiales
Concepte
Concours Medical
Congressional Quarterly Weekly Report
Connecticut Law Review
Connecticut Medicine
Contemporary Review
Contraception

Cornell Law Review
The Criminal Law Reports: Supreme Court Proceedings
Critic
Critica
Critical List
Cross Currents
Current Medical Research and Opinion
Cytogenetics and Cell Genetics

Daily Telegraph
Danish Medical Bulletin
Demography
Denver Journal of International Law and Policy
Department of State Bulletin
Dermatologica
Deutsche Gesundheitswesen
Deutsch Medizinische Wochenschrift
Diabetes
Dial
Dialogue
Discussion
Dissent
Dissertation Abstracts International
La Documentation Catholique
Drug Topics

ETC; A Review of General Semantics
East African Medical Journal
Economic Botany
Economic History Review
Economic Development and Cultural Change
Economie et Humanisme
The Economist
Educational Broadcasting International
Egyptian Dental Journal
Emergency Medicine
Encounter
Endocrinologia Japonica
Endocrinologie
Endocrinology

Endokrinologie
Engage/Social Action
Environmental Affairs
Environmental Science and Technology
Esquire
Ethics
European Journal of Cancer
European Journal of Clinical Investigation
European Journal of Clinical Pharmacology
European Urology
Exceptional Parent
Experientia
Experimental Aging Research

FDA Consumer
FDA Drug Bulletin
Family and Community Health
Family Coordinator
Family Law Quarterly
Family Planning Perspectives
Far East Economic Review
Farm Journal
Farmakologiya i Toksikologiya
Federal Register
Federation Proceedings
Fertility and Sterility
Folia Endocrinologica Japonica
Food Research Institute Studies
Fordham Urban Law Journal
Fortschritte der Medizin
Fortschritte der Neurologie, Psychiatrie und ihrer Grenzgebiete
Fortschritte du Medizin
Forum
French Historical Studies
Frontiers
Frontiers of Hormone Research
Furrow

Gaceta Medica de Mexico
Gallup Opinion Index

Gastroenterologie Clinique et Biologique
Gastroenterology
Gastrointestinal Radiology
Geburtshilfe und Frauenheilkunde
General Pharmacology
Genetika
Genus
George Washington Law Review
Ginecologia y Obstetricia de Mexico
Ginekologia Polaska
Glamour
Good Housekeeping
Guardian
Gynaekologische Rundschau
Gynecologic Oncology
Gynecologie

Haemostasis
Harefauh
Harper's Bazaar
Hastings Center Report
Hawaii Medical Journal
Headache
Health and Social Work
Health Bulletin
Health Education
Health Education Monographs
Health–PAC Bulletin
Health Visitor
Hereditas
Hippokrates
Hiroshima Journal of Medical Sciences
Histopathology
Hofstra Law Review
Homiletic and Pastoral Review
Hong Kong Nursing Journal
Horizon
Hormone and Metabolic Research
Hormone Research
Hormones and Behavior
Hospital Administration in Canada
Hospital and Community Psychiatry

Hospital Progress
Hospitals; Journal of the American Hospital Association
Human Behavior
Human Genetics
Human Organization
Human Pathology
Human Rights
The Humanist

IPPF Medical Bulletin (International Planned Parenthood Federation)
Illinois Medical Journal
Indian Journal of Biochemistry and Biophysics
Indian Journal of Experimental Biology
Indian Journal of Medical Research
Indian Journal of Medical Sciences
Indian Journal of Pediatrics
Indian Journal of Physiology and Pharmacology
Indian Journal of Public Health
Indian Pediatrics
Indiana Law Journal
Industry of Free China (Taipei)
Infirmière Canadienne
Intellect
Interciencia
International Journal for Vitamin and Nutrition Research
International Journal of Bio-Medical Computing
International Journal of Dermatology
International Journal of Fertility
International Journal of Gynaecology and Obstetrics
International Journal of Health Education
International Journal of Psychiatry in Medicine
International Surgery
Internist
Investigative Urology
Irish Journal of Medical Science
Irish Medical Journal
Israel Annals of Psychiatry
Israel Journal of Medical Sciences

JAMA; Journal of the American Medical Association
JOGN; Journal of Obstetric, Gynecologic and Neonatal Nursing
The John Marshall Journal of Practice and Procedure
Josanpu Zasshi
Journal de Chirurgie
Journal de Gynecologie, Obstetrique et Biologie de la Reproduction
Journal d'Urologie et de Nephrologie
Journal for Scientific Study of Religion
Journal of Abnormal Psychology
Journal of Advertising Research
Journal of the American College Health Association
Journal of the American Health Care Association
Journal of the American Optometric Association
Journal of Applied Physiology
Journal of Applied Social Psychology
Journal of the Arkansas Medical Society
Journal of Biosocial Science
Journal of Bone and Joint Surgery
Journal of the Canadian Association of Radiologists
Journal of Chemical Education
Journal of Clinical Endocrinology and Metabolism
Journal of Clinical Microbiology
Journal of Clinical Pathology
Journal of Clinical Psychiatry
Journal of College Student Personnel
Journal of Community Health
Journal of Comparative Physiology and Psychology
Journal of Criminal Law and Criminology
Journal of Current Social Issues
Journal of Development Studies
Journal of Economic History
Journal of the Egyptian Medical Association
Journal of Endocrinology
Journal of Family History
Journal of Family Law
Journal of Family Practice
Journal of Family Welfare
Journal of the Florida Medical Association
Journal of Health and Social Behavior
Journal of Health Politics, Policy and Law
Journal of the History of Ideas

Journal of Homosexuality
Journal of the Indian Medical Association
Journal of the Indiana State Medical Association
Journal of Infectious Diseases
Journal of International Medical Research
Journal of the Kentucky Medical Association
Journal of Laboratory and Clinical Medicine
Journal of Legal Medicine
Journal of Lipid Research
Journal of the Louisiana State Medical Society
Journal of the Maine Medical Association
Journal of Marketing
Journal of Marketing Research
Journal of Marriage and the Family
Journal of Medical Association of Georgia
Journal of the Medical Association of the State of Alabama
Journal of the Medical Association of Thailand
Journal of Medical Ethics
Journal of Medical Genetics
Journal of the Medical Society of New Jersey
Journal of Medicinal Chemistry
Journal of Medicine
Journal of the National Cancer Institute
Journal of Nervous and Mental Disease
Journal of Neurochemistry
Journal of Nurse-Midwifery
Journal of Nursing
Journal of Nutrition
Journal of Obstetrics and Gynaecology of India
Journal of Pharmaceutical Sciences
Journal of Philosophy
Journal of Population
Journal of Postgraduate Medicine
Journal of Psychology
Journal of Psychosomatic Research
Journal of Reproduction and Fertility
Journal of Reproductive Medicine
Journal of School Health
Journal of Sex and Marital Therapy
Journal of Sex Research
Journal of Social History
Journal of Social Psychology
Journal of Sociology and Social Welfare

Journal of Steroid Biochemistry
Journal of the Tennessee Medical Association
Journal of Toxicology and Environmental Health
Journal of Urology
Journal of Youth and Adolescence
Judicature
Juvenile Justice Digest

Kango
Kardiologiia
Katilolehti
Klinika Oczna
Klinische Monatsblaetter fuer Augenheilkunde
Klinische Wochenschrift
Kokyu Io Junkan

Lakartidningen
Lancet
Law and Contemporary Problems
Law Quarterly Review
Learning
Legal Aspects of Medical Practice
Legal Medicine Annual
Life Sciences
Lijecnicki Vjesnik
Linacre Quarterly
Liquorian
Listening
Louvain Studies
Loyola Law Review
Loyola University of Chicago Law Journal

MCN; American Journal of Maternal-Child Nursing
McCalls
Maclean's
Mademoiselle
Majority Report
Manchester Medical Gazette
Marriage

Materia Medica Polono
Medical and Pediatric Oncology
Medical Aspects of Human Sexuality
Medical Biology
Medical Care
Medical Education
Medical Hypotheses
Medical Journal of Australia
Medical Journal of Malaysia
Medical Letter on Drugs and Therapeutics
Medical Times
Medical Trial Technique Quarterly
Medical World News
Medicina
Medicine
Medicine, Science and the Law
Medicinski Pregled
Meditsinskaia Sestra
Medizinische Klinik
Medizinische Welt
Mental Health and Society
Mental Retardation
Metabolism
Methods of Information in Medicine
Midwives Chronicle
Milbank Memorial Fund Quarterly
Militant
Military Medicine
Minerva Chirurgica
Minerva Ginecologia
Minerva Medica
Modern Law Review
Molecular and Cellular Endocrinology
Month
Ms Magazine
Muenchener Medizinische Wochenschrift

Narodno Zdravije
Nation
National Catholic Reporter
National Review

Nature
Naturwissenschaften
Nederlands Tijdschrift voor Geneeskunde
Neuroendocrinology
New England Journal of Medicine
New Humanist
New Physician
New Republic
New Scholasticism
New Scientist
New Society
New Statesman
New Times
New York Law School Law Review
New York Review of Books
New York State Journal of Medicine
The New York Times Magazine
New Zealand Medical Journal
New Zealand Nursing Forum
Newsweek
Nichidai Izaku Zasshi
Nippon Funin Gakkai Zasshi
Nippon Hinyokika Gakkai Zasshi
Nippon Naibunpi Gakkai Zasshi
North Carolina Medical Journal
Northern Kentucky Law Review
Northwestern University Law Review
Nouvelle Presse Medicale
Nurse in Israel
Nurse Practitioner
Nurses Drug Alert
Nursing Care
Nursing Forum
The Nursing Journal of Singapore
Nursing Mirror and Midwives' Journal
Nursing News
Nursing Research
Nursing Times
Nutrition Reviews

Observer

Obstetrical and Gynecological Survey
Obstetricia y Ginecologia Latino-Americanas
Obstetrics and Gynecology
Obstetrics and Gynecology Annual
Occupational Health Nursing
Oeffentliche Gesundheitswesen
Off Our Backs
Ohio Northern University Law Review
Ophthalmic Seminars
Origins
Orvosi Hetilap
Osservatore Romano
Other Woman
Our Sunday Visitor

Paediatrie und Paedologie
Pain
Panminerva Medica
Parents
Parents' Magazine
Pathology Annual
Pathology Research and Practice
Patient Care
Patologia e Clinica Ostetricia e Ginecologica
Pediatric Annals
Pediatric Clinics of North America
Pediatric Nursing
Pediatrics
Pediatriya Akusherstvo i Hinekolohiya
People
People (London)
Perceptual and Motor Skills
Perinatal Care
Personalist
Personality and Social Psychology Bulletin
Perspective on Politics
Pharmacology, Biochemistry and Behavior
Philippine Journal of Public Administration
The Philosophical Quarterly
Philosophical Studies
Philosophy and Public Affairs

Radical America
Readers Digest
Redbook
Regan Report on Nursing Law
Reproduccion
Res Publica
Research Communications in Chemical Pathology and Pharmacology
Research in Reproduction
Revista Brasileira de Pesquisas Medicas e Biologicas
Revista Chilena de Obstetricia y Ginecologia
Revista Clinica Espanola
Revista Colombiana de Obstetricia y Ginecologia
Revista de Medicina Interna [Neurologie, Psikiatrie]
Revista Eclesiastica Brasileira
Revista Medica de Chile
Revista Medico-Chirurgicala a Societatii de Medici si Naturalisti din Iasi
Revue Francaise de Gynecologie et d'Obstetrique
Revue Medicale de la Suisse Romande
Revue Tunisienne de Sciences Sociales
Rinsho Shinkeigaku
Rivista di Patalogia Nervosa e Mentale
Rivista di Servigio Sociale
Rivista Italiana di Ginecologia
Rivista Venezolana de Filosof

SPM; Salud Publica de Mexico
Sairaanhoitaja
Saskatchewan Law Review
Saturday Review
Sbornik Lekarsky
Scandinavian Journal of Gastroenterology
Schweizer Archiv fuer Neurologie, Neurochirurgie und Psychiatrie
Schweizer Archiv fur Tierheilkunde
Schwestern Revue
Science
Science for the People
Science News
Scottish Medical Journal

Theology Today
Therapeutische Umschau
Therapia Hungarica
Theriogenology
Thought
Tidsskrift for den Norske Laegeforening
Tieraerztliche Praxis
Tijdschrift vor Ziekenverpleging
Time
Today's Parish
Toxicology
Trial
Tulane Law Review
Tulsa Law Journal
Tunisie Medicale

Ugeskrift For Laeger
Union Medicale du Canada
University of Cincinnati Law Review
University of Miami Law Review
University of Pennsylvania Law Review
University of Pittsburgh Law Review
University of Richmond Law Review
University of San Francisco Law Review
Upsala Journal of Medical Sciences
Urban Affairs Quarterly
Urologe
Urology
U. S. Catholic
U. S. Medicine
U. S. News and World
U. S. A. Today

Vardfacket
Verhandlungen der Anatomischen Gesellschaft
Verhandlungen der Deutschen Gesellschaft fuer Kreislauffors-
    chung
Veterinary Record
Victimology: An International Journal
Victorian Studies
Villanova Law Review

Virchows Archiv. Abt. A. Pathologische Anatomie-Pathology
Virginia Medicine
Vital Health Statistics
Vogue
Voprosy Okhrany Materinstva i Detstva

WHO Bulletin
WHO Technical Report Series
Wall Street Journal
War on Hunger
Washington University Law Quarterly
West Indian Medical Journal
West Virginia Medical Journal
Western Political Quarterly
Wiadomosci Lekarskie
Wiadomosci Parazytologiczne
Wiener Medizinische Wochenschrift
Wisconsin Medical Journal
Women Health
Womens Press
Women's Rights Law Reporter
World Development
World Health
World of Irish Nursing
Worldmission

Yale Journal of Biology and Medicine

Zeitschrift fuer Ernaehrungswissenschaft
Zeitschrift fuer Urologie und Nephrologie
Zeitschrift fur Aerztliche Fortbildung
Zeitschrift fur Geburtschilfe und Perinatologie
Zeitschrift fur die Gesamte Hygiene und Ihre Grenzgebiete
Zentralblatt fuer Allgemeine Pathologie und Pathologische Anatomie
Zentralblatt fur Gynaekologie
Zentralblatt fuer Veterinaermedizine. [B]

SUBJECT HEADING INDEX

xxxi

BOOKS, GOVERNMENT PUBLICATIONS, AND MONOGRAPHS

ABORTO DI STATO, STRAGE DELLE INNOCENTI/A CURA DEL COLLETTIVO INTERNAZIONALE FEMMINISTA. Venezia: Marsilio, 1976.

L'ABORTO IN ITALIA: Fenomenologia Dell'aborto: Riflessione Morale, Giuridica e Pastorale. Bologna: Edizioni dehoniane, 1975.

L'ABORTO NELLE SENTENZE DELLE CORTI COSTITU-ZIONALI: USA, AUSTRIA, FRANCIA E REPUBBLICA FEDERALE TEDESCA. Milano: A. Giuffrè, 1976.

ABORTO: PRIMO CRIMINE. Padova: Associazione difesa famiglia, 1975.

Alan Guttmacher Institute. ABORTION 1974-1975: NEED & SERVICES IN THE UNITED STATES EACH STATE & METROPOLITAN AREA: A REPORT by Christopher Tietze, et al. New York: The Institue, 1976.

Alexander, N. J. "Immunological Aspecsts of Vasectomy," in IMMUNOLOGICAL INFLUENCE ON HUMAN FERTILITY, ed. by B. Boettcher. Sydney: Academic Press, 1977, pp. 125-128.

Archiprete, Kaye, et al. THE ABORTION BUSINESS: A Report on Free-Standing Abortion Clinics. Cambridge, Massachusetts: Women's Research Action Project, 1977.

Arisi, Emilio. ABORTO E CONTROLLO DELLE NASCITE:

CONTRACCEZIONE E CONSULTORI FAMILIARI. Roma: Editori riuniti, 1976.

Asian Regional Research Seminar on Psychosocial Aspects of Abortion, Kathmandu, 1974. PSYCHOSOCIAL ASPECTS OF ABORTION IN AISA: Proceedings of the Asian Regional Research Seminar on Psychosocial Aspects of Abortion, Kathmandu, Nepal, 26-29 November, 1974. Kathmandu: Family Planning Association of Nepal; Washington: Transnational Family Research Program, American Institutes for Research, 1975.

Baum, Herbert Mark. A Comparison of the factors influencing husband and wife decisions about contraception. Johns Hopkins University, 1978 (Ph.D. dissertation).

Belenky, Mary Field. Conflict and development: a longitudinal study of the impact of abortion decisions on moral judgements of adolescent and adult women, Harvard University, 1978 (Ed.D. dissertation).

Berendes, H. W. "Methods of Family Planning and the Risk of Low Birth Weight," in THE EPIDEMIOLOGY OF PREMATURITY, ed. by D. M. Reed, et al. Baltimore: Urban and Schwarzenberg, 1977, pp. 281-189.

Bernstein, H. N. "Ocular Side-Effects of Drugs," in DRUGS AND OCULAR TISSUES, ed. by S. Dikstein. Basel: Karger, 1977, pp. 560-643.

Berrigan, F. J. A MANUAL ON MASS MEDIA IN POPULATION AND DEVELOPMENT. New York: United Nations, 1977.

Bertone, T., et al. DISCUSSIONE SULL'ABORTO. Roma: LAS, 1975.

Blázquez, Niceto. EL ABORTO: NO MATARAS. Madrid: Biblioteca de Autores Cristianos, 1977.

Bonte, J. "Endocrine Factors, Including Antiovulatory Steroids, Favoritn Bresast Disease," in GYNECOLOGY AND OB-

STETRICS, ed. by L. Castelazo-Ayala, et al. Amsterdam: Excerpta Medica, 1977, pp. 139-154.

Brody, Baruch A. ABORTION AND THE SANCTITY OF HUMAN LIFE: A Philosophical View. Cambridge, Massachusetts: MIT Press, 1975.

California. Bureau of Maternal and Child Health. INDUCED ABORTION IN CALIFORNIA. Sacramento, State of California, Department of Health, Bureau of Maternal and Child Heatlh, 1977.

Chandrasekhar, Scripati. ABORTION IN A CROWDED WORLD: The Problem of Abortion With Special Reference to India. London: Allen & Unwin, 1974.

Civil Liberties Union, Montréal, Québec. LA SOCIÉTÉ QUÉBÉCOIS FACE A FAVORTEMENT. Montréal: Leméac, 1974.

Cliquet, R. L., et al. FROM INCIDENTAL TO PLANNED PARENTHOOD: Results of the Second National Fertility Survey in Belgium. Leiden: Netherlands Interuniversity Demographic Institute, 1976.

Cohen, H. "Abortion and the Quality of Life," in FEMINISM AND PHILOSOPHY, ed. by Mary V-Braggin, et al. Towata, New Jersey: Rowman & Littlefield, 1977, pp. 429-440.

Coleman, Samuel J. Induced Abortion and Contraceptive Method Choice Among Urban Japanese Marrieds. Columbia University, 1978 (Ph.D. dissertation).

"Computerized Screening for Medical, Psychiatric and Social Problems—Review of the Technique and Results in 1296 Consecutive Applications for Therapeutic Abortions," in SYSTEMS SCIENCE IN HEALTH CARE, ed. by A. M. Coblentz, et al. London: Taylor & Francis, 1977, pp. 67-74.

Daube, D. "The Duty of Procreation," in CLASSICAL ASSOCIATION PROCEEDINGS, Volume 74 (1977), pp. 10-25.

Desgouet, Christian. LE PLAISIR SEXUEL, EST-CE UN DROIT? Paris: Levain, 1975.

DIRECTORY OF PROVIDERS OF FAMILY PLANNING AND ABORTION SERVICES 1977. New York: Alan Guttmacher Institute, 1977.

Duda, Gunther. ABTREIBUNG, JA ODER NIEN? Pähl: Verlag Hohe Warte von Bebenbury, 1973.

English, J. "Abortion and the Concept of a Person," in FEMIN-ISM AND PHILOSOPHY, ed. by M. V-Braggin, et al. Towata, New Jersey: Rowman & Littlefield, 1977, pp. 417-428.

Eschenbach, D. A. "Sexually Transmitted Diseases: Recent Developments," in GYNECOLOGY AND OBSTETRICS, ed. by L. Castelazo-Ayalo, et al. Amsterdam, Excerpta Medica, 1977, pp. 195-203.

Fairweather, Eugene, et al. THE RIGHT TO BIRTH: Some Christian Views on Abortion. Toronto: Anglican Book Centre, 1976.

Family Planning Association of Great Britain. CLINIC HAND-BOOK. London: The Association, 1975.

Floyd, Mary K., comp. ABORTION BIBLIOGRAPHY FOR 1976. Troy, New York: Whitston Publishing, 1978.

Gordon, Sol, et al., eds. SEXUALITY TODAY AND TOMOR-ROW: Contemporary Issues in Human Sexuality. North Scituate, Massachusetts: Duxbury Press, 1976.

Great Britain. Parliament. House of Commons. Select Committee on the Abortion (Amendment) Bill. SPECIAL REPORTS AND MINUTES OF EVIDENCE OF THE SELECT COM-MITTEE ON THE ABORTION (AMENDMENT) BILL. Session 1974-75. Together With the Proceedings of the Committee. London: H.M.S.O., 1976.

Hammerstein, J. "Hormonal Contraception and Future Pregnancies," in GYNECOLOGY AND OBSTETRICS, ed. by

4

L. Castelazo-Ayala, et al. Amsterdam: Excerpta Medica, 1977, pp. 96-109.

Harris, Harry. PRENATAL DIAGNOSIS AND SELECTIVE ABORTION. London: Nuffield Provincial Hospitals Trust, 1974.

Hess, E. V., et al. "Immunological Consequences of Human Vasectomy," in IMMUNOLOGICAL INFLUENCE ON HUMAN FERTILITY, ed. by B. Boettcher. Sydney: Academic Press, 1977, pp. 329-332.

Ibrahim, Ahman. LAW AND POPULATION IN MALAYSIA. Medford, Massachusetts: Fletcher School of Law and Diplomacy, Tufts University, 1977.

Inter-governmental Coordinating Committee, Southeast Asia Regional Cooperation in Family and Population Planning. Expert Group Working Committee on Sterilization and Abortion. STERILIZATION AND ABORTION PROCEDURES: Proceedings of the First Meeting of the IGCC Expert Group Working Committee on Sterilization and Abortion Held in Penang, Malaysia, during 3-5 January 1973. Kuala Lumpur: Inter-governmental Coordinating Committee, Southeast Asian Regional Cooperation in Family and Population Planning, 1973.

Jann, Edmund D. THE ABORTION DECISION OF FEBRUARY 25, 1975 OF THE FEDERAL CONSTITUTIONAL COURT. FEDERAL REPUBLIC OF GERMANY. Washington: Library of Congress, Law Library, 1975.

Kalmar, Roberta, ed. ABORTION: The Emotional Implications. Dubuque, Iowa: Kendall/Hunt Publishing Company, 1977.

Komitee für Straffreie Abtreibung. MEINUNGEN, ARGUMENTE, STELLUNGNAHMEN ZUR ABTREIBUNGSFRAGE. Wien: Olga Makomaski, 1975.

Koop, C. THE RIGHT TO LIVE, THE RIGHT TO DIE. Wheaton, Illinois: Tyndale House Publishers, 1976.

Leisner, Walter, et al. DAS RECHT AUF LEBEN: Untersuchungen zu Artikel 2,2 des Grundgesetzes für die Brundesrepublik Deutschland. Hannover: Niedersächsische Landeszentrale für Politische Bildung, 1976.

López, Riocerezo, et al. CRIMINALES DE LA PAZ: (lucha contra el aborto). Madrid: Studium, 1974.

Lyle, Katherine Ch'iu, et al, eds. INTERNATIONAL FAMILY-PLANNING PROGRAMS, 1966-1975: A Bibliography. University, Alabama: University of Alabama Press, 1977.

McCormick, Mary Lillian. Contraceptive experience and associated personality valuables. Boston University, 1978 (Ph.D. dissertation).

Marini, Emilio. ABORTIREI, MA. Pinerolo: Alzani, 1976.

Masnick, G. S. "Fecundability and Contraceptive Opportunities," in NUTRITION AND HUMAN REPRODUCTION, ed. by W. H. Mosley. New York: Plenum Press, 1978, pp. 313-323.

Melvin, Edward J. THE LEGAL PRINCIPLES OF THE FOUNDING FATHERS AND THE SUPREME COURT: A Survey of the Historical Background of the Pro-Abortion Decisions Handed Down by the Supreme Court in 1973 and 1976. Jenkintown: Pro Life Coalition of Pennsylvania, 1977.

Mindick, Burton. Personality and local psychological correlates of success or failure in contraception: a longitudinal predictive study. Claremont University, 1978 (PhD. dissertation).

Moreira, Morvan de Mello, et al. BRAZIL. New York: Population Council, 1978.

Morgentaler, Henry. HENRY MORGENTALER: Un Entrecien Avec Catherine Germain et Sylvie Dupont. Outremont: Éditions l'Étincelle; Montréal: distributeur, Messageries Prologue, 1976.

Neme, B. "Post-Abortion infections," in GYNECOLOGY AND OBSTETRICS, ed. by L. Castelazo-Ayala, et al. Amsterdam:

Excerpta Medica, 1977, pp. 253-261.

Neubardt, Selig, et al. TECHNIQUES OF ABORTION. 2d ed. Boston: Little, Brown, 1977.

Nicholson, S. T. "The Roman Catholic Doctrine of Therapeutic Abortion," in FEMINISM AND PHILOSOPHY, ed. by M. V-Braggin. Towata, New Jersey: Rowman & Littlefield, 1977, pp. 385-407.

Nofziger, Margaret. A COOPERATIVE METHOD OF NATURAL BIRTH CONTROL. Summertown, Tennessee: Book Publishing Company, 1976.

Nolen, William. A. THE BABY IN THE BOTTLE: An Investigative Review of the Edelin Case and Its Larger Meanings for the Controversy Over Abortion Reform. New York: Coward, 1978.

Ohno, S., et al. "The X and Y Chromosomes: Mechanism of Sex Determination," in MOLECULAR HUMAN CYTOGENET-ICS, ed. by R. S. Sparkes, et al. New York: Academic Press, 1977, pp. 294-303.

O'Neill, John Stafford. FETUS-IN-LAW. Dunedin: Independent Publishing Company, 1976.

ORGANIZACION, ADMINISTRACION Y EVALUACION DE LOS PROGRAMAS DE PLANIFICACION FAMILIAR: Memoria Del Seminario Realizado en el Centro Interamericano de Estudios de Seguridad Socail Del 21 Noviembre al 2 de Diciembre de 1977. Mexico City: Centro Interamericano de Estudios de Seguridad Social, 1978.

Osteria, T. S. "Variations in Fertility With Breast-Feeding Practice and Contraception in Urban Filipino Women: Implications for a Nutrition Program," in NUTRITION AND HU-MAN REPRODUCTION, ed. by W. H. Mosley. New York: Plenum Press, 1978, pp. 411-432.

Pages, Fanchon. GUIDE PRATIQUE DE L'AVORTEMENT LEGAL ET DE LA CONTRACEPTION. Paris: Mercure de

France, 1976.

Partito dell ademocrazia cristiana. Gruppo parlamentare alla Camera dei depatati. LIBRO BIANCO SULL'ABORTO: Cronaca di un Dramma Della Coscienze Italiana: documenti dei Dibattiti Parlamentari Nella VI e Nella VII Legislatura. Milano: Rusconi, 1977.

Pelriae, Eleanor Wright. MORGENTALER: The Doctor Who Couldn't Turn Away. Agincourt, Ontario: Gage, 1975.

Prasad, A. S., et al. "The Effect of Oral Contraceptives on Micronutrients," in NUTRITION AND HUMAN REPRODUCTION, ed. by W. H. Mosely. New York: Plenum Press, 1978, pp. 61-85.

Rappapart, E., et al. "One Step Forward, Two Steps Backward: Abortion and Ethical Theory," in FEMINISM AND PHILOSOPHY, ed. by M. V-Braggin. Towata, New Jersey: Rowman & Littlefield, 1977, pp. 408-416.

Rauch, Andrea. QUESTO ABORTO NO S'HA DA FARE. Firenze: Guaraldi, 1975.

Raynaud, J. P., et al. "Estrogen and Progestin Receptors in Human Breast Cancer," in PROGESTERONE RECEPTORS IN NORMAL AND NEOPLASTIC TISSUES, ed. by W. L. McGuire, et al. New York: Raven Press, 1977, pp. 171-191.

Right to Life Association. South Australia Division. Research Committee. RESEARCH LIBRARY BIBLIOGRAPHY, SUMMER 1974-75. Everard Park, S. A.: The Committee, 1975.

Rogers, E. M. "Netword Analysis of the Diffusion of Innovations: Family Planning in Korean Villages," in COMMUNICATION RESEARCH—A HALF CENTURY APPRAISAL, by D. Lerner, et al. Honolulu: University Press of Hawaii, 1977, pp. 117-147.

Rutledge, Mark Spicer. The effects of counseling on university women requesting abortion. Northern Illinois University,

1978 (Ed.D. dissertation).

Sagrera, Martin. ?CRIMEN O DERECHO?: Sociologia Del Aborto. Buenos Aires: Editorial Libería El Lorraine, 1975.

Schnabel, Paul. ABORTUS IN NEDERLAND: Rapport Van de Permanente Registratie Poliklinische Abortus Nederland 1974: Een Analyse Van Abortus Provocatus als Sociaal Verschijnsel. Den Haag: Stimezo-Nederland, 1976?

Schrömbgens, Gerhard E. DIE FRUCHTSCHADENSINDIKA-TION ZUM SCHWANGERSCHAFTSABBRUCH. s.l.: s.n., 1976.

Shivers, C. A. "The Zona Pellucida as a Possible Target in Immunocontraception," in IMMUNOLOGICAL INFLUENCE ON HUMAN FERTILITY, ed. by B. Boettcher. Sydney: Academic Press, 1977, pp. 13-24.

Simpson, John P. ABORTION AND MERCY KILLING. Memphis: Pearl Publications, 1977.

Singh, S., et al. ABORTION LAW IN INDIA: PAST AND PRESENT. Chandigarh: Family Planning Association of India, Haryana Branch, 1976.

Skowronski, Marjory. ABORTION AND ALTERNATIVES. Millbrae, California: Les Femmes Publishers, 1977.

Smith, C. THE FETAL RIGHT TO LIFE ARGUMENT. Silver Spring, Maryland: Citizenship Enterprises, 1977.

Smith, Elizabeth Mary. Psycho-social correlates of regular contraceptive use in young unmarried women. Washington University, 1978 (Ph.D. dissertation).

Srikantan, K. S. THE FAMILY PLANNING PROGRAM IN THE SOCIOECONOMIC CONTEXT. New York: Population Council, 1977.

Steinhoff, Patricia G., et al. ABORTION POLITICS: The Hawaii Experience. Honolulu: University Press of Hawaii, 1977.

9

Stycos, J. M. "Some Minority Opinion on Birth Control," in POPULATION POLICY AND ETHICS. New York: Halsted Press, 1977, pp. 169-196.

Sulovic, V., et al. "Population of B and T lymphocytes and Lymphocyte Blast Transformation Test in Spontaneous and Missed Abortions in the First Trimester of Pregnancy," in IMMUNOLOGICAL INFLUENCE ON HUMAN FERTILITY, ed. by B. Boettcher. Sydney: Academic Press, 1977, pp. 323-328.

Tarrab, Gilbert. LA POLÉMIQUE QUÉBÉCOISE AUTOUR DE LA QUESTION DE L'AVORTEMENT ET L'AFFAIRE MORGENTALER. Montréal: Éditions Aquila, 1975.

Tumboh-Oeri, A. G., et al. "Cell-Mediated Immunity to Spermatozoa Following Vasectomy," in IMMUNOLOGICAL INFLUENCE ON HUMAN FERTILITY, ed. by B. Boettcher. Syndey: Academic Press, 1977, pp. 199-204.

United Nations. Department of Economic and Social Affairs. METHODS OF MEASURING THE IMPACT OF FAMILY PLANNING PROGRAMMES ON FERTILITY: PROBLEMS AND ISSUES. New York: United Nations, 1978.

U.N. Fund for Population Activities. THE ENGLISH-SPEAKING CARIBBEAN. New York: The Fund, 1978.

—. POPULATION AND MUTUAL SELF-RELIANCE. New York: The Fund, 1978.

—. WOMEN, POPULATION AND DEVELOPMENT. New York: The Fund, n.d.

United States. Bureau of the Census. Population Division. TRENDS IN CHILDSPACING, JUNE 1975. Washington, D.C.: GPO, 1978.

United States. Commission on Civil Rights. Wyoming Advisory Committee. ABORTION SERVICES IN WYOMING: A Report. Washington: The Commission, 1977.

United States. Congress. House. Committee on the Judiciary. Subcommittee on Civil and Constitutional Rights. PRO-POSED CONSTITUTIONAL AMENDMENTS ON ABOR-TION: Hearings Before the Subcommittee on Civil and Constitutional Rights of the Committee on the Judiciary. House of Representatives, Ninety-fourth Congress, second session. Washington: GPO, 1976.

United States. Congress. House. Select Committee on Population. FERTILITY AND CONTRACEPTION IN AMERICA: Hearings: v. 1, February 21-June 16, 1978, Domestic Fertility Trends and Family Planning Services. Washington: GPO, 1978.

—. POPULATION AND DEVELOPMENT: Overview of Trends, Consequences, Perspectives, and Issues: Hearings: v. 1, April 18-20, 1978. Washington: GPO, 1978.

United States. Congress. Senate. Committee on Human Resources. Subcommittee on Child and Human Development. FAMILY PLANNING SERVICES AND POPULATION RE-SEARCH ACT EXTENSION OF 1978: Hearing, February 24 1978, on S. 2522, to amend Title X of the Public Health Service Act to Extend Appropriations Authorizations for Five Fiscal Years. Washington: GPO, 1978.

United States. Congress. Senate. Committee on the Judiciary. Subcommittee on Constitutional Amendments. ABORTION HEARINGS BEFORE THE SUBCOMMITTEE ON CONSTI-STUTIONAL AMENDMENTS OF THE COMMITTEE ON THE JUDICIARY. United States Senate. Ninety-third Congress, second session. Ninety-fourth Congress, first session. Washington: GPO, 1974-1976.

United States. Congress. Senate. Select Committee on Small Business. Subcommittee on Monopoly and Anticompetitive Activities. COMPETITIVE PROBLEMS IN THE DRUG INDUSTRY: The Risks and Benefits of Oral Contraceptives; Summary and Analysis; a Summary Analysis and Discussion of Issues Highlighted During the 1970 Hearings on Oral Contraceptives (Competitive Problems in the Drug Industry, parts 15, 16, and 17), with a Reivew of Current Findings and

Subsequent Federal Government Actions Relating to These Drugs. Washington: Library of Congress, 1978.

United States. National Center for Health Statistics. Division of Health Resources Utilization Statistics. BACKGROUND AND DEVELOPMENT OF THE NATIONAL REPORTING SYSTEM FOR FAMILY PLANNING SERVICES. Washington: GPO, 1978.

United States. National Center for Health Statistics. Division of Vital Statistics. UTILIZATION OF FAMILY PLANNING SERVICES BY CURRENTLY MARRIED WOMEN 15-44 YEARS OF AGE, UNITED STATES, 1973. Washington: GPO, 1977.

Universidad Nacional Pedro Henríquez Urena. Centro de Investigaciones. Unidad de Estudios Sociales. ESTUDIO DEL ABORTO EN 200 MUJERES EN LA REPUBLICA DOMINICAN. Santo Domingo: UNPHU, 1975.

Vanessendelft, Will Ray. A history of the association for voluntary sterilization: 1935-1964. University of Minnesota, 1978 (Ph.D. dissertation).

Veatch, Robert M., ed. POPULATION POLICY AND ETHICS: The American Experience. New York: Halsted Press, 1977.

Veenhoven, R. NEDERLANDERS OVER ABORTUS: Meningen Over Beëindiging van Leven Bij Abortus, Euthanasie, Oorlogsvoering en Bestaffing. Den Haag: Vereniging Stimezo Nederland, 1975?

Verhagen, Carla. RUTGERSHUIZEN: HOE ERVAREN KLIENTEN DE RUTGERSHUIZEN? Zeist: NISSO, 1975.

Viola, Carmelo R. ABORTO: Perchè Deve Decidere la Donna; Con Saggi Sulla Pornografia, Sulla Prostituzione e Sul Femminismo.

—. ABORTO: Pellegrini, 1977.

VOLUNTARY STERILIZATION, 1976. Washington: Population Crisis Committee, 1976.

Weisheit, Eldon. SHOULD I HAVE AN ABORTION? St. Louis: Concordia Publishing House, 1976.

Weissman, I., et al. "Large Migrating Hepatic Adenoma Associated With Use of Oral Contraceptives," in GYNECOLOGY AND OBSTETRICS, ed. by L. Castelazo-Ayala, et al. Amsterdam: Excerpta Medica, 1977.

Weström, L., et al. "Epidemiology, Etiology, and Prognosis of Acute Salpingitis: A Study of 1,457 Laparoscopically Verified Cases," in NONGONOCOCCAL URETHRITIS AND RELATED INFECTIONS, ed. by D. Hobson, et al. Washington: American Society for Microbiology, 1977, pp. 84-90.

Woody, Jeanine. ABORTION? Houston: Hunter Ministries Publishing Company, 1977.

ZUR ENTWICKLUNG DES GESUNDHEITSWESENS IN DER DDR. Bonn: Gesamtdt, Inst., Bundesant f. Gesamtdt. Aufgaben, 1975.

PERIODICAL LITERATURE

TITLE INDEX

AF's interim abortion policy waiting for Hill action, by R. Sanders, et al. AIR FORCE TIMES 39:2, October 16, 1978.

Aborting Medicaid, by P. C. Sexton. DISSENT 24:355, Fall, 1977.

Abortion, ed. by R. W. Jenson. DIAL 17:89-120, Spring, 1978.

Abortion [laws and practices throughout the world]. PEOPLE (London) 5(2):4-21, 1978.

Abortion [letter], by A. C. Somerville. NEW ZEALAND MEDICAL JOURNAL 86(594):201, August 24, 1977.

Aborton, adoption, or motherhood: an empirical study of decision-making during pregnancy, by M. B. Bracken, et al. AMERICAN JOURNAL OF OBSTETRICS AND GYNECOLOGY 130(3):251-262, February 1, 1978.

Abortion after ten years, by G. Sinclair, et al. NEW HUMANIST 93:157-160, Spring, 1978.

Abortion agreement ends funding deadlock, by M. E. Eccles. CONGRESSIONAL QUARTERLY WEEKLY REPORT 35:2547-2550, December 10, 1977.

Abortion alert, by G. Steinem. MS 6:118, November, 1977.

Abortion and conscientious objection, by C. Caffarra. OS-

SERVATORE ROMANO 40(549):4-5, October 5, 1978.

Abortion and contraceptives in France, by E. Salomonsson. VARDFACKET 1(17):14-15, September 22, 1977.

Abortion and control, by J. Turner. NEW SOCIETY p. 490, March 2, 1978.

Abortion and euthanasia; violation of the right to life, by J. Bernardin. OSSERVATORE ROMANO 50(507):8-9, December 15, 1977.

Abortion and fairness. PROGRESSIVE 41:9, September, 1977.

Abortion and feminism in Italy: women against church and state, by E. Cantaron. RADICAL AMERICA 10(6):8-29, November-December, 1976.

Abortion and the human brain, by J. B. Blumenfield. PHILO-SOPHICAL STUDIES 32:251-268, October, 1977.

Abortion and Irish women: social elements of women usually resident in the Republic of Ireland whose pregnancies were terminated during 1973, 1974 and up to May 22, 1975 through pregnancy advisory service, London, by R. S. Rose. SOCIAL STUDIES 6:71-119, November, 1977.

Abortion and lesbianism: issues of controversy, by D. L. Martin. LEARNING 6:34, May-June, 1978.

Abortion and medical ethics, by D. Callahan. ANNALS OF THE AMERICAN ACADEMY OF POLITICAL AND SOCIAL SCIENCE 437(12):116, May, 1978.

Abortion and men, by J. Cham. McCALLS 105:53, June, 1978.

Abortion and men: excerpt from the ambivalence of abortion, by L. B. Francke. ESQUIRE 84:55-80, January, 1978.

Abortion and moral safety, by J. R. Greenwell. CRITICA 9:35-48, December, 1977.

Abortion and politics, by E. Doerr. HUMANIST 36:42-43, March-April, 1976.

Abortion and pregnancy screening, by T. Smith. JOURNAL OF MEDICAL ETHICS 4(2):99, June, 1978.

Abortion and privacy: a woman's right to self determination. SOUTHWESTERN UNIVERSITY LAW REVIEW 10:173-193, 1978.

Abortion and rape [letter], by P. Barry-Martin. NEW ZEA-LAND MEDICAL JOURNAL 86(598):397, October 26, 1977.

Abortion and the "Right to Life": facts, fallacies, and fraud. HUMANIST 38(4):18, July-August, 1978.

Abortion and tinkering, by G. Schedler. DIALOGUE 17:122-125, 1978.

Abortion bills pending, by J. Marino. NATIONAL CATHOLIC REPORTER 14:5, August 11, 1978.

Abortion, birth control, and sex ratio in England and Wales [letter], by R. Cruz-Coke. 2(8087):480, August 26, 1978.

Abortion counseling at the Boulder Valley Clinic, by L. Weber, et al. FRONTIERS 1(2):34-39, 1975.

Abortion deaths and social class [letter], by C. Tietze. LANCET 1(7982):469, August 21, 1976.

Abortion debate. JOURNAL OF CURRENT SOCIAL ISSUES 15:74-75, Spring, 1978.

Abortion: the debate goes on; limiting medicaid funds for abortions. AMERICA 137:2, July 2, 1977.

Abortion debate in Australia, by D. Strangman. OSSERVA-TORE ROMANO 49(506):6-8, December 8, 1977.

Abortion: democracy dies with man, by C. Caffarra. OSSERVA-

TORE ROMANO 11(468):11-12, March 17, 1977.

Abortion double standard; medicaid vs. health insurance coverage. NEW REPUBLIC 177:12, October 15, 1977.

Abortion fight goes to HEW; House approves some funding. NATIONAL CATHOLIC REPORTER 14:4, December 16, 1977.

Abortion funding. CHRISTIANITY TODAY 22:40, December 30, 1977.

Abortion funding: legal and moral questions [letter], by A. Altman. HASTINGS CENTER REPORT 8(2):4+, April, 1978.

Abortion: how members voted in 1977, by M. E. Eccles. CONGRESSIONAL QUARTERLY WEEKLY REPORT 36:258-267, February 4, 1978.

Abortion: huge majority would grant right to abortion, but circumstances and stage of pregnancy are determinants. GALLUP OPINION INDEX pp. 25-29, April, 1978.

Abortion in the balance, by M. C. Stenshoel. DIAL 17:89-94, Spring, 1978.

Abortion in the early stage of pregnancy and prostaglandin, by N. Shimada. JOSANPU ZASSHI 32(1):53, January, 1978.

Abortion in France: women and the regulation of family size 1800-1914, by A. McLaren. FRENCH HISTORICAL STUDIES 10:461-485, Spring, 1978.

Abortion in Italy, by M. Hammond. COMMONWEAL 105: 420-421, July 7, 1978.

Abortion in the United States, 1976-1977, by J. D. Forrest, et al. FAMILY PLANNING PERSPECTIVES 10:271-279, September-October, 1978.

Abortion induced by prostaglandin F 2 alpha in risk patients, by E. Ehrig, et al. ZENTRALBLATT FUER GYNAEKOLO-GIE 100(14):921-925, 1978.

Abortion: the inhuman suppression of the weakest; message on the approval of the law on abortion, by G. Colombo. OS-SERVATORE ROMANO 7(464):7+, February 17, 1977.

Abortion: an inspection into the nature of human life and potential consequences of legalizing its destruction, by H. T. Krimmel, et al. UNIVERSITY OF CINCINNATI LAW REVIEW 46:725-821, 1977.

Abortion is always wrong; excerpt from the right to live; the right to die, by C. Koop. SIGN 58:20-23, September, 1978.

Abortion issue: how both sides are helping poor women, by B. Delatiner. McCALLS 105:58-59, April, 1978.

Abortion issue may snag pregnancy benefits fill, by J. Geisel. BUSINESS INSURANCE 12:14, March 20, 1978.

Abortion: the issue no one wanted, so Catholics took it on; an analysis, by M. Winiarski. NATIONAL CATHOLIC REPORTER 14:1+, February 24, 1978+.

Abortion key issue in senate race; showdown in Minnesota, by M. Papa. NATIONAL CATHOLIC REPORTER 14:3, September 14, 1978.

Abortion language and logic, by R. A. Hipkiss. ETC. A REVIEW OF GENERAL SEMANTICS 33:207-212, June, 1976.

Abortion law in Canada: a need for reform. SASKATCHEWAN LAW REVIEW 42:221-250, 1977-1978.

Abortion law reform [letter], by J. Bury. BRITISH MEDICAL JOURNAL 1(6128):1698-1299, June 24, 1978.

Abortion methods: morbidity, costs and emotional impact. 1. The effect of delay and method choice on the risk of abortion morbidity, by W. Cates, Jr., et al. FAMILY PLANNING

PERSPECTIVES 9:266-268+, November-December, 1977.

—. 2. Costs of treating abortion-related complications, by S. D. Von Allmen, et al. FAMILY PLANNING PERSPECTIVES 9(6):273-276, November-December, 1977.

—. 3. Emotional impact of D&E vs. instillation, by J. B. Rooks, et al. FAMILY PLANNING PERSPECTIVES 9(6):276-277, November-December, 1977.

Abortion need and services in the United States, 1974-1975, by E. Weinstock, et al. FAMILY PLANNING PERSPECTIVES 8:58-80, March-April, 1976.

Abortion 1978 [editorial]. NEW ZEALAND MEDICAL JOURNAL 87(610):285-286, April 26, 1978.

Abortion of early pregnancy on an outpatient basis using Silastic 15(S)-15-methyl prostaglandin F2alpha vaginal devices, by S. L. Corson, et al. FERTILITY AND STERILITY 28(10): 1056-1062, October, 1977.

Abortion or the unwanted child: a choice for a humanistic society, by J. W. Prescott. THE HUMANIST 35(2):11-15, March-April, 1975.

Abortion: our differences are making us forget what we have in common. GLAMOUR 76:56, October, 1978.

Abortion programs in New York City: services, policies, and potential health hazards, by R. C. Lerner, et al. THE MILBANK MEMORIAL FUND QUARTERLY 52(1):15-38, Winter, 1974.

Abortion regarded as contraception [letter]. LANCET 2(8041): 765-766, October 8, 1977.

—, by M. Beaconsfield. LANCET 2(8039):666-667, September 24, 1977.

Abortion: rules for debate, by R. A. McCormick. AMERICA 139:26-30, July 15, 1978.

Abortion services: time for a discussion of marketing policies, by H. S. Gitlow. JOURNAL OF MARKETING 42:71-82, April, 1978.

Abortion—State Statute—Constitutionality. THE CRIMINAL LAW REPORTER: COURT DECISIONS AND PROCEEDINGS 22(10):2223, December 7, 1977.

Abortion statutes after *Danforth:* an examination. JOURNAL OF FAMILY LAW 15:3537-3566, 1977.

Abortion: a study of the perceptions of sixty abortion applicants and twenty service givers in Denver, Colorado, by N. B. Fisher. DISSERTATION ABSTRACTS INTERNATIONAL 37(5-A):3184, November, 1976.

Abortion: subjective attitudes and feelings, by E. W. Freeman. FAMILY PLANNING PERSPECTIVES 10:150-155, May-June, 1978.

Abortion: 10 years after, by P. Davies. DAILY TELEGRAPH p. 17, May 3, 1978.

Abortion under attack. NEWSWEEK, 91(23):36, June 5, 1978.

—, by S. Fraker, et al. NEWSWEEK 91:36-37+, June 5, 1978; Same abr. with title War against abortion. READERS DIGEST 113:179-182, September, 1978.

Abortion: an unresolved moral problem, by G. Cosby. DIALOGUE 1978.

Abortion: an unsettled issue, by L. Dolby. ENGAGE/SOCIAL ACTION 5:49-50, December, 1977.

Abortion: unspeakable crime; moral choices in contemporary society, by J. Connery. NATIONAL CATHOLIC REPORTER 13:33, February 18, 1977.

Abortion U.S.A., by C. Francome. NEW SOCIETY pp. 197-198, April 27, 1978.

Abortion: the viewpoint of potential consumers, by M. H. Hamrick, et al. JOURNAL OF THE AMERICAN COLLEGE HEALTH ASSOCIATION 26(3):136-139, December, 1977.

Abortion: the wages of sin? ECONOMIST 265:36, December 10, 1977.

Abortion: who says there oughta be a law? by L. Cisler. MAJORITY REPORT 6:8, October 30-November 12, 1976.

Abortion: why the issue has not disappeared, by C. Francome. POLITICAL QUARTERLY 49:217-222, April, 1978.

Abortion: with particular reference to the developing role of counselling, by J. Hildebrand. BRITISH JOURNAL OF SOCIAL WORK 7(1):3-24, Spring, 1977.

Abortion: the world scene, by J. A. Loraine. CONTEMPORARY REVIEW 232:92-96, February, 1978.

Abortion: yesterday, today, and tomorrow [editorial], by B. S. Johnson. HEALTH AND SOCIAL WORK 3(1):3-7, February, 1978.

The abortionist, by R. Engel. OUR SUNDAY VISITOR 66:6-7, April 23, 1978.

Abortions and admissions; medical schools, by P. H. Connolly. COMMONWEAL 105:551-552, September 1, 1978.

Abortions increase during '76. U. S. MEDICINE 14(12):4, June 15, 1978.

Abortions 1976, by A. F. Frit Jofsson. LAKARTIDNINGEN 75(19):1907-1908, May 10, 1978.

Abortion's quantum advance, by J. A. Loraine. ATLAS 25:56, September, 1978.

Abortive act, by S. Walker. GUARDIAN p. 9, October 24, 1978.

Absence of capillary microangiopathy in oral contraceptive users with glucose intolerance, by J. W. Goldzieher, et al. OBSTETRICS AND GYNECOLOGY 51(1):89-92, January, 1978.

Absorption of stable isotopes of iron, copper, and zinc during oral contraceptives use, by J. C. King, et al. AMERICAN JOURNAL OF CLINICAL NUTRITION 31(7):1198-1203, July, 1978.

Acceptance of abortion among white Catholics and Protestants, 1962 and 1975, by W. A. McIntosh, et al. JOURNAL OF SCIENTIFIC STUDY OF RELIGION 16:295-303, September, 1977.

Access vs. Abuse: editorial page article on the use of sterilization as a method of birth control and the problems arising from its increasing popularity. POLITICS AND PEOPLE 2(16): 20-23.

The achieved small family: early fertility transition in an African city. STUDIES IN FAMILY PLANNING, 8(12):302, January, 1978.

Acid-base balance immediately after administration of an oral contraceptive, by C. Pilot, et al. ARCHIV FUER GYNAEKOLOGIE 223(3):221-231, October 28, 1977.

Acromegaly and articular lesions caused by contraceptives, by G. Nagyhegyi, et al. ORVOSI HETILAP 119(2):91-93, January 8, 1978.

Actinomyces infection associated with intra-uterine device, by M. C. Santa, et al. JOURNAL OF THE MEDICAL ASSOCIATION OF THE STATE OF ALABAMA 47(11):31-33, May, 1978.

Actinomycetes-like organisms in wearers of intrauterine contraceptive devices [letter], by R. D. Luff, et al. AMERICAN JOURNAL OF OBSTETRICS AND GYNECOLOGY 129(4): 476-477, October 15, 1977.

Action for wrongful life. Law for the nurse superviosr, by

H. Creighton. SUPERVISOR NURSE 8(4):12-15, April, 1977.

Action now for promoting the responsible paternity. REVISTA BRASILEIRA DE PESQUISAS MEDICAS E BIOLOGICAS 10(6):434-437, December, 1977.

Action of d-norgestrel (post-coital and minidosis) on the content of the diesterase enzyme in the human endometrium, by R. Nicholson, et al. OBSTETRICIA Y GINECOLOGIA LATINO AMERICANAS 34(11-12):406-409, November-December, 1976.

The activated factor X-antithrombin III reaction rate: a measure of the increased thrombotic tendency induced by estrogen-containing oral contraceptives in rabbits, by S. N. Gitel, et al. HAEMOSTASIS 7(1):10-18, 1978.

Acute dyserythropoiesis due to folic acid deficiency revealing celiac disease. Apropos of a case in a woman under prolonged oral contraception, by P. Veyssier, et al. ANNALES DE MEDECINE INTERNE 128(10):789-792, October, 1977.

Acute ophthalmologic complications during the use of oral contraceptives, by S. Friedman, et al. CONTRACEPTION 10:685, 1974; abstracted in OBSTETRICAL AND GYNECOLOGICAL SURVEY 30:451-452, 1975.

Acute renal failure as a complication of hypertonic saline abortion in a kidney allograft recipient, by A. Carvallo, et al. CLINICAL NEPHROLOGY 8(5):491-493, November, 1977.

Addition to the bibliographic citations in our work "Use of Microsurgical Technics in Reconstructive Surgery of the Fallopian Tubes" [letter], by L. Beck. GEBURTSHILFE UND FRAUENHEILKUNDE 38(5):398, May, 1978.

Address to the National Catholic Conference of Bishops of the United States of America; role as bishops today, by J. Bernardin. OSSERVATORE ROMANO 2(511):5-6, January 12, 1978.

Adjudicating what Yoder left unresolved: religious rights for minor children after Danforth (Planned Parenthood of Cent. Mo. v. Danforth, 96 Sup Ct 2831) and Carey (Carey v. Population Servs. Int. 97 Sup Ct 2010). UNIVERSITY OF PENNSYLVANIA LAW REVIEW 126:1135-1170, May, 1978.

Administration of prostaglandins by various routes for induction of abortion. Merits and demerits, by U. Krishna, et al. PROSTAGLANDINS 15(4):685-693, April, 1978.

Administrative incongruence and authority conflict in four abortion clinics, by W. M. Hern, et al. HUMAN ORGANIZATION 36:376-383, Winter, 1977.

Adolescent contraceptors: follow-up study, by J. E. Morgenthau, et al. NEW YORK STATE JOURNAL OF MEDICINE 77: 928-931, May, 1977.

Adolescent fertility in Hawaii: implications for planning, by L. Stringfellow, et al. HAWAII MEDICAL JOURNAL 37(4): 105-113, April, 1978.

Adolescent health services and contraceptive use, by E. H. Mudd, et al. AMERICAN JOURNAL OF ORTHOPSYCHIATRY 48:495-504, July, 1978.

Adolescent males, fatherhood, and abortion, by A. A. Rothstein. JOURNAL OF YOUTH AND ADOLESCENCE 7:203-214, June, 1978.

Adolescent parents: a special case of the unplanned family, by J. A. Bruce. THE FAMILY COORDINATOR 27(1):75-78, January, 1978.

Adoption of modern health and family planning practices in a rural community of India, by S. K. Sandhu, et al. INTERNATIONAL JOURNAL OF HEALTH EDUCATION 20(4): 240-247, October-December, 1977.

Adrenal necrosis following abortion, by R. H. Young, et al. IRISH JOURNAL OF MEDICAL SCIENCE 146(10):340-

342, October, 1977.

Advances and perspectives of gynecology, by A. F. Mendizabal. OBSTETRICIA Y GINECOLOGIA LATINO-AMERICANAS 33(5-6):191-202, May-June, 1975.

The advantages of the extra-amniotic transcervical instillation of rivanol in therapeutic abortions, by W. Haensel, et al. GE-BURTSHILFE UND FRAUENHEILKUNDE 37(12):1050-1054, December, 1977.

The advent of legal abortion and surgical abortion techniques, by P. T. Wilson. MEDICAL TRIAL TECHNIQUE QUAR-TERLY 22(3):241-278, Winter, 1976.

Adverse effects of steroid sex hormones, by I. Hirschler. ORVOSI HETILAP 118(34):2061-2063, August 21, 1977.

After Humanae Vitae. TABLET 232:723-724, July 29, 1978.

After "Humane Vitae": a decade of "lively debate," by C. E. Curran. HOSPITAL PROGRESS 59(70:84-89, July, 1978.

After the pill? GUARDIAN p. 11, July 14, 1978.

Again: juriprudence problems in voluntary sterilization, by G. H. Schlund. GEBURTSHILFE UND FRAUENHEILKUNDE 38(8):587-590, August, 1978.

Against abortion: a Protestant proposal, by G. Meilaender. LINACRE 45:165-178, May, 1978.

Age at first coitus and choice of contraceptive method: pre-liminary report on a study of factors related to cervical neoplasia, by C. Gary, et al. SOCIAL BIOLOGY 22:255-260, August, 1975.

Agreement and dissent mark Humanae Vitae Conference, in Milan, Italy, by J. Mather. OUR SUNDAY VISITOR 67:3, July 16, 1978.

Agreement rates between oral contraceptive users and prescribers in relation to drug use histories, by P. D. Stolley, et al. AMERICAN JOURNAL OF EPIDEMIOLOGY 107(3): 226-235, March, 1978.

Akron gets restrictive abortion measure; in Ohio, by J. Petosa. NATIONAL CATHOLIC REPORTER 14:20, March 10, 1978.

Alpha-fetoprotein (AFP) levels in maternal serum in 115 patients with spontaneous abortion, by G. Lidjork, et al. ACTA OBSTETRICIA ET GYNECOLOGICA SCANDINAVICA (69):50-53, 1977.

Alpha-fetoprotein, HPL, ostriol and SP1 concentrations in prostaglandin-induced mid-trimester abortions, by M. Cornely, et al. GEBURTSHILFE UND FRAUENHEIL-KUNDE 38(6):446-451, June, 1978.

Alpha-1-antitrypsin (Pi)-types in recurrent miscarriages, by D. Aarskog, et al. CLINICAL GENETICS 13(1):81-84, January, 1978.

Alpha1-antitrypsin, protein marker in oral contraceptive-associated hepatic tumors, by P. E. Palmer, et al. AMERICAN JOURNAL OF CLINICAL PATHOLOGY 68(6):736-739, December, 1977.

Alternatives to female sterilization, by S. S. Ratnam, et al. INTERNATIONAL JOURNAL OF GYNAECOLOGY AND OBSTETRICS 15(1):88-92, 1977.

Ambulatory abortion, by O. S. Slepykh, et al. PEDIATRIYA, AKUSHERSTVO I HINEKOLOHIYA (5):60-63, September-October, 1977.

Ambulatory care following pregnancy interruption in a rural district, by B. Zerning, et al. ZEITSCHRIFT FUR DIE GESAMTE HYGIENE UND IHRE GRENZGEBIETE 24(5): 392-394, May, 1978.

Ameba trophozoites in cervico-vaginal smear of a patient using an intrauterine device. A case report, by R. E. McNeill, et al.

ACTA CYTOLOGICA 22(2):91-92, March-April, 1978.

América Latina: actividades desarrolladas por los programas de planificación de la familia, 1975, by Z. Soto G. CENTRO LATINOAMERICANO DE DEMOGRAFÍA. BOLETÍN DEMOGRÁFICO.

American Nurses' Association Division on maternal and child health nursing practice: statement on abortion. COLORADO NURSE 78:19, October, 1978.

Amniotic fluid embolism and disseminated intravascular coagulation after evacuation of missed abortion, by W. B. Stromme, et al. OBSTETRICS AND GYNECOLOGY 42 (1 Suppl): 76S-80S, July, 1978.

Analysis of recent decisions involving abortions, by P. Geary. CATHOLIC LAWYER 23:237-242, Summer, 1978.

Analysis of spontaneous abortiveness, child mortality, and of inborn developmental defects in two population series from Horná Nitra, by A. Gencík, et al. BRATISLAVSKE LEKARSKE LISTY 69(6):678-687, June, 1978.

Analyst biases in KAP surveys: a cross-cultural comparison, by J. W. Ratcliffe. STUDIES IN FAMILY PLANNING 7:322, November, 1976.

Anesthesia in induced abortion by intravenous administration of sombrevin and fentanyl, by V. I. Rogovskoi, et a. AKUSHERSTVO I GINEKOLOGIIA (12):51, December, 1977.

Animal in vivo studies and in vitro experiments with human tubes for end-to-end anastomotic operation by a CO_2-laser technique, by F. Klink, et al. FERTILITY AND STERILITY 30(1):100-102, July, 1978.

Another alternative to the pill; encase oval, by J. Chan. McCALLS 104:40, January, 1978.

Another storm brewing over abortion: in Congress and elsewhere, tempers run high on easing or stiffening curbs on public funding of a highly controversial operation. U. S. NEWS 85:63, July 24, 1978.

Antenatal injury and the rights of the foetus, by T. D. Campbell, et al. PHILOSOPHICAL QUARTERLY 28:17-30, January, 1978.

Antiabortion amendment fails, by G. Hildebrand. MILITANT 40(19):2, May 16, 1976.

Anti-abortion forces see Akron's consent law as exploding myths; in Ohio, by J. Petosa. NATIONAL CATHOLIC REPORTER 14:32, March 17, 1978.

Anti-abortion "Guerilla Warfare" aimed at forcing parental consent opposed by health care coalition. JUVENILE JUS-TICE DIGEST 6:19, October 13, 1978.

Anti abortion vote courted, by I. Silber. GUARDIAN 28(49):4, September 29, 1976.

Anti-Catholicism becomes counter-attack strategy of pro-abortionists in nation, by R. Shaw. OUR SUNDAY VISITOR 66:2, February 19, 1978.

Antifertility mode of action of alpha-chlorohydrin-interaction with glyceraldehyde-3-phosphate-dehydrogenase [proceedings], by N. A. Dickinson, et al. BRITISH JOURNAL OF PHARMACOLOGY 61(3):456P, November, 1977.

Anti-implantation action of a medicated intrauterine delivery system (MIDS), by D. L. Moyer, et al. CONTRACEPTION 16(1):39-49, July, 1977.

An approach to the analysis of menstrual patterns in the critical evaluation of contraceptives, by G. Rodriguez, et al. STUDIES IN FAMILY PLANNING 7:42-51, February, 1976.

Approval of depo-provera for contraception denied. FDA DRUG BULLETIN 8(2):10-11, March-April, 1978.

Archidonic acid and other free fatty acid changes during abortion

29

induced by prostaglandin F2alpha, by P. L. Ogburn, Jr., et al. AMERICAN JOURNAL OF OBSTETRICS AND GYNE-COLOGY 130(2):188-193, January 15, 1978.

Archbishop Quiin asks pro-life advocates to show respect for life in every way. OUR SUNDAY VISITOR 66:3, February 5, 1978.

Are we 25 votes away from losing the Bill of Rights. . .and the rest of the Constitution? by L. C. Wohl. MS 6:46-49+, February, 1978.

Argument heard: abortion—state statures—fetal viability. THE CRIMINAL LAW REPORTER: SUPREME COURT PRO-CEEDINGS 24(3):4050-4051, October 18, 1978.

Artificial abortion and perinatal medicine, by H. Kirchhoff. GEBURTSHILFE UND FRAUENHEILKUNDE 37(10): 849-856, October, 1977.

Assay of long-acting contraceptive steroid formulations in rab-bits, by K. Fotherby, et al. CONTRACEPTION 17(4):365-373, April, 1978.

Assessment of human chorionic gonadotropin (HCG) levels during luteal phase in women using intrauterine contracep-tion, by J. M. Aubert, et al. CONTRACEPTION 16(6):557-562, December, 1977.

Assessment of ovarian function in perimenopausal women after stopping oral contraceptives, by R. A. Donald, et al. BRITISH JOURNAL OF OBSTETRICS AND GYNAECOLOGY 85(1): 70-73, January, 1978.

The association between oral contraception and hepatocellular adenoma—a preliminary report, by J. B. Rooks, et al. INTER-NATIONAL JOURNAL OF GYNAECOLOGY AND OBSTE-TRICS 15(2):143-144, 1977.

Asymptomatic liver cell adenomas. Another case of resolution after discontinuation of oral contraceptive use, by W. L. Ramseur, et al. JAMA; JOURNAL OF THE AMERICAN

MEDICAL ASSOCIATION 239(16):1647-1648, April 21, 1978.

Attitude towards family planning (a study of impatient attendants), by G. M. Char, et al. INDIAN JOURNAL OF PUBLIC HEALTH 21(2):89-94, April-June, 1977.

Attitudes of adolescent males toward abortion, contraception, and sexuality, by E. Vadies, et al. SOCIAL WORK HEALTH CARE 3:169-174, Winter, 1977.

Attitudes of nurses to providing contraceptive services for youth, by E. S. Herold, et al. CANADIAN JOURNAL OF PUBLIC HEALTH 68(4):307-310, July-August, 1977.

Attitudes toward abortion: a comparative analysis of correlates for 1973 and 1975, by T. C. Wagenaar. JOURNAL OF SOCIOLOGY AND SOCIAL WELFARE 4(6):927-944, June, 1977.

Attitudes toward abortion in Thailand: a survey of senior medical students, by S. Varakamin, et al. STUDIES IN FAMILY PLANNING 8:288-293, November, 1977.

Attitudes towards family size and family planning in rural Ghana-Danfa project: 1972 survey findings, by D. W. Belcher, et al. JOURNAL OF BIOSOCIAL SCIENCE 10(1): 59-79, January, 1978.

L'augmentation des avortements déclarés en France, by G. Duchene. LA DOCUMENTATION CATHOLIQUE 74:893, October 16, 1977.

Autoantibodies following vasectomy, by J. Y. Bullock, et al. JOURNAL OF UROLOGY 118(4):604-606, October, 1977.

Avoiding tough abortion complication: a live baby. MEDICAL WORLD NEWS 18:83, November 14, 1977.

Away from the ivory tower, by N. Arko, et al. NEW PHYSICIAN 26(12):26-28, December, 1977.

BMA and the Abortion Act [letter], by D. Flint. BRITISH MEDICAL JOURNAL 1(6125):1490, June 3, 1978.

Babies' revenge. ECONOMIST 266:58, January 7, 1978.

Background and development of the National Reporting System for Family Planning Services, by B. J. Haupt. VITAL HEALTH STATISTICS (13):i-iii, 1-64, April, 1978.

Bacteriologic culture results obtained before and after elective midtrimester urea abortion, by R. T. Burkman, et al. CONTRACEPTION 17(6):513-521, June, 1978.

Balneotherapy as prophylaxis in aborted pregnancy by I. F. Perfil'eva, et al. AKUSHERSTVO I GINEKOLOGIIA (7):41-44, July, 1978.

Barrier contraceptive practice and male infertility as related factors to breast cancer in married women, by A. N. Gjorgov. MEDICAL HYPOTHESES 4(2):79-88, March-April, 1978.

Beal v. Doe (97 Sup Ct 2366), Maher v. Roe (97 Sup Ct 2376), and non-therapeutic abortions: the state does not have to pay the bill. LOYOLA UNIVERSITY OF CHICAGO. LAW JOURNAL 9:288-311, Fall, 1977.

Behavior of the C-reactive protein in short and long-term application of various hormonal contraceptives, by G. Klinger, et al. ZENTRALBLATT FUER GYNAEKOLOGIE 100(3):167-172, 1978.

The behavior of serum total protein and proten fractions during the use of various hormonal contraceptives, by G. Klinger, et al. DEUTSCHE GESUNDHEITSWESEN 32(51):2418-2423, 1977.

Behavioural consequences of vasectomy in the mouse, by R. J. Aitken, et al. EXPERIENTIA 33(10):1396-1397, October 15, 1977.

Beliefs regarding the consequences of birth control among black, colored, Indian, and white South Africans, by J. Barling, et al. JOURNAL OF SOCIAL PSYCHOLOGY 105:149-150, June, 1978.

Beneficial effects of ascorbic acid in vasectomized rats, by N. J. Chinoy, et al. INDIAN JOURNAL OF EXPERIMENTAL BIOLOGY 15(10):821-824, October, 1977.

The benefit of lactation amenorrhea as a contraceptive, by F. Hefnawi, et al. INTERNATIONAL JOURNAL OF GYNAE-COLOGY AND OBSTETRICS 15(1):60-62, 1977.

The benefits and risks of IUD use, by L. B. Tyrer. INTERNA-TIONAL JOURNAL OF GYNAECOLOGY AND OBSTE-TRICS 15(2):150-152, 1977.

Benign hepatic lesions in women taking oral contraceptives, by T. J. Davis, et al. GASTROINTESTINAL RADIOLOGY 2(3):213-219, December 20, 1977.

Benign intracranial hypertension and thrombosis of the venous sinuses during contraceptive treatment: anatomo-clinical and neuroradiological observations, by M. Baldini, et al. RI-VISTA DI PATALOGIA NERVOSA E MENTALE 98(3): 185-190, May-June, 1977.

Benign liver-cell tumor and intra-abdominal hemorrhage follow-ing administration of oral contraceptives, by F. Hofstädter, et al. MUNCHENER MEDIZINISCHE WOCHENSCHRIFT 120(6):899-900, June 30, 1978.

Beratung in Sachen 218; ethische anmerkungen zur gestaltung des in der reforth des 218 vorgesehenen beratungssystems, by P. Schmitz. STIMMEN DER ZEIT 195:48-56, January, 1977.

Berdyansk mud treatment of inflammatory gynecological di-seases occurring after abortion in a subacute stage, by L. I. Bero, et al. PEDIATRIYA, AKUSHERSTVO I GINEKOLO-HIYA (2):53-54, 1978.

Better bargains than Hong Kong's, by L. Mathews. GUARDIAN

33

p. 9, December 5, 1978.

Between guilt and gratification: abortion doctors reveal their feelings, by N. Rosen. NEW YORK TIMES MAGAZINE pp. 70-71+, April 17, 1977.

Beyond morals, rights of abortion issue, by R. Cohen. ENGAGE /SOCIAL ACTION 6:28-29, April, 1978.

Bibliography of population theories and studies. POPULATION INDEX 43(2):244, April, 1977.

Bibliography of society, ethics and the life sciences: supplement for 1977-78, by S. Sollitto, et al. HASTINGS CENTER RE-PORT (Suppl):1-26, 1977-1978.

The Billings birth regulation method; a successful experience in Korea, by M. McHugh, Sr. CHRIST TO THE WORLD 21:325-331, November 5, 1976.

Binding of norgestrel to receptor proteins in the human endometrium and myometrium, by J. P. Uniyal, et al. JOURNAL OF STEROID BIOCHEMISTRY 8(11):1183-1188, November, 1977.

Bioavailability of norethindrone in human subjecsts, by R. A. Okerholm, et al. EUROPEAN JOURNAL OF CLINICAL PHARMACOLOGY 13(1):35-39, March 17, 1978.

Biochemical effects of treatment with oral contraceptive steroids on the dopaminergic system of the rat, by S. Algeri, et al. NEUROENDOCRINOLOGY 22(4):343-351, 1976.

Biochemical studies on oxytocinase activities of human endometrium, uterine fluid and plasma, by S. Ganguly, et al. INDIAN JOURNAL OF MEDICAL RESEARCH 66(1):43-48, July, 1977.

Bioethics/case of the fetus, by P. Singer. NEW YORK REVIEW OF BOOKS 23(13):33, August 5, 1976.

Biological antithrombin III levels [letter], by R. L. Bick. JAMA;

JOURNAL OF THE AMERICAN MEDICAL ASSOCIATION 239(4):296, January 23, 1978.

Biological profile of Centchroman—a new post-coital contraceptive, by V. P. Kamboj, et al. INDIAN JOURNAL OF EXPERIMENTAL BIOLOGY 15(12):1144-1150, December, 1977.

Biological properties of interceptive agents from Aristolochia indica Linn, by A. Pakrashi, et al. INDIAN JOURNAL OF MEDICAL RESEARCH 66(6):991-998, December, 1977.

The biomedical research community: its place in consensus development. JAMA; JOURNAL OF THE AMERICAN MEDICAL ASSOCIATION 239(6):485-488, February 6, 1978.

Bipolar cautery for laparoscopic sterilization, by E. Gregersen, et al. ACTA OBSTETRICA ET GINECOLOGICA SCANDINAVICA 57(2):169-171, 1978.

The bipolar needle for vasectomy. I. Experience with the first 1000 cases, by S. S. Schmidt, et al. FERTILITY AND STERILITY 29(6):676-680, June, 1978.

Birth control clinics in the city of Birmingham—a geographical study, by B. D. Giles, et al. SOCIAL SCIENCE AND MEDICINE 11(14-16):763-772, November, 1977.

Birth control in India: the carrot and the rod? by L. C. Landman. FAMILY PLANNING PERSPECTIVES 9:101-110, May-June, 1977.

Birth control in young females, by U. Fritsche, et al. ZEITSCHRIFT FUR AERZTLICHE FORTBILDUNG (Jena) 72(6):282-286, March 15, 1978.

Birth control motivation—what does it mean? by A. Chamberlain. HEALTH VISITOR 51:374-377, October, 1978.

Birth control nightmare; intra-uterine device, by S. Vaughan. GOOD HOUSEKEEPING 187:56+, July, 1978.

Birth control: once-a-month pill, by M. Jeffery. HARPER'S BAZAAR (3201):24, August, 1978.

Birth control: what's new, safe and foolproof, by L. Pembrook. PARENTS MAGAZINE 52:74+, November, 1977.

Birth planning success: motivation and contraceptive method [based on interviews, Summer, 1971, with a stratified sample of 422 black and 939 white urban wives in the East North Central United States], by P. Cutright, et al. FAMILY PLANNING PERSPECTIVES 10:43-48, January-February, 1978.

Birth planning values and decisions: the prediction of fertility, by B. D. Townes, et al. JOURNAL OF APPLIED SOCIAL PSYCHOLOGY 7:73-88, January-March, 1977.

Birth rate and birth control in Sweden 1962-1976, by O. Meirik, et al. LAKARTIDNINGEN 75(6):426-427+, February 8, 1978.

The birth rate in Singapore, by W. Neville. POPULATION STUDIES 32:113-133, March, 1978.

Birthright; saving a mother, saving a life, by C. Anthony. OUR SUNDAY VISITOR 67:6, May 21, 1978.

Births averted in Singapore during 1966-1975, by A. J. Chen, et al. SINGAPORE STATISTICS BULLETIN 6:57-70, December, 1977.

The bishop: transformed into a servant of the word; excerpt from the homily at the ordination of Bishop Thomas C. Kelly, by J. Bernardin. ORIGINS 7:160, August 25, 1977.

Bishops' committee asks for sterilization rules. OUR SUNDAY VISITOR 66:4, March 12, 1978.

Bishops echo Vatican sterilization stance, by M. Winiarski. NATIONAL CATHOLIC REPORTER 14:3, December 2, 1977.

Black ministers' attitudes toward population size and birth control, by J. Irwin, et al. SOCIOLOGICAL ANALYSIS 38: 252-257, Fall, 1977.

Bleeding and serum d-norgestrel, estradiol and progesterone patterns in women using d-norgestrel subdermal polysiloxane capsules for contraception, by D. E. Moore, et al. CONTRACEPTION 17(4):315-328, April, 1978.

Blessing and a curse; the pill, by J. Webb. MACLEANS 91:55-58+, April 17, 1978.

Blood and malignant diseases as indications for pregnancy interruption, by W. F. Jungi. INTERNIST 19(5):279-283, May, 1978.

Blood coagulation disorders in the course of interrupted advanced pregnancy, by M. Uszyński, et al. GINEKOLOGIA POLASKA 48(9):809-812, September, 1977.

Blood coagulation studies of therapeutic abortion induced by 15-methyl-prostaglandin F2 alpha, by R. During, et al. ZENTRALBLATT FUER GYNAEKOLOGIE 99(22):1361-1365, 1977.

Blood pressure response to estrogen-progestin oral contraceptive after pregnancy-induced hypertension, by J. A. Pritchard, et al. AMERICAN JOURNAL OF OBSTETRICS AND GYNECOLOGY 129(7):733-739, December 1, 1977.

Blood serum lipids and cholesterol of the ewe during intravaginal pessary treatment, by P. K. Pareek, et al. ZENTRALBLATT FUER VETERINAERMEDIZINE 24(7):605-607, September, 1977.

Bloodless castrator [letter], by A. V. Clarke-Lewis. VETERINARY RECORD 101(11):215, September 10, 1977.

Bone response to termination of oestrogen treatment, by R. Lindsay, et al. LANCET 1(8078):1325-1327, June 24, 1978.

Books and babies: hope and a deadline [to have or not to have children], by D. F. Tannen. MOVING OUT 6(2):24-26, 1976.

Bowel obstruction and perforation with an intraperitoneal loop intrauterine contraceptive device, by J. D'Amico, et al. AMERICAN JOURNAL OF OBSTETRICS AND GYNE-COLOGY 129(4):461-462, October 15, 1977.

Brazilian elites and population policy [attitudes toward government involvement in population planning of 269 influential public figures who were interviewed in 1972-73], by P. McDonough, et al. POPULATION AND DEVELOPMENT REVIEW 3:377-401, December, 1977.

Breakthrough in Papua New Guinea, by J. C. Abecede. WORLD HEALTH :8-17, October, 1977.

Bringing the sexual revolution home: Planned Parenthood's five-year plan, by M. Schwartz. AMERICA 138:114-116, February 18, 1978; Reply by R. Elliot, 139:241-243, October 14, 1978; Rejoinder 139:243-245, October 14, 1978.

British studies indicate increase in risks. PEOPLE 5(1):22, 1978.

A broader perspective on Humanae Vitae, by J. Quinn. ORIGINS 8:10-12, May 25, 1978.

CO2-hysteroscopy, a method for the removal of occult intra-uterine devices (proceedings), by J. Mohr, et al. ARCHIV FUR GYNAEKOLOGIE 224(1-4):31-32, July 29, 1977.

Calculating the risks, by C. Doyle. OBSERVER p. 11, October 8, 1978.

Califano seeks Congress' okay for teenage pregnancy program. JUVENILE JUSTICE DIGEST 6:13, July 7, 1978.

Call to reflection, by R. G. Hoyt. CHRISTIANITY AND CRISIS 37:253-255, October 31, 1977; DISCUSSION 37:264-266+, November 14, 1977+.

Campaign for natural birth control methods, by M. Nagura. JOSANPU ZASSHI 32(1):62-63, January, 1978.

The campaign in favour of abortion in Italy; declarations of the Hierarchy; two messages of the Italian bishops. CHRIST TO THE WORLD 22:283-285, November 4, 1977.

Campus contraception bitter pill, by P. Edmonds. NATIONAL CATHOLIC REPORTER 13:5-6, December 24, 1976.

Can the first pregnancy of a young adolescent be prevented? a question which must be answered, by M. Baizerman. JOURNAL OF YOUTH AND ADOLESCENCE 6:343-351, December, 1977.

Can 291 popes be wrong? [abortion], by S. Morse. MAJORITY REPORT 7:3, August 6-19, 1977.

Canadian woman doesn't make headlines but her work brings help to mothers; Birthright International, by C. Anthony. OUR SUNDAY VISITOR 66:2, January 8, 1978.

Carbonic anhydrase activity in human cervical mucus and its response to various contraceptives regimes, by E. N. Chantler, et al. BRITISH JOURNAL OF OBSTETRICS AND GYNAECOLOGY 84(9):705-707, September, 1977.

Carcadian variations of plasma delta4-androstenedione in normal and castrated adult males, by D. De Aloysio, et al. ACTA EUROPAEA FERTILITATIS 8(2):175-184, June, 1977.

Cardinal Vicar of Rome on new abortion law; approved by the Chamber of Deputies on 21 January, 1977, by U. Poletti. OSSERVATORE ROMANO 7(464):2, February 17, 1977.

Cardiovascular accidents caused by estroprogestational contraceptives and lipid anomalies in blood circulation, by J. L. de Gennes, et al. ANNALES L'ENDOCRINOLOGIE 38(6): 447-448, 1977.

Cardiovascular birth defects and antenatal exposure to female sex hormones, by O. P. Heinonen, et al. NEW ENGLAND

JOURNAL OF MEDICINE 296:67-70, January 13, 1977.

Cardiovascular complications of oral contraceptives, by N. M. Kaplan. ANNUAL REVIEW OF MEDICINE 29:31-40, 1978.

Cardiovascular diseases as indications for pregnancy interruption, by K. Kochsiek, et al. INTERNIST 19(5):269-272, May, 1978.

Cardiovascular effects of oral contraceptives, by P. D. Stolley, et al. SOUTHERN MEDICAL JOURNAL 71(7):821-824, July, 1978.

Carey (Carey v. Population Serv. Int. 97 Sup Ct 2010) kids and contraceptives: privacy's problem child. UNIVERSITY OF MIAMI LAW REVIEW 32:750-762, June, 1978.

Carey v. Population Services International (97 Sup Ct 2010): closing the curtain on Comstockery. BROOKLYN LAW REVIEW 44:565-597, Spring, 1978.

Carey v. Population Services International (97 Sup Ct 2010): an extension of the right of privacy. OHIO NORTHERN UNIVERSITY LAW REVIEW 5:167-174, January, 1978.

Carey v. Population Servs. Int. 97 Sup Ct. 2010. HUMAN RIGHTS 6:311-313, Spring, 1977.

Caring for the rape victim, by D.H. Chase. BULLETIN OF THE AMERICAN PROTESTANT HOSPITAL ASSOCIATION 41(2):20-24, 1977.

Carter and abortion, by C. Tucker. SATURDAY REVIEW 4:64, September 17, 1977.

—, by A. Wilcox. MILITANT 40(36):12, September 24, 1976.

Carter/Ford join antiabortion drive, by G. Hildebrand. MILITANT 40(36):15, September 24, 1976.

A case control study of carcinoma of the ovary, by M. L. Newhouse, et al. BRITISH JOURNAL OF PREVENTIVE AND SOCIAL MEDICINE 31(3):148-153, September, 1977.

A case-control study of uterine perforations documented at laparoscopy, by M. K. White, et al. AMERICAN JOURNAL OF OBSTETRICS AND GYNECOLOGY 129(6):623-625, November 15, 1977.

The case for injectables, by M. Jones. PEOPLE 4(4):25-28, 1977.

Case of ovarian pregnancy following insertion of a pessary, by F. Buchholz, et al. MEDIZINISCHE WELT 29(2):59-60, January 13, 1978.

Case report on a retinal complication in long-term-therapy with oral hormonal contraceptives, by H. Huismans. KLINISCHE MONATSBLAETTER FUER AUGENHEILKUNDE 171(5): 781-786, November, 1977.

Castration methods and their potential cost [letter], by P. A. Mullen. VETERINARY RECORD 101(19):391, November 5, 1977.

Catching up with Joe O'Rourke; rebel with many causes, by J. Deedy. CRITIC 36:16-17, Spring, 1978.

Catecholamines during therapeutic abortion induced with intra-amniotic prostaglandin F2alpha, by W. E. Brenner, et al. AMERICAN JOURNAL OF OBSTETRICS AND GYNE-COLOGY 130(2):178-187, January 15, 1978.

Catecholamines in discrete areas of the hypothalamus of obese and castrated male rats, by J. A. Cruce, et al. PHARMA-COLOGY, BIOCHEMISTRY AND BEHAVIOR 8(3):287-289, March, 1978.

A Catholic hospital and natural family planning, by R. Kambic, et al. HOSPITAL PROGRESS 59(4):70-73, April, 1978.

Catholic hospital ban on sterilization reaffirmed. OUR SUN-DAY VISITOR 66:1, December 11, 1977.

Catholic hospitals and sterilization, by W. Smith. LINACRE QUARTERLY 44:107-116, May, 1977.

Catholicism and human sexuality; Lenten series, by R. McBrien. NATIONAL CATHOLIC REPORTER 14:9, February 17, 1978.

Causes of clinic drop-out among Iranian pill users, by C. F. Lee, et al. JOURNAL OF BIOSOCIAL SCIENCE 10(1):7-15, January, 1978.

Causes of high teenage birth rate. Youngs drug products corporation. INTELLECT 106:437-438, May, 1978.

Cell-mediated immunity in pregnant patients with and without a previous history of spontaneous abortions, by G. Garewal, et al. BRITISH JOURNAL OF OBSTETRICS AND GYNAECOLOGY 85(3):221-224, March, 1978.

Cell-mediated immunity in vasectomized rhesus monkeys, by B. J. Wilson, et al. FERTILITY AND STERILITY 28(12): 1349-1355, December, 1977.

Cell-mediated immunity to spermatozoa following vasectomy, by A. G. Tumboh-Oheri, et al. THERIOGENOLOGY 8(4): 166, October, 1977.

Centchroman—a post-coital contraceptive agent, by N. Anand, et al. INDIAN JOURNAL OF EXPERIMENTAL BIOLOGY 15(12):1142-1130, December, 1977.

Cerclage in the prevention of spontaneous abortion and premature labor. Experiences at the "Boris Kidrić" in health institute 1966-1975, by L. Janković. NARODNO ZDRAVIJE 32(11-12):525-528, November-December, 1976.

Cerebrovascular diseases in women receiving oral contraceptives: report of three cases, by J. Ogata, et al. RINSHO SHINKEI-GAKU 17(7):465-471, July, 1977.

Cervical cancer: pill seems safe for most women but those with dysplasia may have higher risk. FAMILY PLANNING PER-

SPECTIVES 10(3):165-166, May-June, 1978.

Cervical carcinoma and the pill [letter], by H. J. Collette, et al. LANCET 1(8061):441-442, February 25, 1978.

Cervical factor in fertility regulation, by M. Elstein. ADVANCES IN EXPERIMENTAL MEDICINE AND BIOLOGY 89:371-387, 1977.

Cervical mucus. A new dimension for family planning, by J. J. McCarthy, Jr. JOURNAL OF THE FLORIDA MEDICAL ASSOCIATION 65(1):22-24, January, 1978.

Cervical neoplasia and the pill [letter]. LANCET 2(8042):825-826, October 15, 1977.

Cervical rape: dilators vs. laminaria [abortion], by M. Roos. OFF OUR BACKS 7:17-18, April, 1977.

A change but Spain stays mostly the same, by M. Jones. GUARDIAN p. 9, August 17, 1978.

Change in the adrenal cortex of rats in stress after hypophysectomy, thyroidectomy and castration, by B. Ia. Ryzhavski. ARKHIV ANATOMII, GISTOLOGII I EMBRIOLOGII 74(4):40-46, April, 1978.

Changes in antithrombin III levels in pregnancy, labour and in women on the contraceptive pill, by E. M. Essien. AFRICAN JOURNAL OF MEDICAL SCIENCES 6(3):109-113, September, 1977.

Changes in the extensibility of the cervix of the rat in late pregnancy produced by prostaglandin F2alpha, ovariectomy and steroid replacement [proceedings], by M. Hollingsworth, et al. BRITISH JOURNAL OF PHARMACOLOGY 61(3): 501P-502P, November, 1977.

Changes in the kidneys and upper urinary passages due to hormonal contraceptives, by T. D. Datuashvili. SOVETSKAYA MEDITZINA (11):65-69, November, 1977.

Changes in menstrul cycle length and regularity after use of oral contraceptives, by R. N. Taylor, Jr., et al. INTERNATIONAL JOURNAL OF GYNAECOLOGY AND OBSTETRICS 15(1):55-59, 1977.

Changes in serum high density lipoproteins in women on oral contraceptive drugs, by R. M. Krauss, et al. CLINICA CHIMICA ACTA 80(3):465-470, November 1, 1977.

Changes in serum lipids during treatment with norgestrel, oestradiol-valerate and cycloprogynon, by F. H. Nielsen, et al. ACTA OBSTETRICIA ET GYNECOLOGICA SCANDINAVICA 56(4):367-370, 1977.

Changes in the structure and function of the testes and epididymides in vasectomized rams, by B. M. Perera. FERTILITY AND STERILITY 29(3):354-359, March, 1978.

Changes in tubal sterilization through the years 1955-1975 (proceedings), by F. H. Hepp, et al. ARCHIV FUR GYNAEKOLOGIE 224(1-4):38-39, July 29, 1977.

Changes of glucose tolerance and blood lipid level in women as a result of administration of oral contraceptives, by Z. Kh. Zaripova, et al. VOPROSY OKHRANY MATERINSTVA I DETSTVA 22(10):68-69, October, 1977.

Changes of serum hormone concentrations during oral contraception using monohormonal and combination preparations (proceedings), by J. Nevinny-Stickel, et al. ARCHIV FUR GYNAEKOLOGIE 224(1-4):27-29, July 29, 1977.

Changes of unspecific immune parameters (CH50E, C3, C4, C3A, lysozyme, CRP at the end of 2-year use of a synthetic sex steroid drug, by A. Stelzner, et al. DEUTSCHE GESUNDHEITSWESEN 33(29):1381-1385, 1978.

Changing contraceptive patterns: a global perspective. POPULATION BULLETIN 32(3):1, August, 1977.

Changing contraceptive practices in the U. S. married couples, 1965 and 1975. Population reference bureau. SOCIAL

EDUCATION 42:43-44, January, 1978.

The changing law on sterilization, by A. H. Bernstein. HOS-PITALS 52(3):36+, February 1, 1978.

Changing views of abortion, by T. C. Wagenaar, et al. HUMAN BEHAVIOR 7:58, March, 1978.

Characteristics of the hypophyseal-ovarian relationship in miscarriage, by E. S. Kononova, et al. AKUSHERSTVO I GINEKOLOGIIA (8):37-40, August, 1977.

Characteristics of patients requesting reversal of sterilization, by P. Thomson, et al. BRITISH JOURNAL OF OBSTETRICS AND GYNAECOLOGY 85(3):161-164, March, 1978.

Characteristics of vasectomy patients at a family planning clinic, by R. J. Gandy. JOURNAL OF BIOSOCIAL SCIENCE 10(2):125-132, April, 1978.

Characterization of progesterone receptor in human uterine cytosol with a synthetic progestin, norgestrel [proceedings], by A. K. Srivastava, et al. JOURNAL OF ENDOCRINOLOGY 77(2):22P-23P, May, 1978.

Chemical control of human fertility. ENVIRONMENTAL SCIENCE AND TECHNOLOGY 12:258-259, March, 1978.

Chemical sterilization of male dogs: synergistic action of alpha-chlorohydrin (U-5897) with danazol on the testes and epididymides of dog, by V. P. Dixit. ACTA EUROPAEA FERTILITATIS 8(2):167-173, June, 1977.

Chemical sterilization of male langurs: synergistic action of alpha-chlorohydrin (U-5897) with methallibure (ICI, 33828) on the testes and epididymides of Presbytis entellus entellus Dufresne, by V. P. Dixit. ENDOKRINOLOGIE 69(2):157-163, July, 1977.

Chile: experiencia con un sistema de estadísticas de servicio para un programa materno-infantil y de planificación de la familia. CENTRO LATINOAMERICANO DE DEMOGRAFÍA. BOLE-

TÍN DEMOGRÁFICO (159):47, November, 1977.

Choice of contraceptives, by T. Luukkainen. KATILOLEHTI 83(6):230-233, June, 1978.

Choice of oral contraceptives for a large family planning program, by C. N. Wells. JOURNAL OF THE ARKANSAS MEDICAL SOCIETY 75(2):85-88, July, 1978.

Choking on the pill, by M. S. Kennedy. NEW TIMES 11:68, August 7, 1978.

Choosing sides, by E. Yeo. JOURNAL OF CURRENT SOCIAL ISSUES 15:76-78, Spring, 1978.

Christian morality and scientific humanism; the thought of Saint Thomas in Humanae Vitae, by M. Ciappi. OSSERVATORE ROMANO 21(530):7-8, May 25, 1978.

Christians faced with the legalization of abortion; reprint from La civiltà cattolica, May 20, 1978. OSSERVATORE ROMANO 24(533):9-11, June 15, 1978.

Chromatographic separation of multiple renin substrates in women: effect of pregnancy and oral contraceptives, by D. B. Gordon, et al. PROCEEDINGS OF THE SOCIETY FOR EXPERIMENTAL BIOLOGY AND MEDICINE 156(3):461-464, December, 1977.

Chromosomal aberrations in couples with habitual abortion, by M. Lancet, et al. HAREFUAH 94(2):67-69, January 15, 1978.

Chromosome abnormalities: a major cause of birth defects, stillbirth and spontaneous abortion, by R. G. Worton. CANADIAN MEDICAL ASSOCIATION JOURNAL 117(8):849+, October 22, 1977.

Chromosome analysis in baboons born following the use of potential, postovulatory, fertility-inhibiting steroids, by Z. A. Jemilev, et al. ZENTRALBLATT FUER GYNAEKOLOGIE 100(6):337-340, 1978.

Chromosome anomalies in cases of habitual abortions, by K. H. Breuker, et al. GEBURTSHILFE UND FRAUENHEIL-KUNDE 38(1):11-17, January, 1978.

Chromosome changes and congenital malformations after use of estroprogestogens, by A. Pardini, et al. RIVISTA ITALIANA DE GINECOLOGIA 57(3):195-203, May-June, 1976.

Chromosomes in familial primary sterility and in couples with recurrent abortions and stillbirths, by A. Rosenmann, et al. ISRAEL JOURNAL OF MEDICAL SCIENCES 13(11): 1131-1133, November 1977.

Chromosomes in miscarriage [letter] , by M. A. Leversha, et al. AMERICAN JOURNAL OF OBSTETRICS AND GYNE-COLOGY 130(2):245-246, January 15, 1978.

Chronic alcoholism and increased number of spontaneous abortions, by S. Moskovic. SRPSKI ARHIV ZA CELOKUPNO LEKARSTVO 105(2):157-162, February, 1977.

Chronic cytomegaloviral infection as the cause of recurrent abortions, by K. Kouba, et al. CESKOSLOVENSKA GYNE-KOLOGIE 43(1):15-20, March, 1978.

Church loses birth control war, by C. Westoff. HUMAN BE-HAVIOR 7:38, April, 1978.

Cigarette smoking and spontaneous abortion. BRITISH MEDI-CAL JOURNAL 1:259-260, February 4, 1978.

Circulating levels of norethindrone in women with a single silastic implant, by V. Goyal, et al. CONTRACEPTION 17(4):375-382, April, 1978.

The class conflict over abortion [class differences in attitudes toward abortion and the family] , by P. Skerry. PUBLIC INTEREST pp. 69-84, Summer, 1978.

Classic Pages in Obstetrics and Gynecology. The effects of progesterone and related compounds on ovulation and early development in the rabbit: Gregory Pincus and Min Chuch

In: Acta Physiologica Latinoamericana, vol. 3, pp. 177-83, 1953, by G. Pincus, et al. AMERICAN JOURNAL OF OBSTETRICS AND GYNECOLOGY 132(2):215-216, September 15, 1978.

Classical approaches, by L. P. Wilkinson. ENCOUNTER 50:22-32, April, 1978.

A clinical and angiographic study of occlusions of the posterior cerebral artery with special reference to the pathogenetic role of oral contraceptives and nicotine-abuse, by D. Kühne, et al. FORTSCHRITTE DER NEUROLOGIE, PSYCHIATRIE UND IHRER GRENZGEBIETE 46(1):1-28, January, 1978.

Clinical and hematogenic considerations on 2 cases of cerebral venous thrombosis occuring during the use of oral estro-progestational preparations, by J. Galimberti, et al. ANNALI DELL' OSPEDALE MARIA VITTORIA DI TORINO 19(7-12):183-193, July-December, 1976.

Clinical aspects of a new, very low dose combination contraceptive, by D. Mladenović, et al. FORTSCHRITTE DER MEDIZIN 96(13):723-726, April 6, 1978.

Clinical, bacteriological and histological studies following several years of IUD use for contraception, by P. Wolke, et al. ZENTRALBLATT FUER GYNAEKOLOGIE 99(14):880-883, 1977.

Clinical course and pathogenesis of oral contraceptive hypertension, by J. Girndt, et al. MEDIZINISCHE KLINIK 72(41): 1680-1684, October 14, 1977.

The clinical efficacy of the repeated transcervical instillation of quinacrine for female sterilization, by J. Zipper, et al. INTERNATIONAL JOURNAL OF GYNAECOLOGY AND OBSTETRICS 14(6):499-502, 1976.

Clinical evaluation of an oral contraceptive combination with a low dosage of estrogens and progestanes and their correlation in a group of women using intrauterine device, by A. Rinaldi.

REVISTA CHILENA DE OBSTETRICIA Y GINECOLOGIA 42(1):34-40, 1977.

Clinical evaluation on spira-ring, by M. Nagano, et al. NIPPON FUNIN GAKKAI ZASSHI 23(2):104-110, April 1, 1978.

Clinical experience with the intrauterine progesterone contraceptive system, by B. B. Pharriss. JOURNAL OF REPRODUCTIVE MEDICINE 20(3):155-165, March, 1978.

Clinical performance and endocrine profiles with contraceptive vaginal rings containing a combination of estradiol and d-norgestrel, by D. R. Mishell, Jr., et al. AMERICAN JOURNAL OF OBSTETRICS AND GYNECOLOGY 130(1):55-62, January 1, 1978.

Clinical performances and endocrine profilles with contraceptive vaginal rings containing d-norgestrel, by D. R. Mishell, Jr., et al. CONTRACEPTION 16(6):625-636, December, 1977.

Clinical pharmacokinetics of rifampicin, by G. Acocella. CLINICAL PHARMACOKINETICS 3(2):108-127, March-April, 1978.

The clinical, radiologic, and pathologic characterization of benign hepatic neoplasms. Alleged association with oral contraceptives, by D. M. Knowles, 2d, et al. MEDICINE 57(3):223-237, May, 1978.

Clinical report—a case of a failed abortion, by J. Barchilon. MEDICAL TRIAL TECHNIQUE QUARTERLY 24:257-289, Winter, 1978.

Clinical study of intrauterine contraceptives, by L. A. Parshina, et al. AKUSHERSTVO I GINEKOLOGIIA (12):39-40, December, 1977.

Clinical trial with a combination of 150 mcg of d-norgestrel and 30 mcg of ethinylestradiol. Its metabolic effects, by A. V. Moggia, et al. OBSTETRICIA Y GINECOLOGIA LATINO-AMERICANAS 34(11-12):384-397, November-December, 1976.

Clinical trial with subdermal implants of the progestin R-2323, by S. Diaz, et al. CONTRACEPTION 16(2):155-165, August, 1977.

A clinicopathologic study of steroid-related liver tumors, by W. M. Christopherson, et al. AMERICAN JOURNAL OF SURGICAL PATHOLOGY 1(1):31-41, March, 1977.

Clip sterilization failures, by A. M. Mroueh. CONTRACEPTION 16(1):19-27, July, 1977.

Closing down family planning clinics [letter], by P. Thompson. BRITISH MEDICAL JOURNAL 1(6104):53, January 7, 1978.

Clostridial sepsis after abortion with PGF2alpha and intracervical laminaria tents—a case report, by S. L. Green, et al. INTERNATIONAL JOURNAL OF GYNAECOLOGY AND OBSTETRICS 15(4):322-324, 1978.

Coagulation changes following vasectomy: a study in primates, by C. T. Kisker, et al. FERTILITY AND STERILITY 29(5):543-545, May, 1978.

Code board mulls contraceptive ads, by C. Coates. ADVERTISING AGE 49:54, May 29, 1978.

Code of ethics: abortion referral [letter]. CANADIAN MEDICAL ASSOCIATION JOURNAL 118(8):888+, April 22, 1978.

The cold sterilization of abortion cannulae, by M. R. Spence, et al. INTERNATIONAL JOURNAL OF GYNAECOLOGY AND OBSTETRICS 15(4):369-372, 1978.

Collagen bands: a new vaginal delivery system for contraceptive steroids, by A. Victor, et al. CONTRACEPTION 16(2):125-135, August, 1977.

College women's attitudes and expectations concerning menstrual-related changes, by J. Brooks, et al. PSYCHOSOMATIC MEDICINE 39(5):288-298, September-October, 1977.

College women's use of gynecological health services: implications for consumer health education, by R. H. Needle. HEALTH EDUCATION 9:10-11, March-April, 1978.

Combination of ovulation method and diaphragm [letter], by J. F. Cattanach. MEDICAL JOURNAL OF AUSTRALIA 2(14):478, October 1, 1977.

Comments received on excess deaths from restricting Medicaid funds for abortions [letter], by S. Wallenstein. AMERICAN JOURNAL OF PUBLIC HEALTH 68(3):270-272, March, 1978.

Communicating through satisfied adopters of female sterilization. STUDIES IN FAMILY PLANNING 8(8):205, August, 1977.

Community size, public attitudes, and population-policy preferences, by D. A. Caputo. URBAN AFFAIRS QUARTERLY 13:207-222, December, 1977.

The comparative actions of luoxymesterone and testosterone on sexual behavior and accessory sexual glands in castrated rabbits, by A. Agmo. HORMONES AND BEHAVIOR 9(2):112-119, October, 1977.

Comparative clinical trial of two oral contraceptives with a low-estrogen content, by S. Koetsawang, et al. JOURNAL OF THE MEDICAL ASSOCIATION OF THAILAND 60(8): 368-373, August, 1977.

Comparative effects of oestrogen and a progestogen on bone loss in postmenopausal women, by R. Lindsay, et al. CLINICAL SCIENCE AND MOLECULAR MEDICINE 54(2):193-195, February, 1978.

The comparative effects of a synthetic and a "natural" oestrogen on the haemostatic mechanism in patients with primary amenorrhoea, by J. L. Toy, et al. BRITISH JOURNAL OF OBSTETRICS AND GYNAECOLOGY 85(5):359-362, May, 1978.

Comparative metabolism of 17alpha-ethynyl steroids used in

oral contraceptives, by R. E. Ranney. JOURNAL OF TOXI-COLOGY AND ENVIRONMENTAL HEALTH 3(1-2):139-166, September, 1977.

Comparative risk of death from legally induced abortion in hospitals and nonhospital facilities, by D. A. Grimes, et al. OBSTETRICS AND GYNECOLOGY 51(3):323-326, March, 1978.

Comparative studies of the ethynyl estrogens used in oral contra-ceptives: effects with and without progestational agents on plasma androstenedione, testosterone, and testosterone bind-ing in humans, baboons, and beagles, by J. W. Goldzieher, et al. FERTILITY AND STERILITY 29(4):388-396, April, 1978.

Comparative studies of the ethynyl estrogens used in oral contra-ceptives: effects with and without progestational agents on plasma cortisol and cortisol binding in humans, baboons, and beagles,by J. W. Goldzieher, et al. FERTILITY AND STERILITY 28(11):1182-1190, November, 1977.

A comparative study of health status of children whose parents have undergone family planning operations with those whose parents were not, by P. R. Choudhary, et al. INDIAN PEDIATRICS 15(1):13-18, January, 1978.

A comparative study of immunisation status of children whose parents had undergone family planning operations with those whose parents were not, by P. R. Choudhary, et al. INDIAN PEDIATRICS 15(3):229-232, March, 1978.

A comparative study of three low dose progestogens, chlorma-dinone acetate and norethisterone, as oral contraceptives, by D. F. Hawkins, et al. BRITISH JOURNAL OF OBSTE-TRICS AND GYNAECOLOGY 84(9):708-713, September, 1977.

Comparison between the combined pill and intrauterine device in nulliparae under the age of 19, by M. Lie, et al. TIDS-SHRIFT FOR DE NARSKE LAEGEFORENING 98(12): 614-617, April 30, 1978.

Comparison between the use of oral contraceptives and the incidence of surgically confirmed gallstone disease, by K. H. Leissner, et al. SCANDINAVIAN JOURNAL OF GASTROENTEROLOGY 12:893-896, 1977.

A comparison of D & C and vacuum aspiration for performing first trimester abortion, by T. H. Lean, et al. INTERNATIONAL JOURNAL OF GYNAECOLOGY AND OBSTETRICS 14(6):481-486, 1976.

Comparison of the effects of contraceptive steroid formulations containing two doses of estrogen on pituitary function, by J. Z. Scott, et al. FERTILITY AND STERILITY 30(2): 141-145, August, 1978.

Comparison of effects of ingestion of Si on the content of Ca and Mg of different tissues of female rats norml or receiving oral oestrogen-gestogens, by Y. Charnot, et al. ANNALES D'ENDOCRINOLOGIE 38(6):377-378, 1977.

A comparison of the falope ring and laparoscopic tubal cauterization, by J. S. Ziegler, et al. JOURNAL OF REPRODUCTIVE MEDICINE 20(4):237-238, April, 1978.

Comparison of norinyl and combination-5, by A. R. Khan, et al. BANGLADESH MEDICAL RESEARCH COUNCIL BULLETIN 3(2):108-116, December, 1977.

Comparison of plasma hormone changes using a "conventional" and a "paper" pill formulation of a low-dose oral contraceptive, by S. E. Morris, et al. FERTILITY AND STERILITY 29(3):296-303, March, 1978.

A comparison of primary dysmenonhoea and intrauterine device related pain, by A. E. Reading, et al. PAIN 3(3):265-276, June, 1977.

Comparison of strokes in women of childbearing age in Rochester, Minnesota and Bakersfield, California, by T. P. Comer, et al. ANGIOLOGY 26(4):351-355, April, 1975.

Comparison of vaginal cytologic effects and blood elimination curves of different oestrogen drugs, by E. Hempel, et al. ARCHIV FUER GESCHWULSTFORSCHUNG 47(5):479-484, 1977.

Comparison of women seeking early and late abortion, by W. L. Fielding, et al. AMERICAN JOURNAL OF OBSTETRICS AND GYNECOLOGY 131(3):304-310, June 1, 1978.

Compensation for failure of sterilization? by W. Barnikel. GEBURTSHILFE UND FRAUENHEILKUNDE 37(10): 881, October, 1977.

Complete gynecology services in a community college; not an impossible dream! by L. R. Caldwell. JOURNAL OF THE AMERICAN COLLEGE HEALTH ASSOCIATION 26:345+, June, 1978.

Complication of laparoscopic tubal banding procedure: case report, by J. G. Bell, et al. AMERICAN JOURNAL OF OBSTETRICS AND GYNECOLOGY 131(8):908-910, August 15, 1978.

Complications and late sequelae of contraception including sterilization (proceedings), by J. Hammerstein. ARCHIV FUR GYNAEKOLOGIE 224(1-4):1-24, July 29, 1977.

A component analysis of recent fertility decline in Singapore. STUDIES IN FAMILY PLANNING 8(11):282, November, 1977.

Components method for measuring the impact of a family planning program on birth rates, by J. D. Teachman, et al. DEMOGRAPHY 15:113-129, February, 1978.

Compulsory sterilization: the change in India's population policy, by K. Gulhati. SCIENCE 195:1300-1305+, March, 1977.

Concerning a rare inconvenience occurring to women wearing intrauterine devices: missing tails, by F. Carollo, et al. PATOLOGIA E CLINICA OSTETRICIA E GINECOLOGICA 6(3):146-152, May-June, 1978.

Concerning the relation between the use of oral contraceptives and the development of primary malignant tumours of the liver, by I. Hantak, et al. BRATISLAVSKE LEKARSKE LISTY 68(5):613-619, November, 1977.

The con-con drive: constitutional convention sought on abortion ban, by L. B. Weiss. CONGRESSIONAL QUARTERLY SERVICE. WEEKLY REPORT 36:1677-1679, July 1, 1978.

Conditions of fertility decline in developing countries, 1965-75 [the effect of socioeconomic conditions and family planning programs; based on conference paper], by W. P. Mauldin, et al. STUDIES IN FAMILY PLANNING 9:89-147, May, 1978.

The condom and gonorrhoea, by D. Barlow. LANCET 2(8042): 811-813, October 15, 1977.

Condom market—what direction now? AMERICAN DRUG-GIST 177:23-24+, March, 1978.

Condom urinals, by S. D. Lawson, et al. NURSING MIRROR AND MIDWIVES JOURNAL 145(22):19-21, December 1, 1977.

Confidentiality and interagency communication: effect of the Buckley amendment, by E. A. Drake, et al. HOSPITAL AND COMMUNITY PSYCHIATRY 29(5):312-315, May, 1978.

The conflict between work and family in hospital medicine, by F. R. Elliot. HEALTH BULLETIN 36(3):128-130, May, 1978.

Conflict of loyalties: hippocratic or hypocratical? by R. Higgs. JOURNAL OF MEDICAL ETHICS 4:42-44, March, 1978.

Confusion about New Zealand abortion? [letter], by H. C. McLaren. BRITISH MEDICAL JOURNAL 1(6128):1697, June 24, 1978.

Congenital heart disease and prenatal exposure to exogenous

sex hormones, by D. T. Janerich, et al. BRITISH MEDICAL JOURNAL 6068:1058-1060, April 23, 1977.

Congress votes to restrict military abortion payments, by J. Castelli. OUR SUNDAY VISITOR 67:5, August 27, 1978.

Conjugal role definitions, value of children and contraceptive practice, by P. L. Tobin. SOCIOLOGICAL QUARTERLY 17:314-322, Summer, 1976.

Connecticut physicians attitudes toward abortion, by G. L. Pratt, et al. AMERICAN JOURNAL OF PUBLIC HEALTH 66: 288-289, March, 1976.

Connecticut's OB/GYN's on abortion: a two year follow-up study, by G. Affleck, et al. CONNECTICUT MEDICINE 42(3):179-182, March, 1978.

Conscience, infallibility, and contraception, by J. M. Finnis. MONTH 11:410-417, December, 1978.

Conscientious objection of doctors keeps Italian abortion law smouldering, by C. Savitsky. OUR SUNDAY VISITOR 67:1, August 27, 1978.

Consent and sterilization, by G. Sharpe. CANADIAN MEDICAL ASSOCIATION JOURNAL 118(5):591-593, March 4, 1978.

Consequences of the contraceptive mentality; the prophetic witness of Humanae Vitae, by K. Whitehead. OSSERVATORE ROMANO 25(534):5-8, June 22, 1978.

Consistency between fertility attitudes and behaviour: a conceptual model, by S. B. Kar. POPULATION STUDIES 32:173-185, March, 1978.

Constitutional law—aborttion—no requirement to provide Medicaid funds for nontherapeutic abortions under title XIX of the social security act of 1965 or the fourteenth amendment. TULANE LAW REVIEW 52:179-188, December, 1977.

Constitutional law—freedom of the press—prohibition of abor-

tion referral service advertising held unconstitutional. COR-
NELL LAW REVIEW 61:640+, April, 1976.

Constitutional law—minors' access to contraceptives—the right
to privacy, due process and the first amendment. NEW
YORK LAW SCHOOL LAW REVIEW 23:777-790, 1978.

Constitutional law—a state cannot: (1) abridge privacy rights of
minors under sixteen by denying them access to nonprescription contraceptives (2) burden privacy rights by permitting only licensed pharmacists to distribute and sell contraceptives (3) totally prohibit advertisement and display
of contraceptive products. JOURNAL OF FAMILY LAW
16:639-652, 1977-1978.

Constitutional law: state funding of nontherapeutic abortions—
Medicaid plans—equal protection—right to choose an abortion. AKRON LAW REVIEW 11:345-358, Fall, 1977.

Constitutionality of mandatory parental consent in the abortion
decision of a minor: Bellotti II [Baird v. Attorney General
(Bellotti II) (Mass) 360 N E 2d 288] in perspective. NORTH-
ERN KENTUCKY LAW REVIEW 4:323-344, 1977.

Consultants or colleagues: the role of US population advisors in
India, by M. Minkler. POPULATION AND DEVELOPMENT
REVIEW 3:403-419, December, 1977.

Consumer reactions to contraceptive purchasing, by W. A. Fisher,
et al. PERSONALITY AND SOCIAL PSYCHOLOGY
BULLETIN 3(2):293-296, Spring, 1977.

Contact lens tolerance and oral contraceptives, by A. De Vries
Reilingh, et al. ANNALS OF OPHTHALMOLOGY 10(7):
947-952, July, 1978.

Contextual and ideological dimensions of attitudes toward discretionary abortion, by B. K. Singh, et al. DEMOGRAPHY
15:381-388, August, 1978.

A "Contingency Plan" of economic incentive to limit U.S. reproduction. ENVIRONMENTAL AFFAIRS 6(3):301, 1978.

Continued pregnancy after failed first trimester abortion, by W. L. Fielding, et al. OBSTETRICS AND GYNECOLOGY 52(1):56-58, July, 1978.

Continued use of contraception among Philippine family planning acceptors: a multivariate analysis, by J. F. Phillips. STUDIES IN FAMILY PLANNING 9:182-192, July, 1978.

Continuing the discussion: how to argue about abortion [rejoinder to B. Harrison], by J. T. Burtchaell. CHRISTIANITY AND CRISIS 37:313-316, December 26, 1977.

—, [Reply to R. Hoyt and J. T. Burtchaell], by V. Lindermayer, et al. CHRISTIANITY AND CRISIS 37:316-318, December 26, 1977.

—, II [Reply to J. Burtchaell, with rejoinder, pp. 313-316], by B. Harrison. CHRISTIANITY AND CRISIS 37:311-313, December 26, 1977.

Contraception, by D. R. Mishell, Jr. AMERICAN JOURNAL OF DISEASES OF CHILDREN 132(9):912-920, September, 1978.

—, by P. T. Wilson, et al. MEDICAL TRIAL TECHNIQUE QUARTERLY 24(1):45-60, Summer, 1977.

Contraception and the adolescent female, by C. Poole. JOURNAL OF SCHOOL HEALTH 46:475-479, October, 1976.

Contraception and arterial hypertension, by P. Corvol, et al. ACQUISITIONS MEDICALES RECENTES :177-180, 1977.

Contraception and the college freshman, by R. H. Neelde, et al. HEALTH EDUCATION 8:23-24, March-April, 1977.

Contraception and family planning, by E. C. Miller. ZEITSCHRIFT FUR AERZTLICHE FORTBILDUNG (Jena) 71(22):1041-1045, November 15, 1977.

Contraception and fertility. Analysis of 1090 pregnancies, by A. Cervantes, et al. GINECOLOGIA Y OBSTETRICIA DE

MEXICO 43(256):56-68, February, 1978.

Contraception and the infallibility of the ordinary magisterium, by J. C. Ford, et al. THEOLOGICAL STUDIES 39:258-312, June, 1978.

Contraception and pregnancy in the young female hypertensive patient, by F. A. Finnerty, Jr. PEDIATRIC CLINICS OF NORTH AMERICA 25(1):119-126, February, 1978.

Contraception and VD handbook, by J. E. Rodgers. MADE-MOISELLE 84:103-105, August, 1978.

Contraception: an antipregnancy vaccine? SCIENCE 200:1258, June 16, 1978.

—, by J. L. Marx. SCIENCE 200:1258, June 16, 1978.

Contraception et avortement, by S. Luoni. LA DOCUMENTA-TION CATHOLIQUE 74:643-645, July 3, 1977.

Contraception in the adolescent, by R. M. Schwartz. PEDI-ATRIC ANNALS 7(3):189-194, March, 1978.

Contraception in adolescents, by I. Rey-Stocker. REVUE MEDI-CALE DE LA SUISSE ROMANDE 97(6):322-331, June, 1977.

Contraception in cardiac patients, by R. Taurelle, et al. JOUR-NAL DE GYNECOLOGIE, OBSTETRIQUE ET BIOLOGIE DE LA REPRODUCTION 7(1):111-118, January, 1978.

Contraception in children and adolescents, by M. Sas. FORT-SCHRITTE DU MEDIZIN 96(14):747-748, April 13, 1978.

Contraception in youths, by D. Mühlnickel. DEUTSCHE GE-SUNDHEITSWESEN 32(41):1944-1946, 1977.

Contraception, infallibility and the ordinary magisterium; a summary of some major elements of the argument made by Ford and Grisez, by R. Shaw. HOMILETIC AND PASTORAL REVIEW 78:9-19, July, 1978.

Contraception: methods of those in the know; fertility control: how to cut the dangers, by M. Weber. VOGUE 168:210, August, 1978.

Contraception: pills and IUDs Part 1. PERINATAL CARE 2:13-18, April, 1978.

Contraception—retrospect and prospect, by M. J. Harper. PROGRESS IN DRUG RESEACH 21:293-407, 1977.

Contraception, sterilisation and abortion [editorial]. NEW ZEALAND MEDICAL JOURNAL 85(588):428-429, May 25, 1977.

Contraception, sterilisation and abortion in New Zealand. NEW ZEALAND MEDICAL JOURNAL 85(588):441-445, May 25, 1977.

Contraception through progesterone-containing intrauterine device (IUD), by J. R. Strecker. HIPPOKRATES 48(4):413-414, November, 1977.

The contraception-to-conception ratio: a tool for measuring success of family planning programs in reaching very young teenagers, by J. D. Shelton. ADVANCES IN PLANNED PARENTHOOD 13(1):1-6, 1978.

Contraception. When avoiding pregnancy is the issue, ed. by H. A. Wade. PATIENT CARE 12:252-253+, September 15, 1978.

Contraception: when should barrier methods be recommended; by C. Lauritzen MUENCHENER MEDIZINISCHE WOCHENSCHRIFT 120(37):1180, September 15, 1978.

Contraception—why failures? by J. R. Taylor. CANADIAN JOURNAL OF HOSPITAL PHARMACY 29(5):150-151, September-October, 1976.

Contraception with a new vaginal suppository (Patentex Oval), by T. Weber, et al. UGESKRIFT FOR LAEGER 139(40): 2397-2398, October 3, 1977.

Contraception with a norethisterone-releasing IUD. Plasma levels of norethisterone and its influence on the ovarian function, by C. G. Nilsson, et al. CONTRACEPTION 17(2):115-122, February, 1978.

Contraception with a normophasic agent, by H. Kopera. WIENER MEDIZINISCHE WOCHENSCHRIFT 127(18):573-577, October 10, 1977.

Contraceptive agents and cardiovascular diseases, by N. Lisin, et al. BRUXELLES-MEDICALE 57(11):499-502, November, 1977.

Contraceptive choices for Latin American women, by P. H. Hass, et al. POPULI 3(4):14-24, 1976.

Contraceptive counseling for the younger adolescent woman: a suggested solution to the problem, by M. O. Robbie. JOGN; JOURNAL OF OBSTETRIC, GYNECOLOGIC AND NEO-NATAL NURSING 7(4):29-33, July-August, 1978.

Contraceptive effectiveness: misleading statistics, by J. J. Lieberman. AMERICAN BIOLOGY TEACHER 39:503, November, 1977.

Contraceptive effectivess warning issued: spiermicide, Encare Oval. FDA CONSUMER 12:4, September, 1978.

The contraceptive effects of a new low-dose combination type oral contraceptive, by H. Kallio, et al. CURRENT MEDI-CAL RESEARCH AND OPINION 5(6):444-449, 1978.

Contraceptive efficiency of triphasic inhibitors, by W. H. Schneider, et al. MEDIZINISCHE KLINIK 72(48):2081-2085, December 2, 1977.

Contraceptive failure among married women in the United States, 1970-1973, by B. Vaughan, et al. FAMILY PLANN-ING PERSPECTIVES 9:251-258, November-December, 1977.

Contraceptive method continuation according to type of provider, by R. F. Einhorn, et al. AMERICAN JOURNAL OF PUBLIC HEALTH 67:1157-1164, December, 1977.

Contraceptive patterns and premarital pregnancy among women aged 15-19 in 1976, by M. Zelnik, et al. FAMILY PLANNING PERSPECTIVES 10:135-142, May-June, 1978.

Contraceptive practice after women have undergone "spontaneous" abortion in Indonesia and Sudan, by H. Rushwan, et al. INTERNATIONAL JOURNAL OF GYNAECOLOGY AND OBSTETRICS 15(3):241-249, 1977.

Contraceptive practice among hospital attendants, by G. M Dhar, et al. INDIAN JOURNAL OF PUBLIC HEALTH 21(1):8-15, January-March, 1977.

Contraceptive practices: in an adolescent health center, by A. Morgenthau, et al. NEW YORK STATE JOURNAL OF MEDICINE 76:1311-1315, August, 1976.

Contraceptive services for adolescents: an overview, by J. G. Dryfoos, et al. FAMILY PLANNING PERSPECTIVES 10:233-235+, July-August, 1978.

Contraceptive sponge fights VD, too. MEDICAL WORLD NEWS 18:29, October 17, 1977.

Contraceptive steroids and breast cancer [letter], by B. A. Stoll. BRITISH MEDICAL JOURNAL 1(6123):1350-1351, May 20, 1978.

Contraceptive steroids and liver lesions, by C. R. Garcia, et al. JOURNAL OF TOXICOLOGY AND ENVIRONMENTAL HEALTH 3(1-2):197-206, September, 1977.

Contraceptive studies are faulty, Msgr. McHugh says. OUR SUNDAY VISITOR 66:2, December 11, 1977.

Contraceptive tablets and liver adenoma, by B. Westerholm. LAKARTIDNINGEN 74(34):2803, August 24, 1977.

A contraceptive that's absorbable [birth control pellet for men or women]. MEDICAL WORLD NEWS 18:30, June 13, 1977.

Contraceptive usage and other characteristics of 440 pregnant teenage patients at MCG in 1975, by V. McNamara, et al. JOURNAL OF THE MEDICAL ASSOCIATION OF GEORGIA 66(9):689-693, September, 1977.

Contraceptive use, by J. E. Anderson, et al. NEW YORK STATE JOURNAL OF MEDICINE 77:933-937, May, 1977.

Contraceptive use and pregnancy planning in the Hutt Valley, by S. S. Poh, et al. NEW ZEALAND MEDICAL JOURNAL 85(584):217-220, March 23, 1977.

Contraceptive use in the United States, 1973-1976, by K. Ford. FAMILY PLANNING PERSPECTIVES 10:264-269, September-October, 1978.

Contraceptive use: prevalence among married women in Albany, New York, health region, 1974, by J. E. Anderson, et al. NEW YORK STATE JOURNAL OF MEDICINE 77:933-937, May, 1977.

Control of fertility with potentiated intrauterine devices, by G. Gozzi, et al. PATOLOGIA E CLINICA OSTETRICIA E GINECOLOGICA 5(1):32-36, 1977.

A controlled study of the effect of oral contraceptives on migraine, by R. E. Ryan, Sr. HEADACHE 17(6):250-252, January, 1978.

A controlled trial of antiemetics in abortion by PGF2alpha and laminaria, by A. F. Kaul, et al. JOURNAL OF REPRODUCTIVE MEDICINE 20(4):213-218, April, 1978.

Coping with pregnancy resolution among never-married women, by M. B. Bracken, et al. AMERICAN JOURNAL OF ORTHOPSYCHIATRY 48:320-334, April, 1978.

The copper intrauterine device and its mode of action, by G. Oster, et al. NEW ENGLAND JOURNAL OF MEDICINE

293:432-438, August 28, 1975.

Coronary thrombosis on oral contraception, by A. Barrillon, et al. NOUVELLE PRESSE MEDICALE 6(31):2758-2760, September 24, 1977.

Le corps paramédical face au planning familial [based on questionnaire survey of midwives, nurses and other medical workers], by S. Sahli. REVUE TUNISIENNE DE SCIENCES SOCIALES 14(50-51):283-291, 1977.

Correlates of contraceptive behavior among unmarried U. S. college students, by K. G. Foreit, et al. STUDIES IN FAMILY PLANNING 9:169-174, June, 1978.

Correlates of field-worker performance in the Indonesian family planning program: a test of the homophily-heterophily hypothesis, by R. Repetto. STUDIES IN FAMILY PLANNING 8:19+, January, 1977.

Costs of treating abortion-related complications, by S. D. Von Allmen, et al. FAMILY PLANNING PERSPECTIVES 9: 273-276, November-December, 1977.

—. 2, by S. D. Von Allmen, et al. FAMILY PLANNING PERSPECTIVES 9:273-276, November-December, 1977.

Counseling women for tubal sterilization, by E. Barron, et al. HEALTH AND SOCIAL WORK 3:48-58, February, 1978.

Counselling of patients requesting an abortion, by J. L. Dunlop. PRACTITIONER 220(1320):847-852, June, 1978.

Course of pregnancy and the state of the intrauterine fetus after the use of various contraceptive agents, by M. Ia. Martynshin, et al. VOPROSY OKHRANY MATERINSTVA I DETSTVA 22(9):60-62, September, 1977.

Court blocked sterilization of a retarded minor, by W. A. Regan. HOSPITAL PROGRESS 59(5):96+, May, 1978.

Court's abortion decisions flawed, by E. Melvin. OUR SUNDAY

VISITOR 65:1+, January 23, 1977.

Criteria for choosing oral contraceptives in Tunisia, by R. Chadi. TUNISIE MEDICALE 55(4):269-272, July-August, 1977.

A critique of rules proposed by the Department of Health, Education and Welfare. Sterilization restrictions, by H. C. Moss. JOURNAL OF THE INDIANA STATE MEDICAL ASSOCIATION 71(4):390-392, April, 1978.

Cruelty of morality; abortion views of J. Carter. NATION 225:68, July 23, 1977.

Current practice concerning time of IUD insertion, by M. K. White, et al. IPPF MEDICAL BULLETIN 11(6):1-3, December, 1977.

Cytogenetic studies on couples with habitual abortions (proceedings), by K. H. Breuker, et al. ARCHIV FUR GYNAEKOLOGIE 224(1-4):186-187, July 29, 1977.

Cytogenetic studies on women during and following the use of hormonal contraceptives, by R. Müller, et al. ZENTRALBLATT FUER GYNAEKOLOGIE 100(6):347-354, 1978.

Cytogenetic study in early spontaneous abortion, by H. Takahara, et al. HIROSHIMA JOURNAL OF MEDICAL SCIENCES 26(4):291-296, 1977.

A cytogenetic study of spontaneous abortions in Hawaii, by T. J. Hassold, et al. ANNALS OF HUMAN GENETICS 41(4): 443-454, May, 1978.

Cytogenetics of aborters and abortuses, by T. Kajii, et al. AMERICAN JOURNAL OF OBSTETRICS AND GYNECOLOGY 131(1):33-38, May 1, 1978.

Cytogenetics of recurrent abortions, by D. W. Heritage, et al. FERTILITY AND STERILITY 29(4):414-417, April, 1978.

Cytologic detection and clinical significance of actinomyces israelii in women using intrauterine contraceptive devices, by M. R. Spence, et al. AMERICAN JOURNAL OF OBSTE-TRICS AND GYNECOLOGY 131(3):295-298, June 1, 1978.

Cytological evaluation of long term effect of Lippes loop and copper IUDs, by J. S. Misra, et al. INDIAN JOURNAL OF MEDICAL RESEARCH 66(6):942-945, December, 1977.

Cytophotometric DNA-measurements in abortion, by W. P. Kunze. PATHOLOGY RESEARCH AND PRACTICE 162(3):253-262, July, 1978.

DHEW proposes 30-day waiting period for sterilizations; no funds for under 21s, contraceptive hysterectomies. FAMILY PLANNING PERSPECTIVES 10(1):39-40, January-February, 1978.

DoD progressing on long journey, by V. McKenzie. U. S. MEDI-CINE 14(2):19-22, January 15, 1978.

DOD walks thin line on abortions, by T. Philpott. AIR FORCE TIMES 39:2, September 24, 1978.

Dalkon Shield perforation of the uterus and urinary bladder with calculus formation: case report, by E. Neutz, et al. AMERI-CAN JOURNAL OF OBSTETRICS AND GYNECOLOGY 130(7):848-849, April 1, 1978.

The Danfa family planning program in rural Ghana, by D. A. Ampofo, et al. STUDIES IN FAMILY PLANNING 7:266-274, October, 1976.

Danse macabre: Hyde amendment, by M. Kinsley. NEW RE-PUBLIC 177:13+, November 19, 1977.

Daycare Pomeroy sterilisation by the vaginal route, by V. J. Hart-field. NEW ZEALAND MEDICAL JOURNAL 85(584):223-225, March 23, 1977.

Death after legally induced abortion. A comprehensive approach for determination of abortion-related deaths based on record linkage, by J. D. Shelton, et al. PUBLIC HEALTH REPORTS

93(4):375-378, July-August, 1978.

Deaths among pill users in Britain. IPPF MEDICAL BULLETIN 11(5):1-2, October, 1977.

Deaths caused by pulmonary thromboembolism after legally induced abortion, by A. M. Kimball, et al. AMERICAN JOURNAL OF OBSTETRICS AND GYNECOLOGY 132(2): 169-174, September 15, 1978.

A decade of change in abortion law: 1967-77 [throughout the world]. PEOPLE (London) 5(2):1, 1978.

A decade of international change in abortion law: 1967-1977, by R. J. Cook, et al. AMERICAN JOURNAL OF PUBLIC HEALTH 68:637-651, July, 1978.

Declaration of the Italian Episcopal Conference after the law on abortion. OSSERVATORE ROMANO 25(534):4, June 22, 1978.

Defective sterility after vasectomy, by T. Christensen, et al. UGESKRIFT FOR LAEGER 140(21):1236, May 22, 1978.

Definitive contraception and contraceptive responsibility (on the psychic situation in voluntary sterilization in men and women—results of psychologic-psychiatric research), by P. Petersen. PSYCHIATRISCHE PRAXIS 5(1):35-43, February, 1978.

Delay in the diagnosis of cervical cancer in patients using hormonal contraceptives and IUDs, by H. H. Büttner, et al. ZEITSCHRIFT FUR AERZTLICHE FORTBILDUNG 71(23):1129-1130, December 1, 1977.

Delayed adverse effects of contraceptives. ORVOSI HETILAP 119(20):1257-1261, May 14, 1978.

Delayed-baby boom: its meaning; increasing numbers of women are deciding to have their first child after years of marriage; their decisions promise major changes for both society and individual lives, by L. J. Lord. U. S. NEWS 84:39-41,

February 20, 1978.

Demographic and contraceptive innovators: a study of transitional African society, by J. C. Caldwell, et al. JOURNAL OF BIOSOCIAL SCIENCE 8:347-366, October, 1976.

Demographic and socio-economic characteristics of choosing vasectomy, by M. A. Parsons, et al. JOURNAL OF BIOSOCIAL SCIENCE 10(2):133-139, April, 1978.

A demographic assessment of family planning programs: a bibliographic essay, by J. A. Ross, et al. POPULATION INDEX 44:8-27, January, 1978.

Demographic evaluation of Taiwan's family planning program [conference paper], by T. H. Sun. INDUSTRY OF FREE CHINA 49:11-27+, May, 1978+.

Demographic impact of family planning programme in Singur area, West Bengal, by A. K. Chakraborty, et al. INDIAN JOURNAL OF PUBLIC HEALTH 21(1):38-43, January-March, 1977.

Denial of public funds for nontherapeutic abortions. CONNECTICUT LAW REVIEW 10:487-510, Winter, 1978.

Depo-provera as a contraceptive measure [letter], by P. B. Combrink. SOUTH AFRICAN MEDICAL JOURNAL 53(11):388, March 18, 1978.

Depo-provera (injectable contraceptive), a review by M. Smith. SCOTTISH MEDICAL JOURNAL 23(3):233-236, July, 1978.

Desexing birth control, by J. M. Stycos. FAMILY PLANNING PERSPECTIVES 9(6):286-292, November-December, 1977.

Detachment of the uterine cervix in association with induced midtrimester abortion, by R. T. Burkman, et al. AMERICAN JOURNAL OF OBSTETRICS AND GYNECOLOGY 129(5):585-586, November 1, 1977.

The detection and measurement of D-norgestrel in human milk using Sephadex LH 20 chromatography and radioimmunoassay, by M. J. Thomas, et al. STEROIDS 30(3):349-361, September, 1977.

Determination of antithrombin III (chromogenic substatres) and FDP in women in treatment with oral estroprogestin agents, by A. Gibelli, et al. MINERVA MEDICA 69(18): 1241-1244, April 14, 1978.

Determination of plasma concentration of D-norgestrel during a one year follow-up in women with a D-norgestrel-releasing IUD, by C. G. Nilsson, et al. CONTRACEPTION 17(6): 569-573, June, 1978.

Determination of the plasma gonadotropins FSH, LH and LMTH in patients treated with estroprogestogens, by A. Segre, et al. MINERVA GINECOLOGIA 30(3):157-165, March, 1978.

Determination of pregnancy duration following terminated hormonal contraception, by G. Klinger, et al. ZENTRALBLATT FUER GYNAEKOLOGIE 99(26):1629-1632, 1977.

Developing a clinic strategy appropriate to community family planning needs and practices: an experience in Lagos, Nigeria, by A. Bamisaiye, et al. STUDIES IN FAMILY PLANNING 9(2-3):44-48, February-March, 1978.

Development of knowledge concerning the early diagnosis of pregnancy, by G. Gentile. RIVISTA ITALIANA DI GINECOLOGIA 57(4-6):305-321, July-December, 1976.

Development of a long-acting vaginal suppository for termination of 2d trimester pregnancy and for preoperative cervical dilatation, by M. Bygdeman, et al. LAKARTIDNINGEN 74(46):4107-4109, November 16, 1977.

The development of neo-Malthusianism in Flanders, by Ph. van Praag. POPULATION STUDIES 32:467-480, November, 1978.

Development of the oral contraceptives, by M. C. Chang. AMER-

ICAN JOURNAL OF OBSTETRICS AND GYNECOLOGY 132(2):217-219, September 15, 1978.

Developments in family planning overseas. 2, by P. Hewitt. AUSTRALASIAN NURSES JOURNAL 7(11):34-37, June, 1978.

Developments in family planning overseas. An account of family planning education programmes in Britain, Italy, Hong Kong, Malaysia and Singapore. Part one—Britain, by P. Hewitt. AUSTRALASIAN NURSES JOURNAL 7(10): 32-35+, May, 1978.

Diabetes mellitus and endocrine diseases as indications for pregnancy interruption, by R. Petzoldt, et al. INTERNIST 19(5):284-286, May, 1978.

Diaphragms, by J. Coburn. MADEMOISELLE 84(11):68, November, 1978.

Dietary folate intake and concentration of folate in serum and erythrocytes in women using oral contraceptives, by G. J. Pietarinen, et al. AMERICAN JOURNAL OF CLINICAL NUTRITION 30:375-380, March, 1977.

Differences and delay in the decision to seek induced abortion among Black and White women, by M. B. Bracken, et al. SOCIAL PSYCHIATRY 12(2):57-570, April, 1977.

The differences between having one and two children, by D. Knox, et al. THE FAMILY COORDINATOR 27:1, January 23-25, 1978.

Differences between physicians and nurses in providing family planning services: findings from a Bogota clinic, by R. F. Einhorn, et al. STUDIES IN FAMILY PLANNING 9(2-3): 35-38, February-March, 1978.

Differential approach to the treatment of threatened abortion, by Iu. F. Borisova, et al. SOVETSKAYA MEDITZINA (9):100-103, September, 1977.

Differential fertility by intelligence: the role of birth planning, by J. R. Udry. SOCIAL BIOLOGY 25(1):10-14, Spring, 1978.

Differential fertility by sterilized and non-sterilized couples, by E. R. Ram, et al. JOURNAL OF FAMILY WELFARE 23:45-50, December, 1976.

Differentiation of factor C-LHIH and the synthetic contraceptive polypeptide, H-Thr-Pro-Arg-Lys-OH, by D. Chang, et al. BIOCHEMICAL AND BIOPHYSICAL RESEARCH COMMUNICATIONS 65(4):1208-1213, August 18, 1975.

Difficulties with intrauterine anticonception envisaged from the aspect of work-ability, by J. Petros, et al. CESKOSLOVENSKA GYNEKOLOGIE 43(4):274-276, May, 1978.

Diffuse bilateral retinal periphlebitis in a young woman taking contraceptives, by C. Gervais, et al. BULLETIN DES SOCIETES D'OPHTHALMOLOGIE DE FRANCE 77(2):191-192, February, 1977.

La diffusion des méthodes modernes de contraception: une étude dans une consultation hospitalière, by H. Leridon, et al. POPULATION 32(4-5):777-785, 1977.

The diffusion of abortion facilities in the northeastern United States, 1970-1976, by N. F. Henry. SOCIAL SCIENCE AND MEDICINE 12(1D):7-15, March, 1978.

Dilatation and curettage for termination of second-trimester pregnancy [letter], by S. Fribourg. AMERICAN JOURNAL OF OBSTETRICS AND GYNECOLOGY 130(4):505-506, February 15, 1978.

The dilemma of family planning in a North Indian state, by B. D. Misra, et al. STUDIES IN FAMILY PLANNING 7:66-74, March, 1976.

Directions for classification and indications of oral contraceptives, by J. P. d'Ernst, et al. PRAXIS 66(50):1620-1627, December 13, 1977.

Disseminated intravascular coagulation syndrome after vacuum curettement for first trimester abortion, by A. S. Goss, Jr. SOUTHERN MEDICAL JOURNAL 71(8):967-968, August, 1978.

Dissenters barred from symposium: Humanae Vitae, by J. Coleman. NATIONAL CATHOLIC REPORTER 14:24-25, August 11, 1978.

Distribution of oral contraceptives: legal changes and new concepts of preventive care, by R. J. Cook. AMERICAN JOURNAL OF PUBLIC HEALTH 66:590+, June, 1976.

Divisive issue: debate over abortion heats up in state capitols as some legislators seek a constitutional ban, by J. Spivak. WALL STREET JOURNAL 191:40, January 26, 1978.

Do Catholics have constitutional rights? COMMENTARY 105:771-773, December 8, 1978.

Do-it-yourself abortions available through new technology that's here, by R. Shaw. OUR SUNDAY VISITOR 66:3, May 7, 1978.

The doctor and the new ethical code; abortion law in Italy, by D. Tettamanzi. OSSERVATORE ROMANO 27(536):8-9, July 6, 1978.

Doctor must pay damages, child-rearing expenses for failed vasectomy, by J. F. Eisberg. LEGAL ASPECTS OF MEDICAL PRACTICE 6(3):48-49, March, 1978.

Doctors and the global population crisis, by J. A. Loraine. BRITISH MEDICAL JOURNAL 2(6088):691-693, September 10, 1977.

Doctors have varied reactions to abortion. OUR SUNDAY VISITOR 66:3, May 29, 1977.

Does implantation occur in the presence of an IUD? by B. B. Saxena, et al. RESEARCH IN REPRODUCTION 10(3):1-2, May, 1978.

Does the pill kill? women over 35 are now being steered gently a-
way from the pill; where's the research on its ever more popular alternative? ECONOMIST 265:10-11, October, 15, 1977.

Does the risk of radiodiagnostic examination at the beginning of
pregnancy justify pregnancy termination? by P. Magnin, et
al. NOUVELLE PRESSE MEDICALE 6(30):2655-2658,
September 17, 1977.

Does sterilization prevent pelvic infection? by S. N. Jahh. JOUR-
NAL OF REPRODUCTIVE MEDICINE 20(5):289-290,
May, 1978.

Does your mother know. . .? by A. Torres. FAMILY PLANN-
ING PERSPECTIVES 10:280-282, September-October,
1978.

Don't kill babies before they're born. . .kill them afterwards, by
J. Wells. U. S. CATHOLIC 43:41, September, 1978.

Doses-related effects of lynestrenol on ovulation, by M. A. Pizarro, et al. REPRODUCTION 3(3-4):193-205, July-December, 1976.

Double uterine perforation with Dalkon Shield intrauterine device, by E. Hakim-Elahi. NEW YORK STATE JOURNAL
OF MEDICINE 76:567-569, April, 1976.

Dream recall and the contraceptive pill, by P. Sheldrake, et al.
JOURNAL OF NERVOUS AND MENTAL DISEASE 163(1):
59-60, 1976.

Drug file: abortion deaths from anesthesia, by E. M. Goldstein.
TRIAL 13(6):11, June, 1977.

Drug file: the pill—the problems continue: from dysplasia to cancer; birth defects; heart disease, by E. M. Goldstein. TRIAL
13(8):10, August, 1977.

Drug-induced abortion in early pregnancy with intravaginally administered (15S)-15-methyl-prostaglandin F2 alpha methylester (15-S-PGF2 alpha) (proceedings), by J. H. Duenhoelter, et

ARCHIV FUR GYNAEKOLOGIE 224(1-4):268-269, July 29, 1977.

Drug induced sterility (editorial), by H. Pedersen. UGESHRIFT FOR LAEGER 139(40):2399-2400, October 3, 1977.

Drug interactions with oral contraceptives. IPPF MEDICAL BULLETIN 12(4):1, August, 1978.

Drug noxae as indications for pregnancy interruption, by D. Neubert. INTERNIST 19(5):304-309, May, 1978.

Drugs, depo proverba ban appealed, by M. Fisk. TRIAL 14(11): 17, November, 1978.

Drugs, IUD studies prompt concern, by M. Fisk. TRIAL 14(5): 56, May, 1978.

Drugs: the pill and MI, by M. Fisk. TRIAL 14(6):22-23, June, 1978.

Drugs: survey results on tumors and the pill, by M. Fisk. TRIAL 14(1):16, January, 1978.

Due process and equal protection: constitutional implications of abortion notice and reporting requirements. BOSTON UNIVERSITY LAW REVIEW 56:522-541, May, 1976.

The dynamics of anti-abortionism, by J. Noonan, Jr. CATHOLIC MIND 76:7-13, May, 1978.

Dynamics of contraceptive failures, by W. G. Cobliner, et al. JOURNAL OF PSYCHOLOGY 94:153-162, November, 1976.

Dysplasias of uterine cervix: epidemiological aspects: role of age at first coitus and use of oral contraceptives, by A. Meisels, et al. CANCER 40(6):3076-3081, December, 1977.

The e.p.t. do-it-yourself early pregnancy test. MEDICAL LETTER ON DRUGS AND THERAPEUTICS 20(8):39-40, April 21, 1978.

The earliest influence of contraception on the incidence of conception, by O. Norgaard. UGESKRIFT FOR LAEGER 139(42):2537-2539, October 17, 1977.

Early artificial termination of pregnancy by Karman's method, by D. Vasilev. AKUSHERSTVO I GINEKOLOGIIA 17(2): 98-103, 1978.

Early experience in contraception with a new progestogen, by J. A. McEwan, et al. CONTRACEPTION 16(4):339-350, October, 1977.

Early first-trimester abortion induction by silastic vaginal devices for continuous release of 15(S)=15-methyl prostaglandin F2alpha methyl ester, by J. Robins. FERTILITY AND STERILITY 28(10):1048-1055, October, 1977.

East Asia review, 1976-77, ed. by S. M. Keeny. STUDIES IN FAMILY PLANNING 9:233-254, September, 1978.

Economic variables and the decision to have additional children: evidence from the survey of economic opportunity, by D. Snyder. AMERICAN ECONOMIST 22:12-16, Spring, 1978.

Ectopic pregnancies during use of low-dose progestogens for oral contraception, by P. Liukko, et al. CONTRACEPTION 16(6):575-580, December, 1977.

Ectopic pregnancies, IUD's and abortion [letter], by I. Sivin. CONTRACEPTION 17(6):575-582, June, 1978.

Ectopic pregnancy and the pill [letter], by D. B. Weiss, et al. LANCET 2(7978):196-197, July 24, 1976.

Ectopic pregnancy following tubal sterilization, by S. Kumar, et al. CANADIAN MEDICAL ASSOCIATION JOURNAL 119(2):156-157, July 22, 1978.

Ectopic pregnancy rates in IUD users [letter], by R. Azner, et al. BRITISH MEDICAL JOURNAL 1(6115):785-786, March 25, 1978.

Education in health and family planning to nurses and midwives, by W. Haddad. JOURNAL DE GYNECOLOGIE, OBSTE-TRIQUE ET BIOLOGI DE LA REPRODUCTION 7(2):307-311, March, 1978.

Education in marital hygiene and popular professional literature, by V. Wynnyczuk. CASOPIS LEKARU CESKYCH 116(33): 1033-1034, August 19, 1977.

Effect of abortion on obstetric patterns, by R. Beard, et al. BRITISH MEDICAL JOURNAL 2(6089):765-766, September 17, 1977.

Effect of an ayurvedic preparation on peripheral parameters of the menstrual cycle, by J. Joshi, et al. INDIAN JOURNAL OF MEDICAL RESEARCH 66(1):39-42, July, 1977.

Effect of castration and testosterone administration on the neuromuscular junction in the levator ani muscle of the rat, by Hanzilíková, et al. CELL AND TISSUE RESEARCH 189(1): 155-166, May 18, 1978.

Effect of castration and testosterone treatment on catecholamine metabolism in ventral prostates of normal and chemically sympathectomized rats, by R. B. Rastogi, et al. CANADIAN JOURNAL OF PHYSIOLOGY AND PHARMACOLOGY 55(5):1015-1022, October, 1977.

The effect of castration, thyroidectomy and haloperidol upon the turnover rates of dopamine and norepinephrine and the kinetic properties of tyrosine hydroxylase in discrete hypothalamic nuclei of the male rat, by J. S. Kizer, et al. BRAIN RESEARCH 146(1):95-107, May 5, 1978.

Effect of chronic administration of testosterone enanthate on sperm production and plasma testosterone, follicle-stimulating hormone, and luteinizing hormone levels: a preliminary evaluation of a possible male contraceptive, by E. Steinberger, et al. FERTILITY AND STERILITY 28(12):1320-1328, December, 1977.

Effect of chronic treatment with an estrogen-progestogen combination on beta adrenergic-induced thirst, by T. N. Thrasher, et al. PHARMACOLOGY, BIOCHEMISTRY AND BE-HAVIOR 8(2):177-183, February, 1978.

Effect of a contraceptive steroid combination of the "serum acti-vation" of lipoprotein lipase in rats, by A. Bizzi, et al. BIO-CHEMICAL PHARMACOLOGY 27(5):795-797, March 1, 1978.

Effect of contraceptive steroids on arginine-stimulated glucagon and insulin secretion in women. III. Medroxyprogesterone acetate, by P. Beck, et al. METABOLISM 26(11):1193-1198, November, 1977.

Effect of copper intrauterine contraceptive device on the estro-gen & progesterone uptake in ovariectomized rat uterus, by M. Ghosh, et al. INDIAN JOURNAL OF EXPERIMENTAL BIOLOGY 15(6):477-478, June, 1977.

Effect of cyproterone acetate on hair growth, sebaceous secre-tion and endocrine parameters in a hirsute subject, by F. J. Ebling, et al. BRITISH JOURNAL OF DERMATOLOGY 97(4):371-381, October, 1977.

Effect of cyproterone acetate on skin surface lipids, by D. Fanta, et al. ACTA DERMATO-VENEREOLOGICA 58(1):85-87, 1978.

Effect of d-norgestrel on LH levels and ovulation in the rhesus monkey, by N. E. Reame, et al. CONTRACEPTION 16(5):499-505, November, 1977.

The effect of daily norethisterone (0.35 mg) on cervical mucus and on urinary LH, pregnanediol and oestrogen levels, by M. Elstein, et al. BRITISH JOURNAL OF OBSTETRICS AND GYNAECOLOGY 83(2):165-168, February, 1976.

The effect of delay and method choice on the risk of abortion morbidity, by W. Cates, Jr., et al. FAMILY PLANNING PERSPECTIVES 9(6):266-268+, November-December, 1977.

Effect of estrogens on the liver. Case presentation, by R. Dahl. GASTROENTEROLOGY 75(3):517, September, 1978.

Effect of ethinyl oestradiol and megestrol acetate on carbohydrate metabolism in rabbits, by B. B. Gaitonde, et al. INDIAN JOURNAL OF MEDICAL RESEARCH 66(2);223-235, August, 1977.

Effect of ethinyloestradiol on protein, nucleic acids and nucleases in the rat liver, by M. A. Mukundan, et al. INDIAN JOURNAL OF MEDICAL RESEARCH 66(6):946-949, December, 1977.

Effect of ethynodiol diacetate with ethinyl estradiol on the mammary glands of rhesus monkeys: a preliminary report, by V. A. Drill, et al. JOURNAL OF THE NATIONAL CANCER INSTITUTE 60(5):1169-1170, May, 1978.

Effect of ethynylestradiol on biliary excretion of bile acids, phosphatidylcolines, and cholesterol in the bile fistula rat, by F. Kern, Jr., et al. JOURNAL OF LIPID RESEARCH 18(5):623-234, September, 1977.

The effect of 15-methyl-prostaglandin F2 alpha administered intramuscularly to induce abortion in the first half of pregnancy (proceedings), by U. Haller, et al. ARCHIV FUR GYNAEKOLOGIE 224(1-4):266-268, July 29, 1977.

Effect of general and local anaesthesia on blood loss during and after therapeutic abortion, by B. R. Moller. ACTA OBSTETRICIA ET GYNECOLOGICA SCANDINAVICA 57(2): 133-136, 1978.

Effect of group level variables on fertility in a rural Indian sample, by R. Anker. JOURNAL OF DEVELOPMENT STUDIES 14:63-76, October, 1977.

Effect of intrauterine contraception on nonspecific reactivity of the female body, by R. S. Baryshkina, et al. AKUSHERSTVO I GINEKOLOGIIA (12):34-36, December, 1977.

Effect of intrauterine device on ovarian function, by S. Chander, et al. THERIOGENOLOGY 8(5):271-278, November, 1977.

The effect of intrauterine devices containing zinc and copper on their levels in serum, by S. O. Anteby, et al. FERTILITY AND STERILITY 29(1):30-34, January, 1978.

The effect of kind of carbohydrate in the diet and use of oral contraceptives on metabolism of young women. I. Blood and urinary lactate, uric acid, andphosphorus, by J. L. Kelsay, et al. AMERICAN JOURNAL OF CLINICAL NUTRITION 30(12):2016-2022, December, 1977.

Effect of liberalized abortion on maternal mortality rates [letter], by W. Cates, Jr., et al. AMERICAN JOURNAL OF OBSTETRICS AND GYNECOLOGY 130(3):372-374, February 1, 1978.

The effect of ligation or separation between the intrauterine device of horn and adjacent ovary on implantation in the hamster, by W. J. Bo, et al. FERTILITY AND STERILITY 29(3):351-353, March, 1978.

The effect of long-term oral oestriol succinate therapy on the skin of castrated women, by R. Punnonen, et al. ANNALES CHIRURGIAE ET GYNAECOLOGIAE FENNIAE 66(4): 214-215, 1977.

Effect of long term vasectomy on the secretory function of the epididymis in rat, by Q. Jehan, et al. INDIAN JOURNAL OF EXPERIMENTAL BIOLOGY 15(7):553-554, July, 1977.

The effect of a low dose progestagen on the trace metal content and disulphide and sulphydryl groups in cervical mucus, by B. Daunter, et al. CONTRACEPTION 17(1):35-40, January, 1978.

Effect of low zinc intake and oral contraceptive agents on nitrogen utilization and clinical findings in young women, by F. M. Hess, et al. JOURNAL OF NUTRITION 107(12): 2219-2227, December, 1977.

Effect of the menstrul cycle, oral contraception and pregnancy of forearm blood flow, venous distensibility and clotting factors, by R. Fawer, et al. EUROPEAN JOURNAL OF CLINICAL PHARMACOLOGY 13(4):251-257, June 19, 1978.

Effect of menstrual hygiene (tampons vs pads) and of the form of contraception on pH and bacterial infection of the vagina, by E. G. Loch, et al. FORTSCHRITTE DER MEDIZIN 95(44):2653-2656+, November 24, 1977.

Effect of a new service on women's abortion experience, by S. Treloar, et al. JOURNAL OF BIOSOCIAL SCIENCE 9(4): 417-427, October, 1977.

Effect of norethindrone acetate released from a single silastic implant on serum FSH, LH, progesterone and estradiol-17beta of women druing first eight months of treatment, by S. A. Rahman, et al. CONTRACEPTION 16(5):487-497, November, 1977.

Effect of norethisterone oenanthate on serum gonadotrophin levels, by K. Fotherby, et al. CONTRACEPTION 16(6): 591-604, December, 1977.

Effect of oral alanine loads on plasma amino acids in oral contraceptive users and control women, by C. Potera, et al. AMERICAN JOURNAL OF CLINICAL NUTRITION 31(5):794-798, May, 1978.

The effect of oral contraceptive agents on plasma vitamin A in the human and the rat. NUTRITION REVIEWS 35(9):245-248, September, 1977.

Effect of oral contraceptive on blood coagulation and blood fibrinolysis, by V. Sharma. JOURNAL OF OBSTETRICS AND GYNAECOLOGY OF INDIA 27(4):567-575, August, 1977.

The effect of an oral contraceptive on serum lipoproteins and skinfold thickness in young women, by H. J. van der Steeg, et al. CONTRACEPTION 16(1):29-38, July, 1977.

The effect of oral contraceptives and of bromocriptine upon pituitary stimulation by LH-RH and TRH, by J. S. Dericks-Tan, et al. CONTRACEPTION 17(1):79-86, January, 1978.

Effect of oral contraceptives on the blood lipid level, by E. V. Zhemerikina, et al. KARDIOLOGIIA 17(9):104-108, September, 1977.

Effect of oral contraceptives on the capacity to stimulate plasma renin activity and plasma aldosterone, by F. Klumpp, et al. MEDIZINISCH WELT 29(6):228-231, February 10, 1978.

Effect of oral contraceptives on plasma androgenic steroids and their precursors, by M. Fern, et al. OBSTETRICS AND GYNECOLOGY 51(5):541-544, May, 1978.

Effect of oral contraceptives on the psyche and on sexuality, by G. Nahrendorf, et al. ZENTRALBLATT FUER GYNAE-KOLOGIE 100(10):632-637, 1978.

Effect of oral contraceptives on sebum excretion rate, by R. J. Pye, et al. BRITISH MEDICAL JOURNAL 2(6102):1581-1582, December 17, 1977.

The effect of oral contraceptives on serum immunoglobuims, by D. Shouval, et al. HAREFUAH 94(2):49-51, January 15, 1978.

Effect of ovarectomy of femals and oestrogen administration to males during the neonatal critical period on salt intake in adulthood in rats, by J. Krecek. PHYSIOLOGIA BOHEMO-SLOVACA 27(1):1-5, 1978.

The effect of ovariectomy on the responsiveness of preoptic-septal neurons to microelectrophoresed estrogen, by M. J. Kelly, et al. NEUROENDOCRINOLOGY 25(4):204-211, 1978.

Effect of ovulation inhabitors on the course of hereditary spontaneous hypertension of the rat (SH rats), by A. Samizadeh, et al. MEDIZINISCHE WELT 29(6):225-227, February 10, 1978.

The effect of oxytocin on hypertonic saline abortion, by B. Sandström, et al. ACTA OBSTETRICIA ET GYNECOLOGICA SCANDINAVICA (66):129-131, 1977.

Effect of papaya (Carica papaya linn) on pregnancy and estrous cycle in albino rats of Wistar strain, by M. Gopalakrishnan, et al. INDIAN JOURNAL OF PHYSIOLOGY AND PHARMACOLOGY 22(1):66-70, January-March, 1978.

Effect of paramethasone acetate on women with secondary amenorrhea: a preliminary report, by V. Cortés-Gallegos, et al. FERTILITY AND STERILITY 29(4):402-406, April, 1978.

The effect of pregnancy and two different contraceptive pills on serum lipids and lipoproteins in a woman with a type III hyperlipoproteinaemia pattern, by D. P. Muller, et al. BRITISH JOURNAL OF OBSTETRICS AND GYNAECOLOGY 85(2):127-133, February, 1978.

Effect of pregnancy on liver tumor associated with oral contracptives, by d. R. Kent, et al. OBSTETRICS AND GYNECOLOGY 51(2):148-151, February, 1978.

The effect of prepuberal castration on the development of the nuclear sizes of the neurons in the hypothalamic nuclei of feamale rats, by H. Morishita, et al. BRAIN RESEARCH 146(2):388-391, May 12, 1978.

Effect of Pulsatilla administered pituitary extracts of ovariectomized donor rats on the ovaries, uteri & thyroids of normally cycling recipients, by S. Prasad, et al. INDIAN JOURNAL OF EXPERIMENTAL BIOLOGY 16(3):289-293, March, 1978.

Effect of quinestrol on plasma lipids in women, by M. M. Abdel Kader, et al. ACTA BIOLOGICA ET MEDICA GERMANICA 36(9):1285-1287, 1977.

The effect of recent FDA legislation on contraceptive development and safety, by R. P. Dickey. INTERNATIONAL JOURNAL OF GYNAECOLOGY AND OBSTETRICS

15(2):111-114, 1977.

Effect of recent medicaid decisions on a constituional right: abortions only for the rich? FORDHAM URBAN LAW JOURNAL 6:687-710, Spring, 1978.

Effect of S-adenosyl-L-methionine on ethynylestradiol-induced impairment of bile flow in female rats, by G. Stramentinoli, et al. EXPERIENTIA 33(10):1361-1362, October 15, 1977.

The effect of sex hormones on peripheral immunity in patients with advanced breast cancer, by C. R. Franks, et al. CLINI-CAL ONCOLOGY 4(1):19-24, March, 1978.

Effect of steroid contraceptive drug treatment on the catecholamine metabolism in the guinea pig central nervous system, by F. Ponzio, et al. MEDICAL BIOLOGY 55(4):224-227, August, 1977.

Effect of steroidal contraception on lipid factors and liver function tests, by S. M. Shahani, et al. JOURNAL OF OBSTE-TRICS AND GYNAECOLOGY OF INDIA 27(1):95-101, February, 1977.

The effect of subcutaneous administration of oestrogens on plasma oestrogen levels and tumour incidence in female rats, by M. A. Blankenstein, et al. EUROPEAN JOURNAL OF CANCER 13(12):1437-1443, December, 1977.

Effect of a subdermal silastic implant containing norethindrone acetate on human lactation, by U. Seth, et al. CONTRA-CEPTION 16(4):383-398, October, 1977.

The effect of subsidized family planning services on reproductive behavior in the United States: 1969-1974, by J. R. Udry, et al. DEMOGRAPHY 13:463-478, November, 1976.

The effect of synthetic gestagens on progesterone formation in vitro in human placenta of early pregnancy, by A. Saure, et al. JOURNAL OF REPRODUCTION AND FERTILITY 51(2):369-373, November, 1977.

The effect of two progestins on human endometrial enzymes and trace elements, by J. Jelínek, et al. ACTA ENDOCRINOLOGICA 88(3):580-588, July, 1978.

The effect of various doses of oral oestradiolvalerate and oestriol-succinate on urine calcium/creatinine, serum FSH and endometrium in castrated women, by L. Rauramo, et al. ACTA OBSTETRICIA ET GYNECOLOGICA SCANDINAVICA 56(4):363-368, 1977.

Effect of vasectomy on hepatic drug metabolism, by D. E. Cook. EXPERIENTIA 34(3):315-316, March 15, 1978.

Effectiveness of contraception in Belgium: results of the Second National Fertility Survey, 1971 (Nego ii), by R. L. Cliquet, et al. JOURNAL OF BIOSOCIAL SCIENCE 9(4):403-416, October, 1977.

Effectiveness of a programmed instruction module on oral contraceptives, by M. K. Guimei. NURSING RESEARCH 26(6):452-455, November-December, 1977.

Effectiveness of the use of contraception in the voluntary family planning program of the Instituo Mexicano del Seguro Social, by J. García Peña, et al. SPM: SALUD PUBLICA DE MEXICO 19(5):655-663, September-October, 1977.

The effects of anti-androgenic agents on metabolism and biosynthesis of testosterone (I): testosterone metabolic regulation in the liver and the biosynthesis in the testes on rats treated with chlormadinone acetate, by S. Honma, et al. FOLIA ENDOCRINOLOGICA JAPONICA 63(5):703-718, March 20, 1977.

Effects of castration and androgen replacement on acid phosphatase activity in the adult rat prostate gland, by M. P. Tenniswood, et al. JOURNAL OF ENDOCRINOLOGY 77(3):301-308, June, 1978.

Effects of castration and testosterone, dihydrotestosterone or oestradiol replacement treatment in neonatal rats on mounting behaviour in the adult, by P. Södersten, et al. JOURNAL

OF ENDOCRINOLOGY 76(2):251-260, February, 1978.

Effects of castration and testosterone treatment on sex specific orientation in the male rat, by J. Hetta, et al. ACTA PHYSIOLOGICA SCANDINAVICA (453):47-62, 1978.

Effects of castration on the mechanical response to motor nerve stimulation of the rat vas deferens [proceedings], by D. P. Gilmore, et al. BRITISH JOURNAL OF PHARMACOLOGY 61(3):473P-474P, November, 1977.

Effects of castration on serum LH and FSH concentrations in male guinea-pigs, by D. Croix. JOURNAL OF REPRODUCTION AND FERTILITY 51(1):149-151, September, 1977.

Effects of Centchroman on the ovary & uterus of unilaterally ovariectomized rats, by J. K. Datta, et al. INDIAN JOURNAL OF EXPERIMENTAL BIOLOGY 15(12):1154-1156, December, 1977.

Effects of copper intravasal device on the fertility of rat, by N. K. Sud, et al. INDIAN JOURNAL OF MEDICAL RESEARCH 65(6):812-816, June, 1977.

Effects of danazol on gonadotropin secretion after ovariectomy in rats, by J. A. Milchez-Martinez, et al. CONTRACEPTION 17(3):283-290, March, 1978.

The effects of ergosterol on the response of female chicks to oral oestrogens and progestogens, by G. P. Webb, et al. BRITISH POULTRY SCIENCE 18(5):543-545, September, 1977.

Effects of estradiol benzoate, estrone, and propionates of testosterone or dihydrotestosterone on sexual and related behaviors of ovariectomized Rhesus monkeys, by K. Wallen, et al. HORMONES AND BEHAVIOR 9(3):228-248, December, 1977.

Effects of estrogens on the liver, by F. R. Simmon. GASTROENTEROLOGY 75(3):512-514, September, 1978.

Effects of ethinyl estradiol on hepatic microsomal proteins and the turnover of cytochrome P-450, by M. Mackinnon, et al. JOURNAL OF LABORATORY AND CLINICAL MEDICINE 90(6):1096-1106, December, 1977.

The effects of intramuscular injections of 15(S)-15-methyl prostaglandin F2alpha in failed abortions, by N. H. Lauersen, et al. FERTILITY AND STERILITY 28(10):1044-1047, October, 1977.

Effects of long-acting steroid contraceptives on ovarian and uterine histology of rats, by Harun-Ar-Rashid, et al. BANGLADESH MEDICAL RESEARCH COUNCIL BULLETIN 3(1):46-51, June, 1977.

Effects of low-oestrogen oral contraceptives [letter], by T. W. Meade. LANCET 1(8059):332, February 11, 1978.

The effects of medroxyprogesterone on dentofacial development in males with idiopathic isosexual precocity, by F. A. Catalanotto, et al. ANGLE ORTHODONTIST 48(2):106-113, April, 1978.

Effects of medroxyprogesterone on the liver function and drug metabolism of patients with primary biliary cirrhosis and chronic active hepatitis, by E. A. Sotaniemi, et al. JOURNAL OF MEDICINE 9(2):117-128, 1978.

Effects of mestranol on blood pressure and norepinephrine in young normotensive and genetically hypertensive rats, by G. M. Lew. GENERAL PHARMACOLOGY 9(3):163-166, 1978.

Effects of oral and intrauterine administration of contraceptives on the uterus, by W. B. Ober. HUMAN PATHOLOGY 8(5):513-527, September, 1977.

Effects of an oral contraceptive on hepatic size and antipyrine metabolism in premenopausal women, by M. Homeida, et al. CLINICAL PHARMACOLOGY AND THERAPEUTICS 24(2):228-232, August, 1978.

Effects of oral contraceptives on tryptophan metabolism and
vitamin B6 requirements in women, by R. R. Brown, et al.
ACTA VITAMINOLOGICA ET ENZYMOLOGICA 29(1-6):
151-157, 1975.

Effects of oral hormonal contraceptive in the adolescent, by V.
Ruiz Velasco, et al. OBSTETRICIA Y GINECOLOGIA
LATINO-AMERICANAS 35(7-8):217-224, July-August,
1977.

Effects of ovariectomy and estradiol injection on nuclear structures of endometrial epithelial cells, by G. H. Vázquez-Nin,
et al. ACTA ANATOMICA 102(3):308-318, 1978.

Effects of ovariectomy and estradiol replacement therapy upon
the sexual and aggressive behavior of the greater galago
(Galago crassicaudatus crassicaudatus), by A. F. Dixson.
HORMONE RESEARCH 10(1):61-70, February, 1978.

Effects of ovariectomy and treatment with progesterone or
oestradiol-17 beta on the secretion of insulin by the perfused
rat pancreas, by S. Senzen. JOURNAL OF ENDOCRINOLO-
GY 78(1):153-154, July, 1978.

Effects of the Progestasert on the menstrual pattern, ovarian
steroids and endometrium, by L. S. Wan, et al. CONTRA-
CEPTION 16(4):417-434, October, 1977.

The effects of psychological preparation on pain at intrauterine
device insertion, by J. R. Newton, et al. CONTRACEPTION
16(5):523-532, November, 1977.

Effects of quingestanol acetate on the histology, histochemistry
and ultrastructure of the endometrium, by C. E. Flowers,
et al. JOURNAL DE GYNECOLOGIE, OBSTETRIQUE
ET BIOLOGIE DE LA REPRODUCTION 6(8):1139-1157,
December, 1977.

Effects of smoking and oral contraceptives on plasma and whole
blood viscosity. Rheologic studies on normal subjects, by
H. Leonhardt, et al. MEDIZINISCHE WELT 29(21):880-
883, May 26, 1978.

Effects of social disincentive policies on fertility behavior in Singapore, by S. B. Tan, et al. AMERICAN JOURNAL OF PUBLIC HEALTH 68(2):119-124, February, 1978.

Effects of steroids on serum lipids and serum cholesterol binding reserve, by M. S. Roth, et al. AMERICAN JOURNAL OF OBSTETRICS AND GYNECOLOGY 132(2):151-156, September 15, 1978.

The effects of sulpiride on plasma LH, FSH, and progesterone in women during the reproductive years. Role of hyperprolactinism in ovulation disorders, by J. Buvat, et al. JOURNAL DE GYNECOLOGIE, OBSTETRIQUE ET BIOLOGIE DE LA REPRODUCTION 7(1):5-18, January, 1978.

Effects of testrosterone replacement on the recovery from increased emotionality, produced by septal lesions in prepubertal castrated male rats, by I. Lieblich, et al. PHYSIOLOGY AND BEHAVIOR 18(6):1159-1164, June, 1977.

Effects of various factors on selection for family planning status and natural fecundability: a simulation study, by J. C. Barrett. DEMOGRAPHY 15:87-98, February, 1978.

Effects of vasectomy and antisperm antibodies on human seminal fluid deoxyribonucleic acid polymerase activity, by S. S. Witkin, et al. FERTILITY AND STERILITY 29(3):314-319, March, 1978.

The effects of vasectomy on the testis and accessory sex glands of the Hartlye strain guinea pig, by J. S. Jhunjhunwala, et al. INVESTIGATIVE UROLOGY 15(3):200-204, November, 1977.

Effects, on the endometrium, of a new oral contraceptive: Physiostat, by P. Delacroix. REVUE FRANCAISE DE GYNECOLOGIE ET D'OBSTETRIQUE 72(7-9):583-585, July-September, 1977.

The efficiency of menstrual regulation as a method of fertility control, by J. Bongaarts, et al. STUDIES IN FAMILY PLANNING 8(10):268-272, October, 1977.

Elective surgery and the contraceptive pill (editorial), by A. Eldor, et al. HAREFUAH 94(2):93, January 15, 1978.

Electrical activity of the rat uterus during early pregnancy and abortion, by A. Talo, et al. ACTA PHYSIOLOGICA SCANDINAVICA 100(3):377-381, July, 1977.

Electrolyte studies after intra-amniotic instillation of 20 per cent sodium chloride, by R. V. Bhatt, et al. INDIAN JOURNAL OF MEDICAL RESEARCH 67:589-592, April, 1978.

Eleven years on, by M. Stott. GUARDIAN p. 9, February 21, 1978.

Embryonic development in consecutive specimens from recurrent spontaneous abortions, by B. J. Poland, et al. AMERICAN JOURNAL OF OBSTETRICS AND GYNECOLOGY 130(5): 512-515, March 1, 1978.

Emotional disturbance in unplanned versus planned children, by G. Singer, et al. SOCIAL BIOLOGY 23:254-259, August, 1976.

An emperical argument against abortion, by J. Newman. NEW SCHOLASTICISM 51:384-395, Summer, 1977.

Enacting religious beliefs in a pluralistic society, by F. S. Jaffe. HASTINGS CENTER REPORT 8:14-16, August, 1978.

The encare oval. MEDICAL LETTER ON DRUGS AND THERAPEUTICS 20(6):29-30, March 24, 1978.

Endocoagulation: a new and completely safe medical current for sterilization, by K. Semm. INTERNATIONAL JOURNAL OF FERTILITY 22(4):238-242, 1977.

Endocrine changes and symptomatology after oophorectomy in premenopausal women, by S. Chakravarti, et al. BRITISH JOURNAL OF OBSTETRICS AND GYNAECOLOGY 84(10):769-775, October, 1977.

Endometrial cytology and copper containing intrauterine devices, by W. Hasting, et al. FORTSCHRITTE DER MEDIZIN 96(7):311-314, February 16, 1978.

Endometrial histology and progesterone levels in women using norethindrone acetate implants for contraception, by D. Takkar, et al. CONTRACEPTION 17(2):103-113, February, 1978.

Endometrial histology with oral contraceptives, by R. Baveja, et al. JOURNAL OF OBSTETRICS AND GYNAECOLOGY OF INDIA 27(2):195-197, April, 1977.

Endometrial morphology of women using a d-norgestrel-releasing intrauterine device, by C. G. Nilsson, et al. FERTILITY AND STERILITY 29(4):397-401, April, 1978.

Endometrial ossification following an abortion, by M. Waxman, et al. AMERICAN JOURNAL OF OBSTETRICS AND GYNECOLOGY 130(5):587-588, March 1, 1978.

Endometrial prostaglandin F content in women wearing non-medicated or progestin-releasing intrauterine devices, by A. Scommegna, et al. FERTILITY AND STERILITY 29(5): 500-504, May, 1978.

Epidemiological relationship between steroid hormones and liver lesions, by E. Mahboubi, et al. JOURNAL OF TOXICOLOGY AND ENVIRONMENTAL HEALTH 3(1-2):207-218, September, 1977.

Epidemiological study of cases undergoing medical termination of pregnancy, by N. Kishor, et al. JOURNAL OF THE INDIAN MEDICAL ASSOCIATION 68(6):116-119, March 16, 1977.

Epidemiology of uterine cervicocarcinoma, by L. Barberis, et al. MINERVA GINECOLOGIA 30(4):291-298, April, 1978.

Epilepsy and contraception, by A. Fanard, et al. ACTA OBSTETRICA Y GINECOLOGICA HISPANA-LUSITANA 25(6):311-317, June, 1977.

Equity in abortion services, by R. Roemer. AMERICAN JOURNAL OF PUBLIC HEALTH 68:629-631, July, 1978.

Erotic imagery and self-castration in transvestism/transsexualism: a case report, by D. P. van Kammen, et al. JOURNAL OF HOMSEXUALITY 2(4):359-366, Summer, 1977.

Erroneous clinical diagnosis of leg vein thrombosis in women on oral contraceptives, by R. W. Barnes, et al. OBSTETRICS AND GYNECOLOGY 51(5):556-558, May, 1978.

Erythema nodosum and oral contraceptives [letter], by A. Taaffe, et al. BRITISH MEDICAL JOURNAL 2(6098): 1353, November 19, 1977.

Erythema nodosum associated with pregnancy and oral contraceptives, by S. Bombardieri, et al. BRITISH MEDICAL JOURNAL 6075:1509-1510, June 11, 1977.

Estimating the effects of contraceptive use on fertility: techniques and findings from the 1974 Philippine National Acceptor Survey. STUDIES IN FAMILY PLANNING 9(6):150, June, 1978.

—, by J. E. Laing. STUDIES IN FAMILY PLANNING 9:150-162, June, 1978.

Estimating the incidence of induced abortion in Italy, by I. Figa Talamanca. GENUS 32(1-2):91-108, 1976.

Estimating the number of illegal abortions, by C. Francome. JOURNAL OF BIOSOCIAL SCIENCE 9(4):467-479, October, 1977.

Estradiol and pregnanidiol excretion in threatening miscarriages in late period of pregnancy depending on the cause of miscarriage, by N. G. Kosheleva, et al. VOPROSY OKHRANY MATERINSTVA I DETSTVA 22(7):70-73, July, 1977.

Estrogen metabolism in normal and neoplastic endometrium, by E. Gurpide, et al. AMERICAN JOURNAL OF OBSTETRICS AND GYNEKOLOGY 129(7):809-816, December 1,

1977.

Estrogen profiles of premenopausal women with breast cancer, by P. Cole, et al. CANCER RESEARCH 38(3):745-748, March, 1978.

Estrogen/progestogen-exposure and fetal effects, by J. G. Forsberg. TIDSSKRIFT FOR DEN NORSKE LAEGEFORENING 97(30):1583-1584, October 30, 1977.

Estrogen-progestogen treatment enhances the ovulatory response to clomiphene in amenorrheic patients, by E. Gitsch, et al. FERTILITY AND STERILITY 29(2):159-163, February, 1978.

Estrogen treatment in tall girls, by N. Kuhn, et al. OBSTETRICAL AND GYNECOLOGICAL SURVEY 32(7):604-605, September, 1977.

Estrogens and blood pressure, by M. H. Weinberger. JOURNAL OF THE INDIANA STATE MEDICAL ASSOCIATION 70(12):925-926, December, 1977.

Estrogens and experimental atherosclerosis in the baboon (Papio cynocephalus), by H. C. McGill, Jr., et al. CIRCULATION 56(4 Pt 1):657-662, October, 1977.

Estrogens for contraception and menopause, by L. B. Tyrer, et al. NURSES DRUG ALERT 1:169-180, December, 1977.

Estrus control with gestagens, by H. J. Ficus. TIERAERZTLICHE PRAXIS 5(4):521-524, 1977.

Ethical values in anesthesia and intensive care (7): A hospital chaplain's view of abortion, euthanasia and the ethical aspects of suicide, by I. Stenäs. LAKARTIDNINGEN 75(4):224-225, January 25, 1978.

Ethinyl estradiol administration and plasma steroid concentrations in ovariectomized women, by D. K. Mahajan, et al. AMERICAN JOURNAL OF OBSTETRICS AND GYNECOLOGY 130(4):398-402, February 15, 1978.

Ethinyl estradiol in human milk and plasma after oral administration, by S. Nilsson, et al. CONTRACEPTION 17(2):131-139, February, 1978.

Ethinyl estradiol may lead to malignancy [letter], by E. Eichner. AMERICAN JOURNAL OF OBSTETRICS AND GYNECOLOGY 130(4):506-508, February 15, 1978.

Etiological and pathogenetic factors in aborted pregnancy, by N. K. Moskvitina, et al. AKUSHERSTVO I GINEKOLOGIIA (7):31-35, July, 1978.

Etre évêque demain? by R. Bouchex. LE SUPPLEMENT 124: 93-104, February, 1978.

Eugenic sterilization statutes: a constitutional re-evaluation. JOURNAL OF FAMILY LAW 14(2):280+, 1975.

The Euiryong experiment: a Korean innovation in household contraceptive distribution, by C. B. Park, et al. STUDIES IN FAMILY PLANNING 8:67, March, 1977.

Evacuation of retained products of conception in a treatment room and without general anaesthesia, by G. M. Filshie, et al. BRITISH JOURNAL OF OBSTETRICS AND GYNAE-COLOGY 84(7):514-516, July, 1977.

Evaluating family planning program effectiveness and efficiency, by S. L. Gehrz, et al. STUDIES IN FAMILY PLANNING 6(2):37-44, 1975.

Evaluation of a balloon dialtor to augment midtrimester abortion, by M. Borten, et al. AMERICAN JOURNAL OF OBSTETRICS AND GYNECOLOGY 130(2):156-159, January 15, 1978.

An evaluaton of intramuscular progesterone for the diagnosis of early pregnancy, by D. Vengadasalam, et al. JOURNAL OF REPRODUCTIVE MEDICINE 20(5):260-264, May, 1978.

Evaluation of a new direct latex agglutination tube test (UCG-Macrotube) for pregnancy, by T. K. Mukherjee, et al.

AMERICAN JOURNAL OF OBSTETRICS AND GYNE-
COLOGY 131(6):701-702, July 15, 1978.

Evaluation of the "Quick test" a direct latex agglutination test
for pregnancy, by M. Sathanandan, et al. CEYLON MEDI-
CAL JOURNAL 22(2):110-113, June, 1977.

Evaluation of the results concerning radioimmunologically active
human-chorionic gonadotrophin (RIA HCG) in the serum of
women with imminent abortions, by M. Talas, et al. CESKO-
SLOVENSKA GYNEKOLOGIE 43(5):344-347, June, 1978.

Evaluation of sequelae of tubal ligation, by R. J. Stock. FER-
TILITY AND STERILITY 29(2):169-174, February, 1978.

The evaluation of sex chromatin number of newborns of mothers
using oral contraceptives prior to conception, by R. Vajda.
THERAPIA HUNGARICA 25(4):166-168, 1977.

Evaluation of a single dose schedule of 15 (S) 15 methyl PGF2
alpha methyl ester suppository for the termination of 10-14
weeks of pregnancy, by G. Kinra, et al. CONTRACEPTION
17(5):455-464, May, 1978.

Evaluation of single-stitch tubal ligation in postpartum women,
by P. V. Mehta, et al. OBSTETRICS AND GYNECOLOGY
51(5):567-568, May, 1978.

An evaluation of studies concerning reproduction after first
trimester induced abortion, by C. J. Hogue. INTERNA-
TIONAL JOURNAL OF GYNAECOLOGY AND OBSTE-
TRICS 15(2):167-171, 1977.

Les évêques italiens et l'avortement. LA DOCUMENTATION
CATHOLIQUE 74:523-524, June 5, 1977.

The evolution of family planning in an African city: Ibadan,
Nigeria, by J. C. Caldwell, et al. POPULATION STUDIES
31:487-507, November, 1977.

Evolution of the pituitary gonadotropins and ovarian steroids
during progestational treatment begun on the 10th day of

the cycle (10 mg/day Lynestrenol), by D. Dargent, et al. GYNECOLOGIE 29(1):73-76, 1978.

Evolution of the properties of semen immediately following vasectomy, by P. Jouannei, et al. FERTILITY AND STERILITY 29(4):435-441, April, 1978.

Examination of contraceptive perceptions and usage among Los Angeles County women, by B. B. Houser, et al. CONTRA-CEPTION 18(1):7-18, July, 1978.

Examining the intrafamily decision-making process with respect to contraceptive behavior, by P. E. Downs. DISSERTATION ABSTRACTS INTERNATIONAL 37(8-A):4377-4378, February, 1977.

Exceeding all expectancies, by R. Tasker. FAR EAST ECO-NOMIC REVIEW 101:23-25, August 25, 1978.

Excess mortality and the pill, by H. M. Carey. MEDICAL JOUR-NAL OF AUSTRALIA 1(3):153-154, February 11, 1978.

—, [letter], by T. Dwyer, et al. MEDICAL JOURNAL OF AUSTRALIA 1(6):335-336, March 25, 1978.

Exclusion de la procréation selon le droit matrimonial ecclesial, by N. Picard. STUDIA CANONICA 10(1):37-74, 1976.

Existence of an ejaculatory-like reaction in ewe ovariectomized and treated with androgens in adulthood, by C. Fabre. HOR-MONES AND BEHAVIOR 9(2):150-155, October, 1977.

Exogenous hormones, reproductive history, and breast cancer, by P. E. Sartwell, et al. JOURNAL OF THE NATIONAL CANCER INSTITUTE 59(6):1589-1592, December, 1977.

Experience in using POPSIM in a family planning simulation ex-periment, by R. C. Treadway. SIMULATION AND GAMES 9:159-172, June, 1978.

The experience of abortion, by R. Schmidt. NEW SOCIETY pp. 242-244, February 2, 1978.

Experience with medroxyprogesterone acetate (Depo-Provera) as an injectable contraceptive, by S. P. Ellinas. INTERNATIONAL JOURNAL OF GYNAECOLOGY AND OBSTETRICS 15(2):145-149, 1977.

Experience with modern inert IUDs to date: a review and comments, by L. Keith, et al. JOURNAL OF REPRODUCTIVE MEDICINE 20(3):125-132, March, 1978.

Experience with the trans-uterine tubal coagulation with high frequency current and the thermo method under hysteroscopic control, by D. Neubüser, et al. GEBURTSHILFE FRAUENHEILKUNDE 37(9):809-812, September, 1977.

Experience with the tupla-clip for tubal sterilization by laparoscopy, by J. Babenerd, et al. GEBURTSHILFE FRAUENHEILKUNDE 38(4):299-303, April, 1978.

Experiences from a school counseling bureau, by H. Sjöström. LAKARTIDNINGEN 75(21):2130-2131, May 24, 1978.

Experiences in 9 patient/family education workshops, by J. P. Lovegren, et al. JOURNAL OF THE AMERICAN HEALTH CARE ASSOCIATION 4(1):18-21, January, 1978.

Experiences with the preventive use of herparin in septic abortion, by R. Schwarz. ZENTRALBLATT FUER GYNAEKOLOGIE 100(8):487-489, 1978.

Experiences with tubal sterilization using bipolar electrocoagulation (proceedings), by H. A. Hirsch, et al. ARCHIV FUR GYNAEKOLOGIE 224(1-4):39, July 29, 1977.

Experiences with vaginal tubal sterilization using Kroener's fimbriectomy (proceedings), by G. Scholtes. ARCHIV FUR GYNAEKOLOGIE 224(1-4):42, July 29, 1977.

Experimental and clinical data on Cyclabil, by W. H. Schneider, et al. ACTA OBSTETRICIA ET GYNECOLOGICA SCANDINAVICA (65):39-43, 1977.

Experimental trial of the tri-cycle pill [letter], by E. Elliott.

BRITISH MEDICAL JOURNAL 2(6093):1025-1026, October 15, 1977.

Experimentation in family planning delivery systems: an overview. STUDIES IN FAMILY PLANNING 8(12):302, December, 1977.

—, by R. Cuca, et al. STUDIES IN FAMILY PLANNING 8(12):302-310, December, 1977.

Experiments with polyacetyl tube clips in the rabbit (proceedings), by K. Diedrich, et al. ARCHIV FUR GYNAEKOLOGIE 224(1-4):45-46, July 29, 1977.

Experts question new IUD warning [on warning not to insert IUD after child birth or abortion till involution is complete because of a claimed increase in perforation and expulsion. MEDICAL WORLD NEWS 18:13, November 28, 1977.

Extra-amniotic prostaglandin E2 and intravenousoxytocin in termination of mid-trimester pregnancy and the management of missed abortion and hydatiform mole, by H. Arshat. MEDICAL JOURNAL OF MALAYSIA 31(3):220-225, March, 1977.

FDA denies approval of Depo-Provera in U.S. for contraception; risks outweigh benefits. FAMILY PLANNING PERSPECTIVES 10(3):163, May-June, 1978.

FDA establishes new patient information requirements for birth control pills. OCCUPATIONAL HEALTH NURSING 26:42-43, April, 1978.

FDA said that, contrary to Eaton-Merz Lab claim, Encare oval, a widely used non-prescription contraceptive, doesn't seem to be any more effective than similar products sold by competitors. WALL STREET JOURNAL p. 2, July 13-29.

FDA studies of estrogen, progestogens, and estrogen/progestogen comginations in the dog and monkey, by R. G. Geil, et al. JOURNAL OF TOXICOLOGY AND ENVIRONMENTAL HEALTH 3(1-2):179-193, September, 1977.

FP/MIS: a management information system for a community family planning clinic, by J. Herson, et al. MEDICAL CARE 15(5): , May, 1977.

Fabrication and testing of vaginal contraceptive devices designed for release of prespecified dose levels of steroids, by F. G. Burton, et al. CONTRACEPTION 17(3):221-230, March, 1978.

Face to face with abortion, by G. La Pira. OSSEIVATORE ROMANO 12(521):9-10, March 23, 1978.

Factors affecting contraceptive practices of high school and college-age students, by R. H. Needle. JOURNAL OF SCHOOL HEALTH 47:340-345, June, 1977.

Factors affecting pituitary gonadotropin function in users of oral contraceptive steroids, by J. A. Scott, et al. AMERICAN JOURNAL OF OBSTETRICS AND GYNECOLOGY 130(7):817-821, April 1, 1978.

Factors in the decision to obtain voluntary sterilization: the choice of a male versus a female procedure, by M. P. Clark. DISSERTATION ABSTRACTS INTERNATIONAL 37(5-A):3210, November, 1976.

Factors influencing contraceptive behavior of single college students, by J. W. Maxwell, et al. JOURNAL OF SEX AND MARITAL THERAPY 3(4):265-273, Winter, 1977.

Failed abortion in a septate uterus, by C. R. McArdle. AMERICAN JOURNAL OF OBSTETRICS AND GYNECOLOGY 131(8):910, August 15, 1978.

Failed tubal sterilization as an etiologic factor in ectopic tubal pregnancy, by L. H. Honoré, et al. FERTILITY AND STERILITY 29(5):509-511, May, 1978.

Failure to cause abortion in cows wih intravenous sodium iodide treatement [letter], by H. P. Riemann, et al. JOURNAL OF THE AMERICAN VETERINARY ASSOCIATION 172(10):1147, May 15, 1978.

Failures of contraceptive practice, by J. Robins. NEW YORK STATE JOURNAL OF MEDICINE 76:361-365, March, 1976.

Falope-ring: a laparoscopic sterilization. Technical handling, action and experiences, by J. A. Balmer, et al. PRAXIS 66(41):1314-1320, October 11, 1977.

Falope ring tubal ligation, by A. B. Lalonde. AMERICAN JOURNAL OF OBSTETRICS AND GYNECOLOGY 130(5): 567-568, March 1, 1978.

Familia y esclavitud en Aristoles, by A. J. Cappelletti. REVISTA VENEZOLANA DE FILOSAF pp. 7-44, 1977.

La famille tunisienne et la contraception: données et motivations, by S. Sahli. REVUE TUNISIENNE DE SCIENCES SOCIALES 14(48-49):161-175, 1977.

Family law: contraception: a brief legal history, by H. F. Pilpel. TRIAL 13(12):16-17+, December, 1977.

Family limitation and the English demographic revolution: a simulation approach, by N. F. R. Crafts, et al. JOURNAL OF ECONOMIC HISTORY 36:598-623, September, 1976.

Family limitation in pre-industrial England, by E. A. Wrigley. ECONOMIC HISTORY REVIEW 19:82-109, April, 1966; Reply with rejoinder by R. B. Morrow, 31:419-436, August, 1978.

Family limitation in pre-industrial England: a reappraisal, by R. B. Morrow. ECONOMIC HISTORY REVIEW 31:419-428, August, 1978.

Family nurse practitioner in health services center for employees in industry, by R. R. Bauer, et al. OCCUPATIONAL HEALTH NURSING 26(2):11-14, February, 1978.

Family planning, by T. Svendsby. SYKEPLEIEN 65(6):337, April 20, 1978.

Family planning clinic "dropouts", by O. F. Moore, et al. NURSE PRACTITIONER 3:14+, July-August, 1978.

Family planning. Contraception: foams, mechanical devices, Part 1, by R. A. Hatcher, et al. PERINATAL CARE 2:21-23+, March, 1978.

Family planning costs [letter], by R. F. Martin. BRITISH MEDICAL JOURNAL 1(6106):180, January 21, 1978.

Family planning education as an integral part of day care services in Korea, by K. Sung. STUDIES IN FAMILY PLANNING 9:71-74, April, 1978.

Family planning in China. NURSING TIMES 74:62, March 9, 1978.

—, by W. Wen. INDIAN JOURNAL OF PEDIATRICS 44(350): 78-80, March, 1977.

Family planning in genetic services, by J. O. Hof. SOUTH AFRICAN NURSING JOURNAL 44:23, November, 1977.

Family planning in Hong Kong. AUSTRALASIAN NURSES JOURNAL 7(4):43, November, 1977.

Family planning in Mauritius: a national survey, by C. R. Hein. STUDIES IN FAMILY PLANNING 8(12):316-320, December, 1977.

Family planning in the Philippines: assessment of program implementation [based on conference paper], by A. P. Varela. PHILIPPINE JOURNAL OF PUBLIC ADMINISTRATION 20:236-260, July, 1976.

Family planning in a sample of Edinburgh women, by D. R. Hannay, et al. HEALTH BULLETIN (Edinburgh) 35(6): 326-329, November, 1977.

Family planning needs and services in nonmetropolitan areas, by T. H. Firpo, et al. FAMILY PLANNING PERSPECTIVES 8:231-248, September-October, 1976.

Family planning needs urgent attention. NURSING NEWS 1:1-2, June, 1978.

Family planning opinion leadership in the United States, by A. A. Fisher. INTERNATIONAL JOURNAL OF HEALTH EDUCATION 21(2):98-106, 1978.

Family planning program activity and patient enrollment rates in the United States, 1969 and 1971. DEMOGRAPHY 14(2): 213, May, 1977.

Family planning program: big strides in 10 years: 26% of repro-ductive-age Filipinos now enrolled; 1980 target is 35%. WAR ON HUNGER 11:16-19, December, 1977.

Family planning programs found to be a major factor behind sharp fertility declines in Latin America and Asia. FAMILY PLANNING PERSPECTIVES 10(1):41-42, January-February, 1978.

Family planning programs in Britain, German Federal Republic, Denmark and Sweden, with the implications for Canada, by E. S. Smith. CANADIAN JOURNAL OF PUBLIC HEALTH 68(5):369-374, September-October, 1977.

Family-planning services [letter]. LANCET 2(7939):819-820, October 25, 1975.

Family planning services for persons handicapped by mental retardation, by H. P. David, et al. AMERICAN JOURNAL OF PUBLIC HEALTH 66:1053-1057, November, 1976.

Family planning under the magnifying glass (with special refer-ence to the elections in India), by F. M. de Villiers. SOUTH AFRICAN NURSING JOURNAL 44(10):25-27, October, 1977.

Family practice: teaching new docs old tricks, by J. Lukomnik. HEALTH—PAC BULLETIN (80):1-2+, January-February, 1978.

Family spacing and limitation: acceptable and effective techniques-still in the future? by D. M. Potts. PROCEEDINGS OF THE ROYAL SOCIETY OF LONDON; BIOLOGICAL SCIENCES 199(1134):129-144, October 19, 1977.

Family spacing and limitation. Applying family planning in rural communities, by P. Senanayake. PROCEEDINGS OF THE ROYAL SOCIETY OF LONDON; BIOLOGICAL SCIENCES 199(1134):115-127, October 19, 1977.

Fatal amniotic fluid embolism during induced abortion, 1972-1975, by D. A. Grimes, et al. SOUTHERN MEDICAL JOURNAL 70(11):1325-1326, November, 1977.

Fatal outcome of an hepatic adenoma following short term oral contraceptive use, byA. W. Blayney, et al. IRISH MEDICAL JOURNAL 70(15):455-456, October 21, 1977.

Fatal uterine rupture during oxytocin-augmented, saline-induced abortion, by D. A. Grimes, et al. AMERICAN JOURNAL OF OBSTETRICS AND GYNECOLOGY 130(5):591-593, March 1, 1978.

Fate of spermatozoa in the male: I. Quantitation of sperm accumulation after vasectomy in the rabbit, by H. D. Moore, et al. BIOLOGY OF REPRODUCTION 18(5):784-790, June, 1978.

—. II. Absence of a specific sperm disposal mechanism in the androgen-deficient hamster and rabbit, by P. D. Temple-Smith, et al. BIOLOGY OF REPRODUCTION 18(5):791-798, June, 1978.

Fecundability following the discontinuation of IUD use among Taiwanese women, by A. K. Jain, et al. JOURNAL OF BIOSOCIAL SCIENCE 9:137-152, April, 1977.

Federal controls and local realities, by D. H. Hitt. BULLETIN OF THE AMERICAN PROTESTANT HOSPITAL ASSOCIATION 42(1):14-15+, Spring, 1978.

Federal financial participation in state claims for abortions. FEDERAL REGISTER 43(23):4571-4582, February 2, 1978.

Fellowship theme: fools for Christ? by E. Curtin, Jr. NATION-
AL CATHOLIC REPORTER 14:3, April 14, 1978.

Female hygiene and nursing care. Induced abortion today and
yesterday, by H. T. Ng. JOURNAL OF NURSING 24(2):
1-4, April, 1977.

Female sex hormones and thrombosis. Epidemiological aspects,
by M. P. Vessey, et al. BRITISH MEDICAL BULLETIN
34(2):157-162, May, 1978.

Female status and fertility behaviour in a metropolitan urban
area of Bangladesh, by R. H. Chaudhury. POPULATION
STUDIES 32:261-273, July, 1978.

Female sterilization by laparoscopy: a comparative study of
tubal occlusion with electrocoagulation and spring-loaded
clip with one-year follow-up, by S. Koetsawang, et al.
ANNALES CHIRURGIAE ET GYNAECOLOGIAE FEN-
NIAE 66(5):240-246, 1977.

Female sterilization in Aberdeen: preliminary findings, by S.
Teper. POPULATION STUDIES 32:549-566, November,
1978.

Female sterilization in small camp settings in rural India, by R.
V. Bhatt, et al. STUDIES IN FAMILY PLANNING 9(2-3):
39-43, February-March, 1978.

Female sterilization: training for rural service, by K. Chatura-
chinda, et al. INTERNATIONAL PLANNED PARENT-
HOOD FEDERATION MEDICAL BULLETIN 12(2):1-3,
April, 1978.

Female sterilization using the tubal ring, by R. Quiñones, et al.
INTERNATIONAL JOURNAL OF GYNAECOLOGY AND
OBSTETRICS 14(6):489-493, 1976.

Feminist doctor discusses birth control, by K. Emmot. OTHER
WOMAN 4(5):15, September, 1976.

Fertilisation in women with intrauterine devices [letter], by

C. G. Nilsson, et al. LANCET 2(8048):1126, November 26, 1977.

Fertility after stopping different methods of contraceptions, by M. P. Vessey, et al. BRITISH MEDICAL JOURNAL 1(6108): 265-267, February 4, 1978.

Fertility and family planning in rural northern Thailand, by S. Shevasunt, et al. STUDIES IN FAMILY PLANNING 9:212-221, August, 1978.

Fertility awareness as a method of conception control, by H. Klaus. NURSING TIMES 74:63-64, January 12, 1978.

Fertility control in man: the history of contraception from antiquity to the present, by L. P. Bengtsson. LAKARTID-NINGEN 74(51):4598-4600, December 21, 1977.

Fertility control services for adolescents: access and utilization, by F. S. Jaffe, et al. FAMILY PLANNING PERSPECTIVES 8(4):   , July-August, 1976.

Fertility control through steroid hormones used as contraceptives in the woman, by J. Zañartn, et al. REVISTA MEDICA DE CHILE 103(1):52-60, January, 1975.

Fertility decline and birth control in the People's Republic of China, by J. S. Aird. POPULATION AND DEVELOPMENT REVIEW 4:225-254, June, 1978.

Fertility in the rhesus monkey following long-term inhibition of ovarian function with danazol, by H. P. Schane, et al. FER-TILITY AND STERILITY 29(6):692-694, June, 1978.

Fertility mortality migration and family planning in the Yemen Arab Republic, by J. Allman, et al. POPULATION STUDIES 32:159-171, March, 1978.

Fertility news: some Texas discoveries; reversal of tubal steriliza-tion; research by Carlton Eddy, by A. Brewer. VOGUE 168:152, May, 1978.

Fetal abnormalities after abortion [letter], by C. B. Goodhart. BRITISH MEDICAL JOURNAL 1(6123):1351, May 20, 1978.

Fetal and maternal indications for considering abortion, by R. C. Juberg. SOUTHERN MEDICAL JOURNAL 71(1):50-57+, January, 1978.

Fetus papyraceus in twin pregnancy, by E. J. Livnat, et al. OBSTETRICS AND GYNECOLOGY 51 (1 Suppl):41s-45s, January, 1978.

Fibrinolytic activity in utero and bleeding complications with intrauterine contraceptive devices, by J. Bonnar, et al. BRITISH JOURNAL OF OBSTETRICS AND GYNECOLOGY 83(2):160-164, February, 1976.

Fibrocystic breast disease in oral-contraceptive users. A histopathological evaluation of epithelial atypia, by V. A. LiVolsi, et al. NEW ENGLAND JOURNAL OF MEDICINE 299(8):381-385, August 24, 1978.

A field study of the choice and continuity of use of three contraceptive methods in a rural area of Thailand. JOURNAL OF BIOSOCIAL SCIENCE 10(2):209, April, 1978.

15(S)15-methyl prostaglandin F2alpha for termination of very early human pregnancy. A comparative study of a single intramuscular injection and vaginal suppositories, by P. Fylling, et al. PROSTAGLANDINS 14(4):785-790, October, 1977.

50 years ago—1927—the 1st demonstration of chorionic gonadotropin in the urine of pregnant women by Aschheim and Zondek, by G. Göretzlehner, et al. ZENTRALBLATT FUER GYNAEKOLOGIE 100(10:638-641, 1978.

The fight for life can be won: good news from Britain for prolife, by D. Finlay. OUR SUNDAY VISITOR 65:1+, December 5, 1976.

Fight over abortions—heating up again. U. S. NEWS AND

WORLD 83:68, December 19, 1977.

Fighting sterilization abuse, by J. Herman. SCIENCE FOR THE PEOPLE 9:17-19, January-February, 1977.

Firm in condemning the abominable crime; abortion. OSSERVA-TORE ROMANO 7(516):4, February 16, 1978.

The first month in family practice residency training, by J. N. Dunn. JOURNAL OF FAMILY PRACTICE 6(5):1105-1106, May, 1978.

First pregnancies to women aged 15-19: 1976 and 1971, by M. Zelnick, et al. FAMILY PLANNING PERSPECTIVES 10(1):11-20, January-February, 1978.

First results with a new prostaglandin E2-derivate, by M. Schmidt-Gollwitzer, et al. GEBURTSHILFE UND FRAU-ENHEILKUNDE 37(12):1030-1038, December, 1977.

5 studies: no apparent harmful effect from legal abortion on sub-sequent pregnancies; D&C is possible exception. FAMILY PLANNING PERSPECTIVES 10(1):34-35, January-Febru-ary, 1978.

Flushing of the vas deferens during vasectomy [letter], by A. J. Robson, et al. CANADIAN MEDICAL ASSOCIATION JOURNAL 118(7):770-771, April 8, 1978.

Focal nodular hyperplasia of the live and oral contraceptives, by H. Gögler, et al. CHIRURG 49(3):172-179, March, 1978.

Focal nodular hyperplasia of the liver: nucleographic and ultra-sonic findings, by J. Cassoff, et al. JOURNAL OF THE CANADIAN ASSOCIATION OF RADIOLOGISTS 29(3): 199-200, September, 1978.

Focus on family planning, by J. Christiansen. SAIRAANHOI-TAJA 53(22):30-31, November 22, 1977.

Folic acid deficiencey, the "pill" and the withheld anamnesis, by D. E. Mendes de Leon. NEDERLANDS TIJDSCHRIFT VOOR GENEESKUNDE 122(5):146-150, February 4, 1978.

A follow-up of 72 cases referred for abortion, by A. Gillis. MENTAL HEALTH AND SOCIETY 2(3-6):212-218, 1975.

For a human society aware of its own rights and duties; our yes to life, by R. D'Andrea. OSSERVATORE ROMANO 23(532):6-7, June 8, 1978.

For women who wonder about birth control, by E. R. Dobell. REDBOOK 15(4):64, August, 1978.

Forced sterilization, by B. Levin. TIMES p. 14, November 7, 1978.

Forced sterilization in India: a disregard of spiritual values, by J. Emanuel. WORLDMISSION 27:56-58, Winter, 1976-1977.

Forecasting demand for abortions: the experience of a New York city clinic, by R. Oppenheim, et al. AMERICAN JOURNAL OF ECONOMICS AND SOCIOLOGY 37:177-178, April, 1978.

Forensic and surgical guidelines for male sterilization, by P. Carl, et al. UROLOGE 16(5):298-301, September, 1977.

480 million in suits against Dalkon. WOMENS PRESS 6(4):8, July, 1976.

The fourth Korean child: the effect of son preference on subsequent fertility, by C. B. Park. JOURNAL OF BIOSOCIAL SCIENCE 10(1):95-106, January, 1978.

The fragmented intrauterine device: an unusual complication of a Lippes loop, by K. A. Burry, et al. FERTILITY AND STERILITY 29(2):218-219, February, 1978.

The freedom of choice of a girl—a dilemma which the doctor falls into. Nurses' dilemmas, by K. Miwa. KANGO 30(1):

26-32, January, 1978.

Frequency of chromosomal abnormalities in miscarriages and perinatal deaths, by E. D. Alberman, et al. JOURNAL OF MEDICAL GENETICS 14(5):313-315, October, 1977.

Frequency of endocrine problems in repeated spontaneous aborttion, by A. M. Serban. ENDOCRINOLOGIE 16(1):55-59, January-March, 1978.

Fresh battle on abortion, by D. A. Williams, et al. NEWSWEEK 91:32, February 6, 1978.

From the files of the KMA Maternal Mortality Study Committee, by J. W. Greene, Jr. JOURNAL OF THE KENTUCKY MEDICAL ASSOCIATION 76(3):134-135, March, 1978.

From stigma to sterilization: eliminating the retarded in American law, by R. Sherlock. LINACRE QUARTERLY 45:116-134, May, 1978.

Fromino-glutamic acid (Figlu) excretion and abortion, by S. Friedman, et al. PANMINERVA MEDICA 19(4):271-274, July-August, 1977.

A further case of a 22;22 Robertsonian translocation associated with recurrent abortions, by M. Mameli, et al. HUMAN GENETICS 41(3):359-361, April 24, 1978.

Further comments on "contraceptive hormones and congenital heart disease" [letter], by J. R. Miller, et al. TERATOLOGY 17(3):359-360, June, 1978.

Further ethical considerations in induced abortion. JOGN NURSING 7:53-55, May-June, 1978.

Further studies on a new bioassay of progestational activity (traumatic deciduoma formation in immature rats), by Z. S. Madjerek, et al. ACTA MORPHOLOGICA NEERLANDO-SCANDINAVICA 15(1):65-74, February, 1977.

Further studies on the restoration of estrogen-induced sexual receptivity in ovariectomized mice treated with dihydro-testosterone: effects of progesterone, dihydroprogesterone and LH-RH, by W. G. Luttge, et al. PHARMACOLOGY, BIOCHEMISTRY AND BEHAVIOR 7(6):563-566, December, 1977.

Future of abortion rights: Houston was never like this, by E. B. Stengel. ENGAGE/SOCIAL ACTION 6:27-31, February, 1978.

Future orientation, perception of population problems and birth planning behavior, by D. O. Jorgenson. PERCEPTUAL AND MOTOR SKILLS 46(2):501-502, April, 1978.

GI reaction to oral contraceptives. NURSES DRUG ALERT 2:86-87, July, 1978.

Gas exchange and acid-base status during the normal human menstrual cycle and in subjects taking oral contraceptives [proceedings], by J. A. Milne, et al. JOURNAL OF EN-DOCRINOLOGY 75(3):17P-18P, December, 1977.

Gender of offspring after oral-contraceptive use, by K. Rothman, et al. NEW ENGLAND JOURNAL OF MEDICINE 295: 859-861, October 14, 1976.

General anasthesia for outpatient termination of pregnancy. A prospective analysis of 6 different types of anesthetics, by A. Risbo, et al. UGESKRIFT FOR LAEGER 139(32): 1896-1898, August 8, 1977.

A generalized epileptiform convulsion after intra-amniotic prostaglandin with intravenous oxytocin infusion: a case report, by E. Kaplan. SOUTH AFRICAN MEDICAL JOUR-NAL 53(1):27-29, January 7, 1978.

Genetic aspects of spontaneous abortion, by J. G. Lauritsen. DANISH MEDICAL BULLETIN 24(5):169-189, October, 1977.

Genetically determined pathology of fertility in a population of parental couples having spontaneous (habitual) abortions, by V. P. Kulazhenko, et al. GENETIKA 13(1):138-145, 1977.

Genital actionomycosis and the intrauterine device. Apropos of 3 cases, by J. Hamels. JOURNAL DE GYNECOLOGIE, OBSTETRIQUE ET BIOLOGIE DE LA REPRODUCTION 6(8):1061-1069, December, 1977.

Gestational age limit of twelve weeks for abortion by curettage, by D. A. Grimes, et al. AMERICAN JOURNAL OF OBSTETRICS AND GYNECOLOGY 132(2):207-210, September 15, 1978.

Getting violent, by R. Boeth, et al. NEWSWEEK 91:33, March 13, 1978.

Gonadotrophin response after castration and selective destruction of the testicular interstitium in the normal and aspermatogenic rat, by I. D. Morris, et al. ACTA ENDOCRINOLOGICA 88(1):38-47, May, 1978.

Gonadotropic and ovarian homrone content in the blood of women using intrauterine devices containing copper, by N. B. Antipova, et al. SOVETSKAYA MEDITZINA (6):80-85, June, 1978.

Gonorrhea screening in a prostitute population, by B. O. Leeb, et al. OBSTETRICS AND GYNECOLOGY 51(2):229-232, February, 1978.

Government response to contraceptive and cosmetic health risks, by J. L. Weaver. WOMEN HEALTH 1(2):5-11, March-April, 1976.

Government's plan to destroy the family [New York City guidelines on informed consent for sterilization], by L. Davis. MAJORITY REPORT 6:1+, April 30-May 13, 1977.

Graduate medical students and contraception. Study on a sample of 6th year students at the University of Turin Medical School, by R. Volante, et al. MINERVA GINECOLOGIA 30(7-8):635-640, July-August, 1978.

Group A streptococcal sepsis and arthritis. Origin from an intra-uterine device, by J. D. Brosseau, et al. JAMA; JOURNAL OF THE AMERICAN MEDICAL ASSOCIATION 238(20): 2178, November 14, 1977.

Group struggle in a value field: the comparative performance of New Zealand pressure groups on the question of abortion, 1970-1975, by R. Stone. POLITICAL SCIENCE 29:139-153, December, 1977.

A guide to curable causes of hypertension, by N. M. Kaplan. MEDICAL TIMES 106(5):32-39, May, 1978.

Guide to equipment selection for M/F sterilization procedures, by L. A. Reingold. POPULATION REPORTS (1):M1-34, September, 1977.

Guidelines for dispensing oral contraceptive PPIs [patient package insert]. DRUG TOPICS 122:22, March 15, 1978.

Gynecologic approach to counseling the sexually active young woman, by E. C. Pierson. CLINICAL OBSTETRICS AND GYNECOLOGY 21(1):235-248, March, 1978.

Gynecological care and information; mentally retarded, by L. Cibley. EXCEPTIONAL PARENT 8:9-13, February, 1978.

Gynaecological laparoscopy. The Report of the Working Party of the Confidential Enquiry into Gynaecological Laparo-scopy. BRITISH JOURNAL OF OBSTETRICS AND GY-NAECOLOGY 85(6):401-403, June, 1978.

Gynecology in childhood and adolescence. 2. Surgical interven-tions, contraception for adolescents, legal questions, by H. J. Kümper, et al. FORTSCHRITTE DER MEDIZIN 96(11): 603-608, March 23, 1978.

H.D.L. cholestrol during oral contraception [letter], by R. W. Schade, et al. LANCET 2(8079):40, July 1, 1978.

HEW rules allow funding for natural family planning, by J. Castelli. OUR SUNDAY VISITOR 67:2, October 8, 1978.

HEW's Califano urges debate on moral issues, by J. A. Califano, Jr. HOSPITAL PROGRESS 59(3):71-72+, March, 1978.

Habitual abortion, by R. H. Glass, et al. FERTILITY AND STERILITY 29(3):257-265, 1978.

Haemostatic, lipid, and blood-pressure profiles of women on oral contraceptives containing 50 microgram or 30 microgram oestrogen, by T. W. Meade, et al. LANCET 2(8045):948-951, November 5, 1977.

Hair analysis of trace minerals in human subjects as influenced by age, sex, and contraceptive drugs, by S. B. Deeming, et al. AMERICAN JOURNAL OF CLINICAL NUTRITION 31(7): 1175-1180, July, 1978.

Harmful effects of abortion legislation in United States, by T. Cooke. OSSERVATORE ROMANO 4(461):12, January 27, 1977.

Harvard researcher has second thoughts on use of the pill; Dr. Robert Kistner; reprint from The Cincinnati Enquirer, April 14, 1977. OSSERVATORE ROMANO 22(479):11, June 2, 1977.

Have women abandoned abortion issue, by R. Martlin. MAJORITY REPORT 6(6):12, July 24, 1976.

Hawaii physicians' attitudes and practices regarding reproductive health services for minors, by J. H. Fertel, et al. HAWAII MEDICAL JOURNAL 37(2):41-43, February, 1978.

Hazards seen in male birth control. CRITICAL LIST 1(2):27, March, 1976.

Headache and sex hormone therapy, by L. Dennerstein, et al. HEADACHE 18(3):146-153, July, 1978.

The health belief model as a conceptual framework for explaining contraceptive compliance, by M. E. Katatsky. HEALTH EDUCATION MONOGRAPHS 5(3):232-243, Fall, 1977.

Health care for adolescents. Contraceptive counseling for the younger adolescent woman: a suggested solution to the problem. Part 3, by M. O. Robbie. JOGN; JOURNAL OF OBSTETRIC, GYNECOLOGIC AND NEONATAL NURSING 7:29-33, July-August, 1978.

Health: a cut above the rest [sterilization: vasectomy, laparoscopy, tubal occlusion], by A. Henry. OFF OUR BACKS 7;4, September, 1977.

Health: the family planning factor, by E. Eckholm, et al. INTERCIENCIA 2(4):208-215, 1977.

Hemodynamic effects of oral contraceptives during exercise, by P. Lehtovirta, et al. INTERNATIONAL JOURNAL OF GYNAECOLOGY AND OBSTETRICS 15(1):35-37, 1977.

Hemophilus parainfluenzae peritonitis associated with an intrauterine contraceptive device, by T. E. Gallant, et al. AMERICAN JOURNAL OF OBSTETRICS AND GYNECOLOGY 129(6):702-703, November 15, 1977.

Hemostasis in the Egyptian female in abortion with a case report, by M. Talaat, et al. JOURNAL OF THE EGYPTIAN MEDICAL ASSOCIATION 59(1-2):98-105, 1976.

Hemostatic changes induced by exercise during oral contraceptive use, by A. M. Hedlin, et al. CANADIAN JOURNAL OF PHYSIOLOGY AND PHARMACOLOGY 56(2):316-320, April, 1978.

Hemostatic disorders in acute renal failure post-abortion. Study of 60 cases, by J. C. Sánchez Avalos, et al. MEDICINA 37(Suppl 2):70-86, 1977.

Heparin resistance and decreased hepatic triglyceride hydrolase release during long-term estrogen-progestin treatment, by B. W. Glad, et al. METABOLISM 27(1):53-60, January, 1978.

Hepatic adenoma and oral contraceptives, by J. Hureau, et al. JOURNAL DE CHIRURGIE 114(5):339-350, 1977.

Hepatic peliose, nodular focal hyperplasia of the liver: a propos two cases, by A. El Hafed, et al. ACTA CHIRURGICA BELGICA 76(5):509-514, September-October, 1977.

Hepatic tumors and oral contraceptives, by R. E. Fechner. PATHOLOGY ANNUAL 12(Pt. 1):293-310, 1977.

—, by A. Mallory. GASTROENTEROLOGY 75(517-518, September, 1978.

Hepatic vein thrombosis in a woman taking oral contraceptives: a case report, by C. Hines, Jr., et al. JOURNAL OF THE LOUISIANA STATE MEDICAL SOCIETY 129(8):189-192, August, 1977.

Hepatocellular carcinoma associated with oral contraceptives, by N. Menzies-Gow. BRITISH JOURNAL OF SURGERY 65(5):316-317, May, 1978.

Hepatocellular carcinoma in young women on oral contraceptives [letter], by W. M. Christopherson, et al. LANCET 2(8079):38-39, July 1, 1978.

Hepatocellular carcinoma in a young woman with prlonged exposure to oral contraceptives, by P. N. Gattanell, et al. MEDICAL AND PEDIATRIC ONCOLOGY 4(2):99-103, 1978.

Herpesvirus hominis endometritis in a young woman wearing an intrauterine contraceptive device, by A. A. Abraham. AMERICAN JOURNAL OF OBSTETRICS AND GYNECOLOGY 131(3):340-342, June 1, 1978.

The hidden intrauterine device, by K. Schumann, et al. FORTSCHRITTE DU MEDIZIN 95(41):2505-2509, November 3, 1977.

High court outlaws curbs on contraceptive sales, displays, ads. DRUG TOPICS 121:7+, July 1, 1977.

High court ponders doctors right to kill viable fetus, by R. McMunn. OUR SUNDAY VISITOR 67:1, October 22, 1978.

High inhibitory activity of R 5020, a pure progestin, at the hypothalamic-adenohypophyseal level on gonadotropin secretion, by F. Labrie, et al. FERTILITY AND STERILITY 28(10):1104-1112, October, 1977.

High-performance liquid chromatography of the steroid hormones, by F. A. Fitzpatrick. ADVANCES IN CHROMATOGRAPHY 16:37-73, 1978.

Hindu crush, by S. Rosenhause. GUARDIAN p. 17, May 16, 1978.

Histochemical and electron scanning microscopy studies of the fallopian tube under the influence of various hormones (proceedings), by P. Kugler, et al. ARCHER FUR GYNAEKOLOGIE 224(1-4):82-83, July 29, 1977.

Histological and ultrastructural changes of the endometrium in women using inert and copper-coiled IUDs, by N. Ragni, et al. ACTA EUROPAEA FERTILITATIS 8(3):193-210, September, 1977.

Historical considerations in the development of modern IUD's: patient and device selection and the importance of insertion techniques, by D. R. Mishell, Jr. JOURNAL OF REPRODUCTIVE MEDICINE 20(3):121-124, March, 1978.

The historical meaning of the Humane Vitae controversy, by N. Rigali. CHICAGO STUDIES 15:127-138, Summer, 1976; Reply by R. McCormick. THEOLOGICAL STUDIES 38:57-114, March, 1977; Rejoinder. CHICAGO STUDIES 16:299-308, Fall, 1977.

History of the first oral contraceptive, by V. A. Drill. JOURNAL OF TOXICOLOGY AND ENVIRONMENTAL HEALTH 3(1-2):133-138, September, 1977.

Hormonal changes after vasectomy, by B. S. Setty. INDIAN JOURNAL OF MEDICAL SCIENCES 30(3):109-112, March, 1976.

Hormonal changes in artificial abortion in the 7th-8th weeks of pregnancy, by L. E. Murashko. SOVETSKAYA MEDIT-ZINA (6):75-80, June, 1978.

Hormonal contraception and pregnancy, by A. Spira. JOUR-NAL DE GYNECOLOGIE, OBSTETRIQUE ET BIOLOGIE DE LA REPRODUCTION 6(5):711-712, July-August, 1977.

Hormonal contraception for adolescents? by J. M. Wenderlein. MUENCHENER MEDIZINISCHE WOCHENSCHRIFT 120(37):1193-1198, September 15, 1978.

Hormonal contraception in young girls, by F. Hamvas, et al. OROOSI HETILAP 118(5):3097-3098, December 18, 1977.

Hormonal contraception: perspectives. Part two. Special techniques, by G. P. Wood. JOURNAL OF THE ARKANSAS MEDICAL SOCIETY 74(7):239-241, December, 1977.

Hormonal contraception using the oral depot preparation, Deposition, by D. Vasilev. AKUSHERSTVO I GINEKOLO-GIIA 17(2):147-151, 1978.

Hormonal profile as a prognostic index of early threatened abortion, by L. Jovanovic, et al. AMERICAN JOURNAL OF OBSTETRICS AND GYNECOLOGY 130(3):274-278, February 1, 1978.

Hormone therapy in renal adenocarcinoma, by L. Giuliani, et al. MINERVA CHIRURGICA 32(23-24):1463-1465, December 15-31, 1977.

Hormone use to change normal physiology—is the risk worth it? (editorial), by D. M. Small. NEW ENGLAND JOURNAL OF MEDICINE 294:219-221, January 22, 1976.

Hormones and skin pigmentation in the mammal, by A. J. Thody, et al. INTERNATIONAL JOURNAL OF DERMA-TOLOGY 16(8):657-664, October, 1977.

Hormonic colpocytotest in diagnosis and therapy of some spontaneous abortions, by G. Teleman, et al. REVISTA MEDI-CO-CHIRURGICALA A SOCIETATII DE MEDICI SI

NATURATISTI DIN IASI 81(3):499-504, July-September, 1977.

Hormonoprophylaxis and hormonotherapy in the treatment of endometrial adenocarcinoma by means of medroxyprogesterone acetate, by J. Boute, et al. GYNECOLOGIC ONCOLOGY 6(1):60-75, February, 1978.

Hospital abortions in El Salvador, by T. Monreal, et al. SPM: SALUD PUBLICA DE MEXICO 19(3):387-395, May-June, 1977.

Hospital family planning: collecting information a first step in monitoring the service, by J. McEwan. CONTRACEPTION 2(6): , June, 1975.

Hospitals must prepare for inevitable payment controls, by D. H. Hitt. TIMES 19(4):3-5+, April, 1978.

House bill opposes mandatory abortion coverage but bill now goes to Senate, by J. Castelli. OUR SUNDAY VISITOR 67:2, August 6, 1978.

House says no on abortions, by A. Plattner. AIR FORCE TIMES 39:8, August 21, 1978.

House, Senate deadlock on abortion funds. CONGRESSIONAL QUARTERLY WEEKLY REPORT 35:1640, August 6, 1977.

How attitudes toward abortion are changing. JOURNAL OF POPULATION 1(1):5, Spring, 1978.

How doctors in Bolivia and the Philippines view sterilization, by D. W. MacCorquodale, et al. STUDIES IN FAMILY PLANNING 6:426-428, December, 1975.

How effective is a reversal procedure following a vasectomy? by D. Urquhart-Hay. NEW ZEALAND MEDICAL JOURNAL 86(600):475-477, November 23, 1977.

How men come to hear about vasectomy: evidence from a Man-

chester clinic in the UK, by B. E. Spencer. INTERNATION-
AL JOURNAL OF HEALTH EDUCATION 21(2):112-115,
1978.

How men feel now about contraceptives, by M. D'Antonio.
GLAMOUR 76:101-102+, August, 1978.

How to argue about abortion, by J. C. Bennett, et al. CHRIS-
TIANITY AND CRISIS 37:264-266, November 14, 1977.

How to distinguish 2-phase (sequential) steroid contraceptives,
by J. Presl. CESKOSLOVENSKA GYNEKOLOGIE 43(3):
198-200, April, 1978.

How to handle the rape victim, by A. F. Schiff. SOUTHERN
MEDICAL JOURNAL 71(5):509-511+, May, 1978.

Human potentiality: its moral relevance, by L. L. Thomas.
PERSONALIST 59:266-272, July, 1978.

Human service program design and the family, by J. E. Northman. FAMILY AND COMMUNITY HEALTH 1(2):17-26,
July, 1978.

Humanae Vitae and Catholic mortality, by M. Clappi. OSSER-
VATORE ROMANO 43(552):11, October 26, 1978.

Humanae Vitae and its reception: ecclesiological reflections, by
J. A. Komonchak. THEOLOGICAL STUDIES 39:221-257,
June, 1978.

Humanae Vitae and the sense of the faithful; some questions for
theologians, by A. Greeley. CRITIC 35:14-25, Spring, 1977.

Humanae Vitae defender hits natural birth control; Malcolm
Muggeridge, by J. Pereira. OUR SUNDAY VISITOR 67:2,
August 13, 1978.

Humanae Vitae in context, by D. O'Callaghan. FURROW 28:
230-234, April, 1977.

Humanae Vitae: 1968-1978, by W. Wheeler. OSSERVATORE

ROMANO 37(546):4+, September 14, 1978.

Humanae Vitae: symposium: Humanae Vitae and intrinsic evil, by K. Dwyer, et al. FURROW 28:426-433, July, 1977; Reply by D. O'Callaghan 28:433-434, July, 1977.

Humanae Vitae—Ten years later, by A. Grutka. LINACRE QUARTERLY 45:10-14, February, 1978.

Humanae Vitae ten years later; declaration of the Indian Episcopal Conference, January 17, 1978. THE POPE SPEAKS 23:183-187, November 2, 1978.

Humanae Vitae today; report on a conference held in Milan, 21 to 25 June, by A. McCormack. TABLET 232:674+, July 15, 1978.

The hundred million dollar misunderstanding. . .How much money is being spent on family planning clinic programs in the United States? by J. G. Dryfoos, et al. FAMILY PLANNING PERSPECTIVES 10:144-147, May-June, 1978.

A husband and his unborn child, by R. O'Brien. MONTH 11: 219-220, July, 1978.

Husband-wife agreement about reproductive goals, by L. C. Coombs, et al. DEMOGRAPHY 15(1):57-73, February, 1978.

Hyperosmolar urea for elective midtrimester abortion. Experience in 1,913 cases, by R. T. Burkman, et al. AMERICAN JOURNAL OF OBSTETRICS AND GYNECOLOGY 131(1): 10-17, May 1, 1978.

Hypertension and nephropathy during pregnancy and while taking ovulation inhibitors, by P. Kramer, et al. MEDIZINISCHE KLINIK 73(26):967-977, June 30, 1978.

Hypertension and oral contraceptives [editorial]. BRITISH MEDICAL JOURNAL 1(6127):1570-1571, June 17, 1978.

Hypertension and oral contraceptives (editorial), by B. Westerholm. LAKARTIDNINGEN 75(37):3164, September 13, 1978.

Hypertension due to hormonal contraceptives and estrogens, by W. Oelkers. MUNCHENER MEDIZINISCHE WOCHENSCHRIFT 120(13):439-444, March 31, 1978.

Hypothalamic LH-releasing activity in young and aged intact and gonadectomized rats, by A. E. Miller, et al. EXPERIMENTAL AGING RESEARCH 4(3):145-155, June, 1978.

Hysterectomies: clinical necessity & consent. REGAN REPORT ON NURSING LAW 18:2, December, 1977.

Hysterectomy and sterilisation: changes of fashion and mind [editorial]. BRITISH MEDICAL JOURNAL 2(6089): 715-716, September 17, 1977.

Hysterectomy for pregnancy termination and sterilization, by S. T. DeLee. INTERNATIONAL SURGERY 63(3):176-180, March, 1978.

Hysteroscopic management of intrauterine adhesions, by C. M. March, et al. AMERICAN JOURNAL OF OBSTETRICS AND GYNECOLOGY 130(6):653-657, March 15, 1978.

Hysteroscopic removal of intrauterine contraceptive devices with missing threads, by I. Gupta, et al. INDIAN JOURNAL OF MEDICAL RESEARCH 65(5):661-663, May, 1977.

Hysteroscopic sterilization—a routine method? by V. Rimkus, et al. INTERNATIONAL JOURNAL OF FERTILITY 22(2):121-124, 1977.

IPPF survey: world's contraceptors increased by 35 million; 5 million more in F.P. programs. FAMILY PLANNING PERSPECTIVES 10(3):163-165, May-June, 1978.

IUCDs—a contraindication to removal [letter]. BRITISH MEDICAL JOURNAL 1(6107):237, January 28, 1978.

120

The IUD and endometrial bleeding, by G. Rybo. JOURNAL OF REPRODUCTIVE MEDICINE 20(3):175-182, March, 1978.

IUD and unilateral tubo-ovarian abscess, by J. Srácek. CESKO-SLOVENSKA GYNEKOLOGIE 43(1):52-53, March, 1978.

IUD gangrene of small intestine, by C. J. Barranco. AMERICAN JOURNAL OF SURGERY 135(5):717, May, 1978.

IUD insertions by midwives: five years' experience in Santiago, Chile, by L. Pastene, et al. INTERNATIONAL JOURNAL OF GYNAECOLOGY AND OBSTETRICS 15(1):84-87, 1977.

IUD use effectiveness in an urban Guatemalan clinic, by P. Prior, et al. BULLETIN OF THE PAN-AMERICAN HEALTH ORGANIZATION 11(2):117-124, 1977.

IUD warning. TRIAL 13:6, June, 1977.

I was a pro-life spy at an abortion clinic convention, by J. Scheidler. OUR SUNDAY VISITOR 65:1+, January 30, 1977.

Iatrogenic amenorrhea following the use of estroprogestogens, by A. Pardini, et al. RIVISTA ITALIANA DI GINECOLO-GIA 57(2):121-131, March-April, 1976.

Iatrogenic damage contraception by IUD, by E. Aguilera, et al. REVISTA CHILENA DE OBSTETRICIA Y GINECOLOGIA 42(1):47-48, 1977.

Ideas on the genetic or eugenic indication for interruption [editorial], by H. Berger. PAEDIATRIE UND PAEDOLOGIE 12(4):325-333, 1977.

Identification of ejaculate derived propylamine found in collagen sponge contraceptives, by C. D. Eskelson, et al. BIOMEDICAL MASS SPECTROMETRY 5(3):238-242, March, 1978.

Illegal abortions in the United States: 1972-1974, by W. Cates, Jr., et al. FAMILY PLANNING PERSPECTIVES 8:86-89, April, 1976.

—. FAMILY PLANNING PERSPECTIVES 8(2):86-88+, March-April, 1976.

Illinois Court requires physician to try to save vaible fetus [letter], by D. J. Horan. HOSPITAL PROGRESS 59(6):6+, June, 1978.

Immediate postabortal contraception with a microdose combined preparation: gonadotropin, estradiol and progesterone levels during the last treatment cycle and after discontinuation of oral contraceptives, by P. Lähteenmäki. CONTRACEPTION 17(4):297-307, April, 1978.

Immediate postabortal contraception with a microdose combined preparation: suppression of pituitary and ovarian function and elimination of HCG, by P. Lähteenmäki, et al. CONTRACEPTION 17(2):169-181, February, 1978.

Immediate post-partum insertion of the Antigon, by J. Wiese, et al. ACTA OBSTETRICIA ET GYNECOLOGICA SCANDINAVICA 56(5):509-513, 1977.

Immunologic aspects of vasovasostomy, by S. Friedman. ANDROLOGIA 10(3):251-252, May-June, 1978.

Immunological approaches to fertility regulation, by V. C. Stevens. WHO BULLETIN 56(2):179-192, 1978.

Immunological effects of vasectomy, by W. B. Schill, et al. ANDROLOGIA 10(3):252-254, May-June, 1978.

Immunological mechanism for spontaneous abortion in systemic lupus erythematosus, by B. Breshnihan, et al. LANCET 2(8050):1205-1207, December 10, 1977.

Immunological study on spontaneous abortion in early pregnancy, by H. Amemiya. NICHIDAI IGAKU ZASSHI 36(10):865-876, 1977.

Impact of constitutional law on the protection of unborn human life: some comparative remarks, by E. Benda. HUMAN RIGHTS 6:223-243, Spring, 1977.

Impact of the Malaysian family planning programme on births: a comparison of matched acceptor and non-acceptor birth rates, by J. T. Johnson, et al. POPULATION STUDIES 32:215-230, July, 1978.

Implementation of contraceptive education, by W. L. McNab. HEALTH EDUCATION 8:36, November-December, 1977.

Implementing family planning in a ministry of health: organizational barriers at the state and district levels [Uttar Pradesh, India], by R. S. Simmons, et al. STUDIES IN FAMILY PLANNING 9:22-34, February-March, 1978.

Implications of attitude-behavior studies for population research and action [methodological problems in relating attitudes to family planning behavior], by P. D. Werner. STUDIES IN FAMILY PLANNING 8:294-299, November, 1977.

Importance of correct identification of intrauterine contraceptive device [letter], by R. A. Hatcher, et al. AMERICAN JOURNAL OF OBSTETRICS AND GYNECOLOGY 131(2): 229, May 15, 1978.

The importance of risk factors in cerebrovascular processes while taking oral contraceptives, by W. Holtmann, et al. MUENCHENER MEDIZINISCHE WOCHENSCHRIFT 119(48): 1557-1560, December 2, 1977.

Impressions of the 1977 National Conference on maternal and child welfare and family planning, by M. Fujiwara. JOSANPU ZASSHI 31(9):588-589, September, 1977.

Improving communication: educating families, by L. Greenberg. JOURNAL OF THE AMERICAN HEALTH CARE ASSOCIATION 4(1):21-28, January, 1978.

Improving management through evaluation: techniques and

strategies for family planning programs. STUDIES IN FAMILY PLANNING 9(6):163, June, 1978.

In pursuit of a policy respecting human life, by J. Quinn. OSSERVATORE ROMANO 11(520):9-10, March 16, 1978.

In vitro liver clearance of tritiated estradiol-17beta in the female rat after retrochiasmatic transection and ovariectomy, by C. H. Rodgers, et al. STEROIDS 31(1):151-161, January, 1978.

In-vitro parameters under the influence of pregnancy or anticonception, respectively, by U. Herter, et al. ZEITSCHRIFT FUR AERZTLICHE FORTBILDUNG 71(20):962-963, October 15, 1977.

In vitro steroid metabolic studies in human tests. II: Metabolism of cholesterol, pregnenolone, progesterone, androstenedione and testosterone by testes of an estrogen-treated man, by L. J. Rodriguez-Rigau, et al. STEROIDS 30(6): 729-739, December, 1977.

In-vitro studies on the effect of D-norgestrel and norethisterone acetate on the formation of sex steroids in the human ovary, by P. Schürenkämper, et al. ENDOKRINOLOGIE 71(1): 25-34, February, 1978.

In vitro uptake of oral contraceptive steroids by magnesium trisilicate, by S. A. Khalil, et al. JOURNAL OF PHARMACEUTICAL SCIENCES 67(2):287-289, February, 1978.

In vivo metabolism of norethisterone-3-oxime in rabbits, by F. S. Khan, et al. JOURNAL OF STEROID BIOCHEMISTRY 9(3):229-232, March, 1978.

An in vivo system in man for quantitation of estrogenicity. II. Pharmacologic changes in binding capacity of serum corticosteroid-binding globulin induced by conjugated estrogens, mestranol, and ethinyl estradiol, by D. E. Moore, et al. AMERICAN JOURNAL OF OBSTETRICS

124

AND GYNECOLOGY 130(4):482-486, February 15, 1978.

Inactivation of herpes simplex viruses by nonionic surfactants, by S. S. Asculai, et al. ANTIMICROBIAL AGENTS AND CHEMOTHERAPY 13(4):686-690, April, 1978.

The incidence of cervical cancer and duration of oral contraceptive use, by E. Peritz, et al. AMERICAN JOURNAL OF EPIDEMIOLOGY 106(6):462-469, December, 1977.

Incidence of depressive symptoms in users of the oral contraceptive, by O. Fleming, et al. BRITISH JOURNAL OF PSYCHIATRY 132:431-440, May, 1978.

Incidence of hypertension in the course of taking contraceptives, by F. Wessels, et al. VERHANDLUNGEN DER DEUTSCHEN GESELLSCHAFT FUER KREISLAUF-FORSCHUNG 43:242, 1977.

Incidence of post-abortion psychosis: a prosepctive study, by C. Brewer. BRITISH MEDICAL JOURNAL 6059:476-477, February 19, 1977.

—. OBSTETRICAL AND GYNECOLOGICAL SURVEY 32(7):600-601, September, 1977.

Incidence of side effects of synthetic progestins with different content of estrogenic and gestagenic components, by I. E. Rotkina, et al. AKUSHERSTVO I GINEKOLOGIIA (9): 29-31, September 9, 1977.

Incidence of spontaneous abortion with and without prior administration of ovulation inhibitors based on morphological studies (proceedings), by G. Dallenbach-Hellweg. ARCHIV FUR GYNAEKOLOGIE 224(1-4):25-26, July 29, 1977.

Independence of oral contraceptive-induced changes in glucose tolerance and plasma cortisol levels, by E. J. Cornish, et al. CLINICAL AND EXPERIMENTAL PHARMACY AND

PHYSIOLOGY 2(6):589-592, November-December, 1975.

India, eliminating coercion, makes sharp shift in birth-control policy. NEW YORK TIMES p. 1, October 3, 1977.

India [family planning situation in the wake of the Apr., 1977, elections which swept the Indian national congress from power; eight articles. PEOPLE 5:3-24, November 3, 1978.

India: the great population control experiment, by R. Engel. LINACRE QUARTERLY 43:230-243, November, 1976.

The Indian dilemma: coercive birth control or compulsory pregnancy, by T. Black, et al. CONTEMPORARY REVIEW 233:232-236, November, 1978.

Indian Health Service begins wooing physicians' families, by J. Stacey. AMERICAN MEDICAL NEWS 21(9):7-8, February 27, 1978.

India's compulsory sterilization laws: the human right of family planning. CALIFORNIA WESTERN INTERNATIONAL LAW JOURNAL 8:342-367, Spring, 1978.

India's experience with sterilization programmes, 1965-75: an overview of research results, by M. Nag. JOURNAL OF FAMILY WELFARE 23:3-19, December, 1976.

India's new birth rate target: an analysis, by D. L. Nortman. POPULATION AND DEVELOPMENT REVIEW 4:277-312, June, 1978.

Indication and technic of tubal sterilization by vaginal route. Posterior transverse colpotomy, by J. Salvat, et al. JOURNAL DE GYNECOLOGIE, OBSTETRIQUE, ET BIOLOGIE DE LA REPRODUCTION 6(6):851-859, September, 1977.

Indications and statistics of tubal sterilization using a synthetic clip (proceedings), by W. Bleier. ARCHIV FUR GYNAEKOLOGIE 224(1-4):41-42, July 29, 1977.

Indications for pregnancy interruption due to diseases of the respiratory system, by F. Trendelenburg, et al. INTERNIST 19(5):291-293, May, 1978.

Indications for pregnancy interruption in kidney diseases and hypertension, by H. H. Edel. INTERNIST 19(5):273-278, May, 1978.

Indices of adrenal cortical function in children whose mothers were treated during pregnancy with steroid hormones for habitual abortion, by R. A. Stepanova, et al. VOPROSY OKHRANY MATERINSTVA I DETSTVA 22(9):34-35, September, 1977.

Indigent women and abortion: limitation of the right of privacy in Maher v. Roe (97 Sup Ct 2376). TULSA LAW JOURNAL 13:287-303, 1977.

Indigent women—what rights to abortion? by B. W. Friedman. NEW YORK LAW SCHOOL LAW REVIEW 23:709-741, November 4, 1978.

Indirect measurements of family size preferences of abortion, by J. C. Barrett. JOURNAL OF BIOSOCIAL SCIENCE 9(3): 279-291, July, 1977.

Indonesia's family planning story: success and challenge. POPU-LATION BULLETIN 32(6):53, November, 1977.

Induced abortion, by J. Bouwhuis-Lely. TIJDSCHRIFT VOR ZIEKENVERPLEGING 31(5):217-218, February 28, 1978.

Induced abortion after feeling fetal movements: its causes and emotional consequences, by C. Brewer. JOURNAL OF BIOSOCIAL SCIENCE 10(2):203-208, April, 1978.

Induced abortion and its hazards, by P. Chatterjee. JOURNAL OF THE INDIAN MEDICAL ASSOCIATION 69(8):173-175, October 16, 1977.

Induced abortion and spontaneous abortion: no connection? by J. Kline, et al. AMERICAN JOURNAL OF EPIDEMIOLOGY 107(4):290-298, April, 1978.

127

Induced abortion and subsequent outcome of pregnancy in a series of American women, by J. R. Daling, et al. NEW ENGLAND JOURNAL OF MEDICINE 297(23):1241-1245, December 8, 1977.

Induced abortion in a Ghanaian family, by W. Bleek. AFRICAN STUDIES REVIEW 21:103-120, April, 1978.

Induced abortion in measels? (proceedings), by G. Farkas, et al. ARCHIV FUR GYNAEKOLOGIE 224(1-4):271, July 29, 1977.

Induced abortion in the Republic of Ireland, by R. S. Rose. BRITISH JOURNAL OF CRIMINOLOGY 18:245-254, July, 1978.

Induced abortion. Methods, results and complications, by W. Rummel, et al. FORTSCHRITTE DU MEDIZIN 95(25): 2154-2156, September 22, 1977.

Induced abortion—nurses' role in preventive work: numbers shock us but we do not participate in preventive work, by L. Lindén. SYGEPLEJERSKEN 70(48):10-13+, December 7, 1977.

Induced abortion. The patient's knowledge of the anatomy and physiology of the reproductive organs and possible complications of induced abortion, b A. Tabor, et al. UGESKRIFT FOR LAEGER 139(32):1893-1896, August 8, 1977.

Induced abortion with prostaglandin F2alpha and a new prostaglandin E2 derivative, by W. Lichtenegger. WIENER MEDIZINISCHE WOCHENSCHRIFT 127(17):536-538, Septem-30, 1977.

Induced illegal abortions in Benin City, Nigeria, by S. E. Okojie. INTERNATIONAL JOURNAL OF GYNAECOLOGY AND OBSTETRICS 14(6):517-521, 1976.

Induction of abortion by intrauterine administration of prostaglandin via laparoscopy with concurrent sterilization, by M. Morad, et al. INTERNATIONAL JOURNAL OF GYNAE-

Induction of abortion using a single dose of vaginally administered prostaglandin, by F. Havránek. CESKOLOVENSKA GYNECOLOGIE 43(3):202-203, April, 1978.

Induction of abortion with 15(S)-15-methyl PGF2alpha (Tham) vaginal suppositories, by D. Vengadassalam, et al. INTERNATIONAL JOURNAL OF GYNAECOLOGY AND OBSTETRICS 15(1):93-95, 1977.

Induction of abortion with prostaglandin F2 alpha. Cervix dilatation with 3 mg prostaglandin F2 alpha gel in the 1. trimester. Experiences after 197 induced abortions, by H. Knabe, et al. FORTSCHRITTE DU MEDIZIN 96(7):360-362, February 16, 1978.

Induction of internal abortion, of hydatidiform mole in the 2d and 3d trimesters of pregnancy, with a dead fetus, using transcervical intra-amniotic injection of PGF2 alpha, by E. Rizzuto, et al. MINERVA GINECOLOGIA 29(10):775-800, October, 1977.

Induction of labor in missed abortion, fetal death and vesicular mole, using PFG2 alpha by extra-amniotic intracavitary administration, by A. Paladini, et al. MINERVA GINECOLOGICA 29(12):931-938, December, 1977.

Induction of labour with prostaglandin E2 gel in cases of intrauterine fetal death, by T. H. Lippert, et al. PROSTAGLANDINS 15(3):533-542, March, 1978.

Induction of maternal behaviors in primigravid rats by ovariectomy, hysterectomy, or ovariectomy plus hysterectomy: effect of length of gestation, by R. S. Bridges, et al. HORMONES AND BEHAVIOR 9(2):156-169, October, 1977.

Induction of second-trimester abortion with a single does (40 mg) of intra-amniotic prostaglandin F2a, by E. S. Grech, et al. EAST AFRICAN MEDICAL JOURNAL 54(6):306-313, June, 1977.

Inefficiency of high doses of urokinase in a massive pulmonary embolism. Possible role of an oral contraceptive [letter], by A. Grand, et al. NOUVELLE PRESSE MEDICALE 7(27): 2391, July 1-8, 1978.

Infanticide and abortion in nineteenth-century Britain, by R. Sauer. POPULATION STUDIES 32:81-93, March, 1978.

Infection hazards and complications following the use of IUDs, by W. Böhm, et al. ZENTRALBLATT FUER GYNAE-KOLOGIE 99(24):1484-1488, 1977.

Influence of contraceptive hormones on hair growth [letter], by H. Zaun. DEUTSCH MEDIZENISCHE WOCHENSCHRIFT 103(6):240, February 10, 1978.

Influence of estrogens on atheroma development [editorial]. NOUVELLE PRESSE MEDICALE 6(31):2739-2740, September 24, 1977.

Influence of estrogens on pituitary responsiveness to LHRH and TRH in human, by T. Lemarchand-Béraud, et al. ANNALES D'ENDOCRINOLOGIE 38(6):379-382, 1977.

Influence of fetal sex on the concentration of amniotic fluid testosterone: antenatal sex determination? by H. J. Künzig, et al. ARCHIV FUR GYNAEKOLOGIE 223(2):75-84, September 30, 1977.

Influence of the hippocampus on the luteinizing activity of the adenohypophysis and the contraceptive activity of megastranol, by I. V. Tomilina. FARMAKOLOGIYA I TOKSI-KOLOGIYA 40(3):342-346, May-June, 1977.

Influence of human chorionic gonadotrophin on the response of luteinizing hormone to luteinizing hormone releasing hormone in gonadectomized women, by A. Miyake, et al. JOURNAL OF ENDOCRINOLOGY 74(3):499-500, September, 1977.

Influence of induced abortion on gestational duration in subsequent pregnancies, by J. W. van der Slikke, et al. BRITISH

MEDICAL JOURNAL 1(6108):270-272, February 4, 1978.

The influence of oestroprogestational agents on cervico-facial cutaneous scars, by P. Tailhardat. ANNALES D'OTO-LARYNGOLOGIE ET DE CHIRURGIE CERVICO FACIALE 94(10-11):623-627, October-November, 1977.

Influence of oral contraceptive agents on the concentration of amino acids in leukocytes of supposedly healthy women, by P. Tarallo, et al. CLINICA CHIMICA ACTA 81(3):283-286, December 15, 1977.

Influence of parents, peers, and partners on the contraceptive use of college men and women, by L. Thompson, et al. JOURNAL OF MARRIAGE AND THE FAMILY 40(3): 210, August, 1978.

Influence of progesterone on serotonin metabolism: a possible causal factor for mood changes, by W. Ladisich. PSY-CHONEUROENDOCRINOLOGY 2(3):257-266, 1977.

The influence of thiamin deficiency on the metabolism of the oral contraceptive mestranol [3-methoxy-17-ethynyl-1,3,5(10)-estratrien-17 beta-ol] by female rat liver enzymes, by A. E. Wade, et al. STEROIDS 30(2):275-283, August, 1977.

Influence of vasectomy on development of autoantibodies, by J. D. Wilson, et al. IPPF MEDICAL BULLETIN 11(6):3-4, December, 1977.

Inhibition of hepatic demethylation of aminopyrine by oral contraceptive steroids in humans, by R. Herz, et al. EURO-PEAN JOURNAL OF CLNICAL INVESTIGATION 8(1): 27-30, February, 1978.

Inhibition of the nuclear dihydrotestosterone receptor complex from rat ventral prostate by antiandrogens and stilboestrol, by C. B. Smith, et al. MOLECULAR AND CELLULAR EX-DOCRINOLOGY 10(1):13-20, February-March, 1978.

Inhibition of ovulation by gestagens, by E. Johansson, et al. UPSALA JOURNAL OF MEDICAL SCIENCES (22):16-22,

1978.

Inhibition of ovulation in women by chronic treatment with a stimulatory LRH analogue—a new approach to birth control? by S. J. Nillius, et al. CONTRACEPTION 17(6):537-545, June, 1978.

Inhibition of puerperal lactation by bromocriptine, by R. Rolland, et al. ACTA ENDOCRINOLOGICA 88(216):119-130, 1978.

Inhibition of testosterone-induced sexual behavior in the castrated male rat by aromatase blockers, by G. Morali, et al. HORMONES AND BEHAVIOR 9(3):203-213, December, 1977.

Inhibitory effects of RU 16117, a potent estrogen antagonist, on the estrous cycle in the rat, by L. Ferland, et al. BIOLOGY OF REPRODUCTION 18(1):99-104, February, 1978.

Injectable contraception (medroxyprogesterone acetate) in rural Bangladesh, by L. Parveen, et al. LANCET 2(8045):946-948, November 5, 1977.

Injections of ACTH and HCG into the fetus during midpregnancy legal abortion performed by intraamniotic instillation of prostaglandin. Influence on maternal plasma oestrogens and testosterone, by J. R. Strecker, et al. HORMONE AND METABOLIC RESEARCH 9(5):409-414, September, 1977.

Insurance coverage of abortion, contraception and sterilization [various private health insurance plans; United States], by C. F. Muller. FAMILY PLANNING PERSPECTIVES 10:71-77, March-April, 1978.

Integrating nutritional and family planning education with food services in Korean day care centers—an evaluation, by K. T. Sung. PUBLIC HEALTH REPORTS 93(2):177-185, March-April, 1978.

Integration of family planning and maternal and child health in rural West Africa, by A. K. Neumann, et al. JOURNAL OF BIOSOCIAL SCIENCE 8:161-174, April, 1976.

Integration of health, nutrition, and family planning: the Companiganj project in Bangladesh, by C. McCord. FOOD RESEARCH INSTITUTE STUDIES 16:91-105, November 2, 1977.

Intelligent woman's guide to sex; Supreme Court's decision on use of medicaid for abortions, by J. Coburn. MADEMOISELLE 83:136+, September, 1977.

The interaction of antibiotics with synthetic steroids in the rat [proceedings], by D. J. Back, et al. BRITISH JOURNAL OF PHARMACOLOGY 62(3):441P, March, 1978.

Interaction of antiepileptics, by J. Opavský. CASOPIS LEKARU CESKYCH 116(50):1550-1553, December 16, 1977.

Interaction of drugs and nutrition, by T. K. Basu. JOURNAL OF HUMAN NUTRITION 31(6):449-458, December, 1977.

The interactive effects of induced abortion, inter-pregnancy interval and contraceptive use on subsequent pregnancy outcome, by C. J. Hogue, et al. AMERICAN JOURNAL OF EPIDEMIOLOGY 107(1):15-26, January, 1978.

Interceptive & abortifacient activity of Aristolochia indica L. & possible mode of action, by A. Pakrashi, et al. INDIAN JOURNAL OF EXPERIMENTAL BIOLOGY 15(6):428-430, June, 1977.

Interference of gestagens and androgens with rat uterine oestrogen receptors, by F. Di Carlo, et al. JOURNAL OF ENDOCRINOLOGY 77(1):49-55, April, 1978.

Intermediate objectives for the monitoring of family planning services, by C. A. Corzantes. BULLETIN OF THE PANAMERICAN HEALTH ORGANIZATION 12(1):55-60, 1978.

International Conference on the ovulation method; Melbourne, Australia, by A. McElwain. OSSERVATORE ROMANO 11(520):10, March 16, 1979.

International population programs: should they change local values? by D. Warwick, et al. HASTINGS CENTER REPORT 7(5):17-18, October, 1977.

Interrelationships between circulating levels of estradiol-17 beta, progesterone, FSH and LH immediately after unilateral ovariectomy in the cyclic rat, by R. Welschen, et al. BIOLOGY OF REPRODUCTION 18(3):421-427, April, 1978.

Interruption of early pregnancy with a silastic device containing (15S)-15-methyl prostaglandin F2alpha methyl ester: efficacy and mode of action, by J. H. Duenhoelter, et al. CONTRACEPTION 17(1):51-59, January, 1978.

Interruption of first trimester pregnancy by prostaglandins, by M. Bygdeman, et al. INTERNATIONAL JOURNAL OF GYNAECOLOGY AND OBSTETRICS 15(1):69-72, 1977.

Interruption of pregnancy in alcoholic women, by F. Majewski, et al. DEUTSCHE MEDIZINISCHE WOCHENSCHRIFT 103(21):895-898, May 26, 1978.

Interruption of pregnancy in epileptic women, by R. Schweingruber. PRAXIS 67(23):854-855, June 6, 1978.

Interrutpion of pregnancy in the 2nd trimester through the intra-amniotic instillation of 25% glucose, by V. Krstajić, et al. MEDICINSKI PREGLED 30(7-8):401-403, 1977.

Intraamniotic and intramuscular administration of 15-methyl postaglandin F 2alpha for midtrimester abortion, by C. Bergquist, et al. ACTA OBSTETRICIA ET GYNECOLOGICA SCANDINAVICA (66):19-26, 1977.

Intracranial phlebothrombosis and oral contraceptives: report of 2 cases and review of the literature, by R. Navarro Izquierdo, et al. REVISTA CLINICA ESPANOLA 148(5):479-482, March 15, 1978.

Intracranial venous thrombosis, by J. H. Mateos-Gómez, et al. GACETA MEDICA DE MEXICO 114(1):43-47, January, 1978.

Intraligamentous tumor of the late post-abortion period, by K. Tshibangu, et al. JOURNAL DE GYNECOLOGIE, OBSTETRIQUE ET BIOLOGIE DE LA REPRODUCTION 7(1): 73-75, January, 1978.

Intraperitoneal explosion during female sterilization by laparoscopic electrocoagulation. A case report, by A. A. El-Kady, et al. INTERNATIONAL JOURNAL OF GYNAECOLOGY AND OBSTETRICS 14(6):487-488, 1976.

Intrauterine contraception, by R. P. Rao, et al. AMERICAN FAMILY PHYSICIAN 16(5):177-185, November, 1977.

Intrauterine contraception after induced abortion. A clinical study of immediate or later insertion, by H. P. Sundsbak, et al. TIDSSKRIFT FOR DEN NORSKE LAEGEFORENING 97(34-36):1787-1789, December 10, 1977.

The intrauterine contraceptive device, by B. N. Barwin, et al. CANADIAN MEDICAL ASSOCIATION JOURNAL 118(1): 53-58, January 7, 1978.

Intra-uterine contraceptive devices, by J. Dommisse. SOUTH AFRICAN MEDICAL JOURNAL 42(12):495-496, September 10, 1977.

Intrauterine contraceptive devices (IUD'S), by H. Lehfeldt. ZENTRABLATT FUER GYNAEKOLOGIE 99(24):1473-1483, 1977.

Intrauterine device and ectopic pregnancy, by R. Erkkola, et al. CONTRACEPTION 16(6):569-574, December, 1977.

Intrauterine device and pelvic inflammatory diseases, by L. Thaler, et al. INTERNATIONAL JOURNAL OF FERTILITY 23(1):69-72, 1978.

Intrauterine devices [editorial]. NEW ZELANAD MEDICAL JOURNAL 86(598):387-388, October 26, 1977.

Intrauterine devices and menstrual blood loss. A contraceptive study of eight devices during the first six months of use, by by A. J. Gallegost, et al. CONTRACEPTION 17(2):153-161, February, 1978.

Intrauterine devices for contraception? Results of an inquiry conducted in the BRD in 1976, by W. Stolp, et al. FORT-SCHRITTE DU MEDIZIN 95(39):2347-2352, October 20, 1977.

Intrauterine devides: an invitational symposium, by A. Scommegna. JOURNAL OF REPRODUCTIVE MEDICINE 20(3):119-120, March, 1978.

The intrauterine progesterone contraceptive system, by R. Erickson, et al. ADVANCES IN PLANNED PARENTHOOD 11(4):167-174, 1976.

Intravenous glucose tolerance after 18 months on progestogen or combination-type oral contraceptive, by J. A. Goldman. ISRAEL JOURNAL OF MEDICAL SCIENCES 14(3):324-327, March, 1978.

L'introduction des problèmes de population dans les programmes scolaires [based on questionnaire survey of about 900 students, teachers and parents conducted in 1974], by A. Bouraoui, et al. REVUE TUNISIENNE DE SCIENCES SOCIALES 14(50-51):11-33, 1977.

Introduction: menstrual regulation—the method and the issues, by W. B. Watson. STUDIES IN FAMILY PLANNING 8(10):250-252, October, 1977.

Introduction to the topic of pregnancy interruption, by E. Buchborn. INTERNIST 19(5):257-258, May, 1978.

Investigations of pharmacokinetics of levonorgestrel to specific consideration of a possible first-pass effect in women, by M. Hümpel, et al. CONTRACEPTION 17(3):207-220, March, 1978.

Involuntary sterilization: the latest case, by M. O. Steinfels. PSYCHOLOGY TODAY 11:124, February, 1978.

The irrelevance of religion in the abortion debate, by L. Newton. HASTINGS CENTER REPORT 8:16-17, April, 1978.

Is a bad rep killing the pill? by M. S. Kennedy. NEW TIMES 11(3):68, August 7, 1978.

Is a physician liable for compensation in a voluntary sterilization? by H. Roesch. MEDIZINISCHE KLINIK 72(48): 2094-2098, December 2, 1977.

Is spontaneous respiration sufficient during laparoscopic sterilization under local anesthesia? (proceedings), by W. Dieckmann, et al. ARCHIV FUR GYNAEKOLOGIE 224(1-4): 39-40, July 29, 1977.

Ischemic disease of the small bowel and colon associated with oral contraceptives, by G. G. Ghahremani, et al. GASTROINTESTINAL RADIOLOGY 293):221-228, December 20, 1977.

The issue of the legalization of abortion in Belgium, by B. J. De Clercq. RES PUBLICA 19(2):305-322, 1977.

Issues in contraception: recognizing the reasons for contraceptives non-use and abuse, ty J. L. Tanis. MCN: AMERICAN JOURNAL OF MATERNAL CHILD NURSING 2(6):364-369, November-December, 1977.

Issues in contraception: today's pill and the individual woman, by L. K. Huxall. MCN: AMERICAN JOURNAL OF MATERNAL CHILD NURSING 2(6):359-363, November-December, 1977.

Issues in family practice: medical student and practicing physician perspectives, by J. R. Kimberly, et al. MEDICAL CARE 16(3):214-225, March, 1978.

Italian bishops reaffirm life. OSSERVATORE ROMANO 21(478):11, May 26, 1977.

Italian Episcopal Conference on the law on abortion. OSSERVATORE ROMANO 30(539):12, July 27, 1978.

Italy: three-month wonder. ECONOMIST 267:66, April 22, 1978.

Italy's abortion law [letter], by E. Lombardo. LANCET 2(8082):207-208, July 22, 1978.

Italy's liberal abortion law isn't working and pro-abortionists object, by C. Savitsky. OUR SUNDAY VISITOR 67:2, June 25, 1978.

Jaundice due to gestagens revisited, by H. Reyes, et al. REVISTA MEDICA DE CHILE 106(2):85-90, February, 1978.

Judicial immunity covers malice and procedural errors, court rules, by B. Hoelzel. JUDICATURE 61:10, May, 1978.

Judicial immunity is absolute, by A. Bequai. SECURITY MANAGEMENT 22:9, September, 1978.

Judicial imperialism, by R. M. Byrn. HOSPITAL PROGRESS 58(11):90-97+, November, 1977.

Judiciary: Supreme Court—June 20, 1977 abortion decisions, by M. Fisk. TRIAL 13:8, August, 1977.

Juridicial problems of surgical sterilization, by F. P. Blanc. JOURNAL DE GYNECOLOGIE, OBSTETRIQUES ET BIOLOGIE DE LA REPRODUCTION 6(6):737-747, September, 1977.

Juvenile privacy: a minor's right of access to contraceptives. FORDHAM URBAN LAW JOURNAL 6:371-387, Winter, 1978.

Kentucky law makes abortion more painful; case of Mr. Pitchford, by B. Bishop. NEW TIMES 11:15, October 2, 1978.

Ketamine as the sole anaesthetic agent for laparoscopic sterilization. The effects of premedication on the frequency of adverse clinical reactions, by E. M. Figallo, et al. BRITISH JOURNAL OF ANAESTHESIOLOGY 49(11):1159-1165,

November, 1977.

The Korean mothers' club program, by H. J. Park, et al. STUDIES IN FAMILY PLANNING 7:275-283, October, 1976.

Laboratory pregnancy testing, by G. D. Wasley. NURSING TIMES 74(1):25-27, January 5, 1978.

Lack of association of the development of anti-sperm antibodies and other autoantibodies as a consequence of vasectomy, by P. Crewe, et al. INTERNATIONAL JOURNAL OF FERTILITY 22(2):104-109, 1977.

Lactation—the central control of reproduction, by R. V. Short. CIBA FOUNDATION SYMPOSIA (45):73-86, 1976.

Lactation, fertility, and contraception [editorial]. LANCET 2(7982):407-408, August 21, 1976.

Language differences and the family planning survey, by D. Lucas, et al. STUDIES IN FAMILY PLANNING 8(9): 233-236, September, 1977.

Laparoscopic Falope Ring sterilization. Two years of experience, by D. L. Chatman. AMERICAN JOURNAL OF OBSTETRICS AND GYNECOLOGY 131(3):291-294, June 1, 1978.

Laparoscopic sterilization after "spontaneous" abortion, by A. Quan, et al. INTERNATIONAL JOURNAL OF GYNAECOLOGY AND OBSTETRICS 15(3):258-261, 1977.

Laparoscopic sterilization at an outpatient clinic. PUBLIC HEALTH REPORTS 93(1):55, January-February, 1978.

Laparoscopic sterilization: experience with the Falope-Ring TM, by R. P. Pulliam. WEST VIRGINIA MEDICAL JOURNAL 74(3):49-52, March, 1978.

Laparoscopic sterilization with therapeutic abortion versus sterilization or abortion alone, by A. Weil. OBSTETRICS AND GYNECOLOGY 52(1):79-82, July, 1978.

Laparoscopic tubal sterilization: a report on 300 cases, by J. St. Elmo Hall, et al. WEST INDIAN MEDICAL JOURNAL 26(4):187-196, December, 1977.

Large majority of Americans favor legal abortion, sex education & contraceptive services for teens. FAMILY PLANNING PERSPECTIVES 10(3):159-160, May-June, 1978.

Large migrating hepatic adenoma associated with use of oral contraceptives, by I. Weissman, et al. ILLINOIS MEDICAL JOURNAL 152(6):483-486, December, 1977.

Larger animal testing of an injectable sustained release fertility control system, by J. D. Gresser, et al. CONTRACEPTION 17(3):253-266, March, 1978.

Late complications of female sterilization: a review of the literature and a proposal for further research, by J. E. Rioux. JOURNAL OF REPRODUCTIVE MEDICINE 19(6):329-340, December, 1977.

Late effects of female sterilisation [letter], by A. T. Letchworth, et al. LANCET 2(804):768, October 8, 1977.

—, by M. F. McCann, et al. LANCET 1(8054):37-38, January 7, 1978.

Late sequelae of induced abortion in primigravidae. The outcome of the subsequent pregnancies, by O. Koller, et al. ACTA OBSTETRICIA ET GYNECOLOGICA SCANDINAVICA 56(4):311-317, 1977.

Latin Americans criticize anti-life programs sponsored by United States, by D. Duggan. OUR SUNDAY VISITOR 67:3, July 9, 1978.

Law and the life sciences: abortion and the Supreme Court: round two. HASTINGS CENTER REPORT 6:15+, October, 1976.

The law legalizing abortion in Italy; a declaration of the Italian Episcopal Conference, June 9, 1978. THE POPE SPEAKS

23:263-264, Fall, 1978.

Law-medicine notes. The freedom of medical practice, sterilization, and economic medical philosophy, by W. J. Curran. NEW ENGLAND JOURNAL OF MEDICINE 298(1):32-33, January 5, 1978.

Legal abortion, by L. H. Lee. HONG KONG NURSING JOURNAL :53-54, May, 1977.

Legal abortion in the United States, 1975-1976, by E. Sullivan, et al. FAMILY PLANNING PERSPECTIVES 9:116-137, May-June, 1977.

Legal abortion, Italian style. VICTIMOLOGY: AN INTERNATIONAL JOURNAL 2:1, Spring, 1977.

Legal abortions in an Indian state, by N. B. Rao, et al. STUDIES IN FAMILY PLANNING 8(12):311-315, December, 1977.

Legal abortions, subsidized family planning services, and the U. S. birth dearth, by K. E. Bauman, et al. SOCIAL BIOLOGY 24:183-191, Fall, 1977.

Legal aspects of abortion Der Schwangerschaftsabbruch—rechtlich gesehen. CONCEPTE 13(7):20-26, 1977.

Legal aspects of sex education, by E. H. Kellogg, et al. AMERICAN JOURNAL OF COMPARATIVE LAW 26:573-608, Fall, 1978.

Legal induced abortions in the world. POPULATION 32:175-183, January-Feburary, 1977.

The legal precedents, by M. Bayles. HASTINGS CENTER REPORT 8(3):37-41, June, 1978.

Legal prerequisites for pregnancy interruption due to medical, eugenic and social indications, by W. Spann, et al. INTERNIST 19(5):259-263, May, 1978.

Legalized abortion, by B. Barley. MEDICAL WORLD NEWS 19:53-54+, January 23, 1978.

Legalized abortion: effect on national trends of maternal and abortion-related mortality (1940 through 1976), by W. Cates, Jr., et al. AMERICAN JOURNAL OF OBSTETRICS AND GYNECOLOGY 132(2):211-214, September 15, 1978.

Legislation of education? A practical, effective approach to the problem of informed consent in elective sterilization, by M. C. Boria, et al. ADVANCES IN PLANNED PARENTHOOD 13(1):21-23, 1978.

Let us reconcile, by C. Gallagher. OUR SUNDAY VISITOR 66:14, May 29, 1977.

Lethality in abortions and the ways for its further decrease, by Ia. P. Sol'skii, et al. PEDIATRIYA AKUSHERSTVO I HINEKOLOHIYA (2):47-49, 1978.

Let's quit pretending about birth control; the call to action conference in Detroit, committee on sex and birth control, by F. Wessling. U. S. CATHOLIC 42:29-31, August, 1977.

Lettre pastorale des évêques suisses sur l'avortement; 27-28 août, 1977. DOCUMENTATION CATHOLIQUE 74:891-893, October 16, 1977.

Leukocytes are consistently associated with degenerating embryos in IUD-bearing rhesus monkeys, by P. R. Hurst, et al. NATURE 269(5626):331-33, September 22, 1977.

Levels of contraceptive steroids in breast milk and plasma of lactating women, by B. N. Saxena, et al. CONTRACEPTION 16(6):605-613, December, 1977.

Liability for failure of birth control methods. COLUMBIA LAW REVIEW 26:1187, November, 1976.

The life table according to Chiang as a method for the description and assessment of the efficacy of oral contraceptives,

by C. Wolfrum. METHODS OF INFORMATION IN MEDI-
CINE 16(3):176-181, July, 1977.

Life table analysis of the effectiveness of contraceptive methods
using an APL computer program, by D. L. Cooper, et al.
INTERNATIONAL JOURNAL OF BIO-MEDICAL COM-
PUTING 9(1):1-9, January, 1978.

Lifeline pregnancy care; service giving social, financial and moral
help in Great Britain, by D. Bevan. CLERGY REVIEW
61:441-443, November, 1976.

Ligenous cellulitis associated with an IUD, by A. J. Weiland, et
al. OBSTETRICS AND GYNECOLOGY 51(1 Suppl):485-
515, January, 1977.

Limited patient knowledge as a reproductive risk factor, by S.
M. Johnson, et al. JOURNAL OF FAMILY PRACTICE
6(4):855-862, April, 1978.

A link between abortion future pregnancy problems. OUR
SUNDAY VISITOR 67:2, August 27, 1978.

The link between nutrition and family planning. AUSTRALA-
SIAN NURSES JOURNAL 7(5):16, December, 1977.

Live tumors and oral contraceptives, by D. R. Kent, et al. IN-
TERNATIONAL JOURNAL OF GYNAECOLOGY AND
OBSTETRICS 15(2):137-142, 1977.

The liver and oral contraceptives, by P. Berthelot. ACQUISI-
TIONS MEDICALES RECENTES :33-37, 1977.

Liver-cell adenomas associated with use of oral contraceptives,
by H. A. Edmondson, et al. NEW ENGLAND JOURNAL
OF MEDICINE 294:470-472, February 26, 1976.

Liver cell carcinoma associated with oral contraceptives, by J.
Leclère, et al. ANNALES D'ENDOCRINOLOGIE 38(6):
361-362, 1977.

Liver function in Thai women using different types of hormonal contraceptive agents, by N. Dusitsin, et al. JOURNAL OF THE MEDICAL ASSOCIATION OF THAILAND 61(7): 381-389, July, 1978.

Liver lesions and oral contraceptive steroids, by G. H. Barrows, et al. JOURNAL OF TOXICOLOGY AND ENVIRON-MENTAL HEALTH 3(1-2):219-230, September, 1977.

Liver lesions caused by oral contraceptives. I. Contraceptive-induced hepatosis in 85 women: recommendations for diagnosis and prophylaxis, by J. D. Fengler, et al. DEUTSCHE GESUNDHEITWESEN 33(27):1251-1256, 1978.

Liver tumors and oral contraceptives, by A. H. Ansari, et al. FERTILITY AND STERILITY 29(6):643-650, June, 1978.

Liver tumours associated with the use of contraceptive pills, by J. Terblanche. SOUTH AFRICAN MEDICAL JOURNAL 53(12):439-442, March 25, 1978.

Lo, the poor and sterilized Indian; on the report of the Government Accounting Office, by B. Wagner. AMERICA 136:75, January 29, 1977.

Local proteinase inhibitor concentration in uterine secretions with intrauterine spirals (IUD) in situ (proceedings), by P. F. Tauber, et al. ARCHIV FUR GYNAEKOLOGIE 224(1-4): 32-33, July 29, 1977.

Long-term contraception by a single silastic implant-D containing norethindrone acetate in women: a clinical evaluation, by D. Takkar, et al. CONTRACEPTION 17(4):341-354, April, 1978.

A long-term follow-up study of women using different methods of contraception—an interim report, by M. Vessey, et al. JOURNAL OF BIOSOCIAL SCIENCE 8:373+, October, 1976.

Long-term study of a progestational micropill: 600 mcg nore-thisterone acetate, by F. Robey-Lelièvre, et al. JOURNAL DE GYNECOLOGIE, OBSTETRIQUE ET BIOLOGIE DE

LA REPRODUCTION 7(3):485-497, April, 1978.

A longitudinal study of success versus failure in contraceptive planning. JOURNAL OF POPULATION 1(1):69, Spring, 1978.

Loss of bony tissue in castrated women, by V. Culig. LIJEC-NICKI VJESNIK 100(3):153-158, March, 1978.

Lost intrauterine devices and their localization, by R. P. Rao. JOURNAL OF REPRODUCTIVE MEDICINE 20(4):195-199, April, 1978.

Love, sex, permissiveness, and abortion: a test of alternative models, by A. M. Mirande, et al. ARCHIVES OF SEXUAL BEHAVIOR 5:553-556, November, 1976.

Lowering of H.D.L. cholesterol by oral contraceptives [letter], by S. Roössner. LANCET 2(8083):269, July 29, 1978.

Lutherans and abortion. AMERICA 138:296-297, April 15, 1978.

MLCu 250 in comparison with other intrauterine contraceptive devices (proceedings), by H. Van der Pas, et al. ARCHIV FUR GYNAEKOLOGIE 224(1-4):35-36, July 29, 1977.

A machine to predict ovulation time. MEDICAL WORLD NEWS 18:40, June 13, 1977.

Magisterium and theologians: steps towards dialogue, by J. Bernardin. CHICAGO STUDIES 17:151-158, Summer, 1978.

Mahgoub's operation: a reversible method of sterilization, by S. El Mahgoub. FERTILITY AND STERILITY 29(4):466-467, April, 1978.

The *Majority Report* guide to abortifacient herbs, by V. Cava-Rizzuto, et al. MAJORITY REPORT 7:7-9, August 6-19, 1977.

Making women modern: middle class women and health reform in 19th century America, by R. M. Morantz. JOURNAL OF SOCIAL HISTORY 10:491-507, Summer, 1977.

Male contraception, by L. Westoff. SCIENCE 8(4):12, July, 1976.

Male contraception and family planning: a social and historical review, by L. Diller, et al. FERTILITY AND STERILITY 28(12):1271-1279, December, 1977.

Male involvement in contraceptive decision making: the role of birth control counselors, by P. Scales, et al. JOURNAL OF COMMUNITY HEALTH 3:54-60, Fall, 1977.

Males and morals: teenage contraceptive behavior amid the double standard, by P. Scales. FAMILY COORDINATOR 26(3):211-222, July, 1977.

Malignant arterial hypertension and oral contraceptives. Apropos of 4 cases, by Y. Saint-Hillier, et al. JOURNAL D'UROLOGIE ET DE NEPHROLOGIE 83(9):673-679, September, 1977.

Malignant melanoma and oral contraceptive use among women in California, by V. Beral, et al. BRITISH JOURNAL OF CANCER 36(6):804-809, December, 1977.

Malpractice decisions you should know about. Unsuccessful sterilization worth $462,500. MEDICAL TIMES 105(11): 115, November, 1977.

Mammary nodules in beagle dogs administered investigational oral contraceptive steroids, by R. C. Giles, et al. JOURNAL OF THE NATIONAL CANCER INSTITUTE 60(6): 1351-1364, June, 1978.

Mammary nodules in beagle dogs administered steroids in dogs, by J. H. Weikel, Jr., et al. JOURNAL OF TOXICOLOGY AND ENVIRONMENTAL HEALTH 3(1-2):167-177, September, 1977.

Management of missed abortion and fetal death in utero, by H. el-Damaraway, et al. PROSTAGLANDINS 14(3):583-590, September 1977.

Management of uterine perforation following elective abortion, by S. M. Freiman, et al. OBSTETRICA AND GYNECOLOGY 50(6):647-650, December, 1977.

Many rights to life, by M. Mead. REDBOOK 151:109+, July, 1978.

Maori abortion practices in pre and early European New Zealand, by R. B. Hunton. NEW ZEALAND MEDICAL JOURNAL 86(602):567-570, December 28, 1977.

Marital privacy and family law; a major political and social issue involving the Supreme Court, the Irish Governmet and the Catholic Hierarchy, by J. O'Reilly. STUDIES 66:8-24, September, 1977; Reply by W. Binchy, 66:330-335, Winter, 1977.

Maternal and child health and family planning, by H. C. Taylor, Jr. JOURNAL OF THE MEDICAL ASSOCIATION OF THE STATE OF ALABAMA 45(12):38-45, June, 1976.

Maternal exposure to exogenous progestogen/estrogen as a potential cause of birth defects, by A. H. Nora, et al. ADVANCES IN PLANNED PARENTHOOD 12(3):156-169, 1978.

Maternal plasma alpha-feto-protein in pregnancies terminating in spontaneous abortion, by Z. Habib. BIOLOGY OF THE NEONATE 33(1-2):39-42, 1978.

McLuhan: electronic age a factor in campaign for legal abortion, by E. Moore. NATIONAL CATHOLIC REPORTER 13:16, May 20, 1977.

Meaningful right to abortion for indigent women? LOYOLA LAW REVIEW 24:301-307, Spring, 1978.

Measurement of intrauterine pressure during extra-amnial induced abortion with prostaglandin F2 alpha, by G. Schott, et al. ZENTRALBLATT FUER GYNAEKOLOGIE 100(12): 805-810, 1978.

Measurement of unconjugated testosterone, 5alpha-dihydrotestosterone and oestradiol in human urine, by J. M. Kjeld, et al. CLINICA CHIMICA ACTA 80(2):271-284, October 15, 1977.

Measuring the effectiveness of contraceptive marketing programs: Preethi in Sri Lanka, by J. Davies, et al. STUDIES IN FAMILY PLANNING 8:82-90, April, 1977.

Mechanism for spontaneous abortion in S.L.E. [letter], by N. Amino, et al. LANCET 1(8061):447, February 25, 1978.

Mechanism of action of conjugated estrogens as contraceptives. I. Clinical study, by S. Fuensalida, et al. REVISTA CHILENA DE OBSTETRICIA Y GINECOLOGIA 41(6):333-336, 1976.

Mechanism of action of estradiol valerate. II. Changes in the genital tract of rats castrated and subjected to prolonged treatment, by G. Merlino, et al. ARCHIVIO DI OSTETRICIA E GINECOLOGIA 79(5-6):336-341, August-December, 1974.

Mechanism of action of intrauterine contraceptives, by E. P. Maizel', et al. VOPROSY OKHRANY MATERINSTVA I DETSTVA 22(7):73-76, July, 1977.

The mechanism of antiandrogenic action of chlormadinone acetate, by Y. Ito, et al. NIPPON HINYOKIKA GAKKAI ZASSHI 68(6):537-552, June, 1977.

Mechanism of contraceptive effect of low progestin doses, by V. V. Korkhov, et al. VOPROSY OKHRANY MATERINSTVA I DETSTVA 22(8):89-90, August, 1977.

Mechanism of contraceptive effect with postovulatory estrogen treatment, by T. Koyama, et al. NIPPON NAIBUNPI GAK-

KI ZASSHI 52(11):1053-1062, November 20, 1976.

Mechanism of estrogen-induced saturated bile in the hamster, by G. G. Bonorris, et al. JOURNAL OF LABORATORY AND CLINICAL MEDICINE 90(6):963-970, December, 1977.

Medicaid and the abortion right. GEORGE WASHINGTON LAW REVIEW 44:404-417, March, 1976.

Medicaid-funded abortion: the evidence, the imperatives, by N. M. Welch. VIRGINIA MEDICINE 105(6):463-464, June, 1978.

Medicaid funding for abortions: the Medicaid statute and the equal protection clause. HOFSTRA LAW REVIEW 6:421-443, Winter, 1978.

Medical abortion complications. An epidemiologic study at a mid-Missouri clinic, by D. K. Nemec, et al. OBSTETRICS AND GYNECOLOGY 51(4):433-436, April, 1978.

The medical attitude towards abortion regarded as deviant behavior. BULLETIN DE MEDICINE LEGALE ET DE TOXICOLOGIE MEDICALE 18(5):303-311, 1975.

Medical heroics and the good death, by M. C. Shumiatcher. CANADIAN MEDICAL ASSOCIATION JOURNAL 117(5): 520-522, September 3, 1977.

Medical supervision for contraception: too little or too much? by A. Rosenfield. INTERNATIONAL JOURNAL OF GYNAECOLOGY AND OBSTETRICS 15(2):105-110, 1977.

Medicated intrauterine devices to improve bleeding events, by F. Hefnawi, et al. INTERNATIONAL JOURNAL OF GYNAECOLOGY AND OBSTETRICS 15(1):79-83, 1977.

Medicine/abortion ripoff, by B. Miner. GUARDIAN 28(47):2, September 15, 1976.

Megaloblastic anemia caused by folic acid deficiency following administration of oral contraceptives. Description of 2 clinical cases, by G. Bianco, et al. MINERVA MEDICA 69(22): 1513-1516, May 5, 1978.

Megestrol acetate concentrations in plasma and milk during administration of an oral contraceptive containing 4 mg megestrol acetate to nursing women, by S. Nilsson, et al. CONTRACEPTION 16(6):615-624, December, 1977.

Menstrul induction with vaginal administration of 16,16 dimethyl trans-delta 2-PGE1 methyl ester (ONO 802), by S. M. Karim, et al. PROSTAGLANDINS 14(3):615-616, September, 1977.

Menstrual patterns after laparoscopic sterilization using a spring-loaded clip, by B. A. Lieberman, et al. BRITISH JOURNAL OF OBSTETRICS AND GYNAECOLOGY 85(5):376-380, May, 1978.

Menstrual regulation: the method and the issues. Competing risks of unnecessary procedures and complications, by J. A. Fortney, et al. STUDIES IN FAMILY PLANNING 8(10):257-262, October, 1977.

The menstrual regulation procedure, by L. E. Laufe. STUDIES IN FAMILY PLANNING 8(10):253-256, October, 1977.

Menstrual regulation: risks and "abuses," by W. E. Brenner, et al. INTERNATIONAL JOURNAL OF GYNAECOLOGY AND OBSTETRICS 15(2):177-183, 1977.

Mesenteric vascular occlusion associated with oral contraceptive use, by T. J. Lescher, et al. ARCHIVES OF SURGERY 112(10):1231-1232, October, 1977.

Metabolic studies under administration of oral contraceptives. A review, by S. Hauschildt. ZEITSCHRIFT FUER ERNAEHRUNGSWISSENSCHAFT 17(1):1-18, March, 1978.

Metabolism of ethynyl estrogens, by E. D. Helton, et al. JOURNAL OF TOXICOLOGY AND ENVIRONMENTAL HEALTH 3(1-2):231-241, September, 1977.

Metabolism of an oral tryptophan load by women and evidence against the induction of tryptophan pyrrolase by oral contraceptives, by A. R. Green, et al. BRITISH JOURNAL OF CLINICAL PHARMACOLOGY 5(3):233-241, March, 1978.

Metabolism of 3H-testosterone in epididymis & accessory glands of reproduction in the castrate hamster Mesocricetus auratus, by T. K. Bose, et al. INDIAN JOURNAL OF EXPERIMENTAL BIOLOGY 15(10):852-855, October, 1977.

Methionine metabolism and vitamin B6 status in women using oral contraceptives, by L. T. Miller, et al. AMERICAN JOURNAL OF CLINICAL NUTRITION 31(4):619-625, April, 1978.

Methodist's open letter to Bishop Quinn; United Methodist, by H. L. Boche. CHRISTIAN CENTURY 95:437-438, April 26, 1978.

Methods of laparoscopic sterilization and possible failures, by K. G. Ober. GEBURTSHILFE UND FRAUENHEILKUNDE 38(8):593, August, 1978.

Methods of midtrimester abortion: which is safest? by D. A. Grimes, et al. INTERNATIONAL JOURNAL OF GYNAECOLOGY AND OBSTETRICS 15(2):184-188, 1977.

Methods of sterilization in women, by A. A. Haspels, et al. TIJDSCHRIFT VOR ZIEKENVERPLEGING 31(16):721-724, August 8, 1978.

Metropolitan dominance and family planning in Barbados, by H. R. Jones. SOCIAL AND ECONOMIC STUDIES 26:327-338, September, 1977.

Microrheological studies in healthy subjects. Effect of cigarette smoke and oral contraceptives on erythrocyte flexibility, by H. G. Grigoleit, et al. DEUTSCH MEDIZINSCHE WOCHENSCHRIFT 103(8):339-341, February 24, 1978.

Microsrugery: the new hope for men and women who were

surgically sterilized and now want to have babies, by E. M. Wylie. GOOD HOUSEKEEPING 187:108+, September, 1978.

Microsurgical anastomosis of the rabbit oviduct using 9-0 monofilament polyglycolic acid suture, by J. J. Stangel, et al. FERTILITY AND STERILITY 30(2):210-215, August, 1978.

Microsurgical anastomosis of vas deferens: an experimental study in the rat, by N. Hampel, et al. INVESTIGATIVE UROLOGY 15(5):395-396, March, 1978.

The microsurgical basis of Fallopian tube reconstruction, by E. R. Owen, et al. AUSTRALIAN AND NEW ZEALAND JOURNAL OF SURGERY 47(3):300-305, June, 1977.

Microsurgical reconstruction of the uterin tube in sterilized patients, by E. Diamond. FERTILITY AND STERILITY 28(11):1203-1210, November, 1977.

Microsurgical restoration of fertility [editorial]. MEDICAL JOURNAL OF AUSTRALIA 2(17):552, October 22, 1977.

Microsurgical tubal anastomosis for sterilization reversal, by P. Paterson, et al. MEDICAL JOURNAL OF AUSTRALIA 2(17):560-561, October 22, 1977.

Microsurgical tubocornual anastomosis for reversal of sterilization, by R. M. Winston. OBSTETRICAL AND GYNECOLOGICAL SURVEY 32(7):623-625, September, 1977.

Microsurgical two-layer vasovasostomy: laboratory use of vasectomized segments, by A. M. Belker, et al. FERTILITY AND STERILITY 29(1):48-51, January, 1978.

Microsurgical two-layer vasovasostomy: word of caution, by A. M. Belker, et al. UROLOGY 11(6):616-618, June, 1978.

Microsurgical vasovasostomy: a reliable vasectomy reversal, by E. R. Owen. AUSTRALIAN AND NEW ZEALAND JOURNAL OF SURGERY 47(3):305-309, June, 1977.

Mid-trimester abortion by dilatation and evacuation: a safe and practical alternative, by D. A. Grimes, et al. NEW ENGLAND JOURNAL OF MEDICINE 296:1141-1145, May 19, 1977.

Mid-trimester abortion induced by intravaginal administration of prostaglandin F2 alpha-methylester suppositories, by A. S. van den Bergh, et al. CONTRACEPTION 17(2):141-151, February, 1978.

Midtrimester abortion with urea, prostaglandin F2alpha, laminaria, and oxytocin. A new regimen, by W. B. Wilson, Jr. OBSTETRICS AND GYNECOLOGY 51(6):699-701, June, 1978.

Midtrimester intra-aminotic administration of prostaglandin F2alpha in combination with an hyperosmolar urea solution: effect upon plasma levels of estradiol, progesterone, and human placental lactogen (HPL), by G. Sher, et al. ACTA OBSTETRICIA ET GYNECOLOGICA SCANDINAVICA 57(3):223-225, 1978.

Mid-trimester septic abortion and Escherichia coli septicaemia ina copper IUCD user, by R. A. Sparks, et al. BRITISH MEDICAL JOURNAL 1(6111):481-482, February 25, 1978.

Milder genital herpes with the pill. MEDICAL WORLD NEWS 18:90, April 4, 1977.

Minilaparotomy—more simple and more secure than laparoscopic sterilization, by J. Presl. CESKOSLOVENSKA GYNEKOLOGIE 43(6):448, July, 1978.

Minilaparotomy: safer outpatient sterilization, by R. Skinner, ed. PATIENT CARE 12:148-150+, January 15, 1978.

Minilaparotomy tubal sterilization, by H. F. Sandmire. AMERICAN JOURNAL OF OBSTETRICS AND GYNECOLOGY 131(4):453-459, June 15, 1978.

Minor's right of privacy: limitations on state action after Danforth (Planned Parenthood of Cent. Mo. v. Danforth, 96 Sup Ct 2831) and Carey (Carey v. Population Servs. Int. 97 Sup Ct 2010). COLUMBIA LAW REVIEW 77:1216-1246, December, 1977.

Minors' right to abortion and contraception: prospects for invalidating less than absolute restrictions, by D. Klassel, et al. WOMEN'S RIGHTS LAW REPORTER 4:165-183, Spring, 1978.

Minors' right to litigate privacy interests without parental notice. WASHINGTON UNIVERSITY LAW QUARTERLY 1978: 431-442, Spring, 1978.

Miscarriage: cause and prevention, by S. A. Kaufman. PARENTS MAGAZINE 53:13, May, 1978.

Miscarriages as a cause of spina bifida and anencephaly [letter], by D. I. Rushton. BRITISH MEDICAL JOURNAL 2(6090): 833-834, September 24, 1977.

Misinforming pregnant teenagers, by L. Ambrose. FAMILY PLANNING PERSPECTIVES 10(1):51-53, January-February, 1978.

Missed abortion and uterine contractility, by B. Gustavii. AMERICAN JOURNAL OF OBSTETRICS AND GYNE-COLOGY 130(1):18-19, January 1, 1978.

Misuse and nonuse of contraception, by J. Robins. MEDICAL ASPECTS OF HUMAN SEXUALITY 11(9):127-128, September, 1977.

The model family planning project in Isfahan, Iran, by R. C. Treadway, et al. STUDIES IN FAMILY PLANNING 7:308-321, November, 1976.

A model for health care delivery with an illustration of its application, by P. M. Vacek, et al. MEDICAL CARE 16(7): 547-559, July, 1978.

Modern prospects in the treatment of cancer of the breast and its metastasis. Medroxyprogesterone in massive doses as an alternative to polychemotherapy, by F. Pannuti. MINERVA CHIRURGICA 32(19):1211-1220, October 15, 1977.

Modernism and contraceptive use in Columbia, by W. H. Baldwin, et al. STUDIES IN FAMILY PLANNING 7:80+, March, 1976.

Modulation of the pituitary response to LH-RH by synthetic sex steroids, by T. Iwasaki. NIPPON NAIBUNPI GAKKAI ZASSHI 54(3):255-276, March 20, 1978.

Molecular structure and drug activity. Example: sex hormones, by F. Neumann. NATURWISSENSCHAFTEN 64(8):410-416, August, 1977.

Monitoring of plasma renin activity, renin substrate and aldosterone concentrations during treatment with hormonal contraceptives (proceedings), by H. Kaulhausen, et al. ARCHIV FUR GYNAEKOLOGIE 224(1-4):430-431, July 29, 1977.

Monosomy 21 in a human spontaneous abortus. Morphogenetic disturbances and phenotype at the cellular level, by A. M. Kuliev, et al. HUMAN GENETICS 38(2):137-145, September 22, 1977.

Monsignor McHugh disputes birth control survey. OUR SUNDAY VISITOR 66:2, October 9, 1977.

Monthly variation in conceptions leading to induced abortion, by I. C. Cohen, et al. SOCIAL BIOLOGY 24(3):245-249, Fall, 1977.

Moral teaching, traditional teaching and Humanae Vitae, by J. Selling. LOUVAIN STUDIES 7:24-44, Spring, 1978.

Moral theologians say Humanae Vitae taught truth that can't be changed, by J. C. Ford, et al. OUR SUNDAY VISITOR 67:3, June 18, 1978.

Morbidity and abortions in mothers of children with Dowz's

syndrome, by J. Cernay, et al. BRATISLAVSKE LEKARSKE LISTY 68(5):559-567, November, 1977.

The morning after pill [editorial], by T. Rust. PRAXIS 66(48): 1529-1533, November 29, 1977.

Morphologic alterations in the epithelium of the human oviduct induced by a low dosis gestagen, by U. M. Spornitz, et al. ARCHIV FUR GYNAEKOLOGIE 223(4):269-281, November 29, 1977.

Morphological changes in the placenta and decidua after induction of abortion by extra-amniotic prostaglandin, by H. Fox, et al. HISTOPATHOLOGY 2(2):145-151, March, 1978.

Morphological effects of estrogen on the female rat liver nucleolus, by B. Sheid. EXPERIENTIA 34(7):877-878, July 15, 1978.

Morphometric studies of the human placenta under the influence of sex steroids, by C. Estel, et al. ZENTRALBLATT FUER GYNAEKOLOGIE 99(23):1458-1461, 1977.

Morphometry on the lactating rat's mammary gland after administration of depot estrogen, by O. Low, et al. VERHANDLUNGEN DER ANATOMISCHEN GESELLSCHAFT (71 Pt. 2):1165-1169, 1977.

Mortality among oral-contraceptive users. Royal College of General Practitioners' Oral Contraception Study, by V. Beral. LANCET 2(8041):727-731, October 8, 1977.

Mortality among women participating in the Oxford/Family Planning Association contraceptive study, by M. P. Vessey, et al. LANCET 2(8041):731-733, October 8, 1977.

Mortality and fertility control, by C. Tietze, et al. INTERNATIONAL JOURNAL OF GYNAECOLOGY AND OBSTETRICS 15(2):100-104, 1977.

Mortality and oral contraceptives [editorial]. BRITISH MEDICAL JOURNAL 2(6092):918, October 8, 1977.

Mortality associated with the control of fertility, by C. Tietze, et al. FAMILY PLANNING PERSPECTIVES 8(1):6-14, January-February, 1976.

Mortality associated with the pill [editorial]. LANCET 2(8041):747-748, October 8, 1977.

— [letter]. LANCET 2(8043):879-880, October 22, 1977.

—. LANCET 2(8044):921-922, October 29, 1977.

—. LANCET 2(8046):1023-1024, November 12, 1977.

—, by J. R. Heiby. LANCET 2(8049):1172-1173, December 3, 1977.

—, by M. P. Vessey, et al. LANCET 1(8055):98, January 14, 1978.

Mortality during the use of oral steroid contraceptives—new British studies, by J. Presl. CESKOSLOVENSKA GYNE-KOLOGIE 43(2):134-135, April, 1978.

Mortality enforcement through the criminal law and the modern doctrine of substantive due process, by T. L. Hindes. UNIVERSITY OF PENNSYLVANIA LAW REVIEW 126(2):344-384, 1977.

Mortality, fertility and contraceptive use in Shanghai, by J. Bannister. CHINA QUARTERLY 70:255-295, June, 1977.

Mortality in women on oral contraceptives [letter]. LANCET 2(8041):757-758, October 8, 1977.

—. LANCET 2(8051):1276-1277, December, 17, 1977.

Mortality rates with oral contraception [editorial]. NEW ZEA-LAND MEDICAL JOURNAL 86(601):525, December 14, 1977.

Mortality risk associated with the use of oral contraceptives, by A. K. Jain. STUDIES IN FAMILY PLANNING 8:50-

54, March, 1977.

The most important task of a bishop, by J. Bernardin. ORIGINS 7:369+, December 1, 1977.

Most Italian doctors sign as objectors to abortion. OUR SUNDAY VISITOR 67:3, July 30, 1978.

Most teen girls using contraceptives do so with parental knowledge, study says. JUVENILE JUSTICE DIGEST 6:19, October 13, 1978.

Mother India (continued): after the emergency, the return of democracy; but the return too, of population uncontrol, by K. Singh. ACROSS THE BOARD 15:22-27, January, 1978.

Motherhood by choice; excerpt from Woman's choice, by S. J. Barr, et al. VOGUE 168:246+, March, 1978.

Motivation for vasectomy, by G. Howard. LANCET 1(8063): 546-548, March 11, 1978.

Motivation of sterilization patients: implications for family planning educatin programmes, by M. F. McCann, et al. INTERNATIONAL JOURNAL OF HEALTH EDUCATION 21(1):26-33, 1978.

Motivations for the use of birth control: evidence from West Africa, by H. Ware. DEMOGRAPHY 13:479-494, November, 1976.

Mourning after the night before, by A. L. Gotzsche. GUARDIAN p. 9, May 2, 1978.

Multidisciplinary training in family planning, by D. V. Fairweather, et al. MEDICAL EDUCATION 12(3):205-208, May, 1978.

Multinational comparative clinical evaluation of two long-acting injectable contraceptive steroids: noresthisterone oenanthate and medroxyprogesterone acetate. 2. Bleeding patterns and side effects. CONTRACEPTION 17(5):395-406, May, 1978.

Multiple nodular hyperplasia of liver associated with oral contraceptives, by G. Roschlau. ZENTRALBLATT FUR ALLGEMEINE PATHOLOGIE UND PATHOLOGISCHE ANATOMIE 121(6):517-521, 1977.

Myocardial infarct and oral contraception, by A. Barrillon, et al. ARCHIVES DE MALADIES DU COEUR ET DES VAISSEAUX 70(9):921-928, September, 1977.

Myocardial infarct and oral contraceptives, by M. Baudet, et al. ANNALES DE MEDICINE INTERNE 129(6-7):459-462, June-July, 1978.

Myocardial infarction in women [editorial], by M. O'Rourke. MEDICAL JOURNAL OF AUSTRALIA 1(4):199, February 25, 1978.

Myometrial response to a long-acting vasopressin analogue in early pregnancy, by M. Akerlund, et al. BRITISH JOURNAL OF OBSTETRICS AND GYNAECOLOGY 85(7): 525-529, July, 1978.

Myometrial vascular damage after surgical sterilisation by tubal diathermy, by G. Tregson-Roberts, et al. JOURNAL OF CLINICAL PATHOLOGY 31(7):633-638, July, 1978.

NFP: an idea whose time has come; natural family planning, by S. Overman. OUR SUNDAY VISITOR 67:8-9, June 25, 1978.

NIH research findings: when conception occurs one month after discontinuing the pill, twins are more likely. JAMA; JOURNAL OF THE AMERICAN MEDICAL ASSOCIATION 239(18):1850, May 5, 1978.

Nagaike Clinic, by M. Fujiwara. JOSANPU ZASSHI 31(11): 715, November, 1977.

Narcissim and abortion, by A. M. Ruiz-Mateos Jiménez de Tajada. ACTAS LUSO-ESPANOLAS DE NUROLOGIA Y

PSIQUIATRIA 5(4):241-246, July-August, 1977.

A nation of births, by K. Baker. GUARDIAN p. 12, June 7, 1978.

National Federation of Priests' Councils. A letter on approaches to the abortion issue. CATHOLIC MIND pp. 9-10, March, 1977.

The National Inventory of Family Planning Services: 1975 survey results, by D. L. Morrow. VITAL HEALTH STATISTICS (19):i-iv+, April, 1978.

National right to life, political right interlink, by M. Winiarski. NATIONAL CATHOLIC REPORTER 15:1+, November 10, 1978.

National survey of family growth, cycle I: sample design estimation procedures, and variance estimation, by D. K. French. VITAL HEALTH STATISTICS (76):1-32, January, 1978.

Natural family planning, by C. Norris. NURSING MIRROR 145:29-30, October 27, 1977.

Natural family planning: the Billings method makes good sense, by B. McWilliams. LIQUORIAN 66:16-19, September, 1978.

Natural family planning comes of age, by M. Shivanandan. MARRIAGE 60:18-21, March, 1978.

Natural family planning: different methods, by P. Deibel. MCN: AMERICAN JOURNAL OF MATERNAL-CHILD NURSING 3(3):171-177, May-June, 1978.

Natural family planning draws secular interest. OUR SUNDAY VISITOR 66:3, May 29, 1977.

Natural family planning in America, by L. Kane. OUR SUNDAY VISITOR 67:8-9, June 25, 1978.

Natural methods of family planning [letter], by A. M. Flynn, et al. LANCET 2(7982):418, August 21, 1976.

Nature and uses of congressional power under section five of
the fourteenth amendment to overcome decisions of the
Supreme Court, by I. A. Gordon. NORTHWESTERN UNI-
VERSITY LAW REVIEW 72:656-705, November-December, 1977.

Nature of the ovulation and the state of the preimplantation
fetuses in the experimental administration of hormonal and
neurotropic agents, by V. V. Korkhov, et al. VOPROSY
OKHRANY MATERINSTVA I DETSTVA 23(6):87-88,
June, 1978.

Necessity and the case of Dr. Morgentaler, by L. H. Leigh. THE
CRIMINAL LAW REVIEW pp. 151-158, March, 1978.

Necessity to control endexpiratory CO2-concentration during
laparoscopic sterilisation under general anaesthesia with
controlled ventilation, by E. Voigt. ANAESTHESIST
27(4):219-222, May, 1978.

Neurologic accidents and oral contraceptives, by J. C. Gautier.
SCHWEIZER ARCHIV FUER NEUROLOGIE, NEURO-
CHIRURGIE UND PSYCHIATRIE 120(2):335-338, 1977.

Neurologic diseases as indications for pregnancy interruption,
by U. A. Besinger, et al. INTERNIST 19(5):294-298,
May, 1978.

Never again! Never again? Can we lose our right to abortion? by
R. B. Gratz. MS MAGAZINE 6:54-55, July, 1977.

New abortion legislation: a comparison with professional policy,
by D. Wills. NEW ZEALAND NURSING FORUM 6(1):
12-13, March, 1978.

New abortion rulings (what they really mean), by L. Prinz.
McCALLS 105:111, October, 1977.

A new anti-Catholic bigotry? Editorial page feature article on
anti-Catholicism and issues of abortion and aid to parochial

schools. PERSPECTIVE ON POLITICS 12(14-22):4.

New aspects of contraception by enzyme-directed antibodies, by T. Dietl, et al. ANDROLOGIA 10(3):250-251, May-June, 1978.

The new improved silastic band for ligation of fallopian tubes, by C. L. Lay. FERTILITY AND STERILITY 28(12): 1301-1305, December, 1977.

New leads on contraception. Summarized discussion, by S. J. Segal. UPSALA JOURNAL OF MEDICAL SCIENCES (22):73-74, 1978.

New limits on abortion. TIME 110:12-13, December 19, 1977.

A new perspective on the twentieth-century American fertility swing, by G. S. Masnick, et al. JOURNAL OF FAMILY HISTORY 1:216-243, Winter, 1976.

New phase in the battle, by J. T. Noonan, Jr. NATIONAL REVIEW 30:279, March 3, 1978.

New Pope did not oppose Paul VI on birth control, by J. Maher. OUR SUNDAY VISITOR 67:5, September 10, 1978.

A new role for the nurse; counseling on the subject of abortion, by B. Easterbrook, et al. INFIRMIÈRE CANADIENNE 19(10):35-37, October, 1977.

New warnings on IUDs, by C. M. Rob. GOOD HOUSEKEEP-ING 187:258, September, 1978.

Nine year follow-up of a case of benign liver cell adenoma related to oral contraceptives, by S. Kay. CANCER 40(4): 1759-1760, October, 1977.

1966-1977: a look at the record, by B. Berelson. FAMILY PLANNING PERSPECTIVES 10(1):20-22, January-February, 1978.

Nipping 'em in the bud. NATIONAL REVIEW 30:454, April

14, 1978.

Nitrofurazone: vas irrigation as adjunct in vasectomy, by P. S. Albert, et al. UROLOGY 10(5):450-451, November, 1977.

No abortions, say Italian physicians. CHRISTIAN CENTURY 95:671, July 5, 1978.

No increase of the fibrinolytic activity of the human endometrium by progesterone-releasing IUD (progestasertR), by P. Liedholm, et al. CONTRACEPTION 17(6):531-533, June, 1978.

No surrender on abortion, declare the bishops of Italy, by J. Muthig, Jr. OUR SUNDAY VISITOR 67:5, June 11, 1978.

Non-acceptance of poerperal sterilization. A study, by B. Palaniappan. INTERNATIONAL JOURNAL OF GYNAECOLOGY AND OBSTETRICS 14(6):505-508, 1976.

Non-acceptance of sterilization in women after having two children. . .Singapore, by L. M. Wat. THE NURSING JOURNAL OF SINGAPORE 17:45-47+, November, 1977.

Non-formal education in the developing world: the role of the International audio-visual resource service, by R. Morell. EDUCATIONAL BROADCASTING INTERNATIONAL 10:68-70, June, 1977.

Norethisterone oenanthate as an injectable contraceptive: use of a modified dose schedule, by O. F. Giwa-Osagie, et al. BRITISH MEDICAL JOURNAL 1(6128):1660-1662, June 24, 1978.

Not just doctors' dilemmas, by D. Gould. NEW STATESMAN 95:74, January 20, 1978.

Now it's his turn, by C. Doyle. OBSERVER p. 32, April 30, 1978.

Noxious effect of intrauterine devices (IUD) on the development of concomitant pregnancy, by E. Jaworski. WIADOMOSCI LEKARSKIE 31(3):209-211, February 1, 1978.

Nun on the line for medicaid abortions, by S. Birknell. MS MAGAZINE 6:23, June, 1978.

Nurse-midwife insertion of the copper T in Thailand: performance, acceptance, and programmatic effects, by N. H. Wright, et al. STUDIES IN FAMILY PLANNING 8(9):237-243, September, 1977.

Nurse specialist work in family planning, by M. P. Newton, et al. MIDWIVES CHRONICLE 90(1079):290-291, December, 1977.

Nurses health study, by C. F. Belanger, et al. AMERICAN JOURNAL OF NURSING 78:1039-1040, June, 1978.

Nursing functions: limits on nursing service. Case in point: Wright v. State (351 So. 2d 708-FLA.). REGAN REPORT ON NURSING LAW 18:2, January, 1978.

Nutrition, health, and population in strategies for rural development [policies and programs best suited to promoting self-sustaining economic growth and eliminating poverty], by B. F. Johnston, et al. ECONOMIC DEVELOPMENT AND CULTURAL CHANGE 26:1-23, October, 1977.

L'objection de conscience contre la loi italienne sur l'avortement, by U. Poletti. LA DOCUMENTATION CATHOLIQUE 75:630-632, July 2, 1978.

Observations on birth planning in China, by F. S. Jaffe, et al. FAMILY PLANNING PERSPECTIVES 10:101-108, March-April, 1978.

Observations with Ovidon, by M. Farkas, et al. THERAPIA HUNGARICA 25(3):93-101, 1977.

Obstacles to family planning practice in urban Morocco, by F. Mernissi. STUDIES IN FAMILY PLANNING 6:418-425, December, 1975.

Occupational and environmental risks in and around a smelter in northern Sweden. III. Frequencies of spontaneous abortion, by S. Nordström, et al. HEREDITAS 88(1):51-54, 1978.

Occupational exposure to synthetic estrogens—the need to establish safety standards. AMERICAN INDUSTRIAL HYGIENE ASSOCIATION JOURNAL 39(2):139, February, 1978.

The occupational hazards of formulating oral contraceptives—a survey of plant employees, by J. M. Harrington, et al. ARCHIVES OF ENVIRONMENTAL HEALTH 33(1):12-15, January-February, 1978.

Ocular complications of oral contraceptives, by J. R. Wood. OPHTHALMIC SEMINARS 2(4):371-402, 1977.

Oestradiol and progesterone: soluble receptor levels and metabolism in the uterus of the ovariectomized ewe, by L. Murphy, et al. AUSTRALIAN JOURNAL OF BIOLOGICAL SCIENCES 30(3):225-228, June, 1977.

Oestrogen-associated disease of the renal microcirculation, by K. Jones, et al. CLINICLA SCIENCE AND MOLECULAR MEDICINE 52(1):33-42, January, 1977.

Oestrogen content of oral contraceptives [letter], by M. Briggs, et al. LANCET 2(8050):1233, December 10, 1977.

Of many things; escalating violence over abortion question, by J. O'Hare. AMERICA 138:inside cover, March 11, 1978.

—. CHRISTIANITY TODAY 22:29, April 21, 1978.

Okay, Mr. Califano, consider the alternatives to abortion, by J. O'Reilly. MS MAGAZINE 6:74+, May, 1978.

On abortion, by G. Duchene. OSSERVATORE ROMANO 7(516):11, February 16, 1978.

On abortion; interview by Christianity Today; excerpt from

Christianity Today, April 21, 1978. CATHOLIC DIGEST 42:43-47, September, 1978.

On abortion philosophy [letter], by G. Crum. AMERICAN JOURNAL OF PUBLIC HEALTH 68(3):272, March, 1978.

On IUD package inserts [letter], by W. Cates, Jr. AMERICAN JOURNAL OF PUBLIC HEALTH 68(3):269-270, March, 1978.

On the judgment of the indication of emergency in abortion legislation, by N. Kathke, et al. OEFFENTLICHE GESUND-HEITSWESEN 40(1):20-22, January, 1978.

On paying the price of abortion, by S. E. Allen. MADEMOI-SELLE 84:100+, March, 1978.

On the problems of planned parenthood, by S. Azrieli. NURSE IN ISRAEL 23(94):23-24, November, 1975.

On the proposed legislation dealing with family planning, contraception; statement from the Irish Bishops' Conference. OSSERVATORE ROMANO 17(526):11, April 27, 1978.

On the reanastomosis of fallopian tubes after surgical sterilization, by H. W. Jones, et al. FERTILITY AND STERILITY 29(6):702-704, June, 1978.

On the use of fenoterolhydrobromide in the treatment of imminent abortion, by E. Ruppin, et al. GEBURTSHILFE UND FRAUENHEILKUNDE 38(6):461-467, June, 1978.

On wrongful birth actions, by J. G. Zimmerly. LEGAL ASPECTS OF MEDICAL PRACTICE 6(3):48-49, March, 1978.

100 million reasons why family life must change, by J. Cunningham. GUARDIAN p. 19, December 18, 1978.

One hundred thousand Catholics gather in Milan for a celebration of life; homily, by G. G. Colombo. OSSERVATORE ROMANO 18(475):4, May 5, 1977.

A (1;7) translocation, balanced, from a subject associated with repeated abortion. Respository identification No. GM-1356, by L. G. Jackson, et al. CYTOGENETICS AND CELL GENETICS 21(3):175, 1978.

Only women have babies; proposal for a male-child birth pill, by C. B. Luce. NATIONAL REVIEW 30:824-827, July 7, 1978.

An open assessment of a new low dose oestrogen combined oral contraceptive, by I. Hughes. JOURNAL OF INTERNATIONAL MEDICAL RESEARCH 6(1):41-45, 1978.

Open letter to the president of the medical federation, by L. Reale. OSSERVATORE ROMANO 31(540):7, August 3, 1978.

Open your eyes; note of the Episcopal Commission for the family on abortion. OSSERVATORE ROMANO 7(516): 11, February 16, 1978.

Operating theatres and prevalence of miscarriage [letter], by D. Angus. MEDICAL JOURNAL OF AUSTRALIA 1(12): 657-658, June 17, 1978.

Operation of the abortion law [letter], by M. E. Krass. CANADIAN MEDICAL ASSOCIATION JOURNAL 118(11):1362, June 10, 1978.

Ophthalmological complications after oral contraceptives, by L. Zeydler-Grzedzielewska, et al. KLINIKA OCZNA 48(5):239-242, May, 1978.

Oral contraception after 40: what is said, what is known, by H. Rozenbaum. CONCOURS MEDICAL 100(12):2051-2054, March 25, 1978.

Oral contraception and fertility return. NURSES DRUG ALERT 2:59, June 7, 1978.

Oral contraception—choice of treatment, by B. Law. PRACTITIONER 219(1312):571-578, October, 1977.

167

Oral contraception. Physiologic and pathologic effects, by W. C. Andrews. OBSTETRICS AND GYNECOLOGY ANNUAL 7:325-351, 1978.

Oral contraceptive exposure in a male with a pituitary micro-adenoma: a case report, by G. C. Buchanan, et al. CONTRACEPTION 16(4):351-356, October, 1977.

Oral-contraceptive-induced benign liver tumors—the magnitude of the problem [letter], by H. Jick, et al. JOURNAL OF THE AMERICAN MEDICAL ASSOCIATION 240(9):828-829, September 1, 1978.

Oral contraceptive induced hypertension simulating primary aldosteronism, by C. R. Raj, et al. WISCONSIN MEDICAL JOURNAL 77(5):49-50, May, 1978.

Oral contraceptive labeling. FDA DRUG BULLETIN 8(2):12-13, March-April, 1978.

Oral contraceptive potencies and side effects, by G. S. Berger, et al. OBSTETRICS AND GYNECOLOGY 51(5):545-547, May, 1978.

Oral contraceptive steroids and thrombophlebitis, by A. W. Diddle, et al. JOURNAL OF THE TENNESSEE MEDICAL ASSOCIATION 71(1):22-26, January, 1978.

Oral contraceptive therapy and benign hepatic lesions in females, by J. Zerner, et al. JOURNAL OF THE MAINE MEDICAL ASSOCIATION 69(6):161-164, June, 1978.

Oral-contraceptive use and bacteriuria in a community-based study, by D. Evans, et al. NEW ENGLAND JOURNAL OF MEDICINE 299(10):536-537, September 7, 1978.

Oral contraceptive use and other factors in the standard glucose tolerance test, by J. Wingerd, et al. DIABETES 26(11): 1024-1033, November, 1977.

Oral contraceptive use and venous thromboembolism: absence of an effect of smoking, by D. H. Lawson, et al. BRITISH

168

MEDICAL JOURNAL 2(6089):729-730, September 17, 1977.

Oral contraceptive use: association with frequency of hospitalization and chronic disease risk indicator, by R. Hoover, et al. AMERICAN JOURNAL OF PUBLIC HEALTH 68:335-341, April, 1978.

Oral contraceptive use: epidemiology, by F. A. MacCornack, et al. NEW YORK STATE JOURNAL OF MEDICINE 77: 200-202, February, 1977.

Oral contraceptives, by A. A. Haspels, et al. NEDERLANDS TIJDSCHRIFT VOOR GENEESKUNDE 122(32):1188-1190, August 12, 1978.

Oral contraceptives and ANA positivity [letter], by J. M. Kennedy. ARTHRITIS AND RHEUMATISM 20(8):1567-1569, November-December, 1977.

Oral contraceptives and birth defects, by K. J. Rothman, et al. NEW ENGLAND JOURNAL OF MEDICINE 299(10):522-524, September 7, 1978.

Oral contracetpives and breast disease. An epidemiological study, by J. L. Kelsey, et al. AMERICAN JOURNAL OF EPIDEMIOLOGY 107(3):236-244, March, 1978.

Oral contraceptives and cholangiocarcinoma [letter], by E. F. Ellis, et al. LANCET 1(8057):207, January 28, 1978.

Oral contraceptives and emotional state, by A. Worsley, et al. JOURNAL OF PSYCHOSOMATIC RESEARCH 22(1): 13-16, 1978.

Oral contraceptives and endometrial and cervical cancer, by K. S. Moghissi. JOURNAL OF TOXICOLOGY AND ENVIRONMENTAL HEALTH 3(1-2):243-265, September, 1977.

Oral contraceptives and focal nodular hyperplasia of the liver. Two case reports with electron-microscopic studies, by

M. Balázs, et al. ACTA HEPATO-GASTROENTEROLO-GICA 25(2):111-118, April, 1978.

Oral contraceptives and liver damage under experimental conditions, by M. Beskid, et al. MATERIA MEDICA POLONA 9(3):210-215, July-September, 1977.

Oral contraceptives and malignant hepatoma [letter], by F. Tigano, et al. LANCET 2(7978):196, July 24, 1976.

Oral contraceptives and myocardial infarct, by J. P. Bounhoure, et al. ARCHIVES DE MALADIES DU COEUR ET DES VAISSEAUX 70(7):765-771, July, 1977.

Oral contraceptives and myocardial infarction [editorial], by S. Shapiro. NEW ENGLAND JOURNAL OF MEDICINE 293:195-196, July 24, 1975.

Oral contraceptives and nonfatal myocardial infarction, by H. Jick, et al. JAMA; JOURNAL OF THE AMERICAN MEDICAL ASSOCIATION 239(14):1403-1406, April 3, 1978.

Oral contraceptives and nonfatal stroke in healthy young women, by H. Jick, et al. ANNALS OF INTERNAL MEDICINE 89(1):58-60, July, 1978.

Oral contraceptives and reduced risk of benign breast diseases, by H. Ory, et al. NEW ENGLAND JOURNAL OF MEDICINE 294:419-422, February 19, 1976.

Oral contraceptives and riboflavin nutriture, by K. Guggenheim, et al. INTERNATIONAL JOURNAL FOR VITAMIN AND NUTRITION RESEARCH 47(3):234-235, 1977.

Oral contraceptives and risk of benign tumors of the breast: recent data from the literature, by A. Simard. UNION MEDICALE DU CANADA 106(8):1115-1119, August, 1977.

Oral contraceptives and subarachnoid haemorrhage [letter], by R. Finn, et al. LANCET 2(8089):582, September 9, 1978.

Oral contraceptives and surgical intervention, by H. Rozenbaum. CONCOURS MEDICAL 99(40):6098-6099, October 29, 1977.

Oral contraceptives and their influence on porphyrin concentrations in erythrocytes and urine, by A. Kansky, et al. DERMATOLOGICA 157(3):181-185, 1978.

Oral contraceptives and their relationship to cancer of the breast: a medicolegal problem, by R. K. Clasper. LEGAL MEDICINE ANNUAL :297-313, 1977.

Oral contraceptives and thromboembolic disease, by J. A. Hall, et al. JOURNAL OF THE INDIANA STATE MEDICAL ASSOCIATION 71(4):413-414, April, 1978.

Oral contraceptives and thromboembolism, by K. Sato, et al. KOKYU TO JUNKAN 26(3):212-220, March, 1978.

Oral contraceptives and vitamin B 6, by L. Ovesen. UGESKRIFT FOR LAEGER 140(29):1733-1735, July 17, 1978.

Oral contraceptives—another look [editorial], by P. E. Sartwell. AMERICAN JOURNAL OF PUBLIC HEALTH 68(4):323-325, April, 1978.

Oral contraceptives, blood clotting and thrombosis, by L. Poller. BRITISH MEDICAL BULLETIN 34(2):151-156, May, 1978.

Oral contraceptives: a demographic survey of military dependents, by R. D. Peppler. MILITARY MEDICINE 142(10): 773-777, October, 1977.

Oral contraceptives, hypertension and nephrosclerosis, by J. Girndt. FORTSCHRITTE DU MEDIZIN 96(7):327-332, February 16, 1978.

Oral contraceptives: a possible association with liver tumors and endometrial carcinoma, by F. W. Hanson. ADVANCES IN PLANNED PARENTHOOD 12(2):86-92, 1977.

Oral contraceptives, smoking and nodular hyperplasia of the liver, by J. Lough, et al. CANADIAN MEDICAL ASSOCIATION JOURNAL 118(4):403-404, February 18, 1978.

Oral contraceptives, smoking, migraine, and food alergy [letter], by E. C. Grant. LANCET 2(8089):581-582, September 9, 1978.

Oral contraceptives, thromboembolic disease, and hypertension: a review, by A. Ferguson. JOURNAL OF THE MEDICAL ASSOCIATION OF THE STATE OF ALABAMA 47(3): 49-55, September, 1977.

Oral contraceptives: which one for my patient? by B. R. Speir. JOURNAL OF THE MEDICAL ASSOCIATION OF THE STATE OF ALABAMA 45(11):36-38, May, 1976.

Oral glucose tolerance test in women in relation to menstrual cycle, by U. Peppler, et al. KLINISCHE WOCHENSCHRIFT 56(13):659-669, July 1, 1978.

Ordeal of a divided jury; W. Waddill case. TIME 111:24, May 22, 1978.

Organized family planning services in the United States, 1968-1976, by A. Torres. FAMILY PLANNING PERSPECTIVES 10:83-88, May-April, 1978.

Origin of acrocentric trisomies in spontaneous abortuses, by N. Niikawa, et al. HUMAN GENETICS 40(1):73-78, December 29, 1977.

Ottawa Family Planning Clinic: experience with 3862 registrants, by J. C. Whyte, et al. CANADIAN MEDICAL ASSOCIATION JOURNAL 118(4):401-402, February 18, 1978.

Our Catholic faith: birth control, by R. Hire. OUR SUNDAY VISITOR 66:4-5, December 4, 1977.

Our Catholic faith: the dignity of human life, by R. Hire. OUR SUNDAY VISITOR 66:6, December 11, 1977.

Our Catholic faith: sterilization, by R. Hire. OUR SUNDAY VISITOR 66:10-11, December 18, 1977.

An outcome evaluation of counseling services provided by abortion clinics, by B. J. Kay, et al. MEDICAL CARE 15(10): 858-868, October, 1977.

Outcome of pregnancy in the presence of intrauterine device, by S. Koetsawang, et al. ACTA OBSTETRICIA ET GYNECOLOGICA SCANDINAVICA 56(5):479-482, 1977.

Outpatient termination of pregnancy, by G. M. Filshie, et al. BRITISH JOURNAL OF OBSTETRICS AND GYNAECOLOGY 84(7):509-513, July, 1977.

Outpatient termination of pregnancy in the first trimester during paracervical blockade with Carticain, by A. Gallinat, et al. GEBURTSHILFE UND FRAUENHEILKUNDE 38(2):105-106, February, 1978.

Out-patient therapeutic termination of pregnancy at the University Hospital of the West Indies, by B. S. Sengupta, et al. WEST INDIAN MEDICAL JOURNAL 26(3):157-163, September, 1977.

Ovarian pregnancy. The dubious role of intra-uterine devices [letter], by J. Y. Grall, et al. NOUVELLE PRESSE MEDICALE 7(6):468, February 11, 1978.

Ovariectomy-induced changes in food motivation in the rat, by S. K. Gale, et al. HORMONES AND BEHAVIOR 9(2): 120-129, October, 1977.

An overview of IUD research and implications for the future, by J. Zipper, et al. INTERNATIONAL JOURNAL OF GYNAECOLOGY AND OBSTETRICS 15(1):73-78, 1977.

Ovulation in rhesus monkeys suppressed by intranasal administration of progesterone and norethisterone, by T. C. Anand Kumar, et al. NATURE 270(5637):532-534, December 8, 1977.

Ovulation inhibitors in under age persons, by A. Hollmann. DEUTSCH MEDIZINISCHE WOCHENSCHRIFT 103(32): 1258-1259, August 11, 1978.

The ovulation method of natural family planning, by E. Petschel. MARRIAGE 60:14-15, October 1978.

Oxidative metabolism of the placenta in miscarriage, by M. A. Kampo, et al. PEDIATRIYA AKUSHERSTVO I HINE-KOLOHIYA (1):43-44, January-February, 1978.

PID and the IUD. EMERGENCY MEDICINE 10:170, February, 1978.

Pancreatitis, cholecystitis, incompetent cervix, and premature labor in a habitual aborter: a rare combination, by M. Hochman, et al. AMERICAN JOURNAL OF OBSTETRICS AND GYNECOLOGY 131(8):905-906, August 15, 1978.

Le Pape d'Humanae Vitae, by G. Matagrin. LA DOCUMENTA-TION CATHOLIQUE 75:752, September 3-17, 1978.

Paracervical block in therapeutic abortions [letter], by P. A. Poma. AMERICAN JOURNAL OF OBSTETRICS AND GYNECOLOGY 131(8):915-916, August 15, 1978.

Parent and child—statutory construction and interpretation of sections of a Massachusetts statute which set forth the necessary extent of parental notification, consultation and consent for the performance of an abortion on an unmarried minor. JOURNAL OF FAMILY LAW 16:116-122, November, 1977.

Parental consent abortion statutes: the limits of state power. INDIANA LAW JOURNAL 52:837-850, Summer, 1977.

Partial salpingectomy technique [letter], by W. S. Van Bergen. AMERICAN JOURNAL OF OBSTETRICS AND GYNE-COLOGY 130(2):249, January 15, 1978.

Past, present and future of the surgical sterilization of women, by J. E. Rioux. UNION MEDICALE DU CANADA 107(6):

544-558, June, 1978.

Pastoral letter on abortion, by T. Cahill. OSSERVATORE RO-
MANO 19(476):11, May 12, 1977.

A pastoral letter on sterilization; the Bishops of India. CATHO-
LIC MIND 75:4-6, May, 1977.

Paternidade responsável: algumas antoções, by J. Snoek. RE-
VISTA ECLESIASTICA BRASILEIRA 36:539-544, September, 1976.

Pathogenetic factors in miscarriage and prolonged pregnancy,
by V. N. Kozhevnikov. AKUSHERSTVO I GINEKOLOGIIA
(8):40-42, August, 1977.

Paths to fertility reduction: the "Policy Cube." FAMILY
PLANNING PERSPECTIVES. 9(5):214, September-
October, 1977.

Patient delay in seeking health care: social factors associated with
delayed abortion, by S. J. Guttmacher. DISSERTATION
ABSTRACTS INTERNATIONAL 37(7-A):4652-4653, January, 1977.

Patient education and intrauterine contraceptive—study of two
package inserts, by H. Benson, et al. AMERICAN JOUR-
NAL OF PUBLIC HEALTH 67:446-449, May, 1977.

Patient education through pregnancy counseling: a preventive
approach. . .Gynecology Clinic, Wilce Health Center, Ohio
State University, by L. Meeks, et al. HEALTH EDUCATION
9:42-45, January-February, 1978.

"Patient failure" as a reliability model for the "minipill": a clinical study, by S. Nummi. CURRENT MEDICAL RESEARCH
AND OPINION 5(5):406-411, 1978.

Patient package inserts and oral contraceptives, by H. W. Mayberger, et al. JOURNAL OF LEGAL MEDICINE 5(9):14-
17, September, 1977.

Patients denied abortion at a private early pregnancy termination service in Auckland, by R. B. Hunton. NEW ZEALAND MEDICAL JOURNAL 85(588):424-425, May 25, 1977.

Patients' evaluation of family planning services: the case of innter-city clinics, by K. Sung. STUDIES IN FAMILY PLANNING 8:130, May, 1977.

Patients' rights. Abortion. The right to die. ANNUAL SURVEY OF AMERICAN LAW 1977:535-559, 1977.

Patterns of family building and contraceptive use of middle-class couples, by D. Woodward, et al. JOURNAL OF BIOSOCIAL SCIENCE 10(1):39-58, January, 1978.

Paying for abortion: is the court wrong? by R. Shinn, et al. CHRISTIANITY AND CRISIS 37:202-207, September 19, 1977.

Peers as recruiters: family planning communications of west Malaysian acceptors, by L. M. Berbrugge. JOURNAL OF HEALTH AND SOCIAL BEHAVIOR 19:51-68, March, 1978.

Pelvic abscess and perforation of the sigmoid colen by a segment of benign cystic teratoma: an unusual complication of induced abortion, by F. G. Giustini, et al. JOURNAL OF REPRODUCTIVE MEDICINE 20(5):291-292, May, 1978.

Pelvic abscess in association with intrauterine contraceptive device, by W. C. Scott. AMERICAN JOURNAL OF OBSTETRICS AND GYNECOLOGY 131(2):149-156, May 15, 1978.

Pelvic actinomycosis and the intrauterine contraceptive device. A cyto-histomorphologic study, by R. D. Luff, et al. AMERICAN JOURNAL OF CLINICAL PATHOLOGY 69(6): 581-586, June, 1978.

Pelvic actinomycosis associated with IUCD [letter], by M. Barnham, et al. BRITISH MEDICAL JOURNAL 1(6114):719-720, March 18, 1978.

Pelvic pain and the IUD, by G. E. Trobough. JOURNAL OF RE-
PRODUCTIVE MEDICINE 20(3):167-174, March, 1978.

Pelviscopic sterilization with plastic clips in animal experiments
(rabbits) (proceedings), by E. Brandl, et al. ARCHIV FUR
GYNAEKOLOGIE 224(1-4):43-44, July 29, 1977.

Perforation of the uterus after voluntary termination of pregnancy using the aspiration technique. Two serious cases, by
R. Frydman, et al. JOURNAL DE GYNECOLOGIE OB-
STETRIQUE ET BIOLOGIE DE LA REPRODUCTION
7(3):459-463, April, 1978.

Perforation of the uterus and the urinary bladder with the
Lippes loop, by J. Iglesias, et al. REVISTA CHILENA DE
OBSTETRICIA Y GINECOLOGIA 42(3):149-150, 1977.

Perforation of the uterus as a complication of intrauterine contraception with the Gravigard, by C. D. Brich, et al. UGE-
SHRIFT FOR LAEGER 139(32):1907-1908, August 8,
1977.

Perforation of uterus by Lippes loop. (Case report with brief
review of literature), by S. Agarwal, et al. JOURNAL OF
OBSTETRICS AND GYNAECOLOGY OF INDIA 27(2):
262-265, April, 1977.

Performing second-trimester abortions: rational for inpatient
basis, by G. Stroh, et al. NEW YORK STATE JOURNAL
OF MEDICINE 75:2168-2171, October, 1975.

Persons in the whole sense, by G. M. Atkinson. AMERICAN
JOURNAL OF JURISPRUDENCE 22:86-117, 1977.

Perspectives in evaluating the safety and effectiveness of steroidal
contraceptives in different parts of the world, by J. W. Goldzieher. INTERNATIONAL JOURNAL OF GYNAECOLO-
GY AND OBSTETRICS 15(1):63-68, 1977.

The pharmacist as family planning helpmate, by M. Dolan.
AMERICAN PHARMACY 18(5):40, May, 1978.

The pharmacodynamics and toxicology of steroids and related compounds, by F. Bischoff, et al. ADVANCES IN LIPID RESEARCH 15:61-157, 1977.

Pharmacological activity of progesterone derivatives, by V. V. Korkhov, et al. FARMIKOLOGIYA I TOKSIKOLOGIYA 41(1):55-59, January-February, 1978.

The pharmacological profile of norgestimate, a new orally active progestin, by D. W. Hahn, et al. CONTRACEPTION 16(5): 541-553, November, 1977.

Philosophers and the abortion question, by P. Abbott. POLITICAL THEORY August, 1978.

The philosophical arguments, by R. Neville. HASTINGS CENTER REPORT 8(3):33-37, June, 1978.

Phosphorus-nitrogen compounds. 21. Murine oncolytic and antifertility effect of adamantylaziridine compounds, by L. A. Cates, et al. JOURNAL OF MEDICINAL CHEMISTRY 21(1):143-146, January, 1978.

Physician notes hazards of DES use to prevent pregnancy [letter], by E. F. Diamond. HOSPITAL PROGRESS 59(3):6-10, March, 1978.

Physicians help make rhythm work, by E. F. Keefe. NEW YORK STATE JOURNAL OF MEDICINE 76:205-208, February, 1976.

Physiochemical properties of placental proteins in physiological and interrupted pregnancy, by T. N. Pogorelova. AKUSHERSTVO I GINEKOLOGIIA (7):27-31, July, 1978.

Pigmented skin lesions in babies born to underweight former oral-contraceptive users [letter], by S. Harlap. LANCET 2(8079):39, July 1, 1978.

The pill [letter], by J. Heim. NOUVELLE PRESSE MEDICALE 6(38):3549, November 12, 1977.

The pill and the code, by M. A. Frey. JOURNAL OF FAMILY LAW 15(1):1-26, 1977.

The pill and other methods [letter]. NEW ENGLAND JOURNAL OF MEDICINE 298(2):114, January 12, 1978.

The pill and the rising costs of fertility control, by J. Blake. SOCIAL BIOLOGY 24(4):267-280, Winter, 1977.

Pill as an arthritis preventive. SCIENCE NEWS 113:231, April 15, 1978.

"Pill"—associated liver tumor warrants abstinence from pregnancy. NURSES DRUG ALERT 2:95-96, August, 1978.

Pill brochure stresses smoking warning. FDA CONSUMER 12:3-4, March, 1978.

Pill for birth control, by D. Kolb. JOURNAL OF CHEMICAL EDUCATION 55:591-596, September, 1978.

Pill hazards spark condom sales, by M. Christopher. ADVERTISING AGE 49:3+, January 30, 1978.

Pill-users' strokes are different; angiograms show distinct pattern of abnormalities involving small arteries. MEDICAL WORLD NEWS 18:89, April 4, 1977.

Pill wanes? ECONOMIST 267:26, April 15, 1978.

Pitchfold prosecuted for self-abortion, by A. Scarlet. TIME 112:22, September 11, 1978.

Pituitary and adrenal influences upon spontaneous contractions of uterine horns isolated from ovariectomized or natural estrus rats, by A. L. Gimeno, et al. REPRODUCTION 3(3-4):235-245, July-December, 1976.

Pituitary function in adult males receiving medroxyprogesterone acetate, by W. J. Meyer, 3rd, et al. FERTILITY AND STERILITY 28(10):1072-1076, October, 1977.

Pituitary response to LHRH stimulation in women on oral contraceptives, by L. S. Wan, et al. CONTRACEPTION 17(1): 1-7, January, 1978.

Placental pathology in midtrimester pregnancies interrupted by intra-amniotic injection of hypertonic urea, by S. Segal, et al. BRITISH JOURNAL OF OBSTETRICS AND GYNAECOLOGY 83(2):156-159, February, 1976.

Planitication de la famille et contraception; déclaration des évêques d'Irlande à propos d'un projet de lui. LA DOCUMENTATION CATHOLIQUE 75:424-425, May 7, 1978.

Planned parenthood and childcare, by V. M. Saxdaram, et al. INDIAN PEDIATRICS 15(1):27-32, January, 1978.

The Planned Parenthood Federation of America, by J. O'Hare. AMERICA 138:inside front cover, February 18, 1978.

Planned parenthood: the Planned Parenthood Federation of America, by A. Nevins. OUR SUNDAY VISITOR 66:15, March 12, 1978.

Plant used as means of abortion, contraception, sterilization and fecundation by Paraguayan indigenous people, by P. Arena, et al. ECONOMIC BOTANY 31(3):302-306, 1977.

Plasma concentrations of ethinylestradiol and D-norgestrel during two immediate postabortal oral contraceptive cycles, by P. Lähteenmäki, et al. CONTRACEPTION 17(1):9-17, January, 1978.

Plasma hormone levels and labor in abortion induced with prostaglandin F2 alpha (proceedings), by U. Gethmann, et al. ARCHIV FUR GYNAEKOLOGIE 224(1-4):269-270, July 29, 1977.

Plasma hormone profile of threatened abortion and its prognosis, by I. Miyakawa, et al. INTERNATIONAL JOURNAL OF GYNAECOLOGY AND OBSTETRICS 15(1):12-16, 1977.

Plasma levels of 15(S)15-methyl PGF2alpha following administration via various routes for induction of abortion, by K. Gréen, et al. PROSTAGLANDINS 14(5):1013-1024, November, 1977.

Plasma non-esterified fatty acids, cortisol and glucose in maternal blood during abortion induced with intra-amniotic prostaglandin F2alpha, by H. Ward, et al. BRITISH JOURNAL OF OBSTETRICS AND GYNAECOLOGY 85(5):344-347, May, 1978.

Plasma prolactin levels and contraception: oral contraceptives and intrauterine devices, by W. N. Spellacy, et al. CONTRACEPTION 17(1):71-77, January, 1978.

Plasma prostaglandin concentration and abortifacient effectiveness of a single insertion of a 3 mg 15(S)-methyl-prostaglandin F2a methyl ester vaginal suppository, by C. A. Ballard. CONTRACEPTION 17(4):383-391, April, 1978.

Platelet aggregation and antiovulation agents [letter], by E. E. Ohnhaus. DEUTSCHE MEDIZINISCHE WOCHENSCHRIFT 102(50):1862-1863, December 16, 1977.

Point of view. On the front: nursing and family and community health, by M. L. Kinlein. FAMILY AND COMMUNITY HEALTH 1(1):57-68, April, 1978.

Policy document on family planning. WORLD OF IRISH NURSING 7:7, May, 1978.

The politics of abortion [abortion as a campaign issue in various states; some emphasis on Minnesota], by A. R. Hunt. WALL STREET JOURNAL 192:20, August 15, 1978.

Politics of abortion; Supreme Court decision on medical funding, by P. Steinfels. COMMONWEAL 104:456, July 22, 1977.

Politics of birth control, by D. N. Barrett. U. S. CATHOLIC 43:46-47, January, 1978.

Politics of birth control [India], by B. Kramer. WALL STREET JOURNAL 191:20, May 8, 1978.

Polls: abortion, by C. de Boer. PUBLIC OPINION QUARTER-
LY 41:553-564, Winter, 1977-1978; Reply by R. J. Adamek,
42:411-413, Fall, 1978.

Poor acceptability of "Pill-a-month" contraceptive. High pregnancy and drop-out rates in a small sample, by R. A. Vaidya,
et al. JOURNAL OF POSTGRADUATE MEDICINE 22(4):
176-179, October, 1976.

Pope Paul again reaffirms teaching of Humanae Vitae. OUR
SUNDAY VISITOR 67:1, August 6, 1978.

Pope says Humanae Vitae was painful to issue, our principles
still hold, by J. Muthig, Jr. OUR SUNDAY VISITOR 67:
1, July 9, 1978.

Pope urges natural family planners to help couples follow Church
teaching. OUR SUNDAY VISITOR 66:1, February 26,
1978.

Population and family planning in Thailand. BANGKOK BANK
MONTHLY REVIEW 19:241-247, June, 1978.

Population growth, population organization participants, and the
right of privacy, by L. D. Barnett. FAMILY LAW QUAR-
TERLY 12:37-60, Spring, 1978.

Population policy and family planning [editorial]. INDIAN
JOURNAL OF PUBLIC HEALTH 21(1):1-2, January-
March, 1977.

Positive pregnancy tests at Cowell student health center, by J.
M. Dorman. JOURNAL OF THE AMERICAN COLLEGE
HEALTH ASSOCIATION 26:207-210, February, 1978.

Positive woman or negative man? by H. Klaus. LINACRE
QUARTERLY 43:244-248, November, 1976.

Possibility of burns during laparoscopic tubal sterilization [let-
ter], by T. H. Freilich. AMERICAN JOURNAL OF OB-
STETRICS AND GYNECOLOGY 129(6):708-709, November 15, 1977.

Possible immediate hypersensitivity reaction of the nasal mucosa to oral contraceptives, by Z. Pelikan. ANNALS OF ALLERGY 40(3):211-219, March, 1978.

A possible involvement of adrenaline in the facilitation of lordosis behavior in the ovariectomized rat, by M. Yanase. ENDOCRINOLOGIA JAPONICA 24(5):507-512, October, 1977.

A possible new approach to the treatment of metastatic breast cancer: massive doses of medroxyprogesterone acetate, by F. Pannuti, et al. CANCER TREATMENT REPORTS 62(4):499-504, April, 1978.

A possible role of prostaglandin E1 in the mechanism of action of intrauterine contraceptive device, by R. Das, et al. INDIAN JOURNAL OF MEDICAL RESEARCH 65(3):353-356, March, 1977.

Post-abortal immediate IUD insertion: further experience and a controlled comparison of three devices, by J. A. Ross, et al. CONTRACEPTION 17(3):237-246, March, 1978.

Postabortion insertions of the pleated membrane, by X. Tacla, et al. INTERNATIONAL JOURNAL OF GYNAECOLOGY AND OBSTETRICS 15(3):275-278, 1977.

Postcoital contraception—an appraisal, by W. Rinehart. POPULATION REPORTS (9 Pt. 2):J141-154, January, 1976.

Postcoital contraception in primates. I. Action mechanism of a potential postovulatory fertility-inhibiting substance STS 456 in the baboon (Papio hamadryas), by N. P. Goncharov, et al. ZENTRALBLATT FUER GYNAEKOLOGIE 100(5):263-272, 1978.

Post-coital contraception using d1-norgestrel/ethinyl estradiol combination, by R. P. Smith, et al. CONTRACEPTION 17(3):247-252, March, 1978.

Postcoital contraception using a high-dose depot estrogen (Org 369-2) (proceedings), by A. E. Schindler, et al. ARCHIV

Post-coital contraceptive & uterotrophic effects of Centchroman in mice, by S. R. Munshi, et al. INDIAN JOURNAL OF EXPERIMENTAL BIOLOGY 15(12):1151-1153, December, 1977.

Postcoital hormonal contraception: uses, risks, and abuses, by A. A. Yuzpe. INTERNATIONAL JOURNAL OF GYNAECOLOGY AND OBSTETRICS 15(2):133-136, 1977.

Post-pill amenorrhoea [letter], by K. W. Hancock, et al. BRITISH MEDICAL JOURNAL 1(6104):45, January 7, 1978.

—, by R. P. Shearman. BRITISH MEDICAL JOURNAL 2(6099):1414, November 26, 1977.

Post-"pill" amenorrhoea—cause or coincidence? by H. S. Jacobs, et al. BRITISH MEDICAL JOURNAL 2(6092):940-942, October 8, 1977.

Poststerilization tubal tursion, by B. D. Pujari, et al. INTERNATIONAL SURGERY 63(2):84-86, February, 1978.

Potencies of oral contraceptives [letter], by H. J. Chihal, et al. AMERICAN JOURNAL OF OBSTETRICS AND GYNECOLOGY 130(3):369-371, Febraury 1, 1978.

The potential reduction of medical complications from induced abortion, by R. G. Smith, et al. INTERNATIONAL JOURNAL OF GYNAECOLOGY AND OBSTETRICS 15(4):337-346, 1978.

Pour la défense des plus faibles; lettre pastorale des èvêques belges sur l'avortement juin 1977. LA DOCUMENTATION CATHOLIQUE

Power lines and disembodied women [abortion and sterilization in Latin America], by F. Moira. OFF OUR BACKS 6:10-11, November, 1976.

Power to the papists; on the abortion struggle, by S. Adamo.

Practical control of spontaneous abortion, by J. Barrat. JOURNAL DE BYNECOLOGIE, OBSTETRIQUE ET BIOLOGIE DE LA REPRODUCTION 6(5):695-709, July-August, 1977.

Practice profiles in evaluating the clinical experience of family medicine trainees, by V. Boisseau, et al. JOURNAL OF FAMILY PRACTICE 6(4):801-805, April, 1978.

Preaching on Humanae Vitae; the tenth anniversary of Humanae Vitae, July, 1978, by J. Kppley. HOMILETIC AND PASTORAL REVIEW 78:15-19, March, 1978.

Preclinical evaluation of intrauterine progesterone as a contraceptive agent. I. Local contraceptive effects and their reversal, by R. Hudson, et al. CONTRACEPTION 17(5): 465-474, May, 1978.

—. II. Possible mechanisms of action, by S. A. Tillson, et al. CONTRACEPTION 17(5):475-488, May, 1978.

Prediction of spontaneous abortion by vaginal cytologic smears, by W. Busch. ZENTRALBLATT FUER GYNAEKOLOGIE 100(1):23-33, 1978.

Prediction of success or failure in birth planning: an approach to prevention of individual and family stress, by B. Mindick, et al. AMERICAN JOURNAL OF COMMUNITY PSYCHOLOGY 5(4):447-459, December, 1977.

Predictive factors in emotional response to abortion: King's termination study—IV, by E. M. Belsey, et al. SOCIAL SCIENCE AND MEDICINE 11(2):71-82, January, 1971.

Pregnancy after induced abortion [letter], by D. Trichopoulos. NEW ENGLAND JOURNAL OF MEDICINE 298(22):1261, June 1, 1978.

Pregnancy and the IUD, by J. F. Perlmutter. JOURNAL OF REPRODUCTIVE MEDICINE 20(3):133-138, March, 1978.

Pregnancy counseling and abortion referral for patients in federally funded family planning programs, by J. I. Rosoff. FAMILY PLANNING PERSPECTIVES 8:43-46, January-February, 1976.

Pregnancy following laparoscopic tubal electrocoagulation and division, by A. Shah, et al. AMERICAN JOURNAL OF OBSTETRICS AND GYNECOLOGY 129(4):459-460, October 15, 1977.

Pregnancy in a uterine scar sacculus—an unusual cause of post-abortal haemorrhage. A case report, by J. V. Larsen, et al. SOUTH AFRICAN MEDICAL JOURNAL 53(4):142-143, January 28, 1978.

Pregnancy interruption based on pediatric indications, by J. D. Murken. INTERNIST 19(5):310-314, May, 1978.

Pregnancy, oral hormonal contraception and lipid bile composition, by B. Dökert, et al. DEUTSCH GESUNDHEITSWESEN 33(25):1153-1155, 1978.

Pregnancy, teenagers and the law, 1976, by E. W. Paul, et al. FAMILY PLANNING PERSPECTIVES 8:16-32, January-February, 1976.

Pregnancy termination with the PGE2-analogue SHB 286, by M. O. Pulkkinen. PROSTAGLANDINS 15(1):161-167, January, 1978.

Preliminary note on the use of a flexible intrauterine device, by S. Rugiati, et al. MINERVA GINECOLOGIA 30(1-2):59-64, January-February, 1978.

Preliminary observations on the use of danazol in endometriosis compared to oestrogen/progestogen combination therapy, by A. D. Noble, et al. JOURNAL OF INTERNATIONAL MEDICAL RESEARCH 5(Suppl 3):79-80, 1977.

Premarital contraceptive uses: a test of two models, by J. Delamater, et al. JOURNAL OF MARRIAGE AND THE FAMILY 40:235-247, May, 1978.

Prenatal effects of sex hormones on human male behavior: medroxyprogesterone acetate (MPA), by H. F. Meyer Bahlburg, et al. PSYCHONEUROENDOCRINOLOGY 2(4): 383-390, October, 1977.

Prenatal exposure to medroxyprogesterone acetate (MPA) in girls, by A. A. Ehrhardt, et al. PSYCHONEUROENDOCINOLOGY 2(4):391-398, October, 1977.

Prenatal selection and dermatoglyphic patterns, by W. J. Babler. AMERICAN JOURNAL OF PHYSICAL ANTHROPOLOGY 48:21-27, January, 1978.

The present state of contraceptive counseling and treatment, by B. Baur, et al. GYNAEKOLOGISCHE RUNDSCHAU 17(Suppl 1):131-132, 1977.

Presumptive personhood, by V. Walker. LINACRE QUARTERLY 45:179-186, May, 1978.

Preventing complications due to dilatation by intracervical application of a prostaglandin-gel, by H. Kühnie, et al. GEBURTSHILFE UND FRAUENHEILKUNDE 37(8):675-680, August, 1977.

Preventing unplanned pregnancies, by C. Hawken. MEDICAL JOURNAL OF AUSTRALIA 1(6):344-351, March 25, 1978.

Prevention of endotoxin-induced abortion by treatment of mice with antisera, by F. Rioux-Darrieulat, et al. JOURNAL OF INFECTIOUS DISEASES 137(1):7-13, January, 1978.

The prevention of late psychological sequelae following therapeutic termination of pregnancy. The role of the doctor during consultations, by L. Moor. JOURNAL DE GYNECOLOGIE, OBSTETRIQUE ET DE BIOLOGIE DE LA REPRODUCTION 7(3):465-471, April, 1978.

Prevention of ovarian cystomas by inhibition of ovulation: a new concept, by J. Zajicek. JOURNAL OF REPRODUCTIVE MEDICINE 20(2):114, February, 1978.

Prevention of pregnancy in rabbits using vaginal application of prostaglandin f2alpha, by M. Salomy, et al. FERTILITY AND STERILITY 29(4):456-458, April, 1978.

Prevention of unwanted pregnancy with Yermonil preparation, by Z. Sternadel, et al. GINEKOLOGIA POLASKA 49(2): 139-142, February, 1978.

Primary carcinoma of the liver and long-term administration of oral contraceptives followed by pregnancy, by M. Balázs, et al. DEUTSCHE MEDIZINISCHE WOCHENSCHRIFT 102(41):1472-1474, October 14, 1977.

Primary liver carcinoma; do sex hormones play a role in its pathogenesis? by G. J. Houwert, et al. NEDERLANDS TIJDSCHRIFT VOOR GENEESKUNDE 122(27):965-970, July 8, 1978.

Primary liver tumors and oral contraceptives. Results of a survey, by J. Vana, et al. JAMA; JOURNAL OF THE AMERICAN MEDICAL ASSOCIATION 238(20):2154-2158, November 14, 1977.

Primary or secondary prevention of adolescent pregnancies? by J. F. Jekel. JOURNAL OF SCHOOL HEALTH 47:457-461, October, 1977.

Primary ovarian pregnancy and the intra-uterine contraceptive device. Report of two cases, by A. Golan, et al. SOUTH AFRICAN MEDICAL JOURNAL 52(28):1130-1132, December 31, 1977.

Primary ovarian pregnancy associated with the dalkon shield IUD, by Y. Girard, et al. OBSTETRICS AND GYNECOLOGY 51(1 Suppl):525-555, January, 1977.

Privacy and public funding: Maher v. Roe (97 Sup Ct 2376) as the interaction of Roe v. Wade and Dandridge v. Williams, by D. T. Hardy. ARIZONA LAW REVIEW 18:903-939, 1976.

Probable amniotic fluid embolism during curettage for a missed abortion: a case report, by D. E. Lees, et al. ANESTHESIA AND ANALGESIA 56(5):739-742, September-October, 1977.

The problem of the "lost" IUD (proceedings), by F. H. Hepp. ARCHIV FUR GYNAEKOLOGIE 224(1-4):30-31, July 29, 1977.

The problem of women in penal and correctional institutions, by E. C. Potter. QUARTERLY JOURNAL OF CORRECTIONS 1:4, Fall, 1977.

Problems in evaluating chronic toxicity of contraceptive steroids in dogs, by J. H. Weikel, Jr., et al. JOURNAL OF TOXICOLOGY AND ENVIRONMENTAL HEALTH 3(1-2):167-177, September, 1977.

Problems in the evaluation of contraceptives, by M. Beckmann, et al. GEBURTSHILFE UND FRAUENHEILKUNDE 38(8):640-642, August, 1978.

Problems of male contraception. 2. Male hormonal contraception, post-testicular points of attack, immunization and enzyme inhibition, by W. B. Schill. FORTSCHRITT DU MEDIZIN 96(30):1505-1509, August 10, 1978.

The problems of therapeutic abortion and infanticide, by S. V. Humphries. CENTRAL AFRICAN JOURNAL OF MEDICINE 24(4):77-79, April, 1978.

Problems with IUCD tails [letter], by G. Chamberlain. BRITISH MEDICAL JOURNAL 1(6107):237-, January 28, 1978.

Problems with male contraception. I. Physiological foundations, male contraception (mechanical procedures, contraceptives), by W. B. Schill. FORTSCHRITT DU MEDIZIN 96(29):1447-1451, August 3, 1978.

Problems with the multiple dosage of ovulation inhibitors in peak female athletes, by P. Borckerhoff. MEDIZINISCHE WELT 28(48):1975-1976, December 2, 1977.

Problems with pregnancy vaccination, by R. Pilsworth. NEW SCIENTIST 77:665-667, March 9, 1978.

The production and use of an attitudinal film in birth control education, by E. S. Herold. JOURNAL OF SCHOOL HEALTH 48(5):307-310, May, 1978.

Production of antisera against contraceptive steroids, by N. Kundu, et al. STEROIDS 30(1):85-98, July, 1977.

Professional and public opinion on abortion law proposals, by W. Facer. NEW ZEALAND NURSING FORUM 6(1):13-15, March, 1978.

Profile of women requesting reversal of sterilization, by V. Gomel. FERTILITY AND STERILITY 30(1):39-41, July, 1978.

Profound hypothermia in mammals treated with tetrahydro-cannabinols, morphine, or chlorpromazine, by C. O. Haavik. FEDERATION PROCEEDINGS 36(12):2595-2598, 1977.

Progestagens, blood-clotting, and blood-pressure [letter]. LANCET 2(8047):1085-1086, November 19, 1977.

The progestasert and ectopic pregnancy, by R. Snowden. BRITISH MEDICAL JOURNAL 2(6102):1600-1601, December 17, 1977.

Progesterone antagonism of estradiol-stimulated uterine "induced protein" synthesis, by H. S. Bhakoo, et al. MOLECULAR AND CELLULAR ENDOCRINOLOGY 8(2): 105-120, August, 1977.

Progesterone: effects on investigatory preferences, aggression, and olfaction inorchidectomized, testosterone-treated mice, by M. J. Soares, et al. BEHAVIORAL BIOLOGY 23(2): 260-266, June, 1978.

The progesterone-sensitive period of rat pregnancy: some effects of LHRH and ovariectomy, by R. R. Humphrey, et al. PROCEEDINGS OF THE SOCIETY FOR EXPERIMENTAL

BIOLOGY AND MEDICINE 156(2):345-348, November, 1977.

Progestin treatment in a case of adrenal cortex hyperfunction with cancer of the endometrium, by A. Lanza, et al. MINERVA GINECOLOGIA 30(5):458-459, May, 1978.

Progestogens in prostatic cancer, by L. Denis, et al. EUROPEAN UROLOGY 4(3):162-166, 1978.

Prognostic value of echography in threatened abortion, by D. Gramellini, et al. ATENEO PARMENSE [ACTA BIOMEDICA] 48(3):259-262, 1977.

Prognostic value of the pregnancy zone protein during early pregnancy in spontaneous abortion, by M. G. Damber, et al. OBSTETRICS AND GYNECOLOGY 51(6):677-681, June, 1978.

The prognostic value of serum hCG analysis with the aid of an HCG-receptor assay in patients with imminent abortion (proceedings), by C. Clasen, et al. ARCHIV FUR GYNAE-KOLOGIE 224(1-4):89-90, July 29, 1977.

A program of group counseling for men who accompany women seeking legal abortions, by R. H. Gordon, et al. COMMUNITY MENTAL HEALTH JOURNAL 13:291-295, Winter, 1977.

A project report: follow-up of trained nurse-midwives. . .International Planned Parenthood Federation, by R. Weinstein. JOURNAL OF NURSE-MIDWIFERY 23:36-39, Spring-Summer, 1978.

Prolactin and thyrotropin after stimulation by thyrotropin releasing hormone a study under long-term administration of oral contraceptives, by O. Bellmann, et al. ARCHIV FUR GYNAEKOLOGIE 225(1):31-42, February 22, 1978.

Pro-life aim: pur God on Capitol Hill, by B. Kenkelen. NATIONAL CATHOLIC REPORTER 14:1+, July 14, 1978.

The pro-life fight in England, by J. Nash. OUR SUNDAY VISITOR 66:3, February 12, 1978.

Pro-life largest people's movement in U.S. history, by G. Barmann. OUR SUNDAY VISITOR 66:3, January 15, 1978.

Pro-life leaders agree there is need for ultra-tough strategy in Congress, by R. Shaw. OUR SUNDAY VISITOR 66:2, February 26, 1978.

Pro-life leaders think Edelin reversal could accelerate an amendment. OUR SUNDAY VISITOR 65:2, January 2, 1977.

Pro-life or reflection of conservative ideology? an analysis of opposition to legalized abortion, by D. Granberg. SOCIOLOGY AND SOCIAL RESEARCH 62:414-429, April, 1978.

Pro-life, pro-E.R.A., by J. Loesch. AMERICA 139:435-436, December 9, 1978.

Pro-life target: women's year meetings; Minnesota conference disrupted, by M. Papa. NATIONAL CATHOLIC REPORTER 13:20, June 17, 1977.

Pro-lifers applaud abortion restrictions in Minnesota, by M. Dorsher. OUR SUNDAY VISITOR 66:4, April 9, 1978.

A prophetic witness for Catholics, by J. Garvey. PRIEST 34: 40-42, October, 1978.

A prospective study of psychiatric and menstrual disturbances following tubal ligation, by N. N. Wig, et al. INDIAN JOURNAL OF MEDICAL RESEARCH 66(4):581-590, October, 1977.

Prospects and possibilities of genetic counseling and family planning in the mental health laboratory for adults, by V. Predescu, et al. REVISTA DE MEDICINA INTERNA [NEUROLOGIE, PSIKIATRIE] 23(1):53-58, January-March, 1978.

The prospects for new, reversible male contraceptives [review article with ninety references], by W. J. Bremner, et al. NEW ENGLAND JOURNAL OF MEDICINE 295:1111-1117, November 11, 1976.

Prostaglandin-induced abortion and outcome of subsequent pregnancies: a prospective controlled study, by I. Z. MacKenzie, et al. BRITISH MEDICAL JOURNAL 6095: 1114-1117, October 29, 1977.

Prostaglandins and abortion. I. intramuscular administration of 15-methyl protaglandin F2alpha for induction of abortion in weeks 10 to 20 of pregnancy, by World Health Organization Task Force on the Use of Prostaglandins for the Regulation of Fertility. AMERICAN JOURNAL OF OBSTETRICS AND GYNECOLOGY 129(6):593-596, November 15, 1977.

—. II. Single extra-amniotic administration of 0.92 mg. of 15-methyl prostaglandin F2alpha in Hyskon for termination of pregnancies in weeks 10 to 20 of gestation: an international multicenter study, by World Health Organization Task Force on the Use of Prostaglandins for the Regulation of Fertility. AMERICAN JOURNAL OF OBSTETRICS AND GYNECOLOGY 129(6):597-600, November 15, 1977.

—. III. Comparison of single intra-amniotic injections of 15-methyl prostaglandin F2alpha and prostaglandin F2alpha for termination of second-trimester pregnancy: an international multicenter study, by World Health Organization Task Force on the Use of Prostaglandins for the Regulation of Fertility. AMERICAN JOURNAL OF OBSTETRICS AND GYNECOLOGY 129(6):601-606, November 15, 1977.

Protein secretion of the rat vesicular glands, by R. Vögtle, et al. VERHANDLURGEN DER ANATOMISCHEN GESELL-SCHAFT (71 Pt. 1):571-574, 1977.

Psychiatric aspects of oral contraceptive use, by D. V. Sheehan, et al. PSYCHIATRIC ANNALS 6:81, October, 1976.

Psychiatric indications for pregnancy interruption, by H. Dilling, et al. INTERNIST 19(5):315-321, May, 1978.

Psychiatric sequelae of therapeutic abortions, by J. O. Cavenar, Jr., et al. NORTH CAROLINA MEDICAL JOURNAL 39(2):101-106, February, 1978.

Psychohygienic aspects of modern contraception. Hazards and dangers—results of follow-up examinations, by P. Petersen. MEDIZINISCHE KLINIK 72(48):2089-2093, December 2, 1977.

Psychological adaptation to sterilization (proceedings), by A. Drähne, et al. ARCHIV FUR GYNAEKOLOGIE 224(1-4): 37-38, July 29, 1977.

Psychological consequences of therapeutic abortion, by H. S. Greer, et al. BRITISH JOURNAL OF PSYCHIATRY 128: 74-79, January, 1976.

Psychological correlates of unwanted pregnancy, by G. E. Rader, et al. JOURNAL OF ABNORMAL PSYCHOLOGY 87: 373-376, June, 1978.

Psychological factors involved in request for elective abortion, by M. Blumenfield. JOURNAL OF CLINICAL PSYCHIATRY 39(1):17-25, January, 1978.

Psychological sequelae of sterilization in women in Singapore, by M. C. Cheng, et al. INTERNATIONAL JOURNAL OF GYNAECOLOGY AND OBSTETRICS 15(1):44-47, 1977.

Psychological study on vasectomy, by H. Jablonski. LAKAR-TIDNINGEN 75(26-27):2540-2542, June 28, 1978.

Psychoses following therapeutic abortion, by J. G. Spaulding, et al. AMERICAN JOURNAL OF PSYCHIATRY 135(3): 364-365, March, 1978.

Psychosomatic aspects of abortion: implications for counseling, by M. B. Bracken. JOURNAL OF REPRODUCTIVE MEDICINE 19(5):265-272, November, 1977.

Puberty, privacy, and protection: the risks of children's "rights," by B. C. Hafen. AMERICAN BAR ASSOCIATION JOUR-

NAL 63:1383-1388, October, 1977.

The public health need for abortion statistics, by J. C. Smith, et al. PUBLIC HEALTH REPORTS 93(2):194-197, March-April, 1978.

Pulmonary embolism in a female adolescent with sickle cell trait and oral contraceptive use, by E. P. Hargus, et al. AMERICAN JOURNAL OF OBSTETRICS AND GYNE-COLOGY 129(6):697-698, November 15, 1977.

Pulsatile discharges of luteinizing hormone in the ovariectomized rat during the 24-hour day, by B. D. Soper, et al. NEURO-ENDOCRINOLOGY 23(5):306-311, 1977.

Punitive and tragic; decision to deny public funds for abortion. NATION 225:3-4, July 2, 1977.

Quality v quantity in children [letter], by H. P. Dunn. BRITISH MEDICAL JOURNAL 2(6095):1354, November 19, 1977.

Quantitative histochemical studies of the hypothalamus: dehy-drogenase enzymes following androgen sterilization, by P. M. Packman, et al. NEUROENDOCRINOLOGY 23(6): 330-340, 1977.

Questions of liability in unsuccessful voluntary sterilization, by G. H. Schlund. GEBURTSHILFE UND FRAUENHEIL-KUNDE 37(11):906-908, November, 1977.

RNA polymerase activities in isolated nuclei of guinea pig semi-nal vesicle epithelium: influence of castration and androgen administration, by K. A. Büchi, et al. ANDROLOGIA 9(3):237-246, July-September, 1977.

Rabbi hopes study will decide Jewish stance on abortion. OUR SUNDAY VISITOR 67:3, October 22, 1978.

A rabbi looks at abortion, by C. Lipschitz. OUR SUNDAY VISITOR 65:12-13, April 3, 1977.

Race and abortion: disconfirmation of the genocide hypothesis

195

in a clinical analogue, by B. Crossley, et al. INTERNA-
TIONAL JOURNAL OF PSYCHIATRY IN MEDICINE
8(1):35-42, 1977-1978.

Racial consciousness: a new guise for traditionalism? by B. S.
Roper, et al. SOCIOLOGY AND SOCIAL RESEARCH
62:430-437, April, 1978.

Racism and the availability of family planning services in the
United States, by G. C. Wright, Jr. SOCIAL FORCES 56:
1087-1098, June, 1978.

Radiation exposure as indication for pregnancy interruption, by
F. E. Stieve. INTERNIST 19(5):299-303, May, 1978.

Radioimmanossay study of neurophysins in human plasma,
by A. C. Reinharz, et al. ACTA ENDOCRINOLOGICA
88(3):455-464, July, 1978.

Radioimmunologic testosterone determination: technic and
diagnostic use, by R. Thun, et al. SCHWEIZER ARCHIV
FUR TIERHEILKUNDE 120(4):205-212, April, 1978.

Radioimmunological determination of prolactin following daily
administration of gestagens (proceedings), by J. Thoma,
et al. ARCHIV FUR GYNAEKOLOGIE 224(1-4):410-
411, July 29, 1977.

Radioprotective effect of castration and cyproteron acetate,
by J. Sevcik, et al. SBORNIK LEKARSKY 79(7-8):252-
244, August, 1977.

Rahner on the origin of the soul: some implications regarding
abortion, by J. T. Culleton. THOUGHT June, 1978.

A randomized comparison of the Ypsilon-Y and Lippes loop D
intrauterine devices in parous women, by P. F. Brenner, et
al. OBSTETRICS AND GYNECOLOGY 51(3):327-329,
March, 1978.

A randomized study of 12-mm and 15.9 mm cannulas in mid-
trimester abortion by laminaria and vacuum curettage, by

P. G. Stubblefield, et al. FERTILITY AND STERILITY 29(5):512-517, May, 1978.

Rape [letter], by W. A. Facer. NEW ZEALAND MEDICAL JOURNAL 86(593):152, August 10, 1977.

Rape and abortion [letter], by M. Jackson. NEW ZEALAND MEDICAL JOURNAL 86(596):301-302, September 28, 1977.

A rapid history of contraception, by J. H. Leavesley. AUSTRA-LIAN FAMILY PHYSICIAN 7(6):730-737, June, 1978.

The rat uterine oestrogen receptor in relation to intra-uterine devices and the oestrous cycle [proceedings], by L. Myatt, et al. BIOCHEMICAL SOCIETY TRANSACTIONS 5(5): 1563-1564, 1977.

Rate of abortions and abnormalities following viral hepatitis [letter], by U. Theile. MEDIZINISCHE KLINIK 72(38): 1554, September 23, 1977.

Re: avulsion of the ureter from both ends as a complication of interruption of pregnancy with a vacuum aspirator [letter], by P. M. Papoff. JOURNAL OF UROLOGY 118(6):1073-1074, December, 1977.

Reactions of a large number of laymen in France to the bill on the liberalization of abortion. CHRIST TO THE WORLD 22:286-289, November 4, 1977.

Reactivity of castrated female rats to estrone in alioxan diabetes, by H. Ivanova, et al. PROBLEMY ENDOKRINOLOGII I GORMONOTERAPII 23(5):77-80, September-October, 1977.

A reassessment of menstrual regulation, by J. E. Hodgson. STUDIES IN FAMILY PLANNING 8(10):263-267, October, 1977.

Recanalization rate following methods of vasectomy using inter-position of fascial sheath of vas deferens, by J. O. Esho, et al.

JOURNAL OF UROLOGY 120(2):178-179, August, 1978.

Recent and possible future trends in abortion, by F. Lafitte. JOURNAL OF MEDICAL ETHICS 4(1):25-29, March, 1978.

Recent developments in technology for the control of female fertility, by J. J. Speidel, et al. OBSTETRICS AND GYNECOLOGY ANNUAL 7:397-445, 1978.

Recent progress in the development of long-acting injectables for control of human fertility, by K. R. Laumas. JOURNAL OF OBSTETRICS AND GYNAECOLOGY OF INDIA 27(1): 11-17, February, 1977.

Recent trend in preference of contraceptive methods—ills down, diaphragm on rise, by J. Balog, et al. OBSTETRICAL AND GYNECOLOGICAL SURVEY 33(4):282-283, April, 1978.

Recent trends in contraceptive use in Mexico. STUDIES IN FAMILY PLANNING 8(8):197, August, 1977.

Recent trends in Latin American fertility, by J. M. Stycos. POPULATION STUDIES 32:407-425, November, 1978.

Recent trends in sterilization [England and Wales, 196-75]. POPULATION TRENDS pp. 13-16, Autumn, 1978.

Recognizing the reasons for contraceptive non-use and abuse. Part 2, by J. L. Tanis. MCN; AMERICAN JOURNAL OF MATERNAL-CHILD NURSING 2:364-369, November-December, 1977.

Recommendations from the findings by the RCGP oral contraception study on the mortality risks of oral contraceptive users, by E. V. Kuenssberg, et al. BRITISH MEDICAL JOURNAL 2(6092):947, October 8, 1977.

Reconstructive tubal surgery [letter]. FERTILITY AND STERILITY 28(11):1263-1265, November, 1977.

Redefining the issues in fetal experimentation; reprint from

The Journal of the American Medical Association, July 19, 1976, by E. Diamond. LINACRE QUARTERLY 44:148-154, May, 1977.

Reduced dose of Rh immunoglobulin following first trimester pregnancy termination, by F. H. Stewart, et al. OBSTETRICS AND GYNECOLOGY 51(3):318-322, March, 1978.

Reduced high-density lipoprotein in women aged 40-41 using oral contraceptives. Consultation Bureau Heart Project, by A. C. Arntzenius, et al. LANCET 1(8076):1221-1223, June 10, 1978.

Reduced uterine response to PGF2alpha under oral contraceptives, by S. Shaala, et al. PROSTAGLANDINS 14(3):523-533, September, 1977.

Reduction in incidence of rheumatoid arthritis associated with oral contraceptives. Royal College of General Practitioners' Oral Contraception Study. LANCET 1(8064):569-571, March 18, 1978.

Reduction of mefanamic acid of increased menstrual blood loss associated with intrauterine contraception, by J. Guillebaud, et al. BRITISH JOURNAL OF OBSTETRICS AND GYNAECOLOGY 85(1):53-62, January, 1978.

References to the observation of the postnatal development of the F1-offspring from mice treated with oestrogen during pregnancy, by H. Heinecke, et al. VERHANDLURGEN DER ANATOMISCHEN GESELLSCHAFT (71 Pt. 1):655-658, 1977.

Reflections on some aspects of encyclical Humanae Vitae to which less consideration has been given, by B. de Margerie. 21(530):6-7, May 25, 1978.

Reform of state criminal law and procedure, by B. J. George, Jr. LAW AND CONTEMPORARY PROBLEMS 41:1, Winter, 1977.

La régulation des naissances en Chine, by M. S. Wolfson.

ECONOMIE ET HUMANISME pp. 34-40, November-December, 1977.

La régulation des naissances en Tunisie, by K. Taamallah. POPULATION 33:194-205, November 1, 1978.

Regulatory policy and abortion clinics: implications for planning, by B. J. Kay, et al. JOURNAL OF HEALTH POLITICS, POLICY AND LAW 3(1):43-53, Spring, 1978.

Relation between sex hormone binding globulin and D-norgestrel levels in plasma, by A. Victor, et al. ACTA ENDOCRINO-LOGICA 86(2):430-436, October, 1977.

The relation of body weight to side effects associated with oral contraceptives, by P. P. Talwar, et al. BRITISH MEDICAL JOURNAL 6077:1637-1638, June 25, 1977.

The relation of income to fertility decisions, by E. Mueller, et al. ECONOMIC DEVELOPMENT AND CULTURAL CHANGE 25:325-347, January, 1977.

Relations between human choriongonadotropic hormone (HCG) titres in urine and degree of pregnancy risk, by J. Pakan, et al. BRATISLAVSKE LEKARSKE LISTY 69(2):190-194, February, 1978.

The relationship between oral contraceptives and adolescent sexual behavior, by L. Garres, et al. JOURNAL OF SEX RESEARCH 12(2):133-146, May, 1976.

Relationship between tooth and bone growth in rats after castration and in under hormonal loading, by E. I. Goncharova. STOMATOLOGIIA 57(4):11-14, July-August, 1978.

The relationship of selected demographic variables to the stability of abortion attitudes in college students, by S. E. Wilcox. DISSERTATION ABSTRACTS INTERNATIONAL 37(3-A):1485-1486, September, 1976.

Release of copper from copper-bearing intrauterine contraceptive

devices, by E. Chantler, et al. BRITISH MEDICAL JOUR-
NAL 6082:288-291, July 30, 1977.

Release of copper ions from an intra-vas copper-wire contracep-
tive device, by K. Srivastava, et al. INDIAN JOURNAL OF
PHYSIOLOGY AND PHARMACOLOGY 21(4):387-389,
October-December, 1977.

Religion and the "right to life": correlates of opposition to abortion, by L. R. Petersen, et al. SOCIOLOGICAL ANALYSIS
37(3):243-254, 1976.

Religious, moral, and sociological issues: some basic distinctions,
by B. Brady. HASTINGS CENTER REPORT 8:13, April,
1978.

Removal from the abdominal cavity of an intrauterine device
by culdoscopy, by E. Acota Bendek. REVISTA COLOM-
BINA DE OBSTETRICIA Y GINECOLOGIA 28(2):85-88,
March-April, 1977.

A renewed focus on contraception: signs of a decline in U.S.
sales of the pill point to the need for more research—but also
to new problems in funding such research, by P. Gupte.
POPULI 5(3):45-47, 1978.

Renin-renin substrate kinetic constants in the plasma of normal
and estrogen-treated humans, by W. J. McDonald, et al.
JOURNAL OF CLINICAL ENDOCRINOLOGY AND
METABOLISM 45(6):1297-1304, December, 1977.

Repeat abortions—why more? by C. Tietze. FAMILY PLAN-
NING PERSPECTIVES 10:286-288, September-October,
1978.

Replacement estrogen therapy for menopausal vasomotor flush-
es. Comparison of quinestrol and conjugated estrogens, by
S. B. Baumgardner, et al. OBSTETRICS AND GYNECOLO-
GY 51(4):445-452, April, 1978.

A report from the March for Life, by D. Francis. OUS SUNDAY
VISITOR 65:2, February 6, 1977.

Report of the committee set up by the executive of the Irish Medical Association to advise on the hazards and side-effects of ovulation suppressants. IRISH MEDICAL JOURNAL 17(2 Suppl):1-10, February 17, 1978.

Report of experiences of more than 200 pregnancy interruptions. One year following the reform of Statute 218 of the Criminal Code, by R. Barthel, et al. MEDIZINISCHE WELT 29(1): 20-24, January 6, 1978.

Report of the working party on IUCDs [editorial]. MEDICAL JOURNAL OF AUSTRALIA 2(7):202, August 13, 1977.

Report on a free sterilization service in Natal, by J. H. McMillan, et al. SOUTH AFRICAN MEDICAL JOURNAL 52(24): 978-930, December 3, 1977.

A report on six months experience of committee for the control of abortion, by B. Halpern, et al. MENTAL HEALTH AND SOCIETY 2(3-6):205-211, 1975.

Reproduction and family planning, by M. Manciaux. JOURNAL DE GYNECOLOGIE, OBSTETRIQUE ET BIOLOGIE DE LA REPRODUCTION 7(2):301-302, March, 1978.

Requests for abortion—a psychiatrist's view, by R. Mester. ISRAEL ANNALS OF PSYCHIATRY 14:294+, September, 1976.

Research in family planning, by A. Kessler, et al. WORLD HEALTH :2-39, August-September, 1978.

Respect for life: Jewish and Roman Catholic reflections on abortion and related issues; Los Angeles Catholic-Jewish Respect Life Committee, September, 1977. CATHOLIC MIND 76: 54-64, February, 1978.

Responding to editorial, bishop speaks for unborn, by W. E. McManus. OUR SUNDAY VISITOR 67:3, May 28, 1978.

Response of the epididymis, ductus deferens & accessory glands of the castrated prepubertal rhesus monkey to exogenous administration of testosterone or 5alpha-dihydrotestosterone, by R. Arora-Dinakar, et al. INDIAN JOURNAL OF EXPERIMENTAL BIOLOGY 15(10):829-834, October, 1977.

Response to the letter by Dr. Hodari (Am. J. Obstet. Gynecol. 130:505, 1978) [letter], by S. Fribourg. AMERICAN JOURNAL OF OBSTETRICS AND GYNECOLOGY 131(6):703, July 15, 1978.

Response to the letter by Drs. Wolf and Rubinstein regarding the safety of prostaglandin F2alpha in abortion [letter], by C. W. Tyler, Jr., et al. AMERICAN JOURNAL OF OBSTETRICS AND GYNECOLOGY 131(2):230-231, May 15, 1978.

Responses to advertising contraceptives, by T. R. L. Black, et al. JOURNAL OF ADVERTISING RESEARCH 17:49-56, October, 1977.

Responses to vasectomy performed at different ages in the rat, by G. A. Kinson, et al. RESEARCH COMMUNICATIONS IN CHEMICAL PATHOLOGY AND PHARMACOLOGY 18(3):561-564, November, 1977.

Restoration of fertility by vasovasostomy, by B. Fallon, et al. JOURNAL OF UROLOGY 119(1):85-86, January, 1978.

Results in maintenance of pregnancy after request of interruption (experience at the women's hospital lucerne), by M. Lanz, et al. THERAPEUTISCHE UMSCHAU 35(6):463-473, June, 1978.

Results of in vitro sperm penetration tests in cervical mucus under takings of the sequential oral contraceptive ovanon and sequilar, by K. Bregulla, et al. ARCHIV FUR GYNAEKOLOGIE 223(3):187-193, October 28, 1977.

Results with a new method for objectivation of rheobase measurements in normal pregnancy and risk of miscarriage or premature birth, by H. Fendel, et al. ZEITSCHRIFT FUR GEBURTSCHILFE UND PERINATOLOGIE 181(6):396-401, December, 1977.

Retailers in social program strategy: the case of family planning, by T. R. L. Black, et al. COLUMBIA JOURNAL OF WORLD BUSINESS 12:33-41, Winter, 1977.

Return of ovarian function after abortion, by P. Lähteenmäki, et al. CLINICAL ENDOCRINOLOGY 8(2):123-132, February, 1978.

Reversal of sterilisation [letter], by A. Cartwright. BRITISH MEDICAL JOURNAL 2(6087):641-642, September 3, 1977.

Reversal of sterilization in the male and female. Report of a workshop, by G. I. Zatuchni, et al. CONTRACEPTION 17(5):435-441, May, 1978.

Reversal of sterilization of the female [letter], by R. A. Thatcher. MEDICAL JOURNAL OF AUSTRALIA 1(2):102, January 28, 1978.

A reversible contraceptive action of some 6-chloro-6-deoxy sugars in the male rat, by W. C. Ford, et al. JOURNAL OF REPRODUCTION AND FERTILITY 52(1):153-157, January, 1978.

Rheumatoid arthritis and oral contraceptives [letter], by A. Linos, et al. LANCET 1(8069):871, April 22, 1978.

Rhythm: ideal and reality, by M. Benecke. AMERICA 137: 240-241, October 15, 1977.

Riboflavin deficiency in women taking oral contraceptive agents, by L. J. Newman, et al. AMERICAN JOURNAL OF CLINICAL NUTRITION 31(2):247-249, February, 1978.

Right of the unborn to eternal life threatened by abortion; guaranteed by baptism, by B. de Margerie. OSSERVATORE ROMANO 49(506):6-8, December 8, 1977.

Right to eternal life guaranteed by baptism; victims of abortion; reprint from Esprit et vie, by B. de Margerie. OSSERVATORE ROMANO 16(473):4, April 21, 1977.

The right to fight for life; pastoral letter from the hierarchy of Schotland, by T. Winning, et al. OSSERVATORE ROMANO 50(507):11, December 15, 1977.

Right to life and self-consciousness, by T. D. Sullivan. AMERICA 139:222-224, October 7, 1978.

The right to life in English law; the rights of the unborn and of the woman faced with an unwanted pregnancy. TABLET 232:549+, June 10, 1978.

Right to life: looking at the past to plan for the future; fifth Right to Life Convention, St. Louis, Missouri, June, 1978, by C. Anthony. OUR SUNDAY VISITOR 67:3-4, July 2, 1978.

The right to life; two messages of the Italian Episcopal Conference. THE POPE SPEAKS 22:260-263, November 3, 1977.

Right to privacy expanded: state infringements upon decisions affecting contraception subjected to strict scrutiny. LOYOLA LAW REVIEW 24:149-163, Winter, 1978.

Right without access? Payment for elective abortions after Maher v. Roe (97 Sup Ct 2376). CAPITAL UNIVERSITY LAW REVIEW 7:483-496, 1978.

Rights of fetus uncertain; moral choices in contemporary society, by D. Callahan. NATIONAL CATHOLIC REPORTER 13:32, February 18, 1977.

The risk of dying from legal abortion in the United States, 1972-1975, by W. Cates, Jr., et al. INTERNATIONAL JOURNAL OF GYNAECOLOGY AND OBSTETRICS 15(2):172-176, 1977.

The risk of post-pill amenorrhea: a preliminary report from the Menstruation and Reproduction History Research Program, by G. S. Berger, et al. INTERNATIONAL JOURNAL OF GYNAECOLOGY AND OBSTETRICS 15(2):125-127, 1977.

Risk of pre-term delivery in patients with previous pre-term delivery and/or abortion, by M. J. Keinse, et al. BRITISH JOURNAL OF OBSTETRICS AND GYNAECOLOGY 85(2):81-85, February, 1978.

Risks in laparoscopic sterilization [letter], by J. Leeton, et al. MEDICAL JOURNAL OF AUSTRALIA 1(7):392, April 8, 1978.

Risks of oral contraception [editorial]. SOUTH AFRICAN MEDICAL JOURNAL 52(21):827, November 12, 1977.

Roe v. Wade and In re Quinlan [(NJ) ett A 2d 647] : individual decision and the scope of privacy's constitutional guarantee. UNIVERSITY OF SAN FRANCISCO LAW REVIEW 12: 111-153, Fall, 1977.

Role of arginine-vasopressin (ADH) in the regulation of uterine motility during menstruation, by E. Cobo, et al. REVISTA COLOMBIANA DE OBSTETRICIA Y GINECOLOGIA 28(3):97-115, May-June, 1977.

The role of birth control in the survival of the human race, by R. Wiechert. ANGEWANDTE CHEMIE 16(8):506-513, August, 1977.

Role of counseling in present-day family planning, by K. Sundström-Feigenberg. LAKARTIDNINGEN 75(7):552-557, February 15, 1978.

Role of estro-progestational compounds in myocardial infarct [letter], by T. Darragon. NOUVELLE PRESSE MEDICALE 6(40):3756, November 26, 1977.

The role of the family, by H. L. Tabak. JOURNAL OF THE AMERICAN HEALTH CARE ASSOCIATION 4(5):92-94+, September, 1978.

The role of the family planning association in Hong Kong's fertility decline, by K. C. Chan. STUDIES IN FAMILY PLANNING 7:284+, October, 1976.

Role of the paediatrician in family planning, by D. B. Sharma. INDIAN JOURNAL OF PEDIATRICS 44(356):253-256, September, 1977.

Role of rural-urban income inequality in fertility reductions: cases of Turkey, Taiwan, and Morocco, by A. K. Bhattacharyya. ECONOMIC DEVELOPMENT AND CULTURAL CHANGE 26:117-138, October, 1977.

Rubber chase; double standard for teenage males, by P. Scales. HUMAN BEHAVIOR 7:41, April, 1978.

A safer method for paracervical block in therapeutic abortions, by R. McKenzie, et al. AMERICAN JOURNAL OF OB-STETRICS AND GYNECOLOGY 130(3):317-320, February, 1978.

The safety of combined abortion-sterilization procedure, by M. C. Cheng, et al. AMERICAN JOURNAL OF OBSTETRICS AND GYNECOLOGY 129(5):548-552, November 1, 1977.

Safety of prostaglandin F2alpha in abortion [letter], by J. A. Wolf, et al. AMERICAN JOURNAL OF OBSTETRICS AND GYNECOLOGY 129(8):928-929, December 15, 1977.

Salbutamol and haemorrhage at spontaneous abortions [letter], by P. S. Vinall, et al. LANCET 2(8052-8053):1355, December 24-31, 1977.

Salpingoclasia by laparoscopy with silastic rings, by A. Alvarado Durán, et al. GINECOLOGIA Y OBSTETRICIA DE MEXICO 43(255):7-13, January, 1978.

Salpingo-oophorectomy at the timeof vaginal hysterectomy, by L. E. Smale, et al. AMERICAN JOURNAL OF OBSTETRICS AND GYNECOLOGY 131(2):122-128, May 15, 1978.

Sample attrition in studies of psychosocial sequelae of abortion: how great a problem? by N. E. Adler. JOURNAL OF APPLIED SOCIAL PSYCHOLOGY 6:240-259, July-Septem-

ber, 1976.

The sanctity of life, by C. E. Koop. JOURNAL OF THE MEDI-
CAL SOCIETY OF NEW JERSEY 75(1):62-67, January,
1978.

Says great advances are being made in study of natural family
planning; Lawrence Kane, executive director of the Human
Life and Natural Family Planning Foundation, by S. Overman. OUR SUNDAY VISITOR 66:1, February 26, 1978.

Scanning electron microscopy studies of the internal surface
of the vas deferens in normal and castrated rats, by G. E.
Orlandini, et al. ARCHIVIO ITALIANO DI ANATOMIA E
DI EMBRIOLOGIA 81(4):391-398, 1976.

Schmid still struggles to place contraceptive ads, by M. Christopher. ADVERTISING AGE 49:2+, May 22, 1978.

Sciatica caused by an intrauterine device after silent uterine perforation. A case report, by R. M. Elmer. JOURNAL OF
BONE AND JOINT SURGERY 60(2):265-266, March,
1978.

Screening of substituted nitrobenzene derivatives as postcoital
antifertility agents, by S. K. Garg. INDIAN JOURNAL OF
MEDICAL RESEARCH 66(6):987-990, December, 1977.

A second baby? . . .If yes, when? by E. M. Whelan. AMERICAN
BABY 40:41-42, August, 1978.

Secondary amenorrhea associated with the use of oral contra-
ceptive steroids, by A. W. Diddle, et al. JOURNAL OF THE
TENNESSEE MEDICAL ASSOCIATION 71(7):495-499,
July, 1978.

The secularization of U. S. Catholic birth control practices, by
C. F. Westoff, et al. FAMILY PLANNING PERSPECTIVES
9(5):203-207, September-October, 1977.

Seeking new methods. PEOPLE 4(4):31-32, 1977.

Select committee on abortion [letter]. LANCET 2(7982):424-425, August 21, 1976.

A selected annotated bibliography on midwives and family planning. Part 2, by M. R. Zabrenko, et al. JOURNAL OF NURSE-MIDWIFERY 22:32-38, Fall, 1977.

Selected legal issues in the world population/food equation [problems of an international approach to population problems; based on conference paper], by V. D. Nanda. DENVER JOURNAL OF INTERNATIONAL LAW AND POLICY 7:77-102, Fall, 1977.

Selected recent court decisions, by J. A. Norris, et al. AMERICAN JOURNAL OF LAW AND MEDICINE 3(2):221-244, 1977.

Selection for fertility under gestagen synchronization of estrus in mice, by L. Schüler. GENETIKA 13(5):840-846, 1977.

Selective abortion, by J. M. McLean. MANCHESTER MEDICAL GAZETTE 56(3):66-67, December, 1977.

Self-checking the intrauterine device, by G. Chamberlain. FERTILITY AND STERILITY 28(10):1121-1122, October, 1977.

Self-emasculation: review of the literature, report of a case and outline of the objectives of management, by S. C. Evins, et al. JOURNAL OF UROLOGY 118(5):775-776, November, 1977.

Septic abortion and IUCDs [letter], by R. A. Sparks, et al. BRITISH MEDICAL JOURNAL 1(6120):1141, April 29, 1978.

Sequential aspects of spontaneous abortion: maternal age, parity, and pregnancy compensation artifact, by A. F. Naylor. SOCIAL BIOLOGY 21:195-204, Summer, 1974; Reply by W. H. James, 24:86-89, Spring, 1977.

Serial intramuscular injections of 15 methyl P.G.F.2alpha for

209

second trimester abortions, by R. M. Gharse, et al. JOURNAL OF POSTGRADUATE MEDICINE 23(2):91-94, April, 1977.

Serious complications of oral contraception in insulin-dependent diabetics, by J. M. Steel, et al. CONTRACEPTION 17(4): 291-295, April, 1978.

Serium protein-bound carbohydrate and seromucoid levels during long-acting progestational contraceptive therapy, by F. M. Saleh. CONTRACEPTION 16(4):399-407, October, 1977.

Serum alkaline phosphatase elevation in female rats treated with ethinyl estradiol, by C. Gopinath, et al. TOXICOLOGY 10(1):91-102, May, 1978.

Serum concentration of bile acids in relation to the normal menstrual cycle the administration or oral contraceptives, and pregnancy, by D. E. Jones, et al. AMERICAN JOURNAL OF OBSTETRICS AND GYNECOLOGY 130(5):593, March 1, 1978.

Serum concentration of prolactin, growth hormone, and alpha-fetoprotein under long-term administration of an oral contraceptive containing cyproterone acetate, by O. Bellmann, et al. GEBURTSHILFE UND FRAUENHEILKUNDE 38(7):549-554, July, 1978.

Serum folic level in abortion, by G. P. Dutta. JOURNAL OF THE INDIAN MEDICAL ASSOCIATION 69(7):149-153, October 1, 1977.

Serum gonadotrophins in rats after castration or heat treatment of the testes, by J. H. Aafjes, et al. ACTA ENDOCRINOLOGICA 88(2):260-273, June, 1978.

Serum high-density-lipoprotein cholesterol in women using oral contraceptives, estrogens and progestins, by D. D. Bradley, et al. NEW ENGLAND JOURNAL OF MEDICINE 299(1): 17-20, July 6, 1978.

Serum hormone levels before and two years after vasectomy, by R. E. Johnsonbaugh, et al. CONTRACEPTION 16(6):563-567, December, 1977.

Serum immunoglobulin titer of IgA, IgG and IgM during short- and long-term administration of contraceptive hormones, by G. Klinger, et al. DEUTSCHE GESUNDHEITSWESEN 33(23):1057-1062, 1978.

Serum LH levels in intact & ovariectomized female rats during puberty, by A. Sehgal, et al. INDIAN JOURNAL OF EXPERIMENTAL BIOLOGY 15(3):229-231, March, 1977.

Serum lipids and lipoproteins during treatment with oral contraceptives containing natural and synthetic oestrogens. A controlled double-blind investigation, by E. Bostofte, et al. ACTA ENDOCRINOLOGICA 87(4):855-864, April, 1978.

Serum naphythylamidase isoenzymes during hormonal treatment. Electrophoretic and quantitative studies, by G. Beckman, et al. INTERNATIONAL JOURNAL OF GYNAECOLOGY AND OBSTETRICS 14(6):550-552, 1976.

Serum vitamin B12, serum and red cell folates, vitamin B12 and folic acid binding proteins in women taking oral contraceptives, by S. Areekul, et al. SOUTHEAST ASIAN JOURNAL OF TROPICAL MEDICINE AND PUBLIC HEALTH 8(4): 480-485, December, 1977.

Service statistics: aid to more effective FP program management. POPULATION REPORTS 17:23, November, 1977.

Sessualità, maternità, educazione demografica, by G. Sica. RIVISTA DI SERVIZIO SOCIALE 17:45-54, November 2, 1977.

Severe pelvis peritoneal infections in wearers of IUD. Severe localized genital infection in wearers of IUD, by J. Dueñas, et al. REVISTA CHILENA DE OBSTETRICA Y GINECOLOGIA 42(1):41-43, 1977.

Sex and socialism: the opposition of the French left to birth control in the nineteenth century, by A. McClaren. JOURNAL OF THE HISTORY OF IDEAS 37:475-492, July-September, 1976.

Sex education and family planning clinical for adolescents. BOLETIN MEDICO DE HOSPITAL INFANTILE DE MEXICO 35(3):583-584, May-June, 1978.

Sex hormone binding globulin: binding capacity and studies on the binding of cyproterone acetate and other steroids, by M. Frölich, et al. CLINICA CHIMICA ACTA 87(2): 239-244, July 15, 1978.

Sex-role attitudes and the anticipated timing of the initial stages of family formation among Catholic, by J. W. Wicks, et al. JOURNAL OF MARRIAGE AND THE FAMILY 40(3): 505, August, 1978.

Sex role development and teenage fertility-related behavior, by G. Cvetkovich, et al. ADOLESCENCE 13(50):231-236, Summer, 1978.

Sexual and contraceptive attitudes and behaviour of single attenders at a Dublin family planning clinic, by E. P. Bowman. JOURNAL OF BIOSOCIAL SCIENCE 9(4):429-445, October, 1977.

Sexual attitudes and contraceptive practices, by D. Byrne. U.S.A. TODAY 107:28-30, July, 1978.

Sexual experience, contraceptive usage, and source of contraception among never-married women: Albany (NY) Health Region, by M. Gesche, et al. ADVANCES IN PLANNED PARENTHOOD 12(3):136-139, 1978.

Sexual privacy: access of a minor to contraceptives, abortion, and sterilization without parental consent. UNIVERSITY OF RICHMOND LAW REVIEW 12:221-244, Fall, 1977.

Shame is the best contraceptive. ECONOMIST 269:74, November 25, 1978.

Shifting of the brain stem physiological impedance after ovariectomy and oestradiol implantation in rabbits, by W. Oliskiewicz, et al. ACTA PHYSIOLOGICA POLONICA 28(4): 285-296, July-August, 1977.

Short and long term effects of various contraceptives on ovaries, by A. Sen Gupta, et al. JOURNAL OF OBSTETRICS AND GYNAECOLOGY OF INDIA 27(2):183-187, April, 1977.

Short-term and prolonged treatment with oral contraceptives and liver function, by A. Kulcsár, et al. ARZNEIMITTELFORSCHUNG 27(9):1694-1697, 1977.

Short-term benefits and costs of U.S. family planning programs 1970-1975, by F. Jaffe. FAMILY PLANNING PERSPECTIVES 1(2): , April-May, 1977.

Should one systematically do a liver puncture biopsy during a laparotomy when the patient takes oral contraceptives? [letter], by G. Benhamou, et al. NOUVELLE PRESSE MEDICALE 7(19):1652, May 13, 1978.

Should pro-life people tone down their language? by M. Burson. OUR SUNDAY VISITOR 65:1, February 13, 1977.

Shunning innovation. CHEMICAL WEEK 122:15, May 14, 1978.

Sialic acid & sialidase activity in rat testis & epididymis in relation to age & action of different antifertility agents, by S. Nag, et al. INDIAN JOURNAL OF EXPERIMENTAL BIOLOGY 15(7):510-512, July, 1977.

Sialic acid levels and scanning electronmicroscopy of cervical mucus, by B. Daunter. CONTRACEPTION 17(1):27-34, January, 1978.

Side effects of intrauterine devices, by E. B. Connell. INTERNATIONAL JOURNAL OF GYNAECOLOGY AND OBSTETRICS 15(2):153-156, 1977.

The Silber vasovasostomy: a method of learning the microsurgical technique [letter], by A. A. Carpenter. JOURNAL OF UROLOGY 120(3):388, September, 1978.

Silicone rubber band for laparoscopic tubal sterilization, by A. H. Ansari, et al. FERTILITY AND STERILITY 28(12): 1306-1309, December, 1977.

A simple device for double Falope-Ring application, by T. Kumarasamy. OBSTETRICS AND GYNECOLOGY 52(1): 109-110, July, 1978.

A simple stabilizing clamp for microscopic vasovasostomy, by D. J. Albert, et al. JOURNAL OF UROLOGY 120(1):77, July, 1978.

Simplified classification of spontaneous abortions, by D. I. Rushton. JOURNAL OF MEDICAL GENETICS 15(1):1-9, February, 1978.

Simplified dokumentation and evaluation in abortion patients using data-based medical records, by F. Rössel, et al. ZEN-TRALBLATT FUER GYNAEKOLOGIE 99(18):1089-1096, 1977.

Simultaneous determination using gas chromatography of mestranol and norethisterone in estrogen-progestins combination for oral use, by G. Moretti, et al. BOLLETINO CHIMICO FARMACEUTICO 116(8):463-472, August, 1977.

The Singapore National Family Planning and Population Programme 1966-1975 with particular reference to patterns of response, by F. K. Wan, et al. NURSING JOURNAL OF SINGAPORE 17(2):80-85, November, 1977.

The sinister side of sterilization [editorial]. SOUTH AFRICAN MEDICAL JOURNAL 53(2):38-39, January 14, 1978.

Small-bowel ischaemia and the contraceptive pill [editorial]. BRITISH MEDICAL JOURNAL 1(6104):4, January 7, 1978.

Small dose anti-Rh therapy after first trimester abortion, by L.

Keith, et al. INTERNATIONAL JOURNAL OF GYNAE-
COLOGY AND OBSTETRICS 15(3):235-237, 1977.

Smoking and abortion [letter], by H. E. McKean. NEW ENG-
LAND JOURNAL OF MEDICINE 298(2):113-114, January
12, 1978.

Social and medical trends in female sterilization in Aberdeen,
1951-72, by B. J. Nottage, et al. JOURNAL OF BIOSOCIAL
SCIENCE 9(4):487-500, October, 1977.

Social change and the family: Los Angeles, California, 1850-
1870, by B. Laslett. AMERICAN SOCIOLOGICAL RE-
VIEW 42:268-269, April, 1977.

Social characteristics of diaphragm users in a family planning
clinic, by J. McEwan. JOURNAL OF BIOSOCIAL SCI-
ENCE 10(2):159-167, April, 1978.

Social characteristics of patients attenting a private early pregnancy termination service in Auckland, by R. B. Hunton, et
al. NEW ZEALAND MEDICAL JOURNAL 85(584):220-
222, March 23, 1977.

Social evaluations of a woman with a problem pregnancy: effects of marital status, birth or abortion solution, and sex of
respondents, by D. J. Pope, et al. PSYCHOLOGICAL RE-
PORTS 42:39-47, February, 1978.

Social justice and abortion, by F. X. Meehan. AMERICA 138:
478-481, June 17, 1978.

Social justice must come first, Father Hehir says; bridge the gap
between the Catholic Church's opposition to abortion and
birth control. OUR SUNDAY VISITOR 66:3, March 12,
1978.

Social work attitudes toward birth control for teenagers, by P.
A. Reichelt, et al. COMMUNITY MENTAL HEALTH
JOURNAL 13:352-359, Winter, 1977.

Sociocultural factors affecting acceptance of family planning

215

services by Navajo women, by C. W. Slemenda. HUMAN ORGANIZATION 37:190-194, Summer, 1978.

Socioeconomical characteristics and continuity of patients accepted at the Clinic of Family Planning of the Yucatan University, by D. T. Canto de Cetina, et al. SPM: SALUD PUBLICA DE MEXICO 19(5):685-689, September-October, 1977.

Some contemporary conceptions about the etiology of early abortion, by P. Drác. CESKOSLOVENSKA GYNEKOLOGIE 43(4):286-289, May, 1978.

Some effects of medroxyprogesterone acetate on intermediary metabolism in rat liver, by C. H. Dahm, Jr., et al. LIFE SCIENCES 22(2):165-169, January, 1978.

Some factors related to contraceptive behavior among Wind River Shoshone and Arapahoe females, by T. L. Haynes. HUMAN ORGANIZATION 36:72-75, September, 1977.

Some observations on the use of oral contraception, by M. Hugo. JOURNAL OF NURSE-MIDWIFERY 22(4):10-11, Winter, 1978.

Some reflections on birth control, by R. Westley. LISTENING 12:43-61, Spring, 1977.

Some speculations on the future of marriage and fertility, by C. F. Westoff. FAMILY PLANNING PERSPECTIVES 10(2): 79-83, March-April, 1978.

Sounding Board. Abortions in America: the effects of restrictive funding, by L. R. Berger. NEW ENGLAND JOURNAL OF MEDICINE 298(26):1474-1477, June 29, 1978.

Spacing of children and changing patterns of childbearing, by C. M. Young. JOURNAL OF BIOSOCIAL SCIENCE 9: 201-226, April, 1977.

Special report: for women who wonder about birth control; including doctors' responses to questionnaire, by E. R.

Dobell. REDBOOK 151:64+, August, 1978.

Specific protein synthesis in isolated epithelium of guinea-pig seminal vesicle. Effects of castration and androgen replacement, by C. M. Veneziale, et al. BIOCHEMICAL JOURNAL 166(2):167-173, August 15, 1977.

Sperm agglutinins in seminal plasma and serum after vasectomy: correlation between immunological and clinical findings, by L. Linnet, et al. CLINICAL AND EXPERIMENTAL IMMUNOLOGY 30(3):413-420, December, 1977.

Sperm autoantibodies as a consequence of vasectomy. I. Within 1 year post-operation, by H. W. Hellema, et al. CLINICAL AND EXPERIMENTAL IMMUNOLOGY 31(1):18-29, January, 1978.

Sperm granuloma and reversibility of vasectomy, by S. J. Silber. LANCET 2(8038):588-589, September 17, 1977.

Sperm inhibitors as contraceptives; acrosin inhibitor. SCIENCE NEWS 113:150, March 11, 1978.

Spinal anesthesia for laparoscopic tubal sterilization, by D. Caceres, et al. AMERICAN JOURNAL OF OBSTETRICS AND GYNECOLOGY 131(2):219-220, May 15, 1978.

Splinted vasovasostomy. Comparison of polyglycolic acid and polypropylene sutures, by L. E. Lykins, et al. UROLOGY 11(3):260-261, March, 1978.

Spontaneous abortion and aging of human ova and spermatozoa; also Perinatology begins before conception [editorial], by R. Guerrero, et al. NEW ENGLAND JOURNAL OF MEDICINE 293:473-474+, September 18, 1975.

Spontaneous abortion and fetal abnormality in subsequent pregnancy [letter], by A. J. Gardiner, et al. BRITISH MEDICAL JOURNAL 2(6131):200, July 15, 1978.

Spontaneous abortion and the use of sugar substitutes (saccharin), by J. Kline, et al. AMERICAN JOURNAL OF OB-

STETRICS AND GYNECOLOGY 130(6):708-711, March 15, 1978.

Spontaneous abortion in perspective. A 7-year study, by S. W. Sandler. SOUTH AFRICAN MEDICAL JOURNAL 42(28): 1115-1118, December 31, 1977.

Spontaneous abortion, sex ratio and facial cleft malformations, by J. C. Bear. CLINICAL GENETICS 13(1):1-7, January, 1978.

Spontaneous abortions among women in hospital laboratory [letter], by M. Strandberg, et al. LANCET 1(8060):384-385, February 18, 1978.

Spontaneous extrusion of Hulka-Clemens spring-loaded clips after vaginal hysterectomy: two case reports, by G. H. Barker, et al. BRITISH JOURNAL OF OBSTETRICS AND GYNAECOLOGY 84(12):954-955, December, 1977.

Spontaneous platelet aggregation associated with administration of sex hormones in men and women, by H. Rieger, et al. DEUTSCHE MEDIZINISCHE WOCHENSCHRIFT 102(35):1248-1250, September 2, 1977.

Spontaneous recanalization following vasectomy, by W. B. Schill, et al. MUENCHENER MEDIZINISCHE WOCHEN-SCHRIFT 119(40):1299-1300, October 7, 1977.

Spontaneous recanalization of the vas deferens, by R. P. Jina, et al. INTERNATIONAL SURGERY 62(10):557-558, October, 1977.

Spontaneously regressive ulcerative colitis: the result of contraceptive agents? [letter], by L. Simon, et al. GASTRO-ENTEROLOGIE CLINIQUE ET BIOLOGIQUE 2(4):442-443, April, 1978.

Spouse's right to marital dissolution predicated on the partner's contraceptive surgery. NEW YORK LAW SCHOOL LAW REVIEW 23:99-117, 1977.

Stacy's day at the abortion clinic: Eastern Women's Center clinic, New York City, by B. Dolan. TIME 111:26, April 10, 1978.

Standardized mortality rates associated with legal abortion: United States, 1972-1975, by W. Cates, Jr., et al. FAMILY PLANNING PERSPECTIVES 10:109-112, March-April, 1978.

Starting on the pill [letter], by E. H. Gregson. BRITISH MEDICAL JOURNAL 2(6092):959, October 8, 1977.

State funding of elective abortion: the Supreme Court defers to the legislature. UNIVERSITY OF CINCINNATI LAW REVIEW 46:1003-1009, 1978.

State of the blood coagulation and anticoagulation system in women taking oral contraceptives, by L. V. Terskaia, et al. AKUSHERSTVO I GINEKOLOGIIA (12):41-43, December, 1977.

State of various indicators of the blood coagulation system before and during induced abortion and anesthesia with novocaine and dicain solutions, by A. I. Zherzhov. VOPROSY OKHRANY MATERINSTVA I DETSTVA 23(4):83-84, April, 1978.

State women's meetings. New York, by N. Throop; Massachusetts, by M. Badger; It was a tempest in a uterus [New York women's meeting], by S. Lieberman; The right wing sends in fresh troops [Mormon Church], by B. West. OFF OUR BACKS 7:4-5, August 6-19, 1977.

Statement from the Irish Bishops' Confernece on proposed legislation dealing with family planning and contraception. FURROW 29:525-527, August, 1978.

Statement on the occasion of the tenth anniversary of Humanae Vitae; by Catholic Bishops' Conference of India, 17 January 1978. OSSERVATORE ROMANO 11(520):11, March 16, 1978.

Statements on abortion, by T. Cooke, et al. OSSERVATORE ROMANO 11(520):10, March 16, 1978.

Status of male contraception, by J. E. Davis. OBSTETRICS AND GYNECOLOGY ANNUAL 6:355-369, 1977.

Sterile justice in South Carolina? censure of E. Primus for informing sterilized black women of legal rights, by M. Jordan. BLACK ENTERPRISE 8:11-12, March, 1978.

Sterilisation: the Aberdeen experience, and some broader implications, by S. Teper. JOURNAL OF MEDICAL ETHICS 4(1):18-24, March, 1978.

Sterilisation and its reversal [letter], by J. Guillebad. BRITISH MEDICAL JOURNAL 2(6103):1672, December 24-31, 1977.

Sterilisation failure, by G. J. Hughes. BRITISH MEDICAL JOURNAL 2(6098):1337-1339, November 19, 1977.

Sterilisation of a handicapped child. LAW QUARTERLY REVIEW 92:164-165, April, 1976.

Sterilization. FORUM 2(2):6-13, 1978.

—. GLAMOUR 76:44, January, 1978.

Sterilization and the mentally retarded: HEW's new regulations. Part 2, by P. Urbanus. JOURNAL OF NURSE-MIDWIFERY 23:16, Spring-Summer, 1978.

Sterilization and menstrual disturbances [letter], by L. M. Rubinstein, et al. JAMA; JOURNAL OF THE AMERICAN MEDICAL ASSOCIATION 238(18):1913, October 31, 1977.

Sterilization. April 1-December 31, 1976, gy S. C. Christensen, et al. UGESKRIFT FOR LAEGER 140(16):939, April 17, 1978.

Sterilization by hysterectomy, by J. S. Scott IPPF MEDICAL

BULLETIN 12(1):1-2, February, 1978.

Sterilization by laparoscopy. Use of Yoon's ring, by H. Leyton, et al. REVISTA CHILENA DE OBSTETRICIA Y GINE-COLOGIA 42(3):187-191, 1977.

Sterilization by partial resection of the oviducts via bipolar electrocoagulation, by H. A. Hirsch, et al. GEBURTSHILFE UND FRAUENHEILKUNDE 37(10):869-872, October, 1977.

Sterilization can be moral, by T. Shannon. U. S. CATHOLIC 43:11-12, May, 1978.

Sterilization: Catholic teaching and Catholic practice, by W. May. HOMILETIC AND PASTORAL REVIEW 77:9-22, August-September, 1977; Reply by A. Zimmerman, 78:56-63, June, 1978.

The sterilization controversy examines pivotal issues, by K. O'Rourke. HOSPITAL PROGRESS 58:80-81, August, 1977.

Sterilization: duties of the physician, by Institut für Rechts-medizin der Ludwig-Maximillans-Universität Müchen. GE-BURTSHILFE UND FRAUENHEILKUNDE 38(8):591-592, August, 1978.

Sterilization failures in Singapore: an examination of ligation techniques and failure rates, by M. C. E. Cheng, et al. STUD-IES IN FAMILY PLANNING 8:109, April, 1977.

Sterilization—his or hers, by P. Paterson. MEDICAL JOURNAL OF AUSTRALIA 2(17):571-572, October 22, 1977.

Sterilization: hospitals dodge ban? by B. Kenkelen. NATIONAL CATHOLIC REPORTER 13:1+, October 14, 1977.

Sterilization, how the victims were trapped, by B. Levin. TIMES (London) November 8, 1978, p. 18.

Sterilization—the husband usually decides; research by Margaret

221

Pruitt Clark and others, by J. Gaylin. PSYCHOLOGY TODAY 11:36+, February, 1978.

Sterilization is world's leading contraceptive method. SOCIETY 15:7, May, 1978.

Sterilization: now it's simpler, safer. Reversible? Maybe, by M. L. Schildkraut. GOOD HOUSEKEEPING 186:163-164, January, 1978.

Sterilization of female mentally retarded, by L. Fortier. UNION MEDICALE DU CANADA 107(5):505-506, May, 1978.

Sterilization of the mentally retarded minor. Part 1, by C. Cooper. JOURNAL OF NURSE-MIDWIFERY 23:14-15, Spring-Summer, 1978.

Sterilization of the retarded: in whose interest? by W. Gaylin. HASTINGS CENTER REPORT 8(3):28, June, 1978.

Sterilization of women via suprapublic minilaparotomy, by D. Flodgaard. UGESHRIFT FOR LAEGER 140(13):718-719, March 27, 1978.

Sterilization; pastoral letter. OSSERVATORE ROMANO 7(464):11, February 17, 1977.

Sterilization patterns in a Northern Canadian ppopulation, by J. Cohen, et al. CANADIAN JOURNAL OF PUBLIC HEALTH 69(3):222-224, May-June, 1978.

Sterilization policy for Catholic hospitals; statement by the U. S. Catholic Conference Administrative Board. ORIGINS 7:399-400, December 8, 1977.

Sterilization ruling on legal, not moral, grounds, by T. Barbarie. OUR SUNDAY VISITOR 66:3, August 28, 1977.

Sterilization—the vaginal route revisited, by N. C. Gage. SOUTH AFRICAN MEDICAL JOURNAL 53(16):631-633, April 22, 1978.

Sterilizations 1975-1976, by S. Collatz Christensen, et al. UGE-SHRIFT FOR LAEGER 139(32):1914-1915, August 8, 1977.

Sterilizing the poor, by S. M. Rothman. SOCIETY 14:36-40, January-February, 1977.

Sterilizing the poor and incompetent, by P. Donovan. HASTINGS CENTER REPORT 6:7-17, October, 1976.

Steroid antifertility agents. Ionic complexes of basic derivatives for prolonged action, by A. P. Gray, et al. JOURNAL OF MEDICINAL CHEMISTRY 21(7):712-715, July, 1978.

Steroid contraception and the risk of neoplasia. WHO TECHNICAL REPORT SERIES (619):1-54, 1978.

Steroid hydroxylase induction in cultured human lymphocytes: effects of the menstrual cycle, by W. L. Mason, et al. STEROIDS 31(1):1-7, January, 1978.

A stochastic model for IUCD clinical trials, by H. D. Gupta. INDIAN JOURNAL OF PUBLIC HEALTH 21(2):95-104, April-June, 1977.

Stopping oral contraceptives, by J. Cohen. CONCOURS MEDICAL 100(5):779-780, February 4, 1978.

Storage of proteins in the rough endoplasmic reticulum of human hepatocytes in a patient with normal blood proteins, on oral contraceptives, by A. Porte, et al. VIRCHOWS ARCHIV. ABT. A. PATHOLOGISCHE ANATOMIE-PATHOLOGY 375(3):241-248, September 28, 1977.

Story of the pill, by K. S. Davis. AMERICAN HERITAGE 29:80-91, August, 1978.

Strategy in drug research. Synthesis and study of the progestational and ovulation inhibitory activity of a series of 11beta-substituted-17alpha-ethynyl-4-estren-17beta-ols, by A. J. Broek, et al. STEROIDS 30(4):481-510, October, 1977.

Stromal cell interactions in the rat uterus as influenced by oestrogen and in intrauterine device, by C. M. Wischik, et al. THERIOGENEOLOGY 8(4):144, October, 1977.

Structural modifications in contraceptive steroids altering their metabolism and toxicity, by H. M. Bolt. ARCHIV FUER TOXIKOLOGIE 39(1-2):13-19, December 30, 1977.

Struktur und Funktion des religiösen Aktes. STIMMEN DER ZEIT 195:159-168, March, 1977.

Student volunteers as birth control educators, by R. S. Sanders, et al. JOURNAL OF COLLEGE STUDENT PERSONNEL 19:216-220, May, 1978.

Studies of carbohydrate and lipid metabolism in women using the progesterone-T intrauterine device for six months: blood glucose, insulin, cholesterol, and triglyceride levels, by W. N. Spellacy, et al. FERTILITY AND STERILITY 29(5): 505-508, May, 1978.

Studies on dopamine turnover in ovariectomized or hypophysectomized female rats. Effects of 17 beta-estradiol benzoate, ethynodioldiacetate and ovine prolactin, by F. A. Wiesel, et al. BRAIN RESEARCH 148(2):399-411, June 16, 1978.

Study calls D & E best midtrimester abortion. MEDICAL WORLD NEWS 18:71, January 10, 1977.

Study confirms values of ovulation method, by L. Dolack, Sr. HOSPITAL PROGRESS 69:64-66+, August, 1978.

Study of the behavior of hepatic function and blood coagulation in the course of oral administration of an estroprogestogen in low dosage, by A. R. Pastore, et al. RIVISTA ITALIANA DI GINECOLOGIA 57(3):171-185, May-June, 1976.

Study of folic acid blood levels during estro-progestagen treatment, by R. Karlin, et al. JOURNAL DE GYNECOLOGIE OBSTETRIQUE ET BIOLOGIE DE LA REPRODUCTION 6(4):489-495, June, 1977.

Study of the knowledge, attitude and practice among teenagers in Hawaii related to reproduction, family planning and sexuality, by S. Hancock, et al. HAWAII MEDICAL JOURNAL 37(3):73-75, March, 1978.

A study of new contraceptive acceptors of pills and IUDs at three Bangkok clinics, by R. A. Grossman, et al. CONTRACEPTION 16(1):67-77, July, 1977.

Study of physical & sexual growth of preadolescent & adolescent children of rural Hyderabad and their knowledge attitudes towards human reproduction and family planning, by N. Kishore, et al. INDIAN PEDIATRICS 15(2):147-154, February, 1978.

A study of some socio-demographic characteristics of human sterilization cases in the area coveread by Rural Health Training Centre, Harsola, Indore, by M. C. Mittal, et al. INDIAN JOURNAL OF PUBLIC HEALTH 21(2):65-70, April-June, 1977.

Study of "spontaneous" abortion in Thailand, by S. Koetsawang, et al. INTERNATIONAL JOURNAL OF GYNAECOLOGY AND OBSTETRICS 15(4):361-368, 1978.

Study of the uterine environment in association with intrauterine contraceptive devices, by A. H. Abdel Gawad, et al. CONTRACEPTIVE 16(5):469-485, November, 1977.

A study on the contraceptive effectiveness of a newly designed IUD "FD-1" in Japan, by T. Wagatsuma, et al. CONTRACEPTION 17(1):41-49, January, 1978.

Subsequent pelvic surgery in patients who have undergone tubal sterilization, by D. H. Belsky. JOURNAL OF THE AMERICAN OSTEOPATHIC ASSOCIATION 77(1):36-41, September, 1977.

Successful use of the diaphragm and jelly by a young population: report of a clinical study, by M. E. Lane, et al. FAMILY PLANNING PERSPECTIVES 8:81-85, April, 1976.

Successive spontaneous abortions including one with whole-arm translocation between chromosomes 2, by K. Ohama, et al. HUMAN GENETICS 40(2):221-225, January 19, 1978.

Sudden death from coronary disease in younger women, by H. Althoff. MEDIZINISHCE KLINIK 72(44):1871-1879, November 4, 1977.

Suppression of serum follicle stimulating hormone in intact and acutely ovariecomized rats by porcine follicular fluid, by M. L. Marder, et al. ENDOCRINOLOGY 101(5):1939-1942, November, 1977.

Suppressions of serum testosterone concentrations in men by an oral contraceptive preparation, by J. M. Kjeld, et al. BRITISH MEDICAL JOURNAL 2(6097):1261, November 12, 1977.

The Supreme Court and social change: the case of abortion, by K. A. Kemp, et al. WESTERN POLITICAL QUARTERLY 31(1):19-31, March, 1978.

Supreme Court hearing abortion-related cases, decision to come in the spring, by T. Barbarie. OUR SUNDAY VISITOR 65:2, January 30, 1977.

Supreme Court on minors and contraception; June 9, 1977. ORIGINS 7:65+, June 23, 1977.

Supreme Court report: fourteenth amendment does not require state aid for abortions, by R. L. Young. AMERICAN BAR ASSOCIATION JOURNAL 63:1261-1262, September, 1977.

Supreme Court to review cases on fetal viability, by J. Castelli. HOSPITAL PROGRESS 59(4):18, April, 1978.

The Supreme Court's abortion rulings and social change, by D. W. Brady, et al. SOCIAL SCIENCE QUARTERLY 57:535-546, December, 1976.

Surgeon failed to disclose alternatives to sterilization, by W. A. Regan. HOSPITAL PROGRESS 59(7):98, July, 1978.

Surveillance of spontaneous abortions. Power in environmental monitoring, by J. Kline, et al. AMERICAN JOURNAL OF EPIDEMIOLOGY 106(5):345-350, November, 1977.

A survey of attitude and practice toward family planning of family planning workers in Taiwan, by Y. L. Dah. JOURNAL OF NURSING 24(2):8-16, April, 1977.

A survey of the effects of oral contraceptive patient information, by L. A. Morris, et al. JAMA; JOURNAL OF THE AMERICAN MEDICAL ASSOCIATION 238(23):2504-2508, December 5, 1977.

A survey of fertility and family planning in Atlanta, Georgia, by W. S. Tillack, et al. PUBLIC HEALTH REPORTS 92(5):444-452, September-October, 1977.

Syndenham's chorea: case report of a diagnostic dilemma, by M. P. Weissberg, et al. AMERICAN JOURNAL OF PSYCHOLOGY 135:607-609, May, 1978.

Symposia focus on better birth control. CHEMICAL AND ENGINEERING NEWS 56:6, May 22, 1978.

A symposium—on the report and recommendations of the National Commission for the protection of human subjects of biomedical and behaviorial research; research on the fetus, by R. A. Destro. VILLANOVA LAW REVIEW 22(2):297-299, 1976-1977.

Synergistic effects of ethynylestradiol and noresthisterone on the formation and lengthening of uterine lace in immature rabbits, by Y. Chambon, et al. COMPTES RENDUS DES SEANCES DE LA SOCIETE DE BIOLOGIE ET DE SES FILIALES 171(3):631-635, 1977.

Synergistic effects of prolactin and testosterone in the restoration of rat prostatic epithelium following castration, by S. A. Thompson, et al. ANATOMICAL RECORD 191(1):31-

45, May, 1978.

Synthesis and biological evaluation of 2- and 4-hydroxymestranol, by R. M. Kanojia. STEROIDS 30(3):343-348, September, 1977.

Synthesis of 17beta-D-glucopyranosiduronic acid of 17alpha-ethynylestradiol, by E. D. Helton, et al. JOURNAL OF STEROID BIOCHEMISTRY 9(3):237-238, March, 1978.

Taking up the role of prophets; statement on the fifth anniversary of the U. S. Supreme Court's January 22, 1973, abortion rulings, by J. Quinn. ORIGINS 7:524-526, February 2, 1978.

Target gertility, contraception, and aggregate rates: toward a formal synthesis, by R. D. Lee. DEMOGRAPHY 14(4): 455-479, November, 1977.

Tay-Sachs and related storage disease: family planning, by G. Schneiderman, et al. MENTAL RETARDATION 16:13-15, February, 1978.

A technique of anaesthesia for medical termination of pregnancy, by N. Bose. JOURNAL OF TH EINDIAN MEDICAL ASSOCIATION 69(3):56-58, August 1, 1977.

Techniques of second-trimester abortions, by C. Y. Kawada. CLINICAL OBSTETRICS AND GYNECOLOGY 20(4): 833-847, December, 1977.

Teenage pregnancies: looking ahead to 1984, by C. Tietze. FAMILY PLANNING PERSPECTIVES 10:205-207, July-August, 1978.

Teenage pregnancy: epidemic or statisticl hoax? by J. Kasun. U. S. A. TODAY 107:31-33; Reply by R. Lincoln, pp. 34-37, July, 1978.

Teenage pregnancy: the need for multiple casework services, by S. P. Schnike. SOCIAL CASEWORK 59(7):406-410, July, 1978.

Teenage pregnancy: a second look, by M. Schwartz. OUR SUN-
DAY VISITOR 67:3, September 3, 1978.

Teenage sex and birth control, by E. J. Lieberman. JAMA;
JOURNAL OF THE AMERICAN MEDICAL ASSOCIATION
240(3):275-276, July 21, 1978.

Teenage sterilization in the United States: 1930-1970, by E. A.
Brann, et al. ADVANCES IN PLANNED PARENTHOOD
13(1):24-29, 1978.

Teenagers at risk, by P. Crabbe. NURSING TIMES 73(32):
1229, August 11, 1977.

Teenagers: fertility control behavior and attitudes before and
after abortion, childbearing or negative pregnancy test, by
J. R. Evans. FAMILY PLANNING PERSPECTIVES 8(4):
192-200, July-August, 1976.

Teens have babies, by M. I. Abbott. PEDIATRIC NURSING
4(3):23-26, May-June, 1978.

Ten good reasons not to have children, by E. Peck. HARPER'S
BAZAAR 3203:181, October, 1978.

Ten years later; reflections on the anniversary of Humanae Vitae,
by C. Curran. COMMONWEAL 105:425-430, July 7, 1978.

Terathanasia, by J. Warkany. TERATOLOGY 17(2):187-192,
April, 1978.

Termination of early gestation with a vaginal polysiloxane
device impregnanted with (15S)-15 methyl prostaglandin
F2alpha methylester, by P. F. Brenner, et al. PROSTA-
GLANDINS 14(4):771-777, October, 1977.

Termination of early pregnancy by ONO-802 (16,16-dimethyl-
trans-delta2-PGE1 methyl ester), by S. Takagi, et al. PRO-
STAGLANDINS 14(4):791-798, October, 1977.

Termination of early pregnancy (menstrual induction) with 16-
phenoxy-omega-tetranor PGE2 methylsulfonylamide, by

S. M. Karim, et al. CONTRACEPTION 16(4):377-381, October, 1977.

Termination of mid-term spontaneous and missed abortions by extra-amniotic injection of a single prostaglandin F2alpha dose, by L. Kerekes, et al. THERAPIA HUNGARICA 25(3):102-104, 1977.

Termination of pregnancy in Gisborne, by W. Savage. NURSING FORUM 6(1):5-8, March, 1978.

Territorial aggression of the rat to males castrated at various ages, by K. J. Flannelly, et al. PHYSIOLOGY AND BE-HAVIOR 20(6):785-789, June, 1978.

Testicular function of gerbil (Meriones hurrianae Jerdon) implanted with a copper wire device in vas deferens, by V. P. Dixit, et al. INDIAN JOURNAL OF EXPERIMENTAL BIOLOGY 15(8):653-655, August, 1977.

Testing synergism between ethinyl estradiol and norethisterone on the histamine-induced deciduoma and vaginal mucification of castrated rats, by Y. Chambon, et al. COMPTES RENDUS DES SEANCES DE LA SOCIETE DE BIOLOGIE ET DE SES FILIALES 171(1):192-196, 1977.

Therapeutic abortion in an out-patient clinic. A prospective investigation of complications and patient acceptability, by B. R. Møller, et al. ACTA OBSTETRICIA ET GYNE-COLOGICA SCANDINAVICA 57(1):41-44, 1978.

Therapeutic abortion. The 1975 report from Ulleval Hospital, by F. Jerve, et al. ACTA OBSTETRICIA ET GYNECOLO-GICA SCANDINAVICA 57(3):237-240, 1978.

Therapeutic abortions in the second trimester of pregnancy with prostaglandine gel, by S. Heinzl. GEBURTSHILFE UND FRAUENHEILKUNDE 38(3):220-226, March, 1978.

Therapeutic induction of abortion in the 1st and 2nd trimesters with intramuscular 15-methyl-prostagland F2 alpha, by G. Göretzlehner, et al. ZENTRALBLATT FUER GYNAE-

KOLOGIE 99(22):1356-1360, 1977.

Therapeutic significance of the sequential estrogen-gestagen preparation "Ovara" in gynecologic endocrinology, by R. Prudan, et al. MEDICINSKI PREGLED 30(11-12):585-593, 1977.

Therapy of androgenetic sympatomatology with cyproterone acetate and ethinyl estradiol, by A. E. Schindler, et al. ARCHIV FUR GYNAEKOLOGIE 225(2):103-107, May 12, 1978.

Therapy of androgenization symptoms: double blind study of an antiandrogen preparation (SH B 209 AB) against neogynon, by U. Lachnit-Fixson, et al. MEDIZINISCHE KLINIK 72(45):1922-1926, November 11, 1977.

Therapy of Marchiafava-Micheli's disease: remission under therapy with Lynestrenol, by A. Ruiz-Torres, et al. MEDIZINISCHE KLINIK 73(5):162-167, February 3, 1978.

They made the choice. NEWSWEEK 91:40-41, June 5, 1978.

Thinking about abortion; reasons Christians today give for adopting new beliefs about abortion, by G. Kuykendall. CROSS CURRENTS 27:403-416, Winter, 1978.

Threatened abortion: our point of view, by B. Brigljevic. THERAPEUTISCHE UMSCHAU 35(6):405-409, June, 1978.

3-month therapy cycles for oral contraception? [letter], by C. Lauritzen. DEUTCHE MEDIZINISCHE WOCHENSCHRIFT 102(51):1891, December 23, 1977.

Three-month wonder. ECONOMIST 267:66, April 22, 1978.

Three women with 45,X/46,XX mosaic and multiple spontaneous abortions, by D. Ioan, et al. ENDOCRINOLOGIE 16(2):139-141, April-June, 1978.

Three-year prospective study of carbohydrate metabolism in

231

women using Ovulen, by W. N. Spellacey, et al. SOUTHERN MEDICAL JOURNAL 70(10):1188-1190, October, 1977.

The time course change after castration in short-loop negative feedback control of LH by HCG in women, by A. Miyake, et al. ACTA ENDOCRINOLOGICA 88(1):1-6, May, 1978.

Time horizon effects on product evaluation strategies, by P. Wright, et al. JOURNAL OF MARKETING RESEARCH 14:429-443, November, 1977.

To be or not to be pregnant. MADEMOISELLE 84:86, April, 1978.

To sterilize or not to sterilize, by D. J. Cusine. MEDICINE, SCIENCE AND THE LAW 18(2):120-123, April, 1978.

To which women should antiandrogen-effective ovulation inhibitors be prescribed? (hirsutism, seborrhea, alopecia), by J. R. Strecker. HIPPOKRATES 49(2):200-201, May, 1978.

Tobacco may cause placental separation. MEDICAL WORLD NEWS 18:33-34, May 2, 1977.

Topical uterine anesthesia: a preliminary report, by H. M. Hasson. INTERNATIONAL JOURNAL OF GYNAECOLOGY AND OBSTETRICS 15(3):238-240, 1977.

Torsion of a segment of fallopian tube: a case report of a long-term complication of sterilization by laparoscopic coagulation, by R. J. Stock. JOURNAL OF REPRODUCTIVE MEDICINE 19(4):241-242, October, 1977.

Toxic agents resulting from the oxidative metabolism of steroid hormones and drugs, by E. C. Horning, et al. JOURNAL OF TOXICOLOGY AND ENVIRONMENTAL HEALTH 4(2-3):341-361, March-May, 1978.

Toxic hepatoses due to Gravistat, by C. Metzner, et al. ZEITSCHRIFT FUR DIE GESAMTE HYGIENE UND IHRE GRENZGEBIETE 32(16):407-408, August 15, 1977.

The toxicity of 1-amino-3-chloro-2-propanol hydrochloride (CL88,236) in the rhesus monkey, by R. Heywood, et al. TOXICOLOGY 9(3):219-225, May, 1978.

Toxoplasma antibodies and spontaneous abortion, by D. Lolis, et al. INTERNATIONAL JOURNAL OF GYNAECOLOGY AND OBSTETRICS 15(4):299-301, 1978.

Training family planning personnel in sex counseling and sex education, by S. Price, et al. PUBLIC HEALTH REPORTS 93:328-334, July-August, 1978.

Training in induced abortion by obstetrics and gynecology residency programs, by B. L. Lindheim, et al. FAMILY PLANNING PERSPECTIVES 10:24-28, January-February, 1978.

Training: an integral adjunct to the introduction of newer methods of fertility regulation, by L. E. Laufe, et al. INTERNATIONAL JOURNAL OF GYNAECOLOGY AND OBSTETRICS 15(4):302-306, 1978.

Transient bacteremia due to suction abortion: implications for SBE antibiotic prophylaxis, by R. Ritvo, et al. YALE JOURNAL OF BIOLOGY AND MEDICINE 50(5):471-479, September-October, 1977.

Transient fertility after vasovasostomy, by S. Marshall. UROLOGY 11(5):492-493, May, 1978.

Transitory changes in the heart action with intrauterine contraceptive devices insertion, by S. Salahovi. LIJECNICKI VJESNIK 99(12):747-748, December, 1977.

Translocation of intrauterine contraceptive device, by R. K. Borkotoky, et al. JOURNAL OF THE INDIAN MEDICAL ASSOCIATION 67(6):147-149, September 16, 1976.

Transvaginal sterilization of women—a review, by E. Patek. LAKARTIDNINGEN 75(17):1717-1720, April 26, 1978.

Treatment of advanced adenocarcinoma of the endometrium with melphalan, 5-fluorouracil, and medroxyprogesterone

acetate: a preliminary study, by C. J. Cohen, et al. OBSTE-
TRICS AND GYNECOLOGY 50(4):415-417, October,
1977.

Treatment of the climacteric, by D. J. Hunter. PRACTITIONER
219(1312):564-570, October, 1977.

Treatment of climacteric and postmenopausal women with 17-
beta-oestradiol and norethisterone acetate, by M. Furuhjelm,
et al. ACTA OBSTETRICIA ET GYNECOLOGICA SCAN-
DINAVICA 56(4):351-361, 1977.

The treatment of imminent abortion with monitoring of the
maternal serum HPL level (proceedings), by P. Berle, et al.
ARCHIV FUR GYNAEKOLOGIE 224(1-4):90-91, July
29, 1977.

Treatment of obsessive homosexual pedophilic fantasies with
medroxyprogesterone acetate, by E. R. Pinta. BIOLOGI-
CAL PSYCHIATRY 13(3):369-373, June, 1978.

Treatment of post-pill amenorrhea, by R. P. Dickey. INTER-
NATIONAL JOURNAL OF GYNAECOLOGY AND OBSTE-
TRICS 15(2):128-132, 1977.

Trends in attitudes toward abortion 1972-75, by W. R. Arney.
FAMILY PLANNING PERSPECTIVES 8(3):117-124,
May-June, 1976.

Trends in contraceptive practice: 1965-1973, by C. F. Westoff.
FAMILY PLANNING PERSPECTIVES 8:54-57, March-
April, 1976.

Trends in fertility and family planning in Jordan, by H. Rizk.
STUDIES IN FAMILY PLANNING 8:91-99, April, 1977.

Trends in fertility, family size preferences, and family planning
practice: Taiwan, 1961-76, by T. H. Sun, et al. STUDIES
IN FAMILY PLANNING 9(4):54-70, April, 1978.

Trial of Dr. Waddill, by S. Fraker, et al. NEWSWEEK 91:35,
April 3, 1978.

Tryptophan metabolism, oral contraceptives, and pyridoxine [letter]. LANCET 1(8065):661-662, March 25, 1978.

Tubal ligation in Bangladesh, by J. Calder. NURSING MIRROR 145(24):32-33, December 15, 1977.

Tubal pregnancy distal to complete tubal occlusion following sterilization, by K. G. Metz, et al. AMERICAN JOURNAL OF OBSTETRICS AND GYNECOLOGY 131(8):911-913, August 15, 1978.

Tubal sterilization. Comparative study of 2 approach routes, by G. Magnin, et al. JOURNAL DE GYNECOLOGIE, OB-STETRIQUE ET BIOLOGIE DE LA REPRODUCTION 6(6):861-867, September, 1977.

Tubal sterilization patient care program, by M. A. Hesselbein. AORN JOURNAL 26(5):884-886, November, 1977.

Tubal sterilization. A review, by K. C. Leong. JOURNAL OF THE MAINE MEDICAL ASSOCIATION 69(3):75-80, March, 1978.

Tubal sterilization with a clip applicator under laparoscopic control, by H. Zakut, et al. HAREFUAH 94(9):262-264, May 1, 1978.

Tubo-ovarian actinomycosis and the IUCD, by D. W. Purdie, et al. BRITISH MEDICAL JOURNAL 2(6099):1392, November 26, 1977.

Twins after the pill [letter], by W. H. James. NEW ENGLAND JOURNAL OF MEDICINE 297(18):1015, November 3, 1977.

2-Br-alpha-ergocryptine (Parlodel) in primary and secondary lactation suppression following child-birth or abortion, by H. Gehring, et al. PRAXIS 66(31):985-989, August 2, 1977.

268 medicinal plants used for regulating fertility in various South America countries, by R. Moreno Azorero, et al.

OBSTETRICIA Y GINECOLOGIA LATINO-AMERICANAS 33(9-10):335-348, September-October, 1975.

Two late complications of laparoscopic tubal ligation, by J. W. Georgitis. JOURNAL OF THE MAINE MEDICAL ASSOCIATION 68(10):352-353, October, 1977.

A 2,000-year-old fight for life, by J. McHugh. OUR SUNDAY VISITOR 66:3, January 22, 1978.

Two views on the human life amendment; symposium: abortion: no, amendment: yes, by R. Neuhaus; Abortion: no, amendment: no, by J. Garvey. U. S. CATHOLIC 42:28-31, April, 1977.

Two-year experience with sterilization using the Falopian ring, by V. Chmelik. CESKOSLOVENSKA GYNEKOLOGIE 43(4):293, May, 1978.

2 years of abortion on demand, by H. Sjövall. LAKARTIDNINGEN 75(6):428-433, February 8, 1978.

Types of hepatocellular damage caused by contraceptives, by M. Jasiel, et al. POLSKIE ARCHIWUM MEDYCYNY WEWNETRZNEJ 58(2):161-168, August, 1977.

USCC asks Supreme Court to reverse 1973 abortion ruling. OUR SUNDAY VISITOR 67:1, July 30, 1978.

USCC issues sterilization text. HOSPITAL PROGRESS 59: 26-27, January, 1978.

Ultrasonography in threatened abortion, by C. Smith, et al. OBSTETRICS AND GYNECOLOGY 51(2):173-177, February, 1978.

Ultrasound and semiquantitative chorionic gonadotropin secretin in the diagnosis of abortion, by H. Schillinger, et al. ZENTRALBLATT FUER GYNAEKOLOGIE 100(2):76-83, 1978.

Ultrastructural and enzyme-histochemical alterations of the dog prostate following castration, by C. Hohbach. UROLOGE 16(6):460-465, November, 1977.

Ultrastructural-morphometric investigations on liver biopsies— the influence of oral contraceptives on the human liver, by K. Stahl, et al. ARCHIV FUR GYNAEKOLOGIE 223(3): 205-211, October 28, 1977.

Ultrasturcture of cells in the surface epithelium of the rat uterus during early pregnancy, and the effect of an interauterine device, by P. V. Peplow. THERIOGENOLOGY 8(4):139, October, 1977.

Unborn and the born again; Supreme Court decision on use of state funds to cover abortion costs. NEW REPUBLIC 177: 5-6+, July 2, 1977.

Uncomplicated pregnancy following oral contraceptive-induced liver hepatoma, by J. H. Check, et al. OBSTETRICS AND GYNECOLOGY 51(1 Suppl):28S-29S, July, 1978.

Underutilization, another form of sterilization abuse, by H. A. Stubbs, et al. ADVANCES IN PLANNED PARENTHOOD 12(3):132-135, 1978.

Undoing sterilization, by M. Clark, et al. NEWSWEEK 92:77, July 10, 1978.

The unilateral tubo-ovarian abscess with an IUD, by E. Lo Sin Sjoe, et al. NEDERLANDS TIJDSCHRIFT VOOR GENEE-SKUNDE 122(31):1131-1132, August 5, 1978.

Unilateral tubo-ovarin actinomycosis in the presence of an intrauterine device, by J. F. McCormick, et al. AMERICAN JOURNAL OF CLINICAL PATHOLOGY 68(5):622-626, November, 1977.

U. S. cities shortchange most pregnant teens. FAMILY PLANNING PERSPECTIVES 10(3):167, May-June, 1978.

U. S. restricts abortion, family planning foreign aid; regulations of the U. S. Agency for International Development, by

J. Castelli. OUR SUNDAY VISITOR 66:4, April 30, 1978.

United Way at center of Chicago conflict, by C. Anthony. OUR SUNDAY VISITOR 67:1, October 22, 1978.

University of Minnesota co-sponsors natural family planning seminar, by D. Duggan. OUR SUNDAY VISITOR 67:2, July 23, 1978.

The unmet need for birth control in five Asian countries, by C. F. Westoff. FAMILY PLANNING PERSPECTIVES 10(3):173-181, May-June, 1978.

Unmet needs [main findings of the International planned parenthood federation's worldwide survey of unmet needs in family planning, 1971-76]. PEOPLE (London) 5:25-31, November 3, 1978.

Unwanted and mistimed births in the United States: 1968-1973, by R. H. Weller, et al. FAMILY PLANNING PERSPECTIVES 10:168-172, May-June, 1978.

The unwed mother: a parish approach to the abortion problem, by R. Ranieri. TODAY'S PARISH 10:11-12, October, 1978.

Update on the rhythm method, by N. A. Comer. MADEMOISELLE 84(1):46, January, 1978.

An update on sterilization, by V. Paganelli. LINACRE QUARTERLY 44:12-17, February, 1977.

Urea in the intrauterine space of IUD users, by V. Nesit, et al. CASOPIS LEKARU CESKYCH 116(45):1401-1403, November 11, 1977.

Ureterouterine fistula as a complication of elective abortion, by J. J. Barton, et al. OBSTETRICS AND GYNECOLOGY 52(1 Suppl):81S-84S, July, 1978.

Urinary D-glucaric acid and oral contraceptives, by P. M. Stevens, et al. BRITISH JOURNAL OF CLINICAL PHARMACOLO-

GY 5(6):535-536, June, 1978.

Use-effectiveness and analysis of satisfaction levels with the Billings Ovulation Method: two-year pilot study, by H. Klaus, et al. FERTILITY AND STERILITY 28(10):1038-1043, October, 1977.

Use of anti-Rh-immunoglobulin in abortions, by G. S. Aleskerov. AKUSHERSTVO I GINEKOLOGIIA (11):40-43, November, 1977.

The use of contraceptive pills in treatment of recurrent aphthous ulceration, by S. Sadek, et al. EGYPTIAN DENTAL JOURNAL 21(1):37-42, January, 1975.

Use of contraceptives and sexually transmitted disease among university students, by A. A. Sorensen, et al. JOURNAL OF THE AMERICAN COLLEGE HEALTH ASSOCIATION 26:243-247, April, 1978.

Use of doxycycline in elective first trimester abortion, by R. S. London, et al. SOUTHERN MEDICAL JOURNAL 71(6): 672-673, June, 1978.

Use of high doses of medroxyprogesterone acetate in the palliative treatment of advanced breast cancer. Clinical experience with 44 cases, by D. Amadori, et al. MINERVA MEDICA 68(59):3967-3980, December 1, 1977.

The use of incentives for fertility reduction, by S. M. Wishik. AMERICAN JOURNAL OF PUBLIC HEALTH 68(2): 113-114, February, 1978.

Use of intrauterine devices complicated by trichomonas vaginitis, by M. Cislo, et al. WIADOMOSCI PARAZYTOLOGICZNE 23(5):595-598, 1977.

Use of oral contraceptives, cigarette smoking, and risk of subarachnoid haemorrhage, by D. B. Petitti, et al. LANCET 2(8083):234-235, July 29, 1978.

Use of prostaglandin F2alpha in the management of missed

239

abortion, by H. Foroohav, et al. INTERNATIONAL JOUR-
NAL OF GYNAECOLOGY AND OBSTETRICS 14(6):
541-544, 1976.

Use of prostaglandins in the interruption of pregnancy during
the 1st trimester, by R. Pasargiklian, et al. MINERVA
GINECOLOGIA 29(7-8):591-598, July-August, 1977.

The use of prostaglandins to perform terminations of pregnancy
in the second trimester, by F. V. Thomas, et al. JOURNAL
DE GYNECOLOGIE, OBSTETRIQUE ET BIOLOGIE DE
LA REPRODUCTION 7(1):119-128, January, 1978.

Use of synthetic steroid preparations for hemostasis and normali-
zation of menstrual function in juvenile hemorrhages, by
M. N. Kuznetsova, et al. VOPROSY OKHRANY MATERIN-
STVA I DETSTVA 23(2):77-80, February, 1978.

Using film to inform nurses about teenagers & birth control, by
E. S. Herold, et al. NURSING CARE 10:22-23, November,
1977.

Uterine choriocarcinoma fourteen years following bilateral
tubal ligation, by J. C. Lathrop, et al. OBSTETRICS AND
GYNECOLOGY 51(4):477-488, April, 1978.

Uterine rupture: a complication of midtrimester abortion, by
E. A. Friedman. PROSTAGLANDINS 15(1):187-191,
January, 1978.

Uterotubal implantation and successful pregnancy following
laparoscopic tubal cauterization, by J. R. Musich, et al.
OBSTETRICS AND GYNECOLOGY 50(4):507-509, October, 1977.

Vaginal administration of 15 (S) 15-methyl prostaglandin F2
alpha methyl ester for induction of mid-trimester abortion,
by E. S. Grech, et al. CONTRACEPTION 16(4):327-337,
October, 1977.

Vaginal evacuation [letter], by S. Fribourg. OBSTETRICS AND
GYNECOLOGY 51(6):740, June, 1978.

Vaginal prostaglandin E2 in the management of fetal intrauterine death, by E. M. Southern, et al. BRITISH JOURNAL OF OBSTETRICS AND GYNAECOLOGIE 85(6):437-441, June, 1978.

A vaginal suppository for abortion. MEDICAL LETTER ON DRUGS AND THERAPEUTICS 19(22):89-90, November 4, 1977.

Value of amoxicillin and ampicillin in the treatment of septic abortion (double blind and random comparative studies), by E. López Ortiz, et al. GINECOLOGIA Y OBSTETRICIA DE MEXICO 43(256):123-134, February, 1978.

The value of life, by T. G. Roupas. PHILOSOPHY AND PUBLIC AFFAIRS 7:154-183, Winter, 1978.

A variant chromosome 17 in a mother with repeated abortions and a 46, XY/47, XXY Klinefelter son, by K. H. Gustavson, et al. UPSALA JOURNAL OF MEDICAL SCIENCES 83(2):119-122, 1978.

Variation of food intake and body weight with estrous cycle, ovariectomy, and estradiol benzoate treatment in hamsters (Mesocricetus auratus), by L. P. Morin, et al. JOURNAL OF COMPARATIVE PHYSIOLOGY AND PSYCHOLOGY 9(1):1-6, February, 1978.

Various types of intrauterine devices, by E. B. Connell. MEDICAL ASPECTS OF HUMAN SEXUALITY 11(10):15-16+, October, 1977.

Vas occlusion by tantalum clips and its comparison with conventional vaseactomy in man: reliability, reversibility, and complications, by A. S. Gupta, et al. FERTILITY AND STERILITY 28(10):1086-1089, October, 1977.

Vascular complications of long-term oestrogen therapy, by D. McKay Hart, et al. FRONTIERS OF HORMONE RESEARCH 5:174-191, 1977.

Vascular defects in human endometrium caused by intrauterine contraceptive devices. An electron microscope study, by W. R. Hohman, et al. CONTRACEPTION 16(5):507-522, November, 1977.

Vasectomy and spermatic antibodies, by K. Bandhauer, et al. ZEITSCHRIFT FUER UROLOGIE UND NEPHROLOGIE 70(7):519-522, July, 1977.

Vasectomy and vasectomy reversal, by S. J. Silber. FERTILITY AND STERILITY 29(2):125-140, February, 1978.

Vasectomy: benefits versus risks, by J. E. Davis. INTERNA-TIONAL JOURNAL OF GYNAECOLOGY AND OBSTE-TRICS 15(2):163-166, 1977.

Vasectomy by use of a conservative surgical technic, by J. Eldrup. UGESKRIFT FOR LAEGER 140(16):914-915, April 17, 1978.

Vasectomy in rhesus monkeys. III. Light microscopic studies of testicular morphology, by P. M. Heidger, Jr., et al. UROLO-GY 11(2):148-152, February, 1978.

Vasectomy increases the severity of diet-induced atherosclerosis in Macaca fascicularis, by N. J. Alexander, et al. SCIENCE 201(4355):538-541, August 11, 1978.

Vasectomy reversal: review and assessment of current status, by A. M. Belker, et al. JOURNAL OF THE KENTUCKY MEDICAL ASSOCIATION 75(11):536-537, November, 1977.

Vasectomy sequelae: empirical studies, by E. Jones. JOURNAL OF REPRODUCTIVE MEDICINE 19(5):254-258, November, 1977.

Vasectomy with immediate sterility, by U. H. Jensen, et al. UGESKRIFT FOR LAEGER 140(16):916-917, April 17, 1978.

Vasovagal shock after insertion of intrauterine device [letter], by D. N. Menzies. BRITISH MEDICAL JOURNAL 1(6108):

305, February 4, 1978.

Vasovasostomy and patency rate [letter], by I. D. Sharlip. UROLOGY 11(3):315-316, March, 1978.

Vasovasostomy. Experimental comparative study of polyglycolic acid and polypropylene sutures in the dog, by L. E. Lykins, et al. UROLOGY 10(5):452-455, November, 1977.

Vasovasostomy: the flap technique, by T. J. Fitzpatrick. JOURNAL OF UROLOGY 120(1):78-79, July, 1978.

Vaso-vasostomy, undoing a sterilization, by R. J. Scholtmeijer. NEDELANDS TIJDSCHRIFT VOOR GENEESKUNDE 122(13):417-419, April 1, 1978.

Vatican denounces Italian liberalized abortion law, by J. Mathig, Jr. OUR SUNDAY VISITOR 67:4, June 4, 1978.

Venezuelan birth control policies hit by archbishop; Luis E. Henriquez. OUR SUNDAY VISITOR 67:1, September 24, 1978.

Ventilatory response to medroxyprogesterone acetate in normal subjects: time course and mechanism, by J. B. Skatrud, et al. JOURNAL OF APPLIED PHYSIOLOGY 44(6):393-344, June, 1978.

Verdict in Kentucky; M. Pitchford's abortion trial. NEWSWEEK 92:35-36, September 11, 1978.

Vertigo and the pill [letter], by J. Siegler. BRITISH MEDICAL JOURNAL 2(6099):1416, November 26, 1977.

Very early abortion by prostaglandins, by I. Z. Mackenzie, et al. LANCET 1(8076):1223-1226, June 10, 1978.

Very early induced abortion (overtime treatment), by F. P. Wibaut. NEDERLANDS TIJDSCHRIFT VOOR GENEESKUNDE 121(46):1847-1852, November 12, 1977.

Vesicular stomatitis virus causes abortion and neonatal death in ferrets, by S. C. Suffin, et al. JOURNAL OF CLINICAL MICROBIOLOGY 6(4):437-438, October, 1977.

Victims of an anti-life philosophy; rights of the needy ignored, by J. Sullivan. OUR SUNDAY VISITOR 65:1+, March 6, 1977.

Victorian sex survey, by P. A. David, et al. INTELLECT 106: 276, January, 1978.

Vietnam [family planning programs]. PEOPLE (London) 5:22-27, November 2, 1978.

Vitamin B6 status of Nigerian women using various methods of contraception, by E. M. Wien. AMERICAN JOURNAL OF CLINICAL NUTRITION 31(8):1392-1396, August, 1978.

Vitamin E status of young women on combined-type oral contraceptives, by C. C. Tangney, et al. CONTRACEPTION 17(6):499-512, June, 1978.

Voice changes during hormonal contraception, by I. Krahulec, et al. CESKOSLOVENSKA OTOLARYNGOLOGIE 26(4): 234-237, August, 1977.

Voluntary termination of pregnancy: operational procedure; prevention of peroperative complications. Apropos of 1,000 cases, by M. Rami, et al. JOURNAL DE GYNECOLOGIE, OBSTETRIQUE ET BIOLOGIE DE LA REPRODUCTION 6(8):1171-1182, December, 1977.

Wave of informed consent laws facing tough challenges in court. OUR SUNDAY VISITOR 67:1, September 24, 1978.

A way round Congress. ECONOMIST 268:30, August 12, 1978.

We've won the right to legal abortion, but we're still learning the physical and emotional results, by R. Cherry. GLAMOUR 76:110-111+, January, 1978.

What does the patient know about risks of abortion and what

does the law know? [editorial], by J. Philip. UGESKRIFT
FOR LAEGER 139(32):1919-1920, August 8, 1977.

What I learned marching with N.O.W., by J. M. Shutt. FARM
JOURNAL 101:F1, December, 1977.

What's new in the law: constitutional law. . .parents' rights, by
A. Ashman. AMERICAN BAR ASSOCIATION JOURNAL
64:898-899, June, 1978.

What's new in the law: family planning. . .access to contraceptives, by A. Ashman. AMERICAN BAR ASSOCIATION
JOURNAL 63:857, June, 1977.

When patients "can't" take the pill, by W. S. Freeman. AMER-
ICAN FAMILY PHYSICIAN 17(1):143-149, January,
1978.

Which contraceptive is right for you? GLAMOUR 76:101+,
August, 1978.

Who can't take the pill? by M. Jones. GUARDIAN p. 9, August
30, 1978.

Who is a Catholic; Lenten series, by R. McBrien. NATIONAL
CATHOLIC REPORTER 14:7+, February 10, 1978.

Why the Billings method is permissible, by G. Concetti. CHRIST
TO THE WORLD 21:332-334, November 5, 1976.

Why blame the pill? [letter], by H. A. Mackay. BRITISH MED-
ICAL JOURNAL 1(6120):1141-1142, April 29, 1978.

Why 103 women asked for reversal of sterilisation, by R. M. L.
Winston. BRITISH MEDICAL JOURNAL 6082:305-307,
July 30, 1977.

Why women need late abortions, by C. Brewer. NEW SOCIETY
pp. 208-209, October 26, 1978.

The wider aspects of coercion: much of the current debate on
the use of coercion in population policies has been skewed

by the more negative aspects of a few heavy-handed pro-grammes, by J. P. Wogaman. POPULI 5:39-43, November 1, 1978.

Will church institutions be forced to make medical payments for abortions; excerpt from report to the Administrative Committee of the National Conference of Catholic Bishops, by T. Cooke. ORIGINS 7:577+, March 2, 1978.

Witness says aid funds still promote abortion. OUR SUNDAY VISITOR 66:5, March 12, 1978.

Woman's right, physician's judgment: Commonwealth v. Edelin and a physician's criminal liability for fetal manslaughter, by S. Wagner. WOMEN'S RIGHTS LAW REPORTER 4:97-114, Winter, 1978.

Woman's right to choose, by D. C. Bradley. MODERN LAW REVIEW 41:365-382, July, 1978.

Women at Mexico: beyond family planning acceptors, by A. Germain. FAMILY PLANNING PERSPECTIVES 7(5): 2-11, 1975.

Women slam hospital approach to abortion. HOSPITAL AD-MINISTRATION IN CANADA 20(6):8, June, 1978.

Women who regret sterilisation [letter], by B. Alderman. BRIT-ISH MEDICAL JOURNAL 2)6089):766, September 17, 1977.

Women's organizations: a resource for family planning and de-velopment, by J. Bruce. FAMILY PLANNING PERSPEC-TIVES 8:291, November-December, 1976.

Work forms and methods in family and marriage counseling, by S. I. Markovich. MEDITSINSKAIA SESTRA 36(8):13-17, August, 1977.

Workers sick from pill. CHEMICAL WEEK 120:20, April 13, 1977.

World population: the silent explosion, by M. Green, et al. DEPARTMENT OF STATE BULLETIN 78:45-54, October 1-8, 1978+.

World population situation: problems and prospects. WORLD DEVELOPMENT 5(5-7):395, May-July, 1977.

The world's population problem: possible interventions to reduce fertility, by R. S. McNamara. PUBLIC HEALTH REPORTS 93:124-135, March-April, 1978.

A worldwide population information network: status and goals, by H. K. Kolbe. SPECIAL LIBRARIES 69(7):237-243, July, 1978.

Wrongful birth and emotional distress damages: a suggested approach. UNIVERSITY OF PITTSBURGH LAW REVIEW 38:550-560, Spring, 1977.

X-ray methods of localization of IUD's, by A. Tetti, et al. MINERVA GINECOLOGIA 30(5):390-393, May, 1978.

Yam and the pill, by A. S. Ahl. AMERICAN BIOLOGY TEACHER 40:36-38+, January, 1978.

The year of the child [editorial], by S. Gupta. INDIAN PEDIATRICS 14(4):241-242, April, 1977.

Yes to life, no to abortion; reprint from the publication, Pour la vie naissante, July, 1977, by P. Weber. OSSERVATORE ROMANO 1(510):10-11, January 5, 1978.

The youth reception in Sollentuna, by A. Sedvall. LAKARTIDNINGEN 75(21):2131-2132, May 24, 1978.

PERIODICAL LITERATURE

SUBJECT INDEX

ABORTION (GENERAL)

Abortion [letter], by A. C. Somerville. NEW ZEALAND MEDICAL JOURNAL 86(594):201, August 24, 1977.

Abortion alert, by G. Steinem. MS MAGAZINE 6:118, November, 1977.

Abortion debate. JOURNAL OF CURRENT SOCIAL ISSUES 15:74-75, Spring, 1978.

Abortion regarded as contraception [letter]. LANCET 2(8041):765-766, October 8, 1977.

—, by M. Beaconsfield. LANCET 2(8039):666-667, September 24, 1977.

Abortion: the world scene, by J. A. Loraine. CONTEMPORARY REVIEW 232:92-96, February, 1978.

Comparison of women seeking early and late abortion, by W. L. Fielding, et al. AMERICAN JOURNAL OF OBSTETRICS AND GYNECOLOGY 131(3):304-310, June 1, 1978.

Contraception, sterilisation and abortion [editorial]. NEW ZEALAND MEDICAL JOURNAL 85(588):428-429, May 25, 1977.

The experience of abortion, by R. Schmidt. NEW SOCIETY

pp. 242-244, February 2, 1978.

Legalized abortion, by B. Barley. MEDICAL WORLD NEWS 19:53-54+, January 23, 1978.

Recent and possible future trends in abortion, by F. Lafitte. JOURNAL OF MEDICAL ETHICS 4(1):25-29, March, 1978.

Repeat abortions—why more? by C. Tietze. FAMILY PLANNING PERSPECTIVES 10:286-288, September-October, 1978.

Report of experiences of more than 200 pregnancy interruptions. One year following the reform of Statute 218 of the Criminal Code, by R. Barthel, et al. MEDIZINISCHE WELT 29(1):20-24, January 6, 1978.

A report on six months experience of committee for the control of abortion, by B. Halpern, et al. MENTAL HEALTH AND SOCIETY 2(3-6):205-211, 1975.

Results in maintenance of pregnancy after request of interruption (experience at the women's hospital lucerne), by M. Lanz, et al. THERAPEUTISCHE UMSCHAU 35(6): 463-473, June, 1978.

Select committee on abortion [letter]. LANCET 2(7982): 424-425, August 21, 1976.

Selective abortion, by J. M. McLean. MANCHESTER MEDICAL GAZETTE 56(3):66-67, December, 1977.

AUSTRALIA
Abortion debate in Australia, by D. Strangman. OSSERVA TORE ROMANO 49(506):6-8, December 8, 1977.

BELGIUM
The issue of the legalization of abortion in Belgium, by

BELGIUM
B. J. De Clercq. RES PUBLICA 19(2):305-322, 1977.

CANADA
Abortion law in Canada: a need for reform. SASKATCHE-
WAN LAW REVIEW 42:221-250, 1977-1978.

Canadian woman doesn't make headlines but her work
brings help to mothers; Birthright International, by C.
Anthony. OUR SUNDAY VISITOR 66:2, January
8, 1978.

EL SALVADOR
Hospital abortions in El Salvador, by T. Monreal, et al.
SPM: SALUD PUBLICA DE MEXICO 19(3):387-
395, May-June, 1977.

FRANCE
Abortion and contraceptives in France, by E. Salomonsson.
VARDFACKET 1(17):14-15, September 22, 1977.

Abortion in France: women and the regulation of family
size 1800-1914, by A. McLaren. FRENCH HISTORI-
CAL STUDIES 10:461-485, Spring, 1978.

L'augmentation des avortements déclarés en France, by
G. Duchene. LA DOCUMENTATION CATHOLIQUE
74:893, October 16, 1977.

GERMANY
Beratung in Sachen 218; ethische Anmerkungen zur Ge-
staltung des in der Reform des 218 vorgesehenen
Beratungssystems, by P. Schmitz. STIMMEN DER
ZEIT 195:48-56, January, 1977.

GHANA
Induced abortion in a Ghanaian family, by W. Bleek.
AFRICAN STUDIES REVIEW 21:103-120, April,
1978.

GREAT BRITAIN
Abortion after ten years, by G. Sinclair, et al. NEW HU-
MANIST 93:157-160, Spring, 1978.

Abortion and control, by J. Turner. NEW SOCIETY
p. 490, March 2, 1978.

Abortion, birth control, and sex ratio in England and
Wales [letter], by R. Cruz-Coke. LANCET 2(8087):
480, August 26, 1978.

Abortion: why the issue has not disappeared, by C. Francome. POLITICAL QUARTERLY 49:217-222,
April, 1978.

Eleven years on, by M. Stott. GUARDIAN p. 9, February 21, 1978.

Lifeline pregnancy care; service giving social, financial
and moral help in Great Britain, by D. Bevan. CLER-
GY REVIEW 61:441-443, November, 1976.

Medicine/abortion ripoff, by B. Miner. GUARDIAN
28(47):2, September 15, 1976.

Not just doctors' dilemmas, by D. Gould. NEW STATES-
MAN 95:74, January 20, 1978.

HONG KONG
Better bargins than Hong Kong's, by L. Mathews.
GUARDIAN p. 9, December 5, 1978.

Legal abortion, by K. H. Lee. HONG KONG NURSING
JOURNAL :53-54, May, 1977.

INDIA
Legal abortions in an Indian state, by N. B. Rao, et al.
STUDIES IN FAMILY PLANNING 8(12):311-315,
December, 1977.

IRELAND
Abortion and Irish women: social elements of women usually resident in the Republic of Ireland whose pregnancies were terminated during 1973, 1974 and up to May 22, 1975 through pregnancy advisory service, London, by R. S. Rose. SOCIAL STUDIES 6:71-119, November, 1977.

Induced abortion in the Republic of Ireland, by R. S. Rose. BRITISH JOURNAL OF CRIMINOLOGY 18:245-254, July, 1978.

ITALY
Abortion: democracy dies with man, by C. Caffarra. OSSERVATORE ROMANO 11(468):11-12, March 17, 1977.

Abortion in Italy, by M. Hammond. COMMONWEAL 105:420-421, July 7, 1978.

The campaign in favour of abortion in Italy; declarations of the Hierarchy; two messages of the Italian bishops. CHRIST TO THE WORLD 22:283-286, November 4, 1977.

Conscientious objection of doctors keeps Italian abortion law smouldering, by C. Savitsky. OUR SUNDAY VISITOR 67:1, August 27, 1978.

The doctor and the new ethical code; abortion law in Italy, by D. Tettamanzi. OSSERVATORE ROMANO 27(536):8-9, July 6, 1978.

Estimating the incidence of induced abortion in Italy, by I. Figa Talamanca. GENUS 32(1-2):91-108, 1976.

Les évêques italiens et l'avortement. LA DOCUMENTA-TION CATHOLIQUE 74:523-524, June 5, 1977.

ITALY

Italy: three-month wonder. ECONOMIST 267:66, April 22, 1978.

Italy's abortion law [letter], by E. Lombardo. LANCET 2(8082):207-208, July 22, 1978.

Italy's liberal abortion law isn't working and pro-abortionists object, by C. Savitsky. OUR SUNDAY VISITOR 67:2, June 25, 1978.

The law legalizing abortion in Italy; a declaration of the Italian Episcopal Conference, June 9, 1978. THE POPE SPEAKS 23:263-264, Fall, 1978.

Legal abortion, Italian style. VICTIMOLOGY: AN INTERNATIONAL JOURNAL 2(1):156-157, Spring, 1977.

Most Italian doctors sign as objectors to abortion. OUR SUNDAY VISITOR 67:3, July 30, 1978.

No abortions, say Italian physicians. CHRISTIAN CENTURY 95:671, July 5, 1978.

No surrender on abortion, declare the bishops of Italy, by J. Muthig, Jr. OUR SUNDAY VISITOR 67:5, June 11, 1978.

LATIN AMERICA

Power lines and disembodied women [abortion and sterilization in Latin America], by F. Moira. OFF OUR BACKS 6:10-11, November, 1976.

NEW ZEALAND

Abortion 1978 [editorial]. NEW ZEALAND MEDICAL JOURNAL 87(610):285-286, April 26, 1978.

Abortive act, by S. Walker. GUARDIAN p. 9, October

NEW ZEALAND
   24, 1978.

Confusion about New Zealand abortion? [letter], by H.
   C. McLaren. BRITISH MEDICAL JOURNAL
   1(6128):1697, June 24, 1978.

Contraception, sterilisation and abortion in New Zealand.
   NEW ZEALAND MEDICAL JOURNAL 85(588):
   441-445, May 25, 1977.

Group struggle in a value field: the comparative performance of New Zealand pressure groups on the
   question of abortion, 1970-1975, by R. Stone. PO-
   LITICAL SCIENCE 29:139-153, December, 1977.

Patients denied abortion at a private early pregnancy termination service in Auckland, by R. B. Hunton. NEW
   ZEALAND MEDICAL JOURNAL 85(588):424-
   425, May 25, 1977.

Social characteristics of patients attending a private early
   pregnancy termination service in Auckland, by R. B.
   Hunton, et al. NEW ZEALAND MEDICAL JOUR-
   NAL 85(584):220-222, March 23, 1977.

Termination of pregnancy in Gisborne, by W. Savage.
   NEW ZEALAND NURSING FORUM 6(1):5-8,
   March, 1978.

NIGERIA
   Induced illegal abortions in Benin City, Nigeria, by S. E.
   Okojie. INTERNATIONAL JOURNAL OF GYNAE-
   COLOGY AND OBSTETRICS 14(6):517-521, 1976.

SWITZERLAND
   Lettre pastorale des évéques suisses sur l'avortement; 27-
   28 août, 1977. LA DOCUMENTATION CATHO-
   LIQUE 74:891-893, October 16, 1977.

THAILAND
Attitudes toward abortion in Thailand: a survey of senior
medical students, by S. Varakamin, et al. STUDIES
IN FAMILY PLANNING 8:288-293, November, 1977

UNITED STATES
Abortion in the United States, 1976-1977, by J. D. Forrest, et al. FAMILY PLANNING PERSPECTIVES
10:271-279, September-October, 1978.

Abortion need and services in the United States, 1974-
1975, by E. Weinstock, et al. FAMILY PLANNING
PERSPECTIVES 8:58-80, March-April, 1976.

Abortion U.S.A., by C. Francome. NEW SOCIETY
pp. 197-198, April 27, 1978.

The diffusion of abortion facilities in the northeastern
United States, 1970-1976, by N. F. Henry. SOCIAL
SCIENCE AND MEDICINE 12(1D):7-15, March, 1978

Legal abortion in the United States, 1975-1976, by E.
Sullivan, et al. FAMILY PLANNING PERSPEC-
TIVES 9:116-137, May-June, 1977.

Legal abortions, subsidized family planning services, and
the U.S. birth dearth, by K. E. Bauman, et al. SO-
CIAL BIOLOGY 24:183-191, Fall, 1977.

Sounding Board. Abortions in America: the effects of
restrictive funding, by L. R. Berger. NEW ENG-
LAND JOURNAL OF MEDICINE 298(26):1474-
1477, June 29, 1978.

CONNECTICUT
Connecticut's OB/GYN's on abortion: a two year fol-
low-up study, by G. Affleck, et al. CONNECTI-
CUT MEDICINE 42(3):179-182, March, 1978.

MISSOURI

NEW YORK
Abortion programs in New York City: services, policies, and potential health hazards, by R. C. Lerner, et al. THE MILBANK MEMORIAL FUND QUARTERLY 52(1):15-38, Winter, 1974.

Forecasting demand for abortions: the experience of a New York City clinic, by R. Oppenheim, et al. AMERICAN JOURNAL OF ECONOMICS AND SOCIOLOGY 37:177-178, April, 1978.

OHIO
Akron gets restrictive abortion measures; in Ohio, by J. Petosa. NATIONAL CATHOLIC REPORTER 14:20, March 10, 1978.

ABORTION: ATTITUDES
Abortion, adoption, or motherhood: an empirical study of decision-making during pregnancy, by M. B. Bracken, et al. AMERICAN JOURNAL OF OBSTETRICS AND GYNECOLOGY 130(3):251-262, February 1, 1978.

Abortion and conscientious objection, by C. Caffarra. OSSERVATORE ROMANO 40(549):4-5, October 5, 1978.

Abortion and the human brain, by J. B. Blumenfeld. PHILOSOPHICAL STUDIES 32:251-268, October, 1977.

Abortion and medical ethics, by D. Callahan. ANNALS OF THE AMERICAN ACADEMY OF POLITICAL AND SOCIAL SCIENCE 437:116, May, 1978.

Abortion and men, excerpt from the ambivalence of abortion, by L. B. Francke. ESQUIRE 80:53-60, January, 1978.

Abortion and moral safety, by J. R. Greenwell. CRITICA 9:35-48, December, 1977.

257

Abortion and tinkering, by G. Schedler. DIALOGUE 17: 122-125, 1978.

Abortion: huge majority would grant right to abortion, but circumstances and stage of pregnancy are determinants. GALLUP OPINION INDEX pp. 25-29, April, 1978.

Abortion language and logic, by R. A. Hipkiss. ETC. A REVIEW OF GENERAL SEMANTICS 33:207-212, June, 1976.

Abortion or the unwanted child: a choice for a humanistic society, by J. W. Prescott. THE HUMANIST 35(2):11-15, March-April, 1975.

Abortion: our differences are making us forget what we have in common. GLAMOUR 76:56, October, 1978.

Abortion: rules for debate, by R. A. McCormick. AMERICA 139:26-30, July 15, 1978.

Abortion: a study of the perceptions of sixty abortion applicants and twenty service givers in Denver, Colorado, by N. E. Fisher. DISSERTATION ABSTRACTS INTERNATIONAL 37(5-A):3184, November, 1976.

Abortion: subjective attitudes and feelings, by E. W. Freeman. FAMILY PLANNING PERSPECTIVES 10:150-155, May-June, 1978.

Abortion under attack, by S. Fraker, et al. NEWSWEEK 91:36-37+, June 5, 1978; Same abr. with title War against abortion. READERS DIGEST 113:179-182, September, 1978.

Abortion: an unsettled issue, by L. Dolby. ENGAGE/SOCIAL ACTION 5:49-50, December, 1977.

Abortion: the viewpoint of potential consumers, by M. H.

Hamrick, et al. JOURNAL OF THE AMERICAN COL-
LEGE HEALTH ASSOCIATION 26(3):136-139, December, 1977.

Abortion; the wages of sin? ECONOMIST 265:36, December 10, 1977.

Abortion: who says there oughta be a law? by L. Cisler.
MAJORITY REPORT 6:8, October 30-November 12,
1976.

Anti abortion vote courted, by I. Silber. GUARDIAN
28(49):4, September 29, 1976.

Attitudes toward abortion: a comparative analysis of correlates for 1973 and 1975, by T. C. Wagenaar. JOURNAL
OF SOCIOLOGY AND SOCIAL WELFARE 4(6):927-
944, June, 1977.

Bioethics/case of the fetus, by P. Singer. NEW YORK RE-
VIEW OF BOOKS 23(13):33, August 5, 1976.

Birthright; saving a mother, saving a life, by C. Anthony.
OUR SUNDAY VISITOR 67:6, May 21, 1978.

Black minister's attitudes toward population size and birth
control, by J. Irwin, et al. SOCIOLOGICAL ANALYSIS
38:252-257, Fall, 1977.

Changing views of abortion, by T. C. Wagenaar, et al. HU-
MAN BEHAVIOR 7:58, March, 1978.

Choosing sides, by E. Yeo. JOURNAL OF CURRENT SO-
CIAL ISSUES 15:76-78, Spring, 1978.

The class conflict over abortion [class differences in attitudes toward abortion and the family], by P. Skerry.
PUBLIC INTEREST pp. 69-84, Summer, 1978.

Code of ethics: abortion referral [letter]. CANADIAN MEDICAL ASSOCIATION JOURNAL 118(8):888+, April 22, 1978.

Contextual and ideological dimensions of attitudes toward discretionary abortion, by B. K. Singh, et al. DEMOGRAPHY 15:381-388, August, 1978.

Cruelty of morality; abortion views of J. Carter. NATION 225:68, July 23, 1977.

Differences and delay in the decision to seek induced abortion among black and white women, by M. B. Bracken, et al. SOCIAL PSYCHIATRY 12(2):57-70, April, 1977.

Ethical values in anesthesia and intensive care (7): a hospital chaplain's view of abortion, euthanasia and the ethical aspects of suicide, by I. Stenäs. LAKARTIDNINGEN 75(4):224-225, January 24, 1978.

Firm in condemning the abominable crime; abortion. OSSERVATORE ROMANO 7(516):4, February 16, 1978.

For a human society aware of its own rights and duties; our yes to life, by R. D'Andrea. OSSERVATORE ROMANO 23(532):6-7, June 8, 1978.

Fresh battle on abortion, by D. A. Williams, et al. NEWSWEEK 91:32, February 6, 1978.

Have women abandoned abortion issue, by B. Martlin. MAJORITY REPORT 6(6):12, July 24, 1976.

How attitudes toward abortion are changing. JOURNAL OF POPULATION 1(1):5, Spring, 1978.

How to argue about abortion, by J. C. Bennett, et al. CHRISTIANITY AND CRISIS 37:264-266, November 14, 1977.

Ideas on the genetic or eugenic indication for interruption [editorial], by H. Berger. PAEDIATRIE UND PAEDO-LOGIE 12(4):325-333, 1977.

Indirect measurements of family size preferences and of abortion, by J. C. Barrett. JOURNAL OF BIOSOCIAL SCIENCE 9(3):279-291, July, 1977.

Induced abortion after feeling fetal movements: its causes and emotional consequences, by C. Brewer. JOURNAL OF BIOSOCIAL SCIENCE 10(2):203-208, April, 1978.

Large majority of Americans favor legal abortion, sex education & contraceptive services for teens. FAMILY PLANNING PERSPECTIVES 10(3):159-160, May-June, 1978.

Love, sex, permissiveness, and abortion: a test of alternative models, by A. M. Mirande, et al. ARCHIVES OF SEXUAL BEHAVIOR 5:553-556, November, 1976.

Many rights to life, by M. Mead. REDBOOK 151:109+, July, 1978.

Motherhood by choice; excerpt from Woman's choice, by S. J. Barr, et al. VOGUE 168:246+, March, 1978.

Narcissism and abortion, by A. M. Ruiz-Mateos Jiménez de Tejada. ACTAS LUSO-ESPANOLAS DE NEUROLOGIA Y PSIQUIATRIA 5(4):241-246, July-August, 1977.

On abortion philosophy [letter], by G. Crum. AMERICAN JOURNAL OF PUBLIC HEALTH 68(3):272, March, 1978.

On paying the price of abortion, by S. E. Allen. MADE-MOISELLE 84:100+, March, 1978.

Patient delay in seeking health care: social factors associated with delayed abortion, by S. J. Guttmacher. DISSERTA-

TION ABSTRACTS INTERNATIONAL 37(7-H):4652-4653, January, 1977.

Philosophers and the abortion question, by P. Abbott. POLITICAL THEORY August, 1978.

The philosophical arguments, by R. Neville. HASTINGS CENTER REPORT 8(3):33-37, June, 1978.

Polls: abortion, by C. de Boer. PUBLIC OPINION QUARTERLY 41:553-564, Winter, 1977-1978; Reply by R. J. Adamek, 42:411-413, Fall, 1978.

Predictive factors in emotional response to abortion: King's termination study—IV, by E. M. Belsey, et al. SOCIAL SCIENCE AND MEDICINE 11(2):71-82, January, 1977.

Professional and public opinion on abortion law proposals, by W. Facer. NEW ZEALAND NURSING FORUM 6(1):13-15, March, 1978.

Psychological correlates of unwanted pregnancy, by G. E. Rader, et al. JOURNAL OF ABNORMAL PSYCHOLOGY 87:373-376, June, 1978.

Psychological factors involved in request for elective abortion, by M. Blumenfield. JOURNAL OF CLINICAL PSYCHIATRY 39(1):17-25, January, 1978.

Race and abortion: disconfirmation of the genocide hypothesis in a clinical analogue, by B. Crossley, et al. INTERNATIONAL JOURNAL OF PSYCHIATRY IN MEDICINE 8(1):35-42, 1977-1978.

The relationship of selected demographic variables to the stability of abortion attitudes in college students, by S. E. Wilcox. DISSERTATION ABSTRACTS INTERNATIONAL 37(3-H):1485-1485, September, 1976.

Religious, moral, and sociological issues: some basic distinctions, by B. Brady. HASTINGS CENTER REPORT 8:13, April, 1978.

Social evaluations of a woman with a problem pregnancy: effects of marital status, birth or abortion solution, and sex of respondents, by D. J. Pope, et al. PSYCHOLOGICAL REPORTS 42:39-47, February, 1978.

Trends in attitudes toward abortion 1972-75, by W. R. Arney. FAMILY PLANNING PERSPECTIVES 8(3): 117-124, May-June, 1976.

Woman's right to choose, by D. C. Bradley. MODERN LAW REVIEW 41:365-382, July, 1978.

Women slam hospital approach to abortion. HOSPITAL ADMINISTRATION IN CANADA 20(6):8, June, 1978.

ABORTION: COMPLICATIONS
Acute renal failure as a complication of hypertonic saline abortion in a kidney allograft recipient, by A. Carvallo, et al. CLINICAL NEPHROLOGY 8(5):491-493, November, 1977.

Adrenal necrosis following abortion, by R. H. Young, et al. IRISH JOURNAL OF MEDICAL SCIENCE 146(10): 340-342, October, 1977.

Amniotic fluid embolism and disseminated intravascular coagulation after evacuation of missed abortion, by W. B. Stromme, et al. OBSTETRICS AND GYNECOLOGY 52(1 Suppl):76S-80S, July, 1978.

Arachidonic acid and other free fatty acid changes during abortion induced by prostaglandin F2alpha, by P. L. Ogburn, Jr., et al. AMERICAN JOURNAL OF OBSTETRICS AND GYNECOLOGY 130(2):188-193, January 15, 1978.

Avoiding tough abortion complication: a live baby. MEDI-
CAL WORLD NEWS 18:83, November 14, 1977.

Balneotherapy as prophylaxis in aborted pregnancy, by I. F.
Perfil'eva, et al. AKUSHERSTVO I GINEKOLOGIIA
(7):41-44, July, 1978.

Berdyansk mud treatment of inflammatory gynecological
diseases occurring after abortion in a subacute stage, by
L. I. Bero, et al. PEDIATRIYA, AKUSHERSTVO I
GINEKOLOHIYA (2):53-54, 1978.

Blood and malignant diseases as indications for pregnancy
interruption, by W. F. Jungi. INTERNIST 19(5):279-
283, May, 1978.

Blood coagulation disorders in the course of interrupted
advanced pregnancy, by M. Uszynski, et al. GINE-
KOLOGIA POLASKA 48(9):809-812, September, 1977.

Cervical rape: dilators vs. laminaria [abortion], by M. Roos.
OFF OUR BACKS 7:17-18, April, 1977.

Clinical report—a case of a failed abortion, by J. Barchilon.
MEDICAL TRIAL TECHNIQUE QUARTERLY 24:257-
289, Winter, 1978.

Clostridial sepsis after abortion with PGF2alpha and intracervical laminaria tents—a case report, by S. L. Green,
et al. INTERNATIONAL JOURNAL OF GYNAE-
COLOGY AND OBSTETRICS 15(4):322-324, 1978.

Comparative risk of death from legally induced abortion in
hospitals and nonhospital facilities, by D. A. Grimes,
et al. OBSTETRICS AND GYNECOLOGY 51(3):
323-326, March, 1978.

Costs of treating abortion-related complications, by S. D.
Von Allmen, et al. FAMILY PLANNING PERSPEC-

TIVES 9:273-276, November-December, 1977.

Cytogenetics of aborters and abortuses, by T. Kajii, et al. AMERICAN JOURNAL OF OBSTETRICS AND GYNE-COLOGY 131(1):33-38, May 1, 1978.

Cytophotometric DNA-measurements in abortion, by W. P. Kunze. PATHOLOGY RESEARCH AND PRACTICE 162(3):253-262, July, 1978.

Detachment of the uterine cervix in association with induced midtrimester abortion, by R. T. Burkman, et al. AMER-ICAN JOURNAL OF OBSTETRICS AND GYNECOLO-GY 129(5):585-586, November 1, 1977.

Differential approach to the treatment of threatened abor-tion, by Iu. F. Borisova, et al. SOVETSKAYA MEDIT-ZINA (9):100-103, September, 1977.

Disseminated intravascular coagulation syndrome after vacuum curettement for first trimester abortion, by A. S. Goss, Jr. SOUTHERN MEDICAL JOURNAL 71(8): 967-968, August, 1978.

Effect of abortion on obstetric patterns, by R. Beard, et al. BRITISH MEDICAL JOURNAL 2(6089):765-766, September 17, 1977.

The effect of delay and method choice on the risk of abor-tion morbidity, by W. Cates, Jr., et al. FAMILY PLAN-NING PERSPECTIVES 9(6):266-268+, November-December, 1977.

The effect of 15-methyl-prostaglandin F2 alpha administered intramuscularly to induce abortion in the first half of pregnancy [proceedings], by U. Haller, et al. ARCHIV FUR GYNAEKOLOGIE 224(1-4):266-268, July 29, 1977.

Electrical activity of the rat uterus during early pregnancy and abortion, by A. Talo, et al. ACTA PHYSIOLOGICA SCANDINAVICA 100(3):377-381, July, 1977.

Electrolyte studies after intra-amniotic instillation fo 20 per cent sodium chlorice, by R. V. Bhatt, et al. INDIAN JOURNAL OF MEDICAL RESEARCH 67:589-592, April, 1978.

Endometrial ossification following an abortion, by M. Waxman, et al. AMERICAN JOURNAL OF OBSTETRICS AND GYNECOLOGY 130(5):587-588, March 1, 1978.

Evaluation of the results concerning radioimmunologically active human-chorionic gonadotrophin (RIA HCG) in the serum of women with imminent abortions, by M. Talas, et al. CESKOSLOVENSKA GYNEKOLOGIE 43(5):344-347, June, 1978.

Fetal abnormalities after abortion [letter], by C. B. Goodhart. BRITISH MEDICAL JOURNAL 1(6123):1351, May 20,1978.

5 studies: no apparent harmful effect from legal abortion on subsequent pregnancies; D&C is possible exception. FAMILY PLANNING PERSPECTIVES 10(1):34-35+, January-February, 1978.

Fromino-glutamic acid (Figlu) excretion and abortion, by S. Friedman, et al. PANMINERVA MEDICA 19(4): 271-274, July-August, 1977.

A further case of a 22;22 Robertsonian translocation associated with recurrent abortions, by M. Mameli, et al. HUMAN GENETICS 41(3):359-361, April 24 1978.

Hemostatic disorders in acute renal failure post-abortion. Study of 60 cases, by J. C. Sanchez Avalos, et al. MEDICINA 37(Suppl 2):70-86, 1977.

Incidence of post-abortion psychosis: a prospective study, by C. Brewer. BRITISH MEDICAL JOURNAL 6059: 476-477, February 19, 1977.

—, by C. Brewer. OBSTETRICAL AND GYNECOLOGI-CAL SURVEY 32(7):600-601, September, 1977.

Induced abortion and its hazards, by P. Chatterjee. JOUR-NAL OF THE INDIAN MEDICAL ASSOCIATION 69(8):173-175, October 16, 1977.

Induced abortion. Methods, results and complications, by W. Rummel, et al. FORTSCHRITTE DU MEDIZIN 95(25):2154-2156, September 22, 1977.

Influence of induced abortion on gestational duration in subsequent pregnancies, by J. W. van der Slikke, et al. BRITISH MEDICAL JOURNAL 1(6108):270-272, February 4, 1978.

The interactive effects of induced abortion, inter-pregnancy interval and contraceptive use of subsequent pregnancy outcome, by C. J. Hogue, et al. AMERICAN JOURNAL OF EPIDEMIOLOGY 107(1):15-26, January, 1978.

Intraligamentous tumor of the late post-abortion period, by K. Tshibangu, et al. JOURNAL DE GYNECOLOGIE, OBSTETRIQUE ET BIOLOGIE DE LA REPRODUC-TION 7(1):73-75, January, 1978.

Late sequelae of induced abortion in primigravidae. The outcome of the subsequent pregnancies, by O. Koller, et al. ACTA OBSTETRICIA ET GYNECOLOGICA SCANDINAVICA 56(4):311-317, 1977.

A link between abortion future pregnancy problems. OUR SUNDAY VISITOR 67:2, August 27, 1978.

Management of uterine perforation following elective abor-

tion, by S. M. Freiman, et al. OBSTETRICA AND
GYNECOLOGY 50(6):647-650, December, 1977.

Medical abortion complications. An epidemiologic study at
a mid-Missouri clinic, by D. K. Nemec, et al. OBSTE-
TRICS AND GYNECOLOGY 51(4):433-436, April,
1978.

Morbidity and abortions in mothers of children with Down's
syndrome, by J. Cernay, et al. BRATISLAVSKE LE-
KARSKE LISTY 68(5):559-567, November, 1977.

Pelvic abscess and perforation of the sigmoid colon by a
segment of benign cystic teratoma: an unusual complication of induced abortion, by F. G. Giustini, et al. JOUR-
NAL OF REPRODUCTIVE MEDICINE 20(5):291-292,
May, 1978.

Perforation of the uterus after voluntary termination of pregnancy using the aspiration technique. Two serious cases,
by R. Frydman, et al. JOURNAL DE GYNECOLOGIE,
OBSTETRIQUE ET BIOLOGIE DE LA REPRODUC-
TION 7(3):459-463, April, 1978.

Physiochemical properties of placental proteins in physiological and interrupted pregnancy, by T. N. Pogorelova.
AKUSHERSTVO I GINEKOLOGIIA (7):27-31, July,
1978.

Pituitary and adrenal influences upon spontaneous contractions of uterine horns isolated from ovariectomized or
natural estrus rats, by A. L. Gimeno, et al. REPRODUC-
TION 3(3-4):235-245, July-December, 1976.

Plasma hormone levels and labor in abortion induced with
prostaglandin F2 alpha [proceedings], by U. Gethmann,
et al. ARCHIV FUR GYNAEKOLOGIE 224(1-4):269-
270, July 29, 1977.

Plasma hormone profile of threatened abortion and its prognosis, by I. Miyakawa, et al. INTERNATIONAL JOURNAL OF GYNAECOLOGY AND OBSTETRICS 15(1): 12-16, 1977.

Plasma levels of 15(S)15-methyl PGF2alpha following administration via various routes for induction of abortion, by K. Gréen, et al. PROSTAGLANDINS 14(5):1013-1024, November, 1977.

Plasma non-esterified fatty acids, cortisol and glucose in maternal blood during abortion induced with intra-amniotic prostaglandin F2alpha, by H. Ward, et al. BRITISH JOURNAL OF OBSTETRICS AND GYNECOLOGY 85(5):344-347, May, 1978.

The potential reduction of medical complications from induced abortion, by R. G. Smith, et al. INTERNATIONAL JOURNAL OF GYNAECOLOGY AND OBSTETRICS 15(4):337-346, 1978.

Pregnancy in a uterine scar sacculus—an unusual cause of postabortal haemorrhage. A case report, by J. V. Larsen, et al. SOUTH AFRICAN MEDICAL JOURNAL 53(4): 142-143, January 28, 1978.

Prevention of endotoxin-induced abortion by treatment of mice with antisera, by F. Rioux-Darrieulat, et al. JOURNAL OF INFECTIOUS DISEASES 137(1):7-13, January, 1978.

Probable amniotic fluid embolism during curettage for a missed abortion: a case report, by D. E. Lee, et al. ANESTHESIA AND ANALGESIA 56(5):739-742, September-October, 1977.

Prognostic value of echography in threatened abortion, by D. Gramellini, et al. ATENEO PARMENSE [ACTA BIOMEDICA] 48(3):259-262, 1977.

Psychosomatic aspects of abortion: implications for counseling, by M. B. Bracken. JOURNAL OF REPRODUCTIVE MEDICINE 19(5):265-272, November, 1977.

Re: avulsion of the ureter from both ends as a complication of interruption of pregnancy with a vacuum aspirator [letter], by P. M. Papoff. JOURNAL OF UROLOGY 118(6):1073-1074, December, 1977.

Return of ovarian function after abortion, by P. Lähteenmäki, et al. CLINICAL ENDOCRINOLOGY 8(2):123-132, February, 1978.

The risk of dying from legal abortion in the United States, 1972-1975, by W. Cates, Jr., et al. INTERNATIONAL JOURNAL OF GYNAECOLOGY AND OBSTETRICS 15(2):172-176, 1977.

Sample attrition in studies of psychosocial sequelae of abortion: how great a problem? by N. E. Adler. JOURNAL OF APPLIED SOCIAL PSYCHOLOGY 6:240-259, July-September, 1976.

Serum folic level in abortion, by G. P. Dutta. JOURNAL OF THE INDIAN MEDICAL ASSOCIATION 69(7):149-153, October 1, 1977.

Smoking and abortion [letter], by H. E. McKean. NEW ENGLAND JOURNAL OF MEDICINE 298(2):113-114, January 12, 1978.

State of various indicators of the blood coagulation system before and during induced abortion and anesthesia with novocaine and dicain solutions, by A. I. Zherzhov. VOPROSY OKHRANY MATERINSTVA I DETSTVA 23(4):83-84, April, 1978.

Transient bacteremia due to suction abortion: implications for SBE antibiotic prophylaxis, by R. Ritvo, et al. YALE

JOURNAL OF BIOLOGY AND MEDICINE 50(5):471-479, September-October, 1977.

2-Br-alpha-ergocryptine (Parlodel) in primary and secondary lactation suppression following child-birth or abortion, by H. Gehring, et al. PRAXIS 66(31):985-989, August, 2, 1977.

Ureterouterine fistula as a complication of elective abortion, by J. J. Barton, et al. OBSTETRICS AND GYNECOLOGY 52(1 Suppl):81S-84S, July, 1978.

Uterine rupture: a complication of midtrimester abortion, by E. A. Friedman. PROSTAGLANDINS 15(1):187-191, January, 1978.

Voluntary termination of pregnancy: operational procedure; prevention of preoperative complications. Apropos of 1,000 cases, by M. Rami, et al. JOURNAL DE GYNE-COLOGIE, OBSTETRIQUE ET BIOLOGIE DE LA RE-PRODUCTION 6(8):1171-1182, December, 1977.

What does the patient know about risks of abortion and what does the law know? [editorial], by J. Philip. UGESKRIFT FOR LAEGER 139(32):1919-1920, August 8, 1977.

EGYPT
Hemostasisin the Egyptian female in abortion with a case report, by M. Talaat, et al. JOURNAL OF THE EGYPTIAN MEDICAL ASSOCIATION 59(1-2):98-105, 1976.

ABORTION: COMPLICATIONS: PSYCHOLOGICAL
Abortion methods: morbidity, costs and emotional impact. The effect of delay and method choice on the risk of abortion morbidity. Part 1, by W. Cates, Jr., et al. FAMILY PLANNING PERSPECTIVES 9:266-268+, November-December, 1977.

—. 3. Emotional impact of D&E vs. instillation, by J. B. Rooks, et al. FAMILY PLANNING PERSPECTIVES 9(6):276-277, November-December, 1977.

They made the choice. NEWSWEEK 91:40-41, June 5, 1978.

We've won the right to legal abortion, but we're still learning the physical and emotional results, by R. Cherry. GLAMOUR 76:110-111+, January, 1978.

ABORTION: ECONOMICS
Aborting Medicaid, by P. C. Sexton. DISSENT 24:355, Fall, 1977.

Abortion agreement ends funding deadlock, by M. E. Eccles. CONGRESSIONAL QUARTERLY WEEKLY REPORT 35:2547-2550, December 10, 1977.

Abortion and fairness. PROGRESSIVE 41:9, September, 1977.

Abortion: the debate goes on; limiting medicaid funds for abortions. AMERICA 137:2, July 2, 1977.

Abortion double standard; medicaid vs health insurance coverage. NEW REPUBLIC 177:12, October 15, 1977.

Abortion fight goes to HEW; House approves some funding. NATIONAL CATHOLIC REPORTER 14:4, December 16, 1977.

Abortion funding. CHRISTIANITY TODAY 22:40, December 30, 1977.

Abortion funding: legal and moral questions [letter], by D. D. Clarke. HASTINGS CENTER REPORT 8(2):4+, April, 1978.

Abortion issue: how both sides are helping poor women, by B. Delatiner. McCALLS 105:58-59, April, 1978.

Abortion issue may snag pregnancy benefits bill, by J. Geisel. BUSINESS INSURANCE 12:14, March 20, 1978.

Abortion methods: morbidity, costs and emotional impact. 2. Costs of treating abortion-related complications, by S. D. Von Allmen, et al. FAMILY PLANNING PERSPECTIVES 9(6):273-276, November-December, 1977.

Beal v. Doe (97 Sup Ct 2366), Maher v. Roe (97 Sup Ct 2376), and non-therapeutic abortions: the state does not have to pay the bill. LOYOLA UNIVERSITY OF CHICAGO LAW JOURNAL 9:288-311, Fall, 1977.

Comments received on excess deaths from restricting Medicaid funds for abortions [letter], by S. Wallenstein. AMERICAN JOURNAL OF PUBLIC HEALTH 68(3): 270-272, March, 1978.

Constitutional law—abortion—no requirement to provide Medicaid funds for nontherapeutic abortions under title XIX of the social security act of 1965 or the fourteenth amendment. TULANE LAW REVIEW 52:179-188, December, 1977.

Constitutional law: state funding of nontherapeutic abortions —Medicaid plans—equal protection—right to choose an abortion. AKRON LAW REVIEW 11:345-358, Fall, 1977.

Costs of treating abortion-related complications. Part 2, by S. D. Von Allmen, et al. FAMILY PLANNING PERSPECTIVES 9:273-276, November-December, 1977.

Danse macabre: Hyde amendment, by M. Kinsley. NEW REPUBLIC 177:13+, November 19, 1977.

Denial of public funds for nontherapeutic abortions. CON-NECTICUT LAW REVIEW 10:487-510, Winter, 1978.

Effect of recent medicaid decisions on a constitutional right: abortions only for the rich? FORDHAM URBAN LAW JOURNAL 6:687-710, Spring, 1978.

Federal financial participation in state claims for abortions. FEDERAL REGISTER 43(23):4571-4582, February 2, 1978.

Fight over abortions—heating up again. U. S. NEWS AND WORLD REPORT 83:68, December 19, 1977.

Fresh battle on abortion, by D. A. Williams, et al. NEWS-WEEK 91:32, February 6, 1978.

Hospitals must prepare for inevitable payment controls, by D. H. Hitt. TIMES 19(4):3-5+, April, 1978.

House, Senate deadlock on abortion funds. CONGRES-SIONAL QUARTERLY WEEKLY REPORT 35:1640, August 6, 1977.

Insurance coverage of abortion, contraception and steriliza-tion [various private health insurance plans; United States], by C. F. Muller. FAMILY PLANNING PER-SPECTIVES 10:71-77, March-April, 1978.

Intelligent woman's guide to sex; Supreme Court's decision on use of medicaid for abortions, by J. Coburn. MADE-MOISELLE 83:136+, September, 1977.

Medicaid and the abortion right. GEORGE WASHINGTON LAW REVIEW 44:404-417, March, 1976.

Medicaid-funded abortion: the evidence, the imperatives, by N. M. Welch. VIRGINIA MEDICINE 105(6):463-464, June, 1978.

Medicaid funding for abortions: the Medicaid statute and the equal protection clause. HOFSTRA LAW REVIEW 6: 421-443, Winter, 1978.

New limits on abortion. TIME 110:12-13, December 19, 1977.

New phase in the battle, by J. T. Noonan, Jr. NATIONAL REVIEW 30:279, March 3, 1978.

Punitive and tragic; decision to deny public funds for abortion. NATION 225:3-4, July 2, 1977.

Right without access? Payment for elective abortions after Maher v. Roe (97 Sup Ct 2376). CAPITAL UNIVERSITY LAW REVIEW 7:483-496, 1978.

Sounding Board. Abortions in America: the effects of restrictive funding, by L. R. Berger. NEW ENGLAND JOURNAL OF MEDICINE 298(26):1474-1477, June 29, 1978.

State funding of elective abortion: the Supreme Court defers to the legislature. UNIVERSITY OF CINCINNATI LAW REVIEW 46:1003-1009, 1978.

Supreme Court Report: Fourteenth Amendment does not requie state aid for abortions, by R. L. Young. AMERICAN BAR ASSOCIATION JOURNAL 63:1261-1262, September, 1977.

Unborn and the born again; Supreme Court decision on use of state funds to cover abortion costs. NEW REPUBLIC 177:5-6+, July 2, 1977.

ABORTION: EPIDEMIOLOGY
Epidemiological study of cases undergoing medical termination of pregnancy, by N. Kishore, et al. JOURNAL OF THE INDIAN MEDICAL ASSOCIATION 68(6):116-

119, March 16, 1977.

ABORTION: ETIOLOGY
Etiological and pathogenetic factors in aborted pregnancy, by N. K. Moskvitina, et al. AKUSHERSTVO I GINE-KOLOGIIA (7):31-35, July, 1978.

Some contemporary conceptions about the etiology of early abortion, by P. Drac. CESKOSLOVENSKA GYNE-KOLOGIE 43(4):286-289, May, 1978.

ABORTION: FAILED
Continued pregnancy after failed first trimester abortion, by W. L. Fielding, et al. OBSTETRICS AND GYNECOLO-GY 52(1):56-58, July, 1978.

Failed abortion in a septate uterus, by C. R. McArdle. AMERICAN JOURNAL OF OBSTETRICS AND GYNE-COLOGY 131(8):910, August 15, 1978.

ABORTION: HABITUAL
Chromosomal aberrations in couples with habitual abortion, by M. Lancet, et al. HAREFUAH 94(2):67-69, January 15, 1978.

Chromosome anomalies in cases of habitual abortions, by K. H. Breuker, et al. GEBURTSHILFE UND FRAUEN-HEILKUNDE 38(1):11-17, January, 1978.

Chromosomes in familial primary sterility and in couples with recurrent abortions and stillbirths, by A. Rosen-mann, et al. ISRAEL JOURNAL OF MEDICAL SCI-ENCES 13(11):1131-1133, November, 1977.

Chronic cytomegaloviral infection as the cause of recurrent abortions, by K. Kouba, et al. CESKOSLOVENSKA GYNEKOLOGIE 43(1):15-20, March, 1978.

Cytogenetic studies on couples with habitual abortions

[proceedings], by K. H. Breuker, et al. ARCHIV FUR GYNAEKOLOGIE 224(1-4):186-187, July 29, 1977.

Cytogenetics of recurrent abortions, by D. W. Heritage, et al. FERTILITY AND STERILITY 29(4):414-417, April, 1978.

Embryonic development in consecutive specimens from recurrent spontaneous abortions, by b. J. Poland, et al. AMERICAN JOURNAL OF OBSTETRICS AND GYNECOLOGY 130(5):512-515, March 1, 1978.

Genetically determined pathology of fertility in a population of parental couples having spontaneous (habitual) abortions, by V. P. Kulazhenko, et al. GENETIKA 13(1): 138-145, 1977.

Habitual abortion, by R. H. Glass, et al. FERTILITY AND STERILITY 29(3):257-265, 1978.

A (1;7) translocation, balanced, from a subject associated with repeated abortion. Respository identification No. GM-1356, by L. G. Jackson, et al. CYTOGENETICS AND CELL GENETICS 21(3):175, 1978.

Pancreatitis, cholecystitis, incompetent cervix, and premature labor in a habitual aborter: a rare combination, by M. Hochman, et al. AMERICAN JOURNAL OF OBSTETRICS AND GYNECOLOGY 131(8):905-906, August 15, 1978.

Risk of pre-term delivery in patients with previous pre-term delivery and/or abortion, by M. J. Keirse, et al. BRITISH JOURNAL OF OBSTETRICS AND GYNAECOLOGY 85(2):81-85, February, 1978.

Three women with 45,X/46,XX mosaic and multiple spontaneous abortions, by K. Ioan, et al. ENDOCRINOLOGIE 16(2):139-141, April-June, 1978.

A variant chromosome 17 in a mother with repeated abortions and a 46, XY/47, XXY Klinefelter son, by K. H. Gustavson, et al. UPSALA JOURNAL OF MEDICAL SCIENCES 83(2):119-122, 1978.

ABORTION: HISTORY
Abortion: 10 years after, by P. Davies. DAILY TELEGRAPH p. 17, May 3, 1978.

Abortion: yesterday, today, and tomorrow [editorial], by B. S. Johnson. HEALTH AND SOCIAL WORK 3(1): 3-7, February, 1978.

Female hygiene and nursing care. Induced abortion today and yesterday, by H. T. Ng. JOURNAL OF NURSING 24(2):1-4, April, 1977.

50 years ago—1927—the 1st demonstration of chorionic gonadotropin in the urine of pregnant women by Aschheim and Zondek, by G. Göretzlehner, et al. ZENTRALBLATT FUER GYNAEKOLOGIE 100(10):638-641, 1978.

Infanticide and abortion in nineteenth-century Britian, by R. Sauer. POPULATION STUDIES 32:81-93, March, 1978.

Legalized abortion: effect on national trends of maternal and abortion-related mortality (1940 through 1976), by W. Cates, Jr., et al. AMERICAN JOURNAL OF OBSTETRICS AND GYNECOLOGY 132(2):211-214, September 15, 1978.

Making women modern: middle class women and health reform in 19th century America, by R. M. Morantz. JOURNAL OF SOCIAL HISTORY 10:491-507, Summer, 1977.

Maori abortion practices in pre and early European New

Zealand, by R. B. Hunton. NEW ZEALAND MEDICAL JOURNAL 86(602):567-570, December 28, 1977.

2 years of abortion on demand, by H. Sjövall. LAKARTID-NINGEN 75(6):428-433, February 8, 1978.

ABORTION: ILLEGAL
Estimating the number of illegal abortions, by C. Francome. JOURNAL OF BIOSOCIAL SCIENCE 9(4):467-479, October, 1977.

Illegal abortions in the United States: 1972-1974, by W. Cates, Jr., et al. FAMILY PLANNING PERSPECTIVES 8:86-89, April, 1976.

Medical heroics and the good death, by M. C. Shumiatcher. CANADIAN MEDICAL ASSOCIATION JOURNAL 117(5):520-522, September 3, 1977.

ABORTION: INDUCED
Alpha-fetoprotein, HPL, ostriol and SP1 concentrations in prostaglandin-induced mid-trimester abortions, by M. Cornely, et al. GEBURTSHILFE UND FRAUENHEIL-KUNDE 38(6):446-451, June, 1978.

Artificial abortion and perinatal medicine, by H. Kirchhoff. GEBURTSHILFE UND FRAUENHEILKUNDE 37(10): 849-856, October, 1977.

Differences and delay in decision to seek induced abortion among Black and White women, by m. B. Bracken, et al. SOCIAL PSYCHIATRY 12(2):57-70, 1977.

Female hygiene and nursing care. Induced abortion today and yesterday, by H. T. Ng. JOURNAL OF NURSING 24(2):1-4, April, 1977.

Further ethical considerations in induced abortion. JOGN; JOURNAL OF OBSTETRIC, GYNECOLOGIC AND

NEONATAL NURSING 7:53-55, May-June, 1978.

Hormonal changes in artificial abortion in the 7th-8th weeks of pregnancy, by L. E. Murashko. SOVETSKAYA MEDITZINA (6):75-80, June, 1978.

Induced abortion, by J. Bouwhuis-Lely. TIJDSCHRIFT VOR ZIEKENVERPLEGING 31(5):217-218, February 28, 1978.

Induced abortion and spontaneous abortion: no connection? by J. Kline, et al. AMERICAN JOURNAL OF EPI-DEMIOLOGY 107(4):290-298, April, 1978.

Induced abortion and subsequent outcome of pregnancy in a series of American women, by J. R. Daling, et al. NEW ENGLAND JOURNAL OF MEDICINE 297(23): 1241-1245, December 8, 1977.

Induced abortion in measles? [proceedings], by G. Farkas, et al. ARCHIV FUR GYNAEKOLOGIE 224(1-4):271, July 29, 1977.

Induced abortion—nurses' role in preventive work: numbers shock us but we do not participate in preventive work, by L. Lindén. SYGEPLEJERSKEN 70(48):10-13+, December 7, 1977.

Induced abortion. The patient's knowledge of the anatomy and physiology of the reproductive organs and possible complications of induced abortion, by A. Tabor, et al. UGESKRIFT FOR LAEGER 139(32):1893-1896, August 8, 1977.

Induced abortion with prostaglandin F2alpha and a new prostaglandin E2 derivative, by W. Lichtenegger. WIENER MEDIZINISCHE WOCHENSCHRIFT 127(17):536-538, September 30, 1977.

Induction of abortion by intrauterine administration of prostaglandin via laparoscopy with concurrent sterilization, by M. Morad, et al. INTERNATIONAL JOURNAL OF GYNAECOLOGY AND OBSTETRICS 15(3):256-257, 1977.

Legal induced abortions in the world. POPULATION 32: 175-183, January-February, 1977.

Monthly variation in conceptions leading to induced abortion, by I. C. Cohen, et al. SOCIAL BIOLOGY 24(3): 245-249, Fall, 1977.

Pregnancy after induced abortion [letter], by D. Trichopoulos. NEW ENGLAND JOURNAL OF MEDICINE 298(22):1261, June 1, 1978.

ABORTION: INDUCED: COMPLICATIONS
Fatal amniotic fluid embolism during induced abortion, 1972-1975, by D. A. Grimes, et al. SOUTHERN MEDICAL JOURNAL 70(11):1325-1326, November, 1977.

ABORTION: LAWS AND LEGISLATION
Abortion [laws and practices throughout the world]. PEOPLE (London) 5:4-21, November 2, 1978.

Abortion, ed. by R. W. Jenson. DIAL 17:89-120, Spring, 1978.

Abortion and privacy: a woman's right to self determination. SOUTHWESTERN UNIVERSITY LAW REVIEW 10:173-193, 1978.

Abortion bills pending, by J. Marino. NATIONAL CATHOLIC REPORTER 14:5, August 11, 1978.

Abortion funding: legal and moral questions [letter], by A. Altman. HASTINGS CENTER REPORT 8(2):4+,

April, 1978.

Abortion: how members voted in 1977, by M. E. Eccles. CONGRESSIONAL QUARTERLY WEEKLY REPORT 36:258-267, February 4, 1978.

Abortion in the balance, by M. C. Stenshoel. DIAL 17:89-94, Spring, 1978.

Abortion: an inspection into the nature of human life and potential consequences of legalizing its destruction, by H. T. Krimmel, et al. UNIVERSITY OF CINCINNATI LAW REVIEW 46:725-821, 1977.

Abortion law reform [letter], by J. Bury. BRITISH MEDICAL JOURNAL 1(6128):1698-1699, June 24, 1978.

Abortion—state statute—constitutionality. THE CRIMINAL LAW REPORTER: COURT DECISIONS AND PROCEEDINGS 22(10):2223, December 7, 1977.

Abortion statutes after Danforth: an examination. JOURNAL OF FAMILY LAW 15:3537-3568, 1977.

Abortion's quantum advance, by J. A. Loraine. ATLAS 25:56, September, 1978.

Adjudicating what Yoder left unresolved: religious rights for minor children after Danforth (Planned Parenthood of Cent. Mo. v. Danforth, 96 Sup Ct 2831) and Carey (Carey v. Population Servs. Int. 97 Sup Ct 2010). UNIVERSITY OF PENNSYLVANIA LAW REVIEW 126:1135-1170, May, 1978.

Analysis of recent decisions involving abortions, by P. Geary. CATHOLIC LAWYER 23:237-242, Summer, 1978.

Another storm brewing over abortion: in Congress and elsewhere, tempers run high on easing or stiffening curbs on public funding of a highly controversial operation. U. S. NEWS AND WORLD 85:63, July 24, 1978.

Antiabortion amendment fails, by G. Hildebrand MILITANT 40(15):2, May 14, 1976.

Anti-abortion forces see Akron's consent law as exploding myths; in Ohio, by J. Petosa. NATIONAL CATHOLIC REPORTER 14:32, March 17, 1978.

Are we 25 votes away from losing the Bill of Rights. . .and the rest of the Constitution? by L. C. Wohl. MS MAGAZINE 6:46-49+, February, 1978.

Argument heart: abortion—state statutes—fetal viability. THE CRIMINAL LAW REPORTER: SUPREME COURT PROCEEDINGS 24(3):4050-4051, October 18, 1978.

Beyond morals, rights of abortion issue [reprint], by R. Cohen. ENGAGE/SOCIAL ACTION 6:28-29, April, 1978.

Constitutional law—freedom of the press—prohibition of abortion referral service advertising held unconstitutional. CORNELL LAW REVIEW 61:640+, April, 1976.

Court's abortion decisions flawed, by E. Melvin. OUR SUNDAY VISITOR 65:1+, January 23, 1977.

A decade of change in abortion law: 1967-1977 [throughout the world]. PEOPLE (London) 5:1 folded sheet insert, November 2, 1978.

A decade of international change in abortion law: 1967-1977, by R. J. Cook, et al. AMERICAN JOURNAL OF PUBLIC HEALTH 68:637-651, July, 1978.

Divisive issue: debate over abortion heats up in state capitols as some legislators seek a constitutional ban, by J. Spivak.

WALL STREET JOURNAL 191:40, January 26, 1978.

Due process and equal protection: constitutional implications of abortion notice and reporting requirements. BOSTON UNIVERSITY LAW REVIEW 56:522-541, May, 1976.

Equity in abortion services, by R. Roemer. AMERICAN JOURNAL OF PUBLIC HEALTH 68:629-631, July, 1978.

Federal controls and local realities, by D. H. Hitt. BULLETIN OF THE AMERICAN PROTESTANT HOSPITAL ASSOCIATION 42(1):14-15+, Spring, 1978.

Future of abortion rights: Houston was never like this, by E. B. Stengel. ENGAGE/SOCIAL ACTION 6:27-31, February, 1978.

HEW's Califano urges debate on moral issues, by J. A. Califano, Jr. HOSPITAL PROGRESS 59(3):71-72+, March, 1978.

High court ponders doctors right to kill viable fetus, by R. McMunn. OUR SUNDAY VISITOR 67:1, October 22, 1978.

House bill opposes mandatory abortion coverage but bill now goes to Senate, by J. Castelli. OUR SUNDAY VISITOR 67:2, August 6, 1978.

House syas no on abortions, by A. Plattner. AIR FORCE TIMES 39:8, August 21, 1978.

Impact of constitutional law on the protection of unborn human life: some comparative remarks, by E. Benda. HUMAN RIGHTS 6:223-243, Spring, 1977.

Indigent women and abortion: limitation of the right of

privacy in Maher v. Roe (97 Sup Ct 2376). TULSA LAW JOURNAL 13:287-303, 1977.

Indigent women—what right to abortion? by B. W. Friedman. NEW YORK LAW SCHOOL LAW REVIEW 23:709-741, November 4, 1978.

Judicial imperialism, by R. M. Byrn. HOSPITAL PROGRESS 58(11):90-97+, November, 1977.

Judiciary: Supreme Court—June 20, 1977 abortion decisions, by M. Fisk. TRIAL 13(8):14-16+, August, 1977.

Kentucky law makes abortion more painful; case of M. Pitchford, by B. Bishop. NEW TIMES 11:15, October 2, 1978.

Law and the life sciences: abortion and the Supreme Court: round two. HASTINGS CENTER REPORT 6:15+, October, 1976.

Legal aspects of abortion Der Schwangerschaftsabbruch—rechtlich gesehen. CONCEPTE 13(7):20-26, 1977.

The legal precedents, by M. Bayles. HASTINGS CENTER REPORT 893):37-41, June, 1978.

Meaningful right to abortion for indigent women? LOYOLA LAW REVIEW 24:301-307, Spring, 1978.

Minors' right to abortion and contraception: prospects for invalidating less than absolute restrictions, by D. Klassel, et al. WOMEN'S RIGHTS LAW REPORTER 4:165-183, Spring, 1978.

Mortality enforcement through the criminal law and the modern doctrine of substantive due process, by T. L. Hindes. UNIVERSITY OF PENNSYLVANIA LAW REVIEW 126(2):344-384, 1977.

Nature and uses of congressional power under section five of the fourteenth amendment to overcome decisions of the Supreme Court, by I. A. Gordon. NORTHWESTERN UNIVERSITY LAW REVIEW 72:656-705, November-December, 1977.

Necessity and the case of Dr. Morgentaler, by L. H. Leigh. THE CRIMINAL LAW REVIEW pp. 151-158, March, 1978.

Never again! Never again? Can we lose our right to abortion? by R. B. Gratz. MS MAGAZINE 6:54-55, July, 1977.

New abortion legislation: a comparison with professional policy, by D. Wills. NEW ZEALAND NURSING FORUM 6(1):12-13, March, 1978.

New abortion rulings (what they really mean), by L. Prinz. McCALLS 105:111, October, 1977.

Okay, Mr. Califano, consider the alternatives to abortion. . ., by J. O'Reilly. MS MAGAZINE 6:74+, May, 1978.

On the judgment of the indication of emergency in abortion legislation, by N. Kathke, et al. OEFFENTLICHE GE-SUNDHEITSWESEN 40(1):20-22, January, 1978.

On wrongful birth actions, by J. G. Zimmerly. LEGAL ASPECTS OF MEDICAL PRACTICE 6(3):48-49, March, 1978.

Operation of the abortion law [letter], by M. E. Krass. CANADIAN MEDICAL ASSOCIATION JOURNAL 118(11):1362, June 10, 1978.

Ordeal of a divided jury; W. Waddill case. TIME 111:24, May 22, 1978.

Parent and child—statutory construction and interpretation of sections of a Massachusetts statute which set forth the necessary extent of parental notification, consultation and consent for the performance of an abortion on an unmarried minor. JOURNAL OF FAMILY LAW 16:116-122, November, 1977.

Parental consent abortion statutes: the limits of state power. INDIANA LAW JOURNAL 52:837-850, Summer, 1977.

Patients' rights. Abortion. The right to die. ANNUAL SURVEY OF AMERICAN LAW 1977:535-559, 1977.

Paying for abortion: is the court wrong? by R. Shinn, et al. CHRISTIANITY AND CRISIS 37:202-207, September 19, 1977.

Persons in the whole sense, by G. M. Atkinson. AMERICAN JOURNAL OF JURISPRUDENCE 22:86-117, 1977.

M. Pitchford prosecuted for self-abortion, by A. Scarlet. TIME 112:22, September 11, 1978.

Privacy and public funding: Maher v. Roe (97 Sup Ct 2376) as the interaction of Roe v. Wade and Dandridge v. Williams, by D. T. Hardy. ARIZONA LAW REVIEW 18:903-938, 1976.

Professional and public opinion on abortion law proposals, by W. Facer. NEW ZEALAND NURSING FORUM 6(1):13-15, March, 1978.

Puberty, privacy, and protection: the risks of children's 'rights', by B. C. Hafen. AMERICAN BAR ASSOCIATION JOURNAL 63:1383-1388, October, 1977.

Reform of state criminal law and procedure, by B. J. George, Jr. LAW AND CONTEMPORARY PROBLEMS 4(1):63-

101, Winter, 1977.

The right to life in English law; the rights of the unborn and of the woman faced with an unwanted pregnancy. TABLET 232:549+, June 10, 1978.

Roe v. Wade and In re Quinlan [(NJ) 355 A 2d 647] : individual decision and the scope of privacy's constitutional guarantee. UNIVERSITY OF SAN FRANCISCO LAW REVIEW 12:111-153, Fall, 1977.

The Supreme Court and social change: the case of abortion, by K. A. Kemp, et al. WESTERN POLITICAL QUARTERLY 31(1):19-31, March, 1978.

Supreme Court hearing abortion-related cases, decision to come in the spring, by T. Barbarie. OUR SUNDAY VISITOR 65:2, January 30, 1977.

Supreme Court on minors and contraception; June 9, 1977. ORIGINS 7:65+, June 23, 1977.

Supreme Court Report: New York contraceptive act violates first amendment, by R. L. Young. AMERICAN BAR ASSOCIATION JOURNAL 63:1131-1132, August, 1977.

Supreme Court to review cases on fetal viability, by J. Castelli. HOSPITAL PROGRESS 59(4):18, April, 1978.

The Supreme Court's abortion rulings and social change, by D. W. Brady, et al. SOCIAL SCIENCE QUARTERLY 57:535-546, December, 1976.

Taking up the role of prophets; statement on the fifth anniversary of the U. S. Supreme Court's January 22, 1973, abortion rulings, by J. Quinn. ORIGINS 7:524-526, February 2, 1978.

Trial of Dr. Waddill, by S. Fraker, et al. NEWSWEEK 91: 35, April 3, 1978.

Verdict in Kentucky; M. Pitchford's abortion trial. NEWS-WEEK 92:35-36, September 11, 1978.

Wave of informed consent laws facing tough challenges in court. OUR SUNDAY VISITOR 67:1, September 24, 1978.

What I learned marching with N.O.W., by J. M. Shutt. FARM JOURNAL 101:F1, December, 1977.

Woman's right, physician's judgment: Commonwealth v. Edelin and a physician's criminal liability for fetal manslaughter, by S. Wagner. WOMEN'S RIGHTS LAW REPORTER 4:97-114, Winter, 1978.

Wrongful birth and emotional distress damages: a suggested approach. UNIVERSITY OF PITTSBURGH LAW REVIEW 38:550-560, Spring, 1977.

FRANCE
Reactions of a large number of laymen in France to the bill on the liberalization of abortion. CHRIST TO THE WORLD 22:286-289, November 4, 1977.

GERMANY
Legal prerequisites for pregnancy interruption due to medical, eugenic and social indications, by W. Spann, et al. INTERNIST 19(5):259-263, May, 1978.

GREAT BRITAIN
The fight for life can be won; good news from Britain for pro-life, by D. Finlay. OUR SUNDAY VISITOR 65:1+, December 5, 1976.

A woman's right to choose, by D. C. Bradley. MODERN LAW REVIEW 41:365-382, July, 1978.

ITALY
Three-month wonder. ECONOMIST 267:66, April 22, 1978.

UNITED STATES
Harmful effects of abortion legislation in United States, by T. Cooke. OSSERVATORE ROMANO 4(461): 12, January 27, 1977.

Illinois court requires physician to try to save viable fetus [letter], by D. J. Horan. HOSPITAL PROGRESS 59(6):6+, June, 1978.

A way round Congress. ECONOMIST 268:30, August 12, 1978.

ABORTION: MISSED
Fetus papyraceus in twin pregnancy, by E. J. Livnat, et al. OBSTETRICS AND GYNECOLOGY 51(1 Suppl):41S-45S, January, 1978.

Induction of labor in missed abortion, fetal death and vesicular mole, using PGF2 alpha by extra-amniotic intracavitary administration, by A. Paladini, et al. MINERVA GINECOLOGIA 29(12):931-938, December, 1977.

Management of missed abortion and fetal death in utero, by H. el-Damarawy, et al. PROSTAGLANDINS 14(3):583-590, September, 1977.

Missed abortion and uterine contractility, by B. Gustavii. AMERICAN JOURNAL OF OBSTETRICS AND GYNE-COLOGY 130(1):18-19, January 1, 1978.

ABORTION: MORTALITY AND MORTALITY STATISTICS
Abortion deaths and social class [letter], by C. Tietze. LAN-CET 1(7982):469, August 21, 1976.

Analysis of spontaneous abortiveness, child mortality, and of inborn developmental defects in two population series from Horna Nitra, by A. Gencik, et al. BRATISLAVSKE LEKARSKE LISTY 69(6):678-687, June, 1978.

Comparative risk of death from legally induced abortion in hospitals and nonhospital facilities, by D. A. Grimes, et al. OBSTETRICS AND GYNECOLOGY 51(3):323-326, March, 1978.

Death after legally induced abortion. A comprehensive approach for determination of abortion-related deaths based on record linkage, by J. D. Shelton, et al. PUBLIC HEALTH REPORTS 93(4):375-378, July-August, 1978.

Deaths caused by pulmonary thromboembolism after legally induced abortion, by A. M. Kimball, et al. AMERICAN JOURNAL OF OBSTETRICS AND GYNECOLOGY 132(2):169-174, September 15, 1978.

Drug file: abortion deaths from anesthesia, by E. M. Goldstein. TRIAL 13(6):11, June, 1977.

Effect of liberalized abortion on maternal mortality rates [letter], by W. Cates, Jr., et al. AMERICAN JOURNAL OF OBSTETRICS AND GYNECOLOGY 130(3):372-374, February 1, 1978.

From the files of the KMA Maternal Mortality Study Committee, by J. W. Greene, Jr. JOURNAL OF THE KENTUCKY MEDICAL ASSOCIATION 76(3):134-135, March, 1978.

Lethality in abortions and the ways for its further decrease, by Ia. P. Sol'skii, et al. PEDIATRIYA AKUSHERSTVO I HINEKOLOHIYA (2):47-49, 1978.

Standardized mortality rates associated with legal abortion: United States, 1972-1975, by W. Cates, Jr., et al. FAMILY PLANNING PERSPECTIVES 10:109-112, March-April,

1978.

ABORTION: OUTPATIENT TREATMENT
Abortion of early pregnancy on an outpatient basis using Silastic 15(S)-15-methyl prostaglandin F2alpha vaginal devices, by S. L. Corson, et al. FERTILITY AND STE-RILITY 28(10):1056-1062, October, 1977.

Ambulatory abortion, by O. S. Slepykh, et al. PEDIATRIYA, AKUSHERSTVO I HINEKOLOHIYA (5):60-63, September-October, 1977.

Ambulatory care following pregnancy interruption in a rural district, by B. Zerning, et al. ZEITSCHRIFT FUR DIE GESAMTE HYGIENE UND IHRE GRENZGEBIETE 24(5):392-394, May, 1978.

Outpatient termination of pregnancy, by G. M. Filshie, et al. BRITISH JOURNAL OF OBSTETRICS AND GYNAE-COLOGY 84(7):509-513, July, 1977.

Outpatient termination of pregnancy in the first trimester during paracervical blockade with Carticain, by A. Gallinat, et al. GEBURTSHILFE UND FRAUENHEIL-KUNDE 38(2):105-106, February, 1978.

Out-patient therapeutic termination of pregnancy at the University Hospital of the West Indies, by B. S. Sengupta, et al. WEST INDIAN MEDICAL JOURNAL 26(3): 157-163, September, 1977.

ABORTION: SEPTIC
Experiences with the preventive use of heparin in septic abortion, by R. Schwarz. ZENTRALBLATT FUER GYNAEKOLOGIE 100(8):487-489, 1978.

Prenatal selection and dermatoglyphic patterns, by W. J. Babler. AMERICAN JOURNAL OF PHYSICAL AN-THROPOLOGY 48:21-27, January, 1978.

Septic abortion and IUCDs [letter], by R. A. Sparks, et al. BRITISH MEDICAL JOURNAL 1(6120):1141, April 29, 1978.

Vesicular stomatitis virus causes abortion and neonatal death in ferrets, by S. C. Suffin, et al. JOURNAL OF CLINICAL MICROBIOLOGY 6(4):437-438, October, 1977.

ABORTION: SEPTIC: TECHNIQUES
Value of amoxicillin and ampicillin in the treatment of septic abortion (double blind and random comparative studies), by E. Lopez Ortiz, et al. GINECOLOGIA Y OBSTETRICIA DE MEXICO 43(256):123-134, February, 1978.

ABORTION: SPONTANEOUS
Alpha-fetoprotein (AFP) levels in maternal serum in 115 patients with spontaneous abortion, by G. Lidbjörk, et al. ACTA OBSTETRICIA ET GYNECOLOGICA SCANDINAVICA (69):50-53, 1977.

Alpha-1-antitrypsin (Pi)-types in recurrent miscarriages, by D. Aarskog, et al. CLINICAL GENETICS 13(1):81-84, January, 1978.

Cell-mediated immunity in pregnant patients with and without a previous history of spontaneous abortions, by G. Garewal, et al. BRITISH JOURNAL OF OBSTETRICS AND GYNAECOLOGY 85(3):221-224, March, 1978.

Cerclage in the prevention of spontaneous abortion and premature labor. Experiences at the "Boris Kidric" in health institute 1966-1975, by L. Jankovic. NARODNO ZDRAVIJE 32(11-12):525-528, November-December, 1976.

Characteristics of the hypophyseal-ovarian relationship in miscarriage, by E. S. Kononova, et al. AKUSHERSTVO I GINEKOLOGIIA (8):37-40, August, 1977.

Chromosome abnormalities: a major cause of birth defects, stillbirth and spontaneous abortion, by R. G. Worton. CANADIAN MEDICAL ASSOCIATION JOURNAL 117(8):849+, October 22, 1977.

Chromosomes in miscarriage [letter], by M. A. Leversha, et al. AMERICAN JOURNAL OF OBSTETRICS AND GYNECOLOGY 130(2):245-246, January 15, 1978.

Chronic alcoholism and increased number of spontaneous abortions, by S. Moskovic. SRPSKI ARHIV ZA CELO-KUPNO LEKARSTVO 105(2):157-162, February, 1977.

Cigarette smoking and spontaneous abortion. BRITISH MEDICAL JOURNAL 1:259-260, February 4, 1978.

Cytogenetic study in early spontaneous abortion, by H. Takahara, et al. HIROSHIMA JOURNAL OF MEDICAL SCIENCES 26(4):291-296, 1977.

A cytogenetic study of spontaneous abortions in Hawaii, by T. J. Hassold, et al. ANNALS OF HUMAN GENETICS 41(4):443-454, May, 1978.

Embryonic development in consecutive specimens from recurrent spontaneous abortions, by B. J. Poland, et al. AMERICAN JOURNAL OF OBSTETRICS AND GYNE-COLOGY 130(5):512-515, March 1, 1978.

Frequency of endocrine problems in repeated spontaneous abortion, by A. M. Serban. ENDOCRINOLOGIE 16(1): 55-59, January-March, 1978.

Genetic aspects of spontaneous abortion, by J. G. Lauritsen. DANISH MEDICAL BULLETIN 24(5):169-189, October, 1977.

Hormonic colpocytotest in diagnosis and therapy of some

spontaneous abortions, by G. Teleman, et al. REVISTA
MEDICO-CHIRURGICALA A SOCIETATII DE MEDICI
SI NATURATISTI DIN IASI 81(3):499-504, July-September, 1977.

Immunological mechanism for spontaneous abortion in systemic lupus erythematosus, by B. Breshnihan, et al.
LANCET 2(8050):1205-1207, December 10, 1977.

Immunological study on spontaneous abortion in early pregnancy, by H. Amemiya. NICHIDAI IGAKU ZASSHI
66(10):865-876, 1977.

Incidence of spontaneous abortion with and without prior
administration of ovulation inhibitors based on morphological studies [proceedings] , by G. Dallenbach-Hellweg.
ARCHIV FUR GYNAEKOLOGIE 224(1-4):25-26, July
29, 1977.

Maternal plasma alpha-feto-protein in pregnancies terminating in spontaneous abortion, by Z. Habib. BIOLOGY OF
THE NEONATE 33(1-2):39-42, 1978.

Monosomy 21 in a human spontaneous abortus. Morphogenetic disturbances and phenotype at the cellular level,
by A. M. Kuliev, et al. HUMAN GENETICS 38(2):137-145, September 22, 1977.

On the use of fenoterolhydrobromide in the treatment of
imminent abortion, by E. Ruppin, et al. GEBURT-SHILFE UND FRAUENHEILKUNDE 38(6):461-467,
June, 1978.

Origin of acrocentric trisomies in spontaneous abortuses,
by N. Niikawa, et al. HUMAN GENETICS 40(1):73-78,
December 29, 1977.

Practical control of spontaneous abortion, by J. Barrat.
JOURNAL DE GYNECOLOGIE, OBSTETRIQUE ET

BIOLOGIE DE LA REPRODUCTION 6(5):695-709, July-August, 1977.

Prediction of spontaneous abortion by vaginal cytologic smears, by W. Busch. ZENTRALBLATT FUER GYNAE-KOLOGIE 100(1):23-33, 1978.

Prognostic value of the pregnancy zone protein during early pregnancy in spontaneous abortion, by M. G. Damber, et al. OBSTETRICS AND GYNECOLOGY 51(6):677-681, June, 1978.

The prognostic value of serum hCG analysis with the aid of an HCG-receptor assay in pateints with imminent abortion [proceedings], by C. Clasen, et al. ARCHIV FUR GYNAEKOLOGIE 224(1-4):89-90, July 29, 1977.

Rate of abortions and abnormalities following viral hepatitis [letter], by U. Theile. MEDIZINISCHE KLINIK 72(38): 1554, September 23, 1977.

Salbutamol and haemorrhage at spontaneous abortion [letter], by P. S. Vinall, et al. LANCET 2(8052-8053): 1355, December 24-31, 1977.

Simplified classification of spontaneous abortions, by D. I. Rushton. JOURNAL OF MEDICAL GENETICS 15(1): 1-9, February, 1978.

Spontaneous abortion and aging of human ova and spermatozoa, by R. Guerrero, et al; Perinatology begins before conception [editorial], by F. Hecht, et al. NEW ENG-LAND JOURNAL OF MEDICINE 293:573-575+, September 18, 1975.

Spontaneous abortion and the use of sugar substitutes (saccharin), by J. Kline, et al. AMERICAN JOURNAL OF OBSTETRICS AND GYNECOLOGY 130(6):708-711, March 15, 1978.

Spontaneous abortion in perspective. A 7-year study, by S. W. Sandler. SOUTH AFRICAN MEDICAL JOURNAL 52(28):1115-1118, December 31, 1977.

Successive spontaneous abortions including one with whole-arm translocation between chromosomes 2, by K. Ohama, et al. HUMAN GENETICS 40(2):221-225, January 19, 1978.

Surveillance of spontaneous abortions. Power in environmental monitoring, by J. Kline, et al. AMERICAN JOURNAL OF EPIDEMIOLOGY 106(5):345-350, November, 1977.

Toxoplasma antibodies and spontaneous abortion, by D. Lolis, et al. INTERNATIONAL JOURNAL OF GYNAECOLOGY AND OBSTETRICS 15(4):299-301, 1978.

SWEDEN
Occupational and environmental risks in and around a smelter in northern Sweden. III. Frequencies of spontaneous abortion, by S. Nordström, et al. HEREDITAS 88(1):51-54, 1978.

THAILAND
Study of "spontaneous" abortion in Thailand, by S. Koetsawang, et al. INTERNATIONAL JOURNAL OF GYNAECOLOGY AND OBSTETRICS 15(4): 361-368, 1978.

ABORTION: SPONTANEOUS: COMPLICATIONS
Sequential aspects of spontaneous abortion: maternal age, parity, and pregnancy compensation artifact, by A. F. Naylor. SOCIAL BIOLOGY 21:195-204, Summer, 1974; Reply by W. H. James, 24:86-89, Spring, 1977.

Spontaneous abortion and fetal abnormality in subsequent

pregnancy [letter], by A. J. Gardiner, et al. BRITISH MEDICAL JOURNAL 2(6131):200, July 15, 1978.

Spontaneous abortion, sex ratio and facial cleft malformations, by J. C. Bear. CLINICAL GENETICS 13(1):1-7, January, 1978.

ABORTION: SPONTANEOUS: ETIOLOGY
Spontaneous abortions among women in hospital laboratory [letter], by M. Strandberg, et al. LANCET 1(8060): 384-385, February 18, 1978.

ABORTION: STATISTICS
Abortions increase during '76. U. S. MEDICINE 14(12):4, June 15, 1978.

Abortions 1976, by A. F. Frit Jofsson. LAKARTIDNINGEN 75(19):1907-1908, May 10, 1978.

The public health need for abortion statistics, by J. C. Smith, et al. PUBLIC HEALTH REPORTS 93(2):194-197, March-April, 1978.

Simplified dokumentation and evaluation in abortion patients using data-based medical records, by F. Rössel, et al. ZENTRALBLATT FUER GYNAEKOLOGIE 99(18): 1089-1096, 1977.

UNITED STATES
Standardized mortality rates associated with legal abortion: United States 1972-1975. FAMILY PLANNING PERSPECTIVES 10(2):109-112, March-April, 1978.

ABORTION: TECHNIQUES
Abortion in the early stage of pregnancy and prostaglandin, by N. Shimada. JOSANPU ZASSHI 32(1):53, January, 1978.

Abortion induced by prostaglandin F 2 alpha in risk patients, by E. Ehrig, et al. ZENTRALBLATT FUER GYNAE-KOLOGIE 100(14):921-925, 1978.

Abortion of early pregnancy on an outpatient basis using Silastic 15(S)-15-methyl prostaglandin F2alpha vaginal devices, by S. L. Corson, et al. FERTILITY AND STE-RILITY 28(10):1056-1062, October, 1977.

Administration of prostaglandins by various routes for in-duction of abortion. Merits and demerits, by U. Krishna, et al. PROSTAGLANDINS 15(4):685-693, April, 1978.

The advantages of the extra-amniotic transcervical instilla-tion of rivanol in therapeutic abortions, by W. Haensel, et al. GEBURTSHILFE UND FRAUENHEILKUNDE 37(12):1050-1054, December, 1977.

The advent of legal abortion and surgical abortion tech-niques, by P. T. Wilson. MEDICAL TRIAL TECHNIQUE QUARTERLY 22(3):241-278, Winter, 1976.

Anesthesia in induced abortion by intravenous administra-tion of sombrevin and fentanyl, by V. I. Rogovskoi, et al. AKUSHERSTVO I GINEKOLOGIIA (12):51, Decem-ber, 1977.

Animal in vivo studies and in vitro experiments with human tubes for end-to-end anastomotic operation by a CO2-laser technique, by F. Klink, et al. FERTILITY AND STERILITY 30(1):100-102, July, 1978.

Bacteriologic culture results obtained before and after elec-tive midtrimester urea abortion, by R. T. Burkman, et al. CONTRACEPTION 17(6):513-521, June, 1978.

The cold sterilization of abortion cannulae, by M. R. Spence, et al. INTERNATIONAL JOURNAL OF GYNAE-COLOGY AND OBSTETRICS 15(4):369-372, 1978.

A comparison of D & C and vacuum aspiration for performing first trimester abortion, by T. H. Lean, et al. INTERNATIONAL JOURNAL OF GYNAECOLOGY AND OBSTETRICS 14(6):481-486, 1976.

A controlled trial of antiemetics in abortion by PCG2alpha and laminaria, by A. F. Kaul, et al. JOURNAL OF REPRODUCTIVE MEDICINE 20(4):213-218, April, 1978.

Development of a long-acting vaginal suppository for termination of 2d trimester pregnancy and for preoperative cervical dilatation, by M. Bygdeman, et al. LAKARTID-NINGEN 74(46):4107-4109, November 16, 1977.

Dilatation and curettage for termination of second-trimester pregnancy [letter], by S. Fribourg. AMERICAN JOURNAL OF OBSTETRICS AND GYNECOLOGY 130(4): 505-506, February 15, 1978.

Do-it-yourself abortions available through new technology that's here, by R. Shaw. OUR SUNDAY VISITOR 66:3, May 7, 1978.

Drug-induced abortion in early pregnancy with intravaginally administered (15S)-15-methyl-prostaglandin F2 alpha methylester (15-S-PGF2 alpha) [proceedings], by J. H. Duenhoelter, et al. ARCHIV FUR GYNAEKOLOGIE 224(1-4):268-269, July 29, 1977.

Early artificial termination of pregnancy by Karman's method, by D. Vasilev. AKUSHERSTVO I GINEKOLO-GIIA 17(2):98-103, 1978.

Early first-trimester abortion induction by Silastic vaginal devices for continuous release of 15(S)=15=methyl prostaglandin F2alpha methyl ester, by J. Robbins. FERTILITY AND STERILITY 28(10):1048-1055, October, 1977.

The effect of delay and method choice on the risk of abortion morbidity, by W. Cates, Jr., et al. FAMILY PLANNING PERSPECTIVES 9(6):266-268+, November-December, 1977.

The effect of 15-methyl-prostaglandin F2 alpha administered intramuscularly to induce abortion in the first half of pregnancy [proceedings], by U. Haller, et al. ARCHIV FUR GYNAEKOLOGIE 224(1-4):266-268, July 29, 1977.

Effect of a new service on women's abortion experience, by S. Treloar, et al. JOURNAL OF BIOSOCIAL SCIENCE 9(4):417-427, October, 1977.

The effect of oxytocin on hypertonic saline abortion, by B. Sandström, et al. ACTA OBSTETRICIA ET GYNECOLOGICA SCANDINAVICA (66):129-131, 1977.

Evacuation of retained products of conception in a treatment room and without general anaesthesia, by G. M. Filshie, et al. BRITISH JOURNAL OF OBSTETRICS AND GYNAECOLOGY 84(7):514-516, July, 1977.

Evaluation of a balloon dilator to augment midtrimester abortion, by M. Borten, et al. AMERICAN JOURNAL OF OBSTETRICS AND GYNECOLOGY 130(2):156-159, January 15, 1978.

Evaluation of a single dose schedule of 15 (S) 15 methyl PGF2 alpha methyl ester suppository for the termination of 10-14 weeks of pregnancy, by G. Kinra, et al. CONTRACEPTION 17(5):455-464, May, 1978.

Extra-amniotic prostaglandin E2 and intravenous oxytocin in termination of mid-trimester pregnancy and the management of missed abortion and hydatiform mole, by H. Arshat. MEDICAL JOURNAL OF MALAYSIA 31(3):220-225, March, 1977.

Failure to cause abortion in cows with intravenous sodium iodide treatment [letter], by H. P. Riemann, et al. JOURNAL OF THE AMERICAN VETERINARY ASSO- CIATION 172(10):1147, May 15, 1978.

Fatal uterine rupture during oxytocin-augmented, saline- induced abortion, by D. A. Grimes, et al. AMERICAN JOURNAL OF OBSTETRICS AND GYNECOLOGY 130(5):591-593, March 1, 1978.

15(S)15-methyl prostaglandin F2alpha for termination of very early human pregnancy. A comparative study of a single intramuscular injection and vaginal suppositories, by P. Fylling, et al. PROSTAGLANDINS 14(4):785- 790, October, 1977.

General anasthesia for outpatient termination of pregnancy. A prospective analysis of 6 different types of anesthetics, by A. Risbo, et al. UGESKRIFT FOR LAEGER 139(32): 1896-1898, August 8, 1977.

Gestational age limit of twelve weeks for abortion by curet- tage, by D. A. Grimes, et al. AMERICAN JOURNAL OF OBSTETRICS AND GYNECOLOGY 132(2):207-210, September 15, 1978.

Hyperosmolar urea for elective midtrimester abortion. Ex- perience in 1,913 cases, by R. T. Burkman, et al. AMERICAN JOURNAL OF OBSTETRICS AND GYNE- COLOGY 131(1):10-17, May 1, 1978.

Induced abortion with prostaglandin F2alpha and a new prostaglandn E2 derivative, by W. Lichtenegger. WIENER MEDIZINISCHE WOCHENSCHRIFT 127(17):536-538, September 30, 1977.

Induction of abortion by intrauterine administration of prostaglandin via laparoscopy with concurrent steriliza- tion, by M. Morad, et al. INTERNATIONAL JOURNAL

OF GYNAECOLOGY AND OBSTETRICS 15(3):256-257, 1977.

Induction of abortion using a single dose of vaginally administered prostaglandin, by F. Havranek. CESKOSLO-VENSKA GYNECOLOGIE 43(3):202-203, April, 1978.

Induction of abortion with 15(S)-15-methyl PGF2alpha (Tham) vaginal suppositories, by D. Vengadasalam, et al. INTERNATIONAL JOURNAL OF GYNAECOLOGY AND OBSTETRICS 15(1):93-95, 1977.

Induction of abortion with prostaglandin F2 alpha. Cervix dilatation with 3 mg prostaglandin F2 alpha gel in the 1. trimester. Experiences after 197 induced abortions, by H. Knabe, et al. FORTSCHRITTE DU MEDIZIN 96(7): 360-362, February 16, 1978.

Induction of internal abortion, of hydatidiform mole in the 2d and 3d trimesters of pregnancy, with a dead fetus, using transcervical intra-amniotic injection of PGF2 alpha, by E. Rizzuto, et al. MINERVA GINECOLOGIA 29(10):775-800, October, 1977.

Induction of labour with prostaglandin E2 gel in cases of intrauterine fetal death, by T. H. Lippert, et al. PRO-STAGLANDINS 15(3):533-542, March, 1978.

Induction of second-trimester abortion with a single dose (40 mg) of intra-amniotic prostaglandin F2a, by E. S. Grech, et al. EAST AFRICAN MEDICAL JOURNAL 54(6):306-313, June, 1977.

Injections of ACTH and HCG into the fetus during midpregnancy legal abortion performed by intraamniotic instillation of prostaglandin. Influence on maternal plasma oestrogens and testosterone, by J. R. Strecker, et al. HORMONE AND METABOLIC RESEARCH 9(5):409-414, September, 1977.

Interruption of early pregnancy with a silastic device containing (15S)-15-methyl prostaglandin F2alpha methyl ester: efficacy and mode of action, by J. H. Duenhoelter, et al. CONTRACEPTION 17(1):51-59, January, 1978.

Interruption of first trimester pregnancy by prostaglandins, by M. Bygdeman, et al. INTERNATIONAL JOURNAL OF GYNAECOLOGY AND OBSTETRICS 15(1):69-72, 1977.

Interruption of pregnancy in the 2nd trimester through the intra-amniotic instillation of 25% glucose, by V. Krstajic, et al. MEDICINSKI PREGLED 30(7-8):401-403, 1977.

Intraamniotic and intramuscular administration of 15-methyl prostaglandin F 2alpha for midtrimester abortion, by C. Bergquist, et al. ACTA OBSTETRICIA ET GYNECOLOGICA SCANDINAVICA (66):19-26, 1977.

The *Majority Report* guide to abortifacient herbs, by V. Cava-Rizzuto, et al. MAJORITY REPORT 7:7-9, August 6-19, 1977.

Measurement of intrauterine pressure during extra-amnial induced abortion with prostaglandin F2 alpha, by G. Schott, et al. ZENTRALBLATT FUER GYNAEKOLOGIE 100(12):805-810, 1978.

Mechanism for spontaneous abortion in S.L.E. [letter], by N. Amino, et al. LANCET 1(8061):447, February 25, 1978.

Methods of midtrimester abortion: which is safest? by D. A. Grimes, et al. INTERNATIONAL JOURNAL OF GYNAECOLOGY AND OBSTETRICS 15(2):184-188, 1977.

Mid-trimester abortion by dilatation and evacuation: a safe and practical alternative, by D. A. Grimes, et al. NEW ENGLAND JOURNAL OF MEDICINE 296:1141-1145,

May 19, 1977.

Mid-trimester abortion induced by intravaginal administration of prostaglandin F2 alpha-methylester suppositories, by A. S. van den Bergh, et al. CONTRACEPTION 17(2): 141-151, February, 1978.

Midtrimester abortion with urea, prostaglandin F2alpha, laminaria, and oxytocin. A new regimen, by W. B. Wilson, Jr. OBSTETRICS AND GYNECOLOGY 51(6): 699-701, June, 1978.

Midtrimester intra-amniotic administration of prostaglandin F2alpha in combination with an hyperosmolar urea solution: effect upon plasma levels of estradiol, progesterone, and human placental lactogen (HPL), by G. Sher, et al. ACTA OBSTETRICIA ET GYNECOLOGICA SCANDINAVICA 57(3):223-225, 1978.

Morphological changes in the placenta and decidua after induction of abortion by extra-amniotic prostaglandin, by H. Fox, et al. HISTOPATHOLOGY 2(2):145-151, March, 1978.

Performing second-trimester abortions: rational for inpatient basis, by G. Stroh, et al. NEW YORK STATE JOURNAL OF MEDICINE 75:2168-2171, October, 1975.

Placental pathology in midtrimester pregnancies interrupted by intra-amniotic injection of hypertonic urea, by S. Segal, et al. BRITISH JOURNAL OF OBSTETRICS AND GYNAECOLOGY 83(2):156-159, February, 1976.

Plasma levels of 15(S)15-methyl PGF2alpha following administration via various routes for induction of abortion, by K. Gréen, et al. PROSTAGLANDINS 14(5):1013-1024, November, 1977.

Postabortion insertions of the pleated membrane, by

X. Tacla, et al. INTERNATIONAL JOURNAL OF
GYNAECOLOGY AND OBSTETRICS 15(3):275-278,
1977.

Pregnancy termination with the PGE2-analogue SHB 286,
by M. O. Pulkkinen. PROSTAGLANDINS 15(1):161-
167, January, 1978.

Prostaglandin-induced abortion and outcome of subsequent
pregnancies: a prospective controlled study, by I. Z.
MacKenzie, et al. BRITISH MEDICAL JOURNAL
6095:1114-1117, October 29, 1977.

Prostaglandins and abortion. I. Intramuscular administration
of 15-methyl prostaglandin F2alpha for induction of
abortion in weeks 10 to 20 of pregnancy, by the World
Health Organization Task Force on the Use of Prostaglandins for the Regulation of Fertility. AMERICAN JOUR-
NAL OF OBSTETRICS AND GYNECOLOGY 129(6):
593-596, November 15, 1977.

—. II. Single extra-amniotic administration of 0.92 mg. of
15-methyl prostaglandin F2alpha in Hyskon for termination of pregnancies in weeks 10 to 20 of gestation: an
international multicenter study, by the World Health
Organization Task Force on the Use of Prostaglandins
for the Regulation of Fertility. AMERICAN JOURNAL
OF OBSTETRICS AND GYNECOLOGY 129(6):597-
600, November 15, 1977.

—. III. Comparison of single intra-amniotic injections of 15-
methyl prostaglandin F2alpha and prostaglandin F2alpha
for termination of second-trimester pregnancy: an international multicenter study, by the World Health Organization Task Force on the Use of Prostaglandins for the
Regulation of Fertility. AMERICAN JOURNAL OF
OBSTETRICS AND GYNECOLOGY 129(6):601-606,
November 15, 1977.

A randomized study of 12-mm and 15.9 mm cannulas in midtrimester abortion by laminaria and vacuum curettage, by P. G. Stubblefield, et al. FERTILITY AND STERILITY 29(5):512-517, May, 1978.

Reduced dose of Rh immunoglobulin following first trimester pregnancy termination, by F. H. Stewart, et al. OBSTETRICS AND GYNECOLOGY 51(3):318-322, March, 1978.

Response to the letter by Dr. Hodari (American Journal of Obstetrics and Gynecology 130:505, 1978) [letter], by S. Fribourg. AMERICAN JOURNAL OF OBSTETRICS AND GYNECOLOGY 131(6):703, July 15, 1978.

Response to the letter by Drs. Wolf and Rubinstein regarding the safety of prostaglandin F2alpha in abortion [letter], by C. W. Tyler, Jr., et al. AMERICAN JOURNAL OF OBSTETRICS AND GYNECOLOGY 131(2):230-231, May 15, 1978.

A safer method for paracervical block in therapeutic abortions, by R. McKenzie, et al. AMERICAN JOURNAL OF OBSTETRICS AND GYNECOLOGY 130(3):317-320, February 1, 1978.

The safety of combined abortion-sterilization procedure, by M. C. Cheng, et al. AMERICAN JOURNAL OF OBSTETRICS AND GYNECOLOGY 129(5):548-552, November 1, 1977.

Safety of prostaglandin F2alpha in abortion [letter], by J. A. Wolf, et al. AMERICAN JOURNAL OF OBSTETRICS AND GYNECOLOGY 129(8):928-929, December 15, 1977.

Serial intramuscular injections of 15 methyl P.G.F.2alpha for second trimester abortions, by R. M. Gharse, et al. JOURNAL OF POSTGRADUATE MEDICINE 23(2):91-

94, April, 1977.

Small dose anti-Rh therapy after first trimester abortion, by
L. Keith, et al. INTERNATIONAL JOURNAL OF
GYNAECOLOGY AND OBSTETRICS 15(3):235-237,
1977.

State of various indicators of the blood coagulation system
before and during induced abortion and anesthesia with
novocaine and dicain solutions, by A. I. Zherzhov.
VOPROSY OKHRANY MATERINSTVA DETSTVA
23(4):83-84, April, 1978.

Study calls D & E best midtrimester abortion. MEDICAL
WORLD NEWS 18:71, January 10, 1977.

A technique of anaesthesia for medical termination of pregnancy, by N. Bose. JOURNAL OF THE INDIAN
MEDICAL ASSOCIATION 69(3):56-58, August 1,
1977.

Techniques of second-trimester abortions, by C. Y. Kawada.
CLINICAL OBSTETRICS AND GYNECOLOGY 20(4):
833-847, December, 1977.

Terathanasia, by J. Warkany. TERATOLOGY 17(2):187-
192, April, 1978.

Termination of early gestation with a vaingal polysiloxane
device impregnated with (15S)-15 methyl prostaglandin
F2alpha methylester, by P. F. Brenner, et al. PRO-
STAGLANDINS 14(4):771-777, October, 1977.

Termination of early pregnancy by ONO-802 (16,16-dimethyl-
trans-delta2-PGE1 methyl ester, by S. Takagi, et al.
PROSTAGLANDINS 14(4):791-798, October, 1977.

Termination of early pregnancy (menstrual induction) with
16-phenoxy-omega-tetranor PGE2 methylsulfonylamide,

by S. M. Karim, et al. CONTRACEPTION 16(4):377-381, October, 1977.

Termination of mid-term spontaneous and missed abortions by extra-amniotic injection of a single prostaglandin F2alpha dose, by L. Kerekes, et al. THERAPIA HUNGARICA 25(3):102-104, 1977.

Therapeutic abortions in the second trimester of pregnancy with prostaglandine gel, by S. Heinzl. GEBURTSHILFE UND FRAUENHEILKUNDE 38(3):220-226, March, 1978.

Therapeutic induction of abortion in the 1st and 2nd trimesters with intramuscular 15-methyl-prostaglandin F2 alpha, by G. Göretzlehner, et al. ZENTRALBLATT FUER GYNAEKOLOGIE 99(22):1356-1360, 1977.

Topical uterine anesthesia: a preliminary report, by H. M. Hasson. INTERNATIONAL JOURNAL OF GYNAECOLOGY AND OBSTETRICS 15(3):238-240, 1977.

The treatment of imminent abortion with monitoring of the maternal serum HPL level [proceedings], by P. Berle, et al. ARCHIV FUR GYNAEKOLOGIE 224(1-4):90-91, July 29, 1977.

Ultrasonography in threatened abortion, by C. Smith, et al. OBSTETRICS AND GYNECOLOGY 51(2):173-177, February, 1978.

Ultrasound and semiquantitative chorionic gonadotropin secretin in the diagnosis of abortion, by H. Schillinger, et al. ZENTRALBLATT FUER GYNAEKOLOGIE 100(2):76-83, 1978.

Use of anti-Rh-immunoglobulin in abortions, by G. S. Aleskerov. AKUSHERSTVO I GINEKOLOGIIA (11):40-43, November, 1977.

Use of doxycycline in elective first trimester abortion, by R. S. London, et al. SOUTHERN MEDICAL JOURNAL 71(6):672-673, June, 1978.

Use of prostaglandin F2alpha in the management of missed abortion, by H. Foroohav, et al. INTERNATIONAL JOURNAL OF GYNAECOLOGY AND OBSTETRICS 14(6):541-544, 1976.

Use of prostaglandins in the interruption of pregnancy during the 1st trimester, by R. Pasargiklian, et al. MINERVA GINECOLOGIA 29(7-8):591-598, July-August, 1977.

The use of prostaglandins to perform terminations of pregnancy in the second trimester, by F. V. Thomas, et al. JOURNAL DE GYNECOLOGIE, OBSTETRIQUE ET BIOLOGIE DE LA REPRODUCTION 7(1):119-128, January, 1978.

Vaginal administration of 15 (S) 15-methyl prostaglandin F2 alpha methyl ester for induction of mid-trimester abortion, by E. S. Grech, et al. CONTRACEPTION 16(4): 327-337, October, 1977.

Vaginal evacuation [letter], by S. Fribourg. OBSTETRICS AND GYNECOLOGY 51(6):740, June, 1978.

A vaginal suppository for abortion. MEDICAL LETTER ON DRUGS AND THERAPEUTICS 19(22):89-90, November 4, 1977.

Very early abortion by prostaglandins, by I. Z. Mackenzie, et al. LANCET 1(8076):1223-1226, June 10, 1978.

Very early induced abortion (overtime treatment), by F. P. Wibaut. NEDERLANDS TIJDSCHRIFT VOOR GENEE-SKUNDE 121(46):1847-1852, November 12, 1977.

ABORTION: THERAPEUTIC
Cardiovascular diseases as indications for pregnancy interruption, by K. Kochsiek, et al. INTERNIST 19(5):269-272, May, 1978.

Diabetes mellitus and endocrine diseases as indications for pregnancy interruption, by R. Petzoldt, et al. INTERNIST 19(5):284-286, May, 1978.

Does the risk of radiodiagnositc examination at the beginning of pregnancy justify pregnancy termination? by P. Magnin, et al. NOUVELLE PRESSE MEDICALE 6(30): 2655-2658, September 17, 1977.

Drug noxae as indications for pregnancy interruption, by D. Neubert. INTERNIST 19(5):304-309, May, 1978.

Fatal and maternal indications for considering abortion, by R. C. Juberg. SOUTHERN MEDICAL JOURNAL 71(1): 50-57+, January, 1978.

Indications for pregnancy interruption due to diseases of the respiratory system, by F. Trendelenburg, et al. INTERNIST 19(5):291-293, May, 1978.

Indications for pregnancy interruption in kidney diseases and hypertension, by H. H. Edel. INTERNIST 19(5): 273-278, May, 1978.

Interruption of pregnancy in alcoholic women, by F. Majewski, et al. DEUTSCHE MEDIZINISCHE WOCHENSCHRIFT 103(21):895-898, May 26, 1978.

Interruption of pregnancy in epileptic women, by R. Schweingruber. PRAXIS 67(23):854-855, June 6, 1978.

Laparoscopic sterilization with therapeutic abortion versus sterilization or abortion alone, by A. Weil. OBSTETRICS AND GYNECOLOGY 52(1):79-82, July, 1978.

Neurologic diseases as indications for pregnancy interruption, by U. A. Besinger, et al. INTERNIST 19(5):294-298, May, 1978.

A new role for the nurse; counseling on the subject of abortion, by B. Easterbrook, et al. INFIRMIERE CANADIENNE 19(10):35-37, October, 1977.

Paracervical block in therapeutic abortions [letter], by P. A. Poma. AMERICAN JOURNAL OF OBSTETRICS AND GYNECOLOGY 132(8):915-916, August 15, 1978.

Pregnancy interruption based on pediatric indications, by J. D. Murken. INTERNIST 19(5):310-314, May, 1978.

The problems of therapeutic abortion and infanticide, by S. V. Humphries. CENTRAL AFRICAN JOURNAL OF MEDICINE 24(4):77-79, April, 1978.

Psychiatric indications for pregnancy interruption, by H. Dilling, et al. INTERNIST 19(5):315-321, May, 1978.

Radiation exposure as indication for pregnancy interruption, by F. E. Stieve. INTERNIST 19(5):299-303, May, 1978.

Therapeutic abortion. The 1975 report from Ulleval Hospital, by F. Jerve, et al. ACTA OBSTETRICIA ET GYNECOLOGICA SCANDINAVICA 57(3):237-240, 1978.

Therapeutic abortions in the second trimester of pregnancy with prostaglandine gel, by S. Henzl. GEBURTSHILFE UND FRAUENHEILKUNDE 38(3):220-226, March, 1978.

Therapeutic induction of abortion in the 1st and 2nd trimesters with intramuscular 15-methyl-prostaglandin F2 alpha, by G. Göretzlehner, et al. ZENTRALBLATT FUER GYNAEKOLOGIE 99(22):1356-1360, 1977.

Why women need late abortions, by C. Brewer. NEW SO-
CIETY pp. 208-209, October 26, 1978.

ABORTION: THERAPEUTIC: COMPLICATIONS
Blood coagulation studies of therapeutic abortion induced
by 15-methyl-prostaglandin F2 alpha, by R. During, et
al. ZENTRALBLATT FUER GYNAEKOLOGIE 99(22):
1361-1365, 1977.

Effect of general and local anaesthesia on blood loss during
and after theapeutic abortion, by B. R. Moller. ACTA
OBSTETRICIA ET GYNECOLOGICA SCANDINAVICA
57(2):133-136, 1978.

The prevention of late psychological sequelae following
therapeutic termination of pregnancy. The role of the
doctor during consultations, by L. Moor. JOURNAL
OF GYNECOLOGIE, OBSTETRIQUE ET DE BIOLO-
GIE DE LA REPRODUCTION 7(3):465-471, April,
1978.

Psychiatric sequelae of therapeutic abortions, by J. O.
Cavenar, Jr., et al. NORTH CAROLINA MEDICAL
JOURNAL 39(2):101-106, February, 1978.

Psychological consequences of therapeutic abortion, by H. S.
Greer, et al. BRITISH JOURNAL OF PSYCHIATRY
128:74-79, January, 1976.

Psychoses following therapeutic abortion, by J. G. Spaulding,
et al. AMERICAN JOURNAL OF PSYCHIATRY
135(3):364-365, March, 1978.

ABORTION: THERAPEUTIC: OUTPATIENT TREATMENT
Therapeutic abortion in an out-patient clinic. A prospective
investigation of complications and patient acceptability,
by B. R. Moller, et al. ACTA OBSTETRICIA ET GYNE-
COLOGICA SCANDINAVICA 57(1):41-44, 1978.

ABORTION: THERAPEUTIC: TECHNIQUES
Catecholamines during therapeutic abortion induced with intra-amniotic prostaglandin F2alpha, by W. E. Brenner, et al. AMERICAN JOURNAL OF OBSTETRICS AND GYNECOLOGY 130(2):178-187, January 15, 1978.

ABORTION: THREATENED
Hormonal profile as a prognostic index of early threatened abortion, by L. Jovanovic, et al. AMERICAN JOURNAL OF OBSTETRICS AND GYNECOLOGY 130(3): 274-278, February 1, 1978.

Threatened abortion: our point of view, by B. Brigljevic. THERAPEUTISCHE UMSCHAU 35(6):405-409, June, 1978.

ABORTION AND ADVERTISING

ABORTION AND THE BRITISH MEDICAL ASSOCIATION
BMA and the Abortion Act [letter], by D. Flint. BRITISH MEDICAL JOURNAL 1(6125):1490, June 3, 1978.

ABORTION AND HOMOSEXUALS
Abortion and lesbianism: issues of controversy, by D. L. Martin. LEARNING 6:34, May-June, 1978.

ABORTION AND MALES
Abortion and men, by J. Cham. McCALLS 105:53, June, 1978.

Adolescent males, fatherhood, and abortion, by A. A. Rothstein. JOURNAL OF YOUTH AND ADOLESCENCE 7:203-214, June, 1978.

Attitudes of adolescent males toward abortion, contraception, and sexuality, by E. Vadies, et al. SOCIAL WORK HEALTH CARE 3:169-174, Winter, 1977.

ABORTION AND THE MILITARY
AF's interim abortion policy waiting for Hill action, by R.
Sanders, et al. AIR FORCE TIMES 39:2, October 16,
1978.

Congress votes to restrict military abortion payments, by J.
Castelli. OUR SUNDAY VISITOR 67:5, August 27,
1978.

DoD progressing on long journey, by V. McKenzie. U. S.
MEDICINE 14(1):19-22, January 15, 1978.

DOD walks thin line on abortions, by T. Philpott. AIR
FORCE TIMES 39:2, September 25, 1978.

ABORTION AND NURSES
Action for wrongful life. Law for the nurse supervisor, by
H. Creighton. SUPERVISOR NURSE 8(4):12-15,
April, 1977.

American Nurses' Association Division on maternal and child
health nursing practice: statement on abortion. COLO-
RADO NURSE 78:19, October, 1978.

The freedom of choice of a girl—a dilemma which the doctor
falls into. Nurses' dilemmas, by K. Miwa. KANGO
30(1):26-32, January, 1978.

Induced abortion—nurses' role in preventive work: numbers
shock us but we do not participate in preventive work,
by L. Lindén. SYGEPLEJERSKEN 70(48):10-13+,
December 7, 1977.

A new role for the nurse; counseling on the subject of abortion, by B. Easterbrook, et al. INFIRMIERE CANA-
DIENNE 19(10):35-37, October, 1977.

Nursing functions: limits on nursing service. Case in point:
Wright v. State (351 So. 2d 708-FLA.). REGAN RE-

PORT ON NURSING LAW 18:2, January, 1978.

ABORTION AND PARENTAL CONSENT
Anti-abortion "Guerilla Warfare" aimed at forcing parental
consent opposed by health care coalition. JUVENILE
JUSTICE DIGEST 6(19):4, October 13, 1978.

Constitutionality of mandatory parental consent in the
abortion decision of a minor: Bellotti II [Baird v. Attorney General (Bellotti II) (Mass) 360 N E 2d 288] in
perspective. NORTHERN KENTUCKY LAW REVIEW
4:323-344, 1977.

ABORTION AND PHYSICIANS
Abortion and medical ethics, by D. Callahan. AMERICAN
ACADEMY OF POLITICAL AND SOCIAL SCIENCE
437:116-127, May, 1978.

Away from the ivory tower, by N. Arko, et al. NEW PHY-
SICIAN 26(12):26-28, December, 1977.

Between guilt and gratification: abortion doctors reveal
their feelings, by N. Rosen. NEW YORK TIMES MAGA-
ZINE pp. 70-71+, April 17, 1977.

Connecticut physicians attitudes toward abortion, by G. L.
Pratt, et al. AMERICAN JOURNAL OF PUBLIC
HEALTH 66:288-289, March, 1976.

Doctors have varied reactions to abortion. OUR SUNDAY
VISITOR 66:3, May 29, 1977.

The medical attitude towards abortion regarded as deviant
behavior, by D. Gonin, et al. BULLETIN DE MEDICINE
LEGALE ET DE TOXICOLOGIE MEDICALE 18(5):
303-311, 1975.

Requests for abortion—a psychiatrist's view, by R. Mester.
ISRAEL ANNALS OF PSYCHIATRY 14:294+, Septem-

ber, 1976.

Training in induced abortion by obstetrics and gynecology residency programs, by B. L. Lindheim, et al. FAMILY PLANNING PERSPECTIVES 10:24-28, January-February, 1978.

ABORTION AND POLITICS
Abortion and politics, by E. Doerr. HUMANIST 36:42-43, March-April, 1976.

Abortion key issue in senate race; showdown in Minnesota, by M. Papa. NATIONAL CATHOLIC REPORTER 14:3, September 15, 1978.

Carey v. Population Servs. Int. 97 Sup Ct 2010. HUMAN RIGHTS 6:311-313, Spring, 1977.

Carter and abortion, by C. Tucker. SATURDAY REVIEW 4:64, September 17, 1977.

—, by A. Wilcox. MILITANT 40(36):12, September 24, 1976.

Carter/Ford join antiabortion drive, by G. Hildebrand. MILITANT 40(36):15, September 24, 1976.

The con-con drive: constitutional convention sought on abortion ban, by L. B. Weiss. CONGRESSIONAL QUARTERLY SERVICE WEEKLY REPORT 36:1677-1679, July 1, 1978.

Confidentiality and interagency communication: effect of the Buckley amendment, by E. A. Drake, et al. HOSPITAL AND COMMUNITY PSYCHIATRY 29(5):312-315, May, 1978.

The politics of abortion [abortion as a campaign issue in various states; some emphasis on Minnesota], by A. R. Hunt.

WALL STREET JOURNAL 192:20, August 15, 1978.

Politics of abortion: Supreme Court decision on medicaid funding, by P. Steinfels. COMMONWEAL 104:456, July 22, 1977.

ABORTION AND RAPE
Abortion and rape [letter], by P. Barry-Martin. NEW ZEA-LAND MEDICAL JOURNAL 86(598):397, October 26, 1977.

Caring for the rape victim, by D. H. Chase. BULLETIN OF THE AMERICAN PROTESTANT HOSPITAL ASSOCIA-TION 41(2):20-24, 1977.

How to handle the rape victim, by A. F. Schiff. SOUTHERN MEDICAL JOURNAL 71(5):509-511+, May, 1978.

Rape [letter], by W. A. Facer. NEW ZEALAND MEDICAL JOURNAL 86(593):152, August 10, 1977.

Rape and abortion [letter], by M. Jackson. NEW ZEALAND MEDICAL JOURNAL 86(596):301-302, September 28, 1977.

ABORTION AND RELIGION
Abortion and euthanasia; violation of the right to life, by J. Bernardin. OSSERVATORE ROMANO 50(507): 8-9, December 15, 1977.

Abortion and feminism in Italy: women against church and state, by E. Cantaron. RADICAL AMERICA 10(6):8-27, November-December, 1976.

Abortion and the "Right to Life": facts, fallacies, and fraud. HUMANIST 38(4):18, July-August, 1978.

Abortion: the inhuman suppression of the weakest; message on the approval of the law on abortion, by G. Colombo.

OSSERVATORE ROMANO 7(464):7+, February 17, 1977.

Abortion is always wrong; excerpt from The right to live; the right to die, by C. Koop. SIGN 58:20-23, September, 1978.

Abortion: the issue no one wanted, so Catholics took it on; an analysis, by M. Winiarski. NATIONAL CATHOLIC REPORTER 14:1+, February 24, 1978+.

Abortion: an unresolved moral problem, by G. Cosby. DIALOGUE 1978.

Abortion: unspeakable crime; moral choices in contemporary society, by J. Connery. NATIONAL CATHOLIC REPORTER 13:33, February 18, 1977.

The abortionist, by R. Engel. OUR SUNDAY VISITOR 66: 6-7, April 23, 1978.

Acceptance of abortion among white Catholics and Protestants, 1962 and 1975, by W. A. McIntosh, et al. JOURNAL FOR SCIENTIFIC STUDY OF RELIGION 16: 295-303, September, 1977.

Address to the National Catholic Conference of Bishops of the United States of America; role as bishops today, by J. Bernardin. OSSERVATORE ROMANO 2(511):5-6, January 12, 1978.

Against abortion: a Protestant proposal, by G. Meilaender. LINACRE QUARTERLY 45:165-178, May, 1978.

Agreement and dissent mark Humanae Vitae Conference, in Milan, Italy, by J. Maher. OUR SUNDAY VISITOR 67:3, July 16, 1978.

Antenatal injury and the rights of the foetus, by

T. D. Campbell, et al. PHILOSOPHICAL QUARTERLY 28:17-30, January, 1978.

Anti-Catholicism becomes counter-attack strategy of pro-abortionists in nation, by R. Shaw. OUR SUNDAY VISITOR 66:2, February 19, 1978.

Archbishop Quinn asks pro-life advocates to show respect for life in every way. OUR SUNDAY VISITOR 66:3, February 5, 1978.

The bishop: transformed into a servant of the Word; excerpt from the homily at the ordination of Bishop Thomas C. Kelly, by J. Bernardin. ORIGINS 7:160, August 25, 1977.

A broader perspective on Humanae Vitae, by J. Quinn. ORIGINS 8:10-12, May 25, 1978.

Call to reflection, by R. G. Hoyt. CHRISTIANITY AND CRISIS 37:253-255, October 31, 1977; DISCUSSION 37:264-266+, November 14, 1977+.

Can 291 popes be wrong? [abortion], by S. Morse. MAJORITY REPORT 7:3, August 6-19, 1977.

Cardinal Vicar of Rome on new abortion law; approved by the Chamber of Deputies on 21 January, 1977, by U. Poletti. OSSERVATORE ROMANO 7(464):2, February 17, 1977.

Catching up with Joe O'Rourke; rebel with many causes, by J. Deedy. CRITIC 36:16-17, Spring, 1978.

Christians faced with the legalization of abortion; reprint from La civiltà cattolica, May 20, 1978. OSSERVATORE ROMANO 24(533):9-11, June 15, 1978.

Conflict of loyalties: hippocratic or hypocritical? by

R. Higgs. JOURNAL OF MEDICAL ETHICS 4:42-44, March, 1978.

Continuing the discussion: how to argue about abortion [rejoinder to B. Harrison], by J. T. Burtchaell. CHRISTIANITY AND CRISIS 37:313-316, December 26, 1977.

—. [Reply to R. Hoyt and J. T. Burtchaell], by V. Lindermayer, et al. CHRISTIANITY AND CRISIS 37:316-318, December 26, 1977.

—. II. [Reply to J. Burtchaell, with rejoinder, pp. 313-316], by B. Harrison. CHRISTIANITY AND CRISIS 37:311-313, December 26, 1977.

Contraception et avortement, by S. Luoni. LA DOCUMENTATION CATHOLIQUE 74:643-645, July 3, 1977.

Declaration of the Italian Episcopal Conference after the law on abortion. OSSERVATORE ROMANO 25(534): 4, June 22, 1978.

Dissenters barred from symposium: Humanae Vitae, by J. Coleman. NATIONAL CATHOLIC REPORTER 14:24-25, August 11, 1978.

Do Catholics have constitutional rights? COMMENTARY 105:771-773, December 8, 1978.

Don't kill babies before they're born. . .kill them afterwards, by J. Wells. U. S. CATHOLIC 43:41, September, 1978.

The dynamics of anti-abortionism, by J. Noonan, Jr. CATHOLIC MIND 76:7-13, May, 1978.

An empirical argument against abortion, by J. Newman. NEW SCHOLASTICISM 51:384-395, Summer, 1977.

Enacting religious beliefs in a pluralistic society, by F. S. Jaffe. HASTINGS CENTER REPORT 8:14-16, August, 1978.

Ethical values in anesthesia and intensive care (7): a hospital chaplain's view of abortion, euthanasia and the ethical aspects of suicide, by I. Stenäs. LAKARTIDNINGEN 75(4):224-225, January 25, 1978.

Etre évêque demain? by R. Bouchex. LA SUPPLEMENT 124:93-104, February, 1978.

Face to face with abortion, by G. La Pira. OSSERVATORE ROMANO 12(521):9-10, March 23, 1978.

Fellowship theme: fools for Christ? by E. Curtin, Jr. NATIONAL CATHOLIC REPORTER 14:3, April 14, 1978.

Human potentiality: its moral relevance, by L. L. Thomas. PERSONALIST 59:266-272, July, 1978.

A husband and his unborn child, by R. O'Brien. MONTH 11:219-220, July, 1978.

I was a pro-life spy at an abortion clinic convention, by J. Scheidler. OUR SUNDAY VISITOR 65:1+, January 30, 1977.

In pursuit of a policy respecting human life, by J. Quinn. OSSERVATORE ROMANO 11(520):9-10, March 16, 1978.

The irrelevance of religion in the abortion debate, by L. Newton. HASTINGS CENTER REPORT 8:16-17, April, 1978.

Italian bishops reaffirm life. OSSERVATORE ROMANO 21(478):11, May 26, 1977.

Italian Episcopal Conference on the law on abortion. OS-SERVATORE ROMANO 30(539):12, July 27, 1978.

Latin Americans criticize anti-life programs sponsored by United States, by D. Duggan. OUR SUNDAY VISITOR 67:3, July 9, 1978.

Let us reconcile, by C. Gallagher. OUR SUNDAY VISITOR 66:14, May 29, 1977.

Let's quit pretending about birth control, the Call to Action conference in Detroit, committee on sex and birth control, by F. Wessling. U. S. CATHOLIC 42:29-31, August, 1977.

Lutherans and abortion. AMERICA 138:296-297, April 15, 1978.

Magisterium and theologians: steps towards dialogue, by J. Bernardin. CHICAGO STUDIES 17:151-158, Summer, 1978.

McLuhan: electronic age a factor in campaign for legal abortion, by E. Moore. NATIONAL CATHOLIC REPORTER 13:16, May 20, 1977.

Methodist's open letter to Bishop Quinn: United Methodist, by H. L. Boche. CHRISTIAN CENTURY 95:437-438, April 26, 1978.

Monsignor McHugh disputes birth control survey. OUR SUNDAY VISITOR 66:2, October 9, 1977.

The most important task of a bishop, by J. Bernardin. ORIGINS 7:369+, December 1, 1977.

National Federation of Priests' Councils. A letter on approaches to the abortion issue. CATHOLIC MIND pp. 9-10, March, 1977.

National right to life, political right interlink, by M. Winiarski. NATIONAL CATHOLIC REPORTER 15:1+, November 10, 1978.

A new anti-Catholic bigotry? Editorial page feature article on anti-Catholicism nd issues of abortion and aid to parochial schools. PERSPECTIVE ON POLITICS 12(14-22):4.

Nipping 'em in the bud. NATIONAL REVIEW 30:454, April 14, 1978.

Nun on the line for medicaid abortions, by S. Birknell. MS MAGAZINE 6:23, June, 1978.

L'objection de conscience contre la loi italienne sur l'avortement, by U. Poletti. LA DOCUMENTATION CATHOLIQUE 76:630-632, July 2, 1978.

Of many things; escalating violence over abortion question, by J. O'Hare. AMERICA 138:inside cover, March 11, 1978; Same with title Pro-life militancy. CHRISTIANITY TODAY 22:29, April 21, 1978.

On abortion; interview by Christianity Today; excerpt from Christianity Today, April 21, 1978, by M. Muggeridge. CATHOLIC DIGEST 42:43-47, September, 1978.

On abortion [reprint from Diocesan Bulletin of Saint-Claude; 15 September 1977], by G. Duchene. OSSERVATORE ROMANO 7(516):11, February 16, 1978.

One hundred thousand Catholics gather in Milan for a celebration of life; homily, by G. Colombo. OSSERVATORE ROMANO 18(475):4, May 5, 1977.

Open letter to the president of the medical federation, by L. Reale. OSSERVATORE ROMANO 31(540):7, August 3, 1978.

Open your eyes; note of the Episcopal Commission for the Family on abortion. OSSERVATORE ROMANO 7(516):11, February 16, 1978.

Our Catholic Faith: the dignity of human life, by R. Hire. OUR SUNDAY VISITOR 66:6, December 11, 1977.

Le Pape d'Humanae Vitae, by G. Matagrin. LA DOCU-MENTATION CATHOLIQUE 75:752, September 3-17, 1978.

Pastoral letter on abortion, by T. Cahill. OSSERVATORE ROMANO 19(476):11, May 12, 1977.

Paternidade responsavel: algumas anotacoes, by J. Snoek. REVISTA ECLESIASTICA BRASILEIRA 36:539-544, September, 1976.

Positive woman or negative man? by H. Klaus. LINACRE QUARTERLY 43:244-248, November, 1976.

Pour la défense des plus faibles; lettres pastorale des évêques belges sur l'avortement juin 1977. LA DOCUMENTA-TION CATHOLIQUE

Power to the papists; on the abortion struggle, by S. Adamo. NATIONAL CATHOLIC REPORTER 14:13, March 24, 1978.

Presumptive personhood, by V. Walker. LINACRE QUAR-TERLY 45:179-186, May, 1978.

The problems of therapeutic abortion and infanticide, by S. V. Humphries. CENTRAL AFRICAN JOURNAL OF MEDICINE 24(4):77-79, April, 1978.

Pro-life aim: put God on Capitol Hill, by B. Kenkelen. NATIONAL CATHOLIC REPORTER 14:1+, July 14, 1978.

The pro-life fight in England, by J. Nash. OUR SUNDAY VISITOR 66:3, February 12, 1978.

Pro-life largest people's movement in U. S. history, by G. Barmann. OUR SUNDAY VISITOR 66:3, January 15, 1978.

Pro-life leaders agree there is need for ultratough strategy in Congress, by R. Shaw. OUR SUNDAY VISITOR 66:2, February 26, 1978.

Pro-life leaders think Edelin reversal could accelerate an amendment. OUR SUNDAY VISITOR 65:2, January 2, 1977.

Pro-life or reflection of conservative ideology? an analysis of opposition to legalized abortion, by D. Granberg. SOCIOLOGY AND SOCIAL RESEARCH 62:414-429, April, 1978.

Pro-life, pro-E.R.A., by J. Loesch. AMERICA 139:435-436, December 9, 1978.

Pro-life target: women's year meetings; Minnesota conference disrupted, by M. Papa. NATIONAL CATHOLIC RE- PORTER 13:20, June 17, 1977.

Pro-lifers applaud abortion restrictions in Minnesota, by M. Dorsher. OUR SUNDAY VISITOR 66:4, April 9, 1978.

A prophetic witness for Catholics, by J. Garvey. PRIEST 34:40-42, October, 1978.

Rabbi hopes study will decide Jewish stance on abortion. OUR SUNDAY VISITOR 67:3, October 22, 1978.

A rabbi looks at abortion, by C. Lipschitz. OUR SUNDAY VISITOR 65:12-13, April 3, 1977.

Rahner on the origin of the soul: some implications regarding abortion, by J. T. Culleton. THOUGHT June, 1978.

Redefining the issues in fetal experimentation; reprint from The Journal of the American Medical Association, July 19, 1976, by E. Diamond. LINACRE QUARTERLY 44:148-154, May, 1977.

Religion and the "right to life": correlates of opposition to abortion, by L. R. Petersen, et al. SOCIOLOGICAL ANALYSIS 37(3):243-254, 1976.

A report from the March for Life, by D. Francis. OUR SUNDAY VISITOR 65:2, February 6, 1977.

Respect for life: Jewish and Roman Catholic reflections on abortion and related issues; Los Angeles Catholic-Jewish Respect Life Committee, September, 1977. CATHOLIC MIND 76:54-64, February, 1978.

Responding to editorial, bishop speaks for unborn; Bishop William E. McManus. OUR SUNDAY VISITOR 67:3, May 28, 1978.

Right of the unborn to eternal life threatened by abortion; guaranteed by baptism, by B. de Margerie. OSSERVATORE ROMANO 49(506):6-8, December 8, 1977.

Right to eternal life guaranteed by baptism; victims of abortion; reprint from Esprit et vie, by B. de Margerie. OSSERVATORE ROMANO 16(473):4, April 21, 1977.

The right to fight for life; pastoral letter from the hierarchy of Scotland, by T. Winning, et al. OSSERVATORE ROMANO 50(507):11, December 15, 1977.

Right to life and self-consciousness, by T. D. Sullivan. AMERICA 139:222-224, October 7, 1978.

Right to life: looking at the past to plan for the future; fifth Right to Life Convention, St. Louis, Missouri, June, 1978, by C. Anthony. OUR SUNDAY VISITOR 67:3-4, July 2, 1978.

The right to life; two messages of the Italian Episcopal Conference. THE POPE SPEAKS 22:260-263, November 3, 1977.

Rights of fetus uncertain; moral choices in contemporary society, by D. Callahan. NATIONAL CATHOLIC REPORTER 13:32, February 18, 1977.

The sanctity of life, by C. E. Koop. JOURNAL OF THE MEDICAL SOCIETY OF NEW JERSEY 75(1):62-67, January, 1978.

Should pro-life people tone down their language? by M. Burson. OUR SUNDAY VISITOR 65:1, February 13, 1977.

Social justice and abortion, by F. X. Meehan. AMERICA 138:478-481, June 17, 1978.

Social justice must come first, Father Hehir says; bridge the gap between the Catholic Church's opposition to abortion and birth control. OUR SUNDAY VISITOR 66:3, March 12, 1978.

Some reflections on birth control, by R. Westley. LISTENING 12:43-61, September, 1977.

State women's meetings. New York, by N. Thropp; Massachusetts, by M. Badger; It was a tempest in a uterus [New York women's meeting], by S. Lieberman; The right wing sends in fresh troops [Mormon Church], by B. West. OFF OUR BACKS 7:4-5, August 6-19, 1977.

Statements on abortion, by T. Cooke, et al. OSSERVA-

TORE ROMANO 11(520):10, March 16, 1978.

A symposium—on the report and recommendation of the National Commission for the protection of human subjects of biomedical and behavioral research; research on the fetus, by R. A. Destro. VILLANOVA LAW REVIEW 22(2):297-299, 1976-1977.

Thinking about abortion; reasons Christians today give for adopting new beliefs about abortion, by G. Kuykendall. CROSS CURRENTS 27:403-416, Winter, 1978.

A 2,000-year-old fight for life, by J. McHugh. OUR SUNDAY VISITOR 66:3, January 22, 1978.

Two views on the human life amendment; symposium: abortion: no, amendment: yes, by R. Neuhaus. Abortion: no, amendment: no, by J. Garvey. U. S. CATHOLIC 42:28-31, April, 1977.

USCC asks Supreme Court to reverse 1973 abortion ruling. OUR SUNDAY VISITOR 67:1, July 30, 1978.

United Way at center of Chicago conflict, by C. Anthony. OUR SUNDAY VISITOR 67:1, October 22, 1978.

The unwed mother: a parish approach to the abortion problem, by R. Ranieri. TODAY'S PARISH 10:11-12, October, 1978.

The value of life, by T. G. Roupas. PHILOSOPHY AND PUBLIC AFFAIRS 7:154-183, Winter, 1978.

Vatican denounces Italian liberalized abortion law, by J. Mathig, Jr. OUR SUNDAY VISITOR 67:4, June 4, 1978.

Victims of an anti-life philosophy; rights of the needy ignored, by J. Sullivan. OUR SUNDAY VISITOR 65:1+,

March 6, 1977.

Who is a Catholic; Lenten series, by R. McBrien. NATION-
AL CATHOLIC REPORTER 14:7+, February 10, 1978.

Will Church institutions be forced to make medical payments
for abortions; excerpt from report to the Administrative
Committee of the National Conference of Catholic Bishops, by T. Cooke. ORIGINS 7:577+, March 2, 1978.

Witness says aid funds still promote abortion. OUR SUN-
DAY VISITOR 66:5, March 12, 1978.

Yes to life, no to abortion; reprint from the publication, Pour
la vie naissante, July, 1977, by P. Weber. OSSERVA-
TORE ROMANO 1(510):10-11, January 5, 1978.

ABORTION AND SMOKING
Tobacco may cause placental separation. MEDICAL WORLD
NEWS 18:33-34, May 2, 1977.

ABORTION AND SOCIAL STRATA
Abortion deaths and social class [letter], by C. Tietze. LAN-
CET 1(7982):469, August 21, 1976.

ABORTION AND YOUTH
Attitudes of adolescent males toward abortion, contracep-
tion, and sexuality, by E. Vadies, et al. SOCIAL WORK
HEALTH CARE 3:169-174, Winter, 1977.

Minors' right to abortion and contraception: prospects for
invalidating less than absolute restrictions, by D. Klassel,
et al. WOMEN'S RIGHTS LAW REPORTER 4:165-
183, Spring, 1978.

Sexual privacy: access of a minor to contraceptives, abor-
tion, and sterilization without parental consent. UNI-
VERSITY OF RICHMOND LAW REVIEW 12:221-244,
Fall, 1977.

Supreme court and social change: the case of abortion, by K. A. Kemp, et al. WESTERN POLITICAL QUARTERLY 31:19-31, March, 1978.

ABORTION CLINICS
Administrative incongruence and authority conflict in four abortion clinics, by W. M. Hern, et al. HUMAN ORGANIZATION 36:376-383, Winter, 1977.

Getting violent, by R. Boeth, et al. NEWSWEEK 91:33, March 13, 1978.

An outcome evaluation of counseling services provided by abortion clinics, by B. J. Kay, et al. MEDICAL CARE 15(10):858-868, October, 1977.

Regulatory policy and abortion clinics: implications for planning, by B. J. Kay, et al. JOURNAL OF HEALTH POLITICS, POLICY AND LAW 3(1):43-53, Spring, 1978.

Stacy's day at the abortion clinic; Eastern Women's Center clinic, New York City, by B. Dolan. TIME 111:26, April 10, 1978.

ABORTION COUNSELING
Abortion and men, by J. Cham. McCALLS 105:53, June, 1978.

Abortion and pregnancy screening, by T. Smith. JOURNAL OF MEDICAL ETHICS 4(2):99, June, 1978.

Abortion counseling at the Boulder Valley Clinic, by L. Weber, et al. FRONTIERS 1(2):34-39, 1975.

Abortion: with particular reference to the developing role of counseling, by J. Hildebrand. BRITISH JOURNAL OF SOCIAL WORK 7(1):3-24, Spring, 1977.

Counselling of patients requesting an abortion, by J. L. Dunlop. PRACTITIONER 220(1320):847-852, June, 1978.

ABORTION COUNSELING: MALE
A program of group counseling for men who accompany women seeking legal abortions, by R. H. Gordon, et al. COMMUNITY MENTAL HEALTH JOURNAL 13:291-295, Winter, 1977.

ABORTION EDUCATION
Abortion services: time for a discussion of marketing policies, by H. S. Gitlow. JOURNAL OF MARKETING 42:71-82, April, 1978.

Abortions and admissions: medical schools, by P. H. Connolly. COMMONWEAL 105:551-552, September 1, 1978.

Introduction to the topic of pregnancy interruption, by E. Buchborn. INTERNIST 19(5):257-258, May, 1978.

ABORTION RESEARCH
Advances and perspectives of gynecology, by A. F. Mendizabal. OBSTETRICIA Y GINECOLOGIA LATINO-AMERICANAS 3395-6):191-202, May-June, 1975.

The biomedical research community: its place in consensus development. JAMA: JOURNAL OF THE AMERICAN MEDICAL ASSOCIATION 239(6):485-488, February 6, 1978.

An evaluation of studies concerning reproduction after first trimester induced abortion, by C. J. Hogue. INTERNATIONAL JOURNAL OF GYNAECOLOGY AND OBSTETRICS 15(2):167-171, 1977.

A follow-up of 72 cases referred for abortion, by A. Gillis. MENTAL HEALTH AND SOCIETY 2(3-6):212-218, 1975.

BIRTH CONTROL
Desexing birth control, by J. M. Stycos. FAMILY PLAN-
NING PERSPECTIVES 9(6):286-292, November-
December, 1977.

For women who wonder about birth control, by E. R. Dobell.
REDBOOK 151(4):64, August, 1978.

Immunological approaches to fertility regulation, by V. C.
Stevens. WHO BULLETIN 56(2):179-192, 1978.

Mourning after the night before, by A. Gotzsche. GUAR-
DIAN p. 9, May 2, 1978.

Nutrition, health, and population in strategies for rural
development [policies and programs best suited to promoting self-sustaining economic growth and eliminating
poverty], by B. F. Johnston, et al. ECONOMIC DE-
VELOPMENT AND CULTURAL CHANGE 26:1-23,
October, 1977.

Symposia focus on better birth control. CHEMICAL AND
ENGINEERING NEWS 56:6, May 22, 1978.

To be or not to be pregnant. MADEMOISELLE 84:86,
April, 1978.

The world's population problem: possible interventions to
reduce fertility, by R. S. McNamara. PUBLIC HEALTH
REPORTS 93:124-135, March-April, 1978.

A worldwide population information network: status and
goals, by H. K. Kolbe. SPECIAL LIBRARIES 69(7):
237-243, July, 1978.

AFRICA
Motivations for the use of birth control: evidence from
West Africa, by H. Ware. DEMOGRAPHY 13:479-
494, November, 1976.

ASIA
East Asia review, 1976-77, ed. by S. M. Keeny. STUD-
IES IN FAMILY PLANNING 9:233-254, September,
1978.

BANGLADESH
Female status and fertility behaviour in a metropolitan
urban area of Bangladesh, by R. H. Chaudhury.
POPULATION STUDIES 32:261-273, July, 1978.

100 million reasons why family life must change, by J.
Cunningham. GUARDIAN p. 19, December 18,
1978.

BELGIUM
The development of neo-Malthusianism in Flanders, by
P. van Praag. POPULATION STUDIES 32:467-480,
November, 1978.

BRAZIL
Brazilian elites and population policy [attitudes toward
government involvement in population planning of
269 influential public figures who were interviewed
in 1972-73], by P. McDonough, et al. POPULATION
AND DEVELOPMENT REVIEW 3:377-402, December, 1977.

CHINA
Fertility decline and birth control in the People's Repub-
lic of China, by J. S. Aird. POPULATION AND
DEVELOPMENT REVIEW 4:225-254, June, 1978.

La régulation des naissances en Chine, by M. S. Wolfson.
ECONOMIE ET HUMANISME pp. 34-40, November-December, 1977.

Role of rural-urban income inequality in fertility reductions: case of Turkey, Taiwan, and Morocco, by A. K.
Bhattacharyya. ECONOMIC DEVELOPMENT AND

CHINA
CULTURAL CHANGE 26:117-138, October, 1977.

GREAT BRITAIN
Abortion, birth control, and sex ratio in England and
Wales [letter], by R. Cruz-Coke. LANCET 2(8087):
480, August 26, 1978.

INDIA
Babies' revenge. ECONOMIST 266:58, January 7, 1978.

Birth control in India: the carrot and the rod? by L. C.
Landman. FAMILY PLANNING PERSPECTIVES
9:101-110, May-June, 1977.

Consultants or colleagues: the role of US population advisors in India, by M. Minkler. POPULATION AND
DEVELOPMENT REVIEW 3:403-419, December,
1977.

Effect of group level variables on fertility in a rural
Indian sample, by R. Anker. JOURNAL OF DE-
VELOPMENT STUDIES 14:63-76, October, 1977.

Hindu crush, by S. Rosenhause. GUARDIAN p. 17,
May 16, 1978.

Implementing family planning in a ministry of health:
organizational barriers at the state and district levels
[Uttar Pradesh, India], by R. S. Simmons, et al.
STUDIES IN FAMILY PLANNING 9:22-34, February-March, 1978.

India, eliminating coercion, makes sharp shift in birth-
control policy. NEW YORK TIMES p. 1, October 3,
1977.

The Indian dilemma: coercive birth control or compulsory pregnancy, by T. Black, et al. CONTEMPOR-

INDIA
ARY REVIEW 233:232-236, November, 1978.

Indian Health Service begins wooing physicians' families, by J. Stacey. AMERICAN MEDICAL NEWS 21(9): 7-8, February 27, 1978.

India's new birth rate target: an analysis, by D. L. Nortman. POPULATION AND DEVELOPMENT REVIEW 4:277-312, June, 1978.

Mother India (continued): after the emergency, the return of democracy; but the return, too, of population uncontrol, by K. Singh. ACROSS THE BOARD 15:22-27, January, 1978.

A nation of births, by K. Baker. GUARDIAN p. 12, June 7, 1978.

Politics of birth control [India], by B. Kramer. WALL STREET JOURNAL 191:20, May 8, 1978.

INDONESIA
Exceeding all expectancies, by R. Tasker. FAR EAST ECONOMIC REVIEW 101:23-25, August 25, 1978.

Shame is the best contraceptive. ECONOMIST 269:74, November 25, 1978.

IRELAND
Marital privacy and family law; a major political and social issue involving the Supreme Court, the Irish Government and the Catholic Hierarchy, by J. O'Reilly. STUDIES 66:8-24, September, 1977; Reply by W. Binchy, 66:330-335, Winter, 1977.

KOREA
The Billings birth regulation method; a successful experience in Korea, by M. McHugh, Sr. CHRIST TO

KOREA
THE WORLD 21:325-331, November 5, 1976.

LATIN AMERICA
Recent trends in Latin American fertility, by J. M. Stycos. POPULATION STUDIES 32:407-425, November, 1978.

MOROCCO

NEW ZEALAND
Contraception, sterilisation and abortion in New Zealand. NEW ZEALAND MEDICAL JOURNAL 85(588): 441-445, May 25, 1977.

THE PHILIPPINES
Continued use of contraception among Philippine family planning acceptors: a multivariate analysis, by J. F. Phillips. STUDIES IN FAMILY PLANNING 9:182-192, July, 1978.

SINGAPORE
The birth rate in Singapore, by W. Neville. POPULATION STUDIES 32:113-133, March, 1978.

SPAIN
A change but Spain stays mostly the same, by M. Jones. GUARDIAN p. 9, August 17, 1978.

SOUTH AFRICA
Beliefs regarding the consequences of birth control among black, colored, Indian, and white South Africans, by J. Barling, et al. JOURNAL OF SOCIAL PSYCHOLOGY 105:149-150, June, 1978.

SWEDEN
Birth rate and birth control in Sweden 1962-1976, by O. Meirik, et al. LAKARTIDNINGEN 75(6):426-427+, February 8, 1978.

TUNISIE
La régulation des naissances en Tunisie, by K. Taamallah.
POPULATION 33:194-205, November 1, 1978.

TURKEY

UNITED STATES
Economic variables and the decision to have additional children: evidence from the survey of economic opportunity, by D. Snyder. AMERICAN ECONOMIST 22:12-16, Spring, 1978.

A new perspective on the twentieth-century American fertility swing, by G. S. Masnick, et al. JOURNAL OF FAMILY HISTORY 1:216-243, Winter, 1976.

Premarital contraceptive use: a test of two models, by J. Delamater, et al. JOURNAL OF MARRIAGE AND THE FAMILY 40:235-247, May, 1978.

Racial consciousness: a new guise for traditionalism? by B. S. Roper, et al. SOCIOLOGY AND SOCIAL RESEARCH 62:430-447, April, 1978.

Racism and the availability of family planning services in the United States, by G. C. Wright, Jr. SOCIAL FORCES 56:1087-1098, June, 1978.

UNITED STATES INDIAN
Some factors related to contraceptive behavior among Wind River Shoshone and Arapahoe females, by T. L. Haynes. HUMAN ORGANIZATION 36:72-75, Spring, 1977.

VENEZUELA
Venezuelan birth control policies hit by archbishop; Luis E. Henriquez. OUR SUNDAY VISITOR 67:1, September 24, 1978.

YEMEN
Fertility mortality migration and family planning in the Yemen Arab Republic, by J. Allman, et al. POPU-LATION STUDIES 32:159-171, March, 1978.

BIRTH CONTROL: ATTITUDES
Birth control motivation—what does it mean? by A. Chamberlain. HEALTH VISITOR 51:374-377, October, 1978.

Birth planning values and decisions: the prediction of fertility, by B. D. Townes, et al. JOURNAL OF APPLIED SOCIAL PSYCHOLOGY 7:73-88, January-March, 1977.

Community size, public attitudes, and population-policy preferences, by D. A. Caputo. URBAN AFFAIRS QUARTERLY 13:207-222, December, 1977.

The conflict between work and family in hospital medicine, by F. R. Elliot. HEALTH BULLETIN 36(3):128-130, May, 1978.

Consistency between fertility attitudes and behaviour: a conceptual model, by S. B. Kar. POPULATION STUDIES 32:173-185, March, 1978.

Sex-role attitudes and the anticipated timing of the initial stages of family formation among Catholic, by J. W. Wicks, et al. JOURNAL OF MARRIAGE AND THE FAMILY 40(3):505, August, 1978.

Sexual and contraceptive attitudes and behaviour of single attenders at a Dublin family planning clinic, by E. P. Bowman. JOURNAL OF BIOSOCIAL SCIENCE 9(4): 429-445, October, 1977.

BIRTH CONTROL: HISTORY
Classical approaches, by L. P. Wilkinson. ENCOUNTER 50:22-32, April, 1978.

Sex and socialism: the opposition of the French left to birth control in the nineteenth century, by A. McClaren. JOURNAL OF THE HISTORY OF IDEAS 37:475-492, July-September, 1976.

Victorian sex survey, by P. A. David, et al. INTELLECT 106:276, January, 1978.

BIRTH CONTROL: LAWS AND LEGISLATION
Carey (Carey v. Population Serv. Int. 97 Sup Ct 2010) kids and contraceptives: privacy's problem child. UNIVERSITY OF MIAMI LAW REVIEW 32:750-762, June, 1978.

Carey v. Population Services International (97 Sup Ct 2010): closing the curtain on Comstockery. BROOKLYN LAW REVIEW 44:565-597, Spring, 1978.

—: an extension of the right of privacy. OHIO NORTHERN UNIVERSITY LAW REVIEW 5:167-174, January, 1978.

Minor's right of privacy: limitations on state action after Danforth (Planned Parenthood of Cent. Mo. v. Danforth, 96 Sup Ct 2831) and Carey (Carey v. Population Servs. Int. 97 Sup Ct 2010). COLUMBIA LAW REVIEW 77:1216-1246, December, 1977.

Minor's right to litigate privacy interests without parental notice. WASHINGTON UNIVERSITY LAW QUARTERLY 1978:431-442, Spring, 1978.

Population growth, population organization participants, and the right of privacy, by L. D. Barnett. FAMILY LAW QUARTERLY 12:37-60, Spring, 1978.

Selected legal issues in the world population/food equation [problems of an international approach to population problems; based on conference paper], by V. P. Nanda.

DENVER JOURNAL OF INTERNATIONAL LAW AND
POLICY 7:77-102, Fall, 1977.

Selected recent court decisions, by J. A. Norris, et al. AMER-
ICAN JOURNAL OF LAW AND MEDICINE 3(2):221-
224, 1977.

BIRTH CONTROL: LAWS AND LEGISLATION: IRELAND
Planitication de la famille et contraception; déclaration des
évêques d'Irlande à propos d'un projet de loi. LA DOCU-
MENTATION CATHOLIQUE 75:424-425, May 7, 1978.

Right to privacy expanded: state infringements upon decision affecting contraception subjected to strict scrutiny.
LOYOLA LAW REVIEW 24:149-163, Winter, 1978.

BIRTH CONTROL: NATURAL
Campaign for natural birth control methods, by M. Nagura.
JOSANPU ZASSHI 32(1):62-63, January, 1978.

A Catholic hospital and natural family planning, by R. Kambic, et al. HOSPITAL PROGRESS 59(4):70-73, April,
1978.

NFP: an idea whose time has come; natural family planning,
by S. Overman. OUR SUNDAY VISITOR 67:8-9,
June 25, 1978.

Natural family planning, by C. Norris. NURSING MIRROR
145:29-30, October 27, 1977.

Natural family planning: the Billings method makes good
sense, by B. McWilliams. LIQUORIAN 66:16-19,
September, 1978.

Natural family planning comes of age, by M. Shivanandan.
MARRIAGE 60:18-21, March, 1978.

Natural family planning: different methods, by P. Deibel.

MCN: AMERICAN JOURNAL OF MATERNAL-CHILD
NURSING 3(3):171-177, May-June, 1978.

Natural family planning draws secular interest. OUR SUN-
DAY VISITOR 66:3, May 29, 1977.

Natural family planning in America, by L. Kane. OUR SUN-
DAY VISITOR 67:8-9, June 25, 1978.

Natural methods of family planning [letter], by A. M. Flynn,
et al. LANCET 2(7982):418, August 21, 1976.

The ovulation method of natural family planning, by E.
Petschel. MARRIAGE 60:14-15, October, 1978.

Physicians help make rhythm work, by E. F. Keefe. NEW
YORK STATE JOURNAL OF MEDICINE 76:205-
208, February, 1976.

Pope urges natural family planners to help couples follow
Church teaching. OUR SUNDAY VISITOR 66:1,
February 26, 1978.

Rhythm: ideal and reality, by M. Benecke. AMERICA 137:
240-241, October 15, 1977.

Says great advances are being made in study of natural family
planning; Lawrence Kane, executive director of the Human Life and Natural Family Planning Foundation, by
S. Overman. OUR SUNDAY VISITOR 66:1, February
26, 1978.

University of Minnesota co-sponsors natural family planning
seminar, by D. Duggan. OUR SUNDAY VISITOR 67:2,
July 23, 1978.

Update on the rhythm method, by N. A. Comer. MADE-
MOISELLE 84(1):46, January, 1978.

Use-effectiveness and analysis of satisfaction levels with the Billings Ovulation Method: two-year pilot study, by H. Klaus, et al. FERTILITY AND STERILITY 28(10): 1038-1043, October, 1977.

BIRTH CONTROL: PSYCHOLOGY
Coping with pregnancy resolution among never-married women, by M. B. Bracken, et al. AMERICAN JOURNAL OF ORTHOPSYCHIATRY 48:320-334, April, 1978.

BIRTH CONTROL: TECHNIQUES
Birth control: what's new, safe and foolproof, by L. Pembrook. PARENTS MAGAZINE 52:74+, November, 1977.

A machine to predict ovulation time. MEDICAL WORLD NEWS 18:40, June 13, 1977.

Seeking new methods. PEOPLE 4(4):31-32, 1977.

BIRTH CONTROL AND COLLEGE STUDENTS
College women's use of gynecological health services: implications for consumer health education, by R. H. Needle. HEALTH EDUCATION 9:10-11, March-April, 1978.

Complete gynecology services in a community college; not an impossible dream! by L. R. Caldwell. JOURNAL OF THE AMERICAN COLLEGE HEALTH ASSOCIATION 26:345+, June, 1978.

BIRTH CONTROL AND NURSES
Using film to inform nurses about teenagers and birth control, by E. S. Herold, et al. NURSING CARE 10(11):22-23, November, 1977.

BIRTH CONTROL AND PHYSICIANS
Doctors and the global population crisis, by J. A. Loraine. BRITISH MEDICAL JOURNAL 2(6088):691-693,

September 10, 1977.

Feminist doctor discusses birth control, by K. Emmot. OTHER WOMAN 4(5):15, September, 1976.

BIRTH CONTROL AND POLITICS
The politics of birth control, by D. Barrett. U. S. CATHO-LIC 43:46-47, January, 1978.

BIRTH CONTROL AND RELIGION
After Humanae Vitae. TABLET 232:723-724, July 29, 1978.

After "Humanae Vitae": a decade of "lively debate," by C. E. Curran. HOSPITAL PROGRESS 59(7):84-89, July, 1978.

Catholicism and human sexuality; Lenten series, by R. McBrien. NATIONAL CATHOLIC REPORTER 14:9, February 17, 1978.

Christian morality and scientific humanism; the thought of Saint Thomas in Humanae Vitae, by M. Ciappi. OS-SERVATORE ROMANO 21(530):7-8, May 25, 1978.

Church loses birth control war; study by C. Westoff. HU-MAN BEHAVIOR 7:38, April, 1978.

Conscience, infallibility, and contraception, by J. M. Finnis. MONTH 11:410-417, December, 1978.

Consequences of the contraceptive mentality; the prophetic witness of Humanae Vitae, by K. Whitehead. OSSERVA-TORE ROMANO 25(534):5-8, June 22, 1978.

Contraception and the infallibility of the ordinary magister-ium, by J. C. Ford, et al. THEOLOGICAL STUDIES 39:258-312, June, 1978.

Contraception et avortement, by S. Luoni. LA DOCU-
MENTATION CATHOLIQUE 74:643-645, July 3, 1977.

Contraception, infallibility and the ordinary magisterium; a
summary of some major elements of the argument made
by Ford and Grisez, by R. Shaw. HOMILETIC AND
PASTORAL REVIEW 78:9-19, July, 1978.

Harvard researcher has second thoughts on use of the pill;
Dr. Robert Kistner; reprint from The Cincinnati Enquirer, April 14, 1977. OSSERVATORE ROMANO
22(479):11, June 2, 1977.

The historical meaning of the Humanae Vitae controversy,
by N. Rigali. CHICAGO STUDIES 15:127-138, Summer, 1976; Reply by R. McCormick. THEOLOGICAL
STUDIES 38:57-114, March, 1977; rejoinder CHICAGO
STUDIES 16:299-308, Fall, 1977.

Humanae Vitae and Catholic mortality, by M. Ciappi. OS-
SERVATORE ROMANO 43(552):11, October 26,
1978.

Humanae Vitae and its reception: ecclesiological reflections,
by J. A. Komonchak. THEOLOGICAL STUDIES 39:
221-257, June, 1978.

Humanae Vitae and the sense of the faithful; some questions
for theologians, by A. Greeley. CRITIC 35:14-25,
Spring, 1977.

Humanae Vitae defender hits natural birth control; Malcolm
Muggerdige, by J. Pereira. OUR SUNDAY VISITOR
67:2, August 13, 1978.

Humanae Vitae is context, by D. O'Callaghan. FURROW
28:230-234, April, 1977.

Humanae Vitae: 1968-1978, by W. Wheeler. OSSERVA-

TORE ROMANO 37(546):4+, September 14, 1978.

Humanae Vitae: symposium: Humanae Vitae and intrinsic evil, by K, Dwyer, et al. FURROW 28:426-433, July, 1977; Reply by D. O'Callaghan 28:433-434, July, 1977.

Humanae Vitae—ten years later, by A. Grutka. LINACRE QUARTERLY 45:10-14, February, 1978.

Humanae Vitae ten years later; declaration of the Indian Episcopal Conference, January 17, 1978. THE POPE SPEAKS 23:183-187, November 2, 1978.

Humanae Vitae today; report on a conference held in Milan, 21 to 25 June, by A. McCormack. TABLET 232:674+, July 15, 1978.

Moral teaching, traditional teaching and Humanae Vitae, by J. Selling. LOUVAIN STUDIES 7:24-44, Spring, 1978.

Moral theologians say Humanae Vitae taught truth that can't be chahnged, by J. C. Ford, et al. OUR SUNDAY VISITOR 67:3, June 18, 1978.

New Pope did not oppose Paul VI on birth control, by J. Maher. OUR SUNDAY VISITOR 67:5, September 10, 1978.

Our Catholic Faith: birth control, by R. Hire. OUR SUNDAY VISITOR 66:4-5, December 4, 1977.

Politics of birth control, by D. N. Barret. U. S. CATHOLIC 43:46-47, January, 1978.

Pope Paul again reaffirms teaching of Humanae Vitae. OUR SUNDAY VISITOR 67:1, August 6, 1978.

Pope says Humanae Vitae was painful to issue, our principles still hold, by J. Muthig, Jr. OUR SUNDAY VISITOR 67:1, July 9, 1978.

Preaching on Humanae Vitae; the tenth anniversary of Humanae Vitae, July, 1978, by J. Kippley. HOMILECTIC AND PASTORAL REVIEW 78:15-19, March, 1978.

Reflections on some aspects of encyclical Humanae Vitae to which less consideration has been given, by B. de Margerie. OSSERVATORE ROMANO 21(530):6-7, May 25, 1978.

The secularization of U. S. Catholic birth control practices, by C. F. Westoff, et al. FAMILY PLANNING PERSPECTIVES 9(5):203-207, September-October, 1977.

Statement from the Irish Bishops' Conference on proposed legislation dealing with family planning and contraception. FURROW 29:525-527, August, 1978.

Statement on the occasion of the tenth anniversary of Humanaie Vitae; by Catholic Bishops' Conference on India, 17 January 1978. OSSERVATORE ROMANO 11(520): 11, March 16, 1978.

Struktur und Funktion des religiösen Aktes. STIMMEN DER ZEIT 195:159-168, March, 1977.

Teenage pregnancy: a second look, by M. Schwartz. OUR SUNDAY VISITOR 67:3, September 3, 1978.

Ten years later; reflections on the anniversary of Humanae Vitae, by C. Curran. COMMONWEAL 105:425-430, July 7, 1978.

Why the Billings method is permissible, by G. Concetti. CHRIST TO THE WORLD 21:332-334, November 5, 1976.

The wider aspects of coercion: much of the current debate on the use of coercion in population policies has been skewed by the more negative aspects of a few heavy-handed programmes, by J. P. Wogaman. POPULI 5:39-43, November 1, 1978.

BIRTH CONTROL AND THE RETARDED
Gynecological care and information; mentally retarded, by L. Cibley. EXCEPTIONAL PARENT 8:9-13, February, 1978.

BIRTH CONTROL AND YOUTH
Adolescent fertility in Hawaii: implications for planning, by L. Stringfellow, et al. HAWAII MEDICAL JOURNAL 37(4):104-113, April, 1978.

Causes of high teenage birth rate. Youngs drug products corporation. INTELLECT 106:437-438, May, 1978.

Minor's right of privacy: limitations on state action after Danforth (Planned Parenthood of Cent. Mo. v. Danforth, 96 Sup Ct 2831) and Carey (Carey v. Population Servs. Int. 97 Sup Ct 2010). COLUMBIA LAW REVIEW 77:1216-1246, December, 1977.

Primary or secondary prevention of adolescent pregnancies? by J. F. Jekel. JOURNAL OF SCHOOL HEALTH 47: 457-461, October, 1977.

Social work attitudes toward birth control for teenagers, by P. A.Reichelt, et al. COMMUNITY MENTAL HEALTH JOURNAL 13:352-359, Winter, 1977.

Teenage sex and birth control, by E. J. Lieberman. JAMA: JOURNAL OF THE AMERICAN MEDICAL ASSOCIA-TION 240(3):275-276, July 21, 1978.

U. S. cities shortchange most pregnant teens. FAMILY PLANNING PERSPECTIVES 10(3):167, May-June, 1978.

Using film to inform nurses about teenagers & birth control, by E. S. Herold, et al. NURSING CARE 10:22-23, November, 1977.

BIRTH CONTROL COUNSELING
Family nurse practitioner in health services center for employees in industry, by R. R. Bauer, et al. OCCUPATIONAL HEALTH NURSING 26(2):11-14, February, 1978.

Gynecologic approach to counseling the sexually active young woman, by E. C. Pierson. CLINICAL OBSTETRICS AND GYNECOLOGY 21(1):235-248, March, 1978.

Male involvement in contraceptive decision making: the role of birth control counselors, by P. Scales, et al. JOURNAL OF COMMUNITY HEALTH 3:54-60, Fall, 1977.

The present state of contraceptive counseling and treatment, by B. Baur, et al. GYNAEKOLOGISCHE RUNDSCHAU 17(Suppl 1):131-132, 1977.

BIRTH CONTROL EDUCATION
Limited patient knowledge as a reproductive risk factor, by S. M. Johnson, et al. JOURNAL OF FAMILY PRACTICE 6(4):855-862, April, 1978.

Non-formal education in the developing world: the role of the International audio-visual resource service, by R. Morell. EDUCATIONAL BROADCASTING INTERNATIONAL 10:68-70, June, 1977.

The production and use of an attitudinal film in birth control education, by E. S. Herold. JOURNAL OF SCHOOL HEALTH 48(5):307-310, May, 1978.

Student volunteers as birth control educators, by R. S. Sanders, et al. JOURNAL OF COLLEGE STUDENT

PERSONNEL 19:216-220, May, 1978.

Training: an integral adjunct to the introduction of newer methods of fertility regulation, by L. E. Laufe, et al. INTERNATIONAL JOURNAL OF GYNAECOLOGY AND OBSTETRICS 15(4):302-306, 1978.

CONTRACEPTION: BIBLIOGRAPHIES
Bibliography of population theories and studies. POPULATION INDEX 43(2):224, April, 1977.

Bibliography of society, ethics and the life sciences: supplement for 1977-78, by S. Sollitto, et al. HASTINGS CENTER REPORT (Suppl):1-26, 1977-1978.

CONTRACEPTION AND CONTRACEPTIVES
Consumer reactions to contraceptive purchasing, by W. A. Fisher, et al. PERSONALITY AND SOCIAL PSY-CHOLOGY BULLETIN 3(2):293-296, Spring, 1977.

Examining the intrafamily decision-making process with respect to contraceptive behavior, by P. E. Downs. DISSERTATION ABSTRACTS INTERNATIONAL 37(8-A):5377-5378, February, 1977.

CONTRACEPTION AND CONTRACEPTIVES: HISTORY
Changing contraceptive patterns: a global perspective. POPULATION BULLETIN 32(3):1, August, 1977.

Changing contraceptive practices in the U.S., married couples, 1965 and 1975, by the Population Reference Bureau. SOCIAL EDUCATION 42:43-44, January, 1978.

Fertility control in man: the history of contraception from antiquity to the present, by L. P. Bengtsson. LAKAR-TIDNINGEN 74(51):4598-4600, December 21, 1977.

CONTRACEPTION AND CONTRACEPTIVES: LAWS
Constitutional law—minors' access to contraceptives—the

right to privacy, due process and the first amendment.
NEW YORK LAW SCHOOL LAW REVIEW 23:777-
790, 1978.

Constitutional law—a state cannot: (1) abridge privacy rights
of minors under sixteen by denying them access to non-
prescription contraceptives (2) burden privacy rights by
permitting only licensed pharmacists to distribute and
sell contraceptives (3) totally prohibit advertisement and
display of contraceptive products. JOURNAL OF FAMI-
LY LAW 16:639-652, 1977-1978.

CONTRACEPTION AND CONTRACEPTIVES: RESEARCH
Contraception—retrospect and prospect, by M. J. Harper.
PROGRESS IN DRUG RESEARCH 21:293-407, 1977.

CONTRACEPTION AND CONTRACEPTIVES: TECHNIQUES
The benefit of lactation amenorrhea as a contraceptive, by
F. Hefnawi, et al. INTERNATIONAL JOURNAL OF
GYNAECOLOGY AND OBSTETRICS 15(1):60-62,
1977.

Combination of ovulation method and diaphragm [letter],
by J. F. Cattanach. MEDICAL JOURNAL OF AUS-
TRALIA 2(14):478, October 1, 1978.

Comparison between the combined pill and intrauterine device in nulliparae under the age of 19, by M. Lie, et al.
TIDSSKRIFT FOR DEN NORSKE LAEGEFORENING
98(12):614-617, April 30, 1978.

Contraception: methods of those in the know; fertility control: how to cut the dangers, by M. Weber. VOGUE
168:210, August, 1978.

Contraception: when should barrier methods be recommended? by C. Lauritzen. MUENCHENER MEDIZINISCHE
WOCHENSCHRIFT 120(37):1180, September 15, 1978.

Course of pregnancy and the state of the intrauterine fetus after the use of various contraceptive agents, by M. Ia. Martynshin, et al. VOPROSY OKHRANY MATERINST-VA I DETSTVA 22(9):60-62, September, 1977.

Directions for classification and indications of oral contraceptives, by J. P. d'Ernst, et al. PRAXIS 66(50):1620-1627, December 13, 1977.

The efficiency of menstrual regulation as a method of fertility control, by J. Bongaarts, et al. STUDIES IN FAMILY PLANNING 8(10):268-272, October, 1977.

Study confirms values of ovulation method, by L. Dolack, Sr. HOSPITAL PROGRESS 69:64-66+, August, 1978.

CONTRACEPTION AND CONTRACEPTIVES AND MEN

CONTRACEPTIVE AGENTS
Assay of long-acting contraceptive steroid formulations in rabbits, by K. Fotherby, et al. CONTRACEPTION 17(4):365-373, April, 1978.

Behavior of the C-reactive protein in short and long-term application of various hormonal contraceptives, by G. Klinger, et al. ZENTRALBLATT FUER GYNAEKOLO-GIE 100(3):167-172, 1978.

The behavior of serum total protein and protein fractions during the use of various hormonal contraceptives, by G. Klinger, et al. DEUTSCHE GESUNDHEITSWESEN 32(5):2418-2423, 1977.

Characterization of progesterone receptor in human uterine cytosol with a synthetic progestin, norgestrel [proceedings], by A. K. Srivastava, et al. JOURNAL OF EN-DOCRINOLOGY 77(2):22P-23P, May, 1978.

Clinical aspects of a new, very low dose combination contraceptive, by D. Mladenovic, et al. FORTSCHRITTE DER MEDIZIN 96(13):723-726, April 6, 1978.

Comparative clinical trial of two oral contraceptives with a low—estrogen content, by S. Koetsawang, et al. JOURNAL OF THE MEDICAL ASSOCIATION OF THAILAND 60(8):368-373, August, 1977.

Comparative effects of oestrogen and a progestogen on bone loss in postmenopausal women, by R. Lindsay, et al. CLINICAL SCIENCE AND MOLECULAR MEDICINE 54(2):193-195, February, 1978.

A comparative study of three low does progestogens, chlormadinone acetate, megestrol acetate and norethisterone, as oral contraceptives, by D. F. Hawkins, et al. BRITISH JOURNAL OF OBSTETRICS AND GYNAECOLOGY 84(9):708-713, September, 1977.

Contraception with a normophasic agent, by H. Kopera. WIENER MEDIZINISCHE WOCHENSCHRIFT 127(18): 573-577, October 10, 1977.

Determination of the plasma gonadotropims FSH, LH and LMTH in patients treated with estroprogestogens, by A. Segre, et al. MINERVA GINECOLOGIA 30(3):157-165, March, 1978.

Differentiation of factor C-LHIH and the synthetic contraceptive polypeptide, H-Thr-Pro-Arg-Lys-OH, D. Chang, et al. BIOCHEMICAL AND BIOPHYSICAL RESEARCH COMMUNICATIONS 65(4):1208-1213, August 18, 1975.

Doses-related effects of lynestrenol on ovulation, by M. A. Pizarro, et al. REPRODUCTION 3(3-4):193-205, July-December, 1976.

Early experience in contraception with a new progestogen,

by J. A. McEwan, et al. CONTRACEPTION 16(4):339-350, October, 1977.

Effect of an Ayurvedic preparation on peripheral parameters of the menstrual cycle, by J. Joshi, et al. INDIAN JOURNAL OF MEDICAL RESEARCH 66(1):39-42, July, 1977.

Effect of papaya (Carica papaya linn) on pregnancy and estrous cycle in albino rats of Vistar strain, by M. Gopalakrishnan, et al. INDIAN JOURNAL OF PHYSIOLOGY AND PHARMACOLOGY 22(1):66-70, January-March, 1978.

Experimental and clinical data on Cyclabil, by W. H. Schneider, et al. ACTA OBSTETRICIA ET GYNECOLOGICA SCANDINAVICA (65):39-43, 1977.

FDA studies of estrogen, progestogens, and estrogen/progestogen combinations in the dog and monkey, by R. G. Geil, et al. JOURNAL FO TOXICOLOGY AND ENVIRONMENTAL HEALTH 3(1-2):179-193, September, 1977.

First results with a new prostaglandin E2-derivate, by M. Schmidt-Gollwitzer, et al. GEBURTSHILFE UND FRAUENHEILKUNDE 37(12):1030-1038, December, 1977.

The health belief model as a conceptual framework for explaining contraceptive compliance, by M. E, Katatsky. HEALTH EDUCATION MONOGRAPHS 5(3):232-243, Fall, 1977.

High inhibitory activity of R 5020, a pure progestin, at the hypothalamic-adenohypophyseal level on gonadotropin secretion, by F. Labrie, et al. FERTILITY AND STERILITY 28(10):1104-1112, October, 1977.

High-performance liquid chromatography of the steroid hormones, by F. A. Fitzpatrick. ADVANCES IN CHROMATOGRAPHY 16:37-73, 1978.

Hormonal contraception: perspectives. Part two. Special techniques, by G. P. Wood. JOURNAL OF THE ARKANSAS MEDICAL SOCIETY 74(7):239-241, December, 1977.

Hormonal contraception using the oral depot preparation, Deposiston, by D. Vasilev. AKUSHERSTVO I GINEKOLOGIIA 17(2):147-151, 1978.

Immediate postabortal contraception with a microdose combined preparation: gonadotropin, estradiol and progesterone levels during the last treatment cycle and after discontinuation of oral contraceptives, by P. Lähteenmäki. CONTRACEPTION 17(4):297-307, April, 1978.

Immediate postabortal contraception with a microdose combined preparation: suppression of pituitary and ovarian function and elimination of HCG, by P. Lähteenmäki, et al. CONTRACEPTION 17(2):169-181, February, 1978.

Inhibition of ovulation by gestagens, by E. Johansson, et al. UPSALA JOURNAL OF MEDICAL SCIENCES (22): 16-22, 1978.

Inhibition of ovulation in women by chronic treatment with a stimulatory LRH analogue—a new approach to birth control? by S. J. Nillius, et al. CONTRACEPTION 17(6):537-545, June, 1978.

Inhibition of puerperal lactation by bromocriptine, by R. Rolland, et al. ACTA ENDOCRINOLOGICA 88(216): 119-130, 1978.

Inhibitory effects of RU 16117, a potent estrogen antagonist, on the estrous cycle in the rat, by L. Ferland, et al. BIOLOGY OF REPRODUCTION 18(1):99-104, February, 1978.

Interceptive & abortifacient activity of Aristolochia induca L. & possible mode of action, by A. Pakrashi, et al. INDIAN JOURNAL OF EXPERIMENTAL BIOLOGY 15(6):428-430, June, 1977.

Intravenous glucose tolerance after 18 months on progestogen or comgination-type oral contraceptive, by J. A. Goldman. ISRAEL JOURNAL OF MEDICAL SCIENCES 14(3):324-327, March, 1978.

Introduction: menstrual regulation—the method and the issues, by W. B. Watson. STUDIES IN FAMILY PLANNING 8(10):250-252, October, 1977.

Investigations of pharmacokinetics of levonorgestrel to specific consideration of a possible first-pass effect in women, by M. Hümpel, et al. CONTRACEPTION 17(3):207-220, March, 1978.

Long-term study of a progestational micropill: 600 mcg norethisterone acetate, by F. Robey-Lelièvre, et al. JOURNAL DE GYNECOLOGIE, OBSTETRIQUE ET BIOLOGIE DE LA REPRODUCTION 7(3):485-497, April, 1978.

The mechanism of antiandrogenic action of chlormadinone acetate, by Y. Ito, et al. NIPPON HINYOKIKA GAKKI ZASSHI 68(6):537-552, June, 1977.

Mechanism of contraceptive effect of low progestin doses, by V. V. Korkhov, et al. VOPROSY OKHRANY MATERINSTVA I DETSTVA 22(8):89-90, August, 1977.

Mechanism of contraceptive effect with postovulatory estrogen treatment, by T. Koyama, et al. NIPPON NAIBUNPI

GAKKAI ZASSHI 52(11):1053-1062, November 20, 1976.

Mechanism of estrogen-induced saturated bile in the hamster, by G. G. Bonorris, et al. JOURNAL OF LABORATORY AND CLINICAL MEDICINE 90(6):963-970, December, 1977.

Menstrual induction with vaginal administration of 16,16 dimethyl trans-delta s-PGE1 methyl ester (ONO 802), by S. M. Darim, et al. PROSTAGLANDINS 14(3):615-616, September, 1977.

Menstrual regulation: the method and the issues. Competing risks of unnecessary procedures and complications, by J. A. Fortney, et al. STUDIES IN FAMILY PLANNING 8(10):257-262, October, 1977.

The menstrual regulation procedure, by L. E. Laufe. STUDIES IN FAMILY PLANNING 8(10):253-256, October, 1977.

Menstrual regulation: risks and "abuses", by W. E. Brenner, et al. INTERNATIONAL JOURNAL OF GYNAE-COLOGY AND OBSTETRICS 15(2):177-183, 1977.

Modulation of the pituitary response to LH-RH by synthetic sex steroids, by T. Iwasaki. NIPPON NAIBUNPI GAK-KAI ZASSHI 54(3):255-276, March 20, 1978.

Molecular structure and drug activity. Example: sex hormones, by F. Neumann. NATURWISSENSCHAFTEN 64(8):410-416, August, 1977.

Nature of the ovulation and the state of the preimplantation fetuses in the experimental administration of hormonal and neurotropic agents, by V. V. Korkhov, et al. VO-PROSY OKHRANY MATERINSTVA I DETSTVA 23(6):87-88, June, 1978.

New aspecsts of contraception by enzyme-directed antibodies, by T. Dietl, et al. ANDROLOGIA 10(3):250-251, May-June, 1978.

Observations with Ovidon, by M. Farkas, et al. THERAPIA HUNGARICA 25(3):93-101, 1977.

Perspectives in evaluating the safety and effectiveness of steroidal contraceptives in different parts of the world, by J. W. Goldzieher. INTERNATIONAL JOURNAL OF GYNAECOLOGY AND OBSTETRICS 15(1):63-68, 1977.

Pharmacological activity of progesterone derivatives, by V. V. Korkhov, et al. FARMIKOLOGIYA I TOKSIKOLOGIYA 41(1):55-59, January-February, 1978.

The pharmacological profile of norgestimate, a new orally active progestin, by D.W. Hahn, et al. CONTRACEP-TION 16(5):541-553, November, 1977.

Phosphorus-nitrogen compounds. 21. Murine oncolytic and antifertility effect of adamantylaziridine compounds, by L. A. Cates, et al. JOURNAL OF MEDICINAL CHEM-ISTRY 21(1):143-146, January, 1978.

Physician notes hazards of DES use to prevent pregnancy [letter], by E. F. Diamond. HOSPITAL PROGRESS 59(3):6-10, March, 1978.

A reassessment of menstrual regulation, by J. E. Hodgson. STUDIES IN FAMILY PLANNING 8(10):263-267, October, 1977.

Relation between sex hormone binding globulin and D-norgestrel levels in plasma, by A. Victor, et al. ACTA ENDOCRINOLOGICA 86(2):430-436, October, 1977.

Sperm inhibitors as contraceptives; acrosin inhibitor. SCI-

ENCE NEWS 113:150, March 11, 1978.

Spontaneously regressive ulcerative colitis: the result of contraceptive agents? [letter], by L. Simon, et al. GASTRO-ENTEROLOGIE CLINIQUE ET BIOLOGIQUE 2(4): 442-443, April, 1978.

Steroid antifertility agents. Ionic complexes of basic derivatives for prolonged action, by A. P. Gray, et al. JOURNAL OF MEDICINAL CHEMISTRY 21(7):712-715, July, 1978.

Synthesis and biological evaluation of 2- and 4-hydroxy-mestranol, by R. M. Kanojia. STEROIDS 30(3):343-348, September, 1977.

Synthesis of 17beta-D-glucopyranosiduronic acid of 17alpha-ethynylestradiol, by E. D. Helton, et al. JOURNAL OF STEROID BIOCHEMISTRY 9(3):237-238, March, 1978.

Ventilatory response to medroxyprogesterone acetate in normal subjects: time course and mechanism, by J. B. Skatrud, et al. JOURNAL OF APPLIED PHYSIOLOGY 44(6):393-344, June, 1978.

LATIN AMERICA
268 medicinal plants used for regulating fertility in various South American countries, by R. Moreno Azorero, et al. OBSTETRICIA Y GINECOLOGIA LATINO-AMERICANAS 33(9-10):335-348, September-October, 1975.

PARAGUAY
Plant used as means of abortion, contraception, sterilization and fecundation by Paraguayan indigenous people, by P. Arena, et al. ECONOMIC BOTANY 31(3): 302-306, 1977.

CONTRACEPTIVE AGENTS: COMPLICATIONS
Adverse effects of steroid sex hormones, by I. Hirschler.
ORVOSI HETILAP 118(34):2061-2063, August 21,
1977.

Changes in the kidneys and upper urinary passages due to
hormonal contraceptives, by T. D. Datuashvili. SOVET-
SKAYA MEDITZINA (11):65-69, November, 1977.

Contraceptive agents and cardiovascular diseases, by N. Lisin,
et al. BRUXELLES-MEDICALE 57(11):499-502,
November, 1977.

Contraceptive steroids and breast cancer [letter], by B. A.
Stoll. BRITISH MEDICAL JOURNAL 1(6123):1350-
1351, May 20, 1978.

Effect of chronic treatment with an estrogen-progestogen
combination on beta adrenergic-induced thirst, by T. N.
Thrasher, et al. PHARMACOLOGY, BIOCHEMISTRY
AND BEHAVIOR 8(2):177-183, February, 1978.

Effect of a contraceptive steroid combination of the "serum
activation" of lipoprotein lipase in rats, by A. Bizzi, et al.
BIOCHEMICAL PHARMACOLOGY 27(5):795-797,
March 1, 1978.

Effect of contraceptive steroids on arginine-stimulated glucagon and insulin secretion in women. III. Medroxyprogesterone acetate, by P. Beck, et al. METABOLISM
26(11):1193-1198, November, 1977.

Effect of cyproterone acetate on hair growth, sebaceous
secretion and endocrine parameters in a hirsute subject,
by F. J. Ebling, et al. BRITISH JOURNAL OF DERMA-
TOLOGY 97(4):371-381, October, 1977.

Effect of cyproterone acetate on skin surface lipids, by D.
Fanta, et al. ACTA DERMATO-VENEREOLOGICA

58(1):85-87, 1978.

Effect of d-norgestrel on LH levels and ovulation in the rhesus monkey, by N. E. Reame, et al. CONTRACEPTION 16(5):499-505, November, 1977.

The effect of daily norethisterone (0.35 mg) on cervical mucus and on urinary LH, pregnanediol and oestrogen levels, by M. Elstein, et al. BRITISH JOURNAL OF OBSTETRICS AND GYNAECOLOGY 83(2):165-168, February, 1976.

Effect of estrogens on the liver. Case presentation, by R. Dahl. GASTROENTEROLOGY 75(3):517, September, 1978.

Effect of ethinyl oestradiol and megestrol acetate on carbohydrate metabolism in rabbits, by B. B. Gaitonde, et al. INDIAN JOURNAL OF MEDICAL RESEARCH 66(2): 223-235, August, 1977.

Effect of ethinyloestradiol on protein, nucleic acids and nucleases in the rat liver, by M. A. Mukundan, et al. INDIAN JOURNAL OF MEDICAL RESEARCH 66(6): 946-949, December, 1977.

Effect of ethynodiol diacetate with ethinyl estradiol on the mammary glands of rhesus monkeys: a preliminary report, by V. A. Drill, et al. JOURNAL OF THE NATIONAL CANCER INSTITUTE 60(5):1169-1170, May, 1978.

Effect of ethynylestradiol on bilary excretion of bile acids, phosphatidylcolines, and cholesterol in the bile fistula rat, by F. Kern, Jr., et al. JOURNAL OF LIPID RESEARCH 18(5):623-634, September, 1977.

The effect of a low dose progestagen on the trace metal content and disulphide and sulphydryl groups in cervical mucus, by B. Daunter, et al. CONTRACEPTION 17(1):

35-40, January, 1978.

Effect of norethisterone oenanthate on serum gonadotrophin levels, by K. Fotherby, et al. CONTRACEPTION 16(6): 591-604, December, 1977.

Effect of steroid contraceptive drug treatment on the catecholamine metabolism in the guinea pig central nervous system, by F. Ponzio, et al. MEDICAL BIOLOGY 55(4): 224-227, August, 1977.

Effect of steroidal contraception on lipid factors and liver function tests, by S. M. Shahani, et al. JOURNAL OF OBSTETRICS AND GYNAECOLOGY OF INDIA 27(1):95-101, February, 1977.

Effect of two progestins on human endometrial enzymes and trace elements, by J. Jelinek, et al. ACTA ENDOCRINOLOGICA 88(3):580-588, July, 1978.

Effects of estrogens on the liver, by F. R. Simmon. GASTROENTEROLOGY 75(3):512-514, September, 1978.

Effects of ethinyl estradiol on hepatic microsomal proteins and the turnover of cytochrome P-450, by M. Mackinnon, et al. JOURNAL OF LABORATORY AND CLINICAL MEDICINE 90(6):1096-1106, December, 1977.

Effects of medroxyprogesterone on the liver function and drug metabolism of patients with primary bilary cirrhosis and chronic active hepatitis, by E. A. Sotaniemi, et al. JOURNAL OF MEDICINE 9(2):117-128, 1978.

Effects of mestranol on blood pressure and norepinephrine in young normotensive and genetically hypertensive rats, by G. M. Lew. GENERAL PHARMACOLOGY 9(3): 163-166, 1978.

Effects of quingestanol acetate on the histology, histochemistry and ultrastructure of the endometrium, by C. E. Flowers, et al. JOURNAL DE GYNECOLOGIE, OB-STETRIQUE ET BIOLOGIE DE LA REPRODUCTION 6(8):1139-1157, December, 1977.

Effects of steroids on serum lipids and serum cholesterol binding reserve, by M. S. Roth, et al. AMERICAN JOURNAL OF OBSTETRICS AND GYNECOLOGY 132(2):151-156, September 15, 1978.

Epilepsy and contraception, by A. Fanard, et al. ACTA OBSTETRICA Y GINECOLOGICA HISPANA-LUSI-TANA 25(6):311-317, June, 1977.

Ethinyl estradiol in human milk and plasma after oral administration, by S. Nilsson, et al. CONTRACEPTION 17(2):131-139, February, 1978.

Female sex hormones and thrombosis. Epidemiological aspects, by M. P. Vessey, et al. BRITISH MEDICAL BULLETIN 34(2):157-162, May, 1978.

Further comments on "contraceptive hormones and congenital heart disease" [letter], by J. R. Miller, et al. TERATOLOGY 17(3):359-360, June, 1978.

Further studies on a new bioassay of progestational activity (traumatic deciduoma formation in immature rats), by Z. S. Madjerek, et al. ACTA MORPHOLOGICA NEERLANDS-SCANDINAVICA 15(1):65-74, February, 1977.

Further studies on the restoration of estrogen-induced sexual receptivity in ovariectomized mice treated with dihydrotestosterone: effects of progesterone, dihydroprogesterone and LH-RH, by W. G. Luttge, et al. PHARMACOLOGY, BIOCHEMISTRY AND BEHAVIOR 7(6):563-566, December, 1977.

A generalized epileptiform convulsion after intra-amniotic

363

prostaglandin with intravenous oxytocin infusion: a case report, by E. Kaplan. SOUTH AFRICAN MEDICAL JOURNAL 53(1):27-29, January 7, 1978.

Headache and sex hormone therapy, by L. Dennerstein, et al. HEADACHE 18(3):146-153, July, 1978.

Heparin resistance and decreased hepatic triglyceride hydro-lase release during long-term estrogen-progestin treatment, by B. W. Glad, et al. METABOLISM 27(1):53-60, January, 1978.

Histochemical and electron scanning microscopy studies of the fallopian tube under the influence of various hormones [proceedings], by P. Kugler, et al. ARCHIV FUR GYNAEKOLOGIE 224(1-4):82-83, July 29, 1977.

Hormonal contraception and pregnancy, by A. Spira. JOURNAL DE GYNECOLOGIE, OBSTETRIQUE ET BIOLOGIE DE LA REPRODUCTION 6(5):711-712, July-August, 1977.

Hormones and skin pigmentation in the mammal, by A. J. Thody, et al. INTERNATIONAL JOURNAL OF DERMATOLOGY 16(8):657-664, October, 1977.

In-vitro parameters under the influence of pregnancy or anti-conception, respectively, by U. Herter, et al. ZEITSCHRIFT FUR AERZTLICHE FORTBILDUNG 71(20): 962-963, October 15, 1977.

In vivo metabolism of norethisterone-3-oxime in rabbits, by F. S. Khan, et al. JOURNAL OF STEROID BIOCHEMISTRY 9(3):229-232, March, 1978.

Incidence of side effects of synthetic progestins with different content of estrogenic and gestagenic components, by I. E. Rotkina, et al. AKUSHERSTVO I GINEKOLOGIIA (9):29-31, September 9, 1977.

Indices of adrenal cortical function in children whose mothers were treated during pregnancy with steroid hormones for habitual abortion, by R. A. Stepanova, et al. VOPROSY OKHRANY MATERINSTVA I DETSTVA 22(9):34-35, September, 1977.

Influence of contraceptive hormones on hair growth [letter], by H. Zaun. DEUTSCH MEDIZENISCHE WOCHEN-SCHRIFT 103(6):240, February 10, 1978.

Influence of estrogens on atheroma development [editorial]. NOUVELLE PRESSE MEDICALE 6(31):2739-2740, September 24, 1977.

Influence of estrogens on pituitary responsiveness to LHRH and TRH in human, by T. Lemarchand-Béraud, et al. ANNALES D'ENDOCRINOLOGIE 38(6):379-382, 1977.

Influence of fetal sex on the concentration of amniotic fluid testosterone: antenatal sex determination? by H. J. Kunzig, et al. ARCHIV FUR GYNAEKOLOGIE 223(2): 75-84, September 30, 1977.

Influence of the hippocampus on the luteinizing activity of the adenohypophysis and the contraceptive activity of megastranol, by I. V. Tomilina. FARMAKOLOGIYA I TOKSIKOLOGIYA 40(3):342-346, May-June, 1977.

Influence of human chorionic gonadotrophin on the response of luteinizing hormone to luteinizing hormone releasing hormone in gonadectomized women, by A. Miyake, et al. JOURNAL OF ENDOCRINOLOGY 74(3):499-500, September, 1977.

The influence of oestroprogestational agents on cervico-facial cutaneous scars, by P. Tailhardat. ANNALS D'OTO-LARYNGOLOGIE ET DE CHIRURGIE CERVI-CO FACIALE 94(10-11):623-627, October-November,

1977.

Influence of progesterone on serotonin metabolism: a possible causal factor for mood changes, by W. Ladisich. PSYCHONEUROENDOCRINOLOGY 2(3):257-266, 1977.

Inhibition of the nuclear dihydrotestosterone receptor complex from rat ventral prostate by antiandrogens and stilboestrol, by C. B. Smith, et al. MOLECULAR AND CELLULAR ENDOCRINOLOGY 10(1):13-20, February-March, 1978.

The interaction of antibiotics with synthetic steroids in the rat [proceedings], by D. J. Back, et al. BRITISH JOURNAL OF PHARMACOLOGY 62(3):441P, March, 1978.

Interaction of antiepileptics, by J. Opavsky. CASOPIS LEKARU CESKYCH 116(50):1550-1553, December 16, 1977.

Interaction of drugs and nutrition, by T. K. Basu. JOURNAL OF HUMAN NUTRITION 31(6):449-458, December, 1977.

Interference of gestagens and androgens with rat uterine oestrogen receptors, by F. Di Carlo, et al. JOURNAL OF ENDOCRINOLOGY 77(1):49-55, April, 1978.

Jaundice due to gestagens revisited, by H. Reyes, et al. REVISTA MEDICA DE CHILE 106(2):85-90, February, 1978.

Maternal exposure to exogenous progestogen/estrogen as a potential cause of birth defects, by A. H. Nora, et al. ADVANCES IN PLANNED PARENTHOOD 12(3): 156-169, 1978.

Measurement of unconjugated testosterone, 5alpha-dihydrotestosterone and oestradiol in human urine, by J. M. Kjeld, et al. CLINICA CHIMICA ACTA 80(2):271-284, October 15, 1977.

Mechanism of action of conjugated estrogens as contraceptives. I. Clinical study, by S. Fuensalida, et al. REVISTA CHILENA DE OBSTETRICIA Y GINECOLOGIA 41(6):333-336, 1976.

Metabolism of ethynyl estrogens, by E. D. Helton, et al. JOURNAL OF TOXICOLOGY AND ENVIRONMENTAL HEALTH 3(1-2):231-241, September, 1977.

Monitoring of plasma renin activity, renin substrate and aldosterone concentrations during treatment with hormonal contraceptives [proceedings], by H. Kaulhausen, et al. ARCHIV FUR GYNAEKOLOGIE 224(1-4):430-431, July 29, 1977.

Morphologic alterations in the epithelium of the human oviduct induced by a low dosis gestagen, by U. M. Spornitz, et al. ARCHIV FUR GYNAEKOLOGIE 223(4): 269-281, November 29, 1977.

Mortality and fertility control, by C. Tietze, et al. INTERNATIONAL JOURNAL OF GYNAECOLOGY AND OBSTETRICS 15(2):100-104, 1977.

Mortality associated with the control of fertility, by C. Tietze, et al. FAMILY PLANNING PERSPECTIVES 8(1):6-14, January-February, 1976.

Occupational exposure to synthetic estrogens—the need to establish safety standards. AMERICAN INDUSTRIAL HYGIENE ASSOCIATION JOURNAL 39(2):139, February, 1978.

The pharmacodynamics and toxicology of steroids and related compounds, by F. Bischoff, et al. ADVANCES IN

LIPID RESEARCH 15:61-157, 1977.

Prenatal exposure to medroxyprogesterone acetate (MPA) in girls, by A. A. Ehrhardt, et al. PSYCHONEUROEN-DOCRINOLOGY 2(4):391-398, October, 1977.

Problems in evaluating chronic toxicity of contraceptive steroids in dogs, by J. H. Weikel, Jr., et al. JOURNAL OF TOXICOLOGY AND ENVIRONMENTAL HEALTH 3(1-2):167-177, September, 1977.

Production of antisera against contraceptive steroids, by N. Kundu, et al. STEROIDS 30(1):85-98, July, 1977.

Progestagens, blood-clotting, and blood-pressure [letter]. LANCET 2(8047):1085-1086, November 19, 1977.

Progesterone antagonism of estradiol-stimulated uterine "induced protein" synthesis, by H. S. Bhakoo, et al. MOLECULAR AND CELLULAR ENDOCRINOLOGY 8(2):105-120, August, 1977.

Progesterone: effects on investigatory preferences, aggression, and olfaction inorchidectomized, testosterone-treated mice, by M. J. Soares, et al. BEHAVIORAL BIOLOGY 23(2):260-266, June, 1978.

Progestin treatment in a case of adrenal cortex hyperfunction with cancer of the endometrium, by A. Lanza, et al. MINERVA GINECOLOGIA 30(5):458-459, May, 1978.

Progestogens in prostatic cancer, by L. Denis, et al. EUROPEAN UROLOGY 4(3):162-166, 1978.

Radioimmunological determination of prolactin following daily administration of gestagens [proceedings], by J. Thoma, et al. ARCHIV FUR GYNAEKOLOGIE 224(1-4):410-411, July 29, 1977.

Renin-renin substrate kinetic constants in the plasma of normal and estrogen-treated humans, by W. J. McDonald, et al. JOURNAL OF CLINICAL ENDOCRINOLOGY AND METABOLISM 45(6):1297-1304, December, 1977.

Role of arginine-vasopressin (ADH) in the regulation of uterine motility during menstruation, by E. Cobo, et al. REVISTA COLOMBIANA DE OBSTETRICIA Y GINE-COLOGIA 28(3):97-115, May-June, 1977.

Role of estro-progestational compounds in myocardial infarct [letter], by T. Darragon. NOUVELLE PRESSE MEDI-CALE 6(40):3756, November 26, 1977.

Serium protein-bound carbohydrate and seromucoid levels during long-acting progestational contraceptive therapy, by F. M. Saleh. CONTRACEPTION 16(4):399-407, October, 1977.

Serum naphythylamidase isoenzymes during hormonal treatment. Electrophoretic and quantitative studies, by G. Beckman, et al. INTERNATIONAL JOURNAL OF GYNAECOLOGY AND OBSTETRICS 14(6):550-552, 1976.

Sex hormone binding globulin: binding capacity and studies on the binding of cyproterone acetate and other steroids, by M. Frölich, et al. CLINICA CHIMICA ACTA 87(2): 239-244, July 15, 1978.

Short and long term effects of various contraceptives on ovaries, by A. Sen Gupta, et al. JOURNAL OF OBSTE-TRICS AND GYNAECOLOGY OF INDIA 27(2):183-187, April, 1977.

Some effects of medroxyprogesterone acetate on intermediary metabolism in rat liver, by C. H. Dahm, Jr., et al. LIFE SCIENCES 22(2):165-169, January, 1978.

Spontaneous platelet aggregation associated with administration of sex hormones in men and women, by H. Rieger, et al. DEUTSCH MEDIZINISCHE WOCHENSCHRIFT 102(35):1248-1250, September 2, 1977.

Steroid contraception and the risk of neoplasia. WHO TECHNICAL REPORT SERIES (619):1-54, 1978.

Structural modifications in contraceptive steroids altering their metabolism and toxicity, by H. M. Bolt. ARCHIV FUER TOXIKOLOGIE 39(1-2):13-19, December 30, 1977.

Toxic agents resulting from the oxidative metabolism of steroid hormones and drugs, by E. C. Horning, et al. JOURNAL OF TOXICOLOGY AND ENVIRONMENTAL HEALTH 4(2-3):341-361, March-May, 1978.

Toxic hepatoses due to Gravistat, by C. Metzner, et al. ZEITSCHRIFT FUR DIE GESAMTE HYGIENE UND IHRE GENZGEBIETE 32(16):407-408, August 15, 1977.

CONTRACEPTIVE AGENTS: FEMALE
Approval of depo-provera for contraception denied. FDA DRUG BULLETIN 8(2):10-11, March-April, 1978.

Comparison of Norinyl and Combination-5, by A. R. Khan, et al. BANGLADESH MEDICAL RESEARCH COUNCIL BULLETIN 3(2):108-116, December, 1977.

Effect of ovulation inhibitors on the course of hereditary spontaneous hypertension of the rat (SH rats), by A. Samizadeh, et al. MEDIZINISCHE WELT 29(6):225-227, February 10, 1978.

Effects of the progestasert on the menstrual pattern, ovarian steroids and endometrium, by L. S. Wan, et al. CONTRACEPTION 16(4):417-434, October, 1977.

Estrogens for contraception and menopause, by L. B. Tyrer, et al. NURSES DRUG ALERT 1:169-180, December, 1977.

Fertility control through steroid hormones used as contraceptives in the woman, by J. Zanartn, et al. REVISTA MEDICA DE CHILE 103(1):52-60, January, 1975.

Inactivation of herpes simplex viruses by nonionic surfactants, by S. S. Asculai, et al. ANTIMICROBIAL AGENTS AND CHEMOTHERAPY 13(4):686-690, April, 1978.

Lactation—the central control of reproduction, by R. V. Short. CIBA FOUNDATION SYMPOSIA (45):73-86, 1976.

Lactation, fertility, and contraception [editorial]. LANCET 2(7982):407-408, August 21, 1976.

Preclinical evaluation of intrauterine progesterone as a contraceptive agent. I. Local contraceptive effects and their reversal, by R. Hudson, et al. CONTRACEPTION 17(5): 465-474, May, 1978.

—. II. Possible mechanisms of action, by S. A. Tillson, et al. CONTRACEPTION 17(5):475-488, May, 1978.

Prevention of pregnancy in rabbits using vaginal application of prostaglandin f2alpha, by M. Salomy, et al. FERTILITY AND STERILITY 29(4):456-458, April, 1978.

Prevention of unwanted pregnancy with Yermonil preparation, by Z. Sternadel, et al. GINEKOLOGIA POLASKA 49(2):139-142, February, 1978.

Recent developments in technology for the control of female fertility, by J. J. Speidel, et al. OBSTETRICS AND GYNECOLOGY ANNUAL 7:397-445, 1978.

Strategy in drug research. Synthesis and study of the progestational and ovulation inhibitory activity of a series of
11beta-substituted-17alpha-ethynyl-4-estren-17beta-ols,
by A. J. Broek, et al. STEROIDS 30(4):481-510, October, 1977.

CONTRACEPTIVE AGENTS: FEMALE: COMPLICATIONS
Classic pages in Obstetrics and Gynecology. The effects of
progesterone and related compounds on ovulation and
early development in the rabbit: Gregory Pincus and Min
Chuch Chang. In: Acta physiologica Latinoamericana,
vol. 3, pp. 177-83, 1953, by G. Pincus, et al. AMERI-
CAN JOURNAL OF OBSTETRICS AND GYNECOLO-
GY 132(2):215-216, September 15, 1978.

The comparative effects of a synthetic and a "natural"
oestrogen on the haemostatic mechanism in patients
with primary amenorrhoea, by J. L. Toy, et al. BRITISH
JOURNAL OF OBSTETRICS AND GYNAECOLOGY
85(5):359-362, May, 1978.

Effect of quinestrol on plasma lipids in women, by M. M.
Abdel Kader, et al. ACTA BIOLOGICA ET MEDICA
GERMANICA 36(9):1285-1287, 1977.

The effect of synthetic gestagens on progesterone formation
in vitro in human placenta of early pregnancy, by A.
Saure, et al. JOURNAL OF REPRODUCTION AND
FERTILITY 51(2):369-373, November, 1977.

Effects of estradiol benzoate, estrone, and propionates of
testosterone or dihydrotestosterone on sexual and related behaviors of ovariectomized rhesus monkeys, by
K. Wallen, et al. HORMONES AND BEHAVIOR 9(3):
228-248, December, 1977.

Effects of long-acting steroid contraceptives on ovarian and
uterine histology of rats, by Harun-Ar-Rashid, et al.
BANGLADESH MEDICAL RESEARCH COUNCIL

BULLETIN 3(1):46-51, June, 1977.

The effects of sulpiride on plasma LH, FSH, and progesteroen in women during the reproductive years. Role of hyperprolactinism in ovulation disorders, by J. Buvat, et al. JOURNAL DE GYNECOLOGIE, OBSTETRIQUE ET BIOLOGIE DE LA REPRODUCTION 7(1):5-18, January, 1978.

Epidemiological relationship between steroid hormones and liver lesions, by E. Mahboubi, et al. JOURNAL OF TOXICOLOGY AND ENVIRONMENTAL HEALTH 3(1-2): 207-218, September, 1977.

Epidemiology of uterine cervicocarcinoma, by L. Barberis, et al. MINERVA GINECOLOGIA 30(4):291-298, April, 1978.

Estrogen metabolism in normal and neoplastic endometrium, by E. Gurpide, et al. AMERICAN JOURNAL OF OBSTETRICS AND GYNECOLOGY 129(7):809-816, December 1, 1977.

Estrogen profiles of premenopausal women with breast cancer, by P. Cole, et al. CANCER RESEARCH 38(3):745-748, March, 1978.

Estrogen/progestogen-exposure and fetal effects, by J. G. Forsberg. TIDSSKRIFT FOR DEN NORSKE LAEGEFORENING 97(30):1583-1584, October 30, 1977.

Estrogen-progestogen treatment enhances the ovulatory responce to clomiphene in amenorrheic patients, by E. Gitsch, et al. FERTILITY AND STERILITY 29(2): 159-163, Feburary, 1978.

Estrogens and blood pressure, by M.H. Weinberger. JOURNAL OF THE INDIANA STATE MEDICAL ASSOCIATION 70(12):925-926, December, 1977.

Estrogens and experimental atherosclerosis in the baboon (Papio cynocephalus), by H. C. McGill, Jr., et al. CIR-CULATION 56(4 pt 1):657-662, October, 1977.

Estrus control with gestagens, by H. J. Ficus. TIERAERZT-LICHE PRAXIS 5(4):521-524, 1977.

Exogenous hormones, reproductive history, and breast cancer, by P. E. Sartwell, et al. JOURNAL OF THE NA-TIONAL CANCER INSTITUTE 59(6):1589-1592, December, 1977.

Ethinyl estradiol may lead to malignancy [letter], by E. Eichner. AMERICAN JOURNAL OF OBSTETRICS AND GYNECOLOGY 130(4):506-508, February 15, 1978.

Fertility in the rhesus monkey following long-term inhibition of ovarian function with danazol, by H. P. Schane, et al. FERTILITY AND STERILITY 29(6):692-694, June, 1978.

Hypertension and nephropathy during pregnancy and while taking ovulation inhibitors, by P. Kramer, et al. MEDI-ZINISHCE KLINIK 73(26):967-977, June 30, 1978.

Iatrogenic amenorrhea following the use of estroprogestogens, by A. Pardini, et al. RIVISTA ITALIANA DI GINE-COLOGIA 57(2):121-131, March-April, 1976.

In-vitro studies on the effect of D-norgestrel and norethi-sterone acetate on the formation of sex steroids in the human ovary, by P. Schürenkämper, et al. ENDOKRIN-OLOGIE 71(1):25-34, February, 1978.

Levels of contraceptive steroids in breast milk and plasma of lactating women, by B. N. Saxena, et al. CONTRACEP-TION 16(6):605-613, December, 1977.

Morphological effects of estrogen on the female rat liver nucleolus, by B. Sheid. EXPERIENTIA 34(7):877-878, July 15, 1978.

Morphometric studies of the human placenta under the influence of sex steroids, by C. Estel, et al. ZENTRAL-BLATT FUER GYNAEKOLOGIE 99(23):1458-1461, 1977.

Morphometry on the lactating rat's mammary gland after administration of depot estrogen, by O. Löw, et al. VERHANDLUNGEN DER ANATOMISCHEN GE-SELLSCHAFT (71 pt 2):1165-1169, 1977.

Ovulation in rhesus monkeys suppressed by intranasal administration of progesterone and norethisterone, by T. C. Anand Kumar, et al. NATURE 270(5637):532-534, December 8, 1977.

Platelet aggregation and antiovulation agents [letter], by E. E. Ohnhaus. DEUTSCHE MEDIZINISCHE WOCHEN-SCHRIFT 102(50):1862-1863, December 16, 1977.

Preventing complications due to dilatation by intracervical application of a prostaglandin-gel, by H. Kühnie, et al. GEBURTSHILFE UND FRAUENHEILKUNDE 37(8): 675-680, August, 1977.

Problems with the multiple dosage of ovulation inhibitors in peak female athletes, by P. Borckerhoff. MEDIZIN-ISCHE WELT 28(48):1975-1976, December 2, 1977.

The progesterone-sensitive period of rat pregnancy: some effects of LHRH and ovariectomy, by R. R. Humphrey, et al. PROCEEDINGS OF THE SOCIETY FOR EXPERI-MENTAL BIOLOGY AND MEDICINE 156(2):345-348, November, 1977.

References to the observation of the postnatal development

of the F1-offspring from mice treated with oestrogen during pregnancy, by H. Heinecke, et al. VERHAND- LUNGEN DER ANATOMISCHEN GESELLSCHAFT (71 pt 1):655-658, 1977.

Selection for fertility under gestagen synchronization of estrus in mice, by L. Schüler. GENETIKA 13(5):840- 846, 1977.

Serum alkaline phosphatase elevation in female rats treated with ethinyl estradiol, by C. Gopinath, et al. TOXI- COLOGY 10(1):91-102, May, 1978.

Serum immunoglobulin titer of IgA, IgG and IgM during short- and long-term administration of contraceptive hormones, by G. Klinger, et al. DEUTSCHE GESUND- HEITSWESEN 33(23):1057-1062, 1978.

Sialic acid levels and scanning electronmicroscopy of cervical mucus, by B. Daunter. CONTRACEPTION 17(1):27- 34, January, 1978.

Study of the behavior of hepatic function and blood coagula- tion in the course of oral administration of an estropro- gestogen in low dosage, by A. R. Pastore, et al. RIVISTA ITALIANA DI GINECOLOGIA 57(3):171-185, May- June, 1976.

Study of folic acid blood levels during estro-progestagen treatment, by R. Karlin, et al. JOURNAL DE GYNE- COLOGIE OBSTETRIQUE ET BIOLOGIE DE LA RE- PRODUCTION 6(4):489-495, June, 1977.

Synergistic effects of ethynylestradiol and norethisterone on the formation and lengthening of uterine lace in imma- ture rabbits, by Y. Chambon, et al. COMPTES RENDUS DES SEANCES DE LA SOCIETE DE BIOLOGIE ET DE SES FILIALES 171(3):631-635, 1977.

Types of hepatocellular damage caused by contraceptives, by M. Jasiel, et al. POLSKIE ARCHIWUM MEDYCYNY WEWNETRZNEJ 58(2):161-168, August, 1977.

Voice changes during hormonal contraception, by I. Krahulec, et al. CESKOSLOVENSKA OTOLARYNGOLOGIE 26(4):234-237, August, 1977.

CONTRACEPTIVE AGENTS: FEMALE: THERAPEUTIC
Prevention of ovarian cystomas by inhibition of ovulation: a new concept, by J. Zajicek. JOURNAL OF REPRODUCTIVE MEDICINE 20(2):114, February, 1978.

CONTRACEPTIVE AGENTS: MALE
Inhibition of testosterone-induced sexual behavior in the castrated male rat by aromatase blockers, by G. Morali, et al. HORMONES AND BEHAVIOR 9(3):203-213, December, 1977.

Pituitary function in adult males receiving medroxyprogesterone acetate, by W. J. Meyer, 3d, et al. FERTILITY AND STERILITY 28(10):1072-1076, October, 1977.

Sialic acid & sialidase activity in rat testis & epididymis in relation to age & action of different antifertility agents, by S. Nag, et al. INDIAN JOURNAL OF EXPERIMENTAL BIOLOGY 15(7):510-512, July, 1977.

CONTRACEPTIVE AGENTS: MALE: COMPLICATIONS
The effects of anti-androgenic agents on metabolism and biosynthesis of testosterone (I): testosterone metabolic regulation in the liver and the biosynthesis in the testes on rats treated with chlormadinone acetate, by S. Honma, et al. NIPPON NAIBUNPI GAKKAI ZASSHI 63(5): 703-718, May 20, 1977.

The effects of medroxyprogesterone on dentofacial development in males with idiopathic isosexual precocity, by F. A. Catalanotto, et al. ANGLE ORTHODONTIST 48(2):

106-113, April, 1978.

In vitro steroid metabolic studies in human testes. II: Metabolism of cholesterol, pregnenolone, progesterone, androstenedione and testosterone by testes of an estrogen-treated man, by L. J. Rodriguez-Rigau, et al. STEROIDS 30(6):729-730, December, 1977.

Prenatal effects of sex hormones on human male behavior: medroxyprogesterone acetate (MPA), by H. F. Meyer Bahlburg, et al. PSYCHONEUROENDOCRINOLOGY 2(4):383-390, October, 1977.

The toxicity of 1-amino-3-chloro-2-propanol hydrochloride (CL88,236) in the rehsus monkey, by R. Heywood, et al. TOXICOLOGY 9(3):219-225, March, 1978.

CONTRACEPTIVE AGENTS: PHARMACOLOGY
An in vivo system in man for quantitation of estrogenicity. II. Pharmacologic changes in binding capacity of serum corticosteroid-binding globulin induced by conjugated estrogens, mestranol, and ethinyl estradiol, by D. E. Moore, et al. AMERICAN JOURNAL OF OBSTETRICS AND GYNECOLOGY 130(4):482-486, February 15, 1978.

CONTRACEPTIVE AGENTS: THERAPEUTIC
Estrogen treatment in tall girls, by N. Kuhn, et al. OBSTETRICAL AND GYNECOLOGICAL SURVEY 32(7): 604-605, September, 1977.

Estrogens for contraception and menopause, by L. B. Tyrer, et al. NURSES DRUG ALERT 1:169-180, December, 1977.

Evolution of the pituitary gonadotropins and ovarian steroids during progestational treatment begun on the 10th day of the cycle (10 mg/day Lynestrenol), by D. Dargent, et al. GYNECOLOGIE 29(1):73-76, 1978.

Hormone therapy in renal adenocarcinoma, by L. Giuliani, et al. MINERVA CHIRURGICA 32(23-24):1463-1465, December 15-31, 1977.

Hormone use to change normal physiology—is the risk worth it? [editorial], by D. M. Small. NEW ENGLAND JOURNAL OF MEDICINE 294:219-221, January 22, 1976.

Hormonoprophylaxis and hormonotherapy in the treatment of endometrial adenocarcinoma by means of medroxyprogesterone acetate, by J. Bonte, et al. GYNECOLOGIC ONCOLOGY 6(1):60-75, February, 1978.

Modern prospects in the treatment of cancer of the breast and its metastasis. Medroxyprogesterone in massive doses as an alternative to polychemotherapy, by F. Pannuti. MINERVA CHIRURGICA 32(19):1211-1220, October 15, 1977.

Pill as an arthritis preventive. SCIENCE NEWS 113:231, April 15, 1978.

A possible new approach to the treatment of metastatic breast cancer: massive doses of medroxyprogesterone acetate, by F. Pannuti, et al. CANCER TREATMENT REPORTS 62(4):499-504, April, 1978.

Preliminary observations on the use of danazol in endometriosis compared to oestrogen/progestogen combination therapy, by A. D. Noble, et al. JOURNAL OF INTERNATIONAL MEDICAL RESEARCH 5(Suppl 3):79-80, 1977.

Replacement estrogen therapy for menopausal vasomotor flushes. Comparison of quinestrol and conjugated estrogens, by S. B. Baumgardner, et al. OBSTETRICS AND GYNECOLOGY 51(4):445-452, April, 1978.

Therapeutic significance of the sequential estrogen-gestagen preparation "Ovara" in gynecologic endocrinology, by R. Prudan, et al. MEDICINSKI PREGLED 30(11-12): 585-593, 1977.

Therapy of androgenetic sympatomatology with cyproterone acetate and ethinyl estradiol, by A. E. Schindler, et al. ARCHIV FUR GYNAEKOLOGIE 225(2):103-107, May 12, 1978.

Therapy of androgenization symptoms: double blind study of an antiandrogen preparation (SH B 209 AB) against neogynon, by U. Lachnit-Fixson, et al. MEDIZINISCHE KLINIK 72(45):1922-1926, November 11, 1977.

Therapy of Marchiafava-Micheli's disease: remission under therapy with Lynestrenol, by A. Ruiz-Torres, et al. MEDIZINISCHE KLINIK 73(5):162-167, February 3, 1978.

To which women should antiandrogen-effective ovulation inhibitors be prescribed? (hirsutism, seborrhea, alopecia), by J. R. Strecker. HIPPOKRATES 49(2):200-201, May, 1978.

Treatment of advanced adenocarcinoma of the endometrium with melphalan, 5-fluorouracil, and medroxyprogesterone acetate: a preliminary study, by C. J. Cohen, et al. OB-STETRICS AND GYNECOLOGY 50(4):415-417, October, 1977.

Treatment of the climacteric, by D. J. Hunter. PRACTI-TIONER 219(1312):564-570, October, 1977.

Treatment of climacteric and postmenopausal women with 17-beta-oestradiol and norethisterone acetate, by M. Furuhjelm, et al. ACTA OBSTETRICIA ET GYNE-COLOGICA SCANDINAVICA 56(4):351-361, 1977.

Treatment of obsessive homosexual pedophilic fantasies with

medroxyprogesterone acetate, by E. R. Pinta. BIOLOGI-
CAL PSYCHIATRY 13(3):369-373, June, 1978.

Use of high doses of medroxyprogesterone acetate in the
palliative treatment of advanced breast cancer. Clinical
experience with 44 cases, by D. Amadori, et al. MINER-
VA MEDICA 68(59):3967-3980, December 1, 1977.

Use of synthetic steroid preparations of hemostasis and
normalization of menstrual function in juvenile hemorrhages, by M. N. Kuznetsova, et al. VOPROSY OK-
HRANY MATERINSTVA I DETSTVA 23(2):77-80,
February, 1978.

CONTRACEPTIVE AGENTS: THERAPEUTIC: COMPLICATIONS
Vascular complications of long-term oestrogen therapy, by
D. McKay Hart, et al. FRONTIERS OF HORMONE
RESEARCH 5:174-191, 1977.

CONTRACEPTIVE AGENTS AND MENSTRUATION
Steroid hydroxylase induction in cultured human lymphocytes: effects of the menstrual cycle, by W. L. Mason,
et al. STEROIDS 31(1):1-7, January, 1978.

CONTRACEPTIVE AGENTS AND YOUTH
Hormonal contraception for adolescents? by J. M. Wender-
lein. MUENCHENER MEDIZINISCHE WOCHEN-
SCHRIFT 120(37):1193-1198, September 15, 1978.

Hormonal contraception in young girls, by F. Hamvas, et al.
ORVOSI HETILAP 118(51):3097-3098, December 18,
1977.

CONTRACEPTIVE METHODS
Effect of menstrual hygiene (tampons vs pads) and of the
form of contraception on pH and bacterial infection of
the vagina, by E. G. Loch, et al. FORTSCHRITTE DER
MEDIZIN 95(44):2653-2656+, November 24, 1977.

CONTRACEPTIVES
Abortion regarded as contraception [letter]. LANCET
2(8041):765-766, October 8, 1977.

—, by M. Beaconsfield. LANCET 2(8039):666-667, September 24, 1977.

Choice of contraceptives, by T. Luukkainen. KATILOLEHTI
83(6):230-233, June,1978.

Contraception, by D. R. Mishell, Jr. AMERICAN JOURNAL
OF DISEASES OF CHILDREN 132(9):912-920, September, 1978.

—, by P. T. Wilson, et al. MEDICAL TRIAL TECHNIQUE
QUARTERLY 24(1):45-60, Summer, 1977.

Contraception and family planning, by E. C. Miller. ZEIT-
SCHRIFT FUR AERZTLICHE FORTBILDUNG 71(22):
1041-1045, November 15, 1977.

Contraception. When avoiding pregnancy is the issue, ed. by
H. A. Wade. PATIENT CARE 12:252-253+, September
15, 1978.

Contraceptive efficiency of triphasic inhibitors, by W. H.
Schneider, et al. MEDIZINISCHE KLINIK 72(48):
2081-2085, December 2, 1977.

Contraceptive use, by J. E. Anderson, et al. NEW YORK
STATE JOURNAL OF MEDICINE 77:933-937, May,
1977.

Determination of pregnancy duration following terminated
hormonal contraception, by G. Klinger, et al. ZENTRAL-
BLATT FUER GYNAEKOLOGIE 99(26):1629-1632,
1977.

The earliest influence of contraception on the incidence of

conception, by O. Norgaard. UGESKRIFT FOR LAEGER 139(42):2537-2539, October 17, 1977.

Fertility awareness as a method of conception control, by H. Klaus. NURSING TIMES 74:63-64, January 12, 1978.

International Conference on the ovulation method; Melbourne, Australia, by A. McElwain. OSSERVATORE ROMANO 11(520):10, March 16, 1978.

A long-term follow-up study of women using different methods of contraception—an interim report, by M. Vessey, et al. JOURNAL OF BIOSOCIAL SCIENCE 8: 373+, October, 1976.

Medical supervision for contraception: too little or too much? by A. Rosenfield. INTERNATIONAL JOURNAL OF GYNAECOLOGY AND OBSTETRICS 15(2):105-110, 1977.

Misuse and nonuse of contraception, by J. Robins. MEDICAL ASPECTS OF HUMAN SEXUALITY 11(9):127-128, September, 1977.

New leads on contraception. Summarized discussion, by S. J. Segal. UPSALA JOURNAL OF MEDICAL SCIENCES (22):73-74, 1978.

Problems in the evaluation of contraceptives, by M. Beckmann, et al. GEBURTSHILFE UND FRAUENHEILKUNDE 38(8):640-642, August, 1978.

Shunning innovation. CHEMICAL WEEK 122:15, May 24, 1978.

Target fertility, contraception, and aggregate rates: toward a formal synthesis, by R. D. Lee. DEMOGRAPHY 14(4):455-479, November, 1977.

AFRICA
Demographic and contraceptive innovators: a study of transitional African society, by J. C. Caldwell, et al. JOURNAL OF BIOSOCIAL SCIENCE 8:347-366, October, 1976.

BELGIUM
Effectiveness of contraception in Belgium: results of the Second National Fertility Survey, 1971, by R. L. Cliquet, et al. JOURNAL OF BIOSOCIAL SCIENCE 9(4):403-416, October, 1977.

CHINA
Mortality, fertility and contraceptive use in Shanghai, by J. Bannister. CHINA QUARTERLY 70:255-295, June, 1977.

COLOMBIA
Contraceptive method continuation according to type of provider, by R. F. Einhorn, et al. AMERICAN JOURNAL OF PUBLIC HEALTH 67:1157-1164, December, 1977.

Modernism and contraceptive use in Colombia, by W. H. Baldwin, et al. STUDIES IN FAMILY PLANNING 7:80+, March, 1976.

FRANCE
Abortion and contraceptives in France, by E. Salomonsson. VARDFACKET 1(17):14-15, September 22, 1977.

Absorption of stable isotopes of iron, copper, and zinc during oral contraceptives use, by J. C. King, et al. AMERICAN JOURNAL OF CLINICAL NUTRITION 31(7):1198-1203, July, 1978.

La diffusion des méthodes modernes de contraception: une étude dans une consultation hospitalière, by

FRANCE
   H. Leridon, et al. POPULATION 32:777-785,
   November 4-5, 1977.

INDIA
   Contraceptive practice among hospital attendants, by
   G. M. Dhar, et al. INDIAN JOURNAL OF PUB-
   LIC HEALTH 21(1):8-15, January-March, 1977.

INDONESIA
   Contraceptive practice after women have undergone
   "spontaneous" abortion in Indonesia and Sudan, by
   H. Rushwan, et al. INTERNATIONAL JOURNAL
   OF GYNAECOLOGY AND OBSTETRICS 15(3):
   241-249, 1977.

IRAN
   Causes of clinic drop-out among Iranian pill users, by C.
   F. Lee, et al. JOURNAL OF BIOSOCIAL SCIENCE
   10(1):7-15, January, 1978.

KOREA
   The Euiryong experiment: a Korean innovation in household contraceptive distribution, by C. B. Park, et al.
   STUDIES IN FAMILY PLANNING 8:67, March,
   1977.

LATIN AMERICA
   Contraceptive choices for Latin American women, by P.
   H. Hass. POPULI 3(4):14-24, 1976.

MEXICO
   Recent rends in contraceptive use in Mexico. STUDIES
   IN FAMILY PLANNING 8(8):197, August, 1977.

NIGERIA
   Vitamin B6 status of Nigerian women using various
   methods of contraception, by E. M. Wien. AMERI-
   CAN JOURNAL OF CLINICAL NUTRITION

NIGERIA
31(8):1392-1396, August, 1978.

THE PHILIPPINES
Estimating the effects of contraceptive use on fertility: techniques and findings from the 1974 Philippine national acceptor survey, by J. E. Laing. STUDIES IN FAMILY PLANNING 9:150-162, June, 1978.

SINGAPORE
Births averted in Singapore during 1966-1975, by A. J. Chen, et al. SINGAPORE STATISTICS BULLETIN 6:57-70, December, 1977.

THAILAND
A field study of the choice and continuity of use of three contraceptive methods in a rural area of Thailand. JOURNAL OF BIOSOCIAL SCIENCE 10(2):209, April, 1978.

Liver function in Thai women using different types of hormonal contraceptive agents, by N. Dusitsin, et al. JOURNAL OF THE MEDICAL ASSOCIATION OF THAILAND 61(7):381-389, July, 1978.

TUNISIA
Criteria for choosing oral contraceptives in Tunisia, by R. Chadi. TUNISIE MEDICALE 55(4):269-272, July-August, 1977.

La famille tunisienne et la contraception: données et motivations, by S. Sahli. REVUE TUNISIENNE DE SCIENCES SOCIALES 14(48-49):161-175, 1977.

UNITED STATES
Birth planning success: motivation and contraceptive method [based on interviews, Summer, 1971, with a stratified sample of 422 black and 939 white urban wives in the East North Central United States], by

CONTRACEPTIVES

UNITED STATES
  P. Cutright, et al. FAMILY PLANNING PERSPEC-
  TIVES 10:43-48, January-February, 1978.

  Contraceptive use in the United States, 1973-1976, by
  K. Ford. FAMILY PLANNING PERSPECTIVES
  10:264-269, September-October, 1978.

CALIFORNIA
  Examination of contraceptive perceptions and usage
  among Los Angeles County women, by B. B.
  Houser, et al. CONTRACEPTION 18(1):7-18,
  July, 1978.

NEW YORK
  Contraceptive use: prevalence among married women
  in Albany, New York, health region, 1974, by
  J. E. Anderson, et al. NEW YORK STATE
  JOURNAL OF MEDICINE 77:933-937, May,
  1977.

CONTRACEPTIVES: ADVERTISING
Code board mulls contraceptive ads, by C. Coates. ADVER-
  TISING AGE 49:54, May 29, 1978.

High court outlaws curbs on contraceptive sales, displays,
  ads. DRUG TOPICS 121:7+, July 1, 1977.

Measuring the effectiveness of contraceptive marketing programs: Preethi in Sri Lanka, by J. Davies, et al. STUDIES
  IN FAMILY PLANNING 8:82-90, April, 1977.

Pill hazards spark condom sales, by M. Christopher. AD-
  VERTISING AGE 49:3+, January 30, 1978.

Responses to advertising contraceptives, by T. R. L. Black,
  et al. JOURNAL OF ADVERTISING RESEARCH
  17:49-56, October, 1977.

Retailers in social program strategy: the case of family planning, by T. R. L. Black, et al. COLUMBIA JOURNAL OF WORLD BUSINESS 12:33-41, Winter, 1977.

Schmid still struggles to place contraceptive ads, by M. Christopher. ADVERTISING AGE 49:2+, May 22, 1978.

Time horizon effects on product evaluation strategies, by P. Wright, et al. JOURNAL OF MARKETING RESEARCH 14:429-443, November, 1977.

CONTRACEPTIVES: ATTITUDES

Birth planning success: motivation and contraceptive method [based on interviews, Summer, 1971, with a stratified sample of 422 black and 939 white urban wives in the East North Central United States, by P. Cutright, et al. FAMILY PLANNING PERSPECTIVES 10:43-48, January-February, 1978.

Definitive contraception and contraceptive responsibility (on the psychic situation in voluntary sterilization in men and women—results of psychologic-psychiatric research), by P. Petersen. PSYCHIATRISCHE PRAXIS 5(1):35-43, February, 1978.

How men feel now about contrraceptives, by M. D'Antonio. GLAMOUR 76:101-102+, August, 1978.

Influence of parents, peers, and partners on the contraceptive use of college men and women, by L. Thompson, et al. JOURNAL OF MARRIAGE AND THE FAMILY 40(3): 210, August, 1978.

Issues in contraception: recognizing the reasons for contraceptive non-use and abuse, by J. L. Tanis. MCN: AMERICAN JOURNAL OF MATERNAL-CHILD NURSING 2(6):364-369, November-December, 1977.

Issues in contraception: today's pill and the individual woman, by L. K. Huxall. MCN: AMERICAN JOURNAL OF MATERNAL-CHILD NURSING 2(6):359-363, November-December, 1977.

A renewed focus on contraception: signs of a decline in U. S. sales of the pill point to the need for more research—but also to new problems in funding such research, by P. Gupte. POPULI 5(3):45-47, 1978.

Sexual attitudes and contraceptive practices, by D. Byrne. U. S. A. TODAY 107:28-30, July, 1978.

Sexual experience, contraceptive usage, and source of contraception among never-married women: Albany (NY) Health Region, by M. Gesche, et al. ADVANCES IN PLANNED PARENTHOOD 12(3):136-139, 1978.

THAILAND
A study of new contraceptive acceptors of pills and IUDs at three Bangkok clinics, by R. A. Grossman, et al. CONTRACEPTION 16(1):67-77, July, 1977.

CONTRACEPTIVES: BARRIER
Barrier contraceptive practice and male infertility as related factors to breast cancer in married women, by A. N. Gjorgov. MEDICAL HOPOTHESES 4(2):79-88, March-April, 1978.

Diaphragms, by J. Coburn. MADEMOISELLE 84(11):68, November, 1978.

CONTRACEPTIVES: COMPLICATIONS
Acromegaly and articular lesions caused by contraceptives, by G. Nagyhergyi, et al. ORVOSI HETILAP 119(2): 91-93, January 8, 1978.

British studies indicate increase in risks. PEOPLE 5(1):22, 1978.

Contraception in cardiac patients, by R. Taurelle, et al. JOURNAL DE GYNECOLOGIE, OBSTETRIQUE ET BIOLOGIE DE LA REPRODUCTION 7(1):111-118, January, 1978.

Contraception, sterilisation and abortion [editorial]. NEW ZEALAND MEDICAL JOURNAL 85(588):428-429, May 25, 1977.

Contraceptive steroids and liver lesions, by C. R. Garcia, et al. JOURNAL OF TOXICOLOGY AND ENVIRONMENTAL HEALTH 3(1-2):197-206, September, 1977.

Delayed adverse effects of contraceptives. ORVOSI HETILAP 119(20):1257-1261, May 14, 1978.

Fertility after stopping different methods of contraception, by M. P. Vessey, et al. BRITISH MEDICAL JOURNAL 1(6108):265-267, February 4, 1978.

Government response to contraceptive and cosmetic health risks, by J. L. Weaver. WOMEN HEALTH 1(2):5-11, March-April, 1976.

The interactive effects of induced abortion, inter-pregnancy interval and contraceptive use on subsequent pregnancy outcome, by C. J. Hogue, et al. AMERICAN JOURNAL OF EPIDEMIOLOGY 107(1):15-26, January, 1978.

Psychohygienic aspects of modern contraception. Hazards and dangers—results of follow-up examinations, by P. Petersen. MEDIZINISCHE KLINIK 72(48):2089-2093, December 2, 1977.

Recognizing the reasons for contraceptive non-use and abuse. Part 2, by J. L. Tanis. MCN: AMERICAN JOURNAL OF MATERNAL-CHILD NURSING 2:364-369, November-December, 1977.

CONTRACEPTIVES: FAILURE
Contraception—why failures? by J. R. Taylor. CANADIAN
JOURNAL OF HOSPITAL PHARMACY 29(5):150-
151, September-October, 1976.

Contraceptive effectiveness: misleading statistics, by J. J.
Lieberman. AMERICAN BIOLOGY TEACHER 39:503,
November, 1977.

Contraceptive errectiveness warning issued: spiermicide,
Encare Oval. FDA CONSUMER 12:4, September, 1978.

Contraceptive failure among married women in the United
States, 1970-1973, by B. Vaughan, et al. FAMILY
PLANNING PERSPECTIVES 9:251-258, November-
December, 1977.

Dynamics of contraceptive failures, by W. G. Cobliner, et al.
JOURNAL OF PSYCHOLOGY 94:153-162, November,
1976.

Failures of contraceptive practice, by J. Robins. NEW YORK
STATE JOURNAL OF MEDICINE 76:361-365, March,
1976.

Liability for failure of birth control methods. COLUMBIA
LAW REVIEW 26:1187, November, 1976.

CONTRACEPTIVES: FEMALE
Difficulties with intrauterine anticonception envisaged from
the aspect of work-ability, by J. Petros, et al. CESKO-
SLOVENSKA GYNEKOLOGIE 43(4):274-276, May,
1978.

CONTRACEPTIVES: FEMALE: BARRIER
Recent trend in preference of contraceptive methods—pills
down, diaphragm on rise, by J. Balog, et al. OBSTETRI-
CAL AND GYNECOLOGICAL SURVEY 33(4):282-
283, April, 1978.

Social characteristics of diaphragm users in a family planning clinic, by J. McEwan. JOURNAL OF BIOSOCIAL SCIENCE 10(2):159-167, April, 1978.

Successful use of the diaphragm and jelly by a young population: report of a clinical study, by M. E. Lane, et al. FAMILY PLANNING PERSPECTIVES 8:81-85, April, 1976.

CONTRACEPTIVES: FEMALE: COMPLICATIONS
Age at first coitus and choice of contraceptive method: preliminary report on a study of factors related to cervical neoplasia, by C. G. Merritt, et al. SOCIAL BIOLOGY 22:255-260, August, 1975.

Cervical mucus. A new dimension for family planning, by J. J. McCarthy, Jr. JOURNAL OF THE FLORIDA MEDICAL ASSOCIATION 65(1):22-24, January, 1978.

Contraception and pregnancy in the young female hypertensive patient, by F. A. Finnerty, Jr. PEDIATRIC CLINICS OF NORTH AMERICA 25(1):119-126, February, 1978.

The detection and measurement of D-norgestrel in human milk using Sephadex LH 20 chromatography and radio-immunoassay, by M. J. Thomas, et al. STEROIDS 30(3):349-361, September, 1977.

Late effects of female sterilisation [letter], by A. T. Letchworth, et al. LANCET 2(8041):768, October 8, 1977.

Subsequent pelvic surgery in patients who have undergone tubal sterilization, by D. H. Belsky. JOURNAL OF THE AMERICAN OSTEOPATHIC ASSOCIATION 77(1):36-41, September, 1977.

CONTRACEPTIVES: FEMALE: IUD
Anti-implantation action of a medicated intrauterine delivery system (MIDS), by D. L. Moyer, et al. CONTRACEPTION

16(1):39-49, July, 1977.

Assessment of human chorionic gonadotropin (HCG) levels during luteal phase in women using intrauterine contraception, by J. M. Aubert, et al. CONTRACEPTION 16(6):557-562, December, 1977.

The benefits and risks of IUD use, by L. B. Tyrer. INTERNATIONAL JOURNAL OF GYNAECOLOGY AND OBSTETRICS 15(2):150-152, 1977.

Clinical bacteriological and histological studies following several years of IUD use for contraception, by P. Wolke, et al. ZENTRALBLATT FUER GYNAEKOLOGIE 99(14):880-883, 1977.

Clinical evaluation of an oral contraceptive combination with a low dosage of estrogens and progestanes and their correlation in a group of women using intrauterine device, by A. Rinaldi. REVISTA CHILENA DE OBSTETRICIA Y GINECOLOGIA 42(1):34-40, 1977.

Clinical evaluation on spira-ring, by M. Nagano, et al. NIPPON FUNIN GAKKAI ZASSHI 23(2):104-110, April 1, 1978.

Clinical experience with the intrauterine progesterone contraceptive system, by B. B. Pharriss. JOURNAL OF REPRODUCTIVE MEDICINE 20(3):155-165, March, 1978.

Clinical performance and endocrine profiles with contraceptive vaginal rings containing a combination of estradiol and d-norgestrel, by D. R. Mishell, Jr., et al. AMERICAN JOURNAL OF OBSTETRICS AND GYNECOLOGY 130(1):55-62, January 1, 1978.

Clinical performances and endocrine profilles with contraceptive vaginal rings containing d-norgestrel, by D. R.

Mishell, Jr., et al. CONTRACEPTION 16(6):625-636, December, 1977.

Clinical study of intrauterine contraceptives, by L. A. Parshina, et al. AKUSHERSTVO I GINEKOLOGIIA (12): 39-40, December, 1977.

Collagen bands: a new vaginal delivery system for contraceptive steroids, by A. Victor, et al. CONTRACEPTION 16(2):125-135, August, 1977.

Contraception: pills and IUDs. Part 1. PERINATAL CARE 2:13-18, April, 1978.

Contraception through progesterone-containing intrauterine device (IUD), by J. R. Strecker. HIPPOKRATES 48(4): 413-414, November, 1977.

Contraception with a norethisterone-releasing IUD. Plasma levels of norethisterone and its influence on the ovarian function, by C. G. Nilsson, et al. CONTRACEPTION 17(2):115-122, February, 1978.

Control of fertility with potentiated intrauterine devices, by G. Gozzi, et al. PATOLOGIA E CLINICA OSTETRICIA E GINECOLOGICA 5(1):32-36, 1977.

The copper intrauterine device and its mode of action, by G. Oster, et al. NEW ENGLAND JOURNAL OF MEDICINE 293:432-438, August 28, 1975.

Current practice concerning time of IUD insertion, by M. K. White, et al. IPPF MEDICAL BULLETIN 11(6):1-3, December, 1977.

Does implantation occur in the presence of an IUD? by B. B. Saxena, et al. RESEARCH IN REPRODUCTION 10(3): 1-2, May, 1978.

Double uterine perforation with Dalkon Shield intrauterine device, by E. Hakim-Elahi. NEW YORK STATE JOURNAL OF MEDICINE 76:567-569, April, 1976.

Drugs: IUD studies prompt concern, by M. Fisk. TRIAL 14(5):56, May, 1978.

The Encare oval. MEDICAL LETTER ON DRUGS AND THERAPEUTICS 20(6):29-30, March 24, 1978.

Experience with modern insert IUDs to date: a review and comments, by L. Keith, et al. JOURNAL OF REPRODUCTIVE MEDICINE 20(3):125-132, March, 1978.

Fabrication and testing of vaginal contraceptive devices designed for release of prespecified dose levels of steroids, by F. G. Burton, et al. CONTRACEPTION 17(3):221-230, March, 1978.

Historical considerations in the development of modern IUD's: pateint and device selection and the importance of insertion techniques, by D. R. Mishell, Jr. JOURNAL OF REPRODUCTIVE MEDICINE 20(3):121-124, March, 1978.

Hysteroscopic management of intrauterine adhesions, by C. M. March, et al. AMERICAN JOURNAL OF OBSTETRICS AND GYNECOLOGY 130(6):653-657, March 15, 1978.

Immediate post-partum insertion of the Antigon, by J. Wiese, et al. ACTA OBSTETRICIA ET GYNECOLOGICA SCANDINAVICA 56(5):509-513, 1977.

Intrauterine contraception, by R. P. Rao, et al. AMERICAN FAMILY PHYSICIAN 16(5):177-185, November, 1977.

Intrauterine contraception after induced abortion. A clinical study of immediate or later insertion, by H. P. Sundsbak,

et al. TIDSSKRIFT FOR DEN NORSKE LAEGE-
FORENING 97(34-36):1787-1789, December 10, 1977.

The intrauterine contraceptive device, by B. N. Barwin, et al.
CANADIAN MEDICAL ASSOCIATION JOURNAL
118(1):53-58, January 7, 1978.

Intra-uterine contraceptive devices, by J. Dommisse. SOUTH
AFRICAN MEDICAL JOURNAL 52(12):495-496,
September 10, 1977.

Intrauterine contraceptive devices (IUD'S), by H. Lehfeldt.
ZENTRALBLATT FUER GYNAEKOLOGIE 99(24):
1473-1483, 1977.

Intrauterine devices [editorial]. NEW ZEALAND MEDICAL
JOURNAL 86(598):387-388, October 26, 1977.

Intrauterine devices for contraception? Results of an inquiry
conducted in the BRD in 1976, by W. Stolp, et al.
FORTSCHRITTE DU MEDIZIN 95(39):2347-2352,
October 20, 1977.

Intrauterine devices: an invitational symposium, by A. Scommegna. JOURNAL OF REPRODUCTIVE MEDICINE
20(3):119-120, March, 1978.

MLCu 250 in comparison with other intrauterine contraceptive devices [proceedings], by H. Van der Pas, et al.
ARCHIV FUR GYNAEKOLOGIE 224(1-4):35-36, July
29, 1977.

Mechanism of action of intrauterine contraceptives, by E. P.
Maizel', et al. VOPROSY OKHRANY MATERINSTVA I
DETSTVA 22(7):73-76, July, 1977.

On IUD package inserts [letter], by W. Cates, Jr. AMERI-
CAN JOURNAL OF PUBLIC HEALTH 68(3):269-270,
March, 1978.

An overview of IUD research and implications for the future, by J. Zipper, et al. INTERNATIONAL JOURNAL OF GYNAECOLOGY AND OBSTETRICS 15(1):73-78, 1977.

PID and the IUD. EMERGENCY MEDICINE 10:170, February, 1978.

Patient education and intrauterine contraception—study of two package inserts, by H. Benson, et al. AMERICAN JOURNAL OF PUBLIC HEALTH 67:446-449, May, 1977.

A possible role of prostaglandin E1 in the mechanism of action of intrauterine contraceptive device, by R. Das, et al. INDIAN JOURNAL OF MEDICAL RESEARCH 65(3): 353-356, March, 1977.

Post-abortal immediate IUD insertion: further experience and a controlled comparison of three devices, by J. A. Ross, et al. CONTRACEPTION 17(3):237-246, March, 1978.

Pregnancy and the IUD, by J. F. Perlmutter. JOURNAL OF REPRODUCTIVE MEDICINE 20(3):133-138, March, 1978.

Preliminary note on the use of a flexible intrauterine device, by S. Rugiati, et al. MINERVA GINECOLOGIA 30(1-2): 59-64, January-February, 1978.

A stochastic model for IUCD clinical trials, by H. D. Gupta. INDIAN JOURNAL OF PUBLIC HEALTH 21(2):95-104, April-June, 1977.

A study on the contraceptive effectiveness of a newly designed IUD "FD-1" in Japan, by T. Wagatsuma, et al. CONTRACEPTION 17(1):41-49, January, 1978.

Various types of intrauterine devices, by E. B. Connell.
MEDICAL ASPECTS OF HUMAN SEXUALITY 11(10):
15-16+, October, 1977.

GUATEMALA
IUD use effectiveness in an urban Guatemalan clinic, by
P. Prior, et al. BULLETIN OF THE PAN-AMERICAN
HEALTH ORGANIZATION 11(2):117-124, 1977.

CONTRACEPTIVES: FEMALE: IUD: COMPLICATIONS
Actinomyces infection associated with intra-uterine device,
by M. C. Santa, et al. JOURNAL OF THE MEDICAL
ASSOCIATION OF THE STATE OF ALABAMA 47(11):
31-33, May, 1978.

Actinomycetes-like organisms in wearers of intrauterine con-
traceptive devices [letter], by R. D. Luff, et al. AMERI-
CAN JOURNAL OF OBSTETRICS AND GYNECOLO-
GY 129(4):476-477, October 15, 1977.

Ameba trophozoites in cervico-vaginal smear of a patient
using an intrauterine device. A case report, by R. E.
McNeill, et al. ACTA CYTOLOGICA 22(2):91-92,
March-April, 1978.

Birth control nightmare: intra-uterine device, by S. Vaughan.
GOOD HOSEKEEPING 187:56+, July, 1978.

Blood serum lipids and cholesterol of the ewe during intravaginal pessary treatment, by P. K. Pareek, et al. ZEN-
TRALBLATT FUER VETERINAERMEDIZINE 24(7):
605-607, September, 1977.

Bowel obstruction and perforation with an intraperitoneal
loop intrauterine contraceptive device, by J. D'Amico,
et al. AMERICAN JOURNAL OF OBSTETRICS AND
GYNECOLOGY 129(4):461-462, October 15, 1977.

Case of ovarian pregnancy following insertion of a pessary,

by F. Buchholz, et al. MEDIZINISCHE WELT 29(2): 59-60, January 13, 1978.

A comparison of primary dysmenonhea and intrauterine device related pain, by A. E. Reading, et al. PAIN 3(3): 265-276, June, 1977.

Concerning a rare inconvenience occurring to women wearing intrauterine devices; missing tails, by F. Carollo, et al. PATOLOGIA E CLINICA OSTETRICIA E GINECOLOGICA 6(3):146-152, May-June, 1978.

Dalkon Shield perforation of the uterus and urinary bladder with calculus formation: case report, by E. Neutz, et al. AMERICAN JOURNAL OF OBSTETRICS AND GYNECOLOGY 130(7):848-849, April 1, 1978.

Delay in the diagnosis of cervical cancer in patients using hormonal contraceptives and IUDs, by H. H. Büttner, et al. ZEITSCHRIFT FUR AERZTLICHE FORTBILDUNG 71(23):1129-1130, December 1, 1977.

Determination of plasma concentrations of D-norgestrel during a one year follow-up in women with a D-norgestrel-releasing IUD, by C. G. Nilsson, et al. CONTRACEPTION 17(6):569-573, June, 1978.

Effect of copper intrauterine contraceptive device on the estrogen & progesterone uptake in ovariectomized rat uterus, by M. Ghosh, et al. INDIAN JOURNAL OF EXPERIMENTAL BIOLOGY 15(6):477-478, June, 1977.

Effect of intrauterine contraception on nonspecific reactivity of the female body, by R. S. Baryshkina, et al. AKUSHERSTVO I GINEKOLOGIIA (12):34-36, December, 1977.

Effect of intrauterine device on ovarian function, by S. Chander, et al. THERIOGENEOLOGY 8(5):271-278, November, 1977.

The effect of intrauterine devices containing zinc and copper on their levels in serum, by S. O. Anteby, et al. FERTILITY AND STERILITY 29(1):30-34, January, 1978.

The effect of ligation or separation between the intrauterine device horn and adjacent ovary on implantation in the hamster, by W. J. Bo, et al. FERTILITY AND STERILITY 29(3):351-353, March, 1978.

Effects of oral and intrauterine administration of contraceptives on the uterus, by W. B. Ober. HUMAN PATHOLOGY 8(5):513-527, September, 1977.

Endometrial cytology and copper containing intrauterine devices, by W. Herting, et al. FORTSCHRITTE DER MEDIZIN 96(7):311-314, February 16, 1978.

Endometrial morphology of women using a d-norgestrel-releasing intrauterine device, by C. G. Nilsson, et al. FERTILITY AND STERILITY 29(4):397-401, April, 1978.

Endometrial prostaglandin F content in women wearing nonmedicated or progestin-releasing intrauterine devices, by A. Scommegna, et al. FERTILITY AND STERILITY 29(5):500-504, May, 1978.

Experts question new IUD warning [on warning not to insert IUD after child birth or abortion till involution is complete because of a claimed increase in perforation and expulsion. MEDICAL WORLD NEWS 18:13, November 28, 1977.

Fecundability following the discontinuation of IUD use among Taiwanese women, by A. K. Jain, et al. JOURNAL OF BIOSOCIAL SCIENCE 9:137-152, April, 1977.

Fertilisation in women with intrauterine devices [letter], by C. G. Nilsson, et al. LANCET 2(8048):1126, November

26, 1977.

Fibrinolytic activity in utero and bleeding complications with intrauterine contraceptive devices, by J. Bonnar, et al. BRITISH JOURNAL OF OBSTETRICS AND GYNAECOLOGY 83(2):160-164, February, 1976.

480 million in suits against Dalkon. WOMENS PRESS 6(4): 3, July, 1976.

The fragmented intrauterine device: an unusual complication of a Lippes loop, by K. A. Burry, et al. FERTILITY AND STERILITY 29(2):218-219, February, 1978.

Genital actinomycosis and the intrauterine device. Apropos of 3 cases, by J. Hamels. JOURNAL DE GYNECOLOGIE, OBSTETRIQUE ET BIOLOGIE DE LA REPRODUCTION 6(8):1061-1069, December, 1977.

Gonadotropic and ovarian hormone content in the blood of women using intrauterine devices containing copper, by N. B. Antipova, et al. SOVETSKAYA MEDITZINA (6):80-85, June, 1978.

Group A streptococcal sepsis and arthritis. Origin from an intrauterine device, by J. D. Brosseau, et al. JAMA; JOURNAL OF THE AMERICAN MEDICAL ASSOCIATION 238(20):2178, November 14, 1977.

Hemophilus parainfluenzac peritonitis associated with an intrauterine contraceptive device, by T. E. Gallant, et al. AMERICAN JOURNAL OF OBSTETRICS AND GYNECOLOGY 129(6):702-703, November 15, 1977.

Herpesvirus hominis endometritis in a young woman wearing an intrauterine contraceptive device, by A. A. Abraham. AMERICAN JOURNAL OF OBSTETRICS AND GYNECOLOGY 131(3):340-342, June 1, 1978.

The hidden intrauterine device, by K. Schumann, et al. FORTSCHRITTE DU MEDIZIN 95(41):2505-2509, November 3, 1977.

Histological and ultrastructural changes of the endometrium in women using inert and copper-coiled IUDs, by N. Ragni, et al. ACTA EUROPAEA FERTILITATIS 8(3): 193-210, September, 1977.

Hysteroscopic removal of intrauterine contraceptive devices with missing threads, by J. Gupta, et al. INDIAN JOURNAL OF MEDICAL RESEARCH 65(5):661-663, May, 1977.

IUCDs—a contraindication to removal [letter]. BRITISH MEDICAL JOURNAL 1(6107):237, January 28, 1978.

The IUD and endometrial bleeding, by G. Rybo. JOURNAL OF REPRODUCTIVE MEDICINE 20(3):175-182, March, 1978.

IUD and unilateral tubo-ovarian abscess, by J. Sracek. CESKOSLOVENSKA GYNEKOLOGIE 43(1):52-53, March, 1978.

IUD gangrene of small intestine, by C. J Barranco. AMERICAN JOURNAL OF SURGERY 135(5):717, May, 1978.

Iatrogenic damage contraception by IUD, by E. Aguilera, et al. REVISTA CHILENA DE OBSTETRICIA Y GINECOLOGIA 42(1):47-48, 1977.

Infection hazards and complications following the use of IUDs, by W. Böhn, et al. ZENTRALBLATT FUER GYNAEKOLOGIE 99(24):1484-1488, 1977.

Intrauterine device and pelvic inflammatory diseases, by L. Thaler, et al. INTERNATIONAL JOURNAL OF FERTILITY 23(1):69-72, 1978.

Intrauterine devices and menstrual blood loss. A comparative study of eight devices during the first six months of use, by A. J. Gallegost, et al. CONTRACEPTION 17(2):153-161, February, 1978.

Leukocytes are consistently associated with degenerating embryos in IUD-bearing rhesus monkeys, by P. R. Hurst, et al. NATURE 269(5626):331-333, September 22, 1977.

Ligneous cellulitis associated with an IUD, by A. J. Weiland, et al. OBSTETRICS AND GYNECOLOGY 51(1 Suppl): 485-515, January, 1977.

Long-term contraception by a single silastic implant-D containing norethindrone acetate in women: a clinical evaluation, by D. Takkar, et al. CONTRACEPTION 17(4):341-354, April, 1978.

Lost intrauterine devices and their localization, by R. P. Rao. JOURNAL OF REPRODUCTIVE MEDICINE 20(4): 195-199, April, 1978.

Medicated intrauterine devices to improve bleeding events, by F. Hefnawi, et al. INTERNATIONAL JOURNAL OF GYNAECOLOGY AND OBSTETRICS 15(1):79-83, 1977.

Mid-trimester septic abortion and Escherichia coli septicaemia in a copper IUCD user, by R. A. Sparks, et al. BRITISH MEDICAL JOURNAL 1(6111):481-482, February 25, 1978.

New warnings on IUDs, by C. M. Rob. GOOD HOUSEKEEP-ING 187:258, September, 1978.

No increase of the fibrinolytic activity of the human endometrium by progesterone-releasing IUD (progestasertR), by P. Liedholm, et al. CONTRACEPTION 17(6):531-

533, June, 1978.

Noxious effect of intrauterine devices (IUD) on the development of concomitant pregnancy, by E. Jaworski. WIADOMOSCI LEKARSKIE 31(3):209-211, February 1, 1978.

Nurse-midwife insertion of the copper T in Thailand: performance, acceptance, and programmatic effects, by N. H. Wright, et al. STUDIES IN FAMILY PLANNING 8(9):237-243, September, 1977.

Pelvic abscess in association with intrauterine contraceptive device, by W. C. Scott. AMERICAN JOURNAL OF OBSTETRICS AND GYNECOLOGY 131(2):149-156, May 15, 1978.

Pelvic actinomycosis associated with IUCD [letter], by M. Barnham, et al. BRITISH MEDICAL JOURNAL 1(6114): 719-720, March 18, 1978.

Pelvic actinomycosis and the intrauterine contraceptive device. A cyto-histomorphologic study, by R. D. Luff, et al. AMERICAN JOURNAL OF CLINICAL PATHOLOGY 69(6):581-586, June, 1978.

Pelvic pain and the IUD, by G. E. Trobough. JOURNAL OF REPRODUCTIVE MEDICINE 20(3):167-174, March, 1978.

Perforation of the uterus and the urinary bladder with the Lippes loop, by J. Iglesias, et al. REVISTA CHILENA DE OBSTETRICIA Y GINECOLOGIA 42(3):149-150, 1977.

Perforation of the uterus as a complication of intrauterine contraception with the Gravigard, by C. D. Birch, et al. UGESHRIFT FORLAEGER 139(32):1907-1908, August 8, 1977.

Perforation of uterus by Lippes loop. (Case report with brief review of literature), by S. Agarwal, et al. JOURNAL OF OBSTETRICS AND GYNAECOLOGY OF INDIA 27(2): 262-265, April, 1977.

Plasma prolactin levels and contraception: oral contraceptives and intrauterine devices, by W. N. Spellacy, et al. CONTRACEPTION 17(1):71-77, January, 1978.

Primary ovarian pregnancy and the intra-uterine contraceptive device. Report of two cases, by A. Golan, et al. SOUTH AFRICAN MEDICAL JOURNAL 52(28):1130-1132, December 31, 1977.

Primary ovarian pregnancy associated with the dalkon shield IUD, by Y. Girard, et al. OBSTETRICS AND GYNECOLOGY 51(1 Suppl):525-555, January, 1977.

The problem of the "lost" IUD [proceedings], by F. H. Hepp. ARCHIV FUR GYNAEKOLOGIE 224(1-4):30-31, July 29, 1977.

Problems with IUCD tails [letter], by G. Chamberlain. BRITISH MEDICAL JOURNAL 1(6107):237, January 28, 1978.

The rat uterine oestrogen receptor in relation to intra-uterine devices and the oestrous cycle [proceedings], by L. Myatt, et al. BIOCHEMICAL SOCIETY TRANSACTIONS 5(5):1563-1564, 1977.

Reduction of mefanamic acid of increased menstrual blood loss associated with intrauterine contraception, by J. Guillebaud, et al. BRITISH JOURNAL OF OBSTETRICS AND GYNAECOLOGY 85(1):53-62, January, 1978.

Removal from the abdominal cavity of an intrauterine device by culdoscopy, by E. Acosta Bendek. REVISTA

COLOMBIANA DE OBSTETRICIA Y GINECOLOGICA 28(2):85-88, March-April, 1977.

Report of the working party on IUcDs [editorial]. MEDICAL JOURNAL OF AUSTRALIA 2(7):202, August 13, 1977.

Sciatica caused by an intrauterine device after silent uterine perforation. A case report, by R. M. Elmer. JOURNAL OF BONE AND JOINT SURGERY 60(2):265-266, March, 1978.

Self-checking the intrauterine device, by G. Chamberlain. FERTILITY AND STERILITY 28(10):1121-1122, October, 1977.

Septic abortion and IUCDs [letter], by R. A. Sparks, et al. BRITISH MEDICAL JOURNAL 1(6120):1141, April 29, 1978.

Severe pelvis peritoneal infections in wearers of IUD. Severe localized genital infection in wearers of IUD, by J. Duenas, et al. REVISTA CHILENA DE OBSTETRICIA Y GINECOLOGIA 42(1):41-43, 1977.

Side effects of intrauterine devices, by E. B. Connell. INTERNATIONAL JOURNAL OF GYNAECOLOGY AND OBSTETRICS 15(2):153-156, 1977.

Stromal cell interactions in the rat uterus as influenced by oestrogen and in intrauterine device, by C. M. Wischik, et al. THERIOGENOLOGY 8(4):144, October, 1977.

Studies of carbohydrate and lipid metabolism in women using the progesterone-T intrauterine device for six months: blood glucose, insulin, cholesterol, and triglyceride levels, by W. N. Spellacy, et al. FERTILITY AND STERILITY 29(5):505-508, May, 1978.

Study of the uterine environment in association with intrauterine contraceptive devices, by A. H. Abdel Gawad, et al. CONTRACEPTION 16(5):469-485, November, 1977.

Transitory changes in the heart action with intrauterine contraceptive devices insertion, by S. Salahovi. LIJECNICKI VJESNIK 99(12):747-748, December, 1977.

Translocation of intrauterine contraceptive device, by R. K. Borkotoky, et al. JOURNAL OF THE INDIAN MEDICAL ASSOCIATION 67(6):147-149, September 16, 1976.

Tubo-ovarian actinomycosis and the IUCD, by D. W. Purdie, et al. BRITISH MEDICAL JOURNAL 2(6099):1392, November 26, 1977.

Ultrastructure of eclls in the surface epithelium of the rat uterus during early pregnancy, and the effect of an interuterine device, by P. V. Peplow. THERIOGENOLOGY 8(4):139, October, 1977.

The unilateral tubo-ovarian abscess with an IUD, by E. Lo Sin Sjoe, et al. NEDERLANDS TIJDSCHRIFT VOOR GNEESKUNDE 122(31):1131-1132, August 5, 1978.

Unilateral tubo-ovarin actinomycosis in the presence of an intrauterine device, by J. F. McCormick, et al. AMERICAN JOURNAL OF CLINICAL PATHOLOGY 68(5): 622-626, November, 1977.

Urea in the intrauterine space of IUD users, by V. Nesit, et al. CASOPIS LEKARU CESKYCH 116(45):1401-1403, November 11, 1977.

Use of intrauterine devices complicated by trichomonas vaginitis, by M. Cislo, et al. WIADOMOSCI PARAZYTOLOGICZNE 23(5):595-598, 1977.

Vaginal prostaglandin E2 in the management of fetal intrauterine death, by E. M. Southern, et al. BRITISH JOUR-
NAL OF OBSTETRICS AND GYNAECOLOGIE 85(6):
437-441, June, 1978.

Vascular defects in human endometrium caused by intrauterine contraceptive devices. An election microscope
study, by W. R. Hohman, et al. CONTRACEPTION
16(5):507-522, November, 1977.

Vasovagal shock after insertion of intrauterine device [letter],
by D. N. Menzies. BRITISH MEDICAL JOURNAL
1(6108):305, February 4, 1978.

CONTRACEPTIVES: FEMALE: IUD: COMPLICATIONS:
PSYCHOLOGICAL
The effects of psychological preparation on pain at intra-
uterine device insertion, by J. R. Newton, et al. CON-
TRACEPTION 16(5):523-532, November, 1977.

The progestasert and ecotopic pregnancy, by R. Snowden.
BRITISH MEDICAL JOURNAL 2(6102):1600-1601,
December 17, 1977.

CONTRACEPTIVES: FEMALE: IUD: FAILURE
Ectopic pregnancies, IUD's and abortion [letter], by I.
Sivin. CONTRACEPTION 17(6):575-582, June, 1978.

Ecotopic pregnancy rates in IUD users [letter], by R. Aznar,
et al. BRITISH MEDICAL JOURNAL 1(6115):785-
786, March 25, 1978.

Intrauterine device and ectopic pregnancy, by R. Erkkola,
et al. CONTRACEPTION 16(6):569-574, December,
1977.

Outcome of pregnancy in the presence of intrauterine device,
by S. Koetsawang, et al. ACTA OBSTETRICIA ET
GYNECOLOGICA SCANDINAVICA 56(5):479-482,

1977.

Ovarian pregnancy. The dubious role of intra-uterine devices [letter], by J. Y. Grall, et al. NOUVELLE PRESSE MEDICALE 7(6):468, February 11, 1978.

CONTRACEPTIVES: FEMALE: IUD: LAWS
IUD warning. TRIAL 13(6):4, June, 1977.

CONTRACEPTIVES: FEMALE: IUD: TECHNIQUES
IUD insertions by midwives: five years' experience in Santiago, Chile, by L. Pastene, et al. INTERNATIONAL JOURNAL OF GYNAECOLOGY AND OBSTETRICS 15(1):84-87, 1977.

Importance of correct identification of intrauterine contraceptive device [letter], by R. A. Hatcher, et al. AMERICAN JOURNAL OF OBSTETRICS AND GYNECOLOGY 131(2):229, May 15, 1978.

X-ray methods of localization of IUD's, by A. Tetti, et al. MINERVA GINECOLOGIA 30(5):390-393, May, 1978.

CONTRACEPTIVES: FEMALE: IMPLANTED
Clinical trial with subdermal implants of the progestin R-2323, by S. Diaz, et al. CONTRACEPTION 16(2):155-165, August, 1977.

Effect of norethindrone acetate released from a single silastic implant on serum FSH, LH, progesterone and estradiol-17beta of women during first eight months of treatment, by S. A. Rahman, et al. CONTRACEPTION 16(5):487-497, November, 1977.

The intrauterine progesterone contraceptive system, by R. Erickson, et al. ADVANCES IN PLANNED PARENTHOOD 11(4):167-174, 1976.

CONTRACEPTIVES: FEMALE: IMPLANTED: COMPLICATIONS
Endometrial histology and progesterone levels in women using
norethindrone acetate implants for contraception, by D.
Takkar, et al. CONTRACEPTION 17(2):103-113, February, 1978.

CONTRACEPTIVES: FEMALE: ORAL
After the pill? GUARDIAN p. 11, July 14, 1978.

Agreement rates between oral contraceptive users and prescribers in relation to drug use histories, by P. D. Stolley,
et al. AMERICAN JOURNAL OF EPIDEMIOLOGY
107(3):226-235, March, 1978.

Another alternative to the pill; encore oval, by J. Chan.
McCALLS 105:40, January, 1978.

Birth control: once-a-month pill, by M. Jeffery. HARPER'S
BAZAAR 3201:24, August, 1978.

Blessing and a curse; the pill, by J. Webb. MACLEANS 91:
55-58+, April 17, 1978.

Causes of clinic drop-out among Iranian pill users, by C. F.
Lee, et al. JOURNAL OF BIOSOCIAL SCIENCE 10(1):
7-15, January, 1978.

Chemical control of human fertility. ENVIRONMENTAL
SCIENCE AND TECHNOLOGY 12:258-259, March,
1978.

Choice of oral contraceptives for a large family planning program, by C. N. Wells. JOURNAL OF THE ARKANSAS
MEDICAL SOCIETY 75(2):85-88, July, 1978.

Choking on the pill, by M. S. Kennedy. NEW TIMES 11:68,
August 7, 1978.

Clinical evaluation of an oral contraceptive combination with a low dosage of estrogens and progestanes and their correlation in a group of women using intrauterine device, by A. Rinaldi. REVISTA CHILENA DE OBSTETRICIA Y GINECOLOGICA 42(1):34-40, 1977.

Comparative metabolism of 17alpha-ethynyl steroids used in oral contraceptives, by R. E. Ranney. JOURNAL OF TOXICOLOGY AND ENVIRONMENTAL HEALTH 3(1-2):139-166, September, 1977.

Comparative studies of the ethynyl estrogens used in oral contraceptives: effects with and without progestational agents on plasma cortisol and cortisol binding in humans, baboons, and beagles, by J. W. Goldzieher, et al. FERTILITY AND STERILITY 28(11):1182-1190, November, 1977.

A comparative study of three low dose progestogens, chlormadinone acetate, megestrol acetate and norethisterone, as oral contraceptives, by D. F. Hawkins, et al. BRITISH JOURNAL OF OBSTETRICS AND GYNAECOLOGY 84(9):708-713, September, 1977.

Experimental trial of the tri-cycle pill [letter], by E. Elliott. BRITISH MEDICAL JOURNAL 2(6093):1025-1026, October 15, 1977.

FDA said that, contrary to Eaton-Merz lab claim, encore oval, a widely used nonprescription contraceptives, doesn't seem to be any more effective than similar products sold by competitors. WALL STREET JOURNAL 7:13-29.

Guidelines for dispensing oral contraceptive PPIs [patient package insert]. DRUG TOPICS 122:22, March 15, 1978.

Is a bad rep killing the pill? by M. S. Kennedy. NEW TIMES 11(3):68, August 7, 1978.

Issues in contraception. Today's pill and the individual wo-
man. Part 1, by L. K. Huxall. MCN; AMERICAN JOUR-
NAL OF MATERNAL-CHILD NURSING 2:359-363,
November-December, 1977.

The life table according to Chiang as a method for the description and assessment of the efficacy of oral contraceptives,
by C. Wolfrum. METHODS OF INFORMATION IN
MEDICINE 16(3):176-181, July, 977.

An open assessment of a new low dose oestrogen combined
oral contraceptive, by I. Hughes. JOURNAL OF INTER-
NATIONAL MEDICAL RESEARCH 6(1):41-45, 1978.

Oral contraception—choice of treatment, by B. Law. PRAC-
TITIONER 219(1312):571-578, October, 1977.

Oral contraceptive labeling. FDA DRUG BULLETIN 8(2):
12-13, March-April, 1978.

Oral contraceptive use: epidemiology, by F. A. MacCornack,
et al. NEW YORK STATE JOURNAL OF MEDICINE
77:200-202, February, 1977.

Oral contraceptives, by A. A. Haspels, et al. NEDERLANDS
TIJDSCHRIFT VOOR GENEESKUNDE 122(32):1188-
1190, August 12, 1978.

Oral contraceptives: a demographic survey of military dependents, by R. D. Peppler. MILITARY MEDICINE 142(10):
773-777, October, 1977.

Oral contraceptives: which one for my patient? by B. R.
Spier. JOURNAL OF THE MEDICAL ASSOCIATION
OF THE STATE OF ALABAMA 45(11):36-38, May,
1976.

Patient package inserts and oral contraceptives, by H. W.
Mayberger, et al. JOURNAL OF LEGAL MEDICINE

5(9):14-17, September, 1977.

The pill [letter], by J. Heim. NOUVELLE PRESSE MEDI-CALE 6(38):3549, November 12, 1977.

The pill and the code, by M. A. Frey. JOURNAL OF FAMI-LY LAW 15(1):1-26, 1977.

The pill and other methods [letter]. NEW ENGLAND JOUR-NAL OF MEDICINE 298(2):114, January 12, 1978.

Pill for birth control, by D. Kolb. JOURNAL OF CHEMI-CAL EDUCATION 55:591-596, September, 1978.

Poor acceptability of "Pill-a-month" contraceptive. High pregnancy and drop-out rates in a small sample, by R. A. Vaidya, et al. JOURNAL OF POSTGRADUATE MEDI-CINE 22(4):176-179, October, 1976.

Potencies of oral contraceptives [letter], by H. J. Chihal, et al. AMERICAN JOURNAL OF OBSTETRICS AND GYNECOLOGY 130(3):369-371, February 1, 1978.

Recent trend in preference of contraceptive methods—pills down, diaphragm on rise, by J. Balog, et al. OBSTE-TRICAL AND GYNECOLOGICAL SURVEY 33(4): 282-283, April, 1978.

Some observations on the use of oral contraception, by M. Hugo. JOURNAL OF NURSE-MIDWIFERY 22(4): 10-11, Winter, 1978.

Starting on the pill [letter], by E. H. Gregson. BRITISH MEDICAL JOURNAL 2(6092):959, October 8, 1977.

A survey of the effects of oral contraceptive patient informa-tion, by L. A. Morris, et al. JAMA: JOURNAL OF THE AMERICAN MEDICAL ASSOCIATION 238(23):2504-2508, December 5, 1977.

Three-month wonder. ECONOMIST 267:66, April 22, 1978.

CONTRACEPTIVES: FEMALE: ORAL: COMPLICATIONS
Absence of capillary microangiopathy in oral contraceptive users with glucose intolerance, by J. W. Goldzieher, et al. OBSTETRICS AND GYNECOLOGY 51(1):89-92, January, 1978.

Acid-base balance immediately after administration of an oral contraceptive, by C. Pilot, et al. ARCHIV FUER GYNAEKOLOGIE 223(3):221-231, October 28, 1977.

The activated factor X-antithrombin III reaction rate: a measure of the increased thrombotic tendency induced by estrogen-containing oral contraceptives in rabbits, by S. N. Gitel, et al. HAEMOSTASIS 7(1):10-18, 1978.

Acute dyserythropoiesis due to folic acid deficiency revealing celiac disease. Apropos of a case in a woman under prolonged oral contraception, by P. Veyssier, et al. ANNALES DE MEDECINE INTERNE 128(10):789-792, October, 1977.

Acute ophthalmologic complications during the use of oral contraceptives, by S. Friedman, et al. OBSTETRICAL AND GYNECOLOGICAL SURVEY 30:451-452, 1975.

Alpha1-antirypsin, protein marker in oral contraceptive-associated hepatic tumors, by P. E. Palmer, et al. AMERICAN JOURNAL OF CLINICAL PATHOLOGY 68(6): 736-739, December, 1977.

Assessment of ovarian function in perimenopausal women after stopping oral contraceptives, by R. A. Donald, et al. BRITISH JOURNAL OF OBSTETRICS AND GYNAECOLOGY 85(1):70-73, January, 1978.

The association between oral contraception and hepatocellular adenoma—a preliminary report, by J. B. Rooks, et

al. INTERNATIONAL JOURNAL OF GYNAECOLO-
GY AND OBSTETRICS 15(2):143-144, 1977.

Asymptomatic liver cell adenomas. Another case of resolution after discontinuation of oral contraceptive use, by
W. L. Ramseur, et al. JAMA: JOURNAL OF THE
AMERICAN MEDICAL ASSOCIATION 239(16):
1647-1648, April 21, 1978.

Benign hepatic lesions in women taking oral contraceptives,
by T. J. Davis, et al. GASTROINTESTINAL RADI-
OLOGY 2(3):213-219, December 20, 1977.

Benign intracranial hypertension and thrombosis of the
venous sinuses during contraceptive treatment: anatomo-
clinical and neuroradiological observations, by M. Baldini,
et al. RIVISTA DI PATOLOGIA NERVOSA E MEN-
TALE 98(3):185-190, May-June, 1977.

Benign liver-cell tumor and intra-abdominal hemorrhage
following administration of oral contraceptives, by F.
Hofstädter, et al. MUNCHENER MEDIZINISCHE WO-
CHENSCHRIFT 120(26):899-900, June 30, 1978.

Biological antithrombin III levels [letter], by R. L. Bick.
JAMA: JOURNAL OF THE AMERICAN MEDICAL
ASSOCIATION 239(4):296, January 23, 1978.

Bleeding and serum d-norgestrel, estradiol and progesterone
patterns in women using d-norgestrel subdermal polysiloxane capsules for contraception, by D. E. Moore, et
al. CONTRACEPTION 17(4):315-328, April, 1978.

Blood pressure response to estrogen-progestin oral contraceptive after pregnancy-induced hypertension, by J. A.
Pritchard, et al. AMERICAN JOURNAL OF OBSTE-
TRICS AND GYNECOLOGY 129(7):733-739, December 1, 1977.

Bone response to termination of oestrogen treatment, by R. Lindsay, et al. LANCET 1(8078):1325-1327, June 24, 1978.

CO_2-hysteroscopy, a method for the removal of occult intrauterine devices [proceedings], by J. Mohr, et al. ARCHIV FUR GYNAEKOLOGIE 224(1-4):31-32, July 29, 1977.

Calculating the risks, by C. Doyle. OBSERVER p. 11, October 8, 1978.

Carbonic anhydrase activity in human cervical mucus and its response to various contraceptives regimes, by E. N. Chantler, et al. BRITISH JOURNAL OF OBSTETRICS AND GYNAECOLOGY 84(9):705-707, September, 1977.

Carcadian variations of plasma delta4-androstenedione in normal and castrated adult males, by D. De Aloysio, et al. ACTA EUROPAEA FERTILITATIS 8(2):175-184, June, 1977.

Cardiovascular accidents caused by estroprogestational contraceptives and lipid anomalies in blood circulation, by J. L. de Gennes, et al. ANNALES D'ENDOCRIN-OLOGY 38(6):447-448, 1977.

Cardiovascular birth defects and antenatal exposure to female sex hormones, by O. P. Heinonen, et al. NEW ENGLAND JOURNAL OF MEDICINE 296:67-70, January 13, 1977.

Cardiovascular complications of oral contraceptives, by N. M. Kaplan. ANNUAL REVIEW OF MEDICINE 29:31-40, 1978.

Cardiovascular effects of oral contraceptives, by P. D. Stolley, et al. SOUTHERN MEDICAL JOURNAL 71(7):821-

824, July, 1978.

A case contro study of carcinoma of the ovary, by M. L. Newhouse, et al. BRITISH JOURNAL OF PREVENTIVE AND SOCIAL MEDICINE 31(3):148-153, September, 1977.

A case-control study of uterine perforations documented at laparoscopy, by M. K. White, et al. AMERICAN JOURNAL OF OBSTETRICS AND GYNECOLOGY 129(6): 623-625, November 15, 1977.

Case report on a retinal complication in long-term therapy with oral hormonal contraceptives, by H. Huismans. KLINISCHE MONATSBLAETTER FUER AUGENHEILKUNDE 171(5):781-786, November, 1977.

Cerebrovascular diseases in women receiving oral contraceptives: report of three cases, by J. Ogata, et al. RINSHO SHINKEIGAKU 17(7):465-471, July, 1977.

Cervical cancer: pill seems safe for most women but those with dysplasia may have higher risk. FAMILY PLANNING PERSPECTIVES 10(3):165-166, May-June, 1978.

Cervical caricinoma and the pill [letter], by H. J. Collette, et al. LANCET 1(8061):441-442, February 25, 1978.

Cervical factor in fertility regulation, by M. Elstein. ADVANCES IN EXPERIMENTAL MEDICINE AND BIOLOGY 89:371-386, 1977.

Cervical neoplasia and the pill [letter]. LANCET 2(8042): 825-826, October 15, 1977.

Changes in antithrombia III levels in pregnancy, labour and in women on the contraceptive pill, by E. M. Essien. AFRICAN JOURNAL OF MEDICAL SCIENCES 6(3): 109-113, September, 1977.

Changes in the extensibility of the cervix of the rat in late pregnancy produced by prostaglandin F2alpha, ovariectomy and steroid replacement [proceedings], by M. Hollingsworth, et al. BRITISH JOURNAL OF PHARMACOLOGY 61(3):501P-502P, November, 1971.

Changes in menstrual cycle length and regularity after use of oral contraceptives, by R. N. Taylor, Jr., et al. INTERNATIONAL JOURNAL OF GYNAECOLOGY AND OBSTETRICS 15(1):55-59, 1977.

Changes in serum high density lipoproteins in women on oral contraceptive drugs, by R. M. Krauss, et al. CLINICA CHIMICA ACTA 80(3):465-470, November 1, 1977.

Changes in serum lipids during treatment with norgestrel, oestradiol-valerate and cyploprogynon, by F. H. Nielsen, et al. ACTA OBSTETRICIA ET GYNECOLOGICA SCANDINAVICA 56(4):367-370, 1977.

Changes of glucose toleance and blood lipid level in women as a result of administration of oral contraceptives, by Z. Kh. Zaripova, et al. VOPROSY OKHRANY MATERINSTVA I DETSTVA 22(10):68-69, October, 1977.

Changes of serum hormone concentrations during oral contraception using monohormonal and combination preparations [proceedings], by J. Nevinny-Stickel, et al. ARCHIV FUR GYNAEKOLOGIE 224(1-4):27-29, July 29, 1977.

Changes of unspecific immune parameters (CH50E, C3, C4, C3A, lysozyme, CRP at the end of 2-year use of a synthetic sex steroid drug, by A. Stelzner, et al. DEUTSCHE GESUNDHEITSWESEN 33(29):1381-1385, 1978.

Chromatographic separation of multiple renin substrates in women: effect of pregnancy and oral contraceptives, by D. B. Gordon, et al. PROCEEDINGS OF THE SOCIETY

FOR EXPERIMENTAL BIOLOGY AND MEDICINE 156(3):461-464, December, 1977.

Chromosome analysis in baboons born following the use of potential, postovulatory, fertility-inhibiting steroids, by Z. A. Jemilev, et al. ZENTRALBLATT FUER GY-NAEKOLOGIE 100(6):337-340, 1978.

Chromosome changes and congenital malformations after use of estroprogestogens, by A. Pardini, et al. RIVISTA ITALIANA DI GINECOLOGIA 57(3):195-203, May-June, 1976.

Circulating levels of norethindrone in women with a single silastic implant, by V. Goyal, et al. CONTRACEPTION 17(4):375-382, April, 1978.

A clinical and angiographic study of occlusions of the posterior cerebral artery with special reference to the pathogenetic role of oral contraceptives and nicotine-abuse, by D. Kühne, et al. FORTSCHRITTE DER NEUROLOGIE, PSYCHIATRIE UNE IHRER GRENZGEBIETE 46(1): 1-28, January, 1978.

Clinical and hematogenic considerations of 2 cases of cerebral venous thrombosis occuring during the use of oral estro-progestational preparations, by J. Galimberti, et al. ANNALI DELL' OSPEDALE MARIA VITTORIA DI TORINO 19(7-12):183-193, July-December, 1976.

Clinical course and pathogenesis of oral contraceptive hypertension, by J. Girndt, et al. MEDIZINISCHE KLINIK 72(41):1680-1684, October 14, 1977.

Clinical pharmacokinetics of rifampicin, by G. Acocella. CLINICAL PHARMACOKINETICS 3(2):108-127, March-April, 1978.

The clinical, radiologic, and pathologic characterization of benign hepatic neoplasms. Alleged association with oral contraceptives, by D. M. Knowles, 2d, et al. MEDICINE 57(3):223-237, May, 1978.

Clinical trial with a combination of 150 mcg of d-norgestrel and 30 mcg of ethinylestradiol. Its metabolic effects, by A. V. Moggia, et al. OBSTETRICIA Y GINECOLO-GIA LATINO-AMERICANAS 34(11-12):384-397, November-December, 1976.

A clinicopathologic study of steroid-related liver tumors, by W. M. Christopherson, et al. AMERICAN JOURNAL OF SURGICAL PATHOLOGY 1(1):31-41, March, 1977.

Comparative studies of the ethynyl estrogens used in oral contraceptives: effects with and without progestational agents on plasma androstenedione, testosterone, and testosterone binding in humans, baboons, and beagles, by J. W. Goldzieher, et al. FERTILITY AND STERILI-TY 29(4):388-396, April, 1978.

Comparison between the use of oral contraceptives and the incidence of surgically confirmed gallstone disease, by K. H. Leissner, et al. SCANDINAVIAN JOURNAL OF GASTROENTEROLOGY 12:893-896, 1977.

Comparison of the effects of contraceptive steroid forumula-tions containing two doses of estrogen on pituitary func-tion, by J. Z. Scott, et al. FERTILITY AND STERILI-TY 30(2):141-145, August, 1978.

Comparison of effects of ingestion of Si on the content of Ca and Mg of different tissues of female rats normal or receiving oral oestrogen-gestogens, by Y. Charnot, et al. ANNALES D'ENDOCRINOLOGIE 38(6):377-378, 1977.

Comparison of plasma hormone changes using a "conven-tional" and a "paper" pill formulation of a low-dose oral contraceptive, by S. E. Morris, et al. FERTILITY AND STERILITY 29(3):296-303, March, 1978.

Comparison of strokes in women of childbearing age in Rochester, Minnesota and Bakersfield, California, by T. P. Comer, et al. ANGIOLOGY 26(4):351-355, April, 1975.

Comparison of vaginal cytologic effects and blood elimination curves of different oestrogen drugs, by E. Hempel, et al. ARCHIV FUER GESCHWULSTFORCHUNG 47(5):479-484, 1977.

Concerning the relation between the use of oral contraceptives and the development of primary malignant tumours of the liver, by I. Hantak, et al. BRATISLAVSKE LEKARSKE LISTY 68(5):613-619, November, 1977.

Congenital heart disease and prenatal exposure to exogenous sex hormones, by D. T. Janerich, et al. BRITISH MEDICAL JOURNAL 6068:1058-1060, April 23, 1977.

Contact lens tolerance and oral contraceptives, by A. De Vries Reilingh, et al. ANNALS OF OPHTHALMOLOGY 10(7):947-952, July, 1978.

Contraception and arterial hypertension, by P. Corvol, et al. ACQUISITIONS MEDICALES RECENTES :177-180, 1977.

Contraception and fertility. Analysis of 1090 pregnancies, by A. Cervantes, et al. GINECOLOGIA Y OBSTETRICIA DE MEXICO 43(256):56-68, February, 1978.

The contraceptive effects of a new low-dose combination type oral contraceptive, by H. Kallio, et al. CURRENT MEDICAL RESEARCH AND OPINION 5(6):444-449, 1978.

Contraceptive tablets and liver adenoma, by B. Westerholm.

LAKARTIDNINGEN 73(34):2803, August 24, 1977.

Coronary thrombosis on oral contraception, by A. Barrillon, et al. NOUVELLE PRESSE MEDICALE 6(3):2758-2760, September 24, 1977.

Cytogenetic studies on women during and following the use of hormonal contraceptives, by R. Müller, et al. ZENTRALBLATT FUER GYNAEKOLOGIE 100(6):347-354, 1978.

Cytologic detection and clinical significance of Actinomyces israelii in women using intrauterine contraceptive devices, by M. R. Spence, et al. AMERICAN JOURNAL OF OBSTETRICS AND GYNECOLOGY 131(3):295-298, June 1, 1978.

Cytological evaluation of long term effect of Lippes loop and copper IUDs, by J. S. Misra, et al. INDIAN JOURNAL OF MEDICAL RESEARCH 66(6):942-945, December, 1977.

Deaths among pill users in Britain. IPPF MEDICAL BULLETIN 11(5):1-2, October, 1977.

Delay in the diagnosis of cervical cancer in patients using hormonal contraceptives and IUDs, by H. H. Buttner, et al. ZEITSCHRIFT FUR AERZTLICHE FORTBILDUNG 71(23):1129-1130, December 1, 1977.

Determination of antithrombin III (chromogenic substrates) and FDP in women in treatment with oral estroprogestin agents, by A. Gibelli, et al. MINERVA MEDICA 69(18):1241-1244, April 14, 1978.

Dietary folate intake and concentration of folate in serum and erythrocytes in women using oral contraceptives, by G. J. Pietarinen, et al. AMERICAN JOURNAL OF CLINICAL NUTRITION 30:375-380, March, 1977.

Diffuse bilateral retinal periphlebitis in a young woman taking contraceptives, by C. Gervais, et al. BULLETIN DES SOCIETES D'OPHTHALMOLOGIE DE FRANCE 77(2):191-192, February, 1977.

Does the pill kill? women over 35 are now being steered gently away from the pill; where's the research on its ever more popular alternative? ECONOMIST 265:10-11, October 15, 1977.

Dream recall and the contraceptive pill, by P. Sheldrake, et al. JOURNAL OF NERVOUS AND MENTAL DISEASE 163(1):59-60, 1976.

Drug file: the pill—the problems continue: from dysplaisa to cancer; birth defects; heart disease, by E. M. Goldstein. TRIAL 10(8):10, August, 1977.

Drug interactions with oral contraceptives. IPPF MEDICAL BULLETIN 12(4):1, August, 1978.

Drugs—survey results on tumors and the pill, by M. Fisk. TRIAL 14(1):16, January, 1978.

Dysplasias of uterine cervix: epidemiological aspects: role of age at first coitus and use of oral contraceptives, by A. Meisels, et al. CANCER 40(6):3076-3081, December, 1977.

The effect of kind of carbohydrate in the diet and use of oral contraceptives on metabolism of young women. I. Blood and urinary lactate, uric acid, and phosphorus, by J. L. Kelsay, et al. AMERICAN JOURNAL OF CLINI-CAL NUTRITION 30(12):2016-2022, December, 1977.

Effect of low zinc intake and oral contraceptive agents on nitrogen utilization and clinical findings in young women, by F. M. Hess, et al. JOURNAL OF NUTRITION 107(12):2219-2227, December, 1977.

Effect of the menstrual cycle, oral contraceptive and pregnancy on forearm blood flow, venus distensibility and clotting factors, by R. Fawer, et al. EUROPEAN JOURNAL OF CLINICAL PHARMACOLOGY 13(4):251-257, June 19, 1978.

Effect of oral alanine loads on plasma amino acids in oral contraceptive users and control women, by .C. Potera, et al. AMERICAN JOURNAL OF CLINICAL NUTRITION 31(5):794-798, May, 1978.

The effect of oral contraceptive agents on plasma vitamin A in the human and the rat. NUTRITION REVIEWS 35(9):245-248, September, 1977.

Effect of oral contraceptive on blood coagulation and blood fibrinolysis, by V. Sharma. JOURNAL OF OBSTETRICS AND GYNAECOLOGY OF INDIA 27(4):567-575, August, 1977.

The effect of an oral contraceptive on serum lipoproteins and skinfold thickniss in young women, by H. J. van der Steeg, et al. CONTRACEPTION 16(1):29-38, July,, 1977.

The effect of oral contraceptives and of bromocriptine upon pituitary stimulation by LH-RH and TRH, by J. S. Dericks-Tan, et al. CONTRACEPTION 17(1):79-86, January, 1978.

Effect of oral contraceptives on the blood lipid level, by E. V. Zhemerikina, et al. KARDIOLOGIIA 17(9):104-108, September, 1977.

Effect of oral contraceptives on the capacity to stimulate plasma renin activity and plasma aldosterone, by F. Klumpp, et al. MEDIZINISCHE WELT 29(6):228-231, February 10, 1978.

Effect of oral contraceptives on plasma androgenic steroids and their precursors, by M. Fern, et al. OBSTETRICS AND GYNECOLOGY 51(5):541-544, May, 1978.

Effect of oral contraceptives on sebum excretion rate, by R. J. Pye, et al. BRITISH MEDICAL JOURNAL 2(6102): 1581-1582, December 17, 1977.

The effect of oral contraceptives on serum immunoglouims, by D. Shouval, et al. HAREFUAH 94(2):49-51, January 15, 1978.

The effect of pregnancy and two different contraceptive pills on serum lipids and lipoproteins in a woman with a type III hyperlipoproteinaemia pattern, by D. P. Muller, et al. BRITISH JOURNAL OF OBSTETRICS AND GY-NAECOLOGY 85(2):127-133, February, 1978.

Effect of pregnancy on liver tumor associated with oral con-traceptives, by D. R. Kent, et al. OBSTETRICS AND GYNECOLOGY 51(2):148-151, February, 1978.

Effect of S-adenosyl-L-methionine on ethynylestradiol-induced impairment of bile flow in female rats, by G. Stramentinoli, et al. EXPERIENTIA 33(10):1361-1362, October 15, 1977.

The effect of sex hormones on peripheral immunity in pa-tients with advanced breast cancer, by C. R. Franks, et al. CLINICAL ONCOLOGY 4(1):19-24, March, 1978.

The effect of various doses of oral oestradiolvalerate and oestriolsuccinate on urine calcium/creatinine, serum FSH and endometrium in castrated women, by L. Rauramo, et al. ACTA OBSTETRICIA ET GYNECOLOGICA SCANDINAVICA 56(4):363-368, 1977.

The effects of ergosterol on the response of female chicks to oral oestrogens and progestogens, by G. P. Webb, et al.

BRITISH POULTRY SCIENCE 18(5):543-545, September, 1977.

Effects of low-oestrogen oral contraceptives [letter], by T. W. Meade. LANCET 1(8059):332, February 11, 1978.

Effects of oral and intrauterine administration of contraceptives on the uterus, by W. B. Ober. HUMAN PATHOLOGY 8(5):513-527, September, 1977.

Effects of an oral contraceptive on hepatic size and antipyrine metabolism in premenopausal women, by M. Homeida, et al. CLINICAL PHARMACOLOGY AND THERAPEUTICS 24(2):228-232, August, 1978.

Effects of oral contraceptives on tryptophan metabolism and vitamin B6 requirements in women, by R. R. Brown, et al. ACTA VITAMINOLOGICA ET ENZYMOLOGICA 29(1-6):151-157, 1975.

Effects of oral hormonal contraception in the adolescent, by V. Ruiz Velasco, et al. OBSTETRICIA Y GINECOLOGIA LATINO-AMERICANAS 35(7-8):217-224, July-August, 1977.

Effects of smoking and oral contraceptives on plasma and whole blood viscosity. Rheologic studies on normal subjects, by H. Leonhardt, et al. MEDIZINISHCE WELT 29(21):880-883, May 26, 1978.

Effects, on the endometrium, of a new oral contraceptive: physiostat, by P. Delacroix. REVUE FRANCAISE DE GYNECOLOGIE ET D'OBSTETRIQUE 72(7-9):583-585, July-September, 1977.

Elective surgery and the contraceptive pill [editorial], by A. Eldor, et al. HAREFUAH 94(2):93, January 15, 1978.

Endometrial histology with oral contraceptives, by R. Bevaja,

et al. JOURNAL OF OBSTETRICS AND GYNAE-
COLOGY OF INDIA 27(2):195-197, April, 1977.

Erroneous clinical diagnosis of leg vein thrombosis in women
on oral contraceptives, by R. W. Barnes, et al. OBSTE-
TRICS AND GYNECOLOGY 51(5):556-558, May, 1978.

Erythema nodosum and oral contraceptives [letter], by A.
Taaffe, et al. BRITISH MEDICAL JOURNAL 2(6098):
1353, November 19, 1977.

Erythema nodosum associated with pregnancy and oral contraceptives, by S. Bombardieri, et al. BRITISH MEDI-
CAL JOURNAL 6075:1509-1510, June 11, 1977.

The evaluation of sex chromatin number of newborns of
mothers using oral contraceptives prior to conception, by
R. Vajda. THERAPIA HUNGARICA 25(4):166-168,
1977.

Excess mortality and the pill, by H. M. Carey. MEDICAL
JOURNAL OF AUSTRALIA 1(3):153-154, February
11, 1978.

— [letter], by T. Dwyer, et al. MEDICAL JOURNAL OF
AUSTRALIA 1(6):335-336, March 25, 1978.

Factors affecting pituitary gonadotropin function in users
of oral contraceptive steroids, by J. A. Scott, et al.
AMERICAN JOURNAL OF OBSTETRICS AND GYNE-
COLOGY 130(7):817-821, April 1, 1978.

Fatal outcome of an hepatic adenoma following short term
oral contraceptive use, by A. W. Blayney, et al. IRISH
MEDICAL JOURNAL 70(15):455-456, October 21,
1977.

Fibrocystic breast disease in oral-contraceptive users. A histopathological evaluation of epithelial atypia, by

V. A. LiVolsi, et al. NEW ENGLAND JOURNAL OF MEDICINE 299(8):381-385, August 24, 1978.

Focal nodular hyperplasia of the liver and oral contraceptives, by H. Gögler, et al. CHIRURG 49(3):172-179, March, 1978.

Focal nodular hyperplasia of the liver—nucleographic and ultrasonic findings, by J. Cassoff, et al. JOURNAL OF THE CANADIAN ASSOCIATION OF RADIOLOGISTS 29(3):199-200, September, 1978.

Folic acid deficiency, the "pill" and the withheld anamneis, by D. E. Mendes de Leon. NEDERLANDS TIJDSCHRIFT VOOR GENEESKUNDE 122(5):146-150, February 4, 1978.

Gas exchange and acid-base status during the normal human menstrual cycle and in subjects taking oral contraceptives [proceedings], by J. A. Milne, et al. JOURNAL OF ENDOCRINOLOGY 75(3):17P-18P, December, 1977.

Gender of offspring after oral-contraceptive use, by K. Rothman, et al. NEW ENGLAND JOURNAL OF MEDICINE 295:859-861, October 14, 1976.

A guide to curable causes of hypertension, by N. M. Kaplan. MEDICAL TIMES 106(5):32-39, May, 1978.

H.D.L. cholesterol during oral contraception [letter], by R. W. Schade, et al. LANCET 2(8079):40, July 1, 1976.

Haemostatic, lipid, and blood-pressure profiles of women on oral contraceptives containing 50 microgram or 30 microgram oestrogen, by T. W. Meade, et al. LANCET 2(8045): 948-951, November 5, 1977.

Hair analysis of trace minerals in human subjects as influenced by age, sex, and contraceptive drugs, by S. B. Deeming,

et al. AMERICAN JOURNAL OF CLINICAL NUTRI-
TION 31(7):1175-1180, July, 1978.

Hemodynamic effects of oral contraceptives during exercise,
by P. Lehtovirta, et al. INTERNATIONAL JOURNAL
OF GYNAECOLOGY AND OBSTETRICS 15(1):35-37,
1977.

Hemostatic changes induced by exercise during oral contraceptive use, by A. M. Hedlin, et al. CANADIAN JOUR-
NAL OF PHYSIOLOGY AND PHARMACOLOGY
56(2):316-320, April, 1978.

Hepatic adenoma and oral contraceptives, by J. Hureau, et
al. JOURNAL DE CHIRURGIE 114(5):339-350, 1977.

Hepatic peliose, nodular focal hyperplasia of the liver: a
propos two cases, by A. El Hafed, et al. ACTA CHIRUR-
GICA BELGICA 76(5):509-514, September-October,
1977.

Hepatic tumors and oral contraceptives, by R. E. Fechner.
PATHOLOGY ANNUAL 12(pt 1):293-310, 1977.

—, by A. Mallory. GASTROENTEROLOGY 75(3):517-518,
September, 1978.

Hepatic vein thrombosis in a woman taking oral contraceptives: a case report, by C. Hines, Jr., et al. JOURNAL
OF THE LOUISIANA STATE MEDICAL SOCIETY
129(8):189-192, August, 1977.

Hepatocellulr carcinoma associated with oral contraceptives,
by N. Menzies-Gow. BRITISH JOURNAL OF SUR-
GERY 65(5):316-317, May, 1978.

Hepatocellular carcinoma in young women on oral contraceptives [letter], by W. M. Christopherson, et al. LANCET
2(8079):38-39, July 1, 1978.

Hepatocellular carcinoma in a young woman with prolonged exposure to oral contraceptives, by P. N. Gattanell, et al. MEDICAL AND PEDIATRIC ONCOLOGY 4(2):99-103, 1978.

Hypertension and oral contraceptives [editorial]. BRITISH MEDICAL JOURNAL 1(6127):1570-1571, June 17, 1978.

—, by B. Westerholm. LAKARTIDNINGEN 75(37):3164, September 13, 1978.

Hypertension due to hormonal contraceptives and estrogens, by W. Oelkers. MUNCHENER MEDIZINISCHE WOCHENSCHRIFT 120(13):439-444, March 31, 1978.

The importance of risk factors in cerebrovascular processes while taking oral contraceptives, by W. Holtmann, et al. MUENCHENER MEDIZINISCHE WOCHENSCHRIFT 119(48):1557-1560, December 2, 1977.

In vitro uptake of oral contraceptive steroids by magnesium trisilicate, by S. A. Khalil, et al. JOURNAL OF PHARMACEUTICAL SCIENCES 67(2):287-289, February, 1978.

The incidence of cervical cancer and duration of oral contraceptive use, by E. Peritz, et al. AMERICAN JOURNAL OF EPIDEMIOLOGY 106(6):462-469, December, 1977.

Incidence of depressive symptoms in users of the oral contraceptive, by O. Fleming, et al. BRITISH JOURNAL OF PSYCHIATRY 132:431-440, May, 1978.

Incidence of hypertension in the course of taking contraceptives, by F. Wessels, et al. VERHANDLUNGEN DER DEUTSCHEN GESELLSCHAFT FUER KREISLAUF-FORSCHUNG 43:242, 1977.

Independence of oral contraceptive-induced changes in glucose tolerance and plasma cortisol levels, by E. J. Cornish, et al. CLINICAL AND EXPERIMENTAL PHARMACY AND PHYSIOLOGY 2(6):589-592, November-December, 1975.

Inefficiency of high doses of urokinase in a massive pulmonary embolism. Possible role of an oral contraceptive [letter], by A. Grand, et al. NOUVELLE PRESSE MEDICALE 7(27):2391- July 1-8, 1978.

Influence of oral contraceptive agents on the concentration of amino acids in leukocytes of supposedly healthy women, by P. Tarallo, et al. CLINICA CHIMICA ACTA 81(3):283-286, December 15, 1977.

The influence of thiamin deficiency on the metabolism of the oral contraceptive mestranol [3-methoxy-17-ethynyl-1,35(10)-estratien-17 beta-ol] by female rat liver enzymes, by A. E. Wade, et al. STEROIDS 30(2):275-283, August, 1977.

Inhibition of hepatic demethylation of aminopyrine by oral contraceptive steroids in humans, by R. Herz, et al. EUROPEAN JOURNAL OF CLINICAL INVESTIGATION 8(1):27-30, February, 1978.

Intracranial phlebothrombosis and oral contraceptives: report of 2 cases and review of the literature, by R. Navarro Izquierdo, et al. REVISTA CLINICA EXPANOLA 148(5):479-482, March 15, 1978.

Intracranial venous thrombosis, by J. H. Mateos-Gòmez, et al. GACETA MEDICA DE MEXICO 114(1):43-47, January, 1978.

Intravenous glucose tolerance after 18 months on progestogen or combination-type oral contraceptive, by J. A. Goldman. ISRAEL JOURNAL OF MEDICAL SCIENCES

14(3):324-327, March, 1978.

Ischemic disease of the small bowel and colon associated with oral contraceptives, by G. G. Ghahremani, et al. GASTROINTESTINAL RADIOLOGY 2(3):221-228, December 20, 1977.

Large migrating hepatic adenoma associated with use of oral contraceptives, by I. Weissman, et al. ILLINOIS MEDICAL JOURNAL 152(6):483-486, December, 1977.

Live tumors and oral contraceptives, by D. R. Kent, et al. INTERNATIONAL JOURNAL OF GYNAECOLOGY AND OBSTETRICS 15(2):137-142, 1977.

The liver and oral contraceptives, by P. Berthelot. ACQUISITIONS MEDICALES RECENTES :33-37, 1977.

Liver-cell adenomas associated with use of oral contraceptives, by H. A. Edmondson, et al. NEW ENGLAND JOURNAL OF MEDICINE 294:470-472, February 26, 1976.

Liver cell carcinoma associated with oral contraceptives, by J. Leclère, et al. ANNALES D'ENDOCRINOLOGIE 38(6):361-362, 1977.

Liver lesions and oral contraceptives steroids, by G. H. Barrows, et al. JOURNAL OF TOXICOLOGY AND ENVIRONMENTAL HEALTH 3(1-2):219-230, September, 1977.

Liver lesions caused by oral contraceptives. I. Contraceptive-induced hepatosis in 85 women: recommendations for diagnosis and prophylaxis, by J. D. Fengler, et al. DEUTSCHE GESUNDHEITWESEN 33(27):1251-1256, 1978.

Liver tumors and oral contraceptives, by A. H. Ansari, et al. FERTILITY AND STERILITY 29(6):643-650, June,

1978.

Liver tumours associated with the use of contraceptive pills, by J. Terblanche. SOUTH AFRICAN MEDICAL JOURNAL 53(12):439-442, March 25, 1978.

Malignant arterial hypertension and oral contraceptives. Apropos of 4 cases, by Y. Saint-Hillier, et al. JOURNAL D'UROLOGIE ET DE NEPHROLOGIE 83(9):673-679, September, 1977.

Malignant melanoma and oral contraceptive use among women in California, by V. Beral, et al. BRITISH JOURNAL OF CANCER 36(6):804-809, December, 1977.

Mammary nodules in beagle dogs administered investigational oral contraceptive steroids, by R. C. Giles, et al. JOURNAL OF THE NATIONAL CANCER INSTITUTE 60(6): 1351-1364, June, 1978.

Mammary nodules in beagle dogs administered steroids in dogs, by J. H. Weikel, Jr., et al. JOURNAL OF TOXICOLOGY AND ENVIRONMENTAL HEALTH 3(1-2): 167-177, September, 1977.

Megaloblastic anema caused by folic acid deficiency following administration of oral contraceptives. Description of 2 clinical cases, by G. Bianco, et al. MINERVA MEDICA 69(22):1513-1516, May 5, 1978.

Megestrol acetate concentrations in plasma and milk during administration of an oral contraceptive containing 4 mg megestrol acetate to nursing women, by S. Nilsson, et al. CONTRACEPTION 16(6):615-624, December, 1977.

Mesenteric vascular occlusion associated with oral contraceptive use, by T. J. Lescher, et al. ARCHIVES OF SURGERY 112(10):1231-1232, October, 1977.

Metabolic studies under administration of oral contraceptives. A review, by S. Hauschildt. ZEITSCHRIFT FUER ERNAEHRUNGSWISSENSCHAFT 17(1):1-18, March, 1978.

Metabolism of an oral tryptophan load by women and evidence against the induction of tryptophan pyrrolase by oral contraceptives, by A. R. Green, et al. BRITISH JOURNAL OF CLINICAL PHARMACOLOGY 5(3): 233-241, March, 1978.

Methionine metabolism and vitamin B6 status in women using oral contraceptives, by L. T. Miller, et al. AMERICAN JOURNAL OF CLINICAL NUTRITION 31(4): 619-625, April, 1978.

Microrheological studies in healthy subjects. Effect of cigarette smoke and oral contraceptives on erythrocyte flexibility, by H. G. Grigoleit, et al. DEUTSCH MEDIZINSCHE WOCHENSCHRIFT 103(8):339-341, February, 1978.

Milder genital herpes with the pill. MEDICAL WORLD NEWS 18:90, April 4, 1977.

Mortality among oral-contraceptive users. Royal College of General Practitioners' Oral Contraception Study, by V. Beral. LANCET 2(8041):727-731, October 8, 1977.

Mortality and oral contraceptives [editorial]. BRITISH MEDICAL JOURNAL 2(6092):918, October 8, 1977.

Mortality associated with the pill [editorial]. LANCET 2(8041):747-748, October 8, 1977.

—. LANCET 2(8043):879-880, October 22, 1977.

—. LANCET 2(8044):921-922, October 29, 1977.

—. LANCET 2(8046):1023-1024, November 12, 1977.

—, by J. R. Heiby. LANCET 2(8049):1172-1173, December 3, 1977.

—, by M. P. Vessey, et al. LANCET 1(8055):98, January 14, 1978.

Mortality during the use of oral steroid contraceptives—new British studies, by J. Presl. CESKOSLOVENSKA GYNE-KOLOGIE 43(2):134-135, April, 1978.

Mortality in women on oral contraceptives [letter]. LAN-CET 2(8041):757-758, October 8, 1977.

—. LANCET 2(8051):1276-1277, December 17, 1977.

Mortality rates with oral contraception [editorial]. NEW ZEALAND MEDICAL JOURNAL 86(601):525, December 14, 1977.

Mortality risk associated with the use of oral contraceptives, by A. K. Jain. STUDIES IN FAMILY PLANNING 8:50-54, March, 1977.

Multiple nodular hyperplasia of liver associated with oral contraceptives, by G. Roschlau. ZENTRALBLATT FUER ALLGEMEINE PATHOLOGIE UND PATHO-LOGISCHE ANATOMIE 121(6):517-521, 1977.

Myocardial infarct and oral contraception, by A. Barrillon, et al. ARCHIVES DE MALADIES DU COEUR ET DES VAISSEAUX 70(9):921-928, September, 1977.

—, by M. Baudet, et al. ANNALES DE MEDICINE IN-TERNE 129(6-7):459-462, June-July, 1978.

Myocardial infarction in women [editorial], by M. O'Rourke. MEDICAL JOURNAL OF AUSTRALIA 1(4):199,

February 25, 1978.

Myometrial response to a long-acting vasopressin analogue in early pregnancy, by M. Akerlund, et al. BRITISH JOURNAL OF OBSTETRICS AND GYNAECOLOGY 85(7):525-529, July, 1978.

NIH research findings: when conception occurs one month after discontinuing the pill, twins are more likely. JAMA: JOURNAL OF THE AMERICAN MEDICAL ASSOCIATION 239(18):1850, May 5, 1978.

Neurologic accidents and oral contraceptives, by J. C. Gautier. SCHWEIZER ARCHIV FUER NEUROLOGIE, NEUROCHIRURGIE UND PSYCHIATRIE 120(2):335-338, 1977.

Nine year follow-up of a case of benign liver cell adenoma related to oral contraceptives, by S. Kay. CANCER 40(4):1759-1760, October, 1977.

The occupational hazards of formulating oral contraceptives —a survey of plant employees, by J. M. Harrington, et al. ARCHIVES OF ENVIRONMENTAL HEALTH 33(1): 12-15, January-February, 1978.

Ocular complications of oral contraceptives, by J. R. Wood. OPHTHALMIC SEMINARS 2(4):371-402, 1977.

Oestrogen-associated disease of the renal microcirculation, by K. Jones, et al. CLINICAL SCIENCE AND MOLECULAR MEDICINE 52(1):33-42, January, 1977.

Oestrogen content of oral contraceptives [letter], by M. Briggs, et al. LANCET 2(8050):1233, December 10, 1977.

Ophthalmological complications after oral contraceptives, by L. Zeydler-Grzedzielewska, et al. KLINIKA OCZNA

48(5):239-242, May, 1978.

Oral contraception after 40: what is said, what is known, by H. Rozenbaum. CONCOURS MEDICAL 100(12):2051-2054, March 25, 1978.

Oral contraception and fertility return. NURSES DRUG ALERT 2:59, June 7, 1978.

Oral contraception. Physiologic and pathologic effects, by W. C. Andrews. OBSTETRICS AND GYNECOLOGY ANNUAL 7:325-351, 1978.

Oral contraceptive exposure in a male with a pituitary micro-adenoma: a case report, by G. C. Buchanan, et al. CONTRACEPTION 16(4):351-356, October, 1977.

Oral-contraceptive-induced benign liver tumors—the magnitude of the problem [letter], by H. Jick, et al. JAMA: JOURNAL OF THE AMERICAN MEDICAL ASSOCIATION 240(9):828-829, September 1, 1978.

Oral contraceptive induced hypertension simulating primary aldosteronism, by C. R. Raj, et al. WISCONSIN MEDICAL JOURNAL 77(5):49-50, May, 1978.

Oral contraceptive potencies and side effects, by G. S. Berger, et al. OBSTETRICS AND GYNECOLOGY 51(5):545-547, May, 1978.

Oral contraceptive steroids and thrombophlebitis, by A. W. Diddle, et al. JOURNAL OF THE TENNESSEE MEDICAL ASSOCIATION 71(1):22-26, January, 1978.

Oral contraceptive therapy and benign hepatic lesions in females, by J. Zerner, et al. JOURNAL OF THE MAINE MEDICAL ASSOCIATION 69(6):161-164, June, 1978.

Oral-contraceptive use and bacteriuria in a community-based

study, by D. Evans, et al. NEW ENGALND JOURNAL OF MEDICINE 299(10):536-537, September 7, 1978.

Oral contraceptive use and other factors in the standard glucose tolerance test, by J. Wingerd, et al. DIABETES 26(11):1024-1033, November, 1977.

Oral contraceptive use and venous thromboembolism: absence of an effect of smoking, by D. H. Lawson, et al. BRITISH MEDICAL JOURNAL 2(6089):729-730, September 17, 1977.

Oral contraceptive use: association with frequency of hospitalization and chronic disease risk indicator, by R. Hoover, et al. AMERICAN JOURNAL OF PUBLIC HEALTH 68:335-341, April, 1978.

Oral contraceptives and ANA positivity [letter], by J. M. Kennedy. ARTHRITIS AND RHEUMATISM 20(8): 1567-1569, November-December, 1977.

Oral contraceptives and birth defects, by K. J. Rothman, et NEW ENGLAND JOURNAL OF MEDICINE 299(10): 522-524, September 7, 1978.

Oral contraceptives and breast disease. An epidemiological study, by J. L. Kelsey, et al. AMERICAN JOURNAL OF EPIDEMIOLOGY 107(3):236-244, March, 1978.

Oral contraceptives and cholangiocarcinoma [letter], by E. F. Ellis, et al. LANCET 1(8057):207, January 28, 1978.

Oral contraceptives and emotional state, by A. Worsley, et al. JOURNAL OF PSYCHOSOMATIC RESEARCH 22(1): 13-15, 1978.

Oral contraceptives and endometrial and cervical cancer, by K. S. Moghissi. JOURNAL OF TOXICOLOGY AND ENVIRONMENTAL HEALTH 3(1-2):243-265, September,

1977.

Oral contraceptives and focal nodular hyperplasia of the liver. Two case reports with electron-microscopic studies, by M. Balazs, et al. ACTA HEPATO-GASTROENTEROLO-GICA 25(2):111-118, April, 1978.

Oral contraceptives and liver damage under experimental conditions, by M. Beskid, et al. MATERIA MEDICA POLONA 9(3):210-215, July-September, 1977.

Oral contraceptives and malignant hepatoma [letter], by F. Tigano, et al. LANCET 2(7978):196, July 24, 1976.

Oral contraceptives and myocardial infarct, by J. P. Boun-houre, et al. ARCHIVES DE MALADIES DU COEUR ET DES VAISSEAUX 70(7):765-771, July, 1977.

Oral contraceptives and myocardial infarction [editorial], by S. Shapiro. NEW ENGLAND JOURNAL OF MEDI-CINE 293:195-196, July 24, 1975.

Oral contraceptives and nonfatal myocardial infarction, by H. Jick, et al. JAMA: JOURNAL OF THE AMERICAN MEDICAL ASSOCIATION 239(14):1403-1406, April 3, 1978.

Oral contraceptives and nonfatal stroke in healthy young women, by H. Jick, et al. ANNALS OF INTERNAL MEDICINE 89(1):58-60, July, 1978.

Oral contraceptives and reduced risk of benign breast disease, by H. Ory, et al. NEW ENGLAND JOURNAL OF MEDI-CINE 294:419-422, February 19, 1976.

Oral contraceptives and riboflavin nutriture, by K. Guggen-heim, et al. INTERNATIONAL JOURNAL FOR VITA-MIN AND NUTRITION RESEARCH 47(3):234-235, 1977.

Oral contraceptives and risk of benign tumors of the breast: recent data from the literature, by A. Simard. UNION MEDICALE DU CANADA 106(8):1115-1119, August, 1977.

Oral contraceptives and subarachnoid haemorrhage [letter], by R. Finn, et al. LANCET 2(8089):582, September 9, 1978.

Oral contraceptives and surgical intervention, by H. Rozenbaum. CONCOURS MEDICAL 99(40):6098-6099, October 29, 1977.

Oral contraceptives and their influence on porphyrin concentrations in erythocytes and urine, by A. Kansky, et al. DERMATOLOGICA 157(3):181-185, 1978.

Oral contraceptives and their relationship to cancer of the breast: a medicolegal problem, by R. K. Clasper. LEGAL MEDICINE ANNUAL :297-313, 1977.

Oral contraceptives and thromboembolic disease, by J. A. Hall, et al. JOURNAL OF THE INDIANA STATE MEDICAL ASSOCIATION 71(4):413-414, April, 1978.

Oral contraceptives and thromboembolism, by K. Sato, et al. KOKYU TO JUNKAN 26(3):212-220, March, 1978.

Oral contraceptives and vitamin B 6, by L. Ovesen. UGESKRIFT FOR LAEGER 140(29):1733-1735, July 17, 1978.

Oral contraceptives—another look [editorial], by P. E. Sartwell. AMERICAN JOURNAL OF PUBLIC HEALTH 68(4):323-325, April, 1978.

Oral contraceptives, blood clotting and thrombosis, by L. Poller. BRITISH MEDICAL BULLETIN 34(2):151-156, May, 1978.

Oral contraceptives, hypertension and nephrosclerosis, by J. Girndt. FORTSCHRITTE DU MEDIZIN 96(7):327-332, February 16, 1978.

Oral contraceptives: a possible association with liver tumors and endometrial carcinoma, by F. W. Hanson. ADVANCES IN PLANNED PARENTHOOD 12(2):86-97, 1977.

Oral contraceptives, smoking and nodular hyperplasia of the liver, by J. Lough, et al. CANADIAN MEDICAL ASSOCIATION JOURNAL 118(4):403-404, February 18, 1978.

Oral contraceptives, smoking, migraine, and food alergy [letter], by E. C. Grant. LANCET 2(8089):581-582, September 9, 1978.

Oral contraceptives, thromboembolic disease, and hypertension: a review, by A. Ferguson. JOURNAL OF THE MEDICAL ASSOCIATION OF THE STATE OF ALABAMA 47(3):49-55, September, 1977.

Pigmented skin lesions in babies born to underweight former oral-contraceptive users [letter], by S. Harlap. LANCET 2(8079):39, July 1, 1978.

"Pill"—associated liver tumor warrants abstinence from pregnancy. NURSES DRUG ALERT 2:95-96, August, 1978.

Pill brochure stress smoking warning. FDA CONSUMER 12:3-4, March, 1978.

Pill-users' strokes are different; angiograms show distinct pattern of abnormalities involving small arteries. MEDICAL WORLD NEWS 18:89, April 4, 1977.

Pill wanes? ECONOMIST 267:26, April 15, 1978.

Pituitary response to LHRH stimulation in women on oral contraceptives, by L. W. Wan, et al. CONTRACEPTION 17(1):1-7, January, 1978.

Plasma concentrations of ethinylestradiol and D-norgestrel during two immediate postabortal oral contraceptive cycles, by P. Lähteenmäki, et al. CONTRACEPTION 17(1):9-17, January, 1978.

Plasma prolactin levels and contraception: oral contraceptives and intrauterine devices, by W. N. Spellacy, et al. CONTRACEPTION 17(1):71-77, January, 1978.

Possible immediate hypersensitivity reaction of the nasal mucosa to oral contraceptives, by Z. Pelikan. ANNALS OF ALLERGY 40(3):211-219, March, 1978.

Pregnancy, oral hormonal contraception and lipid bile composition, by B. Dökert, et al. DEUTSCH GESUND-HEITSWESEN 33(25):1153-1155, 1978.

Primary carcinoma of the liver and long-term administration of oral contraceptives followed by pregnancy, by M. Balazs, et al. DEUTSCHE MEDIZINISCHE WOCHEN-SCHRIFT 102(41):1472-1474, October 14, 1972.

Primary liver carcinoma; do sex hormones play a role in its pathogenesis? by G. J. Houwert, et al. NEDERLANDS TIJDSCHRIFT VOOR GENEESKUNDE 122(27): 965-970, July 8, 1978.

Primary liver tumors and oral contraceptives. Results of a survey, by J. Vana, et al. JAMA: JOURNAL OF THE AMERICAN MEDICAL ASSOCIATION 238(20):2154-2158, November 14, 1977.

Prolactin and thyrotropin after stimulation by throtropin releasing hormone a study under long-term administration of oral contraceptives, by O. Bellmann, et al. AR-

CHIV FUR GYNAEKOLOGIE 225(1):31-42, February 22, 1978.

Psychiatric aspects of oral contraceptive use, by D. V. Sheehan, et al. PSYCHIATRIC ANNALS 6:81, October, 1976.

Pulmonary embolism in a female adolescent with sickle cell trait and oral contraceptive use, by E. P. Hargus, et al. AMERICAN JOURNAL OF OBSTETRICS AND GYNE-COLOGY 129(6):697-698, November 15, 1977.

Radioimmanoassay study of neurophysins in human plasma, by A. C. Reinharz, et al. ACTA ENDOCRINOLOGICA 88(3):455-464, July, 1978.

Radioimmunologic testosterone determination: technic and diagnostic use, by R. Thun, et al. SCHWEIZER ARCHIV FUR TIERHEILKUNDE 120(4):205-212, April, 1978.

A randomized comparison of the Ypsilon-Y and Lippes loop D intrauterine devices in parous women, by P. F. Brenner, et al. OBSTETRICS AND GYNECOLOGY 51(3):327-329, March, 1978.

Recommendations from the findings by the RCGP oral contraception study on the mortality risks of oral contraceptive users, by E. V. Kuenssberg, et al. BRITISH MEDICAL JOURNAL 2(6092):947, October 8, 1977.

Reduced high-density lipoprotein in women aged 40-41 using oral contraceptives. Consultation Bureau Heart Project, by A. C. Arntzenius, et al. LANCET 1(8076):1221-1223, June 10, 1978.

Reduced uterine reponse to PGF2alpha under oral contraceptives, by S. Shaala, et al. PROSTAGLANDINS 14(3):523-533, September, 1977.

The relation of body weight to side effects assocaited with oral contraceptives, by P. P. Talwar, et al. BRITISH MEDICAL JOURNAL 6077:1637-1638, June 25, 1977.

Relations between human choriongonadotropic hormone (HCG) titres in urine and degree of pregnancy risk, by J. Pakan, et al. BRATISLAVSKE LEKARSKE LISTY 69(2):190-194, February, 1978.

Release of copper from copper-bearing intrauterine contraceptive devices, by E. Chantler, et al. BRITISH MEDICAL JOURNAL 6082:288-291, July 30, 1977.

Report of the committee set up by the executive of the Irish Medical Association to advise on the hazards and side-effects of ovulation suppressants. IRISH MEDICAL JOURNAL 17(2 Suppl):1-10, February 17, 1978.

Results of in vitro sperm penetration tests in cervical mucus under takings of the sequential oral contraceptive ovanon and sequilar, by K. Bregulla, et al. ARCHIV FUR GYNAEKOLOGIE 223(3):187-193, October 28, 1977.

Rheumatoid arthritis and oral contraceptives [letter], by A. Linos, et al. LANCET 1(8069):871, April 22, 1978.

Riboflavin deficiency in women taking oral contraceptive agents, by L. J. Newman, et al. AMERICAN JOURNAL OF CLINICAL NUTRITION 31(2):247-249, February, 1978.

The risk of post-pill amenorrhea: a preliminary report from the Menstruation and Reproduction History Research Program, by G. S. Berger, et al. INTERNATIONAL JOURNAL OF GYNAECOLOGY AND OBSTETRICS 15(2):125-127, 1977.

Risks of oral contraception [editorial]. SOUTH AFRICAN MEDICAL JOURNAL 52(21):827, November 12, 1977.

Secondary amenorrhea associated with the use of oral contraceptive steroids, by A. W. Diddle, et al. JOURNAL OF THE TENNESSEE MEDICAL ASSOCIATION 71(7):495-499, July, 1978.

Serious complications of oral contraception in insulin-dependent diabetics, by J. M. Steel, et al. CONTRACEPTION 17(4):291-295, April, 1978.

Serum concentration of bile acids in relation to the normal menstrual cycle the administration or oral contraceptives, and pregnancy, by D. E. Jones, et al. AMERICAN JOURNAL OF OBSTETRICS AND GYNECOLOGY 130(5): 593, March 1, 1978.

Serum concentrations of prolactin, growth hormone, and alpha-fetoprotein under long-term administration of an oral contraceptive containing cyproterone acete, by O. Bellmann, et al. GEBURTSHILFE UND FRAUENHEILKUNDE 38(7):549-554, July, 1978.

Serum high-density-lipoprotein cholesterol in women using oral contraceptives, estrogens and progestins, by D. D. Bradley, et al. NEW ENGLAND JOURNAL OF MEDICINE 299(1):17-20, July 6, 1978.

Serum lipids and lipoproteins during treatment with oral contraceptives containing natural and synthetic oestrogens. A controlled double-blind investigation, by E. Bostofte, et al. ACTA ENDOCRINOLOGICA 87(4): 855-864, April, 1978.

Serum vitamin B12, serum and red cell folates, vitamin B12 and folic acid binding proteins in women taking oral contraceptives, by S. Areekul, et al. SOUTHEAST ASIAN JOURNAL OF TROPICAL MEDICINE AND PUBLIC HEALTH 8(4):480-485, December, 1977.

Short-term and prolonged treatment with oral contraceptives

445

and liver function, by A. Kulcsar, et al. ARZNEIMIT-TEL-FORSCHUNG 27(9):1694-1697, 1977.

Should one systematically do a liver puncture biopsy during a laparotomy when the patient takes oral contraceptives? [letter], by G. Benhamou, et al. NOUVELLE PRESSE MEDICALE 7(19):1652, May 13, 1978.

Simultaneous determination using gas chromatography of mestranol and norethisterone in estrogen-progestins combination for oral use, by G. Moretti, et al. BOLLE-TINO CHIMICO FARMACEUTICO 116(8):463-472, August, 1977.

Small-bowel ischaemia and the contraceptive pill [editorial]. BRITISH MEDICAL JOURNAL 1(6104):4, January 7, 1978.

State of the blood coagulation and anticoagulation system in women taking oral contraceptives, by L. V. Terskaia, et al. AKUSHERSTVO I GINEKOLOGIIA (12):41-43, December, 1977.

Stopping oral contraceptives, by J. Cohen. CONCOURS MEDICAL 100(5):779-780, February 4, 1978.

Storage of proteins in the rough endoplasmic reticulum of human hepatocytes in a patient with normal blood proteins, on oral contraceptives, by A. Porte, et al. VIRCHOWS ARCHIV. ABT. A. PATHOLOGISCHE ANATO-MIE-PATHOLOGY 375(3):241-248, September 28, 1977.

Sudden death from coronary disease in younger women, by H. Althoff. MEDIZINISCHE KLINIK 72(44):1871-1879, November 4, 1977.

Sydenham's chorea: case report of a diagnostic dilemma, by M. P. Weissberg, et al. AMERICAN JOURNAL OF PSY-

CHOLOGY 135:607-609, May, 1978.

3-month therapy cycles for oral contraception? [letter] , by C. Lauritzen. DEUTSCHE MEDIZINISCHE WOCHEN-SCHRIFT 102(51):1891, December 23, 1977.

Three-year prospective study of carbohydrate metabolism in women using ovulen, by W. N. Spellacy, et al. SOUTH-ERN MEDICAL JOURNAL 70(10):1188-1190, October, 1977.

Treatment of post-pill amenorrhea, by R. P. Dickey. INTER-NATIONAL JOURNAL OF GYNAECOLOGY AND OB-STETRICS 15(2):128-132, 1977.

Tryptophan metabolism, oral contraceptives, and pyridoxine [letter] . LANCET 1(8065):661-662, March 25, 1978.

Twins after the pill [letter] , by W. H. James. NEW ENG-LAND JOURNAL OF MEDICINE 297(18):1015, November 3, 1977.

Ultrastructural-morphometric investigations on liver biopsies —the influence of oral contraceptives on the human liver, by K. Stahl, et al. ARCHIV FUR GYNAEKOLO-GIE 223(3):205-211, October 28, 1977.

Uncomplicated pregnancy following oral contraceptive-induced liver hepatoma, by J. H. Check, et al. OBSTE-TRICS AND GYNECOLOGY 52(1 Suppl):28S-29S, July, 1978.

Urinary D-glucaric acid and oral contraceptives, by P. M. Stevens, et al. BRITISH JOURNAL OF CLINICAL PHARMACOLOGY 5(6):535-536, June, 1978.

Use of oral contraceptives, cigarette smoking, and risk of subarachnoid haemorrhage, by D. B. Petitti, et al. LAN-CET 2(8083):234-235, July 29, 1978.

Vertigo and the pill [letter] , by J. Siegler. BRITISH MEDI-
CAL JOURNAL 2(6099):1416, November 26, 1977.

Vitamin E status of young women on combined-type oral
contraceptives, by C. C. Tangney, et al. CONTRACEP-
TION 17(6):499-512, June, 1978.

When patients "can't" take the pill, by W. S. Freeman.
AMERICAN FAMILY PHYSICIAN 17(1):143-149,
January, 1978.

Who can't take the pill? by M. Jones. GUARDIAN p. 9,
August 30, 1978.

Why blame the pill? [letter] , by H. A. Mackay. BRITISH
MEDICAL JOURNAL 1(6120):1141-1142, April 29,
1978.

Workers sick from pill. CHEMICAL WEEK 120:20, April
13, 1977.

CONTRACEPTIVES: FEMALE: ORAL: COMPLICATIONS:
PSYCHOLOGICAL
Effect of oral contraceptives on the psyche and on sexuality,
by G. Nahrendorf, et al. ZENTRALBLATT FUER GY-
NAEKOLOGIE 100(10):632-637, 1978.

CONTRACEPTIVES: FEMALE: ORAL: ECONOMICS
The pill and the rising costs of fertility control, by J. Blake.
SOCIAL BIOLOGY 24(4):267-280, Winter, 1977.

CONTRACEPTIVES: FEMALE: ORAL: EDUCATION
Effectiveness of a programmed instruction module on oral
contraceptives, by M. K. Guimei. NURSING RE-
SERACH 26(6):452-455, November-December, 1977.

CONTRACEPTIVES: FEMALE: ORAL: FAILURE
Ectopic pregnancies during use of low-dose progestogens for
oral contraception, by P. Liukko, et al. CONTRACEP-

TION 16(6):575-580, December, 1977.

Ectopic pregnancy and the pill [letter], by D. B. Weiss, et al. LANCET 2(7978):196-197, July 24, 1976.

"Patient failure" as a reliability model for the "minipill": a clinical study, by S. Nummi. CURRENT MEDICAL RESEARCH AND OPINION 5(5):406-411, 1978.

CONTRACEPTIVES: FEMALE: ORAL: HISTORY
History of the first oral contraceptive, by V. A. Drill. JOURNAL OF TOXICOLOGY AND ENVIRONMENTAL HEALTH 3(1-2):133-138, September, 1977.

Story of the pill, by K. S. Davis. AMERICAN HERITAGE 29:80-91, August, 1978.

CONTRACEPTIVES: FEMALE: ORAL: LAWS
Distribution of oral contraceptives: legal changes and new concepts of preventive care, by R. J. Cook. AMERICAN JORUNAL OF PUBLIC HEALTH 66:590+, June, 1976.

Drugs: the pill and MI, by M. Fisk. TRIAL 14(6):22-23, June, 1978.

CONTRACEPTIVES: FEMALE: ORAL: METABOLISM
Comparative metabolism of 17alpha-ethynyl steroids used in oral contraceptives, by R. E. Ranney. JOURNAL OF TOXICOLOGY AND ENVIRONMENTAL HEALTH 3(1-2):139-166, September, 1977.

CONTRACEPTIVES: FEMALE: ORAL: MORTALITY
Excess mortality and the pill [editorial], by R. P. Shearman. MEDICAL JOURNAL OF AUSTRALIA 1(2):75-76, January 28, 1978.

Excess mortality and the pill, by H. M. Carey. MEDICAL JOURNAL OF AUSTRALIA 1(3):153-154, February 11, 1978.

Mortality during the use of oral steroid contraceptives—new British studies, by J. Presl. CESKOSLOVENSKA GYNE-KOLOGIE 43(2):134-135, April, 1978.

Mortality in women on oral contraceptives [letter]. LANCET 2(8051):1276-1277, December 17, 1977.

Mortality rates with oral contraception [editorial]. NEW ZEALAND MEDICAL JOURNAL 86(601):525, December 14, 1977.

Recommendations from the findings by the RCGP oral contraception study on the mortality risks of oral contraceptive users, by E. V. Kuenssberg, et al. BRITISH MEDICAL JOURNAL 2(6092):947, October 8, 1977.

CONTRACEPTIVES: FEMALE: ORAL: PHARMACOLOGY
Binding of norgestrel to receptor proteins in the human endometrium and myometrium, by J. P. Uniyal, et al. JOURNAL OF STEROID BIOCHEMISTRY 8(11): 1183-1188, November, 1977.

Bioavailability of norethindrone in human subjects, by R. A. Okerholm, et al. EUROPEAN JOURNAL OF CLINICAL PHARMACOLOGY 13(1):35-39, March 17, 1978.

Biochemical effects of treatment with oral contraceptive steroids on the dopaminergic system of the rat, by S. Algeri, et al. NEUROENDOCRINOLOGY 22(4):343-351, 1976.

Biochemical studies on oxytocinase activities of human endometrium, uterine fluid and plasma, by S. Ganguly, et al. INDIAN JOURNAL OF MEDICAL RESEARCH 66(1):43-48, July, 1977.

Biological properties of interceptive agents from Aristolochia indica Linn, by A. Pakrashi, et al. INDIAN JOURNAL OF MEDICAL RESEARCH 66(6):991-998, December, 1977.

CONTRACEPTIVES: FEMALE: ORAL: THERAPEUTIC USE
A controlled study of the effect of oral contraceptives on migraine, by R. E. Ryan, Sr. HEADACHE 17(6):250-252, January, 1978.

Lowering of H.D.L. cholesterol by oral contraceptives [letter], by S. Roössner. LANCET 2(8083):269, July 29, 1978.

Reduction in incidence of rheumatoid arthritis associated with oral contraceptives. Royal College of General Practitioners' Oral Contraception Study. LANCET 1(8064): 569-571, March 18, 1978.

The use of contraceptive pills in treatment of recurrent aphthous ulceration, by S. Sadek, et al. EGYPTIAN DENTAL JOURNAL 21(1):37-42, January, 1975.

CONTRACEPTIVES: FEMALE: POST-COITAL
Biological profile of Centchroman—a new post-coital contraceptive, by V. P. Kamboj, et al. INDIAN JOURNAL OF EXPERIMENTAL BIOLOGY 15(12):1144-1150, December, 1977.

Centchroman—a post-coital contraceptive agent, by N. Anand, et al. INDIAN JOURNAL OF EXPERIMENTAL BIOLOGY 15(12):1142-1130, December, 1977.

The morning after pill [editorial], by T. Rust. PRAXIS 66(48):1529-1533, November 29, 1977.

Physician notes hazards of DES use to prevent pregnancy [letter], by E. F. Diamond. HOSPITAL PROGRESS 59(3):6-10, March, 1978.

Postcoital contraception—an appraisal, by W. Rinehart. POPULATION REPORTS 9(pt 2):J141-J154, January, 1976.

Postcoital contraception in primates. I. Action mechanism

of a potential postovulatory fertility-inhibiting substance STS 456 in the baboon (Papio hamadryas), by N. P. Goncharov, et al. ZENTRALBLATT FUER GYNAEKOLOGIE 100(5):263-272, 1978.

Post-coital contraception using d1-norgestrel/ethinyl estradiol combination, by R. P. Smith, et al. CONTRACEPTION 17(3):247-252, March, 1978.

Postcoital contraception using a high-dose depot estrogen (Org 369-2) [proceedings], by A. E. Schindler, et al. ARCHIV FUR GYNAEKOLOGIE 224(1-4):29, July 29, 1977.

Post-coital contraceptive & uterotrophic effects of Centchroman in mice, by S. R. Munshi, et al. INDIAN JOURNAL OF EXPERIMENTAL BIOLOGY 15(12):1151-1153, December, 1977.

Screening of substituted nitrobenzene derivatives as postcoital antifertility agents, by S. K. Garg. INDIAN JOURNAL OF MEDICAL RESEARCH 66(6):987-990, December, 1977.

CONTRACEPTIVES: FEMALE: POST-COITAL: COMPLICATIONS
Action of d-norgestrel (post-coital and mindosis) on the content of the diesterase enzyme in the human endometrium, by R. Nicholson, et al. OBSTETRICIA Y GINECOLOGIA LATINO-AMERICANAS 34(11-12):406-409, November-December, 1976.

Postcoital hormonal contraception: uses, risks, and abuses, by A. A. Yuzpe. INTERNATIONAL JOURNAL OF GYNAECOLOGY AND OBSTETRICS 15(2):133-136, 1977.

Post-pill amenorrhoea [letter], by K. W. Hancock, et al. BRITISH MEDICAL JOURNAL 1(6104):45, January 7,

1978.

—, by R. P. Shearman. BRITISH MEDICAL JOURNAL
2(6099):1414, November 26, 1977.

Post-"pill" amenorrhoea—cause or coincidence? by H. S.
Jacobs, et al. BRITISH MEDICAL JOURNAL 2(6092):
940-942, October 8, 1977.

CONTRACEPTIVES: FEMALE: SUPPOSITORY
Contraception with a new vaginal suppository (Patentex
Oval), by T. Weber, et al. UGESKRIFT FOR LAEGER
139(40):2397-2398, October 3, 1977.

Contraceptive sponge fights VD, too. MEDICAL WORLD
NEWS 18:29, October 17, 1977.

Identification of ejaculate derived propylamine found in col-
lagen sponge contraceptives, by C. D. Eskelson, et al.
BIOMEDICAL MASS SPECTROMETRY 5(3):238-242,
March, 1978.

Plasma prostaglandin concentration and abortifacient effectiveness of a single insertion of a 3 mg 15(S)-methyl-
prostaglandin F2a methyl ester vaginal suppository, by
C. A. Ballard. CONTRACEPTION 17(4):383-391, April,
1978.

CONTRACEPTIVES: FEMALE: TECHNIQUES
Family planning. Contraception: foams, mechanical devices.
Part 1, by R. A. Hatcher, et al. PERINATAL CARE 2:
21-23+, March, 1978.

CONTRACEPTIVES: HISTORY
Male contraception and family planning: a social and histori-
cal review, by L. Diller, et al. FERTILITY AND STE-
RILITY 28(12):1271-1279, December, 1977.

A rapid history of contraception, by J. H. Leavesley. AUS-TRALIAN FAMILY PHYSICIAN 7(6):730-737, June, 1978.

Trends in contraceptive practice: 1965-1973, by C. F. West-off. FAMILY PLANNING PERSPECTIVES 8:54-57, March-April, 1976.

CONTRACEPTIVES: LAWS
Drugs: depo provera ban appealed, by M. Fisk. TRIAL 4(11):17, November, 1978.

The effect of recent FDA legislation on contraceptive development and safety, by R. P. Dickey. INTERNATIONAL JOURNAL OF GYNAECOLOGY AND OBSTETRICS 15(2):111-114, 1977.

Government response to contraceptive and cosmetic health risks, by J. L. Weaver. WOMEN HEALTH 1(2):5-11, March-April, 1976.

What's new in the law: constitutional law. . .parents' rights, by A. Ashman, et al. AMERICAN BAR ASSOCIATION JOURNAL 64:898-899, June, 1978.

CONTRACEPTIVES: LAWS: HISTORY
Family law: contraception: a brief legal history, by H. F. Pilpel. TRIAL 13(12):16-17+, December, 1977.

CONTRACEPTIVES: MALE
Antifertility mode of action of alpha-chlorohydrin—interaction with glyceraldehyde-3-phosphate-dehydrogenase [proceedings], by N. A. Dickinson, et al. BRITISH JOURNAL OF PHARMACOLOGY 61(3):456P, November, 1977.

The condom and gonorrhoea, by D. Barlow. LANCET 2(8042):811-813, October 15, 1977.

Condom market—what direction now? AMERICAN DRUG-
GIST 177:23-24+, March, 1978.

Condom urinals, by S. D. Lawson, et al. NURSING MIR-
ROR AND MIDWIVES JOURNAL 145(22):19-21,
December 1, 1977.

Effect of chronic administration of testosterone enanthate
on sperm production and plasma testosterone, follicle-
stimulating hormone, and luteinizing hormone levels: a
preliminary evaluation of a possible male contraceptive,
by E. Steinberger, et al. FERTILITY AND STERILITY
28(12):1320-1328, December, 1977.

Male contraception, by L. Westoff. SCIENCE 8(4):12, July,
1976.

Male contraception and family planning: a social and historical review, by L. Diller, et al. FERTILITY AND
STERILITY 28(12):1271-1279, December, 1977.

Problems of male contraception. 2. Male hormonal contraception, post-testicular points of attack, immunization
and enzyme inhibition, by W. B. Schill. FORTSCHRITT
DU MEDIZIN 96(30):1505-1509, August 10, 1978.

Problems with male contraception. 1. Physiological foundations, male contraception (mechanical procedures, contraceptives), by W. B. Schill. FORTSCHRITT DU
MEDIZIN 96(29):1447-1451, August 3, 1978.

Release of copper ions from an intra-vas copper-wire contraceptive device, by K. Srivastava, et al. INDIAN JOUR-
NAL OF PHYSIOLOGY AND PHARMACOLOGY
21(4):387-389, October-December, 1977.

A reversible contraceptive action of some 6-chloro-6-deoxy
sugars in the male rat, by W. C. Ford, et al. JOURNAL
OF REPRODUCTION AND FERTILITY 52(1):153-

157, January, 1978.

Status of male contraception, by J. E. Davis. OBSTETRICS AND GYNECOLOGY ANNUAL 6:355-369, 1977.

Testicular function of gerbil (Meriones hurrianae Jerdon) implanted with a copper wire device in vas deferens, by V. P. Dixit, et al. INDIAN JOURNAL OF EXPERI-MENTAL BIOLOGY 15(8):653-655, August, 1977.

CONTRACEPTIVES: MALE: ORAL
Only women have babies; proposal for a male-child birth pill, by C. B. Luce. NATIONAL REVIEW 30:824-827, July 7, 1978.

CONTRACEPTIVES: MALE: ORAL: COMPLICATIONS
Suppression of serum testosterone concentrations in men by an oral contraceptive preparation, by J. M. Kjeld, et al. BRITISH MEDICAL JOURNAL 2(6097):1261, November 12, 1977.

CONTRACEPTIVES: MALE: REVERSAL
The prospects for new, reversible male contraceptives [review article with ninety references], by W. J. Bremner, et al. NEW ENGLAND JOURNAL OF MEDICINE 295:1111-1117, November 11, 1976.

CONTRACEPTIVES: METHODS
Which contraceptive is right for you? GLAMOUR 76:101+, August, 1978.

CONTRACEPTIVES: MORTALITY AND MORTALITY STA-TISTICS
Mortality among women participating in the Oxford/Family Planning Association contraceptive study, by M. P. Vessey, et al. LANCET 2(8041):731-733, October 8, 1977.

CONTRACEPTIVES: ORAL
A contraceptive that's absorbable [birth control pellet for

men or women]. MEDICAL WORLD NEWS 18:30, June 13, 1977.

Directions for classification and indications of oral contraceptives, by J.P. d'Ernst, et al. PRAXIS 66(50):1620-1627, December 13, 1977.

How to distinguish 2-phase (sequential) steroid contraceptives, by J. Presl. CESKOSLOVENSKA GYNEKOLOGIE 43(3):198-200, April, 1978.

Nurses' health study, by C. F. Belanger, et al. AMERICAN JOURNAL OF NURSING 78:1039-1040, June, 1978.

Yam and the pill, by A. S. Ahl. AMERICAN BIOLOGY TEACHER 40:36-38+, January, 1978.

CONTRACEPTIVES: ORAL: EDUCATION
FDA establishes new patient information requirements for birth control pills. OCCUPATIONAL HEALTH NURSING 26:42-43, April, 1978.

CONTRACEPTIVES: ORAL: HISTORY
Development of the oral contraceptives, by M. C. Chang. AMERICAN JOURNAL OF OBSTETRICS AND GYNECOLOGY 132(2):217-219, September 15, 1978.

CONTRACEPTIVES: PARENTERAL
The case for injectables, by M. Jones. PEOPLE 4(4):25-28, 1977.

Contraception: an antipregnancy vaccine? by J. L. Marx. SCIENCE 200:1258, June 16, 1978.

Depo-provea as a contraceptive measure [letter], by P. B. Combrink. SOUTH AFRICAN MEDICAL JOURNAL 53(11):388, March 18, 1978.

Depo-Provera (injectable contraceptive)—a review, by

457

M. Smith. SCOTTISH MEDICAL JOURNAL 23(3):
223-226, July, 1978.

Experience with medroxyprogesterone acetate (Depo-
Provera) as an injectable contraceptive, by S. P. Ellinas.
INTERNATIONAL JOURNAL OF GYNAECOLOGY
AND OBSTETRICS 15(2):145-149, 1977.

Injectable contraception (medroxyprogesterone acetate) in
rural Bangladesh, by L. Parveen, et al. LANCET 2(8045):
946-948, November 5, 1977.

Larger animal testing of an injectable sustained release fertility control system, by J. D. Gresser, et al. CONTRA-
CEPTION 17(3):253-266, March, 1978.

Multinational comparative clinical evaluation of two long-
acting injectable contraceptive steroids: noresthisterone
oenanthate and medroxyprogesterone acetate. 2. Bleeding patterns and side effects. CONTRACEPTION 17(5):
395-406, May, 1978.

Norethisterone oenanthate as an injectable contraceptive: use
of a modified dose schedule, by O. F. Giwa-Osagie, et al.
BRITISH MEDICAL JOURNAL 1(6128):1660-1662,
June 24, 1978.

Problems with pregnancy vaccination, by R. Pilsworth. NEW
SCIENTIST 77:665-667, March 9, 1978.

Recent progress in the development of long-acting injectables
for control of human fertility, by K. R. Laumas. JOUR-
NAL OF OBSTETRICS AND GYNAECOLOGY OF
INDIA 27(1):11-17, February, 1977.

CONTRACEPTIVES: PARENTERAL: COMPLICATIONS
The effect of subcutaneous administration of oestrogens on
plasma oestrogen levels and tumour incidence in female
rates, by M. A. Blankenstein, et al. EUROPEAN JOUR-

NAL OF CANCER 13(12):1437-1443, December, 1977.

Effect of a subdermal silastic implant containing norethindrone acetate on human lactation, by U. Seth, et al. CONTRACEPTION 16(4):383-398, October, 1977.

The effects of intramuscular injections of 15(S)-15-methyl prostaglandin F2alpha in failed abortions, by N. H. Lauersen, et al. FERTILITY AND STERILITY 28(10): 1044-1047, October, 1977.

FDA denies approval of Depo-Provera in U. S. for contraception; risks outweigh benefits. FAMILY PLANNING PERSPECTIVES 10(3):163, May-June, 1978.

CONTRACEPTIVES: TECHNIQUE
Life table analysis of the effectiveness of contraceptive methods using an APL computer program, by D. L. Cooper, et al. INTERNATIONAL JOURNAL OF BIO-MEDICAL COMPUTING 9(1):1-9, January, 1978.

CONTRACEPTIVES AND CHILDREN
Conjugal role definitions, value of children and contraceptive practice, by P. L. Tobin. SOCIOLOGICAL QUARTERLY 17:314-322, Summer, 1976.

CONTRACEPTIVES AND COLLEGE STUDENTS
Campus contraception bitter pill, by P. Edmonds. NATIONAL CATHOLIC REPORTER 13:5-6, December 24, 1976.

College women's attitudes and expectations concerning menstrual-related changes, by J. Brooks, et al. PSYCHOSOMATIC MEDICINE 39(5):288-298, September-October, 1977.

Contraception and the college freshman, by R. H. Needle, et al. HEALTH EDUCATION 8:23-24, March-April, 1977.

Correlates of contraceptive behavior among unmarried U. S. college students, by K. G. Foreit, et al. STUDIES IN FAMILY PLANNING 9:169-174, June, 1978.

Factors affecting contraceptive practices of high school and college-age students, by R. H. Needle. JOURNAL OF SCHOOL HEALTH 47:340-345, June, 1977.

Factors influencing contraceptive behavior of single college students, by J. W. Maxwell, er al. JOURNAL OF SEX AND MARITAL THERAPY 3(4):265-273, Winter, 1977.

Influence of parents, peers, and partners on the contraceptive use of college men and women, by L. Thompson, et al. JOURNAL OF MARRIAGE AND FAMILY 40:481-492, August, 1978.

Use of contraceptives and sexually transmitted disease among university students, by A. A. Sorensen, et al. JOURNAL OF THE AMERICAN COLLEGE HEALTH ASSOCIA-TION 26:243-247, April, 1978.

CONTRACEPTIVES AND ECONOMICS
Insurance coverage of abortion, contraception and steriliza-tion, by C. F. Muller. FAMILY PLANNING PERSPEC-TIVES 10(2):71-77, March-April, 1978.

CONTRACEPTIVES AND EDUCATION
Implementation of contraceptive education, by W. L. McNab. HEALTH EDUCATION 8:36, November-December, 1977.

Legal aspecsts of sex education, by E. H. Kellogg, et al. AMERICAN JOURNAL OF COMPARATIVE LAW 26: 573-608, Fall, 1978.

CONTRACEPTIVES AND MENSTRUATION
An approach to the analysis of menstrual patterns in the

critical evaluation of contraceptives, by G. Rodriguez, et al. STUDIES IN FAMILY PLANNING 7:42-51, February, 1976.

Effect of menstrual hygiene (tampons vs pads) and of the form of contraception on pH and bacterial infection of the vagina, by E. G. Loch, et al. FORTSCHRITTE DER MEDIZIN 95(44):2653-2656+, November 24, 1977.

Effect of paramethasone acetate on women with secondary amenorrhea: a preliminary report, by V. Cortés-Gallegos, et al. FERTILITY AND STERILITY 29(4):402-406, April, 1978.

The efficiency of menstrual regulation as a method of fertility control, by J. Bongaarts, et al. STUDIES IN FAMILY PLANNING 8(10):268-272, October, 1977.

Oral glucose tolerance test in women in relation to menstrual cycle, by U. Peppler, et al. KLINISCHE WOCHEN-SCHRIFT 56(13);659-669, July 1, 1978.

CONTRACEPTIVES AND THE MILITARY
GI reaction to oral contraceptives. NURSES DRUG ALERT 2:86-87, July, 1978.

CONTRACEPTIVES AND NURSES
Attitudes of nurses to providing contraceptive services for youth, by E. S. Herold, et al. JOURNAL OF PUBLIC HEALTH 68(4):307-310, July-August, 1977.

CONTRACEPTIVES AND PHYSICIANS
Graduate medical students and contraception. Study on a sample of 6th year students at the University of Turin Medical School, by R. Volante, et al. MINERVA GINE-COLOGIA 30(7-8):635-640, July-August, 1978.

Issues in family practice: medical student and practicing physician perspectives, by J. R. Kimberly, et al. MEDICAL

CARE 16(3):214-225, March, 1978.

Special report: for women who wonder about birth control; including doctors' responses to questionnaire, by E. R. Dobell. REDBOOK 151:64+, August, 1978.

CONTRACEPTIVES AND RELIGION
Contraceptive studies are faulty, Msgr. McHugh says. OUR SUNDAY VISITOR 66:2, December 11, 1977.

Exclusion de la procréation selon le droit matrimonial ecclésail, by N. Picard. STUDIA CANONICA 10:37-74, November 1, 1976.

On the proposed legislation dealing with family planning, contraception; statement from the Irish Bishops' Conference. OSSERVATORE ROMANO 17(526):11, April 27, 1978.

CONTRACEPTIVES AND VD
Contraception and VD handbook, by J. E. Rodgers. MADEMOISELLE 84:103-105, August, 1978.

Gonorrhea screening in a prostitute population, by B. O. Leeb, et al. OBSTETRICS AND GYNECOLOGY 51(2): 229-232, February, 1978.

The use of contraceptives and sexually transmitted disease among university students, by A. A. Sorensen, et al. JOURNAL OF AMERICAN COLLEGE HEALTH ASSOCIATION 26(5):243-247, April, 1978.

CONTRACEPTIVES AND YOUTH
Adolescent contraceptors: follow-up study, by J. E. Morgenthau, et al. NEW YORK STATE JOURNAL OF MEDICINE 77:928-931, May, 1977.

Adolescent health services and contraceptive use, by E. H. Mudd, et al. AMERICAN JOURNAL OF ORTHOPSY-

CHIATRY 48:495-504, July, 1978.

Attitudes of nurses to providing contraceptive services for youth, by E. S. Herold, et al. CANADIAN JOURNAL OF PUBLIC HEALTH 68(4):307-310, July-August, 1977.

Contraception and the adolescent female, by C. Poole. JOURNAL OF SCHOOL HEALTH 46:475-479, October, 1976.

Can the first pregnancy of a young adolescent be prevented? a question which must be answered, by M. Baizerman. JOURNAL OF YOUTH AND ADOLESCENCE 6:343-351, December, 1977.

Comparison between the combined pill and intrauterine device in nulliparare under the age of 19, by M. Lie, et al. TIDSSKRIFT FOR DEN NORSKE LAEGEFORENING 98(12):614-617, April 30, 1978.

Contraception in the adolescent, by R. M. Schwartz. PEDIATRIC ANNALS 7(3):189-194, March, 1978.

Contraception in adolescents, by I. Rey-Stocker. REVUE MEDICAL DE LA SUISSE ROMANDE 97(6):322-331, June, 1977.

Contraception in children and adolescents, by M. Sas. FORTSCHRITTE DU MEDIZIN 96(14):747-748, April 13, 1978.

Contraception in youths, by D. Mühlnickel. DEUTSCHE GESUNDHEITSWESEN 32(41):1944-1946, 1977.

Contraceptive counseling for the younger adolescent woman: a suggested solution to the problem, by M. O. Robbie. JOGN: JOURNAL OF OBSTETRIC, GYNAECOLOGIC AND NEONATAL NURSING 7(4):29-33, July-August,

1978.

Contraceptive patterns and premarital pregnancy among women aged 15-19 in 1976, by M. Zelnik, et al. FAMILY PLANNING PERSPECTIVES 10:135-142, May-June, 1978.

Contraceptive practices: in an adolescent health center, by J. E. Morgenthau, et al. NEW YORK STATE JOURNAL OF MEDICINE 76:1311-1315, August, 1976.

Contraceptive services for adolescents: an overview, by J. G. Dryfoos, et al. FAMILY PLANNING PERSPECTIVES 10:233-235+, July-August, 1978.

Contraceptive usage and other characteristics of 440 pregnant teenage patients at MCG in 1975, by V. McNamara, et al. JOURNAL OF THE MEDICAL ASSOCIATION OF GEORGIA 66(9):689-693, September, 1977.

Does your mother know. . .? by A. Torres. FAMILY PLANNING PERSPECTIVES 10:280-282, September-October, 1978.

Factors affecting contraceptive practices of high school and college age students, by R. H. Needle. JOURNAL OF SCHOOL HEALTH 47:340-345, June, 1977.

Fertility control services for adolescents: access and utilization, by F. S. Jaffe, et al. FAMILY PLANNING PERSPECTIVES 8(4):   , July-August, 1976.

Gynecology in childhood and adolescent. 2. Surgical interventions, contraception for adolescents, legal questions, by H. J. Kümper, et al. FORTSCHRITTE DER MEDIZIN 96(11):603-608, March 23, 1978.

Health care for adolescents. Contraceptive counseling for the younger adolescent woman: a suggested solution to the problem. Part 3, by M. O. Robbie. JOGN NURSING 7:29-33, July-August, 1978.

Juvenile privacy: a minor's right of access to contraceptives. FORDHAM URBAN LAW JOURNAL 6:371-387, Winter, 1978.

Large majority of Americans favor legal abortion, sex education & contraceptive services for teens. FAMILY PLANNING PERSPECTIVES 10(3):159-160, May-June, 1978.

Males and morals: teenage contraceptive behavior amid the double standard, by P. Scales. FAMILY COORDINATOR 26(3):211-222, July, 1977.

Most teen girls using contraceptives do so with parental knowledge, study says. JUVENILE JUSTICE DIGEST 6(19):3, October 13, 1978.

Ovulation inhibitors in under age persons, by A. Hollmann. DEUTSCH MEDIZINISCHE WOCHENSCHRIFT 103(32):1258-1259, August 11, 1978.

Pulmonary embolism in a female adolescent with sickle cell trait and oral contraceptive use, by E. P. Hargus, et al. AMERICAN JOURNAL OF OBSTETRICS AND GYNECOLOGY 129(6):697-698, November 15, 1977.

The relationship between oral contraceptives and adolescent sexual behavior, by L. Garres, et al. JOURNAL OF SEX RESEARCH 12(2):133-146, May, 1976.

Rubber chase; double standard for teenage males; research by P. Scales. HUMAN BEHAVIOR 7:41, April, 1978.

Sex role development and teenage fertility-related behavior, by G. Cvertkovich, et al. ADOLESCENCE 13(50):231-236, Summer, 1978.

What's new in the law: family planning. . .access to contraceptives, by A. Ashman. AMERICAN BAR ASSOCIATION JOURNAL 63:857, June, 1977.

FAMILY PLANNING
Analyst biases in KAP surveys: a cross-cultural comparison, by J. W. Ratcliffe. STUDIES IN FAMILY PLANNING 7:322, November, 1976.

Birth control in young females, by U. Fritsche, et al. ZEITSCHRIFT FUR AERZTLICHE FORTBILDUNG 72(6): 282-286, March 15, 1978.

Books and babies: hope and a deadline [to have or not to have children], by D. F. Tannen. MOVING OUT 6(2): 24-26, 1976.

Bringing the sexual revolution home: planned parenthood's five-year plan, by M. Schwartz. AMERICA 138:114-116, February 18, 1978; reply by R. Elliot, 139:241-243, October 14, 1978; rejoinder, 139:243-245, October 14, 1978.

Developments in family planning overseas. 2, by P. Hewitt. AUSTRALASIAN NURSES JOURNAL 7(11):34-37, June, 1978.

The differences between having one and two children, by D. Knox, et al. THE FAMILY COORDINATOR 27:1, January 23-25, 1978.

Differential fertility by intelligence: the role of birth planning, by J. R. Udry. SOCIAL BIOLOGY 25(1):10-14, Spring, 1978.

Emotional disturbance in unplanned versus planned children, by G. Singer, et al. SOCIAL BIOLOGY 23:254-259, August, 1976.

Evaluating family planning program effectiveness and efficiency, by S. L. Gehrz, et al. STUDIES IN FAMILY PLANNING 6(2):37-44, 1975.

Experience in using POPSIM in a family planning simulation experiment, by R. C. Treadway. SIMULATION AND GAMES 9:159-172, June, 1978.

Experimentation in family planning delivery systems: an overview, by R. Cuca, et al. STUDIES IN FAMILY PLANNING 8(12):302-310, December, 1977.

Familia y esclavitud en Aristoles, by A. J. Cappelletti. REVISTA VENEZOLANA DE FILOSOF 7:44, 1977.

Family planning, by T. Svendsby. SYKEPLEIEN 65(6): 337, April 20, 1978.

Family planning in genetic services, by J. O. Hof. SOUTH AFRICAN NURSING JOURNAL 44:23, November, 1977.

Family planning needs urgent attention. NURSING NEWS 1:1-2, June, 1978.

Family-planning services [letter]. LANCET 2(7939):819-820, October 25, 1975.

Family spacing and limitation: acceptable and effective techniques-still in the future? by D. M. Potts. PROCEEDINGS OF THE ROYAL SOCIETY OF LONDON; BIOLOGICAL SCIENCES 199(1134):129-144, October 19, 1977.

Focus on family planning, by J. Christiansen. SAIRAAN-HOITAJA 53(22):30-31, November 22, 1977.

Future orientation, perception of population of problems and birth planning behavior, by D. O. Jorgenson. PER-

CEPTUAL AND MOTOR SKILLS 46(2):501-502, April, 1978.

HEW rules allow funding for natural family planning, by J. Castelli. OUR SUNDAY VISITOR 67:2, October 8, 1978.

Health: the family planning factor, by E. Eckholm, et al. INTERCIENCIA 2(4):208-215, 1977.

Hospital family planning: collecting information a first step in monitoring the service, by J. McEwan. CONTRACEP-TION 11(6): , June, 1975.

Human service program design and the family, by J. E. Northman. FAMILY AND COMMUNITY HEALTH 1(2):17-26, July, 1978.

Husband-wife agreement about reproductive goals, by L. C. Coombs, et al. DEMOGRAPHY 15(1):57-73, February, 1978.

IPPF survey: world's contraceptors increased by 35 million; 5 million more in F.P. programs. FAMILY PLANNING PERSPECTIVES 10(3):163-165, May-June, 1978.

Implications of attitude-behavior studies for population research and action [methodological problems in relating attitudes to family planning behavior] , by P. D. Werner. STUDIES IN FAMILY PLANNING 8:294-299, November, 1977.

Impressions of the 1977 National Conference on maternal and child welfare and family planning, by M. Fujiwara. JOSANPU ZASSHI 31(9):588-589, September, 1977.

Improving management through evaluation: techniques and strategies for family planning programs. STUDIES IN FAMILY PLANNING 9(6):163, June, 1978.

Intermediate objectives for the monitoring of family planning sercies, by C. A. Corzantes. BULLETIN OF THE PAN-AMERICAN HEALTH ORGANIZATION 12(1):55-60, 1978.

International population programs: should they change local values? by D. Warwick, et al. HASTINGS CENTER RE-PORT 7(5):17-18, October, 1977.

Limited patient knowledge as a reproductive risk factor, by S. M. Johnson, et al. JOURNAL OF FAMILY PRAC-TICE 6(4):855-862, April, 1978.

The link between nutrition and family planning. AUSTRA-LASIAN NURSES JOURNAL 7(5):16, December, 1977.

A longitudinal study of success versus failure in contraceptive planning. JOURNAL OF POPULATION 1(1):69, Spring, 1978.

Maternal and child health and family planning, by H. C. Taylor, Jr. JOURNAL OF THE MEDICAL ASSOCIATION OF THE STATE OF ALABAMA 45(12):38-45, June, 1976.

A model for health care delivery with an illustration of its application, by P. M. Vacek, et al. MEDICAL CARE 16(7):547-559, July, 1978.

Multidisciplinary training in family planning, by D. V. Fair-weather, et al. MEDICAL EDUCATION 12(3):205-208, May, 1978.

The National Inventory of Family Planning Services: 1975 survey results, by D. L. Morrow. VITAL HEALTH STATISTICS (19):i-iv+, April, 1978.

National survey of family growth, cycle I: sample design, estimation procedures, and variance estimation, by

D. K. French. VITAL HEALTH STATISTICS (76):1-32, January, 1978.

Nurse specialist work in family planning, by M. P. Newton, et al. MIDWIVES CHRONICLE 90(1079):290-291, December, 1977.

On the problems of planned parenthood, by S. Azrieli. NURSE IN ISRAEL 23(94):23-24, November, 1975.

Paths to fertility reduction: the "policy cube." FAMILY PLANNING PERSPECTIVES 9(5):214, September-October, 1977.

Patient education through pregnancy counseling: a preventive approach. . .Gynecology Clinic, Wilce Health Center, Ohio State University, by L. Meeks, et al. HEALTH EDUCATION 9:42-45, January-February, 1978.

Patients' evaluation of family planning services: the case of inner-city clinics, by K. Sung. STUDIES IN FAMILY PLANNING 8:130, May, 1977.

Patterns of family building and contraceptive use of middle-class couples, by D. Woodward, et al. JOURNAL OF BIOSOCIAL SCIENCE 10(1):39-58, January, 1978.

Policy document on family planning. WORLD OF IRISH NURSING 7:7, May, 1978.

Practice profiles in evaluating the clinical experience of family medicine trainees, by V. Boisseau, et al. JOURNAL OF FAMILY PRACTICE 6(4):80-1805, April, 1978.

Prediction of success or failure in birth planning: an approach to prevention of individual and family stress, by B. Mindick, et al. AMERICAN JOURNAL OF COMMUNITY PSYCHOLOGY 5(4):447-459, December, 1977.

Pregnancy counseling and abortion referral for patients in federally funded family planning programs, by J. I. Rosoff. FAMILY PLANNING PERSPECTIVES 8:43-46, January-February, 1976.

Preventing unplanned pregnancies, by C. Hawken. MEDICAL JOURNAL OF AUSTRALIA 1(6):344-351, March 25, 1978.

Prospects and possibilities of genetic counseling and family planning in the mental health laboratory for adults, by V. Predescu, et al. REVISTA DE MEDICINA INTERNA [NEUROLOGIE, PSIKIATRIE] 23(1):53-58, January-March, 1978.

Quality v quantity in children [letter], by H. P. Dunn. BRITISH MEDICAL JOURNAL 2(6095):1354, November 19, 1977.

The relation of income to fertility decisions, by E. Mueller, et al. ECONOMIC DEVELOPMENT AND CULTURAL CHANGE 25:325-347, January, 1977.

Reproduction and family planning, by M. Manciaux. JOURNAL DE GYNECOLOGIE, OBSTETRIQUE ET BIOLOGIE DE LA REPRODUCTION 7(2):301-302, March, 1978.

Research in family planning, by A. Kessler, et al. WORLD HEALTH :2-39, August-September, 1978.

The role of birth control in the survival of the human race, by R. Wiechert. ANGEWANDTE CHEMIE 16(8):506-513, August, 1977.

The role of the family, by H. L. Tabak. JOURNAL OF THE AMERICAN HEALTH CARE ASSOCIATION 4(5):92-94+, September, 1978.

Role of the paediatrician in family planning, by D. B. Sharma. INDIAN JOURNAL OF PEDIATRICS 44(356):253-256, September, 1977.

A second baby?. . .if yes, when? by E. M. Whelan. AMERICAN BABY 40:41-42, August, 1978.

A selected annotated bibliography on midwives and family planning. Part 2, by M. R. Zabarenko, et al. JOURNAL OF NURSE-MIDWIFERY 22:32-38, Fall, 1977.

Service statistics: aid to more effective FP program management. POPULATION REPORTS 17:23, November, 1977.

Some speculations on the future of marriage and fertility, by C. F. Westoff. FAMILY PLANNING PERSPECTIVES 10(2):79-83, March-April, 1978.

Spacing of children and changing patterns of childbearing, by C. M. Young. JOURNAL OF BIOSOCIAL SCIENCE 9:201-226, April, 1977.

Tay-Sachs and related storage diseases: family planning, by G. Schneiderman, et al. MENTAL RETARDATION 16:13-15, February, 1978.

Ten good reasons not to have children, by E. Peck. HARPER'S BAZAAR 3203:181, October, 1978.

Unmet needs [main findings of the international planned parenthood federation's worldwide survey of unmet needs in family planning, 1971-76]. PEOPLE (London) 5:25-31, November 3, 1978.

The use of incentives for fertility reduction, by S. M. Wishik. AMERICAN JOURNAL OF PUBLIC HEALTH 68(2): 113-114, February, 1978.

Women's organizations: a resource for family planning and development, by J. Bruce. FAMILY PLANNING PER-SPECTIVES 8:291, November-December, 1976.

World population: the silent explosion, by M. Green, et al. DEPARTMENT OF STATE BULLETIN 78:45-54, October 1-8, 1978+.

World population situation: problems and prospects. WORLD DEVELOPMENT 5(5-7):395, May-July, 1977.

The year of the child [editorial], by S. Gupta. INDIAN PEDIATRICS 14(4):241-242, April, 1977.

The youth reception in Sollentuna, by A. Sedvall. LAKAR-TIDNINGEN 75(21):2131-2132, May 24, 1978.

AFRICA
The achieved small family: early fertility transition in an African city. STUDIES IN FAMILY PLANNING 8(12):302, January, 1978.

ASIA
The unmet need for birth control in five Asian countries, by C. F. Westoff. FAMILY PLANNING PERSPEC-TIVES 10(3):173-181, May-June, 1978.

BANGLADESH
Integration of health, nutrition, and family planning: the Companiganj project in Bangladesh, by C. McCord. FOOD RESEARCH INSTITUTE STUDIES 16:91-105, November 2, 1977.

BARBADOS
Metropolitan dominance and family planning in Barbados, by H. J. Jones. SOCIAL AND ECONOMIC STUDIES 26:327-338, September, 1977.

BRAZIL
Action now for promoting the responsible paternity. REVISTA BRASILEIRA DE PESQUISAS MEDICAS E BIOLOGICAS 10(6):434-437, December, 1977.

CANADA
Family planning programs in Britain, German Federal Republic, Denmark and Sweden, with the implications for Canada, by E. S. Smith. CANADIAN JOURNAL OF PUBLIC HEALTH 68(5):369-374, September-October, 1977.

Ottawa Family Planning Clinic: experience with 3862 registrants, by J. C. Whyte, et al. CANADIAN MEDICAL ASSOCIATION JOURNAL 118(4):401-402, February 18, 1978.

CHILE
Chile: experiencia con un sistema de estadisticas de servicio para un programa materno-infantil y de plantificacion de la familia, by E. Taucher. CENTRO LATINOAMERICANO DE DEMOGRAFIA. BOLETIN DEMOGRAFICO p. 47, November, 1977.

CHINA
Demographic evaluation of Taiwan's family planning program [conference paper], by T. H. Sun. INDUSTRY OF FREE CHINA 49:11-27, May 15-27, 1978+.

Family planning in China. NURSING TIMES 74:62, March 9, 1978.

—, by W. Wen. INDIAN JOURNAL OF PEDIATRICS 44(350):78-80, March, 1977.

Observations on birth planning in China, 1977, by F. S. Jaffe, et al. FAMILY PLANNING PERSPECTIVES 10:101-108, March-April, 1978.

CHINA
A survey of attitude and practice toward family planning
of family planning workers in Taiwan, by Y. L. Dah.
JOURNAL OF NURSING 24(2):8-16, April, 1977.

Trends in fertility, family size preferences, and family
planning practice: Taiwan, 1961-76, by T. H. Sun, et
al. STUDIES IN FAMILY PLANNING 9(4):54-70,
April, 1978.

GHANA
Attitudes towards family size and family planning in rural
Ghana-Danfa project: 1972 survey findings, by D. W.
Belcher, et al. JOURNAL OF BIOSOCIAL SCIENCE
10(1):59-79, January, 1978.

The Danfa family planning program in rural Ghana, by
D. A. Ampofo, et al. STUDIES IN FAMILY PLAN-
NING 7:266-274, October, 1976.

GREAT BRITAIN
Closing down family planning clinics [letter], by P.
Thompson. BRITISH MEDICAL JOURNAL
1(6104):53, January 7, 1978.

HONG KONG
Family planning in Hong Kong. AUSTRALASIAN
NURSES JOURNAL 7(4):43, November, 1977.

The role of the family planning association in Hong
Kong's fertility decline, by K. C. Chan. STUDIES
IN FAMILY PLANNING 7:284+, October, 1976.

INDIA
Adoption of modern health and family planning practices in a rural community of India, by S. K. Sandhu,
et al. INTERNATIONAL JOURNAL OF HEALTH
EDUCATION 20(4):240-247, October-December,
1977.

INDIA

Attitude towards family planning (a study of impatient attendants), by G. M. Dhar, et al. INDIAN JOURNAL OF PUBLIC HEALTH 21(2):89-94, April-June, 1977.

A comparative study of health status of children whose parents have undergone family planning operations with those whose parents were not, by P. R. Choudhary, et al. INDIAN PEDIATRICS 15(1):13-18, January, 1978.

A comparative study of immunisation status of children whose parents had undergone family planning operations with those whose parents were not, by P. R. Choudhary, et al. INDIAN PEDIATRICS 15(3): 229-232, March, 1978.

Demographic impact of family planning programme in Singur area, West Bengal, by A. K. Chakraborty, et al. INDIAN JOURNAL OF PUBLIC HEALTH 21(1): 38-43, January-March, 1977.

The dilemma of family planning in a North Indian state, by B. D. Misra, et al. STUDIES IN FAMILY PLANNING 7:66-74, March, 1976.

Family planning under the magnifying glass (with special reference to the elections in India), by F. M. de Villiers. SOUTH AFRICAN NURSING JOURNAL 44(10):25-27, October, 1977.

India [family planning situation in the wake of the April, 1977, elections which swept the Indian national congress from power; eight articles]. PEOPLE (London) 5:3-24, November 3, 1978.

India: the great population control experiment, by R. Engel. LINACRE QUARTERLY 43:230-243,

INDIA
November, 1976.

Planned parenthood and childcare, by V. M. Sundaram, et al. INDIAN PEDIATRICS 15(1):27-32, January, 1978.

Population policy and family planning [editorial]. INDIAN JOURNAL OF PUBLIC HEALTH 21(1):1-2, January-March, 1977.

Study of physical & sexual growth of preadolescent & adolescent children of rural Hyderabad and their knowledge attitudes towards human reproduction and family planning, by N. Kishore, et al. INDIAN PEDIATRICS 15(2):147-154, February, 1978.

INDONESIA
Correlates of field-worker performance in the Indonesian family planning program: a test of the homophily-heterophily hypothesis, by R. Repetto. STUDIES IN FAMILY PLANNING 8:19+, January, 1977.

Indonesia's family planning story: success and challenge. POPULATION BULLETIN 32(6:53, November, 1977.

IRAN
The model family planning project in Isfahan, Iran, by R. C. Treadway, et al. STUDIES IN FAMILY PLANNING 7:308-321, November, 1976.

JAPAN
Nagaike Clinic, by M. Fujiwara. JOSANPU ZASSHI 31(11):715, November, 1977.

JORDAN
Trends in fertility and family planning in Jordan, by H. Rizk. STUDIES IN FAMILY PLANNING 8:91-99,

JORDAN
April, 1977.

KOREA
Family planning education as an integral part of day care services in Korea, by K. Sung. STUDIES IN FAMILY PLANNNING 9:71-74, April, 1978.

The fourth Korean child: the effect of son preference on subsequent fertility, by C. B. Park. JOURNAL OF BIOSOCIAL SCIENCE 10(1):95-106, January, 1978.

Integrating nutritional and family planning education with food services in Korean day care centers—an evaluation, by K. T. Sung. PUBLIC HEALTH RE-PORTS 93(2):177-185, March-April, 1978.

The Korean mothers' club program, by H. J. Park, et al. STUDIES IN FAMILY PLANNING 7:275-283, October, 1976.

LATIN AMERICA
Family planning programs found to be a major factor behind sharp fertility declines in Latin America and Asia. FAMILY PLANNING PERSPECTIVES 10(1): 41-42, January-February, 1978.

MALAYSIA
Developments in family planning overseas. Part 2, by P. Hewitt. AUSTRALASIAN NURSES JOURNAL 7:34-37, June, 1978.

Impact of the Malaysian family planning programme on births: a comparison of matched acceptor and non-acceptor birth rates, by J. T. Johnson, et al. POPU-LATION STUDIES 32:215-230, July, 1978.

Peers as recruiters: family planning communications of west Malaysian acceptors, by L. M. Berbrugge.

MALAYSIA
JOURNAL OF HEALTH AND SOCIAL BEHAVIOR
19:51-68, March, 1978.

MAURITIUS
Family planning in Mauritius: a national survey, by C. R.
Hein. STUDIES IN FAMILY PLANNING 8(12):
316-320, December, 1977.

MEXICO
Effectiveness of the use of contraception in the voluntary
family planning program of the Instituo Mexicano del
Serguro Social, by J. Garcia Pena, et al. SPM: SALUD
PUBLICA DE MEXICO 19(5):655-663, September-
October, 1977.

Socioeconomical characteristics and continuity of patients
accepted at the Clinic of Family Planning of the Yucatan University, by D. T. Canto de Cetina, et al. SPM:
SALUD PUBLICA DE MEXICO 19(5):685-689,
September-October, 1977.

Women at Mexico: beyond family planning acceptors, by
A. Germain. FAMILY PLANNING PERSPECTIVES
7(5):2-11, 1975.

MOROCCO
Obstacles to family planning practice in urban Morocco,
by F. Mernissi. STUDIES IN FAMILY PLANNING
6:418-425, December, 1975.

NEW GUINEA
Breakthrough in Papua New Guinea, by J. C. Abcede.
WORLD HEALTH :8-17, October, 1977.

NEW ZEALAND
Contraceptive use and pregnancy planning in the Hutt
Valley, by S. S. Poh, et al. NEW ZEALAND MEDI-
CAL JOURNAL 85(584):217-220, March 23, 1977.

NIGERIA
Developing a clinic strategy appropriate to community
family planning needs and practices: an experience in
Lagos, Nigeria, by A. Bamisaiye, et al. STUDIES IN
FAMILY PLANNING 9(2-3):44-48, February-
March, 1978.

The evolution of family planning in an African city:
Ibadan, Nigeria, by J. C. Caldwell, et al. POPULA-
TION STUDIES 31:487-507, November, 1977.

PHILIPPINES
Family planning in the Philippines: assessment of program implementation [based on conference paper],
by A. P. Varela. PHILIPPINE JOURNAL OF PUB-
LIC ADMINISTRATION 20:236-260, July, 1976.

Family planning program: big strides in 10 years: 26% of
reproductive-age Filipinos now enrolled; 1980 target
is 35%. WAR ON HUNGER 11:16-19, December,
1977.

SCOTLAND
Family planning in a sample of Edinburgh women, by D.
R. Hannay, et al. HEALTH BULLETIN 35(6):326-
329, November, 1977.

SINGAPORE
A component analysis of recent fertility decline in Singapore. STUDIES IN FAMILY PLANNING 8(11):
282, November, 1977.

Effects of social disincentive policies on fertility behavior
in Singapore, by S. B. Tan, et al. AMERICAN JOUR-
NAL OF PUBLIC HEALTH 68(2):119-124, February, 1978.

The Singapore National Family Planning and Population
Programme 1966-1975 with particular reference to

FAMILY PLANNING

SINGAPORE
patterns of response, by F. K. Wan, et al. NURSING
JOURNAL OF SINGAPORE 17(2):80-85, November, 1977.

THAILAND
Components method for measuring the impact of a family planning program on birth rates, by J. D. Teachman, et al. DEMOGRAPHY 15:113-129, February,
1978.

Fertility and family planning in rural northern Thailand,
by S. Shevasunt, et al. STUDIES IN FAMILY PLAN-
NING 9:212-221, August, 1978.

Population and family planning in Thailand. BANGKOK
BANK MONTHLY REVIEW 19:241-247, June,
1978.

TUNISIA
Le corps paramédical face au planning familial [based on
questionnaire survey of midwives, nurses and other
medical workers], by S. Sahli. REVUE TUNISIENNE
DE SCIENCES SOCIALES 14(50-51):283-291,
1977.

L'introduction des problèmes de population dans les
programmes scolaires [based on questionnaire survey
of about 900 students, teachers and parents conducted in 1974], by A. Bouraoui, et al. REVUE
TUNISIENNE DE SCIENCES SOCIALES 14(50-
51):11-33, 1977.

UNITED STATES
Birth control clinics in the city of Birmingham—a geographical study, by B. D. Giles, et al. SOCIAL SCI-
ENCE AND MEDICINE 11(14-16):763-772, November, 1977.

UNITED STATES
Delayed-baby boom: its meaning; increasing numbers of
women are deciding to have their first child after
years of marriage; their decisions promise major
changes for both society and individual lives, by
L. J. Lord. U. S. NEWS AND WORLD 84:39-41,
February 20, 1978.

The effect of subsidized family planning services on reproductive behavior in the United States: 1969-1974,
by J. R. Udry, et al. DEMOGRAPHY 13:463-478,
November, 1976.

Family planning opinion leadership in the United States,
by A. A. Fisher. INTERNATIONAL JOURNAL OF
HEALTH EDUCATION 21(2):98-106, 1978.

Family planning program activity and patient enrollment
rates in the United States, 1969 and 1971. DE-
MOGRAPHY 14(2):213, May, 1977.

Organized family planning services in the United States,
1968-1976, by A. Torres. FAMILY PLANNING
PERSPECTIVES 10:83-88, March-April, 1978.

The Planned Parenthood Federation of America, by J.
O'Hare. AMERICA 138:inside front cover, February 18, 1978.

Social change and the family: Los Angeles, California,
1850-1870, by B. Laslett. AMERICAN SOCIOLOGI-
CAL REVIEW 42:268-269, April, 1977.

GEORGIA
A survey of fertility and family planning in Atlanta,
Georgia, by W. S. Tillack, et al. PUBLIC HEALTH
REPORTS 92(5):444-452, September-October,
1977.

UNITED STATES
HAWAII
Study of the knowledge, attitude and practice among teenagers in Hawaii related to reproduction, family planning and sexuality, by S. Hancock, et al. HAWAII MEDICAL JOURNAL 37(3):73-75, March, 1978.

INDIAN
Sociocultural factors affecting acceptance of family planning services by Navajo women, by C. W. Slemenda. HUMAN ORGANIZATION 37: 190-194, Summer, 1978.

VIETNAM
Vietnam [family planning programs]. PEOPLE (London) 5:22-27, November 2, 1978.

WEST AFRICA
Integration of family planning and maternal and child health in rural West Africa, by A. K. Neumann, et al. JOURNAL OF BIOSOCIAL SCIENCE 8:161-174, April, 1976.

FAMILY PLANNING: BIBLIOGRAPHY
A demographic assessment of family planning programs: a bibliographic essay, by J. A. Ross, et al. POPULATION INDEX 44:8-27, January, 1978.

A selected annotated bibliography on midwives and family planning. Part II, by M. R. Zabarenko, et al. JOURNAL OF NURSE-MIDWIFERY 22(3):32-38, Fall, 1977.

FAMILY PLANNING: DEVELOPING COUNTRIES
Conditions of fertility decline in developing countries, 1965-75 [the effect of socioeconomic conditions and family planning programs; based on conference paper], by W. P. Mauldin, et al. STUDIES IN FAMILY PLANNING 9: 89-147, May, 1978.

FAMILY PLANNING: HISTORY
Family limitation in pre-industrial England, by E. A. Wrigley. ECONOMIC HISTORY REVIEW 19:82-109, April, 1966; Reply with rejoinder by R. B. Morrow, 31:419-436, August, 1978.

Family limitation in pre-industrial England: a reappraisal, by R. B. Morrow. ECONOMIC HISTORY REVIEW 31:419-428, August, 1978.

1966-1977: a look at the record, by B. Berelson. FAMILY PLANNING PERSPECTIVES 10(1):20-22, January-February, 1978.

Unwanted and mistimed births in the United States: 1968-1973, by R. H. Weller, et al. FAMILY PLANNING PERSPECTIVES 10:168-172, May-June, 1978.

FAMILY PLANNING: LAWS AND LEGISLATION
Pregnancy, teenagers, and the law, 1976, by E. W. Paul, et al. FAMILY PLANNING PERSPECTIVES 8(1):16-21, January-February, 1976.

FAMILY PLANNING: RURAL
Family planning needs and services in nonmetropolitan areas, by T. H. Firpo, et al. FAMILY PLANNING PERSPECTIVES 8:231-248, September-October, 1976.

Family spacing and limitation. Applying family planning in rural communities, by P. Senanayake. PROCEEDINGS OF THE ROYAL SOCIETY OF LONDON, BIOLOGICAL SCIENCES 199(1134):115-127, October 19, 1977.

FAMILY PLANNING: STATISTICS
Background and development of the National Reporting System for Family Planning Services, by B. J. Haupt. VITAL HEALTH STATISTICS (13):i-iii+, April, 1978.

FAMILY PLANNING AND NURSES
Differences between physicians and nurses in providing
family planning services: findings from a Bogota clinic,
by R. F. Einhorn, et al. STUDIES IN FAMILY PLAN-
NING 9:35-38, February-March, 1978.

Point of view. On the front: nursing and family and community health, by M. L. Kinlein. FAMILY AND COM-
MUNITY HEALTH 1(1):57-68, April, 1978.

FAMILY PLANNING AND PHARMACISTS
The pharmacist as family planning helpmate, by M. Dolan.
AMERICAN PHARMACY 18(5):40, May, 1978.

FAMILY PLANNING AND PHYSICIANS
Differences between physicians and nurses in providing
family planning services: findings from a Bogota clinic,
by R. F. Einhorn, et al. STUDIES IN FAMILY PLAN-
NING 9(2-3):35-38, February-March, 1978.

Family practice: teaching new docs old tricks, by J. Lukomnik. HEALTH-PAC BULLETIN (80):1-2+, January-
February, 1978.

The first month in family practice residency training, by
J. N. Dunn. JOURNAL OF FAMILY PRACTICE 6(5):
1105-1106, May, 1978.

Hawaii physicians' attitudes and practices regarding reproductive health services for minors, by J. H. Fertel, et al.
HAWAII MEDICAL JOURNAL 37(2):41-43, February,
1978.

FAMILY PLANNING AND RELIGION
The Planned Parenthood Federation of America, by J.
O'Hare. AMERICA 138:inside front cover, February
18, 1978.

Planned parenthood: the Planned Parenthood Federation of

485

America, by A. Nevins. OUR SUNDAY VISITOR
66:15, March 12, 1978.

FAMILY PLANNING AND THE RETARDED
Family planning services for persons handicapped by mental
retardation, by H. P. David, et al. AMERICAN JOUR-
NAL OF PUBLIC HEALTH 66:1053-1057, November,
1976.

FAMILY PLANNING AND YOUTH
Adolescent parents: a special case of the unplanned family,
by J. A. Bruce. THE FAMILY COORDINATOR 27(1):
75-78, January, 1978.

Califano seeks congress' okay for teenage pregnancy program.
JUVENILE JUSTICE DIGEST 6(13):4-5, July 7, 1978.

The contraception-to-conception ratio: a tool for measuring
success of family planning programs in reaching very
young teenagers, by J. D. Shelton. ADVANCES IN
PLANNED PARENTHOOD 13(1):1-6, 1978.

First pregnancies to women aged 15-19: 1976 and 1971, by
M. Zelnick, et al. FAMILY PLANNING PERSPECTIVES
10(1):11-20, January-February, 1978.

Misinforming pregnant teenagers, by L. Ambrose. FAMILY
PLANNING PERSPECTIVES 10(1):51-53, January-
February, 1978.

Pregnancy, teenagers and the law, 1976, by E. W. Paul, et
al. FAMILY PLANNING PERSPECTIVES 8:16-32,
January-February, 1976.

Sex education and family planning clinical for adolescents.
BOLETIN MEDICO DE HOSPITAL INFANTILE DE
MEXICO 35(3):583-584, May-June, 1978.

Teenage pregnancies: looking ahead to 1984, by C. Tietze.

FAMILY PLANNING PERSPECTIVES 10;205-207, July-August, 1978.

Teenage pregnancy: epidemic or statistical hoax? by J. Kasun. U. S. A. TODAY 107:31-33; Reply by R. Lincoln, 34-37, July, 1978.

Teenage pregnancy: the need for multiple casework services, by S. P. Schnike. SOCIAL CASEWORK 59(7):406-410, July, 1978.

Teenagers at risk, by P. Crabbe. NURSING TIMES 73(32): 1229, August 11, 1977.

Teenagers: fertility control behavior and attitudes before and after abortion, childbearing or negative pregnancy test, by J. R. Evans. FAMILY PLANNING PERSPECTIVES 8(4):192-200, July-August, 1976.

Teens having babies, by M. I. Abbott. PEDIATRIC NURS-ING 4(3):23-26, May-June, 1978.

FAMILY PLANNING CLINICS
FP/MIS: a management information system for a community family planning clinic, by J. Herson, et al. MEDICAL CARE 15(5):   , May, 1977.

Family planning clinic "dropouts", by O. F. Moore, et al. NURSE PRACTITIONER 3:14+, July-August, 1978.

FAMILY PLANNING COUNSELING
Experiences from a school counseling bureau, by H. Sjöström. LAKARTIDNINGEN 75(21):2130-2131, May 24, 1978.

Role of counseling in present-day family planning, by K. Sundström-Feigenberg. LAKARTIDNINGEN 75(7): 552-557, February 15, 1978.

Work forms and methods in family and marriage counseling,

by S. I. Markovich. MEDITSINSKAIA SESTRA 36(8):
13-17, August, 1977.

FAMILY PLANNING ECONOMICS
A "contingency plan" of economic incentive to limit U. S.
reproduction. ENVIRONMENTAL AFFAIRS 6(3):
301, 1978.

Family planning costs [letter], by R. F. Martin. BRITISH
MEDICAL JOURNAL 1(6106):180, January 21, 1978.

The hundred million dollar misunderstanding. . .How much
money is being spent on family planning clinic programs
in the United States? by J. G. Dryfoos, et al. FAMILY
PLANNING PERSPECTIVES 10:144-147, May-June,
1978.

Short-term benefits and costs of U. S. family planning programs 1970-75, by F. Jaffe. FAMILY PLANNING PER-
SPECTIVES (2):   , May-April, 1977.

U. S. restricts abortion, family planning foreign aid; regulations of the U. S. Agency for International Development,
by J. Castelli. OUR SUNDAY VISITOR 66:4, April 30,
1978.

FAMILY PLANNING EDUCATION
Developments in family planning overseas. An account of
family planning education programmes in Britain, Italy,
Hong Kong, Malaysia and Singapore. Part one—Britain,
by P. Hewitt. AUSTRALASIAN NURSES JOURNAL
7(10):32-35+, May, 1978.

Education in health and family planning to nurses and mid-
wives, by W. Haddad. JOURNAL DE GYNECOLOGIE,
OBSTETRIQUE ET BIOLOGIE DE LA REPRODUC-
TION 7(2):307-311, March, 1978.

Education in marital hygiene and popular professional literature, by V. Wynnyczuk. CASOPIS LEKARU CESKYCH 116(33):1033-1034, August 19, 1977.

Experiences in 9 patient/family education workshops, by J. P. Lovegren, et al. JOURNAL OF THE AMERICAN HEALTH CARE ASSOCIATION 4(1):18-21, January, 1978.

Improving communication: educating families, by L. Greenberg. JOURNAL OF THE AMERICAN HEALTH CARE ASSOCIATION 4(1):21-28, January, 1978.

Language differences and the family planning survey, by D. Lucas, et al. STUDIES IN FAMILY PLANNING 8(9): 233-236, September, 1977.

Motivation of sterilization patients: implications for family planning education programmes, by M. F. McCann, et al. INTERNATIONAL JOURNAL OF HEALTH EDUCATION 21(1):26-33, 1978.

A project report: follow-up of trained nurse-midwives. . . International Planned Parenthood Federation, by R. Weinstein. JOURNAL OF NURSE-MIDWIFERY 23:36-39, Spring-Summer, 1978.

Sessualità, maternità, educazione demografica, by G. Sica. RIVISTA DI SERVIZIO SOCIALE 17:45-54, November 2, 1977.

Training family planning personnel in sex counseling and sex education, by S. Price, et al. PUBLIC HEALTH REPORTS 93:328-334, July-August, 1978.

FAMILY PLANNING RESEARCH
Effects of various factors on selection for family planning status and natural fecundability: a simulation study, by J. C. Barrett. DEMOGRAPHY 15:87-98, February, 1978.

Family limitation and the English demographic revolution: a simulation approach, by N. F. R. Crafts, et al. JOURNAL OF ECONOMIC HISTORY 36:598-623, September, 1976.

MISCARRIAGES
Estradiol and pregnanldiol excretion in threatening miscarriages in late period of pregnancy depending on the cause of miscarriage, by N. G. Kosheleva, et al. VOPROSY OKHRANY MATERINSTVA I DETSTVA 22(7):70-73, July, 1977.

Frequency of chromosomal abnormalities in miscarriages and perinatal deaths, by E. D. Alberman, et al. JOURNAL OF MEDICAL GENETICS 14(5):313-315, October, 1977.

Miscarriage: cause and prevention, by S. A. Kaufman. PARENTS MAGAZINE 53:13, May, 1978.

Miscarriages as a cause of spina bifida and anencephaly [letter], by D. I. Rushton. BRITISH MEDICAL JOURNAL 2(6090):833-834, September 24, 1977.

Operating theatres and prevalence of miscarriage [letter], by D. Angus. MEDICAL JOURNAL OF AUSTRALIA 1(12):657-658, June 17, 1978.

Oxidative metabolism of the placenta in miscarriage, by M. A. Kampo, et al. PEDIATRIYA AKUSHERSTVO I HINEKOLOHIYA (1):43-44, January-February, 1978.

Pathogenetic factors in miscarriage and prolonged pregnancy, by V. N. Kozhevnikov. AKUSHERSTVO I GINEKOLOGIIA (8):40-42, August, 1977.

Results with a new method for objectivation of rheobase measurements in normal pregnancy and risk of miscarriage or premature birth, by H. Fendel, et al. ZEIT-

SCHRIFT FUR GEBURTSCHILFE UND PERINA-
TOLOGIE 181(6):396-401, December, 1977.

PREGNANCY DIAGNOSIS
Development of knowledge concerning the early diagnosis
of pregnancy, by G. Gentile. RIVISTA ITALIANA DI
GINECOLOGIA 57(4-6):305-321, July-December,
1976.

The e.p.t. do-it-yourself early pregnancy test. MEDICAL
LETTER ON DRUGS AND THERAPEUTICS 20(8):
39-40, April 21, 1978.

An evaluation of intramuscular progesterone for the diagnosis of early pregnancy, by D. Vengadasalam, et al.
JOURNAL OF REPRODUCTIVE MEDICINE 20(5):
260-264, May, 1978.

Evaluation of a new direct latex agglutination tube test
(UCG-Macrotube) for pregnancy, by T. K. Kukherjee,
et al. AMERICAN JOURNAL OF OBSTETRICS AND
GYNECOLOGY 131(6):701-702, July 15, 1978.

Evaluation of the "Quick test" a direct latex agglutination
test for pregnancy, by M. Sathanandan, et al. CEYLON
MEDICAL JOURNAL 22(2):110-113, June, 1977.

Laboratory pregnancy testing, by G. D. Wasley. NURSING
TIMES 74(1):25-27, January 5, 1978.

Positive pregnancy tests at Cowell student health center, by
J. M. Dorman. JOURNAL OF THE AMERICAN COL-
LEGE HEALTH ASSOCIATION 26:207-210, February,
1978.

PROSTAGLANDINS

STERILIZATION
Access vs. abuse: editorial page article on the use of steriliza-

tion as a method of birth control and the problems arising from its increasing popularity. POLITICS AND PEOPLE 2(16-20):3,

Consent and sterilization, by G. Sharpe. CANADIAN MEDICAL ASSOCIATION JOURNAL 118(5):591-593, March 4, 1978.

Contraception, sterilisation and abortion [editorial]. NEW ZEALAND MEDICAL JOURNAL 85(588):428-429, May 25, 1977.

Differential fertility by sterilized and non-sterilized couples, by E. R. Ram, et al. JOURNAL OF FAMILY WELFARE 23:45-50, December, 1976.

Drug induced sterility [editorial], by H. Pedersen. UGESKRIFT FOR LAEGER 139(40):2399-2400, October 3, 1977.

Health: a cut above the rest [sterilization: vasectomy, laparoscopy, tubal occlusion], by A. Henry. OFF OUR BACKS 7:4, September, 1977.

Radioprotective effect of castration and cyproteron acetate, by J. Sevcik, et al. SBORNIK LEKARSKY 79(7-8): 252-255, August, 1977.

Relationship between tooth and bone growth in rats after castration and in under hormonal loading, by E. I. Goncharova. STOMATOLOGIIA 57(4):11-14, July-August, 1978.

Self-emasculation: review of the literature, report of a case and outline of the objectives of management, by S. C. Evins, et al. JOURNAL OF UROLOGY 118(5):775-776, November, 1977.

Sterilization. FORUM 2(2):6-13, 1978.

—. GLAMOUR 76:44, January, 1978.

Sterilization. April 1-December 31, 1976, by S. C. Christensen, et al. UGESKRIFT FOR LAEGER 140(16):939, April 17, 1978.

The sterilization controversy examines pivotal issues, by K. O'Rourke. HOSPITAL PROGRESS 58:80-81, August, 1977.

Sterilization—his or hers, by P. Paterson. MEDICAL JOURNAL OF AUSTRALIA 2(17):571-572, October 22, 1977.

Sterilization: hospitals dodge ban? by B. Kenkelen. NATIONAL CATHOLIC REPORTER 13:1†, October 14, 1977.

Sterilization—the husband usually decides; research by Margaret Pruitt Clark and others, by J. Gaylin. PSYCHOLOGY TODAY 11:36+, February, 1978.

Sterilization is world's leading contraceptive method. SOCIETY 15:7, May, 1978.

Sterilizations 1975-1976, by S. Collatz Christensen, et al. UGESKRIFT FOR LAEGER 139(32):1914-1915, August 8, 1977.

Underutilization, another form of sterilization abuse, by H. A. Stubbs, et al. ADVANCES IN PLANNED PARENTHOOD 12(3):132-135, 1978.

BOLIVIA
How doctors in Bolivia and the Philippines view sterilization, by D. W. MacCorquodale, et al. STUDIES IN FAMILY PLANNING 6:426-428, December, 1975.

CANADA
Sterilization patterns in a Northern Canadian population, by J. Cohen, et al. CANADIAN JOURNAL OF PUBLIC HEALTH 69(3):222-224, May-June, 1978.

GREAT BRITAIN
Recent trends in sterilization [England and Wales, 196-75], by M. Bone. POPULATION TRENDS pp. 13-16, Autumn, 1978.

Sterilisation: the Aberdeen experience, and some broader implications, by S. Teper. JOURNAL OF MEDICAL ETHICS 4(1):18-24, March, 1978.

INDIA
Compulsory sterilization: the change in India's population policy, by K. Gulhati. SCIENCE 195:1300-1305+, March, 1977.

Forced sterilization in India; a disregard of spiritual values, by J. Emanuel. WORLDMISSION 27:56-58, Winter, 1976-1977.

Forced sterilization, by B. Levin. TIMES p. 14, November 7, 1978.

India's compulsory sterilization laws: the human right of family planning. CALIFORNIA WESTERN INTERNATIONAL LAW JOURNAL 8:342-367, Spring, 1978.

India's experience with sterilization programmes, 1965-75: an overview of research results, by M. Nag. JOURNAL OF FAMILY WELFARE 23:3-19, December, 1976.

Sterilization, how the victims were trapped, by B. Levin. TIMES p. 18, November 8, 1978.

INDIA
A study of some socio-demographic chracteristics of hu-
man sterilization cases in the area covered by Rural
Health Training Centre, Harsola, Indore, by M. C.
Mittal, et al. INDIAN JOURNAL OF PUBLIC
HEALTH 21(2):65-70, April-June, 1977.

NATAL
Report on a free sterilization service in Natal, by J. H.
McMillan, et al. SOUTH AFRICAN MEDICAL
JOURNAL 52(24):978-980, December 3, 1977.

NEW ZEALAND
Contraception, sterilisation and abortion in New Zealand.
NEW ZEALAND MEDICAL JOURNAL 85(588):
441-445, May 25, 1977.

THE PHILIPPINES

SINGAPORE
Psychological sequelae of sterilization in women in Singa-
pore, by M. C. Cheng, et al. INTERNATIONAL
JOURNAL OF GYNAECOLOGY AND OBSTE-
TRICS 15(1):44-47, 1977.

UNITED STATES
Lo, the poor and sterilized Indian; on the report of the
Government Accounting Office, by B. Wagner.
AMERICA 136:74, January 29, 1977.

Local proteinase inhibitor concentration in uterine secretions with intrauterine spirals (IUD) in situ [proceed-
ings], by P. F. Tauber, et al. ARCHIV FUR GYNAE-
KOLOGIE 224(1-4):32-33, July 29, 1977.

Sterile justice in South Carolina? censure of E. Primus for
informing sterilized black women of legal rights, by
M. Jordan. BLACK ENTERPRISE 8:11-12, March,
1978.

UNITED STATES INDIAN

STERILIZATION: ATTITUDES
Fighting sterilization abuse, by J. Herman. SCIENCE FOR THE PEOPLE 9:17-19, January-February, 1977.

Hysterectomy and sterilisation: changes of fashion and mind [editorial]. BRITISH MEDICAL JOURNAL 2(6089): 715-716, September 17, 1977.

Non-acceptance of puerperal sterilization. A study, by B. Palaniappan. INTERNATIONAL JOURNAL OF GYNAECOLOGY AND OBSTETRICS 14(6):505-508, 1976.

Non-acceptance of sterilization in women after having two children. . .Singapore, by L. M. Wat. THE NURSING JOURNAL OF SINGAPORE 17:45-47+, November, 1977.

Why 103 women asked for reversal of sterilisation, by R. M. L. Winston. BRITISH MEDICAL JOURNAL 6082:305-307, July 30, 1977.

STERILIZATION: COMPLICATIONS
Change in the adrenal cortex of rats in stress after hypophysectomy, thyroidectomy and castration, by B. Ia. Ryzhavski. ARKHIV ANATOMII, GISTOLOGII I EMBRIOLOGII 74(4):40-46, April, 1978.

Effect of ovarectomy of females and oestrogen administration to males during the neonatal critical period on salt intake in adulthood in rats, by J. Krecek. PHYSIOLOGIA BOHEMOSLOVACA 27(1):1-5, 1978.

Mechanism of action of estradiol valerate. II. Changes in the genital tract of rats castrated and subjected to prolonged treatment, by G. Merlino, et al. ARCHIVIO DI OSTETRICIA E GINECOLOGIA 79(5-6):336-341, August-

December, 1974.

Poststerilization tubal torsion, by B. D. Pujari, et al. INTER-NATIONAL SURGERY 63(2):84-86, February, 1978.

Psychological adaptation to sterilization [proceedings], by A. Drähne, et al. ARCHIV FUR GYNAEKOLOGIE 224(1-4):37-38, July 29, 1977.

The sinister side of sterilization [editorial]. SOUTH AFRICAN MEDICAL JOURNAL 53(2):38-39, January 14, 1978.

Spouse's right to marital dissolution predicated on the partner's contraceptive surgery. NEW YORK LAW SCHOOL LAW REVIEW 23:99-117, 1977.

Studies on dopamine turnover in ovariectomized or hypophysectomized female rats. Effects of 17 beta-estradiol benzoate, ethynodioldiacetate and ovine prolactin, by F. A. Wiesel, et al. BRAIN RESEARCH 148(2):399-411, June 16, 1978.

STERILIZATION: FAILURE
Compensation for failure of sterilization? by W. Barnikel. GEBURTSHILFE UND FRAUENHEILKUNDE 37(10): 881, October, 1977.

Malpractice decisions you should know about. Unsuccessful sterilization worth $462,500. MEDICAL TIMES 105(11): 115, November, 1977.

Questions of liability in unsuccessful voluntary sterilization, by G. H. Schlund. GEBURTSHILFE UND FRAUEN-HEILKUNDE 37(11):906-908, November, 1977.

Sterilisation failure, by G. J. Hughes. BRITISH MEDICAL JOURNAL 2(6098):1337-1339, November 19, 1977.

SINGAPORE
Sterilization failures in Singapore: an examination of ligation techniques and failure rates, by M. C. E. Cheng, et al. STUDIES IN FAMILY PLANNING 8:109, April, 1977.

STERILIZATION: FEMALE
Alternatives to female sterilization, by S. S. Ratnam, et al. INTERNATIONAL JOURNAL OF GYNAECOLOGY AND OBSTETRICS 15(1):88-92, 1977.

Communicating through satisfied adopters of female sterilization. STUDIES IN FAMILY PLANNING 8(8):205, August, 1977.

Counseling women for tubal sterilization, by E. Barron, et al. HEALTH AND SOCIAL WORK 3:48-58, February, 1978.

Does sterilization prevent pelvic infection? by S. N. Hajj. JOURNAL OF REPRODUCTIVE MEDICINE 20(5): 289-290, May, 1978.

Gynaecological laparoscopy. The report of the working party of the confidential enquiry into gynaecological laparoscopy. BRITISH JOURNAL OF OBSTETRICS AND GYNAECOLOGY 85(6):401-403, June, 1978.

Hysterectomy for pregnancy termination and sterilization, by S. T. DeLee. INTERNATIONAL SURGERY 63(3): 176-180, March, 1978.

Induction of abortion by intrauterine administration of prostaglandin via laparoscopy with concurrent sterilization, by M. Morad, et al. INTERNATIONAL JOURNAL OF GYNAECOLOGY AND OBSTETRICS 15(3):256-257, 1977.

Induction of maternal behaviors in primigravid rats by

ovariectomy, hysterectomy, or ovariectomy plus hysterectomy: effect of length of gestation, by R. S. Bridges, et al. HORMONES AND BEHAVIOR 9(2):156-169, October, 1977.

Ketamine as the sole anaesthetic agent for laparoscopic sterilization. The effects of premedication on the frequency of adverse clinical reactions, by E. M. Figallo, et al. BRITISH JOURNAL OF ANAESTHESIOLOGY 49(11):1159-1165, November, 1977.

The new improved silastic band for ligation of fallopian tubes, by C. L. Lay. FERTILITY AND STERILITY 28(12):1301-1305, December, 1977.

Oestradiol and progesterone: soluble recepto levels and metabolism in the uterus of the ovariectomized ewe, by L. Murphy, et al. AUSTRALIAN JOURANL OF BIOLOGICAL SCIENCES 30(3):225-228, June, 1977.

Past, present and future of the surgical sterilization of woment, by J. E. Rioux. UNION MEDICALE DU CANADA 107(6):544-558, June, 1978.

Pelviscopic sterilization with plastic clips in animal experiments (rabbits) [proceedings], by E. Brandl, et al. ARCHIV FUR GYNAEKOLOGIE 224(1-4):43-44, July 29, 1977.

The problem of women in penal and correctional institutions, by E. C. Potter. QUARTERLY JOURNAL OF CORRECTIONS 1(4):9-14, Fall, 1977.

The safety of combined abortion-sterilization procedure, by M. C. Cheng, et al. AMERICAN JOURNAL OF OBSTETRICS AND GYNECOLOGY 129(5):548-552, November 1, 1977.

Serum LH levels in intact & ovariectomized female rats dur-

499

ing puberty, by A. Sehgal, et al. INDIAN JOURNAL OF EXPERIMENTAL BIOLOGY 15(3):229-231, March, 1977.

Sterilization by hysterectomy, by J. S. Scott. IPPF MEDICAL BULLETIN 12(1):1-2, February, 1978.

Sterilization by laparoscopy. Use of Yoon's ring, by H. Leyton, et al. REVISTA CHILENA DE OBSTETRICIA Y GINECOLOGIA 42(3):187-191, 1977.

Sterilization by partial resection of the oviducts via bipolar electrocoagulation, by H. A. Hirsch, et al. GEBURTSHILFE UND FRAUENHEILKUNDE 37(10):869-872, October, 1977.

Sterilization—the vaginal route revisited, by N. C. Gage. SOUTH AFRICAN MEDICAL JOURNAL 53(16):631-633, April 22, 1978.

Tubal sterilization patient care program, by M. A. Hesselbein. AORN JOURNAL 26(5):884-886, November, 1977.

Tubal sterilization. A review, by K. C. Leong. JOURNAL OF THE MAINE MEDICAL ASSOCIATION 69(3):75-80, March, 1978.

Variation of food intake and body weight with estrous cycle, ovariectomy, and estradiol benzoate treatment in hamsters (Mesocricetus auratus), by L. P. Morin, et al. JOURNAL OF COMPARATIVE PHYSIOLOGY AND PSYCHOLOGY 92(1):1-6, February, 1978.

BANGLADESH
Tubal ligation in Bangladesh, by J. Calder. NURSING MIRROR 145(24):32-33, December 15, 1977.

INDIA
Female sterilization in small camp settings in rural India,

INDIA
by R. V. Bhatt, et al. STUDIES IN FAMILY PLAN-
NING 9(2-3):39-43, February-March, 1978.

SCOTLAND
Female sterilization in Aberdeen: preliminary findings,
by S. Teper. POPULATION STUDIES 32:549-566,
November, 1978.

Social and medical trends in female sterilization in
Aberdeen, 1951-72, by B. J. Nottage, et al. JOUR-
NAL OF BIOSOCIAL SCIENCE 9(4):487-500,
October, 1977.

STERILIZATION: FEMALE: COMPLICATIONS
Clip sterilization failures, by A. M. Mroueh. CONTRACEP-
TION 16(1):19-27, July, 1977.

Complication of laparoscopic tubal banding procedure: case
report, by J. G. Bell, et al. AMERICAN JOURNAL OF
OBSTETRICS AND GYNECOLOGY 131(8):908-910,
August 15, 1978.

Complications and the late sequelae of contraception including sterilization [proceedings], by J. Hammerstein.
ARCHIV FUR GYNAEKOLOGIE 224(1-4):1-24, July
29, 1977.

The effect of long-term oral oestriol succinate therapy on the
skin of castrated women, by R. Punnonen, et al. AN-
NALES CHIRURGIAE ET GYNAECOLOGIAE FEN-
NIAE 66(4):214-215, 1977.

The effect of ovariectomy on the responsiveness of preoptic-
septal neurons to microelectrophoresed estrogen, by M.
J. Kelley, et al. NEUROENDOCRINOLOGY 25(4):
204-211, 1978.

The effect of prepuberal castration on the development of

the nuclear sizes of the neurons in the hypothalamic nuclei of female rates, by H. Morishita, et al. BRAIN RESEARCH 146(2):388-391, May 12, 1978.

Effect of Pulsatilla administered pituitary extracts of ovariectomized donor rats on the ovaries, uteri & thyroids of normally cycling recipients, by S. Prasad, et al. INDIAN JOURNAL OF EXPERIMENTAL BIOLOGY 16(3):289-293, March, 1978.

Effects of Centchroman on the ovary & uterus of unilaterally ovariectomized rats, by J. K. Datta, et al. INDIAN JOURNAL OF EXPERIMENTAL BIOLOGY 15(12): 1154-1156, December, 1977.

Effects of danazol on gonadotropin secretion after ovariectomy in rats, by J. A. Vilchez-Martinez, et al. CONTRA-CEPTION 17(3):283-290, March, 1978.

Effects of ovariectomy and estradiol injection on nuclear structures of endometrial epithelial cells, by G. H. Vazquez-Nin, et al. ACTA ANATOMICA 102(3):308-318, 1978.

Effects of ovariectomy and estradiol replacement therapy upon the sexual and aggressive behavior of the greater galago (Galago crassicaudatus crassicaudatus), by A. F. Dixson. HORMONE RESEARCH 10(1):61-70, February, 1978.

Effects of ovariectomy and treatment with progesterone or oestradiol-17 beta on the secretion of insulin by the perfused rat pancreas, by S. Senzen. JOURNAL OF EN-DOCRINOLOGY 78(1):153-154, July, 1978.

Endocrine changes and symptomatology after oophorectomy in premenopausal women, by S. Chakravarti, et al. BRITISH JOURNAL OF OBSTETRICS AND GYNAE-COLOGY 84(10):769-775, October, 1977.

Ethinyl estradiol administration and plasma steroid concentrations in ovariectomized women, by D. K. Mahajan, et al. AMERICAN JOURNAL OF OBSTETRICS AND GYNECOLOGY 130(4):398-402, February 15, 1978.

Evaluation of sequelae of tubal ligation, by R. J. Stock. FERTILITY AND STERILITY 29(2):169-174, February, 1978.

Existence of an ejaculatory-like reaction in ewe ovariectomized and treated with androgens in adulthood, by C. Fabre. HORMONES AND BEHAVIOR 9(2):150-155, October, 1977.

Hypothalamic LH-releasing activity in young and aged intact and gonadectomized rats, by A. E. Miller, et al. EXPERIMENTAL AGING RESEARCH 4(3):145-155, June, 1978.

In vitro liver clearance of tritiated estradiol-17beta in the female rat after retrochiasmatic transection and ovariectomy, by C. H. Rodgers, et al. STEROIDS 31(1):151-161, January, 1978.

Interrelationships between circulating levels of estradiol-17 beta, progesterone, FSH and LH immediately after unilateral ovariectomy in the cyclic rat, by R. Welschen, et al. BIOLOGY OF REPRODUCTION 18(3):421-427, April, 1978.

Intraperitoneal explosion during female sterilization by laparoscopic electrocoagulation. A case report, by A. A. El-Kady, et al. INTERNATIONAL JOURNAL OF GYNAECOLOGY AND OBSTETRICS 14(6):487-488, 1976.

Late effects of female sterilisation [letter], by M. F. McCann, et al. LANCET 1(8054):37-38, January 7, 1978.

Loss of bony tissue in castrated women, by V. Culig. LIJEC-NICKI VJESNIK 100(3):153-158, March, 1978.

Menstrual patterns after laparoscopic sterilization using a spring-loaded clip, by B. A. Lieberman, et al. BRITISH JOURNAL OF OBSTETRICS AND GYNAECOLOGY 85(5):376-380, May, 1978.

Myometrial vascular damage after surgical sterilisation by tubal diathermy, by G. Tregson-Roberts, et al. JOURNAL OF CLINICAL PATHOLOGY 31(7):633-638, July, 1978.

Necessity to control endexpiratory CO_2-concentration during laparoscopic sterilisation under general anaesthesia with controlled ventilation, by E. Voigt. ANAESTHESIST 27(5):219-222, May, 1978.

On the reanastomosis of fallopian tubes after surgical sterilization, by H. W. Jones, et al. FERTILITY AND STERILITY 29(6):702-704, June, 1978.

Ovariectomy-induced changes in food motivation in the rat, by S. K. Gale, et al. HORMONES AND BEHAVIOR 9(2):120-129, October, 1977.

Possibility of burns during laparoscopic tubal sterilization [letter], by T. H. Freilich. AMERICAN JOURNAL OF OBSTETRICS AND GYNECOLOGY 129(6):708-709, November 15, 1977.

A possible involvement of adrenaline in the facilitation of lordosis behavior in the ovariectomized rat, by M. Yanase. ENDOCRINOLOGIA JAPONICA 24(5):507-512, October, 1977.

A prospective study of psychiatric and menstrual disturbances following tubal ligation, by N. N. Wig, et al. INDIAN JOURNAL OF MEDICAL RESEARCH 66(4):

581-590, October, 1977.

Psychological sequelae of sterilization in women in Singapore, by M. C. Cheng, et al. INTERNATIONAL JOURNAL OF GYNAECOLOGY AND OBSTETRICS 15(1):44-47, 1977.

Pulsatile discharges of luteinizing hormone in the ovariectomized rat during the 24-hour day, by B. D. Soper, et al. NEUROENDOCRINOLOGY 23(5):306-311, 1977.

Reactivity of castrated female rats to estrone in alloxan diabetes, by H. Ivanova, et al. PROBLEMY ENDOKRINOLOGII I GORMONOTERAPII 23(5):77-80, September-October, 1977.

Risks in laparoscopic sterilization [letter], by J. Leeton, et al. MEDICAL JOURNAL OF AUSTRALIA 1(7):392, April 8, 1978.

Salpingoclasia by laparoscopy with silastic rings, by A. Alvarado Duran, et al. GINECOLOGIA Y OBSTETRICIA DE MEXICO 43(255):7-13, January, 1978.

Salpingo-oophorectomy at the time of vaginal hysterectomy, by L. E. Smale, et al. AMERICAN JOURNAL OF OBSTETRICS AND GYNECOLOGY 131(2):122-128, May 15, 1978.

Shifting of the brain stem physiological impedance after ovariectomy and oestradiol implantation in rabbits, by W. Oliskiewicz, et al. ACTA PHYSIOLOGICA POLONICA 28(4):285-296, July-August, 1977.

Sterilization and menstrual disturbances [letter], by L. M. Rubinstein, et al. JAMA: JOURNAL OF THE AMERICAN MEDICAL ASSOCIATION 238(18):1913, October 31, 1977.

Suppression of serum follicle stimulating hormone in intact and actuely ovariectomized rats by porcine follicular fluid, by M. L. Marder, et al. ENDOCRINOLOGY 101(5):1939-1942, November, 1972.

Testing synergism between ethinyl estradiol and norethisterone on the histamine-induced deciduoma and vaginal mucification of castrated rats, byY. Chambon, et al. COMPTES RENDUS DES SEANCES DE LA SOCIETE DE BIOLOGIE ET DE SES FILIALES 171(1):192-196, 1977.

The time course change after castration in short-loop negative feedback control of LH by HCG in women, by A. Miyake, et al. ACTA ENDOCRINOLOGICA 88(1):1-6, May, 1978.

Torsion of a segment of fallopian tube: a case report of a long-term complication of sterilization by laparoscopic coagulation, by R. J. Stock. JOURNAL OF REPRO-DUCTIVE MEDICINE 19(4):241-242, October, 1977.

Two late complications of laparoscopic tubal ligation, by J. W. Georgitis. JOURNAL OF THE MAINE MEDICAL ASSOCIATION 68(10):352-353, October, 1977.

Uterine choriocarcinoma fourteen years following bilateral tubal ligation, by J. C. Lathrop, et al. OBSTETRICS AND GYNECOLOGY 51(4):477-488, April, 1978.

STERILIZATION: FEMALE: COMPLICATIONS: BIBLIOG-RAPHY
Late complications of female sterilization: a review of the literature and a proposal for further research, by J. E. Rioux. JOURNAL OF REPRODUCTIVE MEDICINE 19(6):329-340, December, 1977.

STERILIZATION: FEMALE: COMPLICATIONS: PSYCHO-
LOGICAL
Women who regret sterilisation [letter], by B. Alderman.
BRITISH MEDICAL JOURNAL 2(6089):766, Septem-
ber 17, 1977.

STERILIZATION: FEMALE: FAILURE
Ecotopic pregnancy following tubal sterilization, by S.
Kumar, et al. CANADIAN MEDICAL ASSOCIATION
JOURNAL 119(2):156-157, July 22, 1978.

Failed tubal sterilization as an etiologic factor in ectopic
tubal pregnancy, by L. H. Honoré, et al. FERTILITY
AND STERILITY 29(5):509-511, May, 1978.

Pregnancy following laparoscopic tubal electrocoagulation
and division, by A. Shah, et al. AMERICAN JOURNAL
OF OBSTETRICS AND GYNECOLOGY 129(4):459-
460, October 15, 1977.

Tubal pregnancy distal to complete tubal occlusion following
sterilization, by K. G. Metz, et al. AMERICAN JOUR-
NAL OF OBSTETRICS AND GYNECOLOGY 131(8):
911-913, August 15, 1978.

STERILIZATION: FEMALE: LAWS AND LEGISLATION
Hysterectomies: clinical necessity & consent. REGAN
REPORT ON NURSING LAW 18:2, December, 1977.

STERILIZATION: FEMALE: REVERSAL
Addition to the bibliographic citations in our work "Use of
Microsurgical Technics in Reconstructive Surgery of the
Fallopian Tubes" [letter], by L. Beck. GEBURTSHILFE
UND FRAUENHEILKUNDE 38(5):398, May, 1978.

Fertility news: some Texas discoveries: reversal of tubal
sterilization; research by Carlton Eddy, by A. Brewer.
VOGUE 168:152, May, 1978.

The microsurgical basis of Fallopian tube reconstruction, by
E. R. Owen, et al. AUSTRALIAN AND NEW ZEA-
LAND JOURNAL OF SURGERY 47(3):300-305, June,
1977.

Microsurgical reconstruction of the uterin tube in sterilized
patients, by E. Diamond. FERTILITY AND STERILITY
28(11):1203-1210, November, 1977.

Microsurgical tubal anastomosis for sterilization reversal, by
P. Paterson, et al. MEDICAL JOURNAL OF AUS-
TRALIA 2(17):560-561, October 22, 1977.

Microsurgical tubocornual anastomosis for reversal of sterilization, by R. M. Winston. OBSTETRICAL AND GYNE-
COLOGICAL SURVEY 32(7):623-625, September,
1977.

Profile of women requesting reversal of sterilization, by V.
Gomel. FERTILITY AND STERILITY 30(1):39-41,
July, 1978.

Reconstructive tubal surgery [letter]. FERTILITY AND
STERILITY 28(11):1263-1265, November, 1977.

Reversal of sterilization of the female [letter], by R. A.
Thatcher. MEDICAL JOURNAL OF AUSTRALIA
1(2):102, January 28, 1978.

Uterotubal implantation and successful pregnancy following
laparoscopic tubal cauterization, by J. R. Musich, et al.
OBSTETRICS AND GYNECOLOGY 50(4):507-509,
October, 1977.

STERILIZATION: FEMALE: RURAL
Female sterilization: training for rural service, by K. Chatura-
chinda, et al. INTERNATIONAL PLANNED PARENT-
HOOD FEDERATION MEDICAL BULLETIN 12(2):1-
3, April, 1978.

STERILIZATION: FEMALE: TECHNIQUES
Bipolar cautery for laparoscopic sterilization, by E. Gregersen, et al. ACTA OBSTETRIA ET GINECOLOGICA SCANDINAVICA 57(2):169-171, 1978.

The clinical efficacy of the repeated transcervical instillation of quinacrine for female sterilization, by J. Zipper, et al. INTERNATIONAL JOURNAL OF GYNAECOLOGY AND OBSTETRICS 14(6):499-502, 1976.

A comparison of the Falope ring and laparoscopic tubal cauterization, by J. S. Ziegler, et al. JOURNAL OF REPRODUCTIVE MEDICINE 20(4):237-238, April, 1978.

Daycare Pomeroy sterilisation by the vaginal route, by V. J. Hartfield. NEW ZEALAND MEDICAL JOURNAL 85(584):223-225, March 23, 1977.

Evaluation of single-stitch tubal ligation in postpartum women, by P. V. Mehta, et al. OBSTETRICS AND GYNE-COLOGY 51(5):567-568, May, 1978.

Experience with the trans-uterine tubal coagulation with high frequency current and the thermo method under hystero-scopic control, by D. Neubüser, et al. GEBURTSHILFE FRAUENHEILKUNDE 37(9):809-812, September, 1977.

Experience with the tupla-clip for tubal sterilization by laparoscopy, by J. Babenerd, et al. GEBURTSHILFE FRAUENHEILKUNDE 38(4):299-303, April, 1978.

Experiences with tubal sterilization using bipolar electro-coagulation [proceedings], by H. A. Hirsch, et al. AR-CHIV FUR GYNAEKOLOGIE 224(1-4):39, July 29, 1977.

Experiences with vaginal tubal sterilization using Kroener's fimbriectomy [proceedings], by G. Scholtes. ARCHIV FUR GYNAEKOLOGIE 224(1-4):42, July 29, 1977.

Experiments with polyacetyl tube clips in the rabbit [proceedings], by K. Diedrich, et al. ARCHIV FUR GYNAEKOLOGIE 224(1-4):45-46, July 29, 1977.

Factors in the decision to obtain voluntary sterilization: the choice of a male versus a female procedure, by M. P. Clark. DISSERTATION ABSTRACTS INTERNATIONAL 37(5-A):3210, November, 1976.

Falope-ring: a laparoscopic sterilization. Technical handling, action and experiences, by J. A. Balmer, et al. PRAXIS 66(41):1314-1320, October 11, 1977.

Falope ring tubal ligation, by A. B. Lalonde. AMERICAN JOURNAL OF OBSTETRICS AND GYNECOLOGY 130(5):567-568, March 1, 1978.

Female sterilization by laparoscopy: a comparative study of tubal occlusion with electrocoagulation and spring-loaded clip with one-year follow-up, by S. Koetsawang, et al. ANNALES CHIRURGIAE ET GYNAECOLOGIAE FENNIAE 66(5):240-246, 1977.

Female sterilization using the tubal ring, by R. Quinones, et al. INTERNATIONAL JOURNAL OF GYNAECOLOGY AND OBSTETRICS 14(6):489-493, 1976.

Guide to equipment selection for M/F sterilization procedures, by L. A. Reingold. POPULATION REPORTS (1):M1-34, September, 1977.

Hysteroscopic sterilization—a routine method? by V. Rimkus, et al. INTERNATIONAL JOURNAL OF FERTILITY 22(2):121-124, 1977.

Indication and technic of tubal sterilization by vaginal route.

Posterior transverse colpotomy, by J. Salvat, et al. JOUR-
NAL DE GYNECOLOGIE, OBSTETRIQUE, ET BI-
OLOGIE DE LA REPRODUCTION 6(6):851-859,
September, 1977.

Indications and statistics of tubal sterilization using a synthetic clip [proceedings], by W. Bleier. ARCHIV FUR
GYNAEKOLOGIE 224(1-4):41-42, July 29, 1977.

Is spontaneous respiration sufficient during laparoscopic
sterilization under local anesthesia? [proceedings], by
W. Dieckmann, et al. ARCHIV FUR GYNAEKOLOGIE
224(1-4):39-40, July 29, 1977.

Laparoscopic Falope ring sterilization. Two years of experi-
ence, by D. L. Chatman. AMERICAN JOURNAL OF
OBSTETRICS AND GYNECOLOGY 131(3):291-294,
June 1, 1978.

Laparoscopic sterilization after "spontaneous" abortion, by
A. Quan, et al. INTERNATIONAL JOURNAL OF GY-
NAECOLOGY AND OBSTETRICS 15(3):258-261,
1977.

Laparoscopic sterilization at an outpatient clinic. PUBLIC
HEALTH REPORTS 93(1):55, January-February, 1978.

Laparoscopic sterilization: experience with the Falope-
ringTM, by R. P. Pulliam. WEST VIRGINIA MEDICAL
JOURNAL 74(3):49-52, March, 1978.

Laparoscopic tubal sterilization: a report on 300 cases, by J.
St. Elmo Hall, et al. WEST INDIAN MEDICAL JOUR-
NAL 26(4):187-196, December, 1977.

Measurement of intrauterine pressure during extra-amnial
induced abortion with prostaglandin F2 alpha, by G.
Schott, et al. ZENTRALBLATT FUR GYNAEKOLO-
GIE 100(12):805-810, 1978.

Methods of sterilization in women, by A. A. Haspels, et al. TIJDSCHRIFT VOR ZIEKENVERPLEGING 31(16): 721-724, August 8, 1978.

Microsurgical anastomosis of the rabbit oviduct using 9-0 monofilament polyglycolic acid suture, by J. J. Stangel, et al. FERTILITY AND STERILITY 30(2):210-215, August, 1978.

Minilaparotomy—more simple and more secure than laparo-scopic sterilization, by J. Presl. CESKOSLOVENSKA GYNEKOLOGIE 43(6):448, July, 1978.

Minilaparotomy: safer outpatient sterilization, ed. by R. Skinner. PATIENT CARE 12:148-150+, January 15, 1978.

Minilaparotomy tubal sterilization, by H. F. Sandmire. AMERICAN JOURNAL OF OBSTETRICS AND GYNE-COLOGY 131(4):453-458, June 15, 1978.

Silicone rubber band for laparoscopic tubal sterilization, by A. H. Ansari, et al. FERTILITY AND STERILITY 28(12):1306-1309, December, 1977.

A simple device for double Falope-Ring application, by T. Kumarasamy. OBSTETRICS AND GYNECOLOGY 52(1):109-110, July, 1978.

Spinal anesthesia for laparoscopic tubal sterilization, by D. Caceres, et al. AMERICAN JOURNAL OF OBSTE-TRICS AND GYNECOLOGY 131(2):219-220, May 15, 1978.

Spontaneous extrusion of Hulka-Clemens spring-loaded clips after vaginal hysterectomy: two case reports, by G. H. Barker, et al. BRITISH JOURNAL OF OBSTETRICS AND GYNAECOLOGY 84(12):954-955, December, 1977.

Sterilization of women via suprapublic minilaparotomy, by D. Flodgaard. UGESKRIFT FOR LAEGER 140(13): 718-719, March 27, 1978.

Transvaginal sterilization of women—a review, by E. Patek. LAKARTIDNINGEN 75(17):1717-1720, April 26, 1978.

Tubal sterilization. Comparative study of 2 approach routes, by G. Magnin, et al. JOURNAL DE GYNECOLOGIE, OBSTETRIQUE ET BIOLOGIE DE LA REPRODUC- TION 6(6):861-867, September, 1977.

Tubal sterilization with a clip applicator under laparoscopic control, by H. Zakut, et al. HAREFUAH 94(9):262- 264, May 1, 1978.

Two-year experience with sterilization using the Falopian ring, by V. Chmelik. CESKOSLOVENSKA GYNEKOL- OGIE 43(4):293, May, 1978.

STERILIZATION: FEMALE: THERAPEUTIC

STERILIZATION: HISTORY
Changes in tubal sterilization through the years 1955-1975 [proceedings], by F. H. Hepp, et al. ARCHIV FUR GYNAEKOLOGIE 224(1-4):38-39, July 29, 1977.

STERILIZATION: INVOLUNTARY
Involuntary sterilization: the latest case, by M. O. Steinfels. PSYCHOLOGY TODAY 11:124, February, 1978.

Judicial immunity covers malice and procedural errors, court rules, by B. Hoelzel. JUDICATURE 61(10): 485, May, 1978.

Judicial immunity is absolute, by A. Bequai. SECURITY MANAGEMENT 22(9):123, September, 1978.

STERILIZATION: LAWS AND LEGISLATION
Again: juriprudence problems in voluntary sterilization, by
   G. H. Schlund GEBURTSHILFE UND FRAUENHEIL-
   KUNDE 38(8):587-590, August, 1978.

The changing law on sterilization, by A. H. Bernstein. HOS-
   PITALS 52(3):36+, February 1, 1978.

A critique of rules proposed by the Department of Health,
   Education and Welfare. Sterilization restrictions, by H.
   C. Moss. JOURNAL OF THE INDIANA STATE MEDI-
   CAL ASSOCIATION 71(4):390-392, April, 1978.

DHEW proposes 30-day waiting period for sterilizations; no
   funds for under 21s, contraceptive hysterectomies.
   FAMILY PLANNING PERSPECTIVES 10(1):39-40,
   January-February, 1978.

Eugenic sterilization statutes: a constitutional re-evaluation.
   JOURNAL OF FAMILY LAW 14(2):280+, 1975.

Government's plan to destroy the family [New York City
   guidelines on informed consent for sterilization], by L.
   Davis. MAJORITY REPORT 6:1+, April 30-May 13,
   1977.

Juridicial problems of surgical sterilization, by F. P. Blanc.
   JOURNAL DE GYNECOLOGIE OBSTETRIQUES ET
   BIOLOGIE DE LA REPRODUCTION 6(6):737-747,
   September, 1977.

Law-medicine notes. The freedom of medical practice,
   sterilization, and economic medical philosophy, by W. J.
   Curran. NEW ENGLAND JOURNAL OF MEDICINE
   298(1):32-33, January 5, 1978.

Sterilization ruling on legal, not moral, grounds, by T.
   Barbarie. OUR SUNDAY VISITOR 66:3, August 28,
   1977.

To sterilize or not to sterilize? by D. J. Cusine. MEDICINE, SCIENCE AND THE LAW 18(2):120-123, April, 1978.

USCC issues sterilization text. HOSPITAL PROGRESS 59:26-27, January, 1978.

UNITED STATES
From stigma to sterilization: eliminating the retarded in American law, by R. Sherlock. LINACRE QUARTERLY 45:116-134, May, 1978.

STERILIZATION: MALE
Autoantibodies following vaseactomy, by J. Y. Bullock, et al. JOURNAL OF UROLOGY 118(4):604-606, October, 1977.

Behavioural consequences of vasectomy in the mouse, by R. J. Aitken, et al. EXPERIENTIA 33(10):1396-1397, October 15, 1977.

Beneficial effects of ascorbic acid in vasectomized rats, by N. J. Chinoy, et al. INDIAN JOURNAL OF EXPERIMENTAL BIOLOGY 15(10):821-824, October, 1977.

Castration methods and their potential cost [letter], by P. A. Mullen. VETERINARY RECORD 101(19):391, November 5, 1977.

Cell-mediated immunity in vasectomized rhesus monkeys, by B. J. Wilson, et al. FERTILITY AND STERILITY 28(12):1349-1355, December, 1977.

Cell-mediated immunity to spermatozoa following vasectomy, by A. G. Tumboh-Oeri, et al. THERIOGENOLOGY 8(4):166, October, 1977.

Characteristics of vasectomy patients of a family planning clinic, by R. J. Gandy. JOURNAL OF BIOSOCIAL SCIENCE 10(2):125-132, April, 1978.

Chemical sterilization of male dogs: synergistic action of alpha-chlorohydrin (U-5897) with danazol on the testes and epididymides of dog, by V P. Dixit. ACAT EURO-PAEA FERTILITATIS 8(2):167-173, June, 1977.

Chemical sterilization of male langurs: synergistic action of alpha-chlorohydrin (U-5897) with methallibure (ICI, 33828) on the testes and epididymides of Presbytis entellus entellus Dufresne, by V. P. Dixit. ENDOKRINOLOGIE 69(2):157-163, July 1, 977.

The comparative actions of fluoxymesterone and testosterone on sexual behavior and accessory sexual glands in castrated rabbits, by A. Agmo. HORMONES AND BE-HAVIOR 9(2):112-119, October, 1977.

Demographic and socio-economic characteristics of their choosing vasectomy, by M. A. Parsons, et al. JOURNAL OF BIOSOCIAL SCIENCE 10(2):133-139, April, 1978.

Effects of copper intravasal device on the fertility of rat, by N. K. Sud, et al. INDIAN JOURNAL OF MEDICAL RESEARCH 65(6):812-816, June, 1977.

Hazards seen in male birth control. CRITICAL LIST 1(2): 27, March, 1976.

Hormonal changes after vasectomy, by B. S. Setty. INDIAN JOURNAL OF MEDICAL SCIENCES 30(3):109-112, March, 1976.

How men come to hear about vasectomy: evidence from a Manchester clinic in the UK, by B. E. Spencer. INTER-NATIONAL JOURNAL OF HEALTH EDUCATION 21(2):112-115, 1978.

Lack of association of the development of anti-sperm anti-bodies and other autoantibodies as a consequence of vasectomy, by P. Crewe, et al. INTERNATIONAL

JOURNAL OF FERTILITY 22(2):104-109, 1977.

Miscrosurgical two-layer vasovasostomy: laboratory use of vasectomized segments, by A. M. Belker, et al. FERTILITY AND STERILITY 29(1):48-51, January, 1978.

Motivation for vasectomy, by G. Howard. LANCET 1(8063):546-548, March 11, 1978.

Now it's his turn, by C. Doyle. OBSERVER p. 32, April 30, 1978.

Protein secretion of the rat vesicular glands, by R. Vögtle, et al. VERHANDLURGEN DER ANATOMISCHEN GESELLSCHAFT 71(pt 1):571-574, 1977.

Quantitative histochemical studies of the hypothalamus: dehydrogenase enzymes following androgen sterilization, by P. M. Peckman, et al. NEUROENDOCRINOLOGY 23(6):330-340, 1977.

RNA polymerase activities in isolated nuclei of guinea pig seminal vesicle epithelium: influence of castration and androgen administration, by K. A. Büchi, et al. ANDROLOGIA 9(3):237-246, July-September, 1977.

Responses to vasectomy performed at different ages in the rat, by G. A. Kinson, et al. RESEARCH COMMUNICATIONS IN CHEMICAL PATHOLOGY AND PHARMACOLOGY 18(3):561-564, November, 1977.

Specific protein synthesis in isolated epithelium of guinea-pig seminal vesicle. Effects of castration and androgen replacement, by C. M. Veneziale, et al. BIOCHEMICAL JOURNAL 166(2):167-173, August 15, 1977.

Sperm agglutinins in seminal plasma and serum after vasectomy: correlation between immunological and clinical findings, by L. Linnet, et al. CLINICAL AND EXPERI-

MENTAL IMMUNOLOGY 30(3):413-420, December, 1977.

Sperm autoantibodies as a consequence of vasectomy. 1. Within 1 year post-operation, by H. W. Hellema, et al. CLINICAL AND EXPERIMENTAL IMMUNOLOGY 31(1):18-29, January, 1978.

Vasectomy and spermatic antibodies, by K. Bandhauer, et al. ZEITSCHRIFT FUER UROLOGIE UND NEPHRO-LOGIE 70(7):519-522, July, 1977.

Vasectomy: benefits versus risks, by J. E. Davis. INTER-NATIONAL JOURNAL OF GYNAECOLOGY AND OBSTETRICS 15(2):163-166, 1977.

Vasectomy in rhesus monkeys. III. Light microscopic studies of testicular morphology, by P. M. Heidger, Jr., et al. UROLOGY 11(2):148-152, February, 1978.

Vasectomy with immediate sterility, by U. H. Jensen, et al. UGESKRIFT FOR LAEGER 140(16):916-917, April 17, 1978.

Vasovasostomy and patency rate [letter], by I. D. Sharlip. UROLOGY 11(3):315-316, March, 1978.

STERILIZATION: MALE: COMPLICATIONS
Catecholamines in discrete areas of the hypothalamus of obese and castrated male rats, by J. A. Cruce, et al. PHARMACOLOGY, BIOCHEMISTRY AND BEHAVIOR 8(3):287-289, March, 1978.

Changes in the structure and function of the testes and epi-didymides in vasectomized rams, by B. M. Perera. FER-TILITY AND STERILITY 29(3):354-359, March, 1978.

Coagulation changes following vasectomy: a study in pri-mates, by C. T. Kisker, et al. FERTILITY AND STE-

RILITY 29(5):543-545, May, 1978.

Effect of castration and testosterone administration on the neuromuscular junction in the levator ani muscle of the rat, by V. Hanzlikova, et al. CELL AND TISSUE RE-SEARCH 189(1):155-166, May 18, 1978.

Effect of castration and testosterone treatment on catecholamine metabolism in ventral prostates of normal and chemically sympathectomized rats, by R. B. Rastogi, et al. CANADIAN JOURNAL OF PHYSIOLOGY AND PHARMACOLOGY 55(5):1015-1022, October, 1977.

The effect of castration, thyroidectomy and haloperidol upon the turnover rates of dopamine and norepinephrine and the kinetic properties of tyrosine hydroxylase in discrete hypothalamic nuclei of the male rat, by J. S. Kizer, et al. BRAIN RESEARCH 146(1):95-107, May 5, 1978.

Effect of long term vasectomy on the secretory function of the epididymis in rat, by Q. Jehan, et al. INDIAN JOUR-NAL OF EXPERIMENTAL BIOLOGY 15(7):553-554, July, 1977.

Effect of vasectomy on hepatic drug metabolism, by D. E. Cook. EXPERIENTIA 34(3):315-316, March 15, 1978.

Effects of castration and androgen replacement on acid phosphatase activity in the adult rat prostate gland, by M. P. Tenniswood, et al. JOURNAL OF ENDOCRIN-OLOGY 77(3):301-308, June, 1978.

Effects of castration and testosterone, dihydrotestosterone or oestradiol replacement treatment in neonatal rats on mounting behaviour in the adult, by P. Södersten, et al. JOURNAL OF ENDOCRINOLOGY 76(2):251-260, February, 1978.

Effects of castration and testosterone treatment on sex specific orientation in the male rat, by J. Hetta, et al. ACTA PHYSIOLOGICA SCANDINAVICA (453):47-62, 1978.

Effects of castration on the mechanical response to motor nerve stimulation of the rat vas deferens [proceedings], by D. P. Gilmore, et al. BRITISH JOURNAL OF PHAR-MACOLOGY 61(3):473P-474P, November, 1977.

Effects of castration on serum LH and FSH concentrations in male guinea-pigs, by D. Croix. JOURNAL OF RE-PRODUCTION AND FERTILITY 51(1):149-151, September, 1977.

Effects of testrosterone replacement on the recovery from increased emotionality, produced by septal lesions in prepubertal castrated male rats, by I. Lieblich, et al. PHYSIOLOGY AND BEHAVIOR 18(6):1159-1164, June, 1977.

Effects of vasectomy and antisperm antibodies on human seminal fluid deoxyribonucleic acid polymerase activity, by S. S. Witkin, et al. FERTILITY AND STERILITY 29(3):314-319, March, 1978.

The effects of vasectomy on the testis and accessory sex glands of the Hartley strain guinea pig, by J. S. Jhunjhun-wala, et al. INVESTIGATIVE UROLOGY 15(3):200-204, November, 1977.

Evolution of the properties of semen immediately following vasectomy, by P. Jouannet, et al. FERTILITY AND STERILITY 29(4):435-441, April, 1978.

Fate of spermatozoa in the male: 1. Quantitation of sperm accumulation after vasectomy in the rabbit, by H. D. Moore, et al. BIOLOGY OF REPRODUCTION 18(5): 784-790, June, 1978.

—: II. Absence of a specific sperm disposal mechanism in the androgen-deficient hamster and rabbit, by P. D. Temple-Smith, et al. BIOLOGY OF REPRODUCTION 18(5): 791-798, June, 1978.

Gonadotrophin response after castration and selective destruction of the testicular interstitium in the normal and aspermatogenic rat, by I. D. Morris, et al. ACTA ENDOCRINOLOGICA 88(1):38-47, May, 1978.

Immunologic aspects of vasovasostomy, by S. Friedman. ANDROLOGIA 10(3):251-252, May-June, 1978.

Immunological effects of vasectomy, by W. B. Schill, et al. ANDROLOGIA 10(3):252-254, May-June, 1978.

Influence of vasectomy on development of autoantibodies, by J. D. Wilson, et al. IPPF MEDICAL BULLETIN 11(6):3-4, December, 1977.

Metabolism of 3H-testosterone in epididymis & accessory glands of reproduction in the castrate hamster Mesocricetus auratus, by T. K. Bose, et al. INDIAN JOURNAL OF EXPERIMENTAL BIOLOGY 15(10):852-855, October, 1977.

Microsurgical two-layer vasovasostomy: word of caution, by A. M. Belker, et al. UROLOGY 11(6):616-618, June, 1978.

Nitrofurazone: vas irrigation as adjunct in vasectomy, by P. S. Albert, et al. UROLOGY 10(5):450-451, November, 1977.

Psychological study on vasectomy, by H. Jablonski. LAKARTIDNINGEN 75(26-27):2540-2542, June 28, 1978.

Response of the epididymis, ductus deferens & accessory glands of the castrated prepubertal rhesus monkey to

exogenous administration of testosterone or 5alpha-
dihydrotestosterone, by R. Arora-Dinakar, et al. IN-
DIAN JOURNAL OF EXPERIMENTAL BIOLOGY
15(10):829-834, October, 1977.

Scanning electron microscopy studies of the internal surface
of the vas deferens in normal and castrated rats, by G. E.
Orlandini, et al. ARCHIVIO ITALIANO DI ANATOMIA
E DI EMBRIOLOGIA 81(4):391-398, 1976.

Serum gonadotrophins in rats after castration or heat treatment of the testes, by J. H. Aafjes, et al. ACTA EN-
DOCRINOLOGICA 88(2):260-273, June, 1978.

Serum hormone levels before and two years after vasectomy,
by R. E. Johnsonbaugh, et al. CONTRACEPTION 16(6):
563-567, December, 1977.

Synergistic effects of prolactin and testosterone in the
restoration of rat prostatic epithelium following castration, by S. A. Thompson, et al. ANATOMICAL RE-
CORD 191(1):31-45, May, 1978.

Territorial aggression of the rat to males castrated at various
ages, by K. J. Flannelly, et al. PHYSIOLOGY AND BE-
HAVIOR 20(6):785-780, June, 1978.

Ultrastructural and enzyme-histochemical alterations of the
dog prostate following castration, by C. Hohbach.
UROLOGE 16(6):460-465, November, 1977.

Vasectomy increases the severity of diet-induced atherosclerosis in Macaca fasicularis, by N. J. Alexander, et al.
SCIENCE 201(4355):538-541, August 11, 1978.

Vasectomy sequelae: empirical studies, by E. Jones. JOUR-
NAL OF REPRODUCTIVE MEDICINE 19(5):254-258,
November, 1977.

Vasovasostomy. Experimental comparative study of poly-glycolic acid and polypropylene sutures in the dog, by L. E. Lykins, et al. UROLOGY 10(5):452-455, November, 1977.

STERILIZATION: MALE: FAILURE
Defective sterility after vasectomy, by T. Christensen, et al. UGESKRIFT FOR LAEGER 140(21):1236, May 22, 1978.

Doctor must pay damages, child-rearing expenses for failed vasectomy, by J. F. Eisberg. LEGAL ASPECTS OF MEDICAL PRACTICE 6(3):48-49, March, 1978.

Recanalization rate following methods of vasectomy using interposition of fascial sheath of vas deferens, by J. O. Esho, et al. JOURNAL OF UROLOGY 120(2):178-179, August, 1978.

Transient fertility after vasovasostomy, by S. Marshall. UROLOGY 11(5):492-493, May, 1978.

STERILIZATION: MALE: LAWS

STERILIZATION: MALE: REVERSAL
How effective is a reversal procedure following a vasectomy? by D. Urquhart-Hay. NEW ZEALAND MEDICAL JOURNAL 86(600):475-477, November 23, 1977.

Immunologic aspects of vasovasostomy, by S. Friedman. ANDROLOGIA 10(3):251-252, May-June, 1978.

Microsurgical vasovasostomy: a reliable vasectomy reversal, by E. R. Owen. AUSTRALIAN AND NEW ZEALAND JOURNAL OF SURGERY 47(3):305-309, June, 1977.

Restoration of fertility by vasovasostomy, by B. Fallon, et al. JOURNAL OF UROLOGY 119(1):85-86, January, 1978.

Sperm granuloma and reversibility of vasectomy, by S. J. Silber. LANCET 2(8038):588-589, September 17, 1977.

Spontaneous recanalization following vasectomy, by W. B. Schill, et al. MUENCHENER MEDIZINISCHE WO-CHENSCHRIFT 119(40):1299-1300, October 7, 1977.

Spontaneous recanalization of the vas deferens, by R. P. Jina, et al. INTERNATIONAL SURGERY 62(10):557-558, October, 1977.

Vasectomy and vasectomy reversal, by S. J. Silber. FER-TILITY AND STERILITY 29(2):125-140, February, 1978.

Vasectomy reversal: review and assessment of current status, by A. M. Belker, et al. JOURNAL OF THE KENTUCKY MEDICAL ASSOCIATION 75(11):536-537, November, 1977.

Vaso-vasostomy, undoing a sterilization, by R. J. Scholt-meijer. NEDERLANDS TIJDSCHRIFT VOOR GENEE-SKUNDE 122(13):417-419, April 1, 1978.

STERILIZATION: MALE: TECHNIQUES
The bipolar needle for vasectomy. I. Experience with the first 1000 cases, by S. S. Schmidt, et al. FERTILITY AND STERILITY 29(6):676-680, June, 1978.

Bloodless castrator [letter], by A. V. Clarke-Lewis. VET-ERINARY RECORD 101(11):215, September 10, 1977.

Flushing of the vas deferens during vasectomy [letter], by A. J. Rochner, et al. CANADIAN MEDICAL ASSOCIA-TION JOURNAL 118(7):770-771, April 8, 1978.

Forensic and surgical guidelines for male sterilization, by P. Carl, et al. UROLOGE 16(5):298-301, September, 1977.

Microsurgical anastomosis of vas deferens: an experimental study in the rat, by N. Hampel, et al. INVESTIGATIVE UROLOGY 15(5):395-396, March, 1978.

The Silber vasovasostomy: a method of learning the microsurgical technique [letter], by A. A. Carpenter. JOURNAL OF UROLOGY 120(3):388, September, 1978.

A simple stabilizing clamp for microscopic vasovasostomy, by D. J. Albert, et al. JOURNAL OF UROLOGY 120(1): 77, July, 1978.

Splinted vasovasostomy. Comparison of polyglycolic acid and polypropylene sutures, by L. E. Lykins, et al. UROLOGY 11(3):260-261, March, 1978.

Vas occlusion by tantalum clips and its comparison with conventional vasectomy in man: reliability, reversibility, and complications, by A. S. Gupta, et al. FERTILITY AND STERILITY 28(10):1086-1089, October, 1977.

Vasectomy by use of a conservative surgical technic, by J. Eldrup. UGESKRIFT FOR LAEGER 140(16):914-915, April 17, 1978.

Vasovasostomy: the flap technique, by T. J. Fitzpatrick. JOURNAL OF UROLOGY 120(1):78-79, July, 1978.

STERILIZATION: REVERSAL
Characteristics of patients requesting reversal of sterilization, by P. Thomson, et al. BRITISH JOURNAL OF OBSTETRICS AND GYNAECOLOGY 85(3):161-164, March, 1978.

Mahgoub's operation: a reversible method of sterilization, by S. El Mahgoub. FERTILITY AND STERILITY 29(4): 466-467, April, 1978.

Microsurgery: the new hope for men and women who were

surgically sterilized and now want to have babies, by E. M. Wylie. GOOD HOUSEKEEPING 187:108+, September, 1978.

Microsurgical restoration of fertility [editorial]. MEDICAL JOURNAL OF AUSTRALIA 2(17):552, October 22, 1977.

Reversal of sterilisation [letter], by A. Cartwright. BRITISH MEDICAL JOURNAL 2(6078):641-642, September 3, 1977.

Reversal of sterilization in the male and female. Report of a workshop, by G. I. Zatuchni, et al. CONTRACEPTION 17(5):435-441, May, 1978.

Sterilisation and its reversal [letter], by J. Guillebad. BRITISH MEDICAL JOURNAL 2(6103):1672, December 24-31, 1977.

Sterilization: now it's simpler, safer. Reversible? Maybe, by M. L. Schildkraut. GOOD HOUSEKEEPING 186:163-164, January, 1978.

Undoing sterilization, by M. Clark, et al. NEWSWEEK 92: 77, July 10, 1978.

STERILIZATION: TECHNIQUES
Endocoagulation: a new and completely safe medical current for sterilization, by K. Semm. INTERNATIONAL JOURNAL OF FERTILITY 22(4):238-242, 1977.

Ketamine as the sole anaesthetic agent for laparoscopic sterilization. The effects of premedication on the frequency of adverse clinical reactions, by E. M. Figallo, et al. BRITISH JOURNAL OF ANAESTHESIA 49(11): 1159-1165, November, 1977.

Methods of laparoscopic sterilization and possible failures, by

K. G. Ober. GEBURTSHILFE UND FRAUENHEIL-
KUNDE 38(8):593, August, 1978.

Partial salpingectomy technique [letter], by W. S. Van
Bergen. AMERICAN JOURNAL OF OBSTETRICS AND
GYNECOLOGY 130(2):249, June 15, 1978.

STERILIZATION AND CRIMINALS

STERILIZATION AND ECONOMICS
Insurance coverage of abortion, contraception, and steriliza-
tion. FAMILY PLANNING PERSPECTIVES 10(2):71,
March-April, 1978.

STERILIZATION AND THE HANDICAPPED
Sterilisation of a handicapped child. LAW QUARTERLY
REVIEW 91:164-165, April, 1976.

STERILIZATION AND HOMOSEXUALITY
Erotic imagery and self-castration in transvestism/transsexual-
ism: a case report, by D. P. van Kammen, et al. JOUR-
NAL OF HOMOSEXUALITY 2(4):359-366, Summer,
1977.

STERILIZATION AND THE MENTALLY RETARDED
Court blocked sterilization of a retarded minor, by W. A.
Regan. HOSPITAL PROGRESS 59(5):96+, May, 1978.

Sterilization and the mentally retarded: HEW's new regulations. Part 2, by P. Urbanus. JOURNAL OF NURSE-
MIDWIFERY 23:16, Spring-Summer, 1978.

Sterilization of female mentally retarded, by L. Fortier.
UNION MEDICALE DU CANADA 107(5):505-506,
May, 1978.

Sterilization of the mentally retarded minor. Part 1, by
C. Cooper. JOURNAL OF NURSE-MIDWIFERY 23:
14-15, Spring-Summer, 1978.

Sterilization of the retarded: in whose interest? by W. Gaylin. HASTINGS CENTER REPORT 8(3):28, June, 1978.

STERILIZATION AND PHYSICIANS
Is a physician liable for compensation in a voluntary sterilization? by H. Roesch. MEDIZINISCHE KLINIK 72(48): 2094-2098, December 2, 1977.

Sterilization: duties of the physician. GEBURTSHILFE UND FRAUENHEILKUNDE 38(8):591-592, August, 1978.

Surgeon failed to disclose alternatives to sterilization, by W. A. Regan. HOSPITAL PROGRESS 59(7):98, July, 1978.

STERILIZATION AND POVERTY
Sterilizing the poor, by S. M. Rothman. SOCIETY 14:36-40, January-February, 1977.

Sterilizing the poor and incompetent, by P. Donovan. HASTINGS CENTER REPORT 6:7-17, October, 1976.

STERILIZATION AND RELIGION
Bishops' committee asks for sterilization rules. OUR SUNDAY VISITOR 66:4, March 12, 1978.

Bishops echo Vatican sterilization stance, by M. Winiarski. NATIONAL CATHOLIC REPORTER 14:3, December 2, 1977.

Catholic hospital ban on sterilization reaffirmed. OUR SUNDAY VISITOR 66:1, December 11, 1977.

Catholic hospitals and sterilization, by W. Smith. LINACRE QUARTERLY 44:107-116, May, 1977.

Our Catholic faith: sterilization, by R. Hire. OUR SUNDAY VISITOR 66:10-11, December 18, 1977.

A pastoral letter on sterilization: the Bishops of India. CATHOLIC MIND 75:4-6, May, 1977.

Sterilization can be moral, by T. Shannon. U. S. CATHOLIC 43:11-12, May, 1978.

Sterilization: Catholic teaching and Catholic practice, by W. May. HOMILETIC AND PASTORAL REVIEW 77:9-22, August-September, 1977; Reply by A. Zimmerman, 78: 56-63, June, 1978.

Sterilization: pastoral letter. OSSERVATORE ROMANO 7(464):11, February 17, 1977.

Sterilization policy for Catholic hospitals; statement by the U. S. Catholic Conference Administrative Board. ORIGINS 7:399-400, December 8, 1977.

An update on sterilization, by V. Paganelli. LINACRE QUARTERLY 44:12-17, February, 1977.

STERILIZATION AND YOUTH: HISTORY
Teenage sterilization in the United States: 1930-1970, by E. A. Brann, et al. ADVANCES IN PLANNED PARENTHOOD 13(1):24-29, 1978.

STERILIZATION EDUCATION
Legislation of education? A practical, effective approach to the problem of informed consent in elective sterilization, by M. C. Boria, et al. ADVANCES IN PLANNED PARENTHOOD 13(1):21-23, 1978.

AUTHOR INDEX

De Clercq, B. J. 137
Deedy, J. 41
Deeming, S. B. 112
de Gennes, J. L. 39
Deibel, P. 160
Delacroix, P.
Delamater, J. 186
Delatiner, B. 19
DeLee, S. T. 120
de Margerie, B. 199
Denis, L. 191
Dennerstein, L. 112
Dericks-Tan, J. S. 81
d'Ernst, J. P. 71
Desgouet, C. 4
Destro, R. A. 227
de Villiers, F. M. 101
De Vries Reilingh, A. 57
Dhar, G. M. 31, 62
Diamond, E. 152
Diamond, E. F. 178
Diaz, S. 50
Di Carlo, F. 133
Dickey, R. P. 82, 234
Dickinson, N. A. 29
Diddle, A. W. 168, 208
Dieckmann, W. 137
Diedrich, K. 97
Dietl, T. 162
Diller, L. 146
Dilling, H. 193
Dixit, V. P. 45, 230
Dixson, A. F. 87
Dobell, E. R. 107, 216
Doerr, E. 17
Dökert, B. 186
Dolan, B. 219
Dolan, M. 177
Dolby, L. 21
Dommisse, J. 135
Donald, R. A. 30
Donovan, P. 223

Dorman, J. M. 182
Dorsher, M. 192
Downs, P. E. 95
Doyle, C. 38, 163
Drac, P. 216
Drähne, A. 194
Drake, E. A. 55
Drill, V. A. 78, 115
Dryfoos, J. G. 62, 119
Duchene, G. 31, 165
Duda, G. 4
Duenas, J. 211
Duenhoelter, J. H. 73, 134
Duggan, D. 140, 238
Dunlop, J. L. 64
Dunn, H. P. 195
Dunn, J. N. 106
During, R. 37
Dusitsin, N. 143
Dutta, G. P. 210
Dwyer, K. 119
Dwyer, T. 95

Easterbrook, B. 162
Ebling, F. J. 77
Eccles, M. E. 15, 18
Eckholm, E. 113
Edel, H. H. 127
Edmonds, P. 39
Edmondson, H. A. 143
Ehrhardt, A. A. 187
Ehrig, E. 18
Eichner, E. 97
Einhorn, R. F. 61, 70
Eisberg, J. F. 72
el-Damarawy, H. 147
Eldor, A. 89
Eldrup, J. 242
El Hafed, A. 114
El-Kady, A. A. 135
Ellinas, S. P. 96

536

540

542

544

546

549